THE PRINCIPLES OF MORAL
AND CHRISTIAN PHILOSOPHY

VOLUME I
The Principles of Moral Philosophy

NATURAL LAW AND
ENLIGHTENMENT CLASSICS

Knud Haakonssen
General Editor

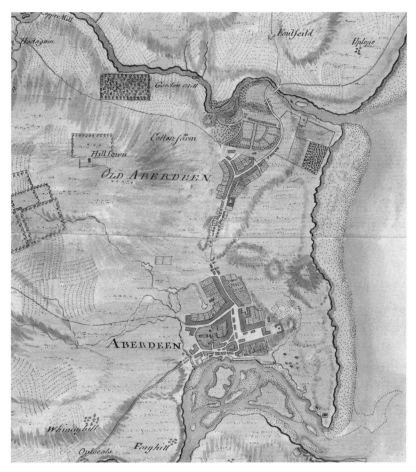

Map of Aberdeen

NATURAL LAW AND
ENLIGHTENMENT CLASSICS

The Principles of Moral and Christian Philosophy

VOLUME I

The Principles of Moral Philosophy

George Turnbull

Edited and with an Introduction by
Alexander Broadie

*Philosophical Works and Correspondence
of George Turnbull*

LIBERTY FUND

Indianapolis

This book is published by Liberty Fund, Inc., a foundation established to encourage study of the ideal of a society of free and responsible individuals.

The cuneiform inscription that serves as our logo and as the design motif for our endpapers is the earliest-known written appearance of the word "freedom" (*amagi*), or "liberty." It is taken from a clay document written about 2300 B.C. in the Sumerian city-state of Lagash.

Introduction, annotations © 2005 Liberty Fund, Inc.

All rights reserved

Printed in the United States of America

09 08 07 06 05 C 5 4 3 2 1
09 08 07 06 05 P 5 4 3 2 1

Cover art and frontispiece are the Aberdeen detail of the William Roy Map, created from 1747 to 1755, and are used by permission of the British Library (Shelfmark Maps C.9.b.21 sheet ½).

Library of Congress Cataloging-in-Publication Data
Turnbull, George, 1698–1748.
The principles of moral and Christian philosophy:
philosophical works and correspondence of George Turnbull
edited and with an introduction by Alexander Broadie.
p.   cm.—(Natural law and enlightenment classics)
Includes bibliographical references.
Contents: v. 1. The principles of moral philosophy.
ISBN 0-86597-455-1 (alk. paper)   ISBN 0-86597-458-6 (pbk.: alk. paper)
ISBN 0-86597-454-3 (set: alk. paper)   ISBN 0-86597-457-8 (set: pbk.: alk. paper)
1. Ethics—Early works to 1800.
2. Christian ethics—Anglican authors—Early works to 1800.
3. Natural law—Religious aspects—Church of England—Early works to 1800.
4. Christianity—Philosophy—Early works to 1800.
I. Broadie, Alexander. II. Title. III. Series.
BJ1012.T82 2005
241'.043—dc22   2004057633

LIBERTY FUND, INC.
8335 Allison Pointe Trail, Suite 300
Indianapolis, Indiana 46250-1684

CONTENTS

Introduction   ix

A Note on the Text   xix

Acknowledgments   xxi

The Principles of Moral Philosophy   I

INTRODUCTION

George Turnbull was born on 11 July 1698, probably in the Scottish town of Alloa in Clackmannanshire where his father was the Church of Scotland parish minister. Turnbull entered Edinburgh University in 1711 and continued his studies there till about 1716, though he did not proceed to graduation until 1721, the year in which he became regent at Marischal College, Aberdeen. The regent's principal task was to instruct a cohort of students in a three-year cycle of studies that included the mathematical and natural sciences, moral philosophy, and natural theology. On becoming regent he inherited a cohort that was already partly through its cycle and that completed it, under Turnbull's instruction, in 1723. His next cohort, which he taught from 1723 until 1726, included Thomas Reid. During his period as regent, Turnbull became the first of a long line of Scottish moralists to speak explicitly about the introduction of the experimental method of reasoning into moral subjects.

Turnbull's teaching had been interrupted by a visit to continental Europe in 1725, when, without the permission of his university, he traveled for a few months in the role of tutor to the Udney family. He was recalled to Marischal and was back at his post by the start of the following year, though in a sense under protest, since he had made it clear in correspondence that, as he put it: "I wish heartily I may be so lucky as to have no more to do with that place."[1] This fragment of autobiography tells

---

1. Quoted in M. A. Stewart, "George Turnbull and educational reform," in *Aberdeen and the Enlightenment,* ed. J. J. Carter and Joan M. Pittock (Aberdeen: Aberdeen University Press, 1987), 95–103; see 97. For much of the biographical information in this introduction I have relied on this article by Stewart and also on Paul

us less about the state of Marischal College than about Turnbull's restless character—it was a restlessness that dominated his life. In 1727 he left his position and received from the college an honorary LLD (doctorate of laws), the first such degree awarded by Marischal.

For the next fifteen years Turnbull held a series of short-term jobs, principally as a private tutor. It was an age when the grand tour was in fashion, marked by educational visits to the great capital cities of Europe, and usually culminating in a stay in Rome. As a private tutor he traveled widely, particularly in the Netherlands, France, Germany, and Italy. For the first five of those fifteen years he was tutor to Andrew Wauchope of Niddry, in which role he took his charge to Edinburgh, Groningen and Utrecht, the Rhineland, and France. But by 1733 he was back in Britain. In that year he matriculated and took his BCL degree (bachelor of civil law) at Exeter College, Oxford, conformed to the Church of England, and evidently cultivated clerical contacts assiduously. During the period 1735–37 he was for part of the time in Italy, again as a private tutor, this time to Thomas Watson, son of Lord Rockingham. Between the years 1727 and 1739 Turnbull had spent far more time outside Scotland than in it, and for a significant part of the period had lived in England. He was a deeply religious man, and in 1739 he was ordained into the Church of England, even though he had been raised in a Scottish Presbyterian family. In 1742 he was appointed rector of the parish of Drumachose in Ireland, an appointment he held until his death in 1748, although he did not spend much time there. His preference for travel reasserted itself; however by then, as we shall see, health considerations may also have played a role. In 1744 he returned to Italy where, among other things, he was involved in the covert gathering of information on exiled Scottish Jacobites.[2]

Turnbull was a prolific writer, with a particular interest in the themes

---

Wood, "George Turnbull (1698–1748)," *Oxford Dictionary of National Biography* (Oxford: Oxford University Press, 2004).

2. For information on his time in Italy see Wood, "George Turnbull."

of morality, religion, and liberal education.[3] His earliest publication was a graduation thesis on the need for moral philosophy to be accepted as a science along with all the other empirical sciences, and to be developed with the aid of the same methodology as that employed for the other sciences.[4] This theme recurs in his writings and is especially conspicuous in the present work.

The relation between the two volumes of *The Principles of Moral and Christian Philosophy* (1740), separately entitled *Principles of Moral Philosophy* and *Christian Philosophy,* respectively, is problematic because the first volume does not declare itself on the title page to be volume one, whereas the second volume does declare itself to be volume two, but only so declares itself in some copies, not all; and where the title page bearing the composite title *The Principles of Moral and Christian Philosophy* does appear in volume two that page has been glued in as a separate leaf and is plainly not part of the original printing plan. The reason for this is almost certainly that John Noon, the publisher of volume two,[5] thought belatedly that Turnbull's new work, *Christian Philosophy,* would have a better chance of commercial success if it were marketed as volume two in relation to the *Principles of Moral Philosophy.* But even if the composite title represents a marketing ploy, there is nonetheless an impressive unity of purpose to the two volumes taken together; in an obvious sense the second takes up and advances the discussion of the first. And there is little doubt that the two volumes were seen by Turnbull himself as two parts of a unitary work.

Furthermore, the first volume ends with an "advertisement" declaring: "So soon as the Author's Health permits, will be published, CHRISTIAN PHILOSOPHY: or, The CHRISTIAN DOCTRINE concerning PROVIDENCE, VIRTUE, and a FUTURE STATE, proved to be

---

3. For the last of these three, see Turnbull's *Observations upon Liberal Education, in All Its Branches* (1742; reprint, ed. Terrence Moore, Indianapolis: Liberty Fund, 2003); also Turnbull's *A Treatise on Ancient Painting* (London, 1740).

4. See *De scientiae naturalis cum philosophia morali conjunctione* (On the unity of natural science and moral philosophy) (Aberdeen, 1723).

5. He was one of the two publishers of volume 1, the other being Andrew Millar. It is not known whether Noon was the initiating bookseller for the first volume.

perfectly agreeable to the PRINCIPLES OF MORAL PHILOSOPHY."
And *Christian Philosophy* does indeed seek to do exactly what the advertisement declares. It is therefore probable that, whatever the publisher's motive for inserting the composite title in some copies of volume
two, the two volumes were, according to the author's intention, a single
book.

In light of the advertisement it might be speculated (without being
strongly urged) that the discrepancy in title pages may be related to Turnbull's poor health; perhaps at the time of going to press with volume one
the publisher was uncertain whether he would ever see the second volume. The nature of his illness is unclear. In a letter to Thomas Birch
dated 7 April 1739, Turnbull had said he had a bad cough and that this
was a new illness; and again on 4 February 1740 to Birch, he described
himself as "seriously ill." It might be conjectured that he was suffering
from bronchitis or tuberculosis, but there is at present insufficient evidence. In the earlier of the two letters he comments that he is revising
"a work which has long lain by me called the Moral philosopher . . ."
and adds that he plans to revise the work that summer.[6] If his publisher
was aware of these medical details, as seems probable, he might well have
been doubtful of his prospects of getting the second volume and consequently did not call the first "volume one"; only belatedly could he
publicly acknowledge the unity of the work by adding the composite
title.

In the preface to volume one Turnbull declares that aside from "a few
things taken from late writers" the work is the substance of several pneumatological discourses that he had read more than twelve years earlier
to students of moral philosophy, and he adds that the lectures were delivered at the time of publication of his two "theses," that is, the public
orations he delivered in 1723 and 1726 on the occasion of the graduation
of his first and second cohorts of students.[7] It is almost certain, therefore,

6. I am grateful to Paul Wood for this information regarding Turnbull's correspondence.

7. *De conjunctione* (Aberdeen, 1723) (see note 4), and *De pulcherrima mundi cum
materialis tum rationalis constitutione* (On the very beautiful constitution of the world
both material and rational) (Aberdeen, 1726).

that the young Thomas Reid heard the lecture-room version of Turnbull's *Principles of Moral Philosophy,* and this points to Turnbull's place in the early stages of the Scottish school of common sense philosophy. But quite aside from the probability that Turnbull had a major influence on Reid, *The Principles of Moral and Christian Philosophy* is of great interest in itself for the doctrines it develops.

Turnbull indicates what he himself regards as his true intellectual context by mentioning some of those who have influenced him. He singles out John Clarke's Boyle lectures, Bishop Berkeley (mainly the *Treatise Concerning the Principles of Human Knowledge*), Lord Shaftesbury's *Characteristicks,* Bishop Butler's *Analogy of Religion,* Alexander Pope's *An Essay on Man* (a work which had just been defended, to Turnbull's delight, by William Warburton, a theologian of whom Turnbull strongly approved), and Francis Hutcheson—"one whom I think not inferior to any modern writer on morals in accuracy and perspicuity, but rather superior to almost all" (p. 14). While, on the basis of Turnbull's own words, he is sometimes said to be particularly indebted to Hutcheson, it should be noted that Turnbull's earliest publication, the graduation oration of 1723, predates Hutcheson's earliest publication by two years and shows Turnbull already well set on the course he was to pursue for the rest of his writing days. The probability is that Turnbull and Hutcheson, educated in the same philosophical-theological canon and relying otherwise on their own native genius, reached rather similar conclusions without either having a great influence on the other.

Shaftesbury may have been a much greater influence on Turnbull than Hutcheson was. Shaftesbury's importance is indicated by Turnbull's early membership in the Rankenian Club (founded 1716 or 1717), an Edinburgh society composed mostly of young men preparing for the church or the law, who were particularly interested in Shaftesbury's ideas and wished to create a forum to discuss them. Shaftesbury's writings were also the focus of attention of the circle of thinkers who gathered round Lord Molesworth in Dublin, and it is therefore of interest that Turnbull, though never a member of the circle, maintained a correspondence with Molesworth on the subject of the relation between liberty, education, and the need to raise standards in the universities.

On the highly informative title page of the *Principles of Moral Philosophy,* Turnbull quotes Sir Isaac Newton's *Opticks* book 3: "And if natural philosophy, in all its parts, by pursuing this method, shall at length be perfected, the bounds of moral philosophy will also be enlarged." In a way this says it all. Turnbull places moral philosophy not outside but within natural philosophy. Natural philosophy is an empirical study of nature pursued by the method of observation and experiment, and for Turnbull, as for Newton, human minds, which are the proper object of the study of moral philosophy, are parts of nature. In that case the moral philosopher should rely on observation and experiment as his principal means of discovering the powers, affections, and operations of the mind. By such means the laws governing the human mind will be laid bare.

Natural philosophy is an investigation into the laws governing the behavior of things in the natural world. The laws are discovered via a search for uniformities in behavior. But Turnbull believes it is possible not only to discover the laws of nature but also to demonstrate their inseparability from a set of values, for the laws play a part in the production of the goodness, beauty, and perfection of the natural world. And the crucial point for Turnbull is that this is true whether we are speaking of the corporeal world or the moral world, that is, the world of spirits, human and otherwise. The principal objective of volume 1 of the *Principles,* therefore, is the identification of the laws of human nature and the demonstration that they serve the good, both the individual good and the good of the whole moral system. Insofar as the laws of nature, so to say, deliver a world that is good and beautiful, and insofar also as the laws are not themselves beings with intellect and will capable of intentionally delivering such a world, they have to be seen as pointing to a divinity beyond the natural world that they structure, a being who does have intellect and will, and who has a providential care for the world he created. The laws are therefore God's instruments created to form a world that measures up as well as any world could to his goodness.

From Turnbull's perspective, indeed, from that of almost every theologian of the Western tradition, the goodness of the world is a very imperfect representation of God's goodness. But though imperfect, it is the best possible for a created world, and it is for this reason that Turnbull repeatedly refers to the world's "perfection." Furthermore, though always aware of the limits of our intellectual powers as we seek insight into the mind of God, Turnbull thinks that progress in this quest is possible because we can make discoveries regarding the natural world and especially regarding the laws of nature as statements of God's intentions for this world. In this sense Turnbull's thinking in the *Principles* is in line with that of his colleague and friend at Marischal College, the mathematician Colin Maclaurin,[8] as well as that of a number of other leading contemporary scientists, who believed that recent scientific discoveries, and particularly those of Newton, constituted the best possible evidence for the existence and the attributes of God. Turnbull holds that in this sense natural science spills over into natural theology, or rather natural theology is one of the facets of natural science, just as—so Turnbull indicates at the start of the *Principles*—natural science spills over into moral philosophy, or rather moral philosophy is one of the facets of natural science. For Turnbull, therefore, the three apparently disparate disciplines constitute a strong unity.

The first law Turnbull identifies is "the law of our power," by which the existence or nonexistence of certain things depends on our will, and here Turnbull refers to the existence, or otherwise, of things whether in our minds only or in the outer world. For by an act of will we produce physical artifacts and we also have ideas—it is a matter of great importance to Turnbull that thoughts are no less subject to our will than are the movements of our limbs. In this sense we have "dominion," though limited, in the corporeal world and the spiritual. Such dominion is a kind of liberty. With dominion over my limbs I am at liberty to move them, and when I exercise that dominion my limbs move not of their own accord but by my determination. Now there is a view that liberty and law are incompatible, for law encroaches upon and thereby constrains the scope of liberty. But Turnbull rejects this and argues, to the contrary, that it is only in a world governed by natural laws that beings such as us can be free. His underlying consideration is that a willed act

---

8. Colin Maclaurin, *An Account of Sir Isaac Newton's Philosophical Discoveries* (London, 1748), ch. 1.

implies both an object at which the agent aims and also an act that is the means by which the object is secured. It is necessary to know enough about how the world works to know what has to be done in order to secure the end willed.

The knowledge in question is scientific since it includes a grasp of the relevant natural laws. Turnbull affirms: "did not fire gently warm and cruelly burn, according to certain fixed laws ascertainable by us, we could not know how to warm ourselves without burning" (p. 58). It is by a like insight into the laws governing the exercise of the mind that we come to acquire much of our knowledge and to contrive our moral improvement. In exercising our liberty, therefore, we use the laws of nature for our own purposes. I know that at a given distance the fire will warm me, not burn me or leave me cold, and I act accordingly. Speaking more generally, the laws of corporeal nature are good insofar as they enable us spiritual beings to realize our aims, all of which embody our values, for if we did not see what we aim at as valuable we would not aim at them.

Formally the same situation obtains with respect to the moral world. For we have dominion over ourselves no less than over things in corporeal nature. We have dominion over our own thinking, for once a thought comes into our head we can determine whether to pursue it or obliterate it, and we can will to start thinking through a given topic. We are therefore just as free in the inner world as in the outer. And in respect of the inner world also, there are laws of nature that we use for our own purposes: "Thus the knowledge of the passions, and their natural bearings and dependencies encrease our power and skill in governing them, by shewing us how they may be strengthned or diminished; directed to proper objects, or taken off from the pursuit of improper ones" (p. 71).

It is with such considerations in mind that Turnbull holds that this "moral anatomy" (i.e., the scientific study of the parts, powers, and affections of the mind) is not only a part, but the most useful part, of "natural philosophy" rightly understood. The goodness of the natural order is spectacularly evident in regard to our perceptual awareness of the world on which we act, and Turnbull comments on the fact that by a very early age we have learned sufficient of the laws concerning the magnitude and distance of objects to be able to judge of such things almost instantaneously. Without a grasp of the relevant laws we would be hopelessly inefficient at getting about in the world. The goodness of these laws is therefore evident.

A final example of a good law among the many that Turnbull spells out is the "law of custom." The repeated conjunction of two ideas produces a habit of mind by which the subsequent occurrence of either idea draws in its train the other. In short, an "association of ideas" is formed by the mind. This law is as much a law of nature as are any of the laws regarding the corporeal world, and it is no less important for us. Indeed, without it we could not live as human beings, and certainly could not attain the level of culture that we reach; for all education is based on our ability to associate ideas one with another, so that ideas are available for instant recall. Without the law of custom, therefore, "we would plainly continue to be in old age, as great novices to the world as we are in our infancy; as incapable to foresee, and consequently as incapable to direct our conduct" (p. 127).[9]

Natural laws are operative throughout the natural world both corporeal and spiritual and, as Turnbull seeks to demonstrate in the *Principles of Moral Philosophy*, all those laws work on behalf of the good, and as such they point to God's providential care for the world he created. Turnbull's philosophy, which has fairly been described as a "providential naturalism,"[10] is strongly argued, and was no doubt found persuasive by many in the two cohorts of students he taught at Marischal.

9. See A. Broadie, "The Association of Ideas: Thomas Reid's Context," *Reid Studies* 5 (2002), 31–53.

10. A phrase first used by David Fate Norton in *From Moral Sense to Common Sense: An Essay on the Development of Scottish Common Sense Philosophy, 1700–1765* (Ph.D. diss., University of California, San Diego, 1966), ch. 6.

A NOTE ON THE TEXT

In preparing Turnbull's text for this edition my approach has been min-
imalist. I have corrected manifest printer's errors but have not modern-
ized Turnbull's eighteenth-century spelling nor corrected what may be
plain spelling mistakes. The 1740 edition contains a list of errata, and I
have silently incorporated the corrections into the text.

I have, however, changed the placement of some footnote markers,
especially where they had been placed before the first word of a quotation. In the original text, Turnbull used repeated alphabetical sequences
to mark his footnotes; but his omissions, repetitions, and interspersed
symbols cause confusion, and so I have chosen to replace his footnote
markers with *a, b,* etc., starting the sequence anew with each page of
this edition. My additions to Turnbull's footnotes are placed in square
brackets within the latter. My own notes are marked by arabic numerals.
I have also altered the placement of the table of contents. In the original
text Turnbull's annotated contents are placed at the end of each volume.
I have moved them to the front of the volumes, where they now precede
their respective texts, and have retained the original page numbers. Page
breaks in the 1740 edition are indicated in this edition by the use of angle
brackets. For example, page 112 of the 1740 edition begins after <112>.

The work includes many Latin quotations. Of these, some are taken
from works that were originally in Latin, others from works that were
translated into Latin from Greek. For the former, I have reproduced
translations from the Loeb Library editions wherever possible. For the
latter, I know of no published translations of the Latin editions. In these
cases I have given my own translations of the Latin translations that
Turnbull used. There are sufficient differences between the Greek text
and the Latin translations to prompt my decision to offer a translation

of the text that Turnbull certainly read, namely the Latin one, rather than the Greek text, which he may not have known except in Latin translation.

Turnbull seems often to have relied on his memory for biblical passages, whether quoted or paraphrased, and I have silently corrected obvious errors of reference. However, it is not always plain whether Turnbull has misidentified a source of a paraphrase or has found a sense that eludes me in the verses at issue. In such cases I have let his references stand. I have used the King James version.

The many quotations from Pope, except for the translations of Homer, are identified in Alexander Pope, *Poetical Works,* edited by Herbert Davis (Oxford: Oxford University Press, 1966). Although there are some verbal differences between the edition Turnbull used and the modern edition, which is based on the Warburton edition of 1751, I have not annotated the differences.

A bibliography of works used in both volumes is found at the end of volume 2.

ACKNOWLEDGMENTS

I am grateful to Åsa Söderman, Richard Stalley, M. A. Stewart, and Paul Wood for help generously given. My thanks are due also to Glasgow University Library, and especially to the staff of the Special Collections Department, for countless acts of assistance during my months-long search for sources. Spec. Coll. was, as ever, a perfect base for me.

I owe a particular debt to Patricia S. Martin. Through her heroic efforts as my research assistant I was able to submit the typescript in good order and on time. Knud Haakonssen's invitation to me to prepare an edition of *The Principles of Moral and Christian Philosophy* provided me with a perfect context for spending many hours of quality time with George Turnbull, a philosopher who has long been one of my favorite thinkers of the Scottish Enlightenment. I am happy to express here my deepest thanks to Professor Haakonssen for the invitation, as well as for his gallant work in taking my typescript forward to publication.

A. Broadie

THE PRINCIPLES OF MORAL PHILOSOPHY

THE
PRINCIPLES
OF

MORAL PHILOSOPHY.

AN

ENQUIRY

Into the wise and good

GOVERNMENT

OF THE

MORAL WORLD.

IN WHICH

The Continuance of Good Administration, and of Due Care about Virtue, for ever, is inferred from present Order in all Things, in that Part chiefly where Virtue is concerned.

By George Turnbull, L.L.D.

And if NATURAL PHILOSOPHY, *in all its Parts, by pursuing this Method, shall at length be perfected, the Bounds of* MORAL PHILOSOPHY *will also be enlarged.*   Newton's Opt. B. III.[1]

Account for Moral, as for Nat'ral Things.   Essay on Man, Ep. I.[2]

LONDON:

Printed for the AUTHOR, and Sold by A. MILLAR, at *Buchanan's* Head, over against St. *Clement's* Church, in the *Strand.* MDCCXL.

---

1. Sir Isaac Newton, *Opticks,* bk. 3, query 31, final par. See Newton, *Opticks: Or, a Treatise on the Reflections, Inflections and Colours of Light,* 4th ed. (1730); reprint, pref. I. Bernard Cohen (New York: Dover Publications, 1952).

2. Pope, *Essay on Man,* I.162.

TO THE

RIGHT HONOURABLE

PHILIP,

Earl of STANHOPE, &c.

This TREATISE is most

humbly Dedicated

By His LORDSHIP's

Most devoted

Humble Servant,

GEORGE TURNBULL.

THE EPISTLE DEDICATORY

My Lord,

I am very sure, that to one of Your truly liberal and virtuous cast of mind, the scope of this Treatise will be very agreeable: Which, to give the shortest view of it I can, is, by endeavouring to account for MORAL, as the great *Newton* has taught us to explain NATURAL Appearances, (that is, by reducing them to good general laws) to shew, that from what we see of perfectly wise and good administration at present with regard to man, as well as all other things constituting the same system, there is sufficient reason to conclude, that the same admirable order shall prevail for ever, and consequently that due care will be taken of virtue, in all its different stages, to all eternity. <ii>

No man, by having the highest opinion of virtue, and of the happiness accruing from rational exercises, and virtuous consciousness, was ever the less inclined to believe a future existence. On the contrary, it will ever be found, that as they who are entirely immersed in gross voluptuousness, and quite strangers to the pure joys virtue alone can give, are the least willing to think of a succeeding life; so they who having a strong sense of the supreme excellence of virtue, highly prefer to what is vulgarly called *pleasure,* the solid, unchanging bliss, with which they feel a well-regulated mind and conformable conduct, so unspeakably to exhilirate the soul even in severe outward distress, are the readiest to embrace and indulge that comfortable opinion and hope, which renders the cause of virtue completely triumphant. The ineffable satisfaction redounding from the exercises of virtuous affections, and the conscience of merit, is a truly divine reward: it comes from our Maker: it is of his appointment: and he who hath so constituted things, must love virtue; and that which he delights in, he will certainly promote to perfect happiness by the properest steps and methods.

We are well authorised to say, that a *virtuous man is the Image of God;* that *he partakes of the divine nature.* And the substantial, un-<iii>fading happiness, which virtue creates, and that augments as it advances and improves, is to us a faint shadow of the divine all-perfect felicity resulting from no other source, but his absolute moral perfection, being of a kind with it: and it is a sure prognostick of that fulness of bliss, which must arise from virtue, when being by due culture brought to great perfection, it shall be placed in circumstances for exerting all its power and excellence suited to such an improved state of it.

Now, My Lord, being convinced of the acceptableness of this Design to Your Lordship, when I offer the work to You, with a heart full of esteem, love and gratitude, as the best pledge of my sincere attachment I can present You with, suffer me but to say one truth: which is, that I never had the pleasure of conversing with Your Lordship, without not only being instructed, but, which is better, without feeling an accession of fresh vigor to that love of truth, liberty, mankind, virtue and religion; Your opinion of my sincere regard to which, procured and preserves me that place in Your friendship, which all who know You, proclaim merit: a friendship which is one of the greatest joys, as well as honours of my life; and to which I am deeply indebted on <iv> many accounts, which I am not at liberty to declare.

Tho' no good man can despise merited praise, yet You shun it even from those whom You know to be incapable of flattering, through a jealousy and watchfulness almost peculiar to Yourself; lest Your mind, whose supreme delight is in doing good, should ever stand in need, in the smallest degree, of any other motive to act the best, the worthiest, the most generous part, besides a thorough-feeling of the excellence of so doing.

> *I am,*
> *My Lord,*
> *Your Lordship's*
> *Most obedient*
> *Humble Servant,*

December,
19. 1739.   George Turnbull

PREFACE <i>

Tho' not a few who are really lovers of, and great proficients in Natural Philosophy, *be not ashamed of the deepest ignorance of the parts and proportions of the human mind, and their mutual relation, connexion and dependency; but reject all such enquiries with an opprobrious sneer as* metaphysick, *meaning by that term of contempt, something quite remote from true philosophy, and all useful or polite learning, to be abandoned by men of genius and taste to* Pedants *and* Sophists.—*Yet it is certain, that the order and symmetry of this inward part is in itself no less real and exact than that of the body. And that this moral anatomy is not only a part, but the most useful part of* Natural Philosophy, *rightly understood, is too evident to need any proof to those who will but take the trouble to consider what* Natural Philosophy, *in its full extent, must mean.*

For, in the first place, it is an enquiry into a real part of nature, which must be carried on in the same way with our researches into our own bodily contexture, or into any other, whether vegetable or animal fabrick. Secondly, 'Tis only by an acurate inspection of this whole, and its constituent parts, that we can come at the knowledge of the means and causes, by which our inward constitution may be rendered or preserved sound and entire; or contrariwise, maimed, distorted, impaired and injured. And yet, in the third place, That it is upon our inward state or temper, our <ii> well-being and happiness, or our uneasiness and misery chiefly depend, must be immediately acknowledged by all who can think; or are in the least acquainted with themselves. To deny it is indeed to assert, that our perceiving or conscious part is not principal in us. Moral Philosophy, *or an enquiry into the frame and connexion of those various powers, appetites and affections, which, by their coalescence and joint-operation, constitute the soul, and its temper, or disposition, may indeed degenerate into a very idle, sophistical, quibling, con-*

tentious logomachy: It hath too often had that miserable fate, thro' the fault of those to whom unhappily people of a more liberal and polite, as well as more useful and solid turn, have principally left it to handle these subjects. But hath not Phisiology *likewise suffered no less cruelly in the same manner? And what other remedy is there in either case, but to treat them both as they ought to be: i.e. as questions of fact or natural history, in which hypotheses assumed at random, and by caprice, or not sufficiently confirmed by experience, are never to be built upon; and in which no words ought to be admitted, till they have had a clear and determinate meaning affixed to them; and withal, in that free, elegant and pleasing way, which we may know from some few examples among the moderns, and from very many among the ancients, not to be incompatible with the profoundest subjects in* Philosophy: *instead of handling them in that insipid, tedious ungainful manner, which having of late more generally prevailed in the schools, far from doing service to* Philosophy, *hath indeed brought it into contempt, and as it were quite banished it from amongst the polite and fashionable part of the world, whose studies are by that means become very trifling, superficial and unmanly*—Mere virtuosoship. <iii>

The great Master, to whose truly marvellous (I had almost said more than human) sagacity and acuracy, we are indebted for all the greater improvements that have been made in Natural Philosophy, *after pointing out in the clearest manner, the only way by which we can acquire real knowledge of any part of nature, corporeal or moral, plainly declares, that he looked upon the enlargement* Moral Philosophy *must needs receive, so soon as* Natural Philosophy, *in its full extent, being pursued in that only proper method of advancing it, should be brought to any considerable degree of perfection, to be the principal advantage mankind and human society would then reap from such science.*

It was by this important, comprehensive hint, I was led long ago to apply myself to the study of the human mind in the same way as to that of the human body, or any other part of Natural Philosophy: *that is, to try whether due enquiry into moral nature would not soon enable us to account for* moral, *as the best of* Philosophers *teaches us to explain* natural *phenomena.*

Now, no sooner had I conceived this idea of moral researches, than I began to look carefully into the better ancients, (into Plato's *works in particular) to know their opinion of human nature, and of the order of the world. And by this research I quickly found, that they had a very firm persuasion of an infinitely wise and good administration, actually prevailing at present throughout the whole of nature, and therefore very likely to prevail for ever, founded, partly, upon what they were able to comprehend in general of order in the government of the sensible world; but chiefly (for they had made no very great advances in what is now commonly called* Natural Philosophy) *upon the great in-<iv>sight they had acquired into the moral constitution of man, by applying themselves to moral enquiries. They were able to discern clearly from thence, that man is very well fitted and qualified for attaining to a very high degree of moral perfection even here; and being satisfied, that such care is taken of virtue, and such provision made for her in this life, as is most proper and best suited to her first state of formation and discipline, they could not entertain any doubts of the kind concern of Heaven about her to be carried on, as may best serve the purpose of general good, by proper steps, for ever.*

And accordingly what I now publish, is an attempt (in consequence of such observations as I have been able to make, or have been led to by others) to vindicate human nature, and the ways of GOD to man, *by reducing the more remarkable appearances in the human system to excellent general laws: i.e. to powers and laws of powers, admirably adapted to produce a very noble species of being in the rising scale of life and perfection.*

And what I think I have proved, by thus endeavouring to account for moral as for natural things, *amounts briefly to this, "That order is kept in man, as well as in the other parts of nature within our observation, constituting the same system: And that from what we clearly see of perfectly wise and good government in all present things, in that part chiefly where virtue is concerned, there is sufficient reason to infer the universal, never-ceasing superintendency of a divine providence, and a future state of complete happiness to the virtuous; or the continuance of perfectly wise and good order in all <v> things, and, which is chief, of due concern about virtue, in all its different stages, for ever and ever."*

In order to conclude a providence, (in the belief of which the chief happiness of thinking persons is absolutely bound up) it is plain, we must first have acurately considered the condition of virtue and vice with respect to this life merely, so as to be able to determine, when, and how far, or in what degrees, and how circumstantiated the one or the other is our present greater good or ill. Now it is only by strictly examining the structure and fabrick of the mind, the frame and connexion of all its powers and affections, and the manner of their operation, that we can ascertain the end and purpose of our being; find out how our moral part either improves or suffers; know what its force is when naturally preserved and maintained in its sound state, and what happens to it in proportion as it is neglected or prostituted, abused or corrupted. Thus, alone, can we with any degree of certainty and assurance say, what is the natural force and tendency of virtue, on the one hand, or the natural influence and result of vice, on the other; or in what manner either of these may work toward our happiness or misery.

But if we set about such an enquiry in the fair impartial way of experiment, and of reasoning from experiment alone, we shall plainly perceive, that as many as the hardships and difficulties are, which virtue has to encounter, struggle with, and surmount in this state; far however, from being quite abandon'd, she is not left without great support and comfort: Nay, that in reality, she is only exposed so far as various trial necessary to her culture and improvement requires; and has a real happiness belonging to her exercises, sufficient to <vi> render her the best and wisest choice even at present, in the opinion of all who make a fair and complete estimate of human life: just so much as leaves room for further hopes in her behalf, by clearly shewing providence to be already most seriously concerned about her, and thoroughly interested on her side in her first probationary state. And therefore the argument for a future life in this treatise, runs in this channel, "There is such provision made for virtue, there is such happiness, such advantages belonging to her, even here in her first state, or at her first setting out in life, as render it highly probable, nay, absolutely certain, that a perfectly kind providential care of her interests begun here, is to be extended to a succeeding life, and perfected hereafter." There is such a foundation laid, nay, such an advancement made here, as plainly points out the nature and scope of that moral

building intended to be carried on to its completion in another state. For
that work or scheme must be advanced gradually, because virtue must be
gradually formed to ripeness and vigour, by means of proper exercises and
trials: And virtue cannot possibly in the nature of things have the happiness
resulting from its exercises, but in proportion as it advances and improves.
Education must precede perfection in the moral, as spring must go before
harvest in the natural world. And moral perfection must be arrived to full
maturity by proper cultivation, before the excellent fruits it can then, and
then only produce, can be reaped and enjoyed. Virtue must be fit to be placed
in the circumstances which alone can render it fully happy, by affording it
proper means and occasions of exerting its complete force and excellence,
before it can be placed in such circumstances; or being so placed, could reap
to <vii> the full, all the advantages of such a situation: but being well pro-
vided for, and duly attended to and supported in its first state of education
and discipline, what reasonable ground of doubt or fear can there be with
regard to its future condition, or its succeeding circumstances in another state,
after it is brought by due culture, step by step, to considerable strength, beauty
and perfection, as virtue must: Gradual improvement to perfection by proper
diligence to cultivate it, being involved in the very notion of virtue and
merit.

I think I need say no more of the design in a Preface. *The variety of*
materials contained in this Essay, *and the order in which it proceeds, may*
be soon seen by casting one's eye on the Contents, *as they are digested into*
a regular summary of the whole. And therefore all that remains to be said
here is, in the first place, that the margine is filled with quotations from
ancient authors, not to make a shew of reading; but because, in reality, the
best observations in this enquiry are taken from some ancient moralist; and
it seem'd to me so much the more necessary to do justice to them on this
occasion by such references, that it hath been so lately asserted, the wisest
ancients had not just notions of God, or of a future state; or, at least, were
not able to produce any conclusive arguments on these important subjects.
But of this opinion I have said enough in my Conclusion. *And therefore I*
shall just say a word of the modern authors from whom I have received the
greatest assistances in this work. I think all of them from whom I have bor-

rowed any thing are referred to in the notes. But the pleasure and advantage
I have reaped from them, render it but justice in me to make more particular
mention of them in this place. <viii>

Some few very good and useful remarks are taken from Dr. John Clark's
excellent Sermons at Boyle's lecture.[3]

I have quoted some very beautiful passages relating to the necessity of gen-
eral laws, and to the wise order of nature appearing in the established con-
nexions between our sensible ideas of different senses, from the philosophical
writings of Dr. Berkley (*Bishop of* Cloyd) *a writer highly esteemed by all*
persons of good taste.[4]

I have used some of Dr. Butler's (*Bishop of* Bristol) *phrases in his dis-*
course on the analogy,[5] &c. *because I thought them very proper, and well*
chosen for the purpose to which they are employed: and this I take to be a
liberty that does not so much as border on plagiarism. Beside that, I am
obliged to the same treatise for several very useful and truly philosophical
observations on human nature. But every intelligent reader, who is ac-
quainted with his excellent sermons, will quickly perceive, that throughout
the whole I am yet more indebted to them. And, indeed, that true method
of enquiring into human nature, which is delineated with such force and
perspicuity of argument in the admirable preface to these divine discourses,
being strictly kept to in them, they make a full vindication of human nature,
and of the ways of God to man. There the natural dignity of human nature,
the real excellence of virtue, the solid happiness it creates, and it alone can

3. The chemist and scholar Robert Boyle (1627–91) provided in his will for the foundation of a series of annual lectures in defense of natural and revealed religion "to prove the truth of the Christian religion against infidels." In 1719 and 1720 John Clarke (1682–1757) delivered the sermons, printed as *An Enquiry into the Cause and Origin of Evil* (London, 1720), and *An Enquiry into the Cause and Origin of Moral Evil* (London, 1721).

4. George Berkeley (1685–1753), philosopher, was bishop of Cloyne from 1734 to 1752. His publications included *An Essay Towards a New Theory of Vision* (1709, 1710, 1732) and *A Treatise Concerning the Principles of Human Knowledge* (1710, 1734).

5. Joseph Butler (1692–1752) was bishop of Bristol from 1738 to 1750, then bishop of Durham. Among his publications were *Fifteen Sermons* (1726) and *The Analogy of Religion, Natural and Revealed, to the Constitution and Course of Nature* (1736).

give, and the indefeasible, unalienable right of moral conscience to maintain the superiority, and govern in the human breast, are set forth in the most forcible convincive manner, with evidence truly irresistible.

I cannot express the vast satisfaction, and equal benefit, with which I have often read the Earl of Shaftsbury's <ix> Characteristicks:[6] *a work that must live for ever in the esteem of all who delight in moral enquiries. There is in his* Essay on virtue and merit, *and his moral* Rapsody, *a complete system of* Moral Philosophy *demonstrated in the strictest manner, which fully secures that first step to revelation, the belief of a Deity and providence. And I cannot possibly account to myself, how it could come about, that a person of great candor and integrity, well acquainted with these writings, and who hath on other occasions shewn such a laudable readiness to do justice to mistaken or wilfully misrepresented authors, should say,* This writer aimed at giving a scheme of virtue without religion,[7] *since he hath on purpose at great length demonstrated the relation which virtue has to piety; and hath there fully proved,* the first not to be complete but in the later; *because* where the later is wanting, there can neither be the same benignity, firmness or constancy; the same good composure of the affections or uniformity of mind. And thus the perfection and height of virtue must be owing to the Belief of a GOD.[8] *These are that incomparable author's own words. 'Tis true, indeed, he hath let fall some things concerning revelation, which have rendered his satisfaction with regard to the evidences of it very doubtful to many. But even with regard to such surmises in his writings, may I not refer it to any candid person, who acts the better part? He, who for the sake of them, thro' the warmth of his zeal, (tho' it be for the best causes) condemns the whole work in the lump; or he who hath been at pains to find out some alleviations and excuses for them? Such a person I know whose*

---

6. Anthony Ashley Cooper, third earl of Shaftesbury (1671–1713). His *Characteristicks of Men, Manners, Opinions, Times* (London, 1711; rev. 1713) included the essays "An Inquiry Concerning Virtue and Merit" and "The Moralists, a Philosophical Rhapsody."

7. Francis Hutcheson, *An Inquiry into the Original of Our Ideas of Beauty and Virtue,* 4th ed. (London, 1738), xix–xx (Liberty Fund edition: Indianapolis, 2004).

8. Shaftesbury, "Virtue," I.iii.3, in *Characteristics,* ed. Klein (Cambridge: Cambridge University Press, 1999), 192.

sincere belief of christianity would not be called into question, were I at liberty to name him: And sure if <x> there be any virtue peculiarly recommended by the christian religion, it is, The charity which is not easily provoked to think evil, but beareth all things, and hopeth all things, *i.e. is disposed to put the most favourable construction upon every thing.*

The writer from whom I have borrowed most, is Mr. Hutcheson, *professor of* Moral Philosophy *in the* University of Glasgow, *a teacher and writer who hath done eminent service to virtue and religion in both ways, and still continues indefatigably so to do.*[9] *But that none of my faults may be imputed to him, it is fit I should apprise my Readers, that in quoting from him I have sometimes taken the liberty, not only to change some of his phrases, but to join places together which lye at some distance in the original; and which is yet a greater freedom, to intermix some things of my own with his reasonings. This his native candor and ingenuity will not only very readily forgive, but immediately attribute to its true cause, which was not any affectation of amending or correcting one whom I think not inferior to any modern writer on morals in accuracy and perspicuity, but rather superior to almost all; but purely, because such changes and additions appeared to me not unnecessary to serve the purpose of my argument.*

The only other author I have to name is Mr. Pope, in his Essay on Man, *which hath been lately defended against the objections of Mr.* Crousaz, *with so much judgment, and such good taste of poetry as well as philosophy, by the very learned, ingenious and worthy author of the divine legation of* Moses.[10] *Never did any poetical work afford me such delight, because none*

---

9. Francis Hutcheson (1694–1746) was appointed professor at Glasgow in 1729, and was professor of moral philosophy 1730–46. The work of his most quoted by Turnbull is *An Essay on the Nature and Conduct of the Passions and Affections, with Illustrations on the Moral Sense* (1728), ed. Aaron Garrett (Indianapolis: Liberty Fund, 2002).

10. Alexander Pope (1688–1744) published a series of moral and philosophical poems in four epistles, *An Essay on Man* (London, 1733–34). Its principal critic was the Swiss professor of logic Jean-Pierre de Crousaz (1663–1750). William Warburton (1698–1779), author of *The Divine Legation of Moses* (1738–41), wrote a series of articles in Pope's defense (1738–39), later published together as *A Vindication of Mr. Pope's Essay on Man* (1742).

ever gave me such deep and useful instruction. As much as I have had occasion by a long course of study in that way to be <xi> *acquainted with the subject, yet that truly philosophical poem is always new to me: the oftner I read it, the more I am charmed with it, and benefited by it.*

This author hath shewn us, that the seemingly most abstruse matters in philosophy, may be rendered, instead of dry and tedious, exceeding pleasing and agreeable. He hath given to this very profound subject, all the charms of poetry, without sacrificing perspicuity to ornament, without wandering from the precision, or breaking the chain of reason. *And tho' I am far from thinking writing in prose upon such philosophical matters, not to be absolutely necessary on many accounts, (otherwise I had not attempted what I have now done) yet I could not chuse but conclude my abstract reasonings with a quotation from him, as far as he goes; which is indeed to the bottom of his subject: because I have often felt,* that principles, precepts or maxims, written in such *harmonious* verse, both strike the reason more strongly at first, and are more easily retained by it afterwards. *And it is impossible for any one to express such profound abstract truths in prose, so shortly as he has done in verse:* Yet nothing is more certain, than that much of the force, as well as grace of arguments or instructions, depends on their conciseness. *What a blessing to society is such a genius! who hath*

> ———— turn'd the tuneful art,
> From sounds to things, from fancy to the heart;
> For Wit's false mirror, held up nature's light;
> Shew'd erring pride, *whatever is, is right.*
> That reason, passion, answer one great aim;
> That true self-love, and social are the same;
> That virtue only makes our bliss below;
> And all our knowledge is, ourselves to know.[11] <xii>

Such a poet, indeed, deserves the ancient venerable name so justly appropriated to poets who employed their muse to truly divine purposes, (divinus,

---

11. Pope, *Essay on Man*, IV.391–98.

sanctus)[a] *and all the honours due to that sacred, highly beneficial character. But as is the heart, so will one's works always be.*

But now that I am speaking of poetry, and its genuine noble ends, I cannot forbear expressing my most ardent wishes, that some genius fit for the glorious task, would give us a Counter-lucretius;[12] *and sing those wonderful harmonies and beauties of nature which have been lately discovered by searching into her order and administration; and the praises of that* Divine man *to whom we are principally beholden for all these momentous discoveries;[13] who may indeed be said, by unraveling the deepest mysteries of nature, and setting her excellent laws in their true light, to have effectually discomfited Atheism and Superstition, and all the gloomy horrors which naturally sprout from the frightful notion of a fatherless world and blind chance, or, which is yet more terrible, the opinion of a malignant administration.*

A certain poet,[14] who is universally confessed to have shewn a most extraordinary genius for descriptive poetry in some of his works, and in all of them a heart deeply impregnated with the warmest love of virtue and man-

---

a. Poetam natura ipsa valere, & mentis viribus excitati, & quasi divíno quodam spiritu inflari. Quare suo jure noster ille Ennius *sanctos* appellat *poetas,* quod quasi Deorum aliquo dono atque munere commendati nobis esse videantur. Sit igitur sanctum hoc poetae nomen quod nulla unquam barbaria violavit.

Cicero pro Archia poeta

[Cicero, *Pro Archia poeta,* viii.18–19: "poetry depends solely upon an inborn faculty, is evoked by a purely mental activity, and is infused with a strange supernal inspiration. Rightly, then, did our great Ennius call poets 'holy,' for they seem recommended to us by the benign bestowal of God. Holy then, let the name of poet be, inviolate hitherto by the most benighted of races!" Cicero, *The Speeches: Pro Archia poeta. . . . ,* trans. N. H. Watts, Loeb Classical Library (London: Heinemann; New York: Putnam, 1923).]

12. Lucretius, or Titus Lucretius Carus (c. 99–52 B.C.). A Roman poet whose book-length poem *De rerum natura* expounds a version of Epicureanism. He held that the human soul is material and that at death we cease to be. We therefore have no need to fear death. Turnbull countered all these doctrines, but since he was not a poet he was not a "counter-Lucretius."

13. "That Divine man" refers to Sir Isaac Newton.

14. "A certain poet" is almost certainly James Thomson (1700–1748), author of *The Seasons* (1730), *Liberty* (1735–36), and *The Castle of Indolence* (1748). See Thomson, *Liberty, The Castle of Indolence, and Other Poems,* ed. James Sambrook (Oxford: Clarendon Press, 1986).

kind, if he chances to cast his eye on this Preface, *as his friendship to me will naturally induce him to do upon* <xiii> *whatever bears my name, I desire he would consider this, as a call upon him from one who highly esteems and sincerely loves him, to set about a work so greatly wanting, and which must gain him immortal honour, by doing vast service to the cause he has most sincerely at heart.*

And what is susceptible of poetical charms, if the beautiful order, and the immense magnificence of nature in all her works be not? There is a person of very uncommon abilities, and equal virtue, from whom, in frequent conversations upon this subject, I have had many very useful hints, but I am not at liberty to name him:[15] *Let me, however, assure him of my warm sense and high value of a friendship so useful to me on many occasions. Let me just add, that tho' this enquiry hath not been very long by me in the shape it now appears, yet it is (a few things taken from late writers excepted) the substance of several* pneumatological *discourses, (as they are called in the school language) read above a dozen years ago to students of* Moral Philosophy,[16] *by way of preparative to a course of lectures,* on the rights and duties of mankind; *at which time were published two* Theses, *in the* University *way, indicating the importance of this philosophy; one upon the connexion between natural and moral philosophy; and the other, upon the manifest evidences and signs of wisdom and good order appearing in the moral as well as the natural world.*[17]

The Corolaries *subjoined to the last part (in which I hope the* Reader *will excuse some repetitions hardly avoidable, since it will appear, that upon the whole I have taken no small pains to diversify things I was often of necessity obliged to repeat) well deserve the attention of all who are seriously*

15. "A person of very uncommon abilities"—the reference is probably to Colin Maclaurin (1698–1746), professor of mathematics at Marischal College, Aberdeen, where he overlapped with Turnbull. He was later appointed to the Edinburgh chair on the recommendation of Newton.

16. Lectures delivered at Marischal College, Aberdeen, where Turnbull was a regent from 1721 to 1727.

17. Turnbull, *Theses philosophicae de scientiae naturalis cum philosophia morali conjunctione* (Aberdeen, 1723), and *Theses academicae de pulcherrima mundi cum materialis tum rationalis constitutione* (Aberdeen, 1726).

concerned about the improvement of true <xiv> philosophy, and right education. To some part of the work carved out in them, shall my studies ever be devoted, in proportion as providence gives me health, leisure and opportunity for carrying them on to advantage. Many who have great abilties for such employments, 'tis to be regreted, are not in the easy circumstances necessary to the pursuit of such serious, profound enquiries. But are there not several, who have both abilities and excellent opportunities, and whose profession loudly calls upon them indefatigably to dedicate themselves to the service of virtue and religion; who wholly neglect these noble ends? Let me therefore address such, together with those, who suitably to their character, very earnestly employ their time, their talents, and all the advantages providence affords them, in recommending and promoting truth, piety, or useful learning, in the words of Cicero, *who was ever engaged, either in useful action, or in teaching virtue and true philosophy.* Quod enim munus reip. afferre, majus, meliusve possumus, quam si docemus atque erudimus juventutem? His praesertim moribus atque temporibus: quibus ita prolapsa est, ut omnium opibus refrenanda, ac coercenda sit.[18] <xv>

---

18. Cicero, *De divinatione,* II.ii.4: "For what greater or better service can I render to the commonwealth than to instruct and train the youth—especially in view of the fact that our young men have gone so far astray because of the present moral laxity that the utmost effort will be needed to hold them in check and direct them in the right way?" Cicero, *De senectute, De amicitia, De divinatione,* trans. William Armstead Falconer, Loeb Classical Library (Cambridge: Harvard University Press; London: Heinemann, 1923).

The Principles of Moral Philosophy

✂ PART I ✂

Human Nature and the ways of GOD to man vindicated, by delineating the general laws to which the principal phenomena in the human system are reducible, and shewing them to be wise and good.

———— Nam sic habetote nullo in genere disputandi magis honeste patefieri, quid sit homini tributum natura, quantam vim rerum optimarum mens humana contineat; cujus muneris colendi, efficiendique causa nati, & in lucem editi simus, quae sit conjunctio hominum, quae naturalis societas inter ipsos. His enim explicatis fons legum & juris inveniri potest.

M. T. Cicero de leg. l. I.[19]

Remember man, the universal cause,
Acts not by partial but by gen'ral laws;
And makes what happiness we justly call,
Subsist, not in the good of one, but all.
There's not a blessing individuals find,
But some way leans and hearken to the kind.

Essay on man, Ep. 4.[20]

---

19. Cicero, *De legibus,* I.v.16: ". . . for you must understand that in no other kind of discussion can one bring out so clearly what nature's gifts to man are, what a wealth of most excellent possessions the human mind enjoys, what the purpose is, to strive after and accomplish which we have been born and placed in this world, what it is that unites men, and what natural fellowship there is among them. For it is only after all these things have been made clear that the origin of law and justice can be discovered." Cicero, *De re publica, De legibus,* trans. Clinton Walker Keyes, Loeb Classical Library (London: Heinemann; New York: Putnam, 1928).

20. Pope, *Essay on Man,* IV.35–40.

19

THE CONTENTS

Digested into a Regular Summary.

PART I

Introduction.

Tho' natural philosophy be distinguished from moral philosophy, yet every enquiry into any part of nature is an enquiry into fact: an enquiry concerning the human mind, its powers, and affections, and their operations, is as much an enquiry into fact, as an enquiry concerning the texture of the human body. *Pages* 1, 2

Natural philosophy is an enquiry into the general laws, according to which all the appearances in the material or sensible world are produced: and into the fitness or goodness of these laws. *p.* 2, 3

It proceeds upon these few following fundamental principles.

I. That the corporeal world cannot be an orderly, regular system, nor by consequence the object of science and imitation, unless it be governed by general laws. *p.* 2, 3, 4

II. Those are justly concluded to be general laws in the material world, which are observed to prevail and operate uniformly in it; and regularly to produce like appearances. *p.* 4, 5, 6

III. Those general laws of the material world are good general laws, which by their steady, uniform operation, produce its good, beauty and perfection in the whole. *p.* 6

Corolary I. No effects of such laws are absolutely evil. *p.* 6, 7

II. Such effects as are reduced to general laws, are accounted for *physically.* *p.* 6

III. They are also accounted for *morally,* if the laws be shewn to be good.

p. 7

IV. Natural philosophy, when it proceeds so far as to account *morally* for appearances in the material world, coincides with moral philosophy.   *p.* 8

When it does not proceed so far, it falls short of its principal use.   *p.* 8, 9

Moral philosophy is an enquiry into the texture and oeconomy of the human mind, its powers, and affections, and the laws according to which these operate or are operated upon: and into the fitness, and goodness of these powers, and affections, and their laws.   *p.* 9

It must presuppose and proceed upon the same fundamental principles as natural philosophy.   *p.* 9

Indeed those principles which have been mentioned as the fundamental principles, or the basis of natural philosophy, are in their nature universal truths or principles.   *p.* 10

And therefore of every system, material or moral, it must be true. I. That unless it be constituted and governed by general laws, it cannot be regular: and consequently it must be absolutely unintelligible.   *p.* 10, 11

II. Those must be received as general laws in a moral as well as a material system, which are found by experience to operate uniformly or invariably in it.   *p.* 11

III. Those are good general laws in a system, moral as well as material, which are conducive by their general operation to the greater good of that system.

p. 11

Corolary I. No effects of such laws are absolutely evil, but good.   *p.* 12

II. Those effects are accounted for *physically* which are reduced to general laws.   *p.* 12

III. They are accounted for *morally* by shewing the laws to be good.   *p.* 12

Hence we see how moral philosophy ought to be carried on, and what is its end and business.   *p.* 13

It is a mistake to imagine, that natural philosophy only can be carried on in that manner: or that it is a material system only which can be governed by general laws. Moral powers, and their exercises, necessarily suppose general laws established with regard to them.   *p.* 13, 14

We are as sure as we can be of any thing by experience and consciousness, that we have a certain sphere of power, activity or dominion.   *p.* 14, 15

But a sphere of activity cannot take place but where general laws obtain.

p. 15

Here some few remarks are made upon the disputes about liberty and necessity: the doctrine of necessity was very properly called by the ancients, *the doctrine of inactivity.*   *p.* 15, 16, 17

The enquiry in which man is chiefly concerned, is the extent of his power or sphere of dominion: accordingly the design of this treatise is to enquire into the powers and affections belonging to human nature, and the laws relative to them.   *p.* 18, 19

This enquiry is carried on in the same way with natural philosophy.
                                                                      p. 19

Accordingly as the one, so the other may proceed in the double manner of analysis and synthesis.   *p.* 20

Hypotheses are not admitted in either, any further than as questions, into the truth or reality of which it is worth while to enquire.   *p.* 20, 21

As natural philosophy proceeds from causes to effects, or from effects to causes, and so is compounded of experiments and reasonings from experience, so moral philosophy in like manner, *&c.*   *p.* 21, 22, 23

The following treatise therefore consists of observations or experiments, and reasonings from experiments about the human mind, in order to give a satisfying answer to this question, "Are all the effects and appearances relative to the constitution of the human mind, effects of faculties, powers, dispositions and affections, which with all the laws and connexions belonging to them, tend to produce good, order, beauty and perfection in the whole?"

Chapter I.

The first general law relative to mankind, is one that extends to, or runs thro' the whole of our constitution and circumstances. It may be called *the law of our power, or activity, or the law of industry.* For, in consequence of it, is it that certain effects depend upon our will, as to their existence and non-existence; and according to it, it is that any goods may be procured, or any evils may be avoided by us; and that, in general, the greatest part of our goods and evils, whether natural or moral, are of our own making or procuring.
                                                                      p. 24

This is matter of universal experience. And were it not so, we would be a very inferior creature to what we now are in consequence of the power allotted to us, natural and moral: we could not be capable of virtue or merit.   *p.* 25

But such a state of things, or such power, supposes general laws to take place with regard to us; or fixed connexions of things. For how otherwise could evils be avoided or goods be procured?   *p.* 26, 27

It is fit to enquire a little more particularly into our sphere of activity, and the laws relating to it.   *p.* 28

First general law. Intelligent power, depends upon knowledge and encreases with it—in the natural—and in the moral world.   *p.* 29, 30

It is because the acquisition of knowledge depends on us, that we have power, or can acquire and augment it.   *p.* 30

Wherefore if knowledge be progressive, intelligent power must likewise be progressive.   *p.* 30, 31

But knowledge cannot but be progressive—whether knowledge by induction from experience—or scientifick, abstract knowledge.   *p.* 31

Knowledge must likewise depend upon our situations for taking in ideas or views.   *p.* 31

But men must be placed in various situations, and therefore they must have various views with respect to the sensible world.   *p.* 32, 33

And with respect to the moral world.   *p.* 33, 34

Knowledge must depend on application to acquire it.   *p.* 35

It must likewise depend upon differences with respect to natural abilities.
                                                                   p. 35

But different abilities are necessary for many reasons.   *p.* 36

Progress in knowledge must depend on social assistances. This likewise is necessary for various reasons.   *p.* 37

These are the most remarkable circumstances or general laws relating to progress in knowledge, and consequently to intelligent power. And all these laws are very fitly established.   *p.* 38

Yet there are several instances of the care and concern of nature about mankind with regard to knowledge, very consistent with these laws of progress.   *p.* 38

Several instances are mentioned.   *p.* 38, 39, 40, 41, 42, 43, 44, 45, 46

But as considerable as these circumstances are, they amount but to a very small share of what nature hath done for us, in order to qualify us for progress in knowledge.   *p.* 46

We have an appetite after knowledge, and progress in it is rewarded by itself, every step our application advances.   *p.* 46

New and uncommon objects wonderfully attract our attention.   *p.* 46

The excellent final cause of this.   *p.* 47

Yet this itch of novelty is for good reasons checked or ballanced by the power of habit or usage over us.   *p.* 47, 48

The mind is exceedingly delighted with comparing ideas, and tracing agreements and differences.   *p.* 48

It is particularly pleased with beautiful objects, or such objects as are regular and have unity of design.   *p.* 49, 50

Thus we are naturally led to enquire after analogies, harmonies and general laws. Nature is beautiful, because nature works always consonant to itself, and by a few simple general laws.   *p.* 50, 51

We have likewise implanted in us by nature a sense of moral beauty; and thus we are naturally led to enquire after the utility, or the good final cause of laws and their operations.   *p.* 51

We are likewise considerably assisted and directed in our researches after knowledge, by the natural delight of our mind in great objects.   *p.* 52, 53

But let us consider a little our faculties, by which we acquire, or lay up and retain knowledge, and have social correspondence.   *p.* 53

The imagination is a most useful power—by it we have memory—it renders us capable of many delightful imitative arts—which is more, it renders us capable of social commerce by discourse—we could not have mutual commerce by discourse about moral objects, were not the moral world analogous to the sensible; so that moral ideas may be pictured to us under sensible images—The right method of teaching any language, would at the same time teach us this beautiful and exceeding useful analogy.   *p.* 54, 55

Moreover, it is by our fancy that our passionate part is touched: truths cannot find their way to the heart but thro' the imagination.   *p.* 56

We are so constituted for very good and wise reasons.   *p.* 56

Imagination is not an ingovernable faculty, as is commonly imagined—but it is much neglected in education.   *p.* 56, 57

The other faculty of our minds that remains to be considered is invention.   *p.* 58

A history of this faculty, and of the phenomena belonging to it is much wanted—Mean time, it is obvious, that invention is the faculty of finding out truths quickly, by ranging or disposing ideas in proper juxta-positions for discovering their relations—Every new juxta-position of ideas discovers some unknown truth—New truths cannot be any other way discovered—It is therefore by exercise that invention is improved.   *p.* 59, 60

In the last place, it becomes easier to make progress in knowledge, in proportion as we make advances in it: and by the help of that science, whose object is science and evidence, properly called *the art of reasoning,* much neglected since *Plato*'s time, tho' clearly delineated and strongly recommended by the great *Verulam.*   *p.* 60, 61

General conclusion concerning our furniture for knowledge; it is very large and noble.   *p.* 61

CHAPTER II.

A second class of laws, those relative to our embodied state, and our connexion with a material world by means of our bodies. *p. 62*

Communication with the material world necessarily supposes dependence on its laws—And natural philosophers have proved these laws to be good. *p. 62, 63*

A material world without being perceived could be of no use. *p. 63*

Without beings capable of enjoying a material world, nature would not be full nor coherent. *p. 64*

And by our commerce with the material world, we receive a great many pleasures of the sensitive kind, which well deserve their place. *p. 64*

Our senses are admirably adjusted to one another, and to our whole frame. *p. 65*

But this is not all; our senses are instruments or means, by which we are capable of many noble sciences and arts,—of natural philosophy. *p. 65*

And of many ingenious imitative arts. *p. 66*

Nor is this all; they are the means, or afford the subjects and occasions of many virtuous exercises,—of many social virtues—And which is principal, they afford our reason and moral conscience subjects to govern and keep in due order—And thus we have a noble dominion to acquire. *p. 67, 68*

But this supposes a moral sense in our mind, which shall be considered in another chapter. *p. 69*

Sensible pains, whence they arise—The law with regard to them is shewn to be good. *p. 69, 70*

Pains are proper and useful monitors. *p. 71*

The only proper ones for us—Nay, we can have no other consistently with the laws relative to knowledge. *p. 72*

But from the necessity there is that bodily appetites should be attended with uneasy sensations arises the necessity of all the other uneasy sensations accompanying our desires, which are called *passions*. *p. 73, 74*

The law of matter makes an infant state of body necessary—And the law of progressive knowledge and power or perfection, makes infant minds necessary—And such bodies and minds are proper mates. *p. 74*

There is a great variety among mankind in respect of mental powers—And this very considerably depends on physical causes,—as is generally owned—It is well worth while to enquire more fully into this phenomenon than hath been yet done. *p. 75, 76, 77*

Mean time, it is evident, that such a dependence is involved in the very idea of union between mind and body. *p.* 78

And it hath very good effects. *p.* 79

True morality, therefore, must consider man as a compound creature, neither merely sensitive nor purely moral,—but, as he really is, *Nexus utriusque mundi.* *p.* 79, 80

All the observations made by naturalists upon the animal oeconomy of the human body, and of other animals, might be inserted here—But the preceeding remarks will prepare every intelligent reader for making a proper use of such, as they occur to them in their reading and studies. The laws relative to our communion with a material world are therefore very fitly chosen.

p. 81

CHAPTER III.

Another class of laws. Those relative to the association of ideas and habits.

p. 81, 82

Both these effects take their rise from one principle.—And they are inseparable, or must go together; if the one take place, the other must likewise take place. The formation of habits supposes association of ideas; and where association of ideas takes place, habits must be contracted. *p.* 82, 83

But whether these effects are reduced to one principle in our nature or not, they do really take place, *i.e.* ideas are associated, and habits are formed by us. And both proceed from a most useful principle in our nature. *p.* 83

Which is really the law of improvement to perfection: for by means of it only do we, or can we arrive at perfection of any kind. *p.* 84

But, in order to treat more fully of so useful and extensive a law of our nature, an associated idea is defined and exemplified, in order to distinguish it from a complex idea. *p.* 85

From the very definition, it is plain, that almost all our ideas have something in them of the associated kind. *p.* 86

This is the necessary effect of a world, governed by general laws, upon minds which have the associating quality, or are capable of forming habits.

p. 86, 87

Accordingly, when we come to philosophize, natural philosophy consists, in a great measure, in separating ideas, which the order of nature hath associated in our mind. *p.* 87

And it is one great business, if not the chief in moral philosophy, to break or separate associations. *p.* 88

Many associations are made by ourselves. But many are inevitably formed in consequence of the order of nature, or the methods in which ideas are independently of us conveyed into our mind.   *p.* 89

What hath been said is no objection against the law of association. For, in general, it is the law of improvement to perfection.   *p.* 90

Several good effects arise from it—Without it we could never become acquainted with the course of nature; every thing would for ever be new to us.   *p.* 91

Unraveling or separating ideas of associations is a very agreeable, rational employment.   *p.* 91

It is in consequence of the law of association, that we are capable of strengthening or diminishing our desires, or of adding to our pleasures, and of alleviating our pains.   *p.* 92

Because desires are excited by ideas, and our power over our ideas lies chiefly in associating and separating.   *p.* 92, 93

Another circumstance with respect to association merits attention—Like ideas are very easily associated. Wit consists in associating—Judgment in separating—Both suppose the law of association to take place—It is therefore in consequence of the law of association, in a great measure, that there are different genius's among mankind—The same law gives rise to an equal diversity of moral characters.   *p.* 93, 94

But so far as temper depends on association of ideas, it depends on ourselves.   *p.* 95

Wit and its instruments, *metaphor and simile,* are associations—Philosophy is separating work—Both may run into extravagances.   *p.* 96

Practical philosophy, or the government of our affections, consists in the assiduous examination of our ideas, fancies and opinions—The chief business of education is to establish early the habit of self-examination.   *p.* 97

Associations cannot be broken by mere refutation of false opinions, but by contrary practice—Were it not so, the law of association would not have its effect.   *p.* 98

I proceed next to consider active habits, properly so called,—from our power of contracting habits, proceed memory,—habitual knowledge, taste of every kind,—and perfection of whatever faculty.   *p.* 99

Instruction and education presuppose the power of habit—How memory may be improved in consequence of this law—We are imitative creatures, but it is in consequence of the law of habits that imitation hath its effect, or example its influence.   *p.* 100, 101

Habit renders that agreeable which was at first disagreeble. *p.* 102

It ballances our natural desire after novelty. *p.* 103

By the law of habit, passive impressions grow weaker in proportion as practical habits are strengthened—instances. *p.* 103

It is in consequence of the law of habits that temper is formed—In consequence of it, we are able to establish in our mind the deliberative habit,—which is self-command, and true moral liberty. *p.* 105

It is therefore this law which renders us capable of liberty, or of being *free agents*. *p.* 106

The laws relating to association of ideas and habits, are therefore good general laws,—an useful corolary. *p.* 107

Chapter IV.

Another class of laws relative to our guiding principle and our moral conduct—Our excellence consists in our having reason and a moral sense to guide our conduct. *p.* 107

It is by our reason, that we rise above merely perceptive beings in the scale of life—It is all our force, or, at least, our chief one. *p.* 108

Reason is our guiding principle, and ought to be exerted as such. *p.* 109, 110

There are two things to be considered with respect to our guiding principle and our rule of conduct—Our sense of right and wrong,—and our sense of happiness—That these two do not disagree, shall be shewn afterwards. *p.* 110

But first let us consider our sense of right and wrong—whether we have such a sense or not is a question of fact—But that we have it is plain, for we are not only capable of electing, but of approving—These two are very different operations. *p.* 111

If we have an approving and disapproving sense, we have a moral sense, or a sense of right and wrong. *p.* 112

What are the qualities which excite approbation or disapprobation—Actions must be done with affection, freedom and reflexion, to excite approbation or condemnation. *p.* 112

Of such actions, veracity, candor, benevolence, *&c.* excite our approbation, and their contraries our disapprobation. *p.* 113, 114

Several arguments to prove we have a moral sense—from analogy,—for we have a sense of beauty in material forms. *p.* 115, 116, 117

—From languages, for they suppose it.   *p.* 118, 119

—From the polite arts, oratory, poetry, painting, *&c.* for they suppose it.
                                                         p. 119, 120

Without supposing it, to account for several phenomena, we must have recourse to very subtle reflexions of which the mind is not capable, and for which it hath not time.   *p.* 121, 122

We can no more be bribed to approve an action, than to assent to a proposition.   *p.* 123

Further reflexions on a moral sense—It is not worth while to dispute about a name, if the thing be owned.   *p.* 124, 125

And it must be owned by all who acknowledge moral differences of actions and characters.   *p.* 125

However, it is proper, nay, necessary to give this sense or faculty in our nature a distinguishing name—This is no less necessary than it is to give distinguishing names to our other senses and faculties.   *p.* 126, 127

That we are determined by pleasure and pain in all our motions, is true in a certain sense—But this general proposition is of little use in philosophy, till our pleasures are distinguished and classed.   *p.* 128

And our moral sense renders us capable of a peculiar set of them, the highest we are susceptible of, or can conceive.   *p.* 129

The cautiousness of the ancient moralists in using the words *good* and *evil* very commendable.   *p.* 130, 131, 132

If we have no moral sense, then we are only capable of computing our external interest or advantage.   *p.* 133

But if we have a moral sense, we are capable of rising higher, and taking in what is worthy and laudable in itself into the account.   *p.* 133, 134

If we would but try ourselves by proper questions, we should soon feel, that we have indeed a moral sense—

And it is absurd to suppose a moral sense, not to be from nature. Art cannot create.   *p.* 134, 135, 136, 137

A moral sense does not suppose innate ideas—But moral ideas are continually haunting our mind—Nature therefore hath not left us quite indifferent to virtue and vice—But our moral sense, like all our other faculties, must depend on our care to improve it.   *p.* 138, 139, 140

Hitherto then we have found our nature to be admirably well constituted with regard to virtue and vice—But, it remains to be enquired, how interest and virtue agree according to the constitution and laws of our nature.
                                                         p. 141

CHAPTER V.

Another class of laws. Those relative to interest, or private and publick good.   *p.* 141

First of all, the several enquiries about morals are classed.   *p.* 142, 143

Next, it is to be observed, that beauty is inseparably connected with utility throughout all nature—It is so in all the imitative arts—Because it is so in nature the standard of truth.   *p.* 144

It is so in our mundan system—and with regard to the bodies of all animals.   *p.* 145

It is so, and must be so with respect to the fabric of the human mind, affections, actions, and characters, and their effects.   *p.* 146

The proof of this must be fetched from the anatomy or texture of the mind—Lord *Shaftsbury*'s reasoning to prove it, is taken notice of as an example how enquiries into the human mind ought to be carried on.   *p.* 147, 148, 149, 150

Another train of reasoning to prove that virtue is private interest—and universally acknowledged to be so.   *p.* 151, 152, 153

Some observations on *Cicero*'s way of ascertaining human perfection and duty,—and then of proving that virtue is in all respects our truest interest.   *p.* 153, 154, 155, 156, 157

An observation upon other ancient arguments to prove that virtue is private good,—we are not made for sensual pleasures, but for those of the mind, or rational ones.   *p.* 158, 159

Man is made for exercise, and to acquire dominion over his mind, and all its appetites—In this our natural greatness of mind consists, and virtue alone can content this natural desire of power, and inclination to extend our capacity. Several observations to illustrate this.   *p.* 160, 161, 162

Some other considerations taken from ancient authors to prove, that virtue is man's supreme, nay, his only happiness,—and that virtue alone can be the reward of virtue.   *p.* 163, 164, 165, 166, 167, 168

Virtue is therefore private interest or good.   *p.* 170, 171

This chapter concludes with some reflexions on the debates among philosophers about the meaning of obligation.   *p.* 171, 172, 173

And then sums up all in a conclusion from the foregoing considerations concerning human nature and its maker, in Lord *Shaftsbury*'s words.   *p.* 174

Chapter VI.

Another class of laws. Those relative to society, or the dependence of human perfection and happiness on social union, and rightly confederated abilities and powers.   *p.* 175

A general view of our social make—Man is in as proper a sense made for society as any machine is for its end.   *p.* 176, 177

The fundamental error of *Hobbs* consists in his considering the desire of power, which is natural to man, as his only natural appetite or instinct.

p. 177

But our natural desire of power, as it is conjoined in our frame with other equally natural desires, is a most noble and useful instinct.   *p.* 178, 179,

180, 181

All our affections, not only the publick ones, but even the private, have a respect to society, and are formed with a view to it.   *p.* 181, 182

Society or variety of social happiness.   *p.* 183, 184

Requires variety of talents and characters.   *p.* 184

The exigences of our animal life require great diversity of powers and talents.   *p.* 185

Moral happiness requires the same diversity—A variety of different tempers and characters is requisite to various reflexions or modifications of social happiness; in like manner, as various textures of bodies are necessary to the different reflexions, refractions, and transmissions of light and heat, in which the beauty of the visible world consists.   *p.* 186, 187

All social virtues suppose mutual dependencies and wants, for they may be all reduced to *giving* and *receiving*.   *p.* 187, 188

Natural diversities make different materials for a variety of good, by our own improvement, or of our own acquisition by right social union.

p. 188, 189

Benevolence or publick affection naturally works in those proper proportions, which the general good of society requires—It operates like attraction in the material world.   *p.* 190

The notion of a publick interest is no sooner formed than due affection arises towards it—And our mind is so fitted by nature to form that notion, that we cannot avoid forming it.   *p.* 191, 192

But benevolence, like other affections, is liable to changes,—it may be diminished or strengthened.   *p.* 192, 193

It is difficult to determine the original force of any affection in our hearts—

But it cannot be asserted, that there is nothing social in our nature, without denying the most evident truths or facts.   *p.* 193, 194, 195

It is absurd to suppose social or any affection produced by art.

p. 196, 197

But it is proper to take notice of something that is yet more peculiarly the result of our social make,—which is the necessary dependence of our happiness and perfection as a kind, on right social union.   *p.* 198, 199

Some states are adjusted to one end, and some to another,—and every moral end, as well as every natural one, hath its natural, proper and necessary means by which alone it can be accomplished.   *p.* 200

Hence it is that politicks is a science,—or that the different effects of different constitutions or different internal principles of government, may be determined.   *p.* 201, 202

But nature could not have dealt more kindly with us than it hath done, by making us social creatures, and by pointing and prompting us to right union in order to our greatest happiness and perfection, as a kind, by our natural disposition to society, and by our moral sense of public good and order.

p. 202

Thus it plainly appears, how well we are constituted for procuring to ourselves that perfection and happiness, which must, in the nature of things, be the result of right union, or well-formed society.   *p.* 202

Chapter VII.

Another class of laws. Those relative to religion. Man is made for religion as well as for virtue.   *p.* 203

He can hardly avoid forming or receiving the idea of a supreme power, upon which he absolutely depends.   *p.* 204

And our moral sense, naturally leads us to ascribe not only intelligence, but the love of order, and the most perfect benignity of temper, to a first or original and independent mind.   *p.* 204, 205

The reasonings which lead us to these conclusions are natural to the human mind, if any sentiments or reasonings can be said to be such; or indeed any instinct or appetite be such.   *p.* 206

Whence then imposture and false religion—It took its rise with tyranny, or was promoted by it.   *p.* 207, 208

But no argument can be brought from hence against a moral sense in our nature.   *p.* 209, 210

Religion is natural to man,—and religious contemplation is a very pleasant exercise.   *p.* 211

And highly improving to virtue.   *p.* 212

But good affections may become too strong and vehement.—The love of mankind may degenerate or be misguided,—and religious admiration is apt to degenerate into certain excesses or extravagancies.   *p.* 212

If any other guide is set up in our mind superior to natural reason, and not to be tried by it, our whole frame is necessarily unhinged.   *p.* 213

But the genuine effects of true well-moderated devotion, are submission to providence, and activity in doing good.   *p.* 214

Thus, we see, we are made for religion as well as for virtue; and that indeed in our nature, religion and virtue are one and the same thing: it is the same disposition of the mind employed contemplatively in admiring and loving supreme virtue, and actively in imitating that model. The sum of religion and virtue, according to reason and revelation, is to love GOD and to love mankind: and these two dispositions must go together.   *p.* 214

CHAPTER VIII.

Here is given a table of the chief phenomena, good and bad belonging to the human system; or resulting from its contexture and situation.   *p.* 215, 216,
                                                                 217

All these phenomena are reducible to the excellent general laws which have been delineated, by which man is fitted and qualified for a very noble end and happiness.   *p.* 217

Wherefore there are no evils, absolutely considered, arising from our frame.   *p.* 218

If we judge in this case as we do in other like ones, we must conclude, that all our powers are given us for a very perfect and noble end.   *p.* 218

Indeed our moral sense cannot possibly be given us for any other reason, but to guide us to the right use of all our powers.   *p.* 218, 219

Our whole frame therefore is good—For all effects reducible to the laws of knowledge, to the laws of our social make, or to any other of the laws of our nature above explained,—must be sufficiently accounted for, if explication of phenomena hath any meaning at all.   *p.* 220

For all the preceeding reasonings about the fitness of laws go on in the same way that is admitted to be good in every other case,—in natural philosophy—The preceeding account of human nature is therefore strictly philosophical.   *p.* 220, 221

A brief recapitulation to prove this.   *p.* 221, 222

General conclusion concerning human nature, that tho' we are not the top of the creation, but are made lower than angels, yet we are crowned with glory and honour, and have a very noble dominion allotted to us, natural and moral.   *p.* 223

Man therefore is made for virtue, whether he is made to last for a short time or for ever—But before we proceed to enquire concerning his duration, it is proper to oppose to the preceeding account of man, such a state of mankind, as it is reasonable to suppose must have been the product of a malignant Creator, who had no sense of nor regard to virtue, or the proper good and perfection of moral beings.   *p.* 224, 225, 226

CHAPTER IX.

Let us now enquire what judgment ought to be formed concerning death— The phenomenon fairly stated—Futurity wisely hid from us.   *p.* 227, 228

Yet we have reason to infer, that death is not a dissolution of our moral powers—It is not analogous to our make to suppose that it is.   *p.* 229

But it is proper to consider this matter very fully and accurately—Our present connexion with a sensible or material world, by means of our bodies, is arbitrary, not necessary.   *p.* 230, 231

We may therefore survive such a connexion,—our perishing totally with our bodies, must be the effect of an arbitrary appointment that it shall be so.   *p.* 232

But there is no reason to apprehend such an annihilating or destroying humour in nature—The destruction of unthinking matter is not properly destruction—Wherefore the destruction of a perceiving being cannot be inferred from the destruction of matter.   *p.* 233

But there is no ground to think any particle of matter is ever destroyed: what we call so, is really but change of form—*a fortiori,* there is no reason to think any perceiving being is destroyed.   *p.* 234

All that can be inferred from death is, That a particular order, in which certain sensations are now conveyed into our minds, then ceases—Whence a destruction of all thinking powers cannot be deduced.   *p.* 234

There is no likeness, no parity between death and total destruction of our being, whatever view we take of it.   *p.* 235

The Objections of *Lucretius* and *Pliny* against immortality, absurdly suppose, that matter can think, or that we are wholly body—The facts only prove

a present dependence of our body and mind according to certain laws of
nature.   *p.* 237

But further, let us consider this is a very good first state for such a progressive being as man—And a first state cannot last always, but must give way
to another.   *p.* 238

It is therefore reasonable to think, that this state only ceases as the first state
of progressive beings ought to do.   *p.* 239

That our death is attended with pain, only proves, that the laws of union
with body continue to operate till the union is quite dissolved.   *p.* 239

There is a plain reason why there should be such a being in the scale of
life—But there is no reason to think it proper, that our present union with a
material world, should always continue, or be the only state in which our
moral powers are placed.   *p.* 240

Nay, it is evident, that union with body and a material world cannot always
last.   *p.* 241, 242

Hence, it is reasonable to conclude, that our moral powers, naturally capable of lasting for ever without wearing out, are only united with bodies for
a time, in order to the fulness of nature, and because it is a very proper first
state for our powers to be formed and improved in.   *p.* 242

Men must live upon earth by successive generations—Our earth could not
be rendered more capacious without altering our whole mundan system—
When our mundan system is able to hold out no longer, there is reason from
analogy to think it shall be succeeded by another proper to succeed to it, perhaps rising out of its ruins.   *p.* 243

But if so, we have yet better reason to think this is but our first state, which
shall be succeeded by one very proper to follow it.   *p.* 244

If mankind cease to be at death, there will necessarily be a void, a chasm
in nature—But we have reason to conclude from experience and analogy, that
fulness and coherence is the end of nature.   *p.* 245

This idea of the universe is natural to the mind; it greatly delights in it—
Wherefore it must be true—fulness in nature can only mean a progress toward
fulness, without any interruption or breach—which cannot be the case if man
is not immortal.   *p.* 246, 247

Hitherto we have only enquired what ought to be inferred from the course
of nature by analogy—But this course proves the Author of nature to be perfectly well disposed.   *p.* 247, 248

Let us therefore consider how the argument will stand, when instead of
nature, or the course of things, we say, the wise and good Author of nature—
Then the argument in the weakest state must stand thus; all looks well, upon

supposition that death is only a period to a first state, but it may be nothing else, nay, it looks like nothing else, and therefore it is probably nothing else.

p. 249

Several considerations add strength to this argument—We can only infer confusion and disorder, from disorder and confusion—But our present state is an excellent first state considered as such: it therefore bespeaks a good orderly future state to succeed it.   *p.* 250, 251

It is no objection against this reasoning that death comes upon men at all ages—For as this is the necessary effect of good present laws, so it may also be requisite to general good in a future state.   *p.* 252, 253

To imagine we are destroyed at death, is to think worse of the Author of nature than we can of any rational creature.   *p.* 253, 254

The greater good of the whole cannot make it necessary—Tis in vain to say, we who know but a small part cannot be judge of the whole.   *p.* 254

For we are able clearly to decide several truths with regard to right administration of a moral whole—As that the world or nature, must, in order to be perfect, be governed by good general laws.   *p.* 255

That no effects of good general laws are evils—That a whole cannot be perfect if any greater quantity of happiness could take place in it—That the good of a moral system ought to be preferred to the good of a merely animal system.   *p.* 256

The greater happiness of moral beings cannot require the destruction of moral powers,—or the discouragement of virtue in a future state,—far less the absolute misery of virtue—Nay, the general good of a moral system must make it necessary, that tried and improved virtue be promoted.   *p.* 257, 258

It cannot require that the present connexions of things should be changed in favour of vice—It cannot require that moral agents should become not such—And far less can it require, that moral agents well disposed and greatly improved, should be pushed backwards, and placed in disadvantageous circumstances for moral exercises, or virtuous improvements, and the enjoyments resulting from them.   *p.* 259

All these reasonings must hold good, if there be order in what we see at present, in that part chiefly wherein virtue is concerned. And if this state really be, as it is, a very proper first state for moral improvement.   *p.* 260

It may be objected, how can a present state be a school to form us for a quite different state—And therefore to clear up all difficulties, a few considerations are added to shew, that our present state is a very proper school for our formation, culture and discipline with regard to any state into which we may pass; however new it may be, or different from the present, and that with respect to our understanding or our will; with respect to science or temper; knowledge or virtue; our rational faculties, or our appetites, affections and passions.   *p.* 261, 262, 263, 264

To ask, why is not virtue completely happy here, or since it is not, why we ought from analogy to conclude a succeeding state of virtue shall be completely happy, is to ask, why the end does not precede the means, or the effect its cause; why education must precede perfection, or spring, harvest. The law here is, that we reap as we sow. And that it is reasonable to think is the universal law throughout moral systems—The law with regard to our future state—And where this law obtains the administration is just, it is perfect.   *p.* 265, 266, 267, 268, 269

Add to all this our natural desire and pre-sentiment of a future state—For there is no instance in nature of any merely animal appetite, or instinct made in vain; or to be disappointed.   *p.* 270, 271

Conclusion.

Man therefore is made (as all the better ancients ever believed and taught) for eternal progress in moral perfection and happiness, proportionally to his care and diligence to improve in it.   *p.* 272

The End of the FIRST PART.

THE CONTENTS

Digested into a Regular Summary.

PART II

Introduction.

How it is proposed to answer all objections.   *Page* 275

All objections which terminate in demanding an impossibility, are absurd.

p. 276

What the ancients meant by the inhability or obliquity of a subject, or necessity of nature.   *p.* 276

Such an inhability or necessity does not suppose any limitation upon the divine, creating power.   *p.* 277

All objections which terminate in demanding a change to the worse, are absurd—They do ultimately terminate in demanding an impossibility.

p. 278, 279

CHAPTER I.

Some objections against man, are really objections against his perfection,— for all our powers, dispositions and affections are so many capacities of perfection and happiness.   *p.* 280

So are all the laws relative to their improvement or degeneracy—The law of habits in particular, which is so extensive.   *p.* 281

The objections against man's imperfections are no less absurd,—they know no stop.   *p.* 282, 283

They really demand a physical impossibility.   *p.* 284

Hence we may see, that the only question concerning man must be, "Whether being naturally qualified for a very noble end, he does not deserve his place in the rising scale of life and perfection?"   *p.* 285

Which he certainly does,—or plainly appears to do, in whatever light we consider his powers and affections.   *p.* 286, 287, 288, 289

Chapter II.

The objection taken from the prevalence of vice considered—Not so much vice in the world as is generally imagined.   *p.* 290

In consequence of the excellent laws of our nature, some vices (morally speaking) are absolutely unavoidable,—because narrow views and wrong affections of ideas, are hardly avoidable.   *p.* 291, 292

But if vice once enters it must spread.   *p.* 292, 293, 294

No objection can be brought from hence which does not terminate in an absurdity.   *p.* 294, 295

Illustration.   *p.* 296, 297

Vices are really but the corruptions, degeneracies, or abuses of good and useful affections.   *p.* 298

Some are misguidances of self-love, which is a very necessary principle in our frame.   *p.* 299

This was the opinion of the best ancient moralists.   *p.* 299

—Who set us an excellent example of the best manner of confutation, even in questions of the greatest importance.   *p.* 300

As does Lord *Shaftsbury* in several instances well worthy our consideration and imitation.   *p.* 301

But more vices are the misguidances or degeneracies of benevolent affections themselves—Instances from *Shaftsbury* to prove this.   *p.* 302, 303, 304, 305

Nature could not possibly have done more to preserve us from degeneracy and corruption, or vice, than it has done,—for the original forces of affections stand right in us.   *p.* 306, 307

Illustration.   *p.* 308, 309, 310

And nature hath given us a guiding principle,—which acquires strength in the properest manner.   *p.* 311, 312

Illustration.   *p.* 313

If it be a perfection to have natural freedom and power, it must be a perfection to have moral freedom and power—But none call the first into question.   *p.* 313, 314, 315

Reason, as such, must depend upon culture.   *p.* 316, 317, 318

We may as well pretend to infer from vices, which prevail among mankind, that there is no such thing as a principle of self-love in our nature, as that there is no such thing as a principle of benevolence in it—But none do the first. *p.* 319

This reasoning applied to ignorance—of the natural—and of the moral world. *p.* 320, 321

This reasoning applied to tyranny. *p.* 322

—and to superstition, which is found to go hand in hand with tyranny. *p.* 323, 324

Without a mixture of good and evil, there could be no place or room for prudence,—that is, for good and bad choice. *p.* 325, 326

Hence we see the necessity of evils,—or, at least, of pleasures far inferior to other pleasures, and so comparatively evils. *p.* 327, 328

Several virtues presuppose not only physical but moral evils. *p.* 329, 330, 331, 332

Every state of the body politic, as well as of the natural body, is incident to particular diseases or vices. *p.* 333

Some reflexions on the vices to which an opulent flourishing state is subject. *p.* 334, 335, 336, 337

Men may chuse their state, but every one hath its natural, necessary attendants and consequences. *p.* 338, 339, 340

Yet in declaiming against these vices several things are misrepresented—Luxury, for example, is declaimed against in a very vague manner. *p.* 341

The polite arts are no part of luxury,—and they do not effeminate a people.—But other arts must be united with them to render a nation equally brave and polite. *p.* 342, 343

Upon the whole, it is virtue alone that is the cement of society—'Tis virtue, and political wisdom, which educe good out of moral evil. *p.* 344

—Even as excrements may be rendered useful. *p.* 345

Supposing vices to be necessary, yet since good may be educed out of them by virtue and political wisdom, the wisdom of the moral world will stand on the same footing as the wisdom of the natural world. *p.* 346

But vices are in no proper sense mechanical effects, but of a very different nature. *p.* 347

CHAPTER III.

The objections taken from physical evils considered.—These evils classed. *p.* 348, 349

Unless there be a mixture of good and evil, there can be no room for right and wrong conduct, prudent and imprudent choice. *p.* 350

Physical evils cannot but take place in a world filled with variety of beings, if each being must have its particular structure subject to general ascertainable laws.   *p.* 351

We must be able to say with assurance, that we have quite exhausted the science of nature, before we can affirm, that several evils we complain of, are absolutely unavoidable by prudence and art.   *p.* 352

But which is of principal consideration, all physical evils proceed from the uniform operation of good general laws.   *p.* 353

Illustration.   *p.* 354

Let those who object against physical evils, as absolute evils, well consider the excellent concatenation of things natural and moral, or how all things hang together in nature.   *p.* 355, 356

An illustration of this taken from an author,—whose principles have no necessary connexion with that kind of reasoning.   *p.* 357, 358, 359

My Lord *Shaftsbury* shews us how such principles ought to be refuted— And his refutation is here inserted, because it is of great moment to my argument, or to prove the sociality of our make.   *p.* 360, 361, 362

Such evils as result from social dependence and union, are really goods.
                                                                          p. 363

Vices punish themselves according to the natural course of things.
                                                                          p. 364

Several goods must fall to the share of the vicious, according to the excellent general law of power and industry.   *p.* 365

(*Here in the marginal notes, a treatise of* Plutarch *is referred to, where this question is fully handled,* "Why the wicked are not visibly punished here in an extraordinary manner?" *He hath quite exhausted that subject: and many of his reasonings coincide with the Scripture-reasons.*)

Vice always produces misery in some manner and degree.—Much more of what is called *misfortune,* is owing to imprudence or vice than is commonly imagined, or, at least, duly attended to—History and poetry prove this.
                                                                     p. 366, 367

Reflexions on the imitative arts to illustrate this.   *p.* 368, 369

In objections against providence, external goods and evils are much overrated.   *p.* 370, 371, 372

External goods depend in general on the law of industry, which is an excellent institution of nature.—But they alone, or without virtue, cannot make man happy—Such is his frame.   *p.* 373, 374, 375

The punishment of vice, as well as the reward of virtue, is wisely left in some measure to society.   *p.* 375, 376

Unless we suppose a mixture of goods and evils dependent on other causes than virtue,—or if we suppose external motives to virtue bestowed in a distinguishing, remarkable manner,—Virtue could not be tried as it ought to be in its first state of education and discipline, and pure love of virtue for its own sake could not be acquired,—for which end we are framed and placed as we are.   *p.* 377, 378

The evils which happen to the virtuous, at the same time that they only happen in consequence of excellent general laws, afford occasions and materials of great virtues,—which are their own reward.   *p.* 379, 380

Some reflexions on the arguments for a future state from what is called *present inequality with respect to virtue and vice.*   *p.* 381

The argument stated in its true light,—and it is indeed demonstrative.
                                                                 p. 382, 383

CHAPTER IV.

A complex view of the objections made against our frame and situation, in which all the parts of our constitution are shewn to be admirably adjusted one to another,—And that no change can be proposed or imagined, which is not either physically absurd,—or morally so,—tending to introduce an alteration much to the worse.   *p.* 385, 386, 387, 388, 389, 390, 391, 392, 393,
                                                                 394, 395, 396

Conclusion.

A review of the manner in which we have proceeded in this enquiry—Why we have not entered into the examination of particular characters.
                                                                 p. 397, 398

It is enough for our purpose to have accounted for all the powers and affections of which all the different characters among mankind are formed,—and for all the laws according to which our affections are variously mixed and compounded, *&c.*   *p.* 399

As in the material world, it is sufficient to delineate the general laws from which phenomena result, so here.   *p.* 400

And as, in the one case, so in the other, so soon as we are able to consider phenomena, as resulting from general laws, which make a whole, we are no more startled at any particular appearances,—but immediately discern order.
                                                                 p. 401

—'Tis to help one to take such an united view of mankind, that is, of the frame and constitution of human nature, that the principal powers and laws of powers belonging to it have been delineated in this Essay.—For this all is accounted for that is to be accounted for; namely, the powers and their laws constituting man, and the circumstances calling them forth into action; or, affording them means, subjects, materials, and occasions of exerting and grat- ifying themselves.   *p.* 402

If the contriver and producer of a system be perfect, the system must be perfect—But many arguments *a priori,* prove the Author of the universe to be an all perfect mind.   *p.* 403

Some observations upon these arguments to shew they are not so abstruse as is said by some, but that they are easy consequences necessarily following from a few self-evident principles.   *p.* 404, 405

Arguments therefore *a priori* and *a posteriori,* exactly agree or tally together, to prove the universal system, of which we are a part, to be perfectly well constituted, and under an infinitely wise and good administration.   *p.* 406

Revelation concurs with them, and is attended with a truly philosophical evidence that proves its truth,—and it makes no encroachment upon the province or exercises of reason.   *p.* 407

Instead of a recapitulation, the Contents being digested into a regular sum- mary to serve that purpose; another view of human nature is laid before the reader, in twelve propositions, which sets the same truths that have been al- ready proved in a light somewhat new.   *p.* 408, 409, 410, 411, 412, 413, 414, 415, 416, 417, 418, 419, 420, 421, 422

An excellent hymn in praise of the creation quoted from an ancient writer.   *p.* 423

A beautiful reasoning about immortality quoted from another.
                                                               p. 424, 425

Some observations on the account given us of a future state by the chris- tian religion.   *p.* 426, 427

The design of this essay being in the text to prove the truth of this prop- osition, "That man is well made for immortal progress in virtue, which is excellently well taken care of and provided for here, and from thence to infer a future happy state for the virtuous"—And by the marginal notes to "prove the antiquity and universality of this persuasion"; some reflexions are made on the opinion of those who assert the ancients were not able to know any thing distinctly of GOD or a future state; or, at least, have produced no con- clusive arguments on these subjects.   *p.* 428, 429, 430, 431, 432

Some Corolaries are added relating to the improvements of moral philosophy and right education, which obviously follow from the sketch of moral philosophy delineated in this essay, and well deserve the serious attention of all who have the best interests of mankind seriously at heart.

p. 433 to the end.

The treatise ends with a quotation from *Cicero,* to prove that unactive knowledge is of little use in comparison of that which prompts to the virtuous activity for which we are made—And another, that contains the substance of what we have proved concerning man, most elegantly expressed from the same Author.

FINIS.

The Principles of Moral Philosophy

<1>

∞ PART I ∞

Introduction

Every one who knows what natural philosophy is, or how it proceeds in its enquiries will easily conceive what moral philosophy must mean; and how it likewise ought to be pursued: for all enquiries into fact, reality, or any part of nature must be set about, and carried on in the same way; and an enquiry into human nature is as much an enquiry into fact, as any question about the frame and texture (for instance) of any plant, or of the human body. <2>

Natural philosophy distinguish'd from moral.

The objects of science are justly divided into corporeal, or sensible ones; and those which not being perceived by the outward senses, but by reflexion on the mind itself and its inward operations, are therefore called intellectual or moral objects. Hence the consideration of the former is stiled Physiology, or Natural philosophy; and that of the other is called Rational, or Moral philosophy. But however philosophy may be divided; nothing can be more evident, than, that the study of nature, whether in the constitution and oeconomy of the sensible world, or in the frame and government of the moral, must set out from the same first principles, and be carried on in the same method of investigation, induction, and reasoning; since both are enquiries into facts or real constitutions.

But both are enquiries into fact or nature.

What is natural philosophy, how is it defined? or, how are its researches carried on? By it is understood an enquiry into the sensible world: that is "into the general laws, according to which its appearances are produced; and into the beauty, order, and good which these general laws

Natural philosophy described.

47

The principles it presupposes and proceeds upon in its enquiries.

produce." And therefore in such an enquiry the following maxims are justly laid down as the foundations on which all its reasonings are built; or as the first principles from which all its conclusions are inferred; and without supposing which it cannot proceed one step.

First principle.

I. That if the corporeal world be not governed by general laws, it cannot be the object of enquiry or science; and far less of imitation by arts, since imitation necessarily presupposes knowledge of the object imitated; and science presupposes a certain determinate object; or fixed ascertainable relations and connexions of things. Upon the contrary supposition the corporeal world must be absolutely unintelligible. Nature, in order to be understood by us, must always speak the same language to us: it <3> must therefore steadily observe the same general laws in its operations, or work uniformly and according to stated, invariable methods and rules. Those terms, order, beauty, general good, and a whole, which are too familiar to philosophers, to need any definition, or explication, plainly include in their meaning, analogy and constancy; uniformity amidst variety; or in other words, the regular observance of general, settled laws in the make and oeconomy, production and operations, or effects of any object to which they are ascribed. Wherever order, fixed connexions, or general laws and unity of design take place, there is certainty in the nature of such objects; and so far therefore knowledge may be acquired. But where these do not obtain, there can be nothing but unconnected independent parts; all must be confusion and disorder; and consequently such a loose disjointed heap of things must be an inexplicable chaos. In one word, science, prudence, government, imitation, and art, necessarily suppose the prevalence of general laws throughout all the objects in nature to which they reach. No being can know itself, project or pursue any scheme, or lay down any maxims for its conduct; but so far as its own constitution is certain; and the connexion of things relative to it are fixed and constant; for so far only, are things ascertainable; and therefore so far only, can rules be drawn from them.

"Nature's[a] operating according to general laws (says a very ingenious

a. Principles of human knowledge. [George Berkeley, *A Treatise Concerning the Principles of Human Knowledge* (1710, 1734). The quote is based mainly on A.151.]

philosopher) is so necessary for letting us into the secret of nature, and for our guidance in the affairs of life, that without it, all reach and compass of thought, all human sagacity could serve to no manner of purpose: it were even impossible there should be any such faculties or powers in the mind. It is <4> this alone, gives us that foresight which enables us to regulate our actions for the benefit of life: and without this, we should be eternally at a loss; we could not know how to act any thing that might procure us the least pleasure, or save us from the least pain. That food nourishes, sleep refreshes, and fire warms us; that to sow in the seed-time, is the way to reap in harvest; that to give application is the way to improve and arrive at perfection in knowledge, or in any moral virtue; and in general, that to obtain such or such ends, such or such means are conducive; all this we know, and only can know, by the observation of the settled laws of nature, without which we should be all in uncertainty and confusion, and a grown man no more know how to manage himself in the affairs of life, than an infant just born."

This first principle in natural philosophy, is therefore indisputable. "That without the prevalence of general laws there can be no order; and consequently no foresight, no science: and that as all appearances in the corporeal world, which are reducible to general laws are explicable, so such as are not, are utterly inexplicable." Or in other words, "such effects as are not always produced in the same way and method, and have always the same consequences and influences, are quite anomalous; they cannot be reduced to any rule or order, and for that reason, no conclusion can be inferred from them." 'Tis only connexions which take place constantly in the same invariable manner that are ascertainable; or that can lay a foundation for science Theoretical or Practical.

II. Now those are justly called by philosophers, general laws in the sensible world. To which many effects are conformable. Or which, in other words, are observed to prevail and operate uni-<5>formly in it; and regularly to produce like appearances. Thus, for instance, gravitation is concluded to be a general law throughout our mundan system, because all bodies are found to have gravity; not one body within the reach of our observation does not shew that quality: but even the most remote ones we are capable of observing, are found to operate according to it; that

Second principle.

is, their appearances are reducible to it, as its natural and necessary effects.

This is very justly inferred, because to say, that analogous, or like appearances are not produced according to the same general law; or that they do not proceed from the same general principle, is indeed to say, that they are and are not analogous. Wherever we find analogy, or similarity of effects, there we find the same law prevailing; or so far do we find particular instances of the same property or law; or of the same method of production and operation[a] in nature. All this is really no more than asserting, for example, that whatever is produced conformably to a known principle, called gravity, is produced conformably to that principle. This second maxim in natural philosophy is therefore likewise indisputable.

"That those are general laws in a system, which prevail and operate uniformly in that system; or to which many effects in it are reducible and none are repugnant." Or in other words, "those effects, however remote from us the objects are, to which they belong, may be justly attributed to that law or property, to which they are reducible, as its natural effects, that is known to be universal, so far as experience can reach; <6> for this very reason that such a known property being sufficient to produce them, is sufficient to account for them."[b]

Third principle.   III. But in the third place, "Those general laws of the corporeal world are good laws, which by their steady and uniform prevalency produce its good, beauty, and perfection in the whole." Thus, for instance, gravitation must be a good general law in the sensible or material world, if its uniform operation be conducive to the greatest good, beauty, and perfection of that system. 'Tis needless to define terms to natural phi-

---

a. Here I multiply words, because all these are used promiscuously by philosophers. See the preface to Sir *Isaac Newton*'s Principia, by *Rog. Cottes,* and the Principia, *Lib.* 3. Regulae philosophandi. [Isaac Newton, *Philosophiae naturalis principia mathematica.* First published in 1687; the second and third editions (1713 and 1726) were produced with the assistance of Roger Cotes (1682–1716), who also wrote a preface. See Newton's *Philosophiae naturalis principia mathematica: The Third Edition (1726) with Variant Readings,* ed. Alexandre Koyré and I. Bernard Cohen, 2 vols. (Cambridge: Cambridge University Press, 1972).]

b. See *Newton*'s Principia, Lib. 3. Regulae philosophandi.

losophers, which are so commonly used by them; and if these terms have any meaning, the following argument must hold good, "All the interests of intelligent beings require that general laws should prevail, so far as they are concerned; nay, without general laws, there could be no union, no general connexion, and consequently no general beauty, good, or perfection, but all must be tumult, incoherence, and disorder." It is therefore absolutely good and fit, that general laws should take place; and those laws must be good in a system, which produce in the sum of things, the greater coherence, order, beauty, good, and perfection of that system.

Now from this it necessarily follows, that no particular effects, which flow from good general laws, can be evils absolutely considered, that is, with regard to the whole. No effect, for example, of gravitation can be evil, if gravitation be a good general law in the sense above explained.

There is therefore a third maxim in philosophy, which is beyond all doubt. "That all the effects of general laws which are good with respect to a <7> whole, are good absolutely considered, or referred to that whole."

General conclusion concerning natural philosophy.

We may then very justly conclude in general, that all effects or appearances in the natural world, are sufficiently explained and accounted for in natural philosophy, which are reduced to good general laws, as so many particular instances of their uniform operation; and that both physically and morally. They are sufficiently explained and accounted for in the physical sense, by being reduced to general laws: for what else is the physical knowledge of a fact in the sensible world, but the knowledge of an effect itself, in its progress, qualities, and influences: or in other words, the knowledge of the manner or order in which it is produced, and in which it operates on other things relating to it; the knowledge of the laws according to which it is produced, works, and is worked upon?

Such effects as are reduced to general laws, are accounted for physically.

"All philosophers acknowledge (says an excellent one) that the first cause, or producer of the sensible world, must be a mind, whose will gives subsistence and efficacy to all its laws and connexions. The difference there is between natural philosophers and other men with regard to their knowledge of natural phenomena, consists not in an exacter knowledge of the efficient cause, that produces them; for that can be no other than

They are accounted for morally, if the laws they are reducible to be good.

the will of a spirit: but only in a greater largeness of comprehension whereby analogies, harmonies, and agreements are discovered in the works of nature and the particular effects are explained, that is, reduced to general laws."

But it is needless to dwell longer on this conclusion, since in the language of all natural philosophers,[a] those effects are reckoned to be fully explained in the physical way, which are shown to be particu-<8>lar instances of a general law that had been already inferred from a sufficient variety of fair and unexceptionable experiments: and those effects only are said to be unexplained, which are not yet reduced to any known law, or the law of which is not yet understood and ascertained.

Such effects are sufficiently explained, and accounted for morally, when they are reduced to general laws which are proved to be good in the whole; because they are thus shown to proceed from laws that are morally good and just.

Natural philosophy in accounting for final causes, coincides with moral philosophy.

Tho' phisiology be distinguished from moral philosophy, yet it was needless to suggest to any class of readers, before we used the words, *beauty, order, good* and *perfection,* that these are terms relative to beings capable of pleasure and pain, and of perceiving good order and beauty; or that laws cannot be said to be good or bad, right or wrong, beautiful or imperfect, but with respect to minds or perceiving beings: for pain or pleasure, good or ill, convenience or inconvenience, beauty or deformity, evidently presuppose perceptive faculties. On the one hand, an unperceiveable world cannot be the object of knowledge, or enjoyment of any kind; and, on the other, 'tis perceiving beings alone that can enjoy, or to whom existence can be happiness. But from this, it follows, that tho' natural philosophy be commonly distinguished from moral; all the conclusions in natural philosophy, concerning the order, beauty, and perfection of the material world, belong properly to moral philosophy; being inferences that respect the contriver, maker, and governor of the world, and other moral beings capable of understanding its wise, good

a. See Sir *Isaac Newton*'s principia. Dr. *John Clark*'s sermons on the origin of evil. The characteristicks, &c.

and beautiful administration, and of being variously affected by its laws and connexions.

In reality, when natural philosophy is carried so far as to reduce phenomena to good general laws, it becomes moral philosophy; and when it stops <9> short of this chief end of all enquiries into the sensible or material world, which is, to be satisfied with regard to the wisdom of its structure and oeconomy; it hardly deserves the name of philosophy in the sense of *Socrates, Plato,* Lord *Verulam,*[21] *Boyle, Newton,* and the other best moral or natural philosophers.[a]

Having thus briefly shown what natural philosophy proposes to do, and upon what foundations it proceeds in establishing any conclusions; let us now see what moral philosophy must be. It is distinguished from phisiology, (as has been observed) because it enquires chiefly about objects not perceiveable by means of our outward organs of sense, but by internal feeling or experience; such as are all our moral powers and faculties, dispositions and affections, the power of comparing ideas, of reasoning or inferring consequences, the power of contracting habits, our sense of beauty and harmony, natural or moral, the desire of society, &c. Even these, however, may very properly be called parts of nature; and by whatever name, they, or the knowledge of them be called, 'tis obvious, that an enquiry about any of them, and the laws and connexions established by the author of nature, with regard to any of them, is as much a question of natural history or of fact, as an enquiry about any of our organs of sense, or about the constitution of any material object whatsoever, and the laws relating to it. And therefore the same principles just mentioned as the foundation of all enquiries and reasonings in natural philosophy, must likewise take place, and be admitted in moral philosophy; that is, in all enquiries and reasonings concerning the human

Moral philosophy described.

It must presuppose and proceed upon the same principles.

a. See Sir *Isaac Newton*'s *Opticks, l.* 3. *p.* 345, and *Plato*'s *Phaedon;* where we see what *Socrates* thought natural philosophy ought to aim at, by what he says of the vanity of the natural philosophy of *Anaxagoras.* [Plato, *Phaedo,* 97C–99E.]

21. Francis Bacon, first Baron Verulam and Viscount St. Albans (1561–1626), English philosopher and statesman, whose works include *The Advancement of Learning* (1605) and *Novum Organum* (1620).

mind, its <10> powers, faculties, dispositions and affections, and the laws relative to them, as well as in all enquiries into the properties of a body.

For these prin-
ciples are of an
universal
nature.

In truth, these principles must necessarily take place in the explication of any piece of nature that can be understood or explained. They are principles of a general nature, which, if they be true in any case, must be universally true; and therefore they must be universally admitted, with regard to every constitution, system or whole, corporeal or incorporeal, natural or moral, that is, body or mind. Whence it results, that with respect to the human mind; to the frame of any mind whatsoever, or in general with respect to any moral system it must be true.[a]

a. How an enquiry into human nature or natural philosophy ought to be carried on, we learn from *Cicero de Finibus*. for tho' in that treatise, different systems are represented and defended, yet it is unanimously agreed amongst all the interlocutors in these dialogues, that the natural end for which man is made, can only be inferred from the consideration of his natural faculties and dispositions as they make one whole; even as we can only know the nature of any animate or inanimate whole; of a vine, for instance, by enquiring into its structure or constitution. This point is argued in all these books at great length. See a fine description of moral philosophy in *Persius Sat. 3.*

> Discite, O miseri, & causas cognoscite rerum
> Quid sumus & quidnam victuri gignimur, ordo
> Quis datus, aut metu qua mollis flexus & unde:
> Quis modus argento, quid fas optare, quid asper
> Utile nummus habet; patriae carisque propinquis
> Quantum elargiri deceat: quam te deus esse
> Jussit, & humana qua parte locatus es in re.

[Persius, *Satires,* III.66–72: "Come and learn, o miserable souls, and be instructed in the causes of things: learn what we are, and for what sort of lives we were born; what place was assigned to us at the start; how to round the turning-post gently, and from what point to begin the turn; what limit should be placed on wealth; what prayers may rightfully be offered; what good there is in fresh-minted coin; how much should be spent on country and on your dear kin; what part God has ordered you to play, and at what point of the human commonwealth you have been stationed." *Juvenal and Persius,* trans. G. G. Ramsay, rev. ed., Loeb Classical Library (London: Heinemann; Cambridge: Harvard University Press, 1940).]

I. That unless it be so constituted and governed, that all the effects and appearances belonging to it, are the effects of general laws, it must be absolutely unintelligible; it must be complete confusion, irregularity and disorder; it cannot have a certain and determinate nature, but must be made up of disanalo-<11>gous, separate, incoherent parts, and operate in a desultory, inconstant manner: that is, it is not a whole; and cannot be the object of government or art, because it cannot be the object of knowledge: for all that can be known of it in such a case, is, that nothing can be ascertained about it; or that it is a *Proteus,* whose changes are without rule, and therefore are absolutely unascertainable.[22]

First principle of moral philosophy.

II. Those must be received as general laws or principles in a moral frame or constitution, which are found by experience to operate uniformly or invariably in that system. Thus, for instance, that habits are contracted by repeated acts, may be justly said to be a general law in our frame, because this law has its effects uniformly and invariably in our natures; or many effects do evidently show a relation to that law as their common source and principle; and not one effect in human nature is repugnant to it; for, in like manner, is gravitation concluded to be a general law in the sensible world.

Second principle.

III. Those must be good principles or laws in the constitution of a mind, or in any moral whole, which are conducive by their steady and uniform operation and prevalency to the greater good, beauty, and perfection of that whole in the sum of things. And therefore no effects which flow from such laws can be evils absolutely considered, or with respect to the whole. Thus the above-mentioned law of habits, must be a good general law in the constitution of the human mind, if its general tendency or influence be contributive to the greater good of the human mind in the sum of things; and no effects of that principle can be absolutely evil; because it is fit and good, that general laws should take place; and those

Third principle.

22. In Greek legend, Proteus was the old man of the sea, who was given the gift of prophecy by the god Poseidon. Proteus assumed different shapes in order to escape prophesying.

must be good general laws, which are good in the whole, or conducive to the greater order, beauty, and perfection of a whole. <12>

Moral effects are sufficiently explained and accounted for physically and morally, by being reduced to good general laws.

From all which it must necessarily follow, that all those effects, with regard to any moral constitution, are fully explained and accounted for physically and morally, which are reduced to such general laws as have been mentioned, as so many particular instances of their uniform and general prevalency.

To know any moral object physically, can be nothing else but to know what it is, and how it is constituted; or to know its parts, and those references of parts to one another, which make it a certain determinate whole, that works and is operated upon in certain determinable ways.

And to know the final cause, or moral fitness of any constitution, can be nothing else, but to know what good end in the sum of things, all its parts, and all their mutual respects, with all the laws and connexions relative to it, tend to produce. In fine, as different beings as a man and a tree are, yet the knowledge of man and the knowledge of a tree must mean the same kind of knowledge; in either case it is to know what the being is, and to what end it is adapted by its make and texture, and in consequence of the laws and connexions upon which it any wise depends.

Hence we see how moral philosophy ought to be pursued, and how it will stand on the same footing with natural philosophy.

All this is too evident to be longer insisted upon. And what is the result of all that has been said? Is it not, that such moral appearances as are reducible to good general laws, will stand upon the same footing in moral philosophy, that those appearances in the natural world do in natural philosophy, which are reducible to good general laws? And that in order to bring moral philosophy, or the knowledge of the moral world, upon the same footing with natural philosophy, or the knowledge of the material world, as it now stands; we must enquire into moral phenomena, in the same manner as we do into physical ones: that is, we must endeavour to find out by experience the good general laws to <13> which they are reducible. For this must hold good in general, that so far as we are able to reduce appearances to a good general law, so far are we able to explain them or account for them. As phenomena which are not the effects of general laws, are in the nature of things absolutely unexplicable; so those which are, can only be explained by reducing them to the general laws of which they are the effects. "Explaining or accounting for phenomena can mean nothing else; it is not indeed now pretended by any philosopher to mean any thing else."

This conclusion manifestly ensues from what has been said. But lest any one should be startled at an attempt to treat effects in the same manner, which are evidently of so different natures, as corporeal and moral effects certainly are; or lest any one should have imagined that general laws can only take place with regard to matter and motion, and consequently, that an essay to explain moral appearances by general laws, must involve in it all the absurdity of an attempt to handle effects, which are not mechanical or material, as if they were such: to prevent all such objections, and to proceed more distinctly and surely in this essay, let us just observe here, that though no two things can be more different than a thinking being and a corporeal one; or than moral powers and operations are from passive unperceiving objects, and their qualities and effects; yet the exercises of all the moral powers, dispositions and affections of minds, as necessarily presuppose an established order of nature, or general laws settled by the Author of nature with respect to them; as the exercises of our bodily senses about qualities and effects of corporeal beings, do with regard to them. As we could neither procure nor avoid, by our will and choice, any sensation of our sight, touch, or any other of our senses, had not nature established a certain order, with respect <14> to the succession or conveyance of our sensations, or the methods in which they are produced in us; so in like manner, we could neither acquire knowledge of any kind, contract habits, or attain to any moral perfection whatsoever; unless the Author of our nature had fixed and appointed certain laws relating to our moral powers, and their exercises and acquisitions. Being able to attain to science, to arts, to vertues, as necessarily presupposes a fixed and appointed road to virtue, &c. as being able to move our hands or limbs, does an established order of nature, with respect to these motions, and the sensations resulting from them, or attainable by them.

A prejudice that may arise from treating natural philosophy in this manner removed.

Moral powers and the exercises of moral powers, necessarily suppose and require general laws.

We are not
more certain
that we have
sensations,
than we are
certain that we
have power, or
a sphere of
activity. We are not more certain, that sensations are conveyed into or impressed upon our minds, by means of certain organs of sensation in a certain order, than we are sure that we have a certain extent of dominion, or a certain sphere of activity and power allotted to us by nature: that is to say, that certain effects, both in the corporeal and moral world, are made to depend, as to their existence or non-existence, upon our will, that they should exist or not exist. That we have such a power, both with regard to several actions of our body and of our mind, is plain matter of experience.

It is not
disputed. There is indeed no dispute about this kind of liberty or dominion belonging to man: but how far it extends, is another question, to be considered afterwards. Now wherever this liberty or dominion obtains, or whatever are its bounds, however wide, or however narrow and stinted it may be, this is certain, that so far as it extends, it necessarily presupposes certain laws of nature relating to it; or to speak more properly, constituting it. For this is no more than saying, that did not fire gently warm and cruelly burn, according to certain fixed laws ascertainable by us, we could not know how to warm ourselves without burning: and by parity of <15> reason, were not knowledge, habits, and moral improve-But power, and
a sphere of
activity, cannot
take place but
where general
laws obtain.ments, acquirable in a certain fixed way, we could not acquire them or attain to them. That is, we could have no liberty, no dominion, no sphere of activity or power, neither in the natural nor moral world: or in other words, either with regard to objects of sense, or moral objects, but upon supposition, that the natural and moral world are governed by general laws; or so far as they are so governed.

  If it could be proved that we have no dominion, no power properly so called, assigned to us by nature, that would not prove us to be mere stocks, mere pieces of mechanism; since even upon that supposition, this essential difference would still remain between material objects and us, that we are conscious, whereas the latter are quite void of perception. But on the other hand, if we really have a certain sphere of activity, in the sense above defined (as we most certainly have to a very considerable extent) this sphere of activity must be allotted to us by our Maker; and it necessarily supposes, so far as it extends, a certain fixed dependance

of objects upon our wills as to their existence or non-existence, conformably to which, and not otherwise, we may exercise that dominion.

The question about liberty and necessity has been violently agitated
among metaphysicians almost in all ages; but it no ways concerns this
present enquiry, that I should enter any further into it than just to observe, 1. That whatever way it may be determined in *abstract metaphysical
speculation,* this fact remains indisputable, that many objects depend
upon our will, as to their existence or non-existence, many objects without the mind as well as in it. And all such objects are εφ ημιν, that is,
they are put by nature within our power, in any sense, that any thing
can be said to be dependent on a being, within its power, or at its option
and disposal. <16> Such ways of speaking are of universal use and extent:
none are more such: but to say that such phrases, received in all languages, and universally understood, have no meaning at all, is to assert
an absurdity no less gross than this; that men may discourse, hold correspondence, and be influenced and determined in their correspondence
with one another, without understanding one another, without any ideas
at all. Common language is built upon fact, or universal feeling. And
every one understands what it is to be free, to have a thing in his power,
at his command, or dependent upon him. It is only such philosophers,
who seeking the knowledge of human nature, not from experience, but
from I know not what subtle theories of their own invention, depart
from common language, and therefore are not understood by others,
and sadly perplex and involve themselves. But, which is more, nothing
can be more certain than that pains and pleasures are the consequences
of certain actions; may be foreseen by us; and may be avoided or obtained accordingly, as we act in such or such a manner. But if this fact,
which is matter of universal experience, be admitted to be true, we are
certainly in respect of all such pains and pleasures, free. That is, having,
or not having them, depends absolutely on our exerting ourselves to have
them or not to have them, according to the connections of nature: so
that, whether the constitution of nature be fortuitous, necessary, or the
free choice of a free being, we are free, and have power; or our happiness
and misery, as far as the connection of these with our actions reaches,

Some remarks on the contro- versy about lib- erty and necessity.

totally depends upon ourselves. If a fact be certain, there is no reasoning against it; but every reasoning, however specious it may be, or rather, however subtle and confounding, if it be repugnant to fact, must be sophistical. And the fact just now mentioned is as <17> certain, as any matter of experience or consciousness can be.

2. Any reasoning from which it follows that men can neither deserve blame nor praise for their actions, and that it is needless for us to take care either to procure goods, or avoid evils, must be false; because it leads to a very absurd and fatal mistake in life and conduct. But truth cannot lead to absurdity or error. For this reason, such arguments were called by the antients λογοι αργοι,[23] *ignavae rationes*[a] Sophisms that lead to

---

a. See *Cicero de fato,* Nec nos impediat illa ignava ratio quae dicitur, appellatur enim αργος λογος, cui si pareamus nihil agamus in vita, &c. So *Plutarch de fato,* Nam istae argutiunculae quae ignava ratio appellantur, revera fallaces sunt conclusiunculae è disputatione de fato tractae. Where the same author observes, that *Fate* properly signifies, Leges quas de universi natura deus sanxit, animis immortalibus praesertim.—Legem appellari comitem naturae universi, secundum quam omnia quae fiant transiguntur.—Ipsum autem Fatum tale esse è natura ejus & appellatione constat. Heimarmene etiam dicitur quasi nexa & consertu lex & sanctio est, quia civili modo constitutum habet quid ex factis consequatur, &c. The ancient phrases to express the liberty of agents are, Liberum nobis esse, in nostra potestate esse, nobis parere, &c. For such actions could one be praised or blamed? [Cicero, *De fato,* xii.28: "Nor shall we for our part be hampered by what is called the 'idle argument'—for one argument is named by the philosophers the *Argos Logos* because if we yielded to it we should live a life of absolute inaction." Cicero, *De oratore, Book III, De fato, Paradoxa Stoicorum, De partitione oratoria,* trans. H. Rackham, Loeb Classical Library (London: Heinemann; Cambridge: Harvard University Press, 1942).

Plutarch, *De fato:* "For these inferences, which are called 'idle talk,' are indeed fallacious arguments arising from the dispute about fate" (574D–E). "Laws which God decreed regarding the nature of the universe and especially regarding immortal souls" (568C). "A law in harmony with the nature of the universe in accordance with which everything that transpires comes to be" (568D). "That fate is such a thing is clear from its nature and name. It is also called Heimarmene because it is bound fastened [the Greek *eiromene,* "unconcatenated"]. And it is a law and a decree because it has determined, as if by civil legislation, what should follow from what has already come to be" (570B). Plutarch, *Omnia quae extant opera* (Paris, 1624); the "ancient phrases" translate as "our being free to," "to be in our power," and "for us to bring about."]

23. "Slothful arguments."

inaction: and they were justly reckoned absurd upon that account; absurd, because to follow them would be sure ruin. If certain pains and pleasures depend upon our manner of acting and exerting ourselves; upon our elections, determinations and pursuits; upon the exercises of our faculties, in consequence of certain fixed connections in nature between our actions and certain effects; then it is our business, because it is our interest, to endeavour to learn these connexions, and to act agreeably to them. And in like manner, if we are so made, that we cannot but approve some actions, and blame others in ourselves and other persons, then is it our proper business to maintain this natural sense of right and wrong, in a sound, uncorrupted state, and to judge <18> and act conformably to it. All principles and reasonings which have an opposite tendency, must be as false as they are pernicious. With respect to our natural disposition to approve or disapprove actions, or our sense of good and ill desert, it necessarily implies in it, or carries along with it, a persuasion of its being in the power of the person blamed or commended, to have done, or not done the action approved or disapproved: for in every instance, when we know a person could not help doing or not doing a thing, we can neither blame nor approve him. Now such a determination of our nature, which necessarily supposes certain actions to be in our power; were no actions really in our power, would be absurd and delusive; which there is no ground from the analogy of nature to suppose, that any disposition or determination in our frame can be.

But it is not my business here to refute the doctrine of *necessity,* or to speak more properly, the doctrine of *inactivity,* (for so was it called by the ancients;) but to shew that freedom, or power, as such, supposes, nay necessarily requires, in order to its subsistence and exercise, established general laws. And this is as evident, as that goods cannot be obtained, nor pains be avoided by us, unless there is a fixed way of getting the one, and shunning the other, which may be foreseen and followed by us.[a]

The enquiry in which man is chiefly interested, is the extent of his dominion, power, or sphere of activity, that he may know how to regulate himself and his actions; not waste his time and powers in vain,

---

a. More is said on this subject in the first Chapter, Law i. of power.

impossible attempts, to gain or change what is absolutely independent of him, but employ himself in the right exercise of his powers, <19> about objects subjected to his will. Accordingly, ancient philosophers have commonly set out in their moral enquiries, by distinguishing and classing the τα εφ ημιν[a] and the τα ουκ εφ ημιν, the objects put by nature in our power, and those that are not. We have an excellent catalogue of them in the beginning of *Epictetus's Enchiridion;* and in the following enquiry, there will be occasion to take notice of the most important branches of our power, in the natural and in the moral world, that is, over external and sensible objects, or over moral and intellectual ones.

An account of the way in which the enquiry into human nature is to be carried on analogously to natural philosophy.

But before I proceed to enquire into any of the general laws relative to human nature, and their effects and final causes; it is necessary, in order to give a clear view of the manner in which it is proposed to carry on that enquiry, and of the strict analogy between natural and moral philosophy, to observe:

That as in natural philosophy, though it would be but building a fine visionary Theory or Fable, to draw out a system of consequences the most accurately connected from mere hypotheses, or upon supposition of the existence and operation of properties, and their laws, which experience does not shew to be really existent; yet the whole of true natural philosophy is not, for that reason, no more than a system of facts discovered by experiment and observation; but it is a mixture of experiments, with reasonings from experiments: so in the same manner, in moral philosophy, though it would be but to contrive a beautiful, elegant romance, to deduce the best coupled system of conclusions concerning human nature from imaginary suppositions, that have no foundation in nature; yet the whole of true moral philosophy, will not, for that reason, be no more than a collection of facts discovered by experience; but it

---

a. See Arrianus and Simplicius on Epictetus. [Epictetus (fl. ca. A.D. 110), a Stoic philosopher, whose *Discourses* have come down to us in the transcript made by his pupil Arrian, or Flavius Arrianus. Arrian also compiled an *Encheiridion* (a handbook) of the teachings of Epictetus. Simplicius (sixth century A.D.) was a Neoplatonist who wrote commentaries on Epictetus and on the *Categories, De anima, De caelo,* and *Physics* of Aristotle.]

likewise will <20> be a mixed science of observations, and reasonings from principles known by experience to take place in, or belong to human nature.

In neither case are hypotheses to be any further admitted, than as questions, about the truth or reality of which it is worth while to enquire; but in both we may proceed in the double method of analysis and synthesis: by the former endeavouring to deduce from some certain select effects, the simple powers of nature, and their laws and proportions; from which, by the latter method, we may infer or resolve the nature of other effects.[a] In both cases equally, as soon as certain powers or laws of nature are inferred from experience, we may consider them, reason about them, compare them with other properties, powers and laws; and these powers being found to be real, whatever conclusions necessarily result from such comparisons or reasonings, must be true concerning them; and do therefore denote as certainly some qualities, properties, attendants or consequents of them, as if these had been immediately discovered by experiment, instead of being deduced by strict reasoning, and

Hypotheses in either are only to be admitted as questions to be enquired into.

But we may proceed in both by analysis and synthesis.

a. See *Cotte*'s Preface to Sir *Isaac Newton's Principia,* and the *Principia,* I. 3. Regulae philosophandi. Qui speculationum suarum fundamentum desumunt ab hypothesibus, etiam si deinde secundum leges mechanicas accuratissime procedant; fabulam quidem elegantem forte & venustam, fabulam tamen concinnare dicendi sunt.—Hypotheses non comminiscuntur, neque in physicam recipiunt nisi ut quaestiones, de quarum veritate disputetur.—Jam illud concedi aequum est quod mathematicis rationibus colligetur & certissime demonstratur.—Certe contra tenorem experimentorum somnia temere, confingenda non sunt, nec a naturae analogia recedendum, &c. [Newton, *Principia.* The passages are from Cotes's preface, par. 3, 4, and 11, and the Regulae philosophandi, regula III: "Those who take the foundation of their speculations from hypotheses, even if they then proceed most rigorously according to mechanical laws, are merely putting together a romance, elegant perhaps and charming, but nevertheless a romance. . . . They do not contrive hypotheses, nor do they admit them into natural science otherwise than as questions whose truth may be discussed. . . . Now, it is reasonable to accept something that can be found by mathematics and proved with the greatest certainty. . . . Certainly idle fancies ought not to be fabricated recklessly against the evidence of experiments, nor should we depart from the analogy of nature." Isaac Newton, *The Principia: Mathematical Principles of Natural Philosophy: A New Translation,* by I. Bernard Cohen and Anne Whitman (Berkeley and London: University of California Press, 1999).]

necessary inference from principles known to be really true by experience: Or if before any property or law was known to be real, perchance many conclusions had been inferred from the very nature or idea of it, compared with other ideas, by necessary consequence; the moment such laws and properties are found < 21 > out to be real, then all the conclusions from them, which were before but mere abstract, hypothetical theories, become real truths, applicable to nature itself, and consequently a key to its operations.

Illustration by examples in natural philosophy.
The thing will be sufficiently plain if we take an example. One may draw several conclusions concerning gravity from the nature of the thing, without knowing that it is an universal law of nature; but the moment it is known to be such, all these abstract conclusions concerning the necessary effects of it in certain circumstances, become instead of mere theories, real truths, that is, real parts of the law of gravity, as far as it extends: or though one had never considered gravity in abstract, or made any necessary deductions from its nature and idea, before it was known to be an universal law of bodies; yet after it is found by experience to be such, if any properties, effects or consequences can be drawn from the very consideration of gravity itself, compared with other properties; all such conclusions, the moment they are found out, may be placed to the account of nature, and deemed parts of the natural law of gravity. Thus if the laws of centripedal forces have been determined with regard to an ellipsis, parabola, hyperbola, &c. it immediately follows, that if bodies move in such or such a curve, such and such must be the laws of their centripedal forces; and *vice versa,* if the laws of the centripedal forces of bodies are found to be such and such, it immediately follows, that such and such must be the nature of the orbits described by bodies that have such and such centripedal forces.

It must be the same in moral philosophy.
In like manner in moral philosophy, whatever can be proved to belong to, result from; or contrary wise, to be repugnant to the very definition of intelligence, volition, affection, habit, or any moral power; and a supposed law of such power will become a part of moral philosophy, so soon as such power is known to exist: or *vice versa,* any ef-< 22 >fects that can only result from such a law, being found by experience to take place,

the law itself must be inferred; and so of course all belonging to that law will come into philosophy, as appertaining to it, and be a key to moral nature and its phenomena, as such. Now of this kind of reasonings in moral philosophy, many instances occur in the following enquiry, almost in every chapter, which for that reason above-mentioned, have the same relation to moral philosophy, that abstract mathematical truths have to natural philosophy, and make part of it in the same way as these do of the latter.

In fine, the only thing in enquiries into any part of nature, moral or corporeal, is not to admit any hypothesis as the real solution of appearances, till it is found really to take place in nature, either by immediate experiment, or by necessary reasonings from effects, that unavoidably lead to it as their sole cause, law, or principle. But all demonstrations which shew that certain moral ideas must have certain relations, that is, certain agreements and disagreements, are in the same way a key to moral nature, that demonstrations relative to the agreements and disagreements of sensible ideas, as gravity, elasticity, circles, triangles, &c. belong, are applicable, or a key to natural philosophy. So that as the explication of the mundan system, being mixed of reasonings and observations, is properly called mixed mathematics, or mixed natural philosophy; so an account of human nature, mixed of principles inferred from immediate observation, and others deduced from such principles, by reasoning from ideas or definitions, may be called mixed moral philosophy, or mixed metaphysics; for demonstrations about moral ideas are commonly called metaphysical. But the word metaphysick having fallen into contempt, instead of calling this treatise mixed principles, or metaphysical principles, I have simply termed it, *The principles of moral philosophy.* I <23> shall not now enquire into the causes that have brought metaphysical reasonings, the name at least, into disrepute: but certainly no one will say, that intelligence, will, affections, or in one word, moral powers, and their relations, are not worth enquiring into, or collecting experiments and reasonings about.

Conclusions concerning moral philosophy.

I have only mentioned all this, to shew how moral philosophy ought to go on, and to forewarn my reader, that he is not to expect in this treatise

The following treatise is

therefore made up partly of observations, or experiments, and of reasonings from the very nature of moral powers.

merely a collection of experiments, but a good deal of reasoning from principles known to be true by experience, to effects; and reciprocally from effects known by experience to be true, to their causes or principles. And whatever may be thought of the execution (which I submit to all candid judges, who are ever rather favourably than severely disposed) sure none can look upon the design to be trifling, who understand what moral powers mean. For if any thing is worth man's attention, it is man himself, that is, his natural powers, end, dignity and happiness.

The chief design of the following enquiry stated.

Having thus dispatched all necessary preliminaries as briefly as I could, the question now to be entered upon is, "*Are all the effects and appearances relative to the constitution of our minds, effects of powers, faculties, dispositions and affections, which with all the laws and connexions belonging to them, tend to produce good, order, beauty and perfection in the whole?*" As in enquiring about the constitution of a horse, for example, it belongs not properly to such a question, whether that animal be superior or inferior to a lion; but that enquiry presupposes the constitutions and ends of both these animals known; so in the present case, the first question is not, whether there are not in nature more noble beings than man; but whether man deserves his place in nature, as being well adapted to a very good and noble end; to a dignity, a per-<24>fection, a happiness, to have fitted and qualified him for which, proves great wisdom and goodness in his Author, the Author of nature.

> *Where all must* full, *or not coherent be;*
> *And all that rises, rise in due* degree;
> *Then in the scale of life and sense, 'tis plain,*
> *There must be* somewhere *such a rank as* man;
> *And all the question (wrangle e'er so long)*
> *Is only this, If God has plac'd him wrong?*
>   Essay on man, Epist. 1.[24]

I shall now endeavour to go through the more remarkable general laws of our constitution, to which the chief appearances relative to mankind seem to be reducible.

24. Pope, *Essay on Man,* I.45–50.

The first thing to be observed with regard to our make and state, is, "That we have a certain sphere of activity." The law of power, or activity.

Whatever disputes there are among philosophers about the freedom of our will, it is universally acknowledged, "That man has in several cases a power to do as he wills or pleases. Thus, if he wills to speak, or be silent, to sit down, or stand, ride, or walk; in fine, if his will changes like a weather-cock, he is able to do as he wills or pleases, unless prevented by some restraint or compulsion. He has also the same power in relation to the actions of his mind, as to those of the body. If he wills or pleases, he can think of this, or that subject, stop short, or pursue his thoughts, deliberate, or defer deliberation; resolve, or suspend his deliberations as he pleases, <25> unless prevented by pain, or a fit of an apoplexy, or some such intervening restraint or compulsion. And this, no doubt, is a great perfection for man to be able in relation both to his thoughts and actions, to do as he wills and pleases in all these cases of pleasure and interest. Had he this power or liberty in all things, he would be omnipotent." And in having this power or liberty to a certain extent, does his superior excellence above the brute creation consist. Were not man so made, he would necessarily be a very low and mean creature in comparison of what he really is; as he is now constituted a free agent; or as he is invested with a certain extent of dominion and efficiency.

The power or dominion of a Being cannot consist in any thing else, but the dependence of certain effects[a] upon its will as to their existence or non-existence. Its sphere of activity, liberty and efficiency is larger or Power consists in dependence of effects upon the will.

a. See the chapter on power in Mr. *Locke's Essay on human Understanding.* [John

It is a perfection to have power.

narrower in proportion to the extent of this dependence on its will; for so far as it reaches does ones command or will reach. Now how far human power or activity extends; or, in other words, what are with respect to man the principal τα εφ ημιν,[25] will appear as we advance in this enquiry. Mean time, it is certainly necessary, in order to our dignity and perfection, that we should have a certain dominion and power in nature assigned to us. This, doubtless, is a greater perfection, than having no power, no command, no sphere of activity. Without power, creatures cannot make any acquisition: being capable of virtue and merit, necessarily presupposes some power or dominion.

Of human power.

It is matter of universal experience, that, in the present state, a large share of what we enjoy or suffer is put in our own power; or, in other words, that pleasure and pain are the natural consequences of our actions. And consequently, the general me-<26>thod of the author of nature, with regard to us, may be justly said to be teaching, or forewarning us by experience in consequence, of having endued us with the capacity of observing the connexions of things, that if we act so and so, we shall

With regard to animal life and its functions.

obtain such enjoyments, and if so and so, we shall have such and such sufferings. That is, the author of nature gives us such and such enjoyments; or makes us feel such and such pains in consequence of our actions. We find, by experience, our maker does not so much as preserve our lives independent of our own care and vigilance to provide for our sustenance, to ward against destruction, and to make a proper use of the means appointed by nature for our safety and well-being. And, in general, all the external objects of our various, natural appetites and affections, can neither be obtained, nor enjoyed without our exerting ourselves in the ways appointed to have them; but, by thus exerting ourselves, we obtain and enjoy those objects in which our natural good

With respect to moral attainments.

consists. In like manner, our progress in knowledge, in any art, or in any virtue, all moral improvements depend upon ourselves: they, with the goods resulting from them, can only be acquired by our own application, or by setting ourselves to acquire them according to the natural methods

---

Locke, *An Essay Concerning Human Understanding,* ed. Peter H. Nidditch (Oxford: Oxford University Press, 1975), bk. 2, ch. 21.]

25. "Things in our power."

of acquiring them. This is really our state; such really is the general law Why it is so.
of our natures.

Now, if it is asked, why the author of nature does not give to mankind
promiscuously such and such perceptions without regard to their actions, or independently of themselves, as nature seems to do with inferior creatures? The answer is obvious, 'Tis because he has made moral
agents as well as lower animals. For it is self-evident, that nothing can
be called a moral attainment or perfection, but what is acquired by one's
own exercise or application to attain to it. There must be a very high and
noble pleasure in considering any quality as one's own acquisition, <27>
which no Beings can have but those who are capable of making improvements and advancements by their own application, or who have a
certain power and dominion in nature by which they can make purchases. Such Beings alone can have the satisfaction of looking upon any
thing as their own; the pleasure of adding to their own happiness, or to
that of others; and of approving themselves for the right use of their
own powers in so doing; which are the highest of all enjoyments. In fine,
without supposing the capacity of foreseeing consequences, and of willing and chusing to act in such and such manners, in order to attain to
certain ends; virtue, merit, good and ill desert have no meaning at all.
The capacity of attaining to certain goods, by our own powers duly exercised and applied, is the very basis of moral perfection. It is in con- Our natural
perfection con-
sequence of our having power to make considerable acquisitions by our sists in our
industry; or by duly exercising our natural faculties, that man rises in the being so
constituted.
scale of life and perfection, as a moral agent capable of virtue and merit,
praise, or blame, above merely perceptive beings, who never act or acquire, but are in all cases passive and acted upon. This is too evident to
be longer insisted upon.

"It is therefore a perfection to have a certain sphere of activity, power,
liberty, or dominion."

II. "But a sphere of power or activity, supposes the prevalence of general Such power
laws, as far as that sphere of power or activity[a] extends." This is as plain, supposes

---

a. Some thing hath been said on this subject already in the *Introduction*. [Subject
discussed above, pp. 48–49.]

nature to be as it is, that goods cannot be obtained, nor pains be avoided by us, unless
governed by there is a fixed way of getting the one, and shuning the other, which may
general laws.
be foreseen and pursued. What is attainable, supposes a capacity and a
certain way of attaining it, and what is evitable, supposes a capacity < 28 >
and a certain way of escaping it. But a capacity and a way of attaining
to; and a capacity and way of escaping certain ends and consequences,
suppose general fixed uniform connexions in nature between certain
manners of acting and certain consequences: that is, they suppose fixed,
uniform and general laws with regard to the exercises of powers or actions. Were there not a certain fixed way of having or avoiding certain
sensations, we could not have them nor avoid them as we will. And, in
like manner, were there not a fixed way of attaining to knowledge, we
could not possibly acquire it: were there not a fixed way of moving the
passions, there could be no art of moving them: were there not a fixed
way of conquering appetites and desires, we could not obtain the command and mastership of them: and so on with regard to all our powers,
dispositions and affections, and their exercises and attainments. The
same Author of nature, who hath conferred certain faculties upon us,
must have established certain laws and connexions with regard to the
exercises of them, and their effects and consequences; otherwise we
could not know how to turn them to any account, how to employ them,
or make any use of them.

Conclusion.   The result of all this is in general, "That we can have no liberty, no
dominion, no sphere of activity and power, natural or moral, unless the
natural and moral world are governed by general laws: or so far only as
they are so governed can any created beings have power or efficiency: so
far only can effects be dependent on their will as to their existence or
non-existence."

We are now to   Now, it being fit that we should have a sphere of activity constituted by
enquire into general laws regulating the dependence of certain effects on our will, it
some of these
general laws only remains to be enquired what these general laws, that make our
which consti- sphere of activity, are; and what their < 29 > consequences are with respect
tute our power. to good or evil, happiness or misery.

III. The first thing remarkable with regard to our sphere of activity is, "that our power and dominion encreases with our knowledge." Our power in the natural world encreases with our knowledge of the natural world. Thus, by the augmentation of our knowledge of the connexions that make the material or sensible world; or, in other words, of the properties of bodies, how much is our empire over sea, air, fire, and every element encreased? when any property of matter becomes known to us, then are we able to render it subservient to some use in life. And therefore in proportion to our advances in the knowledge and imitation of nature, have arts been invented, that are really so many additions to our power and dominion in the sensible world. It is the same with regard to the moral world. All true observations relative to the human mind, its powers and operations, and the connexions of moral objects do in like manner add to our moral dominion; to our empire over ourselves and others. Thus the knowledge of the passions, and their natural bearings and dependencies encrease our power and skill in governing them, by shewing us how they may be strengthned or diminished; directed to proper objects, or taken off from the pursuit of improper ones; in short, how they may be variously regulated so as to answer certain ends. No connexion belonging to the human mind, no law relative to intelligence, or the affections has been discovered, which has not, or may not be made conducive either to the direction of our conduct, or to the improvement of some pleasant and useful art. It is not moral philosophy only, or the science of the conduct of life that depends upon the knowledge of the human mind; oratory, poetry, and all the fine arts which have it for their end and scope to touch the human <30> heart agreeably, do no less depend than morality and politics, upon the science of the human affections, and their natural dependence and ballance.

In general therefore, the increase of knowledge is necessary to the encrease of dominion; or rather, it is really an enlargement of power and property. Power not guided and directed by knowledge is not properly power, it is brute or blind force. But intelligent power can only augment with knowledge, or intelligence. It is therefore because knowledge is dependent on us, or may be acquired by us, that we can have any power, any sphere of activity; were not the acquisition of knowledge dependent

Side notes:

First general law. Intelligent power must depend on knowledge, and encrease with it.

In the natural World.

And in the moral world.

It is because knowledge depends on us that we have or can acquire power.

upon us to a certain degree, we could not have any power at all, nothing could be dependent upon us.

If knowledge be progressive, intelligent power must likewise be so.

IV. But the encrease of our power depends upon the encrease of our knowledge; and therefore, if our knowledge must be successive or progressive, so must our power be. Now, "that knowledge must be progressive is evident beyond all doubt." Being gradually acquired by our application to study nature, take in ideas and compare them, it not only gives us a succession of growing pleasures; but it cannot but be progressive. For, 1. Nature itself, the sole object of all real knowledge, is successive or progressive. What else can direct our conduct, enable us to imitate nature, or to perform any operation in order to attain to any end, but the knowledge of nature's laws? But nature is progressive in all its

Knowledge cannot but be progressive.

productions: and general rules or canons can only be inferred by induction, from the observation of many individuals, or from many experiments about particular objects. Creatures cannot possibly attain to the knowledge of analogies, harmonies and general laws, any other way, than by going over many particular effects which do not all exist at once, but are successive; and by comparing them one with another. 2. And as for abstract or theoretic know-<31>ledge, (as mathematics for instance) which is collected from the comparison of ideas and their relations amongst themselves; that must likewise be progressive; because discoveries made this way are nothing but the different appearances, ideas and their relations offer to the mind in different views or juxta-positions. When the immediate juxta-position of known relations is not sufficient to give the mind the view it desires, but intermediate ideas must be employed in order to make the agreement or disagreement in question appear; then it is plain, however fast the mind may mount, yet it must mount by steps. And even where the immediate juxta-position of ideas, without any intermediate mean of comparison, is sufficient, yet one and the same juxta-position can produce but one view, or one truth. In order to every discovery, there must be a different position of objects; for perceiving truth, is nothing but perceiving the agreement or disagreement of ideas in consequence of some one or other way of placing or disposing them in respect to one another. It is perceiving the relations of ideas by comparing them; and no position can be any other position but that one which it is. In fine, all real knowledge must be progressive, because nature is successive; and the laws of nature can only be gathered from particular effects by induction. And all theoretic knowledge must be progressive, because the mind cannot possibly see ideas in different situations or juxta-positions to one another at one and the same time. That is absolutely impossible with regard to created minds.

"Our knowledge therefore is progressive."

V. "This knowledge, which is in its nature progressive, must depend upon our situations to take in ideas or views." It must be different as these are different, narrow if these be narrow, and proportionably large as these are large and extensive. 1. It is certain, that the knowledge of no being can pos-<32>sibly exceed or go beyond its ideas. Ideas are the materials of knowledge. It cannot therefore extend further than our ideas; and consequently it cannot reach beyond experience, the only source of all our ideas. 2. Now, if it is asked, why men are placed in different situations? it may be answered, 1. It is because men are made for society, which, as shall be proved in its place, requires that men should be placed in different situations for many wise reasons; and with respect to knowledge, and social intercourse in that way, (for that is all that belongs to the present question) there is this obvious good end for it, even that being placed as it were in various points of sight with regard to nature the common object of our contemplation and imitation, men might thus have different prospects or views of the same object to compare one with another, and only be able to make out a tolerably adequate idea of any object by mutual assistance. 2. In whatever situation any man is placed, he may take in ideas that will afford him an exhaustless fund of pleasing contemplation. For what object does not as it were defy our intellect to exhaust it? however far we advance in any enquiry, there will still remain a surplusage of research with regard to its object, that can never be wholly gone through. Every field of speculation widens and enlarges to our view in proportion as we make progress in it. But, 3. Let us consider well what is demanded, when it is asked, why all men are not in the same situations, or precisely equal, or like ones for taking in ideas? For, in reality, it

Knowledge must depend on our situations for taking in ideas or views.

Men must have different situations and views.

amounts to asking, why all different places in nature are not the same: since every different one must be a different point of sight. Now, whatever may be the case with respect to spirits without bodies; corporeal beings cannot penetrate one another and occupy the same space; different bodies must have each its own proper place peculiar to it; and consequently, every embodied being must have its own point of sight, or place of <33> observation, which no other can possess at the same time. 4. Nor is this all, every embody'd being must have its own particular organization distinguished by peculiar differences from that of every other of the same species, tho' similar to them all, in such a manner, that they all are of the same specific sort. And must it not necessarily follow from this, that the sensible world to each individual of the same species, will be just as similar to the sensible world of any other, as their organizations are similar, and just as different as their organizations are different? The external, material world, whether it be called the external cause, or occasion of those sensible ideas and their connexions, which make to each of us what we call the sensible world, is entirely out of the question, when we speak of sensations excited by it in each individual mind according to certain fixed laws. It may be the same, immutable thing in itself. But as for the sensations produced in us from without by means of a material organization, these must be as different as the organizations are, by which they are produced. And it is not more certain, that the organizations of men being so like, that they may be justly said

With respect to the sensible world.

to be specifically the same; our sensations conveyed from without, must likewise be so like, that they may be said to be specifically the same; than it is certain, that our organizations, notwithstanding their specifical agreement, being really so different, that every one is justly said to have a peculiar organization, our sensations conveyed from without must likewise be so different, that every one of us may be said to have different sensations. So that, in reality, there are not only as many different sensible worlds in species, as there are various species of sensitive beings; but there are as many different sensible worlds, as there are different or particular organizations of sensitive beings of any one species. It is similarity amidst vast variety with respect to sensations, and the orders in which they are conveyed, in consequence of simi-<34>larity amidst variety of organizations, that is the foundation of close and intimate intercourse among individuals of the same sensitive species. And the reason why there can only be a remote and very general intercourse among sensitive beings of a different species is, because there can only be a general similarity between their sensations.

VI. But which is yet more, every individual of any species of rational beings, howsoever like it may be specifically to the others of the same species, must however have its own particular fabrick of mind, and peculiar cast of understanding; and consequently, every one must take in views in a manner some what different from every other. The views of every one of the same species will be similar, their fabrick of mind being similar; but their views will likewise be different, every man's complexion, or cast of understanding being different. Similarity of views in consequence of similarity of constitution is all that can constitute the same species of minds; and it will be a sufficient foundation for a close and intimate commerce among beings, that cannot possibly take place among minds differing from one another in species.

In like manner with regard to mental frame and the moral world.

But if every body must have its particular organization, and every mind its particular fabrick, and consequently the sensations, perceptions, ideas, and views of every individual embodied mind must be peculiar; not precisely the same, but different; the only question with regard to our fabrick and situations for receiving or forming ideas, or for taking in and forming views, must be, "Whether there is not such a similarity and agreement amongst us in these, as makes our species capable of very much happiness in the way of social correspondence and intercourse?" Now, that we are so constituted, is very plain; since we are so made, that, notwithstanding all the variety amongst mankind, whether <35> in mental structure or bodily organization, it is hardly possible for us to mistake one another in our correspondence with regard to our sensations conveyed from without; and it is very possible for us to come to a right understanding with one another about all the other objects of our contemplation, enquiry and mutual commerce. But this reasoning will be better understood when we come to consider the effects of our relation to a sensible world by means of our bodies.

Thus then we have seen, that "our knowledge, without which we can have no power, must be progressive, and must depend upon our situation for taking in views or ideas."

VII. But "it must likewise depend upon our application to make progress in it." For, as it hath been shewn, this is the general law with regard to our nature; that the greater part of our happiness, shall be our own purchase. And what depends upon a being's own purchase, must necessarily depend upon its exerting itself with more or less vigour and activity to make that purchase. It is therefore needless to dwell upon this head.

VIII. But there are yet two other remarkable circumstances, with regard to our capacity of making progress in knowledge. 1st. The difference amongst men in point of powers and abilities. 2dly, The dependence of our progress in knowledge upon our situations for receiving assistances by social communication.

It must depend
upon difference
with respect to
natural
abilities. Now as to the first, it will be easily granted that a difference in powers must make a difference with respect to progress in knowledge. And that all men have not equal abilities, for making proficiency in knowledge, is a fact beyond dispute. Wherefore the only remaining question on this head is with regard to the fitness of inequalities among mankind, in respect of powers; but this cannot be called into doubt, without denying the <36> fitness of making man a social creature, or of intending him for society and social happiness: since the interchange of good offices, in which society consists, necessarily supposes mutual dependence in consequence of mutual wants; and not only variety of talents, as well as of tastes, and tempers; but likewise superiority and inferiority, in respect of powers. Without such differences and inequalities, mankind would be, in a great measure, a number of independent individuals: or at least there would be no place for the greater part of those various employments and reciprocal obligations, without which, or some others analogous to them, there can be no community. This is as certain and obvious, as that giving supposes a receiver, as well as a giver; and that giving can only be necessary, where there is something wanted: One cannot

bestow, or give what he has not; and he who is supplied or redressed, must have been in want or distress, previously to the relief received.

As for the other, it is beyond all doubt. For in conversation, how does fancy warm and sprout! It is then that invention is most fertile, and that imagination is most vigorous and sprightly. The best way of getting to the bottom of any subject is by canvassing and sounding it in company: then is an object presented to us by turns in all its various lights, so that one is able, as it were, to see round it. As iron sharpens iron, so does conversation whet wit and invention. Ideas flow faster into the mind, and marshal themselves more easily and naturally into good order in society, than in solitary study. In fine, to be convinced of the happy effects of society in this respect, we need only compare a peasant confined to his hut and herd in the country, with a mechanic of the lowest order in a great city.[a] And when <37> we look into the history of arts and sciences or of mankind in general, nothing is more evident, than that learning of whatever sort, and arts and sciences, never made any great progress but in places of large and extensive commerce. There always was and always will be such a connexion; because men were intended by nature to arrive at perfection in a social way; or by united endeavours. Now as for that fitness, it cannot be called into question no more than the other just mentioned, unless it be said, it is not fit that men should be made for partnership, or for social happiness. For, how can beings be made for society without being so formed as to stand in need of one another; so made as to have pleasure in social communication; and to receive mutual benefits and assistances, or succours from one another in the exercises of their powers; or, unless their perfection and happiness be such a one as can only be acquired by social union and united force? But what relates to society shall be more fully considered in another place.

Progress in knowledge must depend on social assistances.

a. Mr. *Locke on the conduct of the understanding.* [John Locke, *Of the Conduct of the Understanding,* in *Some Thoughts Concerning Education; and, Of the Conduct of the Understanding,* ed. Ruth W. Grant and Nathan Tarcov (Indianapolis and Cambridge: Hackett, 1996), §3.]

Recapitulation. From what hath been said, it is clear, 1. "That it is the general law of our natures with regard to our dominion, power or liberty, that it shall depend upon our progress in knowledge." 2. That it is the general law of our natures with regard to knowledge, "That being in the nature of things progressive, it can only be acquired by experience in proportion to our application, and to our situation for taking in ideas and views, and to our situation for receiving assistances by social communication." So that if men's natural abilities be equal, their progress in knowledge will be in proportion to their situation for receiving ideas, and for receiving assistances by social communication: and if their situations are equal in both these respects, their progress in knowledge will be in proportion to their natural abilities, or their industry and application. But as one's knowledge is, so will his capacity or skill be of employing all his other <38> powers. Intelligent power supposes intelligence or knowledge.

The laws with respect to our intelligent power and progress in knowledge are good. Now all these laws or circumstances relative to knowledge and intelligent action, having been proved to be either necessary or fit; it must follow, that all the phenomena which are reducible to these laws of nature are good, being the effects of good general laws. For without general laws there can be no power or sphere of activity; and all the interests of intelligent beings require, that the laws relative to them be general, that they may be ascertainable by them.

But we shall have yet a clearer view of our make and constitution with respect to knowledge, if we consider a little the faculties and dispositions with which we are provided and furnished for making progress in knowledge.

Instances of the care and concern of nature about us, with regard to knowledge consistently with the preceeding laws. Let us, however, before we go further, observe; that tho' knowledge be progressive and dependent on our diligence and application to improve in it, yet the care of nature about us with regard to knowledge is very remarkable in several instances.

First instance. I. The wisdom and goodness of nature appears with great evidence, in making a part of knowledge, which it is necessary for us to have in our infant state, and before we can think, meditate, compare and reason, as it were unavoidable, or impossible not to be acquired by us insensibly; while, at the same time, knowledge is in the main progressive, and can only be acquired gradually in proportion to our diligence to improve in it. For how soon, how exceeding quickly do we learn by experience to form very ready judgments concerning such laws and connexions in the sensible world, as it is absolutely necessary to our well-being, that we should early know; or be able to judge of betimes with great readiness, or almost instantaneously? How soon do we learn to judge of magnitudes, distances and forms, and of <39> the connexions between the ideas of sight and touch, as far, at least, as the common purposes and conveniencies of life require; in so much, that when we are grown up and begin to reflect, we have quite forgot, how we learned these connexions, and became able to judge of them so readily. Nay, when we come to play the philosopher about them, it is very difficult for us not to confound those ideas, which are however totally distinct from one another, and only connected together by the institution of the Author of nature. It is indeed with wonderful facility that we learn any language in our tender years; but this most useful of all *languages* for us to know, the *language* of nature, as it may very properly be called, is what we learn soonest, and as it were necessarily and insensibly.[a]

II. The wisdom and goodness of nature does no less evidently appear in directing and admonishing us by uneasy sensations to provide necessary supplies for our bodies, and to defend them against what is hurtful to them. For thus, nature teaches and instructs us in the knowledge of what is prejudicial to us, or necessary for our preservation; and how highly inconvenient it would have been, not to be thus admonished by nature, since knowledge must be progressive, and can only be acquired gradually from experience and observation in proportion to our application to ad-

Second instance.

a. See *an essay on vision,* and *a treatise concerning the principles of human knowledge, by the Bishop of* Cloyd. [George Berkeley, *An Essay Towards a New Theory of Vision* (1709, 1710, 1732); and *A Treatise Concerning the Principles of Human Knowledge* (1710, 1734).]

vance in it, is too manifest to need any proof. But of this afterwards in its proper place.

Third instance.   III. The wisdom and goodness of nature likewise discovers itself, in giving us a rule to guide us in our moral conduct, distinct from and antecedent to all our knowledge acquired by reasoning, which is a moral sense of beauty and deformity in affections, <40> actions and characters, by means of which, an affection, action or character, no sooner presents itself to our mind, than it is necessarily approved or disapproved by us. Human nature is not left quite indifferent in the affair of virtue to form itself, observations concerning the advantages and disadvantages of actions, and accordingly to regulate its conduct. Reason must be grown up to very great maturity, and be very considerably improved by exercise and culture, before men can be able to go through those long deductions, which shew some actions to be in the whole advantageous to the agent, and their contraries pernicious. But the Author of nature has much better furnished us for a virtuous conduct than many philosophers seem to imagine, or, at least are willing to grant, by almost as quick and powerful instructions as we have for the preservation of our bodies. He has given us strong affections to be the springs of each virtuous action, and made virtue a lovely form that we might easily distinguish it from its contrary, and be made happy by the pursuit of it. As the Author of nature has determined us to receive by our outward senses, pleasant or disagreeable ideas of objects, according as they are useful or hurtful to our bodies, and to receive from uniform objects the pleasures of beauty and harmony, to excite us to the pursuit of knowledge, and to reward us for it; in the same manner, he has given us a moral sense to direct our actions, and to give us still nobler pleasures; so that while we are only intending the good of others, we undesignedly promote our own greatest private good.[a]

a. See *an Enquiry into the origine of our ideas of beauty,* by Mr. *Hutchinson,* whose words I have here copied. [Francis Hutcheson, *An Inquiry into the Original of Our Ideas of Beauty and Virtue,* II.I.viii.]

IV. The wisdom and goodness of nature shews itself very clearly, in wonderfully adapting our minds to be satisfied with evidence suited to our
external condition and circumstances. We are made <41> for acquiring
knowledge or information concerning the frame of nature, and the connexions of things from experience; but we must in innumerable cases
act upon probability, that is, upon presumptions founded upon analogy
or likeness: and accordingly, in this kind of evidence, we feel great satisfaction and contentment of mind. That we must, in innumerable
cases, act upon probable evidence, is a fact too evident to need any proof;
and that acting upon probable evidence, is acting upon presumptions
founded upon analogy or likeness, will likewise be readily acknowledged
by all who will allow themselves to consider what *probability* means.
That which chiefly constitutes it, is expressed in the word *likely;* that is,[a]
like some known truth or true event; like, in itself, in its evidence, in
some more or fewer of its circumstances. Now, it belongs to the subject
of *logick* to enquire into the nature, the foundation and measure of probability, or to reduce the extent, compass or force of analogical reasoning,
to general observations and rules; and thus to guard against the errors
to which reasoning from analogy is liable; but if we enquire from whence
it proceeds, that likeness should beget that presumption, opinion, or full
conviction, which the human mind is formed to receive from it; and
which it does necessarily produce in every one proportionally to its various degrees. This question contains its own proper and full answer. It is
because the mind is formed to receive satisfaction from it, and acquiesce

---

a. See Dr. *Butler*'s (Bishop of *Bristol*) *Analogy*, &c. where probability is excellently
discoursed of. See *Cicero de inventione rhetorica,* Lib. 1. *probabilis erit narratio, si in
ea videbuntur in esse ea, quae solent apparere in veritate.—Ac veri quidem similis ex his
rationibus esse poterit, &c.—Necessarie demonstrantur, ea quae aliter ac dicuntur, nec
fieri, nec probari possunt,—&c.* [Joseph Butler, *The Analogy of Religion, Natural and
Revealed, to the Constitution and Course of Nature* (1736); Cicero, *De inventione:* "The
narrative will be plausible if it seems to embody characteristics which are accustomed
to appear in real life. . . . Verisimilitude can be secured by following these principles"
(I.xxi.30). ". . . those things are proved irrefutably which cannot happen or be proved
otherwise other than as stated, etc." (I.xxix.44). Cicero, *De inventione. . . .*, trans. H.
M. Hubbell, Loeb Classical Library (London: Heinemann; Cambridge: Harvard
University Press, 1949).]

in it proportionally to its several degrees. And the final cause of this formation is no less evident; since our present state makes our acting upon such evidence <42> necessary. When demonstration is said to force our assent, the meaning is, that by it, we have a clear perception of the necessary agreement or disagreement of certain ideas; an agreement or disagreement that cannot but take place. But where such a necessary agreement or disagreement of ideas cannot be perceived, as it cannot be with respect to any connexions of nature of positive institution, of which sort are, for instance, the connexion between the ideas of sight and touch, and almost all, if not all the connexions of the sensible world. In such cases, nothing but various degrees of likelihood or unlikelihood can be perceived; and such perceptions do not so properly operate upon our understanding producing assent, as upon our temper producing satisfaction and complacency; the contraries of which are wavering and mistrust, or dissidence. But not to seem to dispute about words, let the effect of probability, that is, of likeness, be called an effect upon the understanding, or upon the will; a judgment or a tendency to determine ourselves to act this or the other way, or not to act at all, according to the various force of presumption; yet the effect of it upon the mind cannot be ultimately accounted for, without supposing an aptitude or disposition in our natures to be influenced by presumptions or appearances of likeness. 'Tis the same here, as with regard to the perception of beauty; when we have analysed it into its constituent and concomitant parts; we have in that case a clearer and more adequate notion of it; yet it must still remain true with respect to it, that its constituent and concomitant parts make a perception that affects the mind in a certain manner, merely because the mind is intended and fitted by nature to be so affected by it. We must in all such cases at last come to an ultimate reason, which can be no other than the adjustment of the mind to certain objects. But so far as we see and find our minds suited to our state and circumstances; <43> so far do we see clear proofs of wisdom and goodness in our make and contrivance, or of care and concern about our welfare. 'Tis almost unnecessary to remark here, that to say, the mind often presumes rashly, and makes false judgments about probability, is no more any objection against its right formation in our circumstances with respect to its natural aptitude to be influenced by probability, than it is against certainty and scientific evidence, wherever that is attainable, to say many philosophers have been deceived, and have mistaken absurdities for demonstrations.

V. The care of nature about us, with respect to knowledge, appears by its giving us considerable light into some more necessary parts of knowledge; or, at least, considerable hints and helps for discovering several useful arts, by the operations and productions of inferior animals directed by their natural instincts. For these acting as nature impels them, shew some of us how to build, others to swim, others to dive and fish, some how to spin and weave, some how to cure wounds and diseases, others how to modulate the voice into melody, *&c.* Fifth instance.

This truth is charmingly represented by an excellent poet, in a poem (that must be highly valued while moral science and true harmony are relished in the world) which I shall have frequent occasion to quote.

> *See him from* nature *rising slow* to art!
> *To copy* instinct *then was* reason's *part;*
> *Thus then to man the voice of nature spake—*
> *"Go! from the creatures thy instructions take;*
> *Learn from the birds what food the thickets yield;*
> *Learn from the beasts the physic of the field:* <44>
> *Thy arts of building from the* bee *receive;*
> *Learn of the* mole *to plow, the* worm *to weave;*
> *Learn from the little* nautilus *to sail,*
> *Spread the thin oar and catch the driving gale.*
> *Here too all forms of social union find,*
> *And hence let reason, late instruct mankind:*
> *Here subterranean works and cities see,*
> *The towns aerial on the waving tree.*
> *Learn each small people's genius, policies;*
> *The ants republic, and the realm of bees;*
> *How those in common all their stores bestow,*
> *And anarchy without confusion know,*
> *And these for ever, tho' a monarch reign,*
> *Their sep'rate cells and properties maintain.*

Mark what unvary'd laws preserve their state,
Laws wise as nature, and as fix'd as fate,
In vain thy reason finer webs shall draw,
Entangle justice in her net of law.
And right too rigid, harden into wrong,
Still for the strong too weak, the weak too strong.
Yet go! and thus o'er all the creatures sway,
Thus let the wiser make the rest obey,
And for those arts mere instinct could afford,
Be crown'd as monarchs, or as gods ador'd.
Essay on man, epist. III.[a]

Sixth instance.   VI. Add to this, that as it is from nature only that the real knowledge of
nature can be learned, so the connexions of nature lie open to our view.[b]
It is only because men have wilfully shut their eyes a-<45>gainst nature,
and have vainly set themselves to devise or guess its methods of operation, without taking any assistance from nature itself, that natural knowledge has made such slow advances. Whence it comes about that men
have at any time been misled into the foolish attempt of understanding
nature by any other method, than by attending to it, and carefully observing it, is a question I shall not now enter upon. But so obvious are

a. See *Plutarch de solertia animantium.* [Pope, *Essay on Man,* III.169–98. These
verses by Pope sum up the substance of Plutarch's *De solertia animantium* (or *ani-
malium*), but see especially 966B. Plutarch, *Omnia quae extant opera,* 2 vols. (Paris,
1624).]

b. Artes vero innumerabilis repertae sunt, docente natura, quam imitata ratio, res
ad vitam necessarias sollerter consecuta est. Ipsum autem hominem eadem natura
non solum celeritate mentis ornavit; sed etiam sensus tanquam satellites attribuit &
nuntios: & rerum plurimarum obscuras & necessarias intelligentias enudavit; quasi;
fundamentum scientiae.—*Cicero de legibus,* Lib. 1. [Cicero, *De legibus,* I.viii–ix.26:
"Moreover innumerable arts have been discovered through the teachings of Nature;
for it is by a skilful imitation of her that reason has acquired the necessities of life.
Nature has likewise not only equipped man himself with nimbleness of thought, but
has also given him the senses, to be, as it were, his attendants and messengers; she has
laid bare the obscure and none too [obvious] meanings of a great many things, to
serve as the foundations of knowledge. . . ." Cicero, *De re publica, De legibus,* trans.
Clinton Walker Keyes, Loeb Classical Library (London: Heinemann; New York: Putnam, 1928).]

the greater part of nature's connexions to all those who study nature, that so soon as the right, the only method of getting into its secrets was pursued, great improvements were quickly made in that knowledge; and all discoveries in it, after they are found out, appear so simple and so obvious, that one cannot help wondering how it came about that they were not sooner seen and observed.

Now nature, in order to put us into the right way of coming at real knowledge, has not only implanted in our minds an eager desire or thirst after knowledge, but likewise a strong disposition to emulate all the works of nature that fall more immediately under our cognisance, and in a manner to vie with nature in productions of our own. This disposition to emulate nature, as it adds considerable force to our desire of knowledge, so it serves to assist us in acquiring it; for it necessarily leads and prompts us to copy what is done by nature, and thus makes us attend very closely to the object or phenomenon we would imitate, and try experiments about it; by which means alone, it is obvious, any real knowledge can be acquired. But not only is the knowledge of nature owing to this imitative principle in our minds, together with our desire of knowledge; but hence likewise proceed all the imitative arts, Poetry, Painting, Statuary, &c. Whatever we see performed by nature, we are emulous and restless to perform something like it, and so to rival nature. And hence all the bold and daring efforts of the hu-<46>man mind, in the various ways or arts of imitating, or rather excelling nature.[a]

---

a. See *Aristotle's Poetics*, cap. 4. Nam & imitari, innatum hominibus a pueris est; atque hac re differunt ipsi ab aliis animalibus, quod homo sit animal maxime aptum ad imitandum; primasque rerum perceptiones sibi ipsi faciat per imitationem, non magistrorum praeceptis, sed exemplis aliorum ductus: et gaudere omnes rebus imitatione expressis naturale est veluti picturis, sculpturis & similibus, &c. [Aristotle, *Poetics*, 1248B: "Imitation comes naturally to men from childhood, and in this they differ from other animals because man is an animal especially suited to imitating, and he forms for himself his first notions of things by imitation, led not by the precepts of his teachers but by the examples of others. And it is also natural for everyone to enjoy things that are imitations, such as pictures, sculptures and such like."]

A review of our natural furniture for knowledge. But as considerable as these assistances are which have been mentioned, they amount but to a small share of what nature hath done for us, in order to fit us for progress in knowledge, and the manifold pleasures arising from truth, and the search after it.

Knowledge naturally agreeable to the mind. I. Progress in knowledge is rewarded by itself every step it makes; for darkness is not more disagreeable to the natural eye, than ignorance is to the mind: the breaking in of knowledge upon the understanding, is not less refreshing and chearing than the appearance of day after a gloomy, weary night to a traveller. Every discovery we make; every glimpse of truth, as it begins to dawn upon the mind, gives high delight. And thus every acquisition in science recompences our labour, and becomes a strong incitement to greater application, in order to make further improvements, bring in fresh purchases, and so procure new pleasures to ourselves. The reason of all this can be no other, than that truth or knowledge is naturally as agreeable and satisfactory to the understanding, as light is to the eye; and that there is really implanted in our natures *We have a natural appetite after knowledge.* an appetite after knowledge. It is indeed a mistake to imagine that we have no appetites of the moral kind. The desire of society, and the impatient thirst after knowledge, are as properly appetites, as hunger and thirst, *&c.* The mind of man is naturally anxious and inquisitive; uneasy while it is in the dark about any thing, and anxious to un-<47>derstand it; and when it comes to a satisfactory knowledge of any object, it then looks upon it in a great measure as its own; as subdued by its understanding, and at its command; and thus it triumphs in its own power and force. And the oftner and more intensely this pleasure has been felt, the desire of knowledge waxes stronger and keener. It grows in proportion as it has been exercised and gratified by study and contemplation. But let us observe how this natural desire of knowledge is excited, supported, gratified and directed.[a]

a. See *Cicero de officiis,* Lib. 1. In primis que hominis est propria veri inquisitio, &c. Tantus est igitur innatus in nobis cognitionis amor & scientiae ut nemo dubitare possit, quin ad eas res hominum natura nullo emolumento invitata rapiatur. *De finibus.* Lib. 5. [Cicero, *De officiis,* I.iv.13: "Above all, the search after truth is peculiar

II. New or uncommon objects greatly attract our minds, and give us very high pleasure. Now by this means we are prompted to look out for new ideas, and to give all diligence to make fresh discoveries in science. "Every thing that is new or uncommon (says an excellent writer[a]) raises a pleasure in the imagination, because it fills the soul with an agreeable surprize, gratifies its curiosity, and gives it an idea of which it was not before possessed. We are indeed so often conversant with one set of objects, and tired out with so many repeated shows of the same things, that whatever is new or uncommon, contributes not a little to vary human life, and to divert our minds for a while with the strangeness of its appearance; it serves us for a kind of refreshment, and takes off from that satiety we are apt to complain of, in our usual and ordinary entertainments. It is this that bestows charms on a monster, and makes even the imperfections of nature please us. It is this that recommends variety, <48> when the mind is every instant called off to something new, and the attention not suffered to dwell too long, and waste itself on any particular object. It is this likewise, which improves what is great or beautiful, and makes it afford the mind double entertainment. Groves, fields, meadows, are at any season of the year pleasant to look upon, but never so much as at the beginning of the spring, when they are all new and fresh, with their first gloss upon them, and not yet too much accustomed and familiar to the eye. For this reason there is nothing more enlivens a prospect, than rivers, jetteaus, or falls of water, when the scene is perpetually changing, and entertaining the sight every moment with something that is new: We are quickly tired with looking upon hills and valleys, where every thing continues fixed and settled in the same place and

New or uncommon objects wonderfully attract our attention.

---

to man, etc." Cicero, *De officiis,* trans. Walter Miller, Loeb Classical Library (London: Heinemann; Cambridge: Harvard University Press, 1938). *De finibus,* V.xviii.48: "So great is our innate love of learning and of knowledge, that no one can doubt that man's nature is strongly attracted to these things even without the lure of any profit." Cicero, *De finibus bonorum et malorum,* trans. H. Rackham, Loeb Classical Library (London: Heinemann; New York: Putnam, 1931).]

a. See the essays on the pleasures of imagination, *Spectator,* Vol. 6. [*The Spectator,* nos. 411–21, 1712. The series of eleven papers "on the Pleasures of the Imagination" were written by Joseph Addison (1672–1719). The quote is from no. 412.]

posture; but find our thoughts not a little agitated and relieved at the sight of such objects as are ever in motion, and sliding away from beneath the eye of the beholder."

The final rea-
son or cause
why it is so.

After this description of several effects of novelty, it will be easy to every one to run over many more of the same class in his imagination; and the reason why we are so made, is because we are made for motion and progress: not to stand still, but to go forward and proceed; we are made for encrease, and gradual advancement; and therefore variety is naturally so agreeable, that we cannot be easy without making some new acquirements.

How this itch
of novelty is
checked and
ballanced by
the power of
habit.

But by way of counterpoise in our frame to this useful desire of novelty, and delight in variety, lest it should render us too superficial in our attention to objects, and too rambling and desultory in our quest of knowledge, it is so ordered by our make, that by continuing a little while our attention to the same object, a liking to it is contracted: an object, by being frequently present to our view, be-<49>comes familiar to us, we form an intimacy with it.[a] And thus, as the pleasure of friendship retains us from continually running about in search of new faces, so the habitude of studying in the same train, or of considering the same kind of ideas, by rendring them more agreeable to us, contributes to make us more fixed and steady in our application to the consideration of an object, till we have fully examined it. It prevents our becoming too changeable and unsettled in our pursuit of knowledge, ever to make great advances in any kind of it. Such is the power of habit, which shall be more fully considered afterwards: and hence the sage advice given by philosophers with regard to the choice of one's business or profession in life, "To choose the best, that is, the most advantageous, and custom will make it agreeable."

a. Habit is more fully considered afterwards in a particular chapter.

III. The mind naturally delights in comparing ideas, and in traceing their agreements and disagreements, their resemblances and differences; and it is thus that knowledge is acquired. But which greatly contributes at once to give pleasure to the mind in the pursuit of knowledge, and to direct it to the proper objects and methods of inquiry, is the natural delight of the mind in uniformity amidst variety; or in other words, in unity of design, and the consent of parts to one end. The objects of contemplation that please immediately, or at their first appearance to the mind, are those that are found upon after-examination, to be regular, to have unity, or to make systems easily taken in and comprehended by the mind. Every such form naturally attracts the mind, and is wonderfully agreeable to it. It could not do so, were we not so formed as <50> to receive a particular, distinguishing pleasure from such objects: for whatever pleases, necessarily presupposes an aptitude or disposition in our nature to be agreeably affected by it. Now being so framed as to be naturally and necessarily affected by such objects as have been described, in an agreeable manner, we are thus prompted by nature to delight in the contemplation of such objects, and to seek after them. We are by this means led, impelled and directed to resolve every object into its constituent parts, and to refer these parts to one another, and to their common end; or to consider a thing as a whole, and to look out for its principal meaning scope and intent, and to enquire how that is accomplished; by which means, by the simplest, and those that are merely necessary, or by too complex a way and superfluous toil. It is thus we are led to enquire into nature, trace its analogies and harmonies, or general laws, and to admire its simplicity and frugality. And in like manner in abstract science, as in mathematics, for example, we are conducted by the same principle, to aim at universal conclusions, or such general theorems and canons, as contain in them a great variety of particular cases. It is the same taste that enables us to distinguish what we call ease and grace, whether in external motion, or any composition of wit and genius; namely, our sense of the beauty which consists in the due medium between the *nimium & parum,* the too little and too much; for so the *decorum* is defined by the antients; and all beauty, whether in nature itself,

The natural delight of the mind in beauty.

In natural beauty.

Thus we are led to enquire after analogies and general laws in nature.

or in the arts that imitate nature, ultimately resolves itself into the observance of this maxim, "*Frustra sit per plura quod per pauciora fieri potest.*" Nature is beautiful, because nature "*nihil frustra facit.*"[26] Nature is simple, and we are most aptly contrived to delight in nature, to find out the proper way of studying and imitating it, by <51> our natural delight in the beauty which results from simplicity and regularity.[a]

The natural delight of our mind in moral beauty.

But besides our natural sense of beauty and harmony in material objects, arising from unity amidst variety, we have analogous to it another sense, *viz.* a sense of beauty in affections, actions and characters. Beauty in merely corporeal forms is indeed exceeding entertaining to the mind.

a. This maxim is well explained by Sir *Isaac Newton,* Natura superfluis causis non luxurat. All beauty natural or moral consists in this. See what *Cicero* says of our natural and moral sense of beauty, in the beginning of his first book of Offices; and compare it with several other passages, that in particular, Lib. 1. Cap. 28. where he treats of the *Decorum* at full length. See likewise what he says of the *nimium & parum* ad M. Brutum Orator N. 22. Ed. Schrivelii. See likewise *Theages Pythagoreus, de virtutibus.* Decorum autem est quod esse decet, id quod nec addi quicquam, nec demi postulat, quandoquidem, ipsum quod esse decet est: Indecori vero species duae sunt *nimium & parum.* Illud plus quam decet habet, hoc minus habet, &c. [Newton, *Principia,* Regulae philosophandi, regula I, "[Nature] does not indulge in the luxury of superfluous causes."

Cicero, *De officiis,* I.iv.14; I.xxviii.98–99: "nimium and parum"—"too much" and "too little"; see *Orator,* xxii.73, in Cicero, *Brutus . . . , Orator,* trans. H. M. Hubbell, Loeb Classical Library (London: Heinemann; Cambridge: Harvard University Press, 1939).

Turnbull appears to have used Schrevel's edition of Cicero; see Cicero, *Opera Omnia,* ed. Cornelis Schrevel, 4 vols. (Amsterdam, 1661).

Theages Pythagoreus, *De virtutibus,* in Gale, *Opuscula,* 690: "A right thing is as it should be, not needing anything to be added to it nor subtracted from it, since it is as it should be. Things that are not right are of two kinds, those that are excessive and those that are deficient. Something of the former kind has more than it should, something of the latter has less, etc." All Turnbull's Latin quotes from the Pythagoreans appear to be taken from Gale, ed., *Opuscula mythologica, physica et ethica. Graece et Latine. . . .* (Amsterdam, 1688).]

26. Newton, *Principia,* Regulae philosophandi, regula 1: "What can be done by fewer means is done in vain by more" and "[nature] does nothing in vain." Isaac Newton, *The Principia: Mathematical Principles of Natural Philosophy: A New Translation,* by I. Bernard Cohen and Anne Whitman (Berkeley and London: University of California Press, 1999).

"There is nothing that makes its way more directly to the soul than beauty, which immediately diffuses a secret satisfaction and complacency through the imagination, and gives a finishing to any thing that is great or uncommon. The first discovery of it strikes the mind with secret joy, and spreads a chearfulness and delight through all its faculties."[27] But does not every one feel that beauty of the moral kind is yet more charming and transporting than any corporeal beauty! And what is that, but such a tendency of an action to publick good, as shews generous intention, and benevolent affection in the agent. Now as by the former sense we are impelled and pointed to look out for unity of design, simplicity and consent of parts, and therefore to trace analogies in nature, and to reduce like appearances to general laws; so by the latter, we are prompted and directed to enquire after the goodness and fitness of general laws, that is, their tendency to the good of the whole to which they belong, or which <52> is constituted and regulated by them. This taste of the mind as naturally leads us to such researches as any other appetite impells us to gratify it. And do not these two dispositions in our nature, so analogous to one another, make an excellent provision or assistance for our making progress in knowledge? They naturally point us towards the objects, and methods of enquiring, that will be at once most pleasing and useful. They tell us, as it were, what we ought chiefly to employ our enquiries about, and how we ought to manage them.

Thus we are led to enquire after good final reasons.

IV. To conclude. We are considerably aided and directed in our researches after knowledge, by our natural delight in great objects, or such as wonderfully dilate and expand the mind, and put its grasp to the trial. For thus we are prompted not only to admire the grandeur of nature in general, or in the large and astonishing prospects its immensity affords us; and in the greatness of some particular objects of nature, of an enlivening and sublime kind; but in that greatness of manner which appears every where in its methods of operation, even in the minutest objects of sense; and to copy after this greatness of nature in our imitations

The natural delight of our mind in great objects.

27. *The Spectator,* no. 412, 1712.

of it by arts.^a The mind being naturally great, <53> and fond of power and perfection, delights highly in trying its strength, and in stretching itself, and therefore is exceeding pleased with those objects <54> that dilate it, or give it occasion and excite it to expand itself.

    a. See the *Spectators* upon the pleasures of imagination, Vol. 6, where all these sources of pleasure are handled, novelty, beauty and greatness. See particularly what is there said of the last. By greatness, I do not only mean the bulk of any single object, but the largeness of a whole view, considered as one entire piece. Such are the prospects of an open champain country, a vast uncultivated desart, of huge heaps of mountains, high rocks and precipices, or a wide expanse of waters, where we are not struck with the novelty or beauty of the sight, but with that rude kind of magnificence, which appears in many of these stupendous works of nature. Our imagination loves to be filled with an object, or to grasp at any thing that is too big for its capacity. We are flung into a pleasing astonishment at such unbounded views, and feel a delightful stillness and amazement in the soul at the apprehensions of them. The mind of man naturally hates every thing that looks like a restraint upon it, and is apt to fancy itself under a sort of confinement, when the sight is pent up in a narrow compass, and shortened on every side by the neighbourhood of walls or mountains. On the contrary, a spacious horizon is an image of liberty, where the eye has room to range abroad, to expatiate at large on the immensity of its views, and to lose itself amidst the variety of objects that offer themselves to its observation. He illustrates this remark afterwards by examples from gardening,—from architecture. See what he says there of greatness of manner. In the second place we are to consider greatness of manner in architecture, which has such force upon the imagination, that a small building when it appears, shall give the mind nobler ideas than one of twenty times the bulk, where the manner is ordinary and little. Thus perhaps, a man would have been more astonished with the majestick air that appeared in one of *Lysippus*'s Statues of *Alexander,* though no bigger than the life, than he might have been with mount *Atlas,* had it been cut into the figure of the hero, according to the proposal of *Phidias,* with a river in one hand, and a city in the other. Let any one reflect on the disposition of mind he finds in himself, at his first entrance into the *Pantheon* at *Rome,* and how his imagination is filled with something great and amazing; and at the same time consider how little in proportion he is affected with the inside of a gothic cathedral, though it be five times larger than the other; which can arise from nothing else but the greatness of the manner in the one, and the meanness in the other.—See the observation he adds from Mr. *Freart*'s parallel of the ancient and modern architecture.—Compare with these observations what *Longinus* says *de Sublimitate,* Cap. 35. Naturam non humile nos quoddam, aut contemptum animal reputasse.—Sed invictum una simul & insuperabile mentibus nostris omnis magnae rei, & humanam conditionem excedentis, adeoque divinioris, ingeneravisse desiderium. Atque hinc fieri, ut humanae mentis contemplationi & conjectui ne totus quidam orbis sufficiat, sed ipsos saepenumero ambientis omnia caeli terminos immensa animi agitatione transcendat.—inde intelliget, cui nos rei nati simus. Itaque instinctu illo ducti naturae

Let us now proceed to consider a little some of our faculties or powers, by which we are fitted for knowledge. And here we may observe, 1. That the imagination is a faculty of wonderful use in our frame: it is by this faculty that we have memory, and are able to recal absent objects to our mind, set lovely pictures of them before us, and thus contemplate and examine them, as if they were actually present with us. 2. It is this faculty that renders us capable of many delightful imitative arts, which for that reason are called arts of imagination. Both these facts are too obvious to need any proof. 3. But it is well worth while to remark how it comes about, that imagination is capable of affording us such a vast variety of pleasures, and of inventing so many fine arts, as rhetoric, poetry, painting, &c. for it is evident, that without the imagination these arts would be absolutely unknown to us. Now it has been often observed on that subject, that such is the analogy between sensible and moral objects, that there is none of the latter sort that may not be cloathed with a sensible form or image, and represented to us as it were in a material shape and hue. So true is this, that not only are wit and poetry owned to take place only in consequence of this analogy or resemblance of moral and natural ideas; but even all language is confessed to be originally taken from sen-

The imagination a most useful power.

It is necessary to render us capable of social commerce by discourse.

---

non exiles miramur rivulos, quamvis puro pellucidiores vitro & humanis magis apti sint usibus: verum conspectum vel Danubii vel Rheni resistimus attoniti; maxime omnium ad ipsius intuitum oceani. Ad eundem modum non igniculum aut flammulam, &c. [*The Spectator,* nos. 411–21, 1712. The first quote is from no. 412, the examples from gardening from no. 414, and the quote about architecture is from no. 415. The translation by John Evelyn of Roland Fréart's *Parallele de l'architecture antique et de la moderne* (1650) was first published in 1664.

   Longinus, *De sublimitate,* ch. 35: "that nature did not think we were lowly or contemptible animals, but implanted in our minds an invincible and at the same time indomitable love of everything which is great, which exceeds the human condition and is more divine. And hence it is that the whole world is not sufficient for the contemplation and conjecture of the human mind, which, by a stirring of the soul, often rises beyond the very boundaries of the all-encompassing sky. The mind will thereby understand what it is for which we were born. And, led by an instinct implanted by nature, we do not admire the little streams, although their water is clear and they are more useful to human beings, but we stand in awe at the sight of the Danube or Rhine, and above all at the sight of the ocean. Nor likewise as regards the spark or little flame, etc."]

sible objects, or their properties and effects. But the real truth of the
matter perhaps is not very generally attended to, which is, "That moral
ideas could not at all be expressed by words, if they could not be pictured
to us by means of analogous sensible objects." Not only are those the
best words to express moral objects in oratory or poetry, which suggest
the liveliest, the strongest, the clearest images or pictures of <55> them
derived from sensible forms: but in general, words cannot express any
moral objects, but by exciting pictures of them in our minds. But all
words being originally expressive of sensible qualities, no words can express moral ideas, but so far as there is such an analogy betwixt the natural
and moral world, that objects in the latter may be shadowed forth, pictured or imaged to us by some resemblances to them in the former. It is
imagination therefore that renders us capable of social intercourse and
commerce, even about moral ideas, and their relations, by mutual discourse. And so far as language can go in communicating sentiments, so
far have we an indisputable proof of analogy between the sensible and
the moral world; and consequently of wonderful wisdom and goodness,
in adjusting sensible and moral relations and connexions one to another;
the sensible world to our minds, and reciprocally the connexions of
things relative to our moral powers to the connexions of things that
constitute the sensible world. It is this analogy that makes the beauty,
propriety, and force of words, expressive of moral ideas, by conveying
pictures of them into the mind; so little attended to in teaching languages, whereby the study of language is rendered so jejune and insipid;
whereas, if rightly taught, by it great insight would early be got into one
of the most entertaining and useful parts of knowledge; and that clearly
manifests the wisdom and goodness of nature in our fabric; namely, the
analogy or consent between the moral and natural world, in consequence
of which, words primitively signifying sensible ideas, may convey moral
ones into the mind by analogy.

But whatever may be thought of this assertion, it is plain from the consideration of poetry, oratory, or any of the arts which are capable of
touching or moving the heart agreeably, that nature has given us the
imaginative faculty on purpose to enable us to <56> give warming as

We could not have mutual commerce by discourse, were not the moral world analogous to the natural world.

The right method of teaching language would teach us this analogy.

It is by fancy that our passionate part is reached.

well as enlightening colours to truths; or to embellish, recommend and enforce them upon the mind. For tho' truths may be rendered evident and certain to the understanding by reasoning about them, yet they cannot reach our heart, or bestir our passionate part but by means of the imagination. The fine arts are, indeed, but so many different languages by which truths may be represented, illustrated and recommended to us. And these arts show us the power and use of fancy, by making us feel its influence on the heart, or how directly it makes its way to it. But the moral power of imagination, must be evident to every one who reflects how it is, for instance, that any absent object is able to outweigh a present pleasure in our mind. For how else is it that the remote one receives strength, but by the lively affecting manner in which imagination represents it, so as to render it as it were present, or, at least, tho' absent, so efficacious, that no interveening self-denial, or suffering is sufficient to retard the mind from pursuing it, with the utmost intenseness? 'Tis a lively picture drawn by the fancy that does all this.

Now, if it be asked, why we are so constituted? Perhaps if we had a fuller knowledge of the human mind, we might be able to see many reasons for it: mean time, 'tis sufficient to vindicate nature for having so framed us, that we plainly see, how in consequence of such a constitution, we are able to become *Poets,* in the proper sense of the word, that is, *Creators;* able to vie with nature and rival it; and that to it we owe a vast variety of very noble pleasures, far superior to those of meer sense, even all those which genius, wit, refined fancy, and the fine arts that imitate or contend with nature afford us.

Why we are so constituted.

IV. With regard to imagination, let it be observed, that tho' it be thought by such as have not taken proper pains to form and improve it, a meer <57> rambler, and utterly incapable of governance; yet ancient philosophers have assured us from their experience, "That if habitual temperance be added to just care to cultivate the imagination, and give it a right turn, such a command may be obtained over it, that its employments even in dreams shall not only be pure and chaste, but very regular as well as highly entertaining." It is indeed not to be wondered at, con-

Imagination is not ingovernable.

sidering how egregiously the formation of fancy is neglected in education, that it should be so irregular, desultory and turbulent a faculty,
instead of a pleasant, governable and useful one. Philosophers satisfy
themselves with railing at it, as a pernicious rather than an advantageous
part of our frame; as being instead of an assistant in the pursuit of science, an enemy to truth; a misleader, a sophist, and corrupter: but were
it not capable of being not only regulated, but highly refined and improved by due care, mankind had been utter strangers to all the entertaining and embellishing arts of fancy, which give such lustre, beauty
and taste to human life; to all the ingenious productions of men of wit
and fine imagination: the advances that have been made towards its improvement, to which we owe so many great genius's, and their delightful
productions and compositions, are a sufficient argument, that by timely
care duly persevered in, it might be habituated to order regularity and
wholesome as well as pleasant exercise. Is it to be wondered, that those
whose waking thoughts are so irregular and unprofitable, should have
very idle and impertinent visions in their sleep? But so true is the antient
maxim about the correspondence or analogy between our dreams and
our employments throughout the day, that I believe no temperate man,
much given to study,[a] is not rather entertained <58> than molested by

---

a. Jubet igitur Plato, sic ad somnum proficisci corporibus affectis, ut nihil sit quod
errorem animis, perturbationemque afferat. Ex quo etiam Pythagoricis interdictum
putatur, *ne faba vescerentur,* quod habet inflationem magnam is cibus, tranquilitati
mentis, quaerentis vera contrariam.

Cicero de Divinat, Lib. I. No. 30.

Omnia quae sensu volvuntur vota diurno,
Pectore sopito reddit amica quies;
Me quoque musarum studium sub nocte silenti,
Artibus assuetis sollicitare solet.

[Cicero, *De divinatione,* I.xxx.62–63: "Now Plato's advice to us is to set out for
the land of dreams with bodies so prepared that no error or confusion may assail the
soul. For this reason, it is thought, the Pythagoreans were forbidden to indulge in
beans; for that food produces flatulence and induces a condition at war with a soul
in search of truth."

The four lines of verse are formed by stitching together Claudian, 27 (*Panegyricus
de Sexto Consulatu Honorii Augusti;* Praefatio), lines 1–2 and 11–12. Lines 1–6 and
11–12 are cited as a unity by Addison as the motto of no. 463 of *The Spectator,* Au-

his night reveries, provided he be in a good habit of body. As for the dependence of body and mind, it shall be considered in another place. And the dependence of the imagination upon culture, or our care to improve it, and exercise it rightly, hath been already accounted for, by shewing, that according to the general law of our nature in consequence of which we have dominion, a sphere of activity, and are capable of making acquisitions, and by that means of virtue and merit; the improvement of all our faculties depends on ourselves; and it is the dependence of the improvement of the understanding, reason, imagination, and all our faculties upon our care to improve them, that makes us a species of beings superior to those who have no activity, but only receive sensations from without independently of their own will, choice or foresight.

The other faculty of our minds, that remains to be considered under this article of knowledge, and power, and the laws relative to them, is invention.

Now with respect to it I would observe,

I. That the phenomena of invention appear to us very irregular and whimsical, merely because, for want of a history of them, we cannot reduce them to general laws. Every thing must appear to us casual, anomalous, and as it were detached from nature, while we do not know the general laws on which it depends, or from which it results. And <59> therefore till we be at more pains, than hath yet been taken, to collect a

Invention what it is and how improveable.

---

gust 21, 1712. This may be Turnbull's source. In Broughton's *Mottoes,* the lines are translated as:

What e'er Delights employ our waking Sense,
The Same does fancy to our Dreams Dispence.
My self so close to my gay Studies keep,
That oft I am composing in my Sleep.
                    Thomas Broughton, *The Mottoes of the Spectators,*
        Tatlers and Guardians, translated into English (London, 1735).]

A history of it,
and the phe-
nomena relat-
ing to it, is
much wanted.

history relating to invention, there can be no other reason to call any of them casual and irregular, than there was to call several other phenomena of nature such, while their laws were not known, which now that they are found out, do no more appear to us to be such. On the contrary, there is good reason to think, that the phenomena of invention may have their general laws; since in whatever case almost we have taken right methods of tracing effects to their general laws, such laws have been discovered; and then the effects which before appeared irregular, immediately changed their face, and assumed, as it were, another mein: they now no more seem uncouth and marvelous, but ordinary and according to rule. It is only in the way of experiment, that either the science of the human mind, or of any material system can be acquired. And by the discoveries made in natural philosophy, we know, that no sooner are facts collected, and laid together in proper order, than the true theory of the phenomenon in question presents itself. And hence, we have reason to think, that knowledge of the qualities and operations of bodies, would quickly make very great and profitable advances, far beyond what it has yet arrived to, by pursuing the same method that has brought it to the present degree of perfection. Now when we consider that moral knowledge can only be carried on in the same way, is it any wonder that the human mind is so little known, since men have not studied it with due care, but have rather been more misled in this philosophy, than in natural, by fictitious hypotheses and romantic, visionary theories? For such are all theories that are not the result of well ranged phenomena.

What dis-
covery of new
truths is.

II. But tho, without all doubt, it is highly reasonable to expect very great assistances for the promoti-<60>on and improvement of all sciences and arts from an acurate knowledge of our inventive powers, that is, from a full history of their operations and productions; yet, in the mean time, 'tis plain, that invention is nothing else but the habit acquired by practice of assembling ideas or truths, with facility and readiness, in various positions and arrangements, in order to have new views of them. For no truths can be placed in any position or order with respect to one another, but some agreement or disagreement, some relation or quality of these ideas must appear to the mind. And discovery of a new or unknown relation can be nothing else but the result of placing truths, objects or ideas, in some new or unobserved position. But, if this be the case, then the great business with regard to invention and its improvement, must be to accustom ourselves to look round every idea as it were, and to view it in all possible situations and positions; and to let no truth we know pass, till we have compared it with many others in various respects; not only with such, as are like or a kin to it, but with its seeming contraries, opposites, or disparates. Every different juxtaposition of ideas, will give us a new view of them, that is, discover some unknown truth. And the mind by such exercise alone can attain to readiness, quickness and distinctness, in comparing ideas in order to get knowledge.

And how they are made.

III. Now, this leads me to the last remark I shall make upon our natural furniture for knowledge, which is, that knowledge being progressive and dependent on ourselves; it, by that means, becomes easy to us to make advances in it, in the best and properest way that it can become so, that is, in the way that is qualified to give us the greatest pleasure. For it becomes easier to improve in knowledge, in proportion to the improvements we have made in it. Our inventive, imaginative, comparing and reasoning powers become stronger, more alert, and vigor-<61>ous by proper exercise. The habit of reasoning well, that is, readily and solidly, is acquired by practice in reasoning. And which is more, in consequence of having inured ourselves to accurate thinking, and of having made several advances in science, we become able to form rules to ourselves for our further progress in knowledge in the best, that is, the clearest, quickest, and surest manner. In other words, knowledge may be made easy to us by ourselves, because after we have made some progress in it, after we have exercised our enquiring, comparing and reasoning powers, for some time, about different objects; we can then make enquiring, comparing, reasoning, inventing, and laying truths together in proper order, to bring out new conclusions, the objects of our consideration; and thus we can form a science concerning science and making progress in it. A science, by the by, which ever since *Plato*'s time has been very

How it becomes easier to make progress in knowledge by progress.

And by that science which is properly the art of reasoning.

much neglected in education; and very little cultivated, notwithstanding all Lord *Verulam* has said in his works of its nature and usefulness.[a]

General con-
clusion con-
cerning the
laws of knowl-
edge, and our
natural furni-
ture for it.
Thus then we see how excellently we are furnished[b] by nature for the pleasures of knowledge, and for improving in sciences and arts; so that we may conclude, "That with regard to knowledge, (the foundation of intelligent power, dominion and activity) we are very well constituted; or that all the most important circumstances, or laws relative to our understanding, are very fitly chosen, being necessary to very great goods or perfections." <62>

a. See my Lord *Bacon*'s works, his *Essay on the advancement of learning;* and his *Novum organum. Milton*'s *Letter on education. Plato de republica,* Page 533, 34, 39. Ed. Step. And my *treatise on ancient painting,* Chap. 1. [John Milton, "Of Education," in *Poems, &c upon Several Occasions,* 2d ed. (London, 1673).]

b. See *Cicero de finibus,* l. 5. *de legibus.* l. 1. Animal hoc providum, sagax, multiplex, acutum memor, plenum rationis, & consilii, quem vocamus hominem, praeclara quadam conditione a supremo Deo natum esse, &c. [Cicero, *De legibus,* I.vii.22: ". . . that animal which we call man, endowed with foresight and quick intelligence, complex, keen, possessing memory, full of reason and prudence, has been given a certain distinguished status by the supreme God who created him, etc."]

Let us now consider our relation to the material world, and the reciprocal dependence of our body and mind with the chief effects that result from this source.

I. First, it is evident, that relation to or connexion with a sensible world, must consist in a certain dependence on its laws, so as to be variously affected by them with pleasure and pain; or, a certain bodily organization, by means of which, certain perceptions and affections are excited in the mind. Existence would be thrown away upon a material system, if it were not perceived by minds or enjoyed by them. But the bodily fabric which is necessary to our communication with matter, must necessarily be subject to the laws of that matter. Whatever the frame and structure of it may be, or of whatever materials this body is composed, it must be liable to the common laws, to which the whole material part of the creation, to which it is related, is subject. Now by the late discoveries in natural philosophy, it has been proved, that the centripedal and centrifugal forces which hold our mundan system in that perfect order, which it is so beautiful to behold and contemplate, are the best in every respect that can be imagined: insomuch that no alteration can be supposed with regard to them that would not be attended with much greater irregularities and inconveniencies, than all those put together which result from the present laws.

In like manner, with respect to our earth, gravitation, cohesion, fermentation, to which general principles almost all its phenomena are reducible, have been shewn to be excellent laws, and that no o-<63>thers could be substituted in their room, which would not be exceedingly for

The laws relative to our embodied state, and our connexion with a material world.

Communication with the material world necessarily supposes dependence on its laws.

These laws are good.

This proved by natural philosophers.

the worse. In a word, it has been proved, that our mundan system in all its parts is governed by excellent general laws, in so much that all objections that have been made against its constitution and oeconomy, have either taken their rise from ignorance of its real state and frame, and of the laws by which it is actually governed; and consequently only serve to shew the absurdity of [a] imaginary theories in natural philosophy; or they really terminate in demanding some change greatly to the worse. But such conclusions quite destroy all objections that can be made against our being related to and connected with the sensible world; for to be related to it, and connected with it, without being subject to its laws, is utterly impossible. It is to depend without dependence: it is to be united without any connexion. But a dependence or a connexion that produces greater good in the whole, must be a good dependence. Let us therefore see what goods, advantages or pleasures arise from our having bodies, and being capable of commerce with a material world.

A material world without being perceived could be of no use.

II. But let it be observed before we proceed, that as a material world cannot be said to have order and beauty; or to be wisely contrived, but with respect to beings, who perceive it, and are affected by it; or cannot indeed be created for any end, but so far as perceptive beings have communication with it: so were there not in nature such a kind of beings as we are, nature could not be full or coherent: there would be a chasm or void in nature which could not but render it deformed and imperfect to the view of any being capable of perceiving it; who hath, like us, any idea of richness, fulness, and perfection in nature. For so are we made,

Without beings capable of enjoying a material world, nature would not be full and coherent.

that we cannot repre-<64>sent nature to ourselves as perfect and beautiful, without conceiving it to be full and coherent: we cannot suppose any degree of perfection wanting in the scale of life, that can exist, without being shocked at the thought of such a deficiency, such incompleteness, such a void and breach.

a. See *Discourses on the origine of evil, natural and moral*, by Dr. *John Clark*. [John Clarke, *An Enquiry into the Cause and Origin of Evil* (London, 1720). The whole book deals with this topic, but see especially p. 48.]

III. But not only is such a being as man necessary to make the gradation in nature full and complete; but the sensible pleasures we are susceptible of by means of our bodily organization, or our senses, do well deserve their place in the scale of life and being. The more pleasures a creature is by nature made capable of, the larger provision is certainly made for its happiness: now the enjoyments we are made capable of receiving from a corporeal world, by means of our sensitive organs, are not a few: the variety of them belonging to any of our senses, as for instance, to the sight or ear, is almost innumerable. And all these senses, with all their appurtenances, are admirably adjusted to one another, to our external condition, and to our whole bodily texture, made up of them, and preserved entire by their equal nourishment and sustentation. Thus, for example, our sight, at the same time that it is capable of receiving considerable assistances from artificial instruments, is wonderfully well adapted to judge of magnitudes, distances, and other tangible qualities; it being by contact and motion only, that the mechanism of the body can suffer any injury. In like manner, all our other senses are very well adjusted to one another, and to our situation, as has been often observed by several philosophers. This is delightfully told by our excellent poet already quoted.

By our commerce with a material world we receive a great many pleasures of the sensitive kind.

Our senses are admirably adjusted to one another, and to our whole frame.

> *Why has not man a microscopic eye?*
> *For this plain reason, man is not a fly:* <65>
> *Say, what the use, were finer opticks giv'n?*
> *T' inspect a mite, not comprehend the heav'n.*
> *Or touch, so tremblingly alive all o'er?*
> *To smart and agonize at ev'ry pore.*
> *Or quick effluvia darting thro' the brain?*
> *Die of a rose in aromatic pain.*
> *If nature thunder'd in his opening ears,*
> *And stunn'd him with the music of the spheres,*
> *How would he wish that heav'n had left him still*
> *The whisp'ring zephyr, and the purling rill?*
> *Who finds not providence all good and wise,*
> *Alike in what it gives, and what denies?*
>   Essay on man, Epist. 1.[28]

28. Pope, *Essay on Man*, I.193–206.

But though the pleasures our senses afford us be very many, and far from being despicable in their kind; yet the chief advantages our senses bring us, are, as they are means and instruments of sciences and arts; and the means, occasions and subjects of many excellent virtues.

Our senses are instruments of noble sciences and useful arts.

I. Our communication with the sensible world is not only the source of very considerable enjoyments to us, as sensitive beings; but it is yet a source of more noble pleasures to us, as we are capable of knowledge and imitation.

By our bodily senses, our minds are rendered capable of contemplating, and of imitating by ingenious arts, many parts of a very wonderful system; many parts of a most beautiful disposition and arrangement of infinitely various objects. For how immense is the variety of the sensible world? Can there be a more delightful, or a more capacious field of study and speculation, than what the riches, the simplicity, the grandeur and perfect order of the natural world afford us? What is greater,

Of natural philosophy.

or more elevating, than the contemplation of nature, when we are able to take in large views of it, and comprehend its laws? How agreeably do an-<66>cient philosophers expatiate upon this topic!ᵃ The study of nature, according to them, is the natural food of the soul. And they indeed

a. So *Cicero de natura Deorum,* Lib. 2. Ipse autem homo natus est ad mundum contemplandum & imitandum. Idem *de senectute.* Sed credo, Deos immortalis sparsisse animos in corpora humana, ut essent, qui terras tuerentur, quique caelestium ordinem contemplantes imitarentur eum vitae modo ac constantia.

Academ, Quest. Lib. 2. Est enim animorum ingeniorumque naturale quoddam quasi pabulum, consideratio, contemplatioque naturae, erigimur, altiores fieri videmur, humana despicimus, *&c.* [Cicero, *De natura deorum,* II.xiv.37: ". . . man himself however came into existence for the purpose of contemplating and imitating the world." Cicero, *De natura deorum, Academica,* trans. H. Rackham, Loeb Classical Library (London: Heinemann; New York: Putnam, 1933). *De senectute,* xxi.77: "But I believe that the immortal gods implanted souls in human bodies so as to have beings who would care for the earth and who, while contemplating the celestial order, would imitate it in the moderation and consistency of their lives." Cicero, *De senectute, De amicitia, De divinatione,* trans. William Armstead Falconer, Loeb Classical Library (Cambridge: Harvard University Press; London: Heinemann, 1923). *Academica,* II.xli.127: "For the study and observation of nature affords a sort of natural pasturage for the spirit and intellect; we are uplifted, we seem to become more exalted, we look down on what is human, etc."]

justly placed a great part of man's best happiness in contemplating and imitating the regularity, wisdom, goodness and harmony of the sensible world. They with good reason concluded from the structure of our senses, considered together with our intellectual powers, that we are made, "*Ad mundum contemplandum & imitandum.*"[29] To contemplate, admire and imitate nature. What distinguishes our senses[a] from those of the brutes, is, (as these philosophers have observed) that sense of beauty, order and harmony, with which they are united in our frame, by means of which they are not merely sensitive, but rather rational faculties. For by these outward and inward senses, as they are conjoined in our frame, we are capable of understanding the regularity and wisdom of nature; of investigating its general laws, and admiring the wonderful con-<67>sent of all its various parts to make one beautiful whole. Nor is this all, for we are likewise qualified by them for divers imitative arts, as poetry, painting, statuary, music, architecture, gardening, *&c.* from

And many imitative arts.

a. So *Cicero de nat. Deorum,* Lib. 2. Ad hanc providentiam naturae tam diligentem tamque solertem adjungi multa possunt, e quibus intelligatur, quantae res hominibus a Deo, quamque eximiae tributae sint, qui primum eos humo excitatos, celsos, & erectos constituit, ut Deorum cognitionem, coelum intuentes, capere possent. Sunt enim e terra homines non ut incolae, atque habitatores, sed quasi spectatores superarum rerum, atque caelestium, quarum spectaculum ad nullum aliud genus animantium pertinet. Sensus autem, interpretes, ac nuntii rerum, in capite; tanquam in arce, mirifice ad usus necessarios & facti & collocati sunt—Omnisque sensus hominum multo antecellit sensibus bestiarum. Primum enim oculi in iis artibus, quarum judicium est oculorum, in pictis, fictis, caelatisque formis, &c. [Cicero, *De natura deorum:* "Many further illustrations could be given of this wise and careful providence of nature, to illustrate the lavishness and splendour of the gifts bestowed by the gods on men. First, she has raised them from the ground to stand tall and upright, so that they might be able to behold the sky and so gain a knowledge of the gods. For men are sprung from the earth not as its inhabitants and denizens, but to be as it were the spectators of things supernal and heavenly, in the contemplation whereof no other species of animal participates. Next, the senses, posted in the citadel of the head as the reporters and messengers of the outer world, both in structure and position, are marvellously adapted to their necessary services" (II.lvi.140). "And all the senses of man far excel those of the lower animals. In the first place our eyes have a finer perception of many things in the arts which appeal to the sense of sight, painting, modelling and sculpture, etc." (II.lviii.145).]

29. Cicero, *De natura deorum,* II.xiv.37: "[for the purpose] of contemplating and imitating the world."

which arts do indeed arise pleasures very nearly allied to virtue, very assistant to it; and which, next to its exercises, are our noblest and most pleasing enjoyments.

They are means and subjects of many virtuous exercises.

II. But our senses are yet of further and higher use in our frame, as they afford us means, occasions and materials for exercising many virtues; many kindly, benevolent and generous affections.

Of the social kind.

It is in consequence of our having a corporeal frame, or of being cloathed with bodies, that we are visible, audible, and embraceable one to another; all which are sources of pleasures of a very agreeable kind, as well as of a social nature and tendency. How unembodied spirits have intercourse, is a question we cannot possibly solve; but this is certain, that our mutual correspondence is by means of our bodies. And scarcely will any one object against our frame, merely for our being thus made fit for commerce with one another, by the eyes and touch, and by the faculties of hearing and speech.

And of rational dominion over the sensitive appetites.

But which is yet more, in consequence of our having bodies, various occasions arise of our mutually aiding, relieving, comforting, pleasing and gratifying one another, and of interchanging many good and friendly offices, for which there could not otherwise in the nature of things be room. And not to add more on this head, is not the regulation of our senses, and their appetites after the gratifications suited to them, a most noble exercise for our reason and moral discernment? By this means, our guiding part hath something to guide and govern: subjects committed to its trust, keeping and management; subjects to provide for, and to rule and maintain in decent and good order and <68> discipline. We have therefore, in consequence of our having bodies, a moral dominion committed to us, in which to acquit ourselves honourably, that is, wisely and prudently, or according to truth, reason, and the fitness of things, is certainly the noblest employment we can form any notion of. The spheres or employments of other beings cannot be higher in kind; the difference can only be in species, or rather in degree. For what can be conceived more great or excellent, than to have business of importance to our own happiness, and that of our kind, to manage by reason; subjects to rule and conduct for the good of the whole? And such are we ourselves to ourselves by our make; that is, such are the inferior parts of our constitution, or our bodily appetites, to that which is principal in us, our reason and moral conscience.[a]

Thus therefore, in consequence of our having bodies, we are not only capable of contemplating and imitating the sensible world, and of various other pleasures; but our reason hath very proper practical employment. For thus is it that we are capable of all the virtues which are justly divided by ancient moralists into *Sustenence*[b] and *Abstinence;* or the power of being able to with-hold from the most inviting pleasures, if they be either pernicious in their consequences, or unbecoming our dignity: and the power of suffering any pain with magnanimity, rather than forego our reason, and contradict <69> our moral conscience, by yielding to what these pronounce base and unworthy.

All this, it is plain, supposes a moral sense in our constitution, of which something hath been already said, and that shall afterwards be considered more fully. Mean time, if it be true, that our relation to the sensible world is conducive, or rather necessary to the excellent purposes above-mentioned, it plainly follows, that a reciprocal union between our body and mind, must be morally fit and good.

But this will be yet more evident, if we consider a little some other

a. So *Cicero* and all the ancient moralists. See *Plutarch,* in particular, *de virtute morali.* Plato sensit hominis animam non simplicem esse, aut eodem per omnia modo affectam: sed aliam ejus partem intelligentem esse ac ratiocinatricem qua hominem regi naturae sit conveniens: aliam quae variis motibus obnoxia, bruta, vaga, & incomposita, & suapte natura gubernante opus habeat—quando autem bruta pars contra rationem contendat—Statim animus quasi in duas partes dividitur & manifesta sit discordia. [Plutarch, *De virtute morali:* "Plato thought that the soul of man" (441E) ". . . is not simple, nor is affected in the same way by all things. Instead it has one part which is intelligent and rational by which it is natural that human beings be ruled, and it has another part, one in need of a ruler, a part subject to many impulses, and animal-like, inconstant and lacking orderliness" (442A). "But when the animal part is in contention with reason, the mind is as it were immediately divided into two parts and the discord is plain" (448D). Plutarch, *Omnia quae extant opera,* 2 vols. (Paris, 1624).]

b. See *Epictetus, Arrian* and *Simplicius.* [See above, page 62, note a.]

effects, resulting from this reciprocal connexion, or from our dependence upon the laws of the sensible world, from which we receive so many pleasures, not merely of the sensitive kind.

The general law with respect to sensible pains.

I. It is plain from experience, that with respect to every sensitive being, within the reach of our observation, with respect to ourselves in particular, this is the general law of nature, "That the simple productions of nature, which are useful to us, are also agreeable to us,[a] and the pernicious, or useless, are made disagreeable, or give pain. Our external sensations are, no doubt, often painful, when our bodies are in a dangerous state, when they want supplies of nourishment, or when any thing external would be injurious to them. But if it appears that the general laws are wisely instituted, and it be necessary to the good of a system of agents to be under the influence of general laws, upon which there is occasion for prudence and activity; the particular pains occasioned by a necessary law of sensation, can be no objection against the goodness of the author.

Sensible pains whence they arise.

Now that there is no room for complaint that our external sense of pain is made too acute, must appear from the multitudes we daily see <70> so careless of preserving the blessing of health, of which many are so prodigal as to lavish it away, and expose themselves to external pains for very trifling reasons. Can we repine at the friendly admonitions of nature, joined with some austerity, when we see they are scarce sufficient to restrain us from ruin?" To this let it be added, that the external and superficial parts of our bodies are the most sensible, and cause the greatest pain when they are in any wise hurtfully affected; because they are exposed to many various external objects, and do thus give us immediate notice so soon as they are affected by them; whereas the internal parts being more remote, cannot be so easily come at, and consequently are not liable to so many interruptions from without, and therefore need

a. See *Hutcheson* on the *conduct of the passions,* and Dr. *J. Clark* on the *origine of evil.* [The quote is from Francis Hutcheson, *An Essay on the Nature and Conduct of the Passions. . . .* (1728); ed. Aaron Garrett (Indianapolis: Liberty Fund, 2002), I.VI.iii.]

not such subtle sensation. Thus we experience (say anatomists) that the veins, arteries, bones, and the like, have little or no sensation at all.[a]

II. But further, let it be considered, that of whatever materials a body be composed, or whatever its particular organization may be, it must in the nature of things, be liable to as many disorders as there are means of preventing or disturbing its natural course. In general, upon the supposition of our being capable of agreeable sensation, a proportionable degree of pain must ensue, upon any defect or excess whatsoever: because, if health consist in a certain balance or order, every deviation from that order, must be sickness or disease. Pleasant sensation must be produced in some order and method; that is, in order to it, a body must have a certain texture, and there must be a certain adjustment of external objects to that texture: but the result of this must be, that in a habitation like our earth, not made for any one species of animals, but fitted <71> for a variety of beings, somethings being adjusted to bodies of a different texture from ours, cannot but be contrary in their natures to ours, and so tend to a *solutio continui*[30] in respect of them. This is as plain and as necessary, as it is, that two parts of matter cannot tally, unless they are fitted by their make to one another. In other words, it is necessary in the nature of things, that bodies should have each a particular mechanism fitted for a certain end, or for certain enjoyments: and to every material mechanism, as there must be something congruous, in order to the having agreeable sensations; so in a material world, replenished with various animals, in order to make nature as rich and full with good as possible, some things will of necessity be incongruous, and consequently in some manner and degree pernicious to our particular mechanism, by being fitted to different bodies. For it is impossible but those objects, which are suitable to certain organizations, in order to affect them agreeably,

Several pains the necessary effects of a bodily organization.

a. See Dr. *J. Clark* on the *origine of evil.* [Clarke, *Origin of Evil,* 258–59.]

30. *Solutio continui*—the separation from each other of normally contiguous parts. See Bacon's essay "Of unity in religion" in his *Essays,* which may be Turnbull's source for the phrase. *Sir Francis Bacon: The Essayes or Counsels, Civill and Morall,* ed. M. Kiernan (Oxford: Clarendon Press, 1986).

must be incongruous to organizations of different forms; and being incongruous to them, they must have some tendency to hurt them. This is inevitably the result of the necessity of a thing's having a certain texture, and certain qualities in a determinate degree, in order to its being suitably proportioned or congruous to another certain texture, with its qualities. All things cannot possibly be equally congruous to all different sorts of organization.

Pains are useful and proper monitors.

III. But if our organization be liable to be destroyed or hurted by certain objects, in consequence of the impossibility, "That the same texture should be equally well fitted to all sorts of external impressions, that may happen through the influence of those very laws of matter and motion, which are acknowledged to be necessary to the general good and beauty of the material world, and to our receiving many pleasures of various kinds from it:" if this be <72> the case, it is certainly fit that whatever external object is pernicious, or tends to disturb and hurt the mechanism of our bodies in any considerable degree, should be signified to us by some means or other: Now the method that nature takes is this; "It is generally some pleasant sensation which teaches us what tends to our preservation and well-being; and some painful one which shews us what is pernicious;" "we are directed by uneasy appetites when our bodies stand in need of nourishment;" "and in like manner, it is by a sense of pain excited in us, that we are warned of the dangerous tendency of bruises, wounds, violent labour, and other such hurtful causes."[31]

Now the fitness of our being thus warned and admonished appears, because some warning is necessary; and there can be no other but what has been mentioned, except by knowledge of the natures of things, and their aptitudes to affect us agreeably or hurtfully. But knowledge is in the nature of things progressive, and can only be acquired gradually, as has been shewn, from experience, in proportion to our situation for making observations, and taking in ideas, and to our application to gather knowledge. The knowledge of nature is wisely left to be our own acquisition; and therefore some other warning, even that mentioned by painful sensations, is absolutely necessary to us. It is only some intuitive

---

31. Hutcheson, *Passions*. This is a close paraphrase of passages in I.II.vi.

kind of knowledge of bodies, by immediate inspection (which is hardly conceivable) that could supply the place of admonitions by pain, in order to self-preservation. And if we had such an intuitive knowledge of things as is necessary to this purpose; then no part of knowledge could be left to be our own acquisition by observation and reasoning. For what does not the intuitive knowledge, necessary to be our warner of dangerous applications or approaches to our bodies, include in it? It plainly comprehends in it an intuitive knowledge of our own body, and of all sur-<73>rounding objects to the influences of which it is exposed: that is, it comprehends an intuitive knowledge of the whole of nature. And consequently, having such knowledge (could we, or any creatures possibly have it, as 'tis plain from the nature of knowledge we cannot) is absolutely inconsistent with the dependence of any part of the knowledge of nature upon ourselves; or with such knowledge being in any degree our own acquisition; that is, with any thing's being left to be matter of observation and enquiry to us, or subject of exercise to our reason. All parts of natural or real knowledge are so connected together and involved in one another, that if any part of it were attainable by us otherwise than it now is, no part of it could be attainable, as it now is, *i.e.* by induction, and by reasoning from properties so discovered. And would we not thus be deprived of one of our pleasantest and noblest employments and acquisitions?

IV. Thus then we see the fitness of our being admonished by uneasy sensations of dangers to our bodies of bodily necessities and wants: because thus we are directed and impelled to relieve and preserve ourselves in such a manner, that reason, neither hath, on the one hand, little or no employment; nor, on the other, a very disagreeable and almost insurmountable task. But it is well observed by an excellent philosopher on this head, that when a necessity of adding strong uneasy sensations to one class of appetites appears, there must appear also a like necessity of strengthning the rest in the same mind by like sensations, to keep a just ballance.[32] And thus accordingly, our bodily appetites being for good

From the necessity there is, that bodily appetites should be attended with uneasy sensations arises the necessity of all the other uneasy sensations accompanying our desires which are called Passions.

32. "An excellent philosopher" is Hutcheson. The passage is a paraphrase from *Passions,* I.II.vi.

reasons accompanied with uneasy sensations, our moral desires and affections are strengthened in like manner by uneasy strong sensations to maintain a just balance; so is plainly the Στοργη or natural affection to children, so is compassion or pity to the distressed, and many other mo-<74>ral passions, that thus the public and social ones might not be too weak and feeble in proportion to those which terminate more directly and immediately in the preservation or gratification of our senses. In a constitution, where one degree of force is requisite, a proportionate degree of force in other parts becomes also necessary; otherwise the constituent parts would not bear that proportion to one another, which an equal and sound balance in the whole requires. It is the same here as with regard to antagonist muscles to counterpoise one another in the body.[a]

The laws of matter make an infant state of body necessary. V. Let me just add upon this head, that as for our coming into the world by the way of propagation we now do, and with weak, necessitous, infant bodies: It is a necessary result of the constitution of this material world to which we are related by our bodies; and besides the many good effects of it of the social kind which are very evident, "There is an absolute fitness, that beings made for progress in knowledge, and in every perfection by their own application and industry conjointly with assistances from society, and who consequently must enter upon the world with infant minds, should likewise enter upon it with infant bodies." How very unequally otherwise would our bodies and minds be yoked? How improper companions and mates would they be? As for death, what may be inferred concerning it, shall be considered, when having enquired into all the other principal laws relative to our present state, we are able to take a complete view of it. In the mean time, it is obvious, that death, or the dissolution of our bodily texture, in whatever way it happens, is always the result of our subjection to some of the laws of matter and motion, to which our union with the sensible world necessarily subjects <75> us, and to which are owing all the pleasures we receive from it in our present embodied state.

And the law of progressive perfection makes infant minds necessary.

a. See *Hutcheson, on the conduct of the passions,* in whose words I have given this observation. [The passage footnoted is a paraphrase of Hutcheson, *Passions,* I.VI.iii.]

VI. The other remarkable phenomenon with respect to our union with a material world is, "The dependence of genius, temper, and mental abilities upon the temperature of the body, air, diet, and other such physical causes." That a variety of mental temperatures, turns, dispositions and abilities prevail among mankind, will not be called into doubt. And as it is certain, that different textures of eyes must see differently; or every object must necessarily partake of the colour with which the eye itself is tainted: so variety in temperature, texture and mould, (so to speak) among minds, must necessarily produce great variety of conceptions, sentiments and judgments, and consequently of inclinations, appetites and dispositions. For, such as the soil is, such will the flavour of the fruit be in the natural world; and by like necessity in the moral, all the impressions, sentiments, judgments, and passions of a mind will be correspondent to its prevailing humour and character: they will necessarily partake in some degree of it. And, hence it is, that every man's turn of thinking is as distinguishable as his face or gate from that of every other: there are as few minds as faces that have not very peculiar and distinguishing features.[a]

The dependence of mental powers and dispositions on the body. A great variety in respect of these among mankind.

Now, that differences among minds, in texture and character, abilities and dispositions, are no less necessary to the well-being of society, and variety of beauty and good in it, than differences in complexions and countenances, is very evident at first sight, has been already hinted, and will appear more fully when we come to consider the laws of our nature relative to society. All therefore that belongs to the present question is, how far differences among minds <76> depend upon different textures, and temperaments of bodies, and physical causes, and how and why it is so?

How far that variety arises from and depends on physical causes.

I. I do not indeed pretend, that there may not be a great variety of genius's, characters and abilities among pure, unembodied spirits of the same species: on the contrary, wherever there is community, such di-

a. See what is further said on this Subject, in the Chapter *on the association of ideas*. [John Locke, *An Essay Concerning Human Understanding*, ed. Peter H. Nidditch (Oxford: Oxford University Press, 1975), bk. 2, ch. 33.]

versity is absolutely requisite: a moral, as well as a natural whole, must consist of various parts, fitted by their very differences to one another, and to one common end. But it is manifest that the diversity among mankind in genius, temper and abilities, depends, if not totally, yet to a very great degree and extent, upon bodily constitution and mechanical causes. This is so true, that many philosophers have from hence contended, that all is matter and motion; or that we are wholly body. Such an inference is indeed absurd, but the facts from which it is drawn are beyond all dispute; so palpable are they to every one's feeling and experience. "Each different nation has its national characteristic,[a] not merely in the features of the face and texture of the body, but likewise in temper and turn of mind." "Every man is hot or cold, slow or active, phlegmatic or choleric, lively or dull, amorous and delicate, or dull and insensible, correspondently to the temper of his body, his native climate, &c." "Air and diet change men's dispositions as much as their bodily habit; a disease, or a blow, do not make a greater alteration in the outward than in the inward man." Government, civil policy, and religion more especially, have no doubt a very great influence in <77> forming men's tempers; but, on the other hand, it was never questioned, that the temper of the body, the soil, climate, and many other physical causes have had a very considerable share in originally determining different people into

The great extent of this dependence is generally owned.

a. So *Cicero de lege agraria, contra Rullum.* Non ingenerantur hominibus mores tam a stirpe generis, ac seminis, quam ex iis rebus, quae ab ipsa natura loci, & a vitae consuetudine suppeditantur: quibus alimur, & vivimus. Carthaginienses, fraudulenti, & mendaces, non genere, sed natura loci, &c. See *Barclaii satyricon*, pars quarta, icones animorum, *Charron sur la sagesse.* And *reflexions sur la poesie & la peinture*, Part II. [Cicero, *De lege agraria*, II.xxxv.95: "It is not so much by blood and race that men's characters are implanted in them as by those things which are supplied to us by nature itself to form our habits of life, by which we are nourished and live. The Carthaginians were given to fraud and lying, not so much by race as by the nature of their position, etc." Cicero, *The Speeches*, . . . *De lege agraria*, trans. John Henry Freese, Loeb Classical Library (London: Heinemann; New York: Putnam, 1930).

The other references are to: John Barclay (1582–1621), *Euphormionis Lusinini Satyricon* (1605–7); Pierre Charron (1541–1603), *De la sagesse* (1601); and Abbé Jean-Baptiste Dubos (1670–1742), *Réflexions critiques sur la poésie et sur la peinture* (1719). All of these works appeared in many later editions.]

different forms of government, and distinct establishments with regard to civil and religious policy, by their influences upon genius and temper.

In fine, it is undeniable, that imagination, memory, and the strength of appetites, very much depend upon bodily habit; and, on the other hand, bodily temperature and habit, depend exceedingly on the exercises of the imagination and appetites; upon the employments, habits, and character of the mind. "Let physicians and anatomists, (says an excellent author)[a] explain the several motions of the fluids and solids of the body which accompany any passion; or the temperaments of body, which either make men prone to any passion, or are brought upon us by the long continuance or frequent returns of it. 'Tis only to our purpose, in general, to observe, That probably certain motions of the body do accompany every passion by a fixed law of nature, and alternately, that temperament which is apt to receive or prolong these motions in the body, does influence our passions to heighten or prolong them. Thus a certain temperament may be brought upon the body by its being frequently put into motion by the passions of anger, joy, love or sorrow; and the continuance of this temperament make men prone to these several passions for the future." Were this dependence of the body and mind more studied, and its effects collected and ranged into proper order; no doubt, we would be able to form a better judgment of it, and see further into the good purposes to which it serves; for the greater advances have hitherto been made in any branches of physi-<78>cal philosophy, the more instances do we perceive of excellent contrivance and kind oeconomy.

It is well worth while to enquire more fully into it.

II. Mean time, as the fact, in general, is certain from many experiments, so it is evident, there can be no mutual union of body and mind without reciprocal dependence; and their reciprocal dependence cannot take place without laws, fixing and determining connexions between all the possible changes in the body, and certain correspondent changes in the mind; and alternately between all possible conditions of the mind, and certain correspondent alterations in the bodily part. All this is involved in the very notion of regular and mutual dependence. Consequently the

Mean time, it is evident, that such a dependence is involved in the very idea of union of mind with body.

a. See *Hutcheson on the passions.* [Hutcheson, *Passions,* I.II.vii.]

only question with regard to our present union with a material world by means of our bodies is, 1. Whether, in consequence of these laws, we are not capable of very considerable pleasures, which otherwise could not possibly have place in nature? for did we not exist, in the present embodied state we are now in, the sensible world we are capable of enjoying in so many different ways, as rational as well as sensitive beings, could not exist. And, 2. Whether the pains we suffer, in consequence of this union, be not the necessary effects of the union itself, and the best, that is, the fitest admonitions we can have of what is necessary to our sustenance and well-being? for such pains cannot be called evils with respect to the whole system; but, on the contrary, being the effects of good general laws, are goods. To both which questions a sufficient answer hath been given.

The good consequence of this dependence of our minds on body and physical connexions.

III. To all which let it be added, that from the dependence of our mind upon body and physical causes, there arises this good consequence, "That, whereas the tempers, characters, abilities, and dispositions of our minds, would be utterly unalterable by us, if they were not dependent in that manner upon us; be-<79>ing so dependent, they may in a great measure be changed by our own proper care; or to do so only requires, that we should give due attention to the natural connexions on which they depend; and conformably to them take proper measures to make fit changes." That is to say, changing and reforming our minds, as far as mind depends upon body, depends on ourselves, because it depends upon knowledge of nature we may acquire, and right use of such knowledge. It is often regreted by ancient philosophers,[a] that the dependence

a. See *Plutarch de musica, & de educandis liberis. Plato de legibus & de republica,* passim. See a fine passage to the same purpose, in *Timaeus Locrus de anima mundi.* Ad hos animi impetus, multum adjumenti adferunt corporis temperamenta, &c. See a fine passage to this purpose, in *Cicero de Fato.* Ed. schr. No. 5. Sed haec ex naturalibus causis vitia nasci possunt: extirpari autem & funditus tolli, ut is ipse, qui ad ea propensus fuerit a tantis vitiis avocetur, non est id positum in naturalibus causis, sed in voluntate, studio, disciplina, &c. [Timaeus Locrus, *De anima mundi:* "The

of body and mind, as evidently as its extent discovers itself in many cases, is so little studied and enquired into by philosophers. Were it, say they, more carefully attended to and considered, the medicinal art would extend further than to the body: it would be able to do great services to the mind, by proper applications to the body, or by proper external *regimens* and discipline. Upon this occasion, they have expressed a very high opinion, not only of certain gymnastic exercises, but of the power of music in particular; and seem to think, that very advantageous uses might be made of that art, in several cases, for delivering the mind from disorders; or for purging and refining the passions; calming, quieting, cheering, and strengthning the mind.

But let that be as it will, tho' the science we have now been speaking of (the medicine of the mind, and that part of natural knowledge, from which alone it can be deduced) be very much neglected, yet from what hath been said of the dependence of <80> body and mind, it plainly appears, why the best ancient moralists, as well as the christian religion, recommend severe bodily discipline, in order to form, establish, preserve, and corroborate virtuous habits. Such must the morality be that belongs to beings of our compound make. Precepts not inferred from the human constitution, must be idle and vain, they cannot appertain to us. To forget in directions about our conduct, that we are rational beings, is indeed to forget our most essential and noble part: but, on the other hand, to forget in moral precepts, that we are likewise sensitive, embodied beings, is to leave out in morality, which ought to be founded upon the nature of beings, a very essential and important part of our make. It is therefore no wonder, if such morality prescribes rules to us,

True morality must therefore consider man as a compound creature; or his body and mind as reciprocally dependent.

---

temperaments of the body are a great help to the impulses of the mind." In Gale, ed., *Opuscula mythologica, physica et ethica. Graece et Latine.* . . . (Amsterdam, 1688), 563.

Cicero, *De fato,* V.11: "But it is possible that these defects may be due to natural causes; but their eradication and entire removal, recalling the man himself from the serious vices to which he was inclined, does not rest with natural causes, but with will, effort, training, etc." Cicero, *De oratore, Book III, De fato, Paradoxa Stoicorum, De partitione oratoria,* trans. H. Rackham, Loeb Classical Library (London: Heinemann; Cambridge: Harvard University Press, 1942).]

that are either above our practice, or insufficient to gain that purpose which ought to be the end of all rules relative to our conduct; namely, acting agreeably to our frame, or in a manner becoming our rank and conducive to our happiness. That must necessarily be the case, when our make is not strictly kept in view, in laying down precepts for our observance. Now this is plainly our rank; we are neither wholly moral, nor wholly sensitive beings; but a compound of moral and sensitive powers and affections reciprocally dependent upon one another: man is, as some philosophers have very properly expressed it; *Nexus utriusque mundi*.[33] And the excellence of the christian morality consists in this, that in all its precepts man is considered and advised as such a being.

> *The bliss of man (could pride that blessing find)*
> *Is not to act, or think beyond mankind;*
> *No pow'rs of body, or of soul to share,*
> *But what his nature, and his state can bear.*
> Essay on man, Epist. 1.[34] <81>

General con-clusion con-cerning their laws.
All the observations that have been made by natural philosophers upon the animal oeconomy of the human body, the different bodily oeconomies of other animals suited to their various states, and, in general, upon the wise contrivance and good order of the sensible world might very properly have been collected and inserted here. But the preceeding remarks will prepare every intelligent reader for making a proper use, and seeing the full extent of such observations; and from what has been said, we may justly conclude, "That the laws relating to our embodied state, and our connexion with the material or sensible world, are either necessary or fit: many excellent effects result from them, and none of the effects of good general laws can be evil, absolutely considered, that is, with respect to the whole."

33. "A binding of both worlds."
34. Pope, *Essay on Man*, 1.189–92.

Let us proceed to consider the laws of our nature relative to the association of ideas, and the formation of habits.

There are two things very remarkable in our nature; "The association of
ideas, or the difficulty with which ideas that have been often presented
to the mind together are afterwards disjoined;" and, "The formation of
habits by repeated acts; or a facility in doing, and a propension to reit-
erate the same action contracted by frequent doing it."

These relative
to the associa-
tion of ideas
and habits.

These two effects are very similar or like: they both include in their nature a certain kind of cohesion with the mind, formed by reiterated conjunction or co-existence between objects really separate and distinct
from one another; *i.e.* that do not necessarily co-exist, or are not naturally
parts of one <82> whole. And as they are like to one another, so they
must go together; or neither of them can take place in a mind without
the other. If habits are contracted by repeated acts, ideas will be joined
or mixed by repeated concurrence: and reciprocally, if ideas contract a
sort of coherence by being often joined, habits must be formed by frequent repetition of acts. This is plain. For,

Both these take
their rise from
one principle.

I. Unless the mind were so framed, that ideas frequently presented together to it, should afterwards naturally continue to recal one another,
to blend or return together, habits could not be contracted. Thus, for
instance, the habit of taking snuff, could not take place, did not the
returns of certain perceptions recal the idea and desire of snuff. And the
case must be the same with regard to all other habits; for all habits, of
whatever kind, operate the same way. The reason is, because all actions

of the mind are excited by and employed about ideas; and an action cannot be reiterated, unless its object and motive be revived. A propension to any action is nothing else but the frequent return of a certain desire, which necessarily supposes the equally frequent returns of the ideas which excite it, and are the subject of it: and facility in acting, in like manner, supposes the easy and quick return of the ideas that induce to the action, and are its subject. The formation of habits therefore supposes the association of ideas to take place. But,

II. If association of ideas take place, habits must necessarily be formed by repeated acts. For, if we attend to the matter strictly, we shall immediately find, that the whole course of what is called *action,* or a series of action, (the wills to act or make efforts to act alone excepted) is nothing but a train of passive perceptions or ideas. But ideas, as often as they return, must excite certain affections, and the <83> affections which lead to action, must, as often as they are revived, dispose and excite to act; or, in other words, produce will to act. And if will to act be successful, the train of perceptions called *action,* must succeed; and, by frequently succeeding in this manner, cohesion or association must be formed of this kind, that is, associations that terminate in action must be contracted.

Those effects called the association of ideas and formation of habits, do therefore resolve themselves into the same general law or principle in our nature, which may be called the[a] *law of custom.*

---

a. Thus, for instance, in the whole action of taking snuff, what is there that is active, besides the first will to take it, and the other intermingling volitions to move the hand, open the box, *&c?* The perception, uneasiness, itch, or whatever it is that excites the will to take it, and the moving the hand, opening the box, taking snuff between the fingers, putting it to the nose, drawing it up, and being irritated or pung'd by it; what is there in all these but mere sensation or passion? The whole effect, the volitions to take it, open the box, *&c.* excepted, is but a succession of passive sensations. And it is so with respect to every other active habit, because it is so with respect to every action. There is nothing in any one action besides volition, but sensation or impression. Volition is all that can be called active: and action therefore is nothing else but a train of ideas, subsequent to, or brought into existence by a series of volitions. But volitions are excited or moved by ideas: and therefore associations of ideas exciting volitions, are active habits.

But, whether they are reduced to one or different principles, nothing can be more certain; than that ideas are associated by being frequently conjoined, in such a manner, that it is not easy to prevent their mixing so together as to make one perception, or, at least, their coherence and joint return to the mind; and that habits are formed by repeated acts. Now, nothing can be of greater use in our frames, than the principle or principles from which these effects arise. For, what can be more evident, than that were we not so constituted, we could not attain to perfection in any science, art, or virtue? It <84> would not be in our power to join and unite ideas at our pleasure, to recal past ones, or to lay up a stock of knowledge in our minds to which we could have recourse upon any occasion, and bring forth, as it were, ready money for present use. Nor would it be in our power by all our reiterated acts to become more ready, alert, and expeditious in performing any operation than at our first attempt; but, in every thing, and on every emergence, after ever so much past labour, all our work would constantly be to begin again. In one word, habits are perfected faculties: or faculties perfected by exercise are habits. So that the law of habits is really the *law of improvement to perfection;* and is therefore a most excellent, a most useful law.

All this is very obvious. But so extremely, so universally useful is this part of our frame, that its well worth while to examine it more fully, and take a larger view of its effects. We shall therefore first consider some of the principal phenomena belonging to the association of ideas.

I. And, in order to proceed distinctly, let us be sure that we carry along with us a clear idea of the thing itself.

Sensible ideas or qualities, which by their co-existence make the same object, (as, for instance, it is a particular shape, size, colour, taste, and other combined qualities in the same subject that make a peach) are not said to be associated, because they naturally and really co-exist, or naturally and really make the same object.[a]

Nor is the complex idea which we have of a peach, after having tasted

> **But whatever the cause be, one or more, these effects are certain.**
>
> **Both proceed from a most useful principle.**
>
> **A principle that may justly be called the law of perfection.**
>
> **Associated ideas defined, and distinguished from complex ideas, &c.**

---

a. See *Locke on the human understanding.* The Chapter *on the association of ideas.* [Locke, *Essay,* bk. 2, ch. 33, §5.]

several, that is immediately excited in us by the sight of it, before we touch or taste it, called *an associated idea;* tho' the greater part of it consists of ideas not perceived, but ima-<85>gined; because the qualities imagined do really belong to the peach. We are much indebted to the wonderful quickness of our fancy, in adding several qualities on such occasions to those really perceived, to compleat our ideas. But such supplies, by the imagination to any of our sensible ideas, as intimately as they unite and blend with them, are not called *ideas of association,* because whatever is thus added by the imagination to the perceptions of sense, is a copy of a sensible quality really appertaining to the object perceived.

But, if a peach having been often presented to us on agreeable occasions, should become ever afterwards exceedingly more desireable than before, by recalling to our mind these agreeable circumstances; then is the whole idea of a peach that thus excites our desire and greatly pleases us, compounded of the real qualities of a peach, and of these other delightful ideas not belonging to it, but suggested to, or excited in our imagination by it. Or contrariwise, if a peach which was formerly very agreeable, having been frequently presented to us on melancholly occasions, shall ever afterwards recal to our minds these disagreeable circumstances, and so become hateful to us; then the idea of a peach is compounded of uneasy ideas that overballance all its good and formerly desireable qualities, or that so entirely possess the mind, that there is no room for these qualities to enter into it.

Almost all our ideas have something in them of the associated kind.

In both these and all such cases our ideas are made up of real and associated ingredients, or compounded of parts, some of which do really belong to the object, and others do not, but are added by the mind itself: they are made up of ingredients that have no natural or necessary coherence, but that cohere or are mixed by customary association.

III. The instances that have been given, in order to determine the meaning of association, are indeed <86> but trifling and of little moment. But the thing itself in its full extent is of the greatest consequence. For if we consider our ideas with due attention, and take the trouble to analyse them, we shall find that very few, if any of the ideas, that excite

our warmest and keenest affections, are quite free from associated parts.
The greater number of our perceptions, however agreeable or disagreeable, are of the associated kind in some degree. How many, how very
many of them are like the peaches we have mentioned, chiefly agreeable
or disagreeable in consequence of some things united with them, that
do not belong to them? We can scarcely name any one that offers itself
quite pure and unmixed; or which has no constituent parts of the kind
we are now speaking of. But affections, that is, desires or aversions, will
always be proportioned to the good or evil qualities comprehended in
the ideas by which they are excited.

That few or none of our ideas can escape some mixture by association,
if we are not continually upon our guard to prevent it, is obvious. For
where the law of association takes place, the concomitant circumstances
in which ideas have frequently occurred to the mind, must become constant parts or attendants of these ideas, if we are not assiduously upon
the watch against such association. This is the natural result, or rather
the direct meaning of the law. But, what is the whole frame and course
of nature, or what else indeed can it be but a constant occasion to us of
association, *i.e.* of mixture or coherence of ideas? It cannot but be so,
because no idea can be presented to the mind singly, that is, without
preceeding, concomitant and succeeding circumstances; and in a world
governed by uniform laws, and filled with beings of analogous natures
and employments, no idea can fail of being often presented to the mind
in the same or like circumstances. There are many associations that are
entirely of our own <87> making; but, suppose we made none, it would
be sufficient employment for us, either in order to have true knowledge
or well proportioned affections, to be incessantly upon our guard to prevent the blendings and cohesions of ideas, that the regular course of
things in the world naturally tends, in consequence of the law of association, to form or engender in our minds. Every one who is acquainted
with philosophy, knows, that the great difficulty in attaining to the true
knowledge of things, take its rise from the difficulty of separating ideas
into the parts that naturally belong to one another, and those which are
added by association. For without such analysis, no object can be de-

Where this
necessarily
happens.

It is the neces-
sary effect of
the world's
being governed
by general uni-
form laws.

Natural philos-
ophy consists
in a great
measure, in
separating
associations

which the
order of nature
necessarily pro-
duces in our
minds.
fined, distinguished, nor consequently examined, and so understood. And yet ideas, in consequence of the law of association, must, from the very beginning of our existence, so blend and mix with others totally and essentially distinct from them, that it must become extreamly difficult not to confound together qualities that being different, can never be philosophised about, till we are not only able to distinguish them, but to keep them before the mind without intermingling and quite separate. In reality, the greater part of philosophy consists in separating ideas, that the natural course of things, in consequence of the law of association, hath conjoined, or rather confounded. Many instances might be given to prove this, were it at all necessary. The jangling about beauty among philosophers, whether it is distinct or not from utility, is a sufficient proof of it; and yet into what science does not this dispute necessarily enter? There is no reasoning about poetry, painting, or any of the polite arts, or indeed about morality, without being led into it. But what sufficiently proves it, is the difficulty most persons find in their entrance upon philosophy in distinguishing the qualities perceived by any one sense from those perceived by any other. How few, not very much accustomed to philosophy, are not startled to hear that <88> distance is not an idea of sight, but an idea of touch suggested by ideas of sight! And yet, till this is clearly understood, and the difference is become familiar to the mind, it is impossible to have a clear notion of very many important truths in perspective and optics. But if philosophers find a difficulty arising from the effect of the law of association in analysing ideas; we all find a much greater one from the same source in the conduct of the passions. For here, how difficult, how extreamly difficult is it to

Separating
associations
one great busi-
ness in moral
philosophy.
separate associations early made and long unquestioned? Or, what indeed is the whole of our labour in regulating the passions; in correcting, reforming, or directing them; but an endeavour to render our passions suitable and proportioned to the natures of things, as they are in themselves distinguished from all wrong associations? What else is discipline or government with respect to the love of wealth, of power, of show, of fame; or any one of our desires private or public, but an effort to have just opinions of objects; and so to have affections suitable to their true values? But, how can we have suitable affections till their true values are

known? And, how can the true values of objects be ascertained, till the ideas of them are scrutinized, and every superadded ingredient by association is separated from the qualities that belong to the thing itself? Then only can the objects themselves be understood, or their moments be measured either with respect to quantity or duration.

Now, I say, a great number of those associations, which it is of such importance either in philosophy or moral conduct to be able to distinguish to be such, are the necessary effects of the law of association, in consequence of the natural course of things, which we cannot alter. And it is no otherwise therefore in our power to prevent them, than by constant attendance to the manner in which ideas enter, and so are apt to mix or cohere; or by assiduous prac-<89>tice in examining our ideas daily received. For the circumstances in which ideas are presented to us, are in many instances absolutely independent of us. And yet such is the nature of the law of association, that ideas, ever so few times offered to us in certain circumstances, have a tendency as often as they return, whether by being recalled by our own will, or without being so recalled, to return with more or fewer of the circumstances with which they had formerly occurred. But a late excellent author hath so fully treated of association, so far especially as the conduct of the passions is concerned, that I need not be more particular.[a]

This must needs be the effect of general laws upon minds made likewise to associate ideas.

IV. But perhaps it will be said, that what hath hitherto been suggested, is rather an objection against the law under consideration, than a defence of it. For are not all the difficulties it necessarily involves us in, so many evils or inconveniencies arising from it?

But let us observe the concatenation of things with regard to the human make, or how the several laws of the moral world hang and must hang together. Knowledge must, in the nature of things, be progressive; and our excellence consists in its being acquirable gradually by our own industry to improve in it. The laws of nature make it necessary that we

These difficulties arising from the law of association, are no objections against its fitness.

a. See *Hutcheson on the nature and conduct of the passions.* [Hutcheson, *Passions,* I.iv.]

should come into the world with infant bodies; and the law of progressiveness makes it necessary that we should enter into the world with infant minds; and in this respect, the laws of matter and motion, and the laws of the moral world, are admirably adjusted one to another. But if the law of association likewise take place with these other laws; then, in consequence of all these laws operating together, it is impossible but several associations of ideas must be formed in our minds, before reason is grown up by culture, and we are able to attend to the entrance of our ideas, and the manner <90> in which they associate; that is, mix, join and cohere. The course of nature's laws with respect to the material world, is found, upon enquiry, to be very regular, beautiful and good, the best that can be conceived. But any uniform course of things must produce associations of ideas, in minds where that aptitude called the associating one obtains. Now that the law of association is an excellent law, has been already proved: it is *The law of improvement to perfection*.

But its fitness and goodness will yet more fully appear from the following considerations.

Several good effects of this law.

I. It is plainly in consequence of this law, that we so quickly learn the connexions established by nature between the ideas of different senses, those of the sight and touch, for instance; so as that we are very soon able, even in our infant state, to judge of such appearances and connexions with great facility, ease and quickness, and with as great accuracy as the exigencies of our life require. Those connexions and appearances, by which we judge immediately of magnitudes, distances, forms, and other qualities, may be called the language of nature, signifying these qualities. And it is by means of the law of association, that appearances, found by repeated experience to be connected with effects, do recal those effects to our minds, with which they have been found to be connected, so soon as they recur, or are re-perceived. It is, indeed, in consequence of the law

Without it we could never become acquainted with the course of nature; every thing would for ever be new to us.

of association, that we learn any of the connexions of nature; or that any appearance with its effects, is not as new to us at all times as at first; that is, as unfamiliar to our mind. It is owing to it that any appearance immediately suggests its concomitants and subsequents to us; and that we thus become acquainted with nature, in proportion to the attention we give to the course of <91> things in it; and so are able, by means of one or more perceptions, to recal a great many connected with it, before they appear; or while they are yet at a distance from us, and to be brought about by many intermediate steps. But what could we do, how miserable, how ignorant would we be, without this faculty? without it we would plainly continue to be in old age, as great novices to the world as we are in our infancy; as incapable to foresee, and consequently as incapable to direct our conduct.

But, *secondly,* The examination of our ideas when we are grown up, is a very pleasant employment to us. What can be more entertaining, than to trace our ideas, as far as we can, to their origine; to the various manners of their entrance into our minds; and to resolve them into their constituent parts; and so separate the associated ones from those which by natural and essential coexistence make an object itself. A regular course of things will necessarily produce associations of ideas in minds so formed as to have an associating quality or aptitude. But one of the pleasantest and noblest employments of reasonable beings must consist in studying nature. And studying nature must in a great measure consist in separating our ideas received from experience, into those that are ideas of qualities making particular objects by their co-existence or real combination; and those that are compounded, partly of such really coexisting qualities, and partly of other ideas blended or cohering with them, in consequence of associations formed by their having been often presented to the mind at the same time with other really coexistent qualities. For thus alone can we distinguish connexions in nature that are really inseparable, and make a fixed, regular course or succession of causes and effects, from every thing that does not appertain to such connexions; but however it may be <92> joined to any such in our minds by custom, is no part of them; but is, with respect to them, wholly accidental.

Unravelling ideas of association is a very agreeable employment.

III. Which is yet of greater moment to us; it is by means of the law of association, or of our associating power, that we are able to strengthen or diminish our desires; and to encrease our pleasures, or diminish our

It is in consequence of the law of association, that we

are capable of strengthening or diminishing our desires, of adding to our pleasures, and of alleviating our pains.

pains. For the aggregate of pleasure or pain an idea gives us, will be in proportion to the quantity of pleasure or pain it contains: that is, it is the sum of the pleasures or pains which are its component parts: and our desires or aversions will be stronger or weaker, according as the ideas exciting them are more or less agreeable or disagreeable. Now pleasures associated to an idea will encrease the quantity of agreeableness in that whole complex, blended or mixt idea. And in like manner, pains associated to an idea will encrease the quantity of disagreeableness or uneasiness arising from that whole complex, blended or mixt idea; as parts make up a whole: so that had we not the power of adding to, or taking from our ideas, we could have no power over our affections or desires: for these must always be according to our ideas; but all the power we

Because desires are excited by ideas, and our power over ideas lies chiefly in associating and separating.

can have over ideas is by compounding, associating, and separating. And how great power we have in these respects, almost every virtuous or vicious affection amongst mankind is a proof. For what, on the one hand, are luxurious fancies, excessive love of splendor, voluptuousness, romantic love, and the immoderate lust of power, but extravagant desires, excited by ideas of grandeur and happiness, somehow blended with natural pleasures, and the desires these excite? Or what, on the other hand, are patience, magnanimity, a contented mind, and other such vertues, but affections towards certain natural objects, duly moderated by the consideration of their intrinsic values, and of the strength of desire proportioned to them; by se-<93>parating from them all ideas that tend to encrease desire beyond that due proportion; and by associating to them all the ideas, opinions and judgments, that tend to maintain and preserve desire in a just tone and ballance, with relation to true happiness? How does patience work? How can it work, but by alleviating considerations? And what is it, for instance, makes poverty doubly painful to one, and to another a very supportable state, but different ideas in their minds, connected with mediocrity of circumstances in respect of outward enjoyments, by means of different associations? But indeed Mr. *Hutcheson* hath quite exhausted this subject.[35] We shall therefore only observe further on this head,

35. Hutcheson, *Passions,* I.iv.

IV. That as associations of various sorts must necessarily be formed in the mind, by the natural course of things, absolutely independent of us; so various associations must produce various tempers and dispositions of mind; since every idea, as often as it is repeated, must move the affection it naturally tends to excite; and ideas, with their correspondent affections, often returning, must naturally form inclinations, propensions, or tempers; for temper means nothing else. But with respect to the law of association, there is a circumstance which we have not hitherto taken notice of; (because association strictly considered, is no more but a league, or cohesion, formed by frequent conjunction in the mind) which is very contributive to the formation of various genius's and tempers among mankind; and that circumstance is likeness or resemblance of ideas. Though frequent concurrence be sufficient, as has been observed, to produce the effect called *association,* yet nothing is more certain, than that association is more easily engendered between ideas that have some affinity or likeness, than between those which have no kindred, no resemblance; as we may feel in a thousand instances. Now if we carefully attend to the human mind, we shall find, that the aptitude to as-<94>sociate like ideas which have the smallest resemblances; and the aptitude to separate ideas which have the minutest differences, not only make a very great diversity in minds with respect to genius; but likewise with regard to moral temper. Wit is justly defined to consist in the quick and ready assemblage of such ideas as have any analogy, likeness, or resemblance, especially in those circumstances which are not commonly attended to, so that the resemblance, when it is pointed out, at once strikes by its evidence, and surprizes by its uncommonness. Judgment, on the other hand, is rightly said to lie in nicely distinguishing the disagreements and variances or differences of ideas; those especially which lie more remote from common observation, and are not generally adverted to. The witty person may therefore be said to be one, who hath an aptitude of mind to associate ideas which have any affinity, or rather a ready discernment of the resemblances of ideas, in respects not absolutely glaring to all persons, and yet evident and pleasing to all, when pointed out to their observation by such a quick and acute discerner of likenesses. On the other hand, the man of judgment or discretion (for

Another circumstance with respect to association.

Like ideas are easily associated.

Wit and judgment defined.

But suppose the law of association to take place.

so discretion properly signifies) may be defined to be one who has a particular aptitude to discry differences of all kinds between objects, even the most hidden and remote from vulgar eyes. Now however these different aptitudes may be acquired, or in whatever respects they may be original, cogenial or unacquired; it is manifest that they make a very real difference in character or genius. They have very different effects, and produce very different works; and they presuppose the law of association. The improvement of the one, certainly very much depends upon accustomance to assemble and join; and the improvement of the other upon accustomance to disunite, break and separate.

It is therefore in consequence of the law of association that there are different genius's.

But there is in respect of moral character a parallel variety; some here also are propense to associating, and others to disjoining. Nay as the great variety of genius's <95> may be in general divided into the aptitude to associate, and the aptitude to dissociate: so, perhaps, almost all the different moral characters among mankind may be reduced to the like general division, that is, to the associating and dissociating aptitude. For as a turn to assemble resemblances of different kinds (suppose of the soft and tender, or of the horrible and violent, the serious or ridiculous) makes different species of genius, the epic, comic, tragic, humorous, &c. so dispositions to conjoin ideas of different kinds, will necessarily make an equal variety of moral tempers and characters; the chearful, the melancholy, the cowardly and timorous, or the daring and adventurous, and so forth. But one who naturally delights, or by usage comes to delight, in any one kind of assemblages, will be averse to its opposites: and excessive delight in any one, will become a particular extravagance to be guarded against. In like manner, a turn or propension to disunite ideas admits of as great variety as there is variety of differences to be discerned, and consequently there may be as great a diversity of minds each bent towards distinguishing, as there are separations of various sorts to be made. And every one of these separating propensions, may by over-indulgence run into extravagance; and often does. By pursuing this re-flexion, we may see how far variety of tempers and genius's among mankind depends upon, and may take its rise from the associating power natural to the mind, in consequence of different circumstances calling it forth, or employing it in different ways, or contrariwise, checking it,

It gives rise to an equal diversity of moral characters.

But so far as temper depends on association, it depends on ourselves.

disappointing and thwarting it, and thus obliging the mind to make frequent dissociations; and so using it to the separating practice, till it comes to take delight in it, insomuch that it is ever disposed to act that part, and rather chuses to distinguish than to join, on every occasion. But not to stay longer on this observation, let me only add, that on <96> the one hand, from what has been said of wit, it is plain, that it could not take place, were it not for the associating power of the mind. And how, indeed, do poetry or oratory entertain or agitate, or wherein does their chief excellence consist, whether with respect to soothing and extending the imagination, or bestirring and moving the passions, but in associating the ideas, which being assembled together make agreeable, pleasant, charming, well suited company; in associating ideas which enlighten and set off one another, and by being fitly and closely joined, create great warmth in the mind, or put it into agreeable motion. *Simile* is likeness of ideas, pointed out, as it were, by the finger: and *metaphor* is a resemblance of ideas, that presents itself to the mind without any forewarning, and is doubly agreeable, like good company, by surprizing. On the other hand, from what hath been said of judgment, it is evident that its work supposes likewise the law of association, because it consists in separating; and the philosophical turn being towards scanning, sifting and distinguishing, when carried to excess, must become an enemy to all joining and uniting, as ordinarily happens.

> Metaphor and simile are associations.

> Philosophy is separating work.

> Both may run into extravagances.

But whatever be as to these things, it is certain from the nature of the law now under consideration,

I. That true practical philosophy consists[a] in what it was placed by the ancients: in the assiduous examination of our fancies, ideas or opinions. For <97> by these our desires are guided or influenced: all our desires, whether those which are properly called appetites, having a previous, painful or uneasy sensation, antecedently to any opinion of good in the object; or those which necessarily presuppose an opinion of good and evil in their objects; all our desires, whether after external pleasures, plea-

> Practical philosophy, or the conduct of the affections, consists in the assiduous examination of our ideas, fancies and opinions.

a. See *Epicteti enchiridion,* and *Arrian* and *Simplicius* upon him, and *Marcus Antoninus's meditations, or self-conversation.* This is the self-examination recommended

sures of the imagination, or pleasures of the public and social sense. For this must hold in general concerning all our desires and aversions, that according to the opinion or apprehension of good or evil, the desire or aversion is increased or diminished. Now if this be true, our great interest and concern lies in taking care of our opinions, that they be true and just. This ought to be the whole business of our life; our continual, our daily employment: otherwise we cannot be masters of our desires, or keep them in just and proportionate order. And how happy would it be

Education ought to establish that habit of self-examination.

for men, if education was rightly managed, so as to give us early just notions of things, as far as life is concerned; or but even to establish early in our minds the habit of calling our ideas and opinions daily to a strict account! But all this, it is obvious, supposes a reasonableness and un-reasonableness in associations; or a rule and standard for associating and dissociating. And if it is asked what this rule or standard may be? the answer is, It is the faculty by which we are able to judge both of our happiness, and of what is becoming us, of which we are afterwards to treat, and where it shall be shewn, "That these two, happiness or interest, and becoming or virtue, are the same, or at least inseparably connected." We are to associate and dissociate, join and separate according to that rule; or as our happiness and dignity require.

Associations cannot be bro-ken by mere confutation of false opinions.

II. But, *secondly,* let it be observed, an association is made by joining ideas with one another frequently, and by accustoming ourselves to contemplate <98> them so joined and united. But the confutation of false

---

to us even by the poets, as absolutely necessary to self-command, and true wisdom, or good conduct. So *Horace, Lib.* 1. *Satyr.* 4. And, again, *Epist.* 2. *Lib.* 2. Quocirca mecum loquor, &c. See *Cicero, Tuscul. quest. Lib.* 3. Est igitur causa omnis in opi-nione, nec vero aegritudinis solum, sed etiam reliquarum perturbationum, &c. [For Epictetus, see page 62, note a; for Marcus Antoninus, see *The Meditations of Marcus Aurelius Antoninus,* trans. A. S. L. Farquharson . . . (Oxford: Oxford University Press, 1989). Horace, *Epistles,* II.ii.45: "I talk thus to myself." Horace, *Satires, Epistles and Ars poetica,* trans. H. Rushton Fairclough, Loeb Classical Library (London: Heine-mann; New York: Putnam, 1926). Cicero, *Tusculanae disputationes,* III.xi.24: "It is then wholly in an idea that we find the cause not merely indeed of distress but of all other disturbances as well, etc." Cicero, *Tusculan Disputations,* trans. J. E. King, Loeb Classical Library (London: Heinemann; New York: Putnam, 1927).]

opinions is not sufficient to break an association, so that the desire or passion shall not continue after our understanding has suggested to us that the object is not good, or not proportioned to the strength of the desire. Thus we may observe, that persons who by reasoning have laid aside all opinion of *spirits being in the dark* more than in the light, are still uneasy to be alone in the dark. And it is so in general, with respect to all associations: we must first, indeed, correct the false opinion, from which the unreasonable desire or aversion proceeds: but this is not enough: the association cannot be broken in any case, but, as in that instance just mentioned; by accustoming ourselves to walk in the dark, with the absurdity of the opinion upon which our aversion or fear was formerly founded present to our mind. Ideas which have been long associated, can only be disjoined by frequently acting in opposition to the unreasonable association. Now if it should be enquired why, whereas associations are so easily formed merely by ideas being frequently presented conjunctly to the mind; dissociations however are not brought about without great struggle and difficulty. The reply to this is at hand: were not this the case, the law of association would not gain its end: for it is the difficulty of breaking the association, which is the very end of the law, or produces all its good effects.

But by contrary practice.

Why it is so.

I now proceed to consider some effects, which though habits and association of ideas are really one and the same thing, and really resolve into one principle; yet are in common language called active habits. For by that name are all associations of ideas called, which terminate in what is termed action either of the mind or of the body. Now provided, on this head, we make mention of the most remarkable phenomena belonging to it, it is but of <99> little consequence in what order effects so nearly related to one another are proposed.

Of active habits properly so called.

I. It is in consequence of a propension to do, and a facility and readiness in doing, acquired by repeated exercise called the *Law of habits*, that we have memory and habitual knowledge, learn languages with tolerable ease, attain to grace of body, as in dancing; to a good ear in music, a

Hence memory, habitual knowledge.

Taste of every
kind.

good eye in painting or architecture, and a good taste of any ingenious composition, as in oratory or poetry. For what else is memory, but the power of recalling with facility and quickness ideas and truths we had formerly discovered or perceived? and how is it strengthened or improved but by exercise? Without memory there can be no invention, judgment, nor wit, because without memory ideas cannot be readily and quickly laid together, in order to be compared, that their agreements and resemblances, or disagreements and differences, may be discerned. And what is taste, but the power of judging truly with quickness acquired by frequent consideration and practice: that is, confirmed into habit by

And perfection
of whatever
faculty.

repeated acts? In fine, it is in consequence of this law, or formation of our mind, that the reiterated exercises of any of our faculties are not lost labour, but produce perfection. Attention, judging, reasoning, writing, speaking, composing, in one word, all our powers and actions in their perfection are so many respective habits: and therefore, to ask why the mind is so framed, is to ask, why perfection of any kind is attainable by

Instruction and
education pre-
suppose the
power of habit.

us, or within our power. Instruction and education presuppose this frame of mind in the rules laid down with regard to them: and the effect of education, or early accustomance is well expressed by the common proverb, which calls it, *A second nature.* To exemplify this observation, and at the same time to shew what true *logic* ought to be, and really was among the <100> ancients, I shall just mention two observations of *Cicero,*[a] with regard to the improvement of memory by due exercise. 1. The

a. *Cicero de inventione rhetorica. De oratore, &c.* There is a fine passage to the same purpose, in the *Dissertationes incerti cujusdam pythagorei dorico sermone conscriptae.* Published in a collection of *Greek* tracts, by Mr. *Gale. Dissertation* 5. An virtus & sapientia doceri possent. Sed optimum fuit, & in vitae commoda pulcherrimum inventum memoriae artificium, ad omnia utile.—Hoc autem in eo consistit, primo si animum admodum advertas.—Secundo si mediteris quaecunque audieris.—Tertio si rerum quas audis, imagines reponere noveris, &c. [There is a discussion of exercises for improving memory in Cicero, *De oratore,* II.350–67. Cicero, *De oratore, Books I and II,* trans. E. W. Sutton, completed by H. Rackham, Loeb Classical Library (Cambridge: Harvard University Press; London: Heinemann, 1942). *Dissertationes incerti cuiusdam pythagorei dorico sermone conscriptae:* "Can virtue and wisdom be taught? But the best thing was the art of memory, a very fine device that contributed to the conveniences of life and was useful for everything. The art consists in this, first you concentrate hard, secondly you think about what you've heard, and thirdly you try

way, says he, to be able to retain ideas and judgments, so as to have the use of them always at our command, is to accustom ourselves to attend to things with great closeness and stedfastness; and to ask ourselves before we quit the consideration of any object, whether it is not worth while to store it up in the mind. And if it be, we ought (says he) as it were, formally to charge our memory with the custody of it, for certain particular reasons and uses, to be at the same time laid up in the mind with it. Did we take this method, we should have but little reason to complain of the slipperiness and treachery of memory. But we, it seems, expect it should be strong and perfect, without our taking pains to improve it: that is, we expect a habit to be formed, otherwise than by repeated exercise. 2. What would be of great help to memory, according to the same author, is, not letting any object of importance pass, till we have considered its analogies, relations, and oppositions, with respect to several other objects or truths already of our acquaintance. For by so doing, there necessarily would be, in consequence of the law of habits and association of ideas, various securities for our being able to recal it, in proportion to the variety of analogies, relations, agreements, differences and oppositions to other objects we had observed in it. Technical rules for assist-<101>ing and improving memory, are founded upon the same principle, *viz.* the law of habits. But there is this manifest difference between them, and those rules of *Cicero:* That while, in order to help memory, we are imployed in considering many real analogies and oppositions, we really are at the same time increasing our stock of useful knowledge, and improving our inventive faculty. For does not a great part of science consist in the knowledge of analogies and oppositions among objects? What else is knowledge? And wherein does the perfection of the inventive faculty consist, but in being able to assemble ideas together into proper order, with great facility and quickness, in order to discover hitherto unobserved relations of ideas, by seeing them in new positions?

An observation on memory to illustrate this.

---

to form images of what you have been hearing about." In Gale, ed., *Opuscula mythologica, physica et ethica. Graece et Latine. . . .* (Amsterdam, 1688), 731.]

We are imitative creatures, but it is in consequence of the law of habits, that imitation hath its effect.

II. It is in consequence of the law of habits, that imitation passes into custom, and that example has such powerful influence upon our temper and behaviour. Nature hath wisely made us imitative creatures, *apes,* if I may so speak. But our disposition to imitate would be of no use to us, did not repeated imitations produce habitual conformity to what we imitate. *Quintilian* gives an excellent advice with regard to imitation, when speaking of stage-actors he tells us, that among them it frequently happens, "*imitatio in mores transit.*"[36] He on this occasion sagely advises, for that reason to be extremely cautious, and to take good heed what we allow ourselves to imitate or copy after, in writing or style for instance, but above all in life and manners.

And that example hath influence.

Habit renders that agreeable which was formerly disagreeable.

It is a very remarkable effect of the law of habits, that what is at first very uneasy and disagreeable, becomes by use, or association of ideas and habit, exceeding pleasant and agreeable. Hence it is that we come to like the train of business we have been for some time inured to, however disagreeable <102> it might have been at first. Upon this is founded the ancient sage advice to young people about the choice of a profession in life, "To chuse that which is likeliest to be most advantageous to them, provided they have abilities for it, even though they should have preconceived some prejudice against it, or aversion to it, because custom will make it agreeable."[a] It is owing in some measure to this law of habits, that people of the same business in life, or of the same rank and station, do so readily associate together. It is very fit it should be so on many accounts; but chiefly because people of the same profession will by conversation about their common art, which will naturally be the subject of their discourse, mutually learn from one another, and mutually excite emulation one in another. And so true is the fact, that it is become an universal proverb, *Birds of a feather flock together.*

a. *Plutarch de sanitate tuenda.* [The passage is in Plutarch's *De sanitate tuenda,* 123C; see also his *De tranquillitate animi,* 466F; and *De exilio,* 602B. Plutarch, *Omnia quae extant opera,* 2 vols. (Paris, 1624).]

36. Quintilian, *Institutio oratoria,* I.xi.1: "Frequent imitation develops into habit." Quintilian, *The Orator's Education,* ed. and trans. Donald A. Russell, 5 vols., Loeb Classical Library (Cambridge and London: Harvard University Press, 2001).

We observed before, that a fondness after novelty is necessary in our nature,[a] to spur us to seek after new objects, and new knowledge; but that this desire of novelty is ballanced in our frame by the liking contracted to an object by habitual commerce with it, lest our itch after novelty should render us too unsteady, too desultory, and consequently too superficial and heedless in our attention to an object, to be able to attain to the full knowledge of it. Now it is in consequence of the law of habits, that this liking to an object is formed. By long or frequent conversation with an object, we become more pleased with it: the more narrowly and attentively we have considered it, the more we delight in it; for we find by frequently reasoning about the same object, that it is not new objects only that can afford us fresh entertainment; but that <103> every object is an endless fund of new discoveries: and we at the same time experience, that the more we employ ourselves about the same object, the more easy it becomes to us to make progress in new discoveries about it; and thus a fondness for the same object, or the same train of study, is contracted, so that we are not easily prevailed upon, even by quite new ones, to desert it: or if we are, yet we return to it again with such a relish, as one renews conversation with an old acquaintance he had not seen for some time.

It ballances our natural desire after novelty.

How it does so.

III. But one of the most remarkable advantages of the law of habits is, *(I shall give it in the words of an excellent author),*[b] a power with regard to pleasure and pain in respect of practical habits. As practical habits are formed and strengthned by repeated acts; so passive impressions are found to grow weaker by being repeated on us. Whence it must follow, that active habits may be gradually forming and strengthning by a course of acting upon such and such motives; while excitements themselves are proportionably by degrees becoming less sensible, that is, are continually less and less felt, as the active habits strengthen. Experience confirms this.

By the law of habit passive impressions grow weaker, in proportion as practical habits are strengthned.

a. In the first chapter, upon our furniture for progress in knowledge.

b. Dr. *Butler* (the Bishop of *Bristol*) upon analogy. [Joseph Butler, *The Analogy of Religion, Natural and Revealed, to the Constitution and Course of Nature* (1736), I.V.ii.]

For active principles at the very time they are less lively in perception than they were, are found to be somehow wrought into character and temper, and become more powerful in influencing our practice. Thus Instances. perception of danger is a natural excitement of passive fear, and active caution: and by being inured to danger, habits of the latter are gradually wrought, at the same time that the former gradually lessens. Perception of distress is a natural excitement, passively to pity, and actively to relieve it. But let a man set himself to attend to, enquire out and relieve distressed persons, and he <104> cannot but be less and less affected with the various miseries of human life, with which he must become acquainted: but yet, at the same time, benevolence considered, not as a passion, but as a practical principle of action will strengthen; and whilst he passionately compassionates the distressed less, he will acquire a greater aptitude actively to assist and befriend them. It is the same with all other affections which may be worked by exercise into active principles, and being settled and established as such in the mind, constitute a habitual character or temper that exerts itself calmly and regularly.

'Tis in consequence of the law of habits that temper is formed.

IV. It is indeed, in consequence of the law of habits that temper or character is formed, for tho all the affections of mankind be, and must be originally from nature; and art, or exercise, cannot create, but can only make some change to the better or worse upon what nature hath implanted in our breasts; yet habit is the nurse of all affections: it is by repeated acts that any one is wrought into temper or becomes habitual. Whatever temper we would form, we must do it not merely by enforcing upon our minds, a strong conviction of its usefulness and reasonableness; but chiefly by exerting ourselves to call forth into action the affections which constitute it; by exercising them frequently, or by various acts; and that without intermission till the point is gained; that is, till these affections are become strong, ready to go out into action on any proper occasion; and we have contracted a propension to exert them.

In consequence of that law, we are able to form and

This is the way temper or character is formed. And by this means, it is in our power to change any temper we may have contracted, and to form ourselves to any desireable one. And this leads me to observe, that the chief benefit of the law of habits, is our being able in consequence of it to acquire the *deliberative temper or habit:* that is, the habitual power of enquiring and judging before we choose or <105> act; the opposite to which is the habit of acting precipitately, and in blind, slavish obedience to every fancy or appetite that assails us. Whatever metaphysical janglings there have been about the freedom of our will; our moral dominion, liberty, and mastership of ourselves certainly consist in the established habit of thinking well before we act; insomuch as to be sure of ourselves, that no fancy or appetite shall be able to hurry us away into action, till reason and moral conscience have pronounced an impartial sentence about them. It is this command over ourselves, this empire over our passions, which enables us to put trust or confidence in ourselves, and renders us sure and trust-worthy in society to others. In it do true wisdom and freedom lie. And as it ought to be the chief business of education to form early this deliberative habit and temper in young minds; and the constant employment of every man to preserve and maintain it in due strength; so the only way to attain to it, or uphold it, is, 1. By inculcating upon ourselves the excellence and usefulness of it, and the manifold disadvantages that redound from the want or weakness of it. And, 2. by practicing ourselves in choosing and acting after the deliberative judicious manner; in habituating ourselves to call all sorts of ideas, fancies, and motives to a strict account; or in accustoming whatever opinion or desire claims our pursuit, to give in its reasons at the bar of reason, and to wait patiently its examination and sentence. Thus alone is the right moral temper formed. And these two exercises will be the constant employment of every one, who aims at the improvement and perfection of his mind; or at acting like a rational creature, and with true inward liberty and self-dominion, which, like every other habit, can only be acquired by practice and custom. 'Tis no matter as to the present case, how the will is determined, by motives or by desires, by the last act of the judgment, or by the mind itself, that is, <106> by its own self-motive power. For whatever be the meaning of such phrases, 'tis as certain, that *command* over ourselves is *liberty,* as that being so *enthralled* by any appetite, as not to be able so much as to examine its pretensions before we

establish in our minds the deliberative habit.

Which is self-command and true moral liberty.

How it is established or formed and strengthened.

yield to it; or being so *habituated* to desultoriness and thoughtlessness, and blind rash choice, as not to have it in our power to think or judge before we act, is *vile slavery and impotence.*

It is therefore this law of our nature that renders us capable of liberty or of being free moral agents.

Thus therefore it is really in consequence of the law of habits, that we are capable of liberty, or are free agents.[a]

Now, I think from what has been said of the association of ideas and of habits, we may justly conclude, "That the laws relating to them are of great use in our nature, either necessary, or fitly chosen. And consequently, that no effects which take their rise from them, are evils absolutely considered, or with regard to the whole frame and constitution of the human mind."

Conclusion from the whole.

But there is a truth, which necessarily results from what hath been laid down, that may justly be added to this article, by way of *corolary;* and it is this, "That even in an absolutely perfect constitution of things, where the law of habit and association takes place, if knowledge be progressive, and gradually acquireable in proportion to application to improve in it, and consequently minds must be in an infant state at their

A useful corolary.

---

a. So the ancients define liberty. Soli enim hi vivunt ut volunt, qui quid velle debeant didicerunt. Ineruditae autem & rationis expertes animi incitationes atque actiones exilem quandam ignobilemque voluntatis libertatem multa cum poenitentia conjunctam habent, &c. *Plutarch* de auditione libellus. So *Cicero,* paradox. 5. Quid est enim libertas? potestas vivendi ut velis. Quis igitur vivit, ut vult? nisi qui recta sequitur, qui officio gaudet, cui vivendi via considerata atque provisa est, &c. See a fine description of this moral freedom by *Persius, Satyr.* 5. Libertate opus est, &c. [Plutarch, *De auditione,* 37E: "For only those live as they wish who have learned what they ought to wish. But ignorant and irrational impulses and acts involve a rather meagre and ignoble freedom of will that is conjoined with a good deal of repenting."

Cicero, *Paradoxa Stoicorum,* V.34: "For what is freedom? the power to live as you will. Who then lives as he wills except one who follows the things that are right, who delights in his duty, who has a well-considered path of life mapped out before him, etc." Cicero, *De oratore, Book III, De fato, Paradoxa Stoicorum, De partitione oratoria,* trans. H. Rackham, Loeb Classical Library (London: Heinemann; Cambridge: Harvard University Press, 1942).

Persius, *Satires,* V.73: "What we want is true liberty, etc." *Juvenal and Persius,* trans. G. G. Ramsay, rev. ed., Loeb Classical Library (London: Heinemann; Cambridge: Harvard University Press, 1940).]

entrance upon the world; some associations and habits must be early formed by minds in such a state <107> of things, which ought to be broken, and yet which cannot be broken or dissolved by reason without difficulty and struggling. For it is impossible, but some ideas, by being frequently presented to the mind conjointly must associate, which ought not to be associated; or the association of which is contrary to happiness and reason." But this observation, so plainly follows from what has been proved, that it is needless to dwell longer upon it. I shall therefore but just add, that if any one will pursue it in his own mind through all its consequences, he shall find a solution arising from it to many objections made against the present state of mankind; to those especially which are taken from the prevalence of vice in the world: for wrong opinions must produce wrong choice and action: and yet of most wrong choices, it may be said, *Decipimur specie recti.*[37]

37. Horace, *Ars poetica,* 25: "[We] deceive ourselves by semblance of truth." Horace, *Satires, Epistles and Ars poetica,* trans. H. Rushton Fairclough, Loeb Classical Library (London: Heinemann; New York: Putnam, 1926).

CHAPTER IV

Another class of laws relative to our guiding principle and our moral conduct.

Let us therefore proceed to examine the laws relative to our reason, moral sense, and the rule and standard of our moral conduct with which we are provided and furnished by nature.

We have already considered our constitution with regard to knowledge. But in an enquiry into human nature, it is certainly proper to take

Our excellence consists in our having reason and a moral sense to guide our conduct.

yet a further view of our frame with respect to our moral conduct and guidance; or of the powers we are endued with, to direct us in the management of our affections, and in all our actions; and of the rules or laws nature hath set before us for our measure and guide. Reason, as it relates to our moral conduct, may be defined to be, "Our power of making

What moral reason is.

<108> a just estimate of human life, and its principal end, by connecting things past and to come with what is present; and thus of computing our true interest, and discovering what is best and fittest to do in any case; or contrariwise, what is opposite to our interest, and unbecoming our natural rank and dignity."[a] Now, that we have such a faculty is readily

a. So *Cicero* defines it, in the beginning of the first book of his Offices. Homo autem quod est rationis particeps, per quam consequentia cernit, causas rerum videt, earumque praegressus, & quasi antecessiones non ignorat, similitudines comparat, & rebus presentibus adjungit, atque annectit futuras: facile totius vitae cursum videt, ad eamque degendam praeparat res necessarias, &c. So *de legibus,* l. 1. Etenim ratio qua una praestamus beluis, per quam conjectura valemus, argumentamur, refellimus, disserimus, conficimus aliquid, concludimus—quid est divinius, quae cum adolevit, atque perfecta est, nominatur rite sapientia, &c. [Cicero, *De officiis,* I.iv.11: ". . . while man—because he is endowed with reason, by which he comprehends the chain of consequences, perceives the causes of things, understands the relation of cause to effect and of effect to cause, draws analogies, and connects and associates the present and the future—easily surveys the course of his whole life and makes the necessary preparations for its conduct, etc." Cicero, *De officiis,* trans. Walter Miller, Loeb Classical Library (London: Heinemann; Cambridge: Harvard University Press,

owned: nor does any one hesitate to assert, that our chief excellence above lower animals void of reflexion consists in our having it. 'Tis for this reason we assume to ourselves the name and character of moral agents. We may observe a nice, subtle and uninterrupted gradation in nature from the lowest degree of meer perceptivity to this perfection man is distinguished by, thro' many intermediate steps gradually ascending one above another, without any chasm or void. Thus, nature is full and coherent.

> *Far as creation's ample range extends,*
> *The scale of sensual, mental pow'rs ascends:*
> *Mark how it mounts to man's imperial race,*
> *From the green myriads in the peopled grass!*
> *What modes of sight, between each wide extreme,*
> *The mole's dim curtain, and the lynx's beam:*
> *Of smell the headlong lioness between,*
> *And hound, sagacious on the tainted green;*
> *Of hearing, from the life that fills the flood,*
> *To that which warbles through the vernal wood:*
> *The spider's touch, how exquisitely fine,*
> *Feels at each thread, and lives along the line:*
> *In the nice bee, what sense so subtly true,*
> *From pois'nous herbs extracts the healing dew.* <109>
> *How* instinct *varies! in the groveling swine,*
> *Compar'd half reas'ning elephant with thine.*
> *'Twixt that, and* reason, *what a nice barrier,*
> *For ever sep'rate, yet for ever near:*
> *Remembrance, and reflexion, how ally'd;*
> *What thin partitions sense from thought divide:*
> *And middle natures, how they long to join,*
> *Yet never pass th' insuperable line!*

How we rise in the scale of being by our reason: it is all our force, or at least our chief one.

1938). *De legibus:* ". . . and indeed reason, which alone raises us above the level of the beasts and enables us to draw inferences, to prove and disprove, to discuss and solve problems, and to come to conclusions" (I.x.30). "But what is more divine than reason? And reason, when it is full grown and perfected, is rightly called wisdom" (I.vii.22–23). Cicero, *De re publica, De legibus,* trans. Clinton Walker Keyes, Loeb Classical Library (London: Heinemann; New York: Putnam, 1928).]

> *Without this just* gradation, *could they be*
> *Subjected these to those, or all to thee?*
> *The pow'rs of all subdued by thee alone,*
> *Is not thy reason all those pow'rs in one?*
>
> Essay on man, Epist. 1.[38]

It is our guiding principle, and ought to be exerted as such.

But if reason be acknowledged to be a perfection or power superior in the scale of life to meer sensitive being, the consequence must be, "That reason ought to be upon the throne within us, set up and maintained by us, as the judge and ruler, from which all appetites, fancies, affections and pursuits ought to receive their commands, and to which they ought to be subject and accountable."[a] This seems to need no proof. One may as reasonably ask, why we ought to open our eyes, make use of them, and take care to preserve them from all diseases and imperfections; as why, having reason, we ought to exert it, give it its proper place, and preserve it pure and untainted, and in full possession of its natural right, to guide, direct, and command all our inferior appetites and all our associations. It is as evident, that our appetites and affections are made to be guided by reason, as that reason is a <110> judging power, and as such, our distinguishing, our supreme excellence. If reason be our natural dignity, or that which constitutes us a superior rank of beings above those which have no such governing principle; it must be true, that we only maintain our natural dignity in proportion as reason presides and rules

---

a. Eadem ratio habet in se quiddam amplum atque magnificum ad imperandum magis quam ad parendum accommodatum. *Cicero de finibus,* Lib. 2. No. 14. Duplex enim est vis animorum atque naturae: una pars in appetitu posita est, quae est ορμη graece, quae hominem huc & illuc rapit: altera in ratione, quae docet & explanat quid faciendum fugiendumque sit. Ita fit ut ratio praesit; appetitus vero obtemperet, &c. *Cicero de officiis,* Lib. 1. No. 28 and 29. [Cicero, *De finibus,* II.xiv.46: "Further, reason possesses an intrinsic element of dignity and grandeur, suited rather to require obedience than to render it." Cicero, *De finibus bonorum et malorum,* trans. H. Rackham, Loeb Classical Library (London: Heinemann; New York: Putnam, 1931). *De officiis,* I.xxviii.101: "Now we find that the essential activity of the spirit is twofold: one force is appetite (that is, ορμη, in Greek), which impels a man this way and that; the other is reason, which teaches and explains what should be done and what should be left undone. The result is that reason commands, appetite obeys, etc."]

38. Pope, *Essay on Man,* I.207–32.

within us; and that we fall below the rank of men, in proportion as reason is weak, impotent, over-powered, and unable to act as a ruling or commanding faculty, in truth, to ask, why man is obliged to act according to his reason, or to be ruled by it, is to ask, why reason is reason. It cannot be denied, without asserting, that it is not a higher rank of life to be endowed with it, than to want it; upon which supposition, man is not one step removed in dignity or perfection above meer animals and a gradation or scale of being, are words without any meaning.

But there are two things which deserve our particular attention with regard to our natural capacity and furniture for directing our conduct, or for the regulation of our appetites, desires, affections and actions. "We have a moral sense, or a sense of right and wrong. And we have a sense of interest and happiness." Now if it shall appear, that these two senses do not contradict one another; but that they agree in pointing out to us the same course of management and action; then must it be granted, that our nature is very well constituted with respect to our moral conduct. Were these, indeed, at variance, our frame would be very unaccountable, or rather monstrous; but if virtue and interest be really the same, then is every part of our moral frame consonant to every other part of it; and so it is a good or well composed whole. I have used the word *virtue*, to express what our sense of right and wrong recommends to our choice, because it is universally so used and understood: to use that term, in that sense, is not to beg the question; or to suppose a difference between virtue and vice before we have proved it: it is no <III> more than forewarning, that we are to use *virtue* and *vice,* with these other words *right* and *wrong* in the same sense, because we think these words are very generally employed as equivalent terms. That we have a sense of virtue and vice, or of right and wrong, is now to be proved.

There are two things to be considered with respect to our guiding principle and our rule of conduct.

Our sense of right and wrong.

And our sense of happiness.

That these do not disagree shall be shewn afterwards.

This is a question about fact, and consequently it can only be resolved in the same way, that other faculties or powers may be proved to belong to our nature. But I am apt to think, that every one shall immediately perceive, that he has a moral sense inherent in him, and really inseparable from him; if he will reflect, "Whether he is not so constituted as to be

Our sense of right and wrong, or our moral sense.

necessarily determined by his nature, to approve and disapprove certain affections and actions?" For if that be owned, then are there certain af-

Election distinguished from approbation.

fections and actions which he is necessarily determined by his nature to pronounce *right*, and certain affections and actions which he is necessarily determined by his nature to pronounce *wrong*. The question now under consideration can be no other than whether we have a determination in our nature to approve and disapprove affections and actions; and what we are thus determined to approve and disapprove. For if there are certain affections and actions which we are constantly so determined

We have an approving and disapproving sense.

to approve or disapprove that we cannot chuse but approve the one kind and disapprove the other; then, whatever these may be, they are with respect to us necessary objects or motives, the one kind, to approbation, and the other, to condemnation or disapprobation. Hardly will any one say, that we have no determination to approve or disapprove. "Approbation[a] is a simple idea known by consciousness, which can only be explained by synonimous words, or by concomitant or subsequent circumstances. Approbation of our own action, denotes or is attended with a pleasure in the contemplation of it, and in reflexion upon the affections which inclined us to it. Approba-<112>tion of the action of another is

The qualities that excite approbation or disapprobation.

pleasant, and is attended with love toward the agent. And that the qualities exciting to election, or moving to action, are different from those moving to approbation, every one upon reflexion must feel. For we often do actions which we cannot approve, and approve actions which we omit. We often desire that an agent had omitted an action which we approve, and wish he would do an action which we condemn. Approbation is often employed about the actions of others where there is no room for our election."[b] But if we experience approbation and disapprobation, then must we have an approving and disapproving faculty; a determination to approve and disapprove: and there must likewise be

a. See Mr. *Hutcheson on the passions.* [Francis Hutcheson, *An Essay on the Nature and Conduct of the Passions. . . .* (1728); ed. Aaron Garrett (Indianapolis: Liberty Fund, 2002), II: *Illustrations upon the Moral Sense.*]

b. Our sense of honour and shame supposes this faculty: such affections can only spring from it: they are absolutely unaccountable on any other hypotheses, because they cannot be resolved into any other principle.

objects to excite our approbation, and objects to move our disapprobation. So that the remaining question is, what these objects are?

I. Now it is plain, that we never approve or disapprove, neither with respect to ourselves or others, but when we are sensible an action is done voluntarily, by choice, with reflexion, and without external compulsion or necessity. Thus we neither approve nor disapprove what is done by a brute, an ideot, or changeling; nor even what a rational creature does, not of itself, but when externally forced and compelled. Approbation and disapprobation always suppose their object to be matter of voluntary and free choice and affection. We neither approve nor disapprove ourselves, but when we are conscious that what we do is our own voluntary deed. And with regard to other beings, in like manner, we can neither approve nor disapprove, but when we imagine an action is performed by them with like choice, affection and free-<113>dom, as when we approve or disapprove ourselves for doing or omitting. It is not merely because actions are advantageous or disadvantageous, that we approve or disapprove them; actions must be free, in order to move such sentiments and affections. If they are not, we regard them as the fall of a beam or a tile. This is too evident to be longer insisted upon.

Actions must be done with freedom, affection and reflexion, to excite approbation or condemnation.

II. But of free actions, or actions excited to by affections, and done with reflexion, some cannot be reflected upon without approbation, nor others without dislike and condemnation. Now, what are those, which move our approbation, and by what characteristic are they distinguished from the others? It is experience that must determine this question. And therefore let any one consider,[a] how benevolent actions; how truth, candour,

Of these veracity, candour, benevolence, &c. excite our approbation, and their contraries our disapprobation.

a. See *Cicero* epist. ad Atticum, l. 14. epist. Dolabellae Coss. suo. Nihil est enim, crede mihi virtute formosius, nihil pulchrius, nihil amabilius, &c. *De finibus,* l. 2. Et quoniam eadem natura cupiditatem ingenuit homini veri inveniendi.—His initiis inducti; omnia vera diligimus, id est, fidelia, simplicia, constantiâ: tum vana, falsa, fallentia odimus, ut fraudem perjuriam, malitiam, injuriam, &c. [Cicero, *Letters to Friends,* III.326 (IX.14).4, Cicero to Dolabella; also in *Letters to Atticus,* III.17a: "Nothing, believe me, is more beautiful, fair, and lovable than manly virtue, etc." Cicero, *Letters to Friends,* ed. and trans. D. R. Shackleton Bailey, 3 vols. (Cambridge

veracity, benignity, and such like dispositions, with their proper exertions in action affect us, so soon as we reflect upon them, or contemplate them: and what we think, on the other hand, of their contraries, falshood, dissimulation, treachery, instability, narrowness of mind, selfishness, malice, &c. Creatures capable of reflection, can, nay must make all the affections they experience in their breasts, and by which they are moved to action, the objects of their understanding: they must perceive them, and perceiving them there will naturally and necessarily arise in their minds a new class of affections towards these affections they feel themselves to be moved by. What then are the affections which we experience to accompany the different sorts of affections which have been just mentioned? How do they affect <114> or move us? Are they pleasant to us on reflexion and contemplation, or disagreeable, or do they no way touch or move us; but are we quite neutral and indifferent to them: or when we are agreeably affected by the one sort, and disagreeably affected by the other sort, as we certainly are, whether we will or not, when they are present to our mind, and reflected upon. Is it the same sort of pleasure or pain we perceive when we reflect upon a beautiful and useful plant or an ugly and pernicious one? One or other of these must be said. But surely it will not be affirmed, that we are quite unmoved by such contemplation, and that no affections, whether of the generous or ungenerous kind, do either excite our like or dislike, our approbation or disapprobation; for this would be to assert, that no one character is more agreeable to us than another; but that the mind is equally indifferent to all sorts of characters and tempers. Far less will it be said, that the false, deceitful, mercenary man is agreeable to us; and that the faithful, trusty, and benevolent man moves our hatred. And to say, that tho' we are differently affected by these opposite characters, yet it is no otherwise than as we are differently affected with fruit, for instance, according as it is

---

and London: Harvard University Press, 2001); *Letters to Atticus,* trans. E. O. Winstedt, 3 vols. (London: Heinemann; New York: Putnam, 1912–18). *De finibus,* II.xiv.46: "Nature has also engendered in mankind the desire of contemplating truth. . . . This primary instinct leads us on to love all truth as such, that is, all that is trustworthy, simple and consistent, and to hate things insincere, false and deceptive, such as cheating, perjury, malice and injustice, etc."]

pleasant or disagreeable to our taste, is absurd. For however much we may like or dislike a particular sensation of taste fruit may affect us with; yet surely we do not like and dislike, approve and disapprove fruits, in the same way we like and dislike, approve and disapprove characters. Do we like or approve our generous friend in no other way than we like or dislike our dinner?

But if we are affected by such actions and characters, as have been described, agreeably or disagreeably, in a different way from the agreeable or disagreeable manner in which meats and drinks affect us; then it must follow, that we are fitted and determined by our nature to receive from the consideration of such actions and characters a particular <115> kind of agreeable or disagreeable sentiment, properly expressed by approbation and disapprobation. For this must be true, in general, that no one thing can give us pleasure or pain unless we are fitted by our make to be so affected by it. We could not, for instance, have the pleasures which the modifications of light and colours give to the eye, if we were not so framed as to perceive them and be agreeably affected by them. Now if we are determined by our nature to approve or disapprove characters, in the way that has been mentioned, we may give and ought to give, this aptitude, this determination in our nature a particular distinguishing name to denote it. Let it therefore be called a sense of the difference between actions or characters, or more shortly, a moral sense.

Let us reason about this matter as much as we will, all we can do is but to turn this question into various shapes, *viz.* "Whether we are not necessarily determined to approve the public affections in ourselves or others, which lead to such conduct as promotes the good of our fellow creatures, and to disapprove their opposites; and that immediately, so soon as any one of them is presented to our mind." For the question is about a fact, a part of our constitution; about something felt and experienced within us, in consequence of our frame; and it cannot possibly be decided, but by consciousness, or by attending to our mind, in order to know how we are affected on certain occasions by certain objects. But if any matter of experience merits our attention, this does, and therefore I shall offer the following considerations about it.

Whether we have a moral sense or not, is a question of fact.

Arguments to prove we have it.

I. Did not affections, actions and characters, when they are contemplated by the understanding, and are thus made objects of thought and
reflection, move us agreeably or disagreeably, there would be an analogy
in nature wanting, which we have no reason from nature to think can
be wanting. For there is no-<116>thing more certain, than that all sensible forms, so soon as they are presented to the mind, do affect it with
the agreeable perception of beauty, or the disagreeable perception of
deformity. Some objects of sense do indeed so little affect us, that the
perception produced by their contemplation is scarcely attended to; but
every perception, as such, must be in some degree either pleasant or painful; tho' it is only when perceptions have a considerable degree of pleasure or pain, that they considerably interest us, and we are therefore at
any pains to class them, and give particular names to their effects upon
us. However, setting aside that consideration, it is evident, in fact, with
regard almost to all bodies or subjects of sense, that they give us either
the idea of beauty or deformity according to the different disposition,
measure or arrangement of their several parts. It is the same with respect
to sounds; from every combination of them, there necessarily results
either harmony or discord. Now, did not moral subjects affect us in like
manner with the sense of beauty and deformity, as sensible species or
images of bodies do,[a] there <117> would not be that analogy between

From analogy.

*For we have a
sense of beauty
in sensible
forms.*

a. See *Cicero's offices,* lib. 1. Nec vero illa parva naturae vis rationisque quod unum
hoc animal sentit, quid sit ordo, quid sit quod deceat, in factis dictisque qui modus.
Itaque eorum ipsorum quae adspectu sentiuntur, nullum aliud animal pulchritudinem, venustatem, convenientiam partium sentit; quam similitudinem natura, ra-
tioque ab oculis ad animum transferens, multo etiam magis pulchritudinem; con-
stantiam, ordinem in consiliis factisque conservandam putat, &c. So *de finibus,* lib. 2.
No. 14. and *de finibus,* lib. 5. No. 17. Quid, in motu, & statu corporis nihilne est
quod animadvertendum esse natura judicat? Quemadmodum quis ambulet, sedeat,
qui ductus oris, qui vultus in quoque sit: nihilne est in rebus, quod dignum libero
aut indignum esse putemus? Non odio dignos multos ducimus, qui quodam motu
aut statu videntur naturae legem & modum contempsisse? Et quoniam haec dedu-
cuntur de corpore, quid est, cur non recte pulchritudo etiam ipsa propter se expetenda
ducatur? Nam si pravitatem imminutionemque corporis, propter se fugiendam
putamus, cur non etiam, & fortasse magis, propter se formae dignitatem sequamur—
Quoniam enim natura suis omnibus partibus expleri vult hunc statum expetit, &c.
See *de legibus,* lib. 1. numb. 19. An corporis pravitates, si erint perinsignes, habebunt

the natural and moral world, or between the fabric of our mind with relation to sensible and to moral objects, that one is naturally led to apprehend must take place by the universal analogy of nature to itself observed throughout all its works. No object can indeed be present to the understanding or perceived by it, without affecting it in some manner as an object of the understanding, or as an intelligible species. And therefore every moral object must be fitted to affect the mind with some affection suited to it as a moral species, or an intelligible form. But not to lay any stress at all upon that abstract truth. How can we acknowledge a sense of beauty and deformity with respect to corporeal subjects, and no analogous sense with respect to mental ones? Can we allow the mind to have an eye or an ear for bodily proportions and harmonies; and yet imagine it has no eye or ear by which it can distinguish moral appearances and effects? No sense, whereby it can scan thoughts, and sentiments, and affections, or distinguish the beautiful and deformed, the

---

aliquid offensionis, animi deformitas non habebit? Cujus turpitudo ex ipsis vitiis facillime percipi potest. Quid enim foedius avaritia, quid immanius libidine, quid contemptius timiditate, quid abjectius tarditate & stultitia dici potest, &c. [Cicero, *De officiis,* I.iv.14: "And it is no mean manifestation of Nature and Reason that man is the only animal that has a feeling for order, for propriety, for moderation in word and deed. And so no other animal has a sense of beauty, loveliness, harmony in the visible world; and Nature and Reason, extending the analogy of this from the world of sense to the world of spirit, find that beauty, consistency, order are far more to be maintained in thought and deed, etc." *De finibus,* V.xvii.47: "Again, is there nothing in the movements and postures of the body which Nature herself judges to be of importance? A man's mode of walking and sitting, his particular cast of features and expression—is there nothing in these things that we consider worthy or unworthy of a free man? Do we not often think people deserving of dislike, who by some movement or posture appear to have violated a law or principle of nature? And since people try to get rid of these defects of bearing, why should not even beauty have a good claim to be considered as desirable for its own sake? For if we think imperfection or mutilation of the body things to be avoided for their own sake, why should we not with equal or perhaps still greater reason pursue distinction of form for its own sake? . . . For since our nature aims at the full development of all its parts, she desires . . . that state of body, etc." *De legibus,* I.xix.51: "Are bodily defects, if very conspicuous, to offend us, but not a deformity of character? And yet the baseness of this latter can easily be perceived from the very vices which result from it. For what can be thought of that is more loathsome than greed, what more inhuman than lust, what more contemptible than cowardice, what more degraded than stupidity and folly?"]

harmonious and dissonant, the agreeable and disagreeable in them. Does the bodily eye afford us perceptions of pleasure and pain distinct from the sensations of touch? And has the understanding or eye of the mind, when it is employed about moral forms, no such discernment? Has it no class of pleasures and pains belonging to it, as a seeing or discerning faculty? Are all the pleasures or pains excited in or perceived by the mind, with relation to affections and sentiments, only pleasures and pains of mental touch or feeling, so to speak? Is there nothing of the agreeable and disagreeable kind result-<118>ing from the contemplation of moral subjects, from their visible, *i.e.* intelligible proportions, shapes and textures? Is all, I say, that affects the mind with pain or pleasure of the moral kind merely analogous to our sensible pleasures conveyed by outward touch; and has it, indeed, with respect to moral objects, no class of perceptions analogous to those of the eye; none at all which properly belong to the understanding, and are excited in it by the moral species, in like manner as visible ones affect the sense of seeing? Surely it is contrary to analogy to fancy so. But if there really be any such thing as being affected by the appearances of moral subjects to the understanding as such; in language, which is, and must be originally taken from sensible objects, and their effects upon us, the perceptions conveyed to the understanding by moral forms, will very properly be called by the same names, as the analogous ones produced in us by visible forms; that is, beauty and deformity, regularity and irregularity, proportion and disproportion, *&c.*

From languages, for these suppose it.

II. Language, not being invented by philosophers, but contrived to express common sentiments, or what every one perceives, we may be morally sure, that where universally all languages make a distinction, there is really in nature a difference. Now all languages speak of a beautiful and a deformed, a fair and foul in actions and characters, as well as of advantageousness and disadvantageousness, profitableness and hurtfulness. But all languages which use such words, suppose a moral sense, or a capacity of distinguishing actions and characters from one another, by their appearances to the understanding independently of all their other tendencies, effects or consequences. For at the same time that these words, beauty, deformity, &c. are used, there is in all languages a great variety of other words to express all that can distinguish actions and characters <119> from one another, upon supposition that they are no otherwise different than with relation to their advantageous or disadvantageous effects. Interest, convenience, good, profitable, and innumerable other such terms, and their contraries, sufficiently denote these latter differences; and therefore the words taken from visible perceptions, are quite superfluous, if there are indeed no moral differences discernible by the eye of the mind or understanding, signified by them in distinction from others. But how is it conceiveable that words absolutely superfluous, but founded upon and derived from a supposition of an analogy between visible appearances to the eye and moral appearances to the understanding, could have universally insinuated themselves into all languages, were there no such analogy in nature? Nothing correspondent to the perceptions of beauty and deformity by the eye in material subjects, in immaterial, or moral and intelligible forms to the understanding. This is hardly conceiveable.

III. But to go on. Oratory, poetry, painting, and all the imitative arts, prove the reality of a moral sense: they suppose it, and could not have their agreeable effects upon us, were we not endued with it. If they suppose a sublimity, a beauty, an excellence, a greatness, an irresistable amiableness, in characters[a] absolutely distinct from all the consequences of actions, with regard to profit or loss, advantage or disadvantage; then do they prove a moral sense, or that there are certain actions or characters which we cannot chuse but approve, love and admire; and

From the fine arts, for these suppose it.

a. See *Aristotle's Ars Poet.* and *Longinus.* Archeveque de *Cambray* sur l'eloquence. La tragedie roulât sur deux passions: savoir la terreur, qui doivent donner les suites funestes du vice; & la compassion, qu'inspire la vertue persecutée & patiente, &c. *Dial. 1.* [François de Salignac de la Mothe Fénelon, Archbishop of Cambrai, *Dialogues sur l'éloquence* (1718), I.19–20: "Tragedy runs on two passions; namely terror, which the dark outcome of vice must bring; and compassion, which is inspired by persecuted and long-suffering virtue." (A.B., trans.)]

others which we cannot chuse but disapprove, condemn and abhor, in-
<120>dependently of all other considerations, besides their lovely or vile
forms, their charming and agreeable, or disagreeable and detestable appearances to the understanding. And shall we then, rather than acknowledge such a sense in our make, give up the foundation of all those delightful arts, to which we owe such noble entertainments? Or if we
should be tempted so to do, is it not the utmost length we can go, to
save our being forced to own a moral sense; to say, that though there be
no real amiableness or deformity in moral acts, there is an imaginary one
of full force, upon which these arts work? But what is this but to say,
It must be   that though the thing itself cannot be allowed in nature, yet the imag-
from nature.   ination or fancy of it must be allowed to be from nature: for if there be
such a fancy of full force in our nature that upon it can be raised such
high admiration, warm affection, and transporting approbation by these
arts; whence else can such fancy be, but from nature alone? It is easy to
conceive, if the thing itself, or the imagination of it, be natural, how it
comes about that nothing besides art and strong endeavour, with long
practice, and much violent struggling, can overcome our natural pre-
possession or prevention in favour of this moral distinction, without
which poetry or oratory would in vain attempt to interest our love and
approbation, or excite our aversion and dislike by characters. But if it
be not from nature, art must be able to create; it must be able to do more
than operate upon subjects laid to its hand; it must be able to give existence to what nature knows nothing of, or hath laid no foundation for.

The imitative arts not only prove to us, that we have public affections;
and that these regularly excited and wrought up to certain proper degrees, afford us very noble entertainment in the way of passion or feeling:
but they likewise prove, that characters cannot be exhibited to our view
without effectu-<121>ally moving us; without deeply concerning us in
their fates and fortunes; without exciting our warmest approbation, and
keenest emulation. What else does all that is said of sublimities, great-
The absurdity   ness, beauty, dignity, and loveliness of sentiments, affections, actions,
of supposing it and characters mean? They are indeed words without meaning. And the
is not.   effects they produce in our minds, what are they? In truth, any one who

will but reflect how he is moved by a fine character in a poem, must own these arts are a demonstration, 1. That we are originally so constituted, as that from the moment we come to be tried with sensible objects, pity, love, kindness, generosity, and social affection are brought forth. But how could they be so, if they were not in our nature? Can any art educe from any subject qualities which it has not? 2. That we are so constituted, that the moment we come to be tried by rational objects, and receive unto our mind images or representations of justice, generosity, truth, magnanimity, or any other virtue, we are not able to remain indifferent toward them, but must approve and like them. And indeed it is impossible to imagine, a sensible creature so ill framed and unnatural, as that so soon as he is tried by proper objects, he should have no one good passion towards his kind: no foundation either of compassion, complacency, or kindly affection. And it is equally impossible to conceive a rational creature, coming first to be tried by moral species, or the representations of good and virtuous affections, should have no liking of them, or dislike of their contraries; but be found absolutely neutral, towards whatever is presented to them of that sort. "A soul[a] indeed may as well be without sense as without admiration in the things of which it has any knowledge: coming <122> therefore to a capacity of seeing and admiring in the moral way, it must needs find a beauty and a deformity as well in actions, minds, and tempers, as in figures, sounds, or colours." Let the philosophers, who are for resolving all our publick affections, and all our liking and disliking of actions and characters into certain subtle, nimble reflexions of self-love upon private interest, try whether they can thus account for the love, admiration, esteem and concern excited by a fictitious representation: but if they find the attempt vain here, must it not likewise be so in the original life, from which fictitious representation must be copied, in order to be natural? Sure there is not one nature for life, and another for fiction.

a. See *Shaftsbury's* *essay on virtue,* whose words these are. [Shaftesbury, "Virtue" I.iii.1, in *Characteristics,* ed. Klein (Cambridge: Cambridge University Press, 1999), 178.]

IV. But who can consider human nature, and deny that we have public affections towards the good of others; or assert that all our passions spring from self-love and desire of private advantage; and that we have no moral sense. For take away a moral sense and public desires, how very small a share of our present excitements to action would remain with us? It is owned, that the affections *called* public, make indeed the greater part of our employments; or, that without them we would be almost reduced to absolute indolence. But when they are said not to be really social or public affections, but modes or arts of self-love, how are they accounted for?

How are our natural affection to parents and offspring; our compassion to the distressed; our gratitude, our benevolence; or whatever, in one word, hath the appearance of social in our frame, or of affection to public good: how are they reduced to self-love, but by supposing us, when the objects, which excite these affections are represented to us, immediately to make some very cunning reflexions upon self-interest or private good, which <123> there is neither time for, nor are we conscious of? And can we think that to be true philosophy, or a just account of human nature, which is forced to have recourse to the supposition of many refined subtle reasonings on every occasion, in every honest farmer or peasant? That one consideration is sufficient to refute it, and to shew it to be false and unnatural. But what puts the reality of public affections in our nature, the immediate object of which is the good of others, and of a moral sense by which we are necessarily determined to approve such affections, beyond all doubt, is, that whatever motives there may be from the side of pleasure or interest, by which we may be bribed to do an action; yet we cannot possibly be bribed to approve it contrary to our inward sense: or whatever motives of fear there may be to terrify us from doing an action, yet we cannot be terrified into the approbation of the omission, if it be not really approveable. If a moral sense be owned, the reality of public affections in our nature will be acknowledged; for it is only about actions proceeding from public affections, that there is any dispute as to our determination to approve or disapprove: but if we have no moral sense, agreeably to which we must approve, and contrary to

---

Without supposing or owning it, we must have recourse to very subtle reflexions (of which the mind is not conscious and for which it hath not time) to account for several phenomena; which is absurd.

We can no more be bribed to approve an action, than to assent to a proposition.

which we cannot approve or disapprove; whence comes it about, that though we may be allured, or frighted into doing an action, yet we can neither be allured nor frighted into approving or disapproving an action, no more than we can be bribed or terrified into assenting to a proposition which we perceive to be false; or into refusing our assent to a proposition which we perceive to be true. If that be the case, then approbation or disapprobation depends[a] as absolutely upon the <124> appearances of actions to our minds, as assent and dissent do upon the appearances of propositions to our minds. But that it is so, every one will feel by asking himself, whether an estate can bribe him to approve any degree of villany, though it may perswade him to perpetrate it; or whether he can possibly think treachery, ingratitude, dissimulation or any such actions laudable and approveable in themselves, whatever evils may be averted by them in certain circumstances? Consequences cannot alter the moral differences of actions no more than they can alter the nature of truth and falshood. As a proposition must be true or false in itself, independently of the loss or gain the profession of the belief of it may bring; so actions must be the same in themselves with respect to their moral natures and qualities, with whatever circumstances relative to interest, the doing or not doing may be accompanied. But as truths could not be understood or assented to, had we not a faculty of distinguishing the appearances of truth from falshood; so actions could not be discerned to be morally beautiful and fit, unless we had a faculty of distinguishing the moral differences of actions.

a. Nam ut vera & falsa, ut consequentia & contraria, sua sponte, non aliena judicantur: sic constans & perpetua vitae ratio, quae est virtus, itemque inconstantia, quod est vitium, sua natura probatur. Sed perturbat nos opinionum varietas, hominumque dissentio; & quia non idem contingit in sensibus, &c. *Cicero de legibus. Lib.* I. No. 17. & deinceps. [Cicero, *De legibus,* I.xvii.45–47: "For just as truth and falsehood, the logical and illogical, are judged by themselves and not by anything else, so the steadfast and continuous use of reason in the conduct of life, which is virtue, and also inconstancy, which is vice, [are judged] by their own nature. . . . But we are confused by the variety of men's beliefs and by their disagreements, and because this same variation is not found in the senses, etc."]

Farther reflex-
ions on moral
sense.

But all that relates to a moral sense in our nature, hath been so fully handled by several excellent writers,[a] that I shall only subjoin a few further reflexions upon it, with a view to such philosophers as do not deny the thing, but seem to quarrel with the name; which however will be of considerable use <125> to set our moral sense itself and its usefulness yet in a clearer light.

'Tis not worth
while to dis-
pute about a
name or appel-
lation, if the
thing be
owned.

I. First of all, it is no great matter for the name, if the thing itself in question be acknowledged. And it certainly is by all, who acknowledge the difference between good and evil; however, they may chuse to express that difference by calling it truth, reasonableness, fitness, or by whatever other appellation. For if there is truth, fitness, or reasonableness in actions with regard to us, it is perceivable by us; and if we perceive it, we are capable of perceiving it; that is, we have the faculty requisite to perceiving it, or which enables us to perceive it. Let therefore the capacity or faculty of perceiving moral differences of actions or characters, be called reason, as it is exercised about actions and their moral differences, moral discernment, or moral conscience; we shall not dispute for any word: All we want to establish, is, that as we are capable of distinguishing truth from falsehood, so we are capable of distinguishing good and approveable actions, affections, and characters from bad and disapproveable ones: And that we are not more necessarily determined by our nature, to assent or dissent according to the appearances of things to our understanding, than we are necessarily determined by our make to approve or disapprove affections, actions, and characters, according to their

And it must be
owned by all
who acknowl-
edge moral dif-
ferences of
actions and
characters.

appearances to our understanding. Now as all, who own a necessary and essential difference of the moral kind between any action and its opposite, (as between gratitude, for example, and ingratitude) must own the necessary determination of our minds to approve the one, and disapprove the other, so soon as these moral differences are presented to the

---

a. By *Crouzaz,* in his *traite de beau. Hutcheson* in his *enquiry into the origine of beauty,* and his *illustrations on a moral sense. Shaftsbury* in his *characteristics.* And Dr. *Butler,* Bishop of Bristol, in his *admirable sermons.* [Jean-Pierre de Crousaz, *Traité du beau* (1715); Joseph Butler, *Fifteen Sermons* (1726).]

mind; so every one must be obliged to acknowledge certain necessary and essential differences of actions in the moral kind, resulting necessarily from their natures, <126> according to which the mind must approve or disapprove, so soon as the images of them are represented to it; or he must say that the mind in no case approves or disapproves, but that it is quite a stranger to all such sentiments as these words express. For it is self-evident that if ever approbation and disapprobation be excited, there must be an exciting quality. It is not more true, that when there is election there is some quality exciting to it; than it is necessarily so, that wherever there is approbation, there is a ground, a reason, a motive of approbation, some quality, some appearance to the mind that excites it. As we cannot have or conceive pleasure of any kind, without affection to it, nor alternately affection, without some pleasure towards which it tends; so we cannot conceive delight in approving, without something which creates that delight or complacency; nor alternately any thing fitted to excite delight or complacency felt in approbation, and yet the mind not affected by it in that manner. But it is no uncommon thing to find philosophers asserting propositions which necessarily terminate in affirming, "There may be pleasures without affections, and affections without objects; though hardly will any one philosopher make that assertion in direct terms." I think an excellent philosopher has reduced most of the objections against a moral sense to such conclusions.[a]

II. But if the determination in our nature to approve public affections and virtuous actions, and to disapprove their contraries, be acknowledged, though it is of no importance by what name that determination be expressed; yet it is certainly necessary, that some one should be given it, and fixed to it by philosophers who own the thing. If there is any reason for concluding from the pleasures of <127> harmony we receive by the ear; from the pleasures of light, and colours, and visible beauty we receive by the eye; from the pleasures of truth and knowledge we

However it is proper, nay necessary to give this sense in our natures a distinguishing name.

a. *Hutcheson* in his *illustrations on a moral sense.* [Francis Hutcheson, *An Essay on the Nature and Conduct of the Passions. . . .* (1728), ed. Aaron Garrett (Indianapolis: Liberty Fund, 2002), II: *Illustrations upon the Moral Sense.*]

receive by the exercise of the understanding about speculative matters; or from the pleasures of affection and passion we receive by having our pathetic part agreeably moved and bestirred: If there be any reason to conclude from these perceptions that we really have the faculty of delighting in music, distinct from that of enjoying visible beauty, and both distinct from the faculty of comparing the relations of ideas, and perceiving their agreements or disagreements, and consequently of delighting in truth; and all these distinct from the capacity of receiving pleasures from our affections duly moved (as by a good tragedy for instance): There must be good reason to conclude from the manner in which we are differently affected by the moral appearances of actions and characters, when presented to our mind, either in real life, or by imitation, that we really have a faculty of discerning the moral differences of actions and characters, distinct not only from all our outward senses, but also from the capacity of perceiving the truth and falshood of propositions.

This is no less necessary than it is to give distinguishing names to our other senses and faculties.

And for the same reason that it is not only a proper and distinct way of speaking in philosophy, but a necessary one, to say, we have a sense of harmony, a sense of visible beauty, a capacity of discerning truth from falshood, &c: For the same reason it must not only be a proper and distinct, but a necessary way of speaking in philosophy, to say, that we have a sense of moral beauty and fitness in affections, actions, and characters, as distinct from all these as they are from one another; provided we really are so made, that affections, actions, and characters do necessarily excite our approbation, or dislike and condemnation, according to their moral differences. If there be such a faculty or <128> determination in our nature, it ought to have its distinct name; as well as our other faculties have. We cannot treat of it distinctly no more than of any other of our powers, capacities, and affections, without having some determinate word to express it. But moral sense, moral taste, moral discernment, or moral conscience, well express it; and seem to be the properest phrases in our language, to answer to those used to signify the same determination in our nature by ancient philosophers.[a]

---

a. Δυναμις αγαθοειδης. Sensus decori & honesti, sensus veri ac pulchri, *and sometimes,* sensus communis. So *Juvenal, Satyr* 8. and *Satyr* 15. See *Casaubon, Salmasius,*

III. Some philosophers seem to be excessively fond of the words *pleasure* and *pain,* and to have great satisfaction in repeating over and over again, that it is only pleasure and pain that can excite desire, or move and affect the mind. But though that proposition be very true, when pleasure and pain are taken in a large sense, comprehending all the objects which affect the mind agreeably or disagreeably; yet of what use can it be in philosophy? or, what truths can we discover by its help, till all various sorts of pleasures and pains; that is, all objects which affect the mind agreeably and disagreeably are distinguished and classed, that they may be estimated and apprized? One may as well think of carrying on philosophy distinctly without distinguishing the various pleasures of the senses from one another, because it is the mind perceives them all; and they may for that reason be all called perceptions and pleasures of sense; as think of carrying on philosophy distinctly without distinguishing not only moral pleasures from sensible ones; but the various kinds of moral ones from one another, according to their different values, degrees, <129> and natures. Pleasures of sense, pleasures of imagination, pleasures of contemplation, pleasures of sentiment, and several other classes, that might be named, are all of them but different sorts of pleasures; but because they are different sorts, they ought to be distinguished. Or till they are so, how can they be compared and have their moments determined? If any philosopher asks, "if one can elect or approve without being pleased?" I will answer, "That we cannot be pleased without being pleased." But that election and approbation are as different perceptions or pleasures as any two he can name. If he continues to urge, "That one may say what he will, but one cannot be determined to act but by pleasure, for nothing can please without pleasing." I answer, "Pleasure is pleasure, and nothing can be pleasure but pleasure." But delight in a good action by approbation is as different a pleasure from delight in any advantage it may bring, as pleasure in a picture is from pleasure in music, or as both are

That we are determined by pleasure and pain in all our motions is true in a certain sense.

But this general proposition is of little use in philosophy, till all our pleasures are classed and distinguished.

Gataker. So Horace, *Satyr* 3. l. 16. See Lord *Shaftsbury's Characteristics,* T. 1. *Essay on the freedom of wit and humour.* [Δυναμις αγαθοειδης, "a sense of what's right"; *Sensus decori & honesti*—"the sense of the seemly and of the honest"; *sensus veri ac pulchri*—"a sense of the true and of the beautiful"; Juvenal, *Satires,* viii.73: *sensus communis*—"regard for others." *Juvenal and Persius,* trans. G. G. Ramsay, rev. ed., Loeb Classical Library (London: Heinemann; Cambridge: Harvard University Press, 1940).]

from the pleasure of a dinner, a good picture or a fine tune may procure. Our determination to approve or disapprove actions and characters, renders us capable of a sett of pleasures far superior to any which sense can afford in the most prosperous circumstances of outward enjoyment: and

And our moral sense renders us capable of a peculiar sett of them, the highest we are susceptible of, or can conceive.

it likewise renders us capable of a sett of pains far more insupportable than any we can possibly have from any other quarter. For what pleasures are equal to those of self-approbation, and the conscience of having acted agreeably to the relations of things, to moral beauty and fitness, the dignity and excellency of our nature, and in concert with that amiable temper and disposition of the Author of nature, which appears throughout the whole of his works? And what pains, on the other hand, can be compared with those of a self-condemning mind? But it is our sense of agreeableness and disagreeableness in actions, and our <130> necessary determination to approve or disapprove according to the moral differences of affections and actions, which alone renders us, or can render us sussceptible of these highest of pleasures or pains. They are and must be peculiar to creatures capable of reflecting upon the images of actions and characters, and of approving or disapproving, according to a natural sense of amiableness and its contrary. And in fine, for any one to say, "That he who does good and virtuous actions because he has pleasure in doing them, and an aversion or abhorrence of their contrary, as much pursues his own pleasure as any other person can be said to do, whatever he takes pleasure in; and consequently that all men are equally selfish, though nothing be more true than what the poet tells us, *nec voto vivitur uno.*"ᵃ This is indeed no more than telling us, that pleasure is pleasure. And we shall not scruple to grant them all they demand, provided they will but allow, *First,* That no man can be said to be virtuous, unless he does virtuous deeds from good affections, and with an ap-

a. Mille hominum species, & rerum discolor usus
     Velle suum cuique est, *nec voto, vivitur uno.*
                                                          Persius

[Persius, *Satires,* V.52–53:

     Men are of a thousand kinds, and diverse are the colours of their lives.
     Each has his own desires; no two men offer the same prayers.]

proving sense of what he does. And therefore, *Secondly,* That virtue and vice suppose a determination in our nature to approve the one and to disapprove the other, both which I think have been sufficiently proved.

IV. But after all that has been granted with regard to saying, "That it is always pleasure which determines us to elect or approve;" I believe, all who acknowledge the reality of virtue, if they have attended to the importance or rather necessity of using distinct determinate terms, and keeping closely to definitions, especially in moral philosophy, in order to avoid all ambiguity and collusion; will <131> very readily approve the *cautiousness* of the better ancient moralists, "When they would not allow sensual gratifications, which so often come into competition with virtue and the pure solid satisfaction which virtuous consciousness alone can give, to be called by the same name of pleasure *(bonum,)* nor any pain to be called by the same term evil *(malum)* designed to signify the greatest of all evils and disorders, to avoid any steps towards the introduction of which into the mind, all other pains or evils ought to be undergone with fortitude: even the corruption of the mind by vice." Such caution is very necessary in moral philosophy. And the reasons so often given for it by ancient philosophers, by *Cicero* in particular, in his reasonings against the Epicurean system, in which it was the fundamental and favourite maxim, that all our determinations to act, proceed from pleasure, *Omnia initia agendi à voluptate proficiscuntur;*[39] is beautifully englished to us by an excellent modern philosopher, who was indeed a perfect master of all true ancient learning.[a] "To bring (says he) the satisfactions of the mind, and the enjoyments of reason and judgment under the denom-

The caution of the ancient moralists in using the words good and evil very commendable.

a. See the *Characteristics,* T. 3. and see *Cicero de finibus.* l. 1. and l. 2. At negat Epicurus (hoc enim vestrum lumen est) qui honeste non vivat, jucunde vivere posse. Quasi ego id curem, quid ille aiat aut neget. Illud quaero, quid ei, qui in voluptate summum bonum putet, consentaneum sit dicere, &c. [Shaftesbury, "The Moralists" II.i, in *Characteristics,* ed. Klein, 252; Cicero, *De finibus,* II.xxii.70: "But Epicurus, you will tell me (for this is your strong point), denies that anyone who does not live morally can live pleasantly. As if I cared what Epicurus says or denies! What I ask is, what is it consistent for a man to say who places the Chief Good in pleasure?"]

39. "All origins of action start from desire." This seems to be a paraphrase of a sentence from Cicero, *De finibus,* I.xii.42.

ination of pleasure is only a collusion and a plain receding from the common notion of the word. They deal not fairly with us, who in their philosophical hour admit that for pleasure, which at an ordinary time, and in the common practice of life is so little taken as such. The mathematician who labours at his problem, the bookish man who toils, the artist who endures voluntarily the greatest hardships and fatigues; none of these are said to *follow pleasure.* Nor <132> will the men of pleasure by any means admit them to be of their number. The satisfactions which are purely mental, and depend only on the motion of a *thought,* must in all likelihood be too refined for our *modern Epicures,* who are so taken up with pleasures of a more substantial kind. They who are full of the idea of such a *sensible, solid good,* can have but a slender fancy for the more *spiritual* and *intellectual sort.* But this latter they set up and magnify upon occasion, to save the ignomy which may redound to them from the former: this done, the latter may take its chance, its use is presently at an end. For it is observable, that when men of this sort have recommended the enjoyments of the mind under the title of *pleasure,* when they have thus dignified the word, and included in it whatever is mentally good and honest, they can afterwards suffer it contentedly to slide down again into its own genuine and vulgar sense; whence they raised it only to serve a turn. When pleasure is called in question and attacked, then reason and virtue is called on to her aid, and made principal parts of her constitution. A complicated form appears and comprehends streight all which is generous, beautiful, and honest in human life. But when the attack is over, and the objection once solved, the spectre vanishes: *pleasure* returns again to her former shape; she may even be pleasure still, and have as little concern with dry sober reason, as in the nature of the thing, and according to common understanding she really has. For if this reasonable sort of enjoyment be admitted into the nature of good, how is it possible to admit withal that kind of sensation, which in effect is rather opposite to this enjoyment? 'Tis certain, that in respect of the mind and its enjoyments, the eagerness and irri-<133>tation of mere pleasure is as disturbing, as the importunity and vexation of pain. If either throws the mind off its biass, and deprives it of the satisfaction it takes in its natural exercise and employment, the mind, in this case, must be a sufferer, as well by the one as by the other; if neither does this, there is no harm on either side."

Upon the whole, that we have a moral sense appears, because we have not only the power of examining our appetites and affections, or of computing their tendencies and effects with respect to external hurt or interest, and determining the bounds within which their gratifications must be pursued and regulated, so that none of our pleasures may be too dearly bought:

Hence it is that we are not only capable of computing our advantage and interest;

———— *Nocet empta dolore voluptas.*[40]

But we have also clear ideas of moral order, decency, fitness and unfitness in affections, actions and characters, analogous to our ideas of beauty and regularity in outward forms. For as had we not sensitive appetites and affections towards sensible objects implanted in us by nature, reason could not compare and estimate sensible pleasures; or rather, there would be no such pleasures to estimate and reason about: in like manner, without a sense of moral beauty and fitness, reason could not compare and compute the moral differences of moral objects; or rather, there would be no such objects known to us, for reason to exercise itself about. "It must be true in general, that without appetites, dispositions, faculties and affections suited to particular objects, no one thing could give us more pleasure than another;" and it is fully as true, "That ultimately no other reason can be given why any object pleases us, gives delight, affects us agreeably, or excites our approbation, but that we are so framed by nature; or nature hath so constituted us, and so ap-<134>pointed things." So that if we have ideas of moral differences in affections and actions, there must be a moral sense in our constitution; and if there be, it must be from nature; there must be the same reason to ascribe it to nature, as to attribute any other of our senses or faculties to it.

but likewise of rising higher, and taking in what is worthy and laudable in itself into the account.

On the one hand, if there be no such sense in our make, virtue is

40. Horace, *Epistles,* I.ii.55: "Pleasure bought with pain is harmful." Horace, *Satires, Epistles and Ars poetica,* trans. H. Rushton Fairclough, Loeb Classical Library (London: Heinemann; New York: Putnam, 1926).

really but an empty name; that is, the fitness or approveableness of affections, actions and characters in themselves, is an idle dream that hath
no foundation; but advantage or interest is all that we have to consider
or compute in our determinations. But, on the other side, if there be
really a sense of beauty, fitness, or agreeableness in affections, actions
and characters in themselves, independently of all other considerations,
then it plainly follows that we are made, "Not merely to consider our
private good, or what quantity of external safety, ease, profit, or gratification an action may bring along with it"; but to rise higher in our
contemplation, and chiefly to enquire, "What is fit and becoming,
agreeable, laudable and beautiful in itself "; and thus to ask one's heart
in all consultations about actions. But is it fit, is it becoming, is it good
to do so, whatever advantage may accrue from it?—Or, is it not base, to
whatever dangers not doing it may expose? Shall I betray my trust, treat
my friend ungratefully, forfeit my integrity, desert my country; or do
any such unworthy action, even to save life itself; to gain an uninterrupted succession of sensual joys, or to avoid the most exquisite torments? Without such a sense there can be no foundation for honour
and shame. But such a sense, wherever it takes place, teaches and obliges
to distinguish between life itself, and the causes of living which are worthy of man; or between life and those noble enjoyments arising from a
sense of virtue and merit, without which life is vilely prostituted—
between <135>

It is only by a moral sense we can judge or have a notion of any thing, besides mere external advantage.

——— *Vitam, & propter vitam vivendi perdere causas.*[41]

But we have a nobler relish.

Now in order to be convinced that we have such a sense, let any one but
ask himself, (for it is, as hath been often said, a question that depends
upon inward experience) whether there be not a very wide, a total dif-

And therefore we have a moral sense.

ference, between doing a good action because it is good, or from love
and affection to good, and a thorow feeling of its excellence, and doing
it merely because it will gain him some external advantage or pleasure.

41. Juvenal, *Satires,* VIII.83: "to lose, for the sake of living, all that makes life worth
having."

Let him take the poets catechism, and strictly examine himself and his natural sentiments by it.

Else what foundation have the poet's questions? by which if we try ourselves, our moral sense will soon speak out its real sentiments.

> *Falsus honor juvat, & mendax infamia terret,*
> *Quem, nisi mendosum & mendacem? Vir bonus est quis?*
> *Qui consulta patrum, qui leges juraque servat.* ———
> *Sed videt hunc omnis domus & vicinia tota,*
> *Introrsum turpem, speciosum pelle decora.*
> *Nec furtum feci, nec fugi, si mihi dicat*
> *Servus: habes precium, loris non ureris, aio:*
> *Non hominem occidi: non pasces in cruce corvos.*
> *Sum bonus & frugi: renuit, negat atque Sabellus.*
> *Cautus enim metuit foveam lupus accipiterque,*
> *Suspectos laqueos, & opertum milvus hamum.*
> *Oderunt peccare boni virtutis amore.*
> *Tu nihil admittes in te formidine poenae.*
> *Sit spes fallendi, miscebis sacra profanis.*
>
> Hor. Epist. Lib. I. 16.[42]

Let him ask his heart, whether he can approve himself; or think he will be approved by any being who hath a sense of worth and integrity, however cunning, prudent and sagacious he may be to secure his outward interests; unless he hath a heart that contemns all villany; and would not sacrifice integrity in any one indulgence to the highest plea-<136>sures of sense: The "*jus fasque animo sanctosque recessus mentis & incoctum*

No man can put himself to a proper trial by examination, without feeling he has a moral sense.

---

42. Horace, *Epistles*, I.xvi: "Whom does false honour delight, whom does lying calumny affright, save the man who is full of flaws and needs the doctor?"(39–41). "Yet this very man all his household and all his neighbours see to be foul within, though fair without, under his comely skin. If a slave were to say to me, 'I never stole or ran away' my reply would be, 'You have your reward; you are not flogged.' 'I never killed anyone.' 'You'll hang on no cross to feed crows.' 'I am good and honest.' Our Sabine friend shakes his head and says, 'No, no!' For the wolf is wary and dreads the pit, the hawk the suspected snare, the pike the covered hook. The good hate vice because they love virtue; you will commit no crime because you dread punishment. Suppose there's a hope of escaping detection; you will make no difference between sacred and profane" (44–54).

generoso pectus honesto?"[43] Whether he can chuse but detest all treachery, all villany, all baseness, all dishonesty, however profitable it may be in the ordinary way of sensual appetite and gratification. Whether he can represent to his mind the images of veracity, truth, honesty, benevolence, a sincere, unaffected regard to honour and virtue; and the calm regular presidence of reason and moral conscience in the heart, without approving and loving them. And whether, finally, he can conceive a greater plague than that imprecated by the satyrist's direful curse,

Virtutem videat intabescatque relicta.[44]

To be satisfied of the universality of this sense, let one but try the lowest of mankind in understanding, and fairly representing to him the virtues and vices, bring forth his natural, his first sentiments about them; for he shall find that even the most illiterate have a strong moral sense. *Quae enim natio non comitatem, non benignitatem, non gratum animum & beneficii memorem diligit, quae superbos, quae maleficos, quae crudeles, quae ingratos non aspernatur non odit?*[45]

It is absurd to suppose a moral sense not to be from nature. Indeed, if these sentiments of virtue and vice common to all men, and which none can fully extirpate from their minds, are not from nature, but are the *offspring of flattery upon pride,* and begot by the devices of *cunning politicians;* we are, that is, society is much more indebted to such politics than to nature: for such sentiments are the bond, the cement which holds society together, without which nothing that is truly great or noble could subsist in human life. But how ridiculous is it to ascribe

43. Persius, *Satires,* II.73–74: "A heart rightly attuned towards God and man, a mind pure in its inner depth, and a soul steeped in nobleness and honour."

44. Ibid., III.38: "that he may look on virtue, and pine away because he has lost her."

45. Cicero, *De legibus,* I.31: "For what nation does not love friendliness, benignity, a gracious soul, and the memory of a kindly act? What nation does not despise and hate arrogant people, evildoers, cruel people and ungracious folk?" Cicero, *De re publica, De legibus,* trans. Clinton Walker Keyes, Loeb Classical Library (London: Heinemann; New York: Putnam, 1928).

them to any thing else but nature? For how can custom, education, example, or study, give us new ideas? "They might make us see private advantage <137> in actions whose uselessness did not at first appear; or give us opinions of some tendency of actions to our detriment, by some nice deductions of reason; or by a rash prejudice, when upon the first view of the action we should have observed no such thing: but they never could have made us apprehend actions as amiable or odious, without any consideration of our own advantage."[a] Let such philosophers consider, that it must be a determination previous to reason, which makes us pursue even private good as our end. No end can be intended without desire or affection, and it is nature alone can implant any appetite, any affection or determination in our nature, whether toward private good or publick good; whether toward pleasure of outward sense, or pleasure of inward approbation. It is equally absurd in the natural and moral world, to suppose that art can create; it can only work upon subjects *Art cannot create.* according to their original properties, and the laws of nature's appointment, agreeably to which certain effects may be produced upon them. No art can therefore educe from our natures an affection or determination that is not originally there, no more than art can give bodies a property which they have not.

To assert a determination in our mind to receive the sentiments or simple *A moral sense does not suppose innate ideas.* ideas of approbation or disapprobation from actions so soon as they are presented, antecedent to any opinions of advantage or loss to redound to ourselves from them, is not to assert innate ideas, or innate knowledge; it is only to assert an aptitude or determination in our nature to be affected in a certain manner so soon as they occur to the mind. And this must be true with regard to the mind in respect of every pleasure it receives, that it is fitted by nature to receive it. But it is well worth observing, "That though we have no innate ideas, in the sense now commonly affixed to these words; yet as in the sensible kinds of objects, the

a. See *Hutcheson on the passions.* [This doctrine is dealt with throughout Hutcheson's *Passions,* but see especially section I.]

But moral ideas are continually haunting our mind.

<139> species, the images of bodies, colours and sounds are perpetually moving before our eyes, and acting[a] on our senses, even when we sleep, so in the moral and intellectual kind, the forms and images are no less active and incumbent on the mind at all seasons, and even when the real objects themselves are absent. But in these vagrant characters or pictures of manners, which the mind of necessity figures to itself, and carries still about with it, the heart cannot remain neutral, but constantly takes part with one or other: however false and corrupt it may be within itself, it finds the difference as to beauty and comeliness between one heart and another, one turn of affection, one sentiment, one behaviour from another; and accordingly, in all disinterested cases must approve in some manner what is natural and honest, and disapprove what is dishonest and corrupt." Whether we will or not, moral ideas are always haunting and assaulting us: we must not only shun the world, but shun and avoid ourselves to get entirely rid of them. And let the most hardened, callous wretch, the most abandoned to all sense of honour, shame and integrity that ever existed say, if he dares in a serious conversation with himself approve one vice, or disapprove one virtue, however profitable the one, or disadvantageous the other may be.

Nature therefore hath not left us quite indifferent to virtue and vice.

Thus then we see how we are constituted, with regard to a rule and standard of action, and that nature has not left us quite indifferent to virtue and vice,[b] but hath planted in us a natural sense, <139> which as often as consulted, will not fail to tell us our duty and set us right; and which,

a. See *Shaftsbury's enquiry concerning virtue;* whose words these are. [Shaftesbury, "Virtue" I.ii.3, in *Characteristics,* ed. Klein, 173.]

b. Est quidem vero lex, recta ratio, naturae congruens, diffusa in omneis, constans, sempiterna, quae vocet ad officium jubendo, vetando a fraude deterreat, quae tamen neque probos frustra jubet, aut vetat, nec improbos jubendo aut vetando movet. Huic legi nec obrogari fas est, neque derogari ex hac aliquid licet, neque tota abrogari potest. Nec vero, aut per senatum, aut per populum solvi hac lege possumus. Neque est quaerendus explanator, aut interpres ejus alius: nec erit alia lex Romae, alia Athenis, alia nunc, alia posthac: sed & omnes gentes, & omni tempore, una lex & sempiterna, & immortalis continebit; unusque erit communis quasi magister & imperator omnium deus ille, legis hujus inventor, disceptator, lator cui qui non parebit, ipse se fugiet, ac naturam hominis aspernabitur, atque hoc ipso luet paenas maximas etiamsi

let it be opposed or born down with ever so much violence, or lulled asleep by whatever delusive arts, will often uncalled upon, tell the villain to his face he is such, and bitterly tear his guilty mind with agonizing remorse, terrible beyond expression. And who can bear the horrid pangs of a guilty, self-condemning heart, conscious of the worth and excellence of abandoned virtue, and of the baseness, the enormous baseness of every vice, whatever advantages it may bring? We had therefore good reason to say with respect to knowledge, in the first chapter, that nature hath kindly provided us with a natural sense which leads and prompts us to enquire after good, final causes in the administration of nature, and thus directs us to an enquiry the most assistant to virtuous temper, and of the most pleasing kind; and which at the same time directs us in every case, if we will but consult it, to our duty, or to what is excellent, laudable and praise-worthy in itself, independently of all computations with respect to private good, or interest. This sense is therefore justly said to be engraven on our hearts, innate, original, and universal.

But then such is our excellent make in general, that this rational sense or moral conscience common to all men, must, like all our other faculties, depend for its strength and improvement upon our culture; *But our moral sense, like all our other faculties, must*

---

caetera supplicia, quae putantur, effugerit. *Ciceronis frag. in Lactantio,* Lib. VI. Cap. 8. [Lactantius, *The Divine Institutes,* bk. 6, ch. 8: "There is indeed a true law, right reason, congruent with nature, diffused among all, constant, lasting, which summons us to service by ordering us and deters us from deceit by prohibiting us, which however does not order or forbid worthy people in vain, nor motivates unworthy people by ordering or forbidding them. It is not right that anything of this law should be superseded, nor is it permissible that any of it should be modified. Nor indeed can we be released from it by either the senate or the people. Nor should anyone else be sought who would explain or interpret it. Nor will Rome have one law and Athens another, nor will there be one now and another later. Instead one law, everlasting and undying, will hold for all people and for all time. And one God will be as it were a common master and commander of all. He will be inventor, judge, and proposer of this law. Whoever will not submit to him will put himself to flight and will spurn his nature as a human being. He will thereby suffer the greatest penalty even if he escapes other punishments which are being considered." (A.B., trans.)]

depend on our
own culture
or care to
improve it. <140>[a] upon our care to preserve, to nourish and improve it. Such, as
has been observed, is our frame in general; and therefore, though this
sense can no more be produced by education, where it is wanting, than
an ear for music; yet as the latter, so the former is greatly improveable
by instruction and exercise: both may be rendered less delicate, nay, almost quite dead and insensible; or at least they may be considerably vitiated by wrong practice, by unnatural associations of ideas, through the
influence of bad example, and other depraving methods; but both are
improveable to a great pitch of perfection by proper pains, and both
require cultivation to their improvement. And certainly, with regard to
the latter, it is the great business of education, and the great business
throughout the whole life of every one, to keep it in due exercise, to
preserve it from being corrupted by bad opinions and wrong associations
of ideas, or over-powered by contrary, corrupt, head-strong affections:
and for this reason very often to reflect seriously upon it, as the dignity
of our nature, and to recal to our mind all the motives and considerations
which tend to uphold and corroborate it; to accustom ourselves to review
our actions, and to pass judgments, not only upon what we have done,
but upon what we ought to do in circumstances that may occur: and in
fine, thus to accustom our moral sense to work and act, that it <141>

a. See *Plutarch de liberis educandis.* Quod de artibus & scientiis dicere solemus,
idem & de virtute pronunciandum est; scilicet ad ejus perfectionem tria concurrere
oportere: naturam, rationem & assuefactionem. Natura enim si absque disciplina sit
caeca est. Disciplina si a natura destituatur defecta: exercitatio, his duobus demptis
imperfecta est. Et quemadmodum ad agriculturam, &c.—And therefore he adds, the
moral virtues are very properly expressed in the *Greek* language by a word which
signifies *assuefactio ad virtutem.*
    Cicero de aegritudine lenienda. Tusc. quest. Lib. III. Sunt enim ingeniis nostris
semina innata virtutum: quae si adolescere liceret ipsa nos ad beatam vitam natura
perduceret. [Plutarch, *De liberis educandis,* 2A–B: "We customarily say the same thing
about virtue that we say about the arts and sciences, that is, that three things must
come together if an action is to be perfect, namely nature, reason, and habit. For if
nature lacks learning it is blind, and learning, if lacking what is natural, is imperfect.
Just as with farming etc." Plutarch, *Omnia quae extant opera,* 2 vols. (Paris, 1624).
Cicero, *Tusculanae disputationes,* III.i.2: "The seeds of virtue are inborn in our dispositions and, if they were allowed to ripen, nature's own hand would lead us on to
happiness of life." Cicero, *Tusculan Disputations,* trans. J. E. King, Loeb Classical
Library (London: Heinemann; New York: Putnam, 1927).]

may be rendered by the law of habits habitual to us, and may become larger, and more comprehensive than it can be at first; that is, abler to take in complex ideas, and so to judge of wide and extensive objects: till like a well formed ear or eye, it is capable to judge easily and readily, as well as truly, of any the most complicated piece of harmony. Now nothing is more conducive to such improvement of it, next to exercising it about examples, in judging and pronouncing sentence, (which must be the chief thing) than the philosophical consideration of its analogy to our sense of beauty in material forms, and of the connexion in both cases between beauty and utility. In this sense, and in this sense only, can the love of virtue be taught. But this leads me to enquire, how interest and virtue agree, according to the constitution and laws of our nature. For if it shall be found, that in the moral world, as well as in the natural, utility or advantage is inseparately connected with beauty; then must our frame be an excellent whole. "For hitherto we have found our nature Conclusion. to be admirably well constituted, with regard to virtue and vice, or moral conduct."

ᗩᙢ CHAPTER V ᗩᙢ

Another class
of laws.

Those relative
to interest or
private and
public good.

The several
enquiries about
morals classed.

Let us therefore enquire into the laws of our nature, relative to utility or interest, to private and publick good; the natural end and happiness of every man in particular, and of society or our kind in general.

One of the best modern writers on morals has given us a very accurate division of the chief questions relative to morality.[a] "The first is, to know (says he) whether there are not some actions or affections which obtain the approbation of any spectator or <142> observer, and others which move his dislike and condemnation. Now this question, as every man can answer for himself, so universal experience and history shew that in all nations it is so; and consequently the moral sense is universal. 2. Whether there be any particular quality, which, whenever it is perceived, gains approbation, and the contrary raises disapprobation? Now we shall find this quality to be kind affection or study of the public good of others. And thus the moral senses of men are generally uniform. About these two questions there is little reasoning: we know how to answer them by reflecting on our own sentiments, or by consulting others. 3. But what actions do really evidence kind affections, or do really tend to the greatest public good? About this question is all the special reasoning of those who treat of particular laws of nature, or even civil laws. This is the largest field, and the most useful subject of reasoning, which remains upon every scheme of morals. 4. What are the motives, which even from self-love, would excite each individual to do those actions which are particularly useful. Now it is probable, indeed, no man would approve as virtuous, an action publickly useful, to which the agent was only excited by self-love, without any kind affection: it is also probable,

a. See *Hutcheson on the passions.* [Hutcheson, *Passions,* II.iv.]

174

that no view of interest can raise that kind affection which we approve as virtuous; nor can any reasoning do it, except that which shews some moral goodness, or kind affections in the objects; for this never fails, when it is observed or supposed in any person to raise the love of the observer; so that virtue cannot be taught. Yet since all men have naturally self-love, as well as kind affections, the former may often counteract the latter, or the latter the former: in each case, the agent is in some degree uneasy and unhappy. The first rash views of human affairs often represent private interest as opposite to the public: when it is apprehended self-<143>love may often engage men in public hurtful actions, which their moral sense will condemn, and this is the ordinary course of vice. To represent these motives of self-interest to engage men to publickly useful actions, is therefore the most necessary point in morals." Now this is what I proceed to consider, in order to shew that by the laws of our nature, what the moral sense approves or virtue is private, as well as public good; and what the moral sense disapproves or vice is private as well as public ill.

I. And first of all I would observe, that there is no philosophical subject which affords more pleasure to the mind, than the consideration of the strict union and connexion between beauty and utility prevailing throughout nature,[a] as far as we are able to pry into it; and which there-

> Beauty is inseparably connected with utility throughout all nature.

a. This observation is taken from *Cicero.* See it explained by him at great length, *de oratore,* Lib. 3. No. 45. *Edit. Schrevel.* Sed ut in plerisque rebus incredibiliter hoc natura est ipsa fabricata: sic in oratione; ut ea quae maximam utilitatem in se continerent eadem haberent plurimum vel dignitatis, vel saepe etiam venustatis. Incolumitatis ac salutis, omnium causa videmus hunc statum esse totius mundi atque naturae—Referte nunc animum ad hominum vel etiam caeterorum animantium formam & figuram—linquamus naturam artesque videamus, &c. Compare this passage with what he says, *Orat. ad Marc. Brutum,* No. 22, 23, 24, 25. [Cicero, *De oratore,* III.xlv.178–xlvi.180: "But in oratory as in most matters nature has contrived with incredible skill that the things possessing most utility also have the greatest amount of dignity, and indeed frequently of beauty also. We observe that for the safety and security of the universe this whole ordered world of nature is so constituted. . . . Now carry your mind to the form and figure of human beings or even of the other living creatures. . . . Let us leave nature and contemplate the arts, etc." Cicero, *De oratore, Book III, De fato, Paradoxa Stoicorum, De partitione oratoria,* trans. H. Rackham,

fore must be carefully attended to, and observed in all the arts which imitate nature. It is this union and connexion, (as I have observed in my treatise on *ancient painting*) between beauty and advantage, or utility in all subjects, natural and moral, throughout the whole of nature that renders nature one, or a beautiful coherent analogous system; and for the same reason renders all the sciences and arts one body, or makes them so intimately related and so inseparable one from another.

It is so in all the imitative arts, architecture, painting, *&c.*

Tho' beauty be an agreeable perception excited in us, necessarily and immediately on the first sight or contemplation of certain objects qualified by nature <144> to affect our mind with that pleasing idea; yet when we come to examine these objects attentively, we find, that wherever we perceive beauty, there is truth, proportion, regularity and unity of design to bring about, by a proper variety of parts, one advantageous end: one useful end that could not be accomplished by simpler or fewer means. That is to say, wherever we find beauty we find utility. Whatever is beautiful is advantageous, consonant or well contrived for a good end.

Every one who has any notion of architecture, painting or statuary, will immediately perceive that in all these arts, this connexion is so necessary, so unalterable, that it is not possible to deviate from utility without falling proportionably short of beauty to the sight: or alternately, the rules in architecture which produce beauty are all founded on utility, or necessarily produce it. And in the other arts of design, the truth and beauty of every figure is measured from the perfection of nature in her just adapting every limb and part to the activity, strength, dexterity, and vigour of the particular species designed. Now, what is the reason of

Because it is so in nature the standard of truth.

this? But, because it is so in nature, where universally the proportionate and regular state is the truly prosperous and natural one in every subject. Health of the body is the just proportion, truth and regular course of things, or the sound ballance of parts in our constitution. The same features which produce deformity, create incommodiousness and dis-

---

Loeb Classical Library (London: Heinemann; Cambridge: Harvard University Press, 1942).]

ease. And as it is in the human body, so is it every where throughout It is so in our mundan system. nature. The sound state is the beautiful one. Whence it is justly laid down, by the ancients, as an universal canon with regard to arts and sciences, and with regard also to moral conduct, because it is every where true or an universal law of nature, "That just proportions and beauty are inseparably connected with utility." *Nunquam a vero dividitur utile.*[46] What is <145> beautiful is good and useful, and what is good and useful is beautiful.

Is not the order of our mundan system most transportingly beautiful and pleasant in idea or contemplation? But do not the same general laws which produce that delightful ravishing beauty, order and greatness, likewise tend to the greatest good and advantage of the whole system? What law can be altered without introducing inconveniencies proportionable to irregularity? And what is it that charms us when we survey with rapture the beauty of the mundan system? Is it not the simplicity and the consent of the few laws which hold such a vast complication of mighty orbs in due and advantageous order? And when we contemplate the human body, or any other animal structure; or in general, wherever we see And on the bodies of all animals. beauty and order in nature, what is it we find to be the basis of all that beauty and order which so strongly attracts us?—Is it not the simplicity, the frugality, the analogy, and constancy of nature, in bringing about an useful end; or, in disposing, adjusting, and compounding various parts, so as may best serve a particular good end, without either too little or too much? All that we admire, as has been already observed, is fitly expressed in this general rule observed steadily by nature. *Nil frustra natura facit.*[47,a] Which *frustra* is likewise very well defined <146> by *Frustra fit*

46. "The useful is never separated from the true."

47. Appears as *Natura nihil agit frustra*—"Nature does nothing in vain" in Newton, *Principia,* Regulae philosophandi, regula 1. Isaac Newton, *The Principia: Mathematical Principles of Natural Philosophy: A New Translation,* by I. Bernard Cohen and Anne Whitman (Berkeley and London: University of California Press, 1999).

a. This maxim is well explained by Sir *Isaac Newton,* in these words. "*Superfluis causis non luxuriat.*" See moral beauty explained by *Cicero* in several parts of his *offices:* some of the passages have been already quoted. See what is said of it in the Chapter *of knowledge.* It consists in the middle between the *nimium* and *parum.* There is a *decorum* belonging to every particular character, and therefore to every man; for every

pluribus quod fieri potest paucioribus.[48] And therefore with regard to all arts which imitate nature, poetry, painting, architecture and statuary; and even with regard to all reasonings, arrangements of truths, or demonstrations in the sciences, this is the only rule to attain to beauty, truth and utility.

Denique sit quodvis simplex duntaxat & unum.[49]

It is, and must be so likewise with respect to the fabrick of the human mind, affections, actions, and characters.

Now, as it is with regard to the sensible world, and to all arts and sciences, so is it also with respect to our mental fabrick: its health, soundness, and beauty, consist in the due ballance of all its powers and affections, or in just subordination to a well improved moral sense. This produces moral beauty in affections, in actions, and in character or temper; and this temper is the most advantageous one: It is the sound, the healthful, the natural, the most pleasant state: Every exercise of the affections and powers, in such a constitution is beautiful, and it is pleasant: Agreeable in im-

---

man has his distinguishing peculiar character. This is treated of at large by *Cicero.* But the *decorum* belonging to a virtuous affection or action, consists in its being duly proportioned to its end, neither too little, nor too much; analogously to what is called *ease and grace,* in dancing, in any other exercise, or in any art. All the phrases among the ancients, used to signify the beauty, harmony, and consistency of virtuous manners, are taken from the beauty of sensible forms in nature, or in the arts which imitate nature, music, painting, &c. Such as *Numeros modosque vitae, est modus in rebus. Decorum, quid verumatque decens;* and innumerable such others. So that here we have a clear proof of that analogy between the moral world or moral effects, and the natural world or sensible effects, without which language could not be a moral paintress, or paint moral sentiments, and affections and their effects. [Newton, *Principia,* Regulae philosophandi, regula I: "[Nature] does not indulge in the luxury of superfluous causes." The phrase *nimium et parum*—"excess and defect"—appears in Cicero, *De officiis,* trans. Walter Miller, Loeb Classical Library (London: Heinemann; Cambridge: Harvard University Press, 1938), I.xxv.89. The following Latin phrases are all from Horace: *Numeros modosque vitae*—"the rhythms and measures of life" in *Epistles,* II.ii.144; *est modus in rebus*—"there is a measure in all things" in *Satires,* I.i.106; and *Decorum, quid verumatque decens*—"the correct is right and seemly" in *Epistles,* I.i.11.]
    48. Appears as *frustra fit per plura quod fieri potest per pauciora*—"more causes are in vain when fewer suffice" in Newton, *Principia,* Regulae philosophandi, regula 1.
    49. Horace, *Ars poetica,* 23: "In short, be the work what you will, let it at least be simple and uniform." Horace, *Satires, Epistles and Ars poetica,* trans. H. Rushton Fairclough, Loeb Classical Library (London: Heinemann; New York: Putnam, 1926).

mediate feeling, and good and agreeable in its consequences: every deviation, by whatever affection, from this temper or state, is proportional deformity, disease and suffering. And, finally, in proportion as the mind is nearer to this its perfect state, or further removed from it, so it is in all its exercises more happy or more wretched.

II. To prove this, we must consider the nature of our affections, their operations, and their mutual bearings, dependencies and connexions. The soluti-<147>on to this question must be fetched from the anatomy or structure of the mind, in like manner, as the answer to any questions about the natural, or sound, and advantageous state of the body, must be brought from the science of its oeconomy and texture. Now, my Lord *Shaftsbury*, in his *enquiry concerning virtue*, has fully demonstrated, "That, according to our make and frame, or the laws of our nature, the same affections which work towards public good, work likewise towards private good, and the same affections which work towards public ill work likewise towards private ill."[50] I shall not repeat his arguments to prove this, but 'tis well worth while to take particular notice of the manner in which he proceeds; because its an excellent example of the way in which moral philosophy ought to be carried on, and in which alone indeed it can bring forth solid conclusions.

The proof of this must be fetched from the anatomy or texture of the mind.

First, he takes notice, "that no animal can properly be said to act otherwise, than through affections or passions, such as are peculiar to that animal. For, in convulsive fits, when a creature either strikes himself or others, it is a simple mechanism, an engine or piece of clock-work that acts, and not the animal. Whatsoever then is done or acted by an animal as such, is done only through some affections, as of fear, love, or hatred moving him: and as it is impossible that a weaker passion should overcome a stronger; so it is impossible when the affections or passions are strongest in the main, and form in general the most considerable party

Lord Shaftsbury's reasoning to prove it.

50. This passage seems to be a paraphrase of Shaftesbury, "Virtue" II.i.3, in *Characteristics,* ed. Klein, 196.

either by their force or number, but thither the animal must incline."[51]
"Nothing therefore being properly goodness or illness in a creature, except what is from natural temper; a good creature is such a one as by the natural bent of its temper or affections, is carried presently[52] and immediately, not secondarily and accidentally to good and against ill. And an ill creature is just the contrary, *viz.* one who is wanting in right affections of force enough to <148> carry him directly towards good, and bear him out against ill, or who is carried by other affections directly to ill and against good."[53] 2. "But to proceed, says he, from what is esteemed meer goodness, and lies within the reach and capacity of all sensible creatures, to that which is called *virtue or merit,* and allowed to man only."[54] "In this case alone, it is that we call any creature worthy or virtuous, when it can have the notion of a public interest, and can attain the speculation or science of what is morally good or ill, admirable or blameable, right or wrong. For tho' we may vulgarly call an ill horse vicious, yet we never say of a good one, or of any meer beast, ideot or changeling, that he is worthy or virtuous. So that if a creature be generous, kind, constant, compassionate, yet if he cannot reflect on what he himself does, or sees others do, so as to take notice of what is worthy or honest; and make that notice or conception of worth and honesty to be an object of his affection, he has not the character of being virtuous: for thus, and no otherwise he is capable of having a sense of right and wrong, a sentiment or judgment of what is done, through just, equal, and good affection, or the contrary."[55]

Having thus defined and distinguished goodness and virtue, he observes, that "the affections or passions which must govern the animal, are either, 1. The natural affections which lead to the good of the public. 2. Or the self-affections which lead to the good of the private. 3. Or such, as neither of these, not tending to any good of the public or private;

51. Ibid., 195–96.
52. Shaftesbury, from whom Turnbull is quoting, uses the word "primarily" here, not "presently"; see *Characteristics,* ed. Klein, 171.
53. Shaftesbury, "Virtue" I.ii.2, in *Characteristics,* ed. Klein, 171.
54. Ibid. I.ii.3, 172.
55. Ibid., 173.

but contrariwise: and which may therefore be justly stiled *unnatural affections.*

"So that according as these affections stand, a creature must be either virtuous or vicious, good or ill; the later sort of these affections, 'tis evident, are wholly vicious; the two former may be vicious or virtuous according to their degree. <149>

"It may seem strange, says our author, to speak of natural affections as too strong, or of self-affections as too weak: but to clear this difficulty, we must call to mind, that natural affection may in particular cases be excessive, and in an unnatural degree; as when pity is so overcoming as to destroy its own end, and prevent the succour and relief required: or as when love to the offspring proves such fondness as destroys the parent, and consequently the offspring itself. And, notwithstanding, it may seem harsh to call that unnatural and vicious, which is only an extream of some natural and kind affection; yet it is most certain, that whenever any single good affection of this sort is over great, it must be injurious to the rest, and detract in some measure from their force and natural operation."[56] This he illustrates at great length. "But having shewn what is meant by passions being too high or in too low a degree, and that to have any natural affection too high, and any self-affection too low, tho' it be often approved as virtue, is yet strictly speaking a vice and imperfection; he now comes to the plainer and more essential part of vice, and which alone deserves to be considered as such, that is to say. 1. When either the public affections are weak and deficient. 2. Or the private and self-affections too strong. 3. Or that such affections arise, as are neither of these, nor in any degree tending to the support either of the public or private system.

"Otherwise than this, it is impossible any creature can be such as we call ill or vicious. So that if once we prove that 'tis not the creature's interest to be thus viciously affected, but contrariwise; we shall then have proved, that it is his interest to be wholly good and virtuous in his action and behaviour: our business therefore, says he, will be to prove,

---

56. Shaftesbury, "Virtue" II.i.3, in *Characteristics,* ed. Klein, 196.

"1. That to have the natural, kindly or generous affections strong and powerful towards the good of the public, is to have the chief means and power of <150> self-enjoyment, and that to want them is certain misery and ill. 2. That to have the private or self-affections too strong, or beyond that degree of subordinacy to the kindly and natural, is also miserable. 3. And that to have the unnatural affections, (*viz.* such as are neither founded on the interest of the kind or public, nor of the private person or creature himself) is to be miserable in the highest degree."[57]

Now all these points he has clearly proved, in the way of moral arithmetic, by a full examination of all our affections, private or public, and their effects and consequences. Whence he concludes, that virtue is the good, and vice the ill of every one by our natural constitution. But for his arguments, I must refer the reader to himself. I have only taken notice of his way of proceeding, to shew by this example how enquiries into the human mind ought to be carried on.

Another train of reasoning to prove that virtue is private interest.

That virtue is the natural good, and vice the natural evil of every one, has been evinced by several different ways of reasoning. And I think the few following propositions, which are universally owned to be true, not only amount to a full proof of it, but likewise shew that the truth is universally received and admitted.

1. It will not be disputed, that wherever the natures and connexions of pleasures and pains are fixed, there must be real differences with regard to greater and less; this must hold true in every case, as necessarily as in any one case. If therefore the natures and proportions of moral objects are fixed and determinate things, there must necessarily be in the nature of things with regard to them, as well as any other kinds of quantity, a truth and falshood of the case, a true and a false account or estimation. And therefore with respect to them, it must be our business to attain to as full a knowledge of their true values as we can, in order to make a just judgment or estimation of them. This is prudence: and prudence ne-<151>cessarily supposes wherever it can take place, the natures or moments of things to be ascertainable. 2. But such prudence with regard

---

57. Ibid., 200.

to our moral conduct we can attain to; for, notwithstanding all the diversity there is among mankind in constitution, and consequently in sensibility with respect to sentiments, affections, passions, desires, uneasinesses, and, in one word, sensations of whatever kind, inward or outward; yet there is obviously such a conformity in feeling, and sentiment amongst mankind,[a] that it is unanimously agreed, that there is not only a real satisfaction in every exercise of social and kindly affections, but a pleasure which never cloys or ends in disgust, and which is, in that respect, superior to all the enjoyments of meer sense. And, on the other hand, the unnatural passions, such as hatred, envy, malice, misanthropy, or utter aversion to society, are allowed with universal consent, to produce compleat misery, where they are habitual and wrought into temper.

a. Etenim ratio—certe est communis, doctrina differens, discendi quidem facultate par, nam & sensibus eadem omnia comprehenduntur: & ea quae movent sensus, itidem movent omnium: quaeque in animis imprimuntur; de quibus ante dixi, inchoatae intelligentiae, similiter in omnibus imprimuntur; interpresque est mentis oratio, verbis discrepans, sententiis congruens. Nec est quisquam gentis ullius, qui ducem naturam nactus, ad virtutem pervenire non possit. Nec solum in rectis, sed etiam in pravitatibus insignis est humani generis similitudo. Nam & voluptate capiuntur omnes: quae etsi illecebra turpitudinis, tamen habet quiddam simile naturalis boni. Quae autem natio non comitatem non benignitatem, non gratum animum & beneficii memorem diligit, quae superbos quae maleficos, quae crudeles, quae ingratos non aspernatur? Quibus ex rebus cum omne genus hominum sociatum inter se esse intelligatur, illud extremum est quod recte vivendi ratio meliores efficit. *Cicero de legibus,* Lib. l. No. 11. [Cicero, *De legibus,* I.x.30–xi.32: ". . . and indeed reason . . . is certainly common to us all, and, though varying in what it learns, at least in the capacity to learn it is invariable. For the same things are invariably perceived by the senses, and those things which stimulate the senses, stimulate them in the same way in all men; and those rudimentary beginnings of intelligence to which I have referred, which are imprinted in our minds, are imprinted on all minds alike; and speech, the mind's interpreter, though differing in the choice of words, agrees in the sentiments expressed. In fact, there is no human being of any race who, if he finds a guide, cannot attain to virtue. The similarity of the human race is clearly marked in its evil tendencies as well as in its goodness. For pleasure also attracts all men; and even though it is an enticement to vice, yet it has some likeness to what is naturally good. . . . But what nation does not love courtesy, kindliness, gratitude, and remembrance of favours bestowed? What people does not hate and despise the haughty, the wicked, the cruel, and the ungrateful? Inasmuch as these considerations prove to us that the whole human race is bound together in unity, it follows, finally, that knowledge of the principles of right living is what makes men better."]

But, 3. If that be true, then every step in the nature of things towards
the establishment of bad and unsocial temper, must be a step toward the
introduction of compleat misery into the mind; and contrariwise, every
indulgence of social affection, <152> every virtuous exercise, must be an
advancement toward fixing and settling that benign, generous, good
temper, which is compleat joy, chearfulness and self-contentment; and
therefore is commonly called *the happy temper.* Where there is an absolute degeneracy, a total apostacy from all candor, equity, trust, sociableness, or friendship, there are none who do not see and acknowledge
the misery which is consequent: but the calamity must of necessity hold
proportion with the corruption of the temper. It is impossible that it
can be compleat misery, to be absolutely immoral and inhuman, and yet
be no misery or ill at all to be so in any however little degree. But, besides,
it is beyond all controversy, that habitudes are formed by repeated acts.
Every indulgence therefore to any passion, has a tendency to fix and
settle it in the mind, or to form it into temper and habit. And thus, tho'
there were no considerable ill in any one exercise of immoral affection;
yet it must be contrary to interest, as it necessarily tends in consequence
of the structure of our minds, that is, the dependence of our affections,
to bring on the habitual temper; which is owned to be compleat misery:
so far therefore our prudent part is easily descernible. Now, 4. With respect to all outward conveniencies and advantages, by the unanimous
consent of all mankind, temperance is allowed universally, not only to
be the best preservative of health, without which there can be no enjoyment; but to be necessary, to be able to relish pleasures in the highest
degree; *to be sauce to them,* if one may use that vulgar phrase. *And honesty
is likewise owned to be the best policy:* or the safest, the securest way of
living and acting in society; nay, indeed the only way of securing to ourselves any solid or durable happiness. But these two truths being owned,
they together with the foregoing propositions prove, "That, by the unanimous consent of mankind, founded upon universal experience, it is
prudent to <153> be virtuous, and foolish to be vicious; or that virtue is
the private good of every one, in all views, whether with respect to temper of mind, or outward security and advantage." Indeed such is the
universal agreement among mankind with respect to the good conse-

quences of virtuous behaviour, and the bad ones of every vice, that there is no country in which at all times the chief virtues have not been recommended from the advantages naturally redounding from them; and, on the other hand, almost all vices are condemned on account of the disadvantages naturally resulting from them, by familiar proverbs in every one's mouth? This we shall find to be true, if we but look into the collections of proverbs of different nations. For where, for instance, or in what nation however barbarous, is not cunning distinguished from true prudence; and are not temperance, honesty, faithfulness and generosity or benevolence, strongly inculcated by some very expressive apothegm? Nor can it indeed be otherwise, so plain and evident are the good effects of virtue, and the bad consequences of vice; and so clearly distinguishable is virtue in every case from its contrary.

> *Ask your own heart, and nothing is so plain,*
> *'Tis to mistake them, costs the time and pain.*[58]

But the question we are now upon is of such moment, that it is well worth while to give a short view of some of the different ways ancient philosophers have taken to shew, that virtue is man's natural end; at once his dignity and his happiness.

I. If we would know (says *Cicero*) for what end man is made and fitted, let us analyse his structure, and consider for what end it is adapted; for thus only can we know the end of any constitution, frame, or whole. Now if we look into the frame and constitution of man, and carefully <154> examine its parts and their references to one another, we shall plainly see, says he,[a] that it is fitted for those four virtues, prudence,

The way Cicero *reasons about our natural end, dignity and happiness, shewing that all these must mean the same thing.*

---

58. Pope, *Essay on Man*, II.215–16.

a. *Cicero de officiis, l.* 1. Compare with that *de finibus*, Lib. 2. N. 15. and 34. and *de inventione rhetorica*, Lib. 2. N. 53. where he defines all the virtues. So all the ancients. Virtus enim in cujusque rei natura supremum est & perfectio—tum oculi, in oculi natura, supremum & perfectio; tum hominis, in hominis natura, supremum & perfectio. *Timaeus Locrus de anima mundi.* So *Metopus Pythagoreus, in libro de virtute.* Hominis virtus, est hominis naturae perfectio—nam & equi virtus est ea, quae naturam ejus ad supremum perducit, &c. [Timaeus Locrus, *De anima mundi.* This is in fact in Hippodamus Thurius, *De felicitate:* "For virtue is the highest level and the

benevolence, magnanimity, and moderation, or harmony and decorum; for these four virtues are nothing else but his four most distinguishing natural powers and dispositions, brought by due culture to their perfection. There are, says he, in our constitution, together with the desire of self-preservation, common to all perceptive beings, four distinguishing principles which render man capable of a peculiar dignity, perfection and happiness, superior to what merely perceptive beings can attain to. "The desire of knowledge, or the love of truth, and the capacity of attaining to it; a social disposition, or the love of public good, and the capacity of intending and pursuing it." The desire of power and dominion, *principatus,* or of making ourselves great and able to do much good to ourselves and others, and the capacity of attaining to great esteem, power, and authority among mankind. And lastly, the sense and love of harmony, order, beauty, and consistency in our behaviour, and the capacity of attaining to a regular and orderly administration of our appetites.

These are the endowments, dispositions, and capacities which constitute our distinguishing excellence, or give us a higher rank in being, than the merely sensitive appetites which we have in common with other animals: but if it be so, then must the im-<155>provement of these powers and principles in our nature to the highest pitch of perfection they can be brought to, be our highest end, our duty, our dignity, our happiness, if these words have any meaning at all. And accordingly all the virtues and graces which adorn man, or make him perfect and happy, may be reduced to four, which are nothing else but the best improvements of these our four abovementioned distinguishing powers and principles; prudence, benevolence, magnanimity and moderation. 'Tis these virtues mixing and blending together, which make up the beauty

---

perfection in the nature of everything. The highest level and the perfection of the eye is in the nature of the eye. The highest level and the perfection in a man is in the nature of a man." In Gale, ed., *Opuscula mythologica, physica et ethica. Graece et Latine.* . . . , 660.

"The virtue of a man is the perfection of a man's nature. And the virtue of a horse is that which draws its nature to the highest level, etc." In Gale, *Opuscula,* 684–85.]

and greatness of actions, the beauty and greatness of life, and the proper happiness of man as man: that is, it is in the exercise of these virtues in proportion to their improvement, that all the happiness we can enjoy which is peculiar to us as intelligent rational beings of a higher order than meer sensitive animals consists. This reasoning must be just, if these principles do really take place in our nature; for if they do, they must be placed there, in order to work together jointly in proper proportions, or with forces duly and proportionally regulated and combined; and the perfection of our nature must necessarily consist in their so working; that is, in our taking care that they be all duly improved, and have all of them due exercise. If these principles do really belong to us, then it as necessarily follows that we are made by nature for acquiring and exercising prudence, benevolence, and magnanimity, and for reducing all our sensual appetites into comely and decent order; as that the perfection of any piece of mechanism, must lie in its operating regularly towards the end for which its whole structure consisting of various powers, proportioned to one another, and duly combined, is fitted. It cannot be more true, that the perfection of clockwork consists in its aptitude to measure time regularly, than that the <156> perfection of a being, endowed with the powers and dispositions fitted for acquiring knowledge, perceiving public good with delight and complacency, and for regulating all its appetites and affections, according to a sense of order, fitness, decency, and greatness, must lie in exercising all those powers and dispositions. To acquire these virtues and exercise them is therefore, with regard to man, to follow nature, and live agreeably to it; for it is to follow and live agreeably to his constitution. Virtue is therefore man's natural end or excellence, in any sense that any thing can be said to have a natural end or excellence.

Now having fixed this point, *Cicero,*[a] after explaining fully the several exercises of these powers which by being duly improved to their per-

---

a. See the second book of *the offices,* and the books *de finibus,* where virtue is proved to be happiness. And *Tusc. quaest.* De virtute seipsa contenta. De aegritudine lenienda, &c. ["De virtute seipsa" and "De aegritudine lenienda" refer to books 5 and 3, respectively, of Cicero's *Tusculanae disputationes.*]

fection are the human virtues or duties, and the imperfections to which
these powers are liable, thro' neglect of proper culture and discipline, or
misguidance; he proceeds to shew, that credit, reputation, esteem, love,
power, authority, health, self-enjoyment, and all the advantages of life,
are the natural effects and consequences of prudence, benevolence, fortitude of mind, and rightly moderated appetites; and that every vicious
indulgence or neglect is as dangerous and hurtful, according to the natural course of things, as it is base and contrary to the perfection to which
we are made to attain. And indeed it cannot be disputed, that it is the
real interest of every man to be good, since the villain finds himself
obliged to assume the semblance of virtue; and it is much easier to be
really good, than to act the counterfeit part successfully; for how rarely
is one able to carry on a scheme of villany under a masque, <157> without being discovered; and what are all the advantages of life, if reputation is lost?

> For riches, can they give but to the just
> His own contentment, or another's trust?
> Judges and senates have been bought for gold,
> Esteem and love were never to be sold.
>   Essay on man, Epist. 4.[59]

Virtue is the surest way, according to the natural course of things to
health, safety, peace, esteem, and to all the goods of life: it of itself makes
or causes no unhappiness; it naturally produces no hurtful consequences,
and even from the vicious, virtue commands esteem and respect. But
without the love and esteem of mankind, how miserable must man be![a]
He is a disjointed limb, forlorn and destitute; for no limb is more de-

---

a. That emphatical sentence of *Homer* hath the air of a proverb familiar in his
time.

Never, never, wicked man was wise.
    Odysse. B. 2. L. 320. of *Pope's* trans.

[Homer, *The Odyssey of Homer,* trans. . . . (from the Greek) by Alexander Pope (London: Richards, 1903), II.320.]
    59. Pope, *Essay on Man,* IV.185–88.

pendent on the well-being of the rest, and its union with the whole body, than every man is upon society.

But the main stress of ancient reasoning to prove that virtue is happiness lies upon this, "That man is so made that the pleasures of the mind, *i.e.* of knowledge and virtue, are far superior to those of sense; and that even the best enjoyments of sense are those which the virtuous man receives from his temperate and well regulated gratifications." Not only is it in consequence of our make the highest satisfaction which one can enjoy, to be able to approve our conduct to reason and to a moral sense; but so are we also framed, that social exercises, virtuous affections, and the temperate use of bodily pleasures are the gratifications which afford us the most exquisite touches of joy and satisfac-<158>tion in the way of immediate sensation, and their contraries are really painful. Whatever may be the course of outward circumstances, it is virtue alone that can make truly happy, even in immediate enjoyment, abstracting from all the pleasures of reflection upon good conduct. For external goods or means of happiness are only ministers of true satisfaction to those, whose reason and moral conscience preside over all their pursuits, and prescribe all their enjoyments. This is evident, if we take a complete view of our frame; and to prove it, I think, among many other considerations, the following are sufficient: and they are all taken from ancient writers; for the advantageousness or utility of virtue is no new discovery.

Upon what the arguments of ancient philosophers, to prove that virtue is private good, chiefly turn or depend.

The happiness of an insect or brute can only make an insect or brute happy. A nature with further powers must have further enjoyments. The happiness of a being must be of a kind with its faculties, powers and disposition; or, in one word, with its constitution, because it must result from it. Man therefore, considering the powers and dispositions he is endowed with, must have another happiness, another set of enjoyments in order to be satisfied, than a being merely consisting of senses, without reason, conscience of merit, a public sense and generous affections. It is only a reasonable and moral happiness that can satisfy moral powers and dispositions; so that a man must first divest himself of his moral powers and dispositions before he can be made happy by mere sense alone. 'Tis true, he is not merely made for moral or intellectual happiness, being a

sensitive as well as a rational creature, or a compound of these two natures. But being a compounded being, even his sensitive happiness must be rational as well as sensitive, in order to be fitted to his constitution; that is, his sensitive appetites, and their gratifications must be guided and ruled by his rational part, and partake of it. <159> Accordingly we have many a plain, incontestible experiment of the insufficiency of the most advantageous circumstances of outward enjoyment to make happy. But we have none of unhappiness produced by a well regulated mind, or well governed affections; none of unhappiness produced by the presidence of reason and virtue over our conduct. For how many are extremely happy through virtue, not only in mean but in distressed circumstances; and who are they whom affluence and wealth alone, without any assistance from virtue, have made so much as easy and contented? How tiresome is the circle of mere sensual indulgences to man in consequence of his frame! Let the fretfulness, the peevishness, the spleen, the disgusts of those, who with large estates are strangers to the luxury of doing good witness! All their complaints are so many demonstrations that virtue alone is happiness, and that they who seek it any where else do indeed labour in vain.

We are not made for sensual pleasures, but for them of the mind, or rational pleasures.

If[a] we consider our frame, we shall find that the end of man is not to seek after merely sensual pleasures; but, on the contrary, he is made to raise his mind above them, and to receive more <160> satisfaction from nobly despising them, than from enjoying them in the way of ordinary appetite. It is not only greater, but it is pleasanter because it is greater to

a. Quod si etiam bestiae multa faciant duce suâ, quaeque natura, partim indulgenter, vel cum labore, ut in gignendo, in educando facile appareat, aliud quiddam iis propositum, non voluptatem?—Ergo in bestiis erunt secreta a voluptate humanarum quaedam simulacra virtutum: in ipsis hominibus nisi voluptatis causa virtus nulla erit?—Nos vero, si quidem in voluptate sunt omnia longe multumque superamur a bestiis:—Ad altiora quaedam, & magnificentiora mihi crede, Torquate, nati sumus: nec id ex animi solum partibus, in quibus inest memoria.—Tu autem etiam membra ipsa, sensusque considera: qui tibi ut reliquae corporis partes, non comites solum virtutum, sed ministri etiam videbuntur. Quid si in ipso corpore multa voluptati praeponenda sunt, ut vires, valetudo, velocitas, pulchritudo? Quid tandem in animis censes? De finibus, lib. 2.—Compare lib. 5. Atqui perspicuum est, hominem

contemn all pomp, pageantry, and sensuality, than to possess the means of them. Virtue, in its original signification, means strength of mind, or such firmness as is able to withstand all temptation, whether from the side of enchanting pleasure, or from terrifying pain, rather than contradict our natural sense of what is fit and becoming; and there is not only a pleasure arising from the conscience of such strength of mind upon reflexion which is ineffable, but there is a divine satisfaction in every act of such fortitude.

Some of the ancients divided virtue thus defined into two principal parts or branches,[a] "Being able to deny ourselves any sensible pleasure,

_____

è corpore animoque constare, cum primae sint animi partes, secundae corporis, &c. [Cicero, *De finibus,* II.xxxiii.109–xxxiv.114: "But what if even animals are prompted by their several natures to do many actions conclusively proving that they have some other end in view than pleasure? . . . If animals therefore possess some semblance of the human virtues unconnected with pleasure, are men themselves to display no virtue except as a means to pleasure? . . . As a matter of fact if pleasure be all in all, the lower animals are far and away superior to ourselves. . . . No, Torquatus, believe me, we are born for loftier and more splendid purposes. Nor is this evidenced by the mental faculties alone, including as they do a memory. . . . But I would also have you consider our actual members, and our organs of sensation, which like the other parts of the body you for your part will esteem not as the comrades merely but actually as the servants of the virtues. But if even the body has many attributes of higher value than pleasure, such as strength, health, beauty, speed of foot, what pray think you of the mind?" Compare V.xii.34: "Now it is manifest that man consists of body and mind, although the mind plays the more important part and the body the less." Cicero, *De finibus bonorum et malorum,* trans. H. Rackham, Loeb Classical Library (London: Heinemann; New York: Putnam, 1931).]

a. See *Epictetus* and his *ancient commentators.* See particularly *M. Antoninus Philosophus.* Atqui vide, ne cum omnes recti animi affectiones *virtutes* appellantur, non sit hoc proprium nomen omnium, sed ab ea, quae una ceteris antecellit, omnes nominatae sint. Appellata enim est ex viro virtus: viri autem propria maxime est fortitudo. Cujus munera duo sunt maxima,—mortis dolorisque contemtio. Utendum est igitur his, si virtutis compotis, vel potius si viri volumus esse, quoniam a viris virtus nomen est mutuata. *Cicero Tuscul. Quaest.* lib. 2. No. 18. [Cicero, *Tusculanae disputationes,* II.xviii.43: "And yet, perhaps, though all right-minded states are called virtue, the term is not appropriate to all virtues, but all have got the name from the single virtue which was found to outshine the rest, for it is from the word for 'man' that the word virtue is derived; but man's peculiar virtue is fortitude, of which there are two main functions, namely scorn of death and scorn of pain. These then we must exercise if we wish to prove possessors of virtue, or rather, since the word for 'virtue' is borrowed

if reason or our moral sense forbid the indulgence: being able to withhold from the fairest promises of pleasure, till we have fully considered
their pretensions, and what our moral conscience says of the fitness or
unfitness of the pursuit. And being able, on the other hand, to endure
with magnanimity any pain rather than counteract our sense of honour,
esteem and true merit." And man, instead of being made for voluptuousness, is made for those virtues, *sustinence* and *abstinence.* In exerting
these he feels more sincere delight, than in wallowing in sensuality; because he is made to love power. We cannot have these virtues in perfection, but as all other perfections and habits <161> are acquired, but we
are made to attain to them by exercise and application. Virtue is, and
must be, in the nature of things, a progress. But tho' it be a progress, a
study, a struggle, a violent struggle, in like manner as getting to perfection in any science or art is; yet it is a pleasant exercise, a pleasant struggle
in every step. Man is made for exercise, for making acquisitions by labour
and industry. And therefore exercise is necessary to the welfare and pleasant feeling, so to speak, both of body and mind. And this is the exercise
for which man is best fitted, and in which he feels the highest pleasure,
even the vigorous efforts of his mind to improve his rational powers, to
keep his sensitive appetites in due subjection to reason, or to obtain the
mastership and command of them, and of himself. Virtue is therefore
at the same time, that it is asserted to be man's pleasantest employment,
very justly represented by the ancients as a warfare, as a striving for victory, as contending after perfection, and mounting up towards it. It indeed chiefly consists in conquering our sensual concupiscences; and in
submitting them to the rule and government of reason: but it does not
follow from this, that virtue is not happiness. This brave warfare is at
once our honour and our happiness; For thus alone can the natural greatness of the human mind, or its ardent desire of power, dominion and
independency be satisfied. It is true, virtue is not so delightful in its first
steps, as it becomes in proportion as it improves. We must distinguish
here in the same manner as with regard to any science or art: as there
the first elements are harsh and only afford pleasure to students, because

The virtuous pursuit alone can gratify our natural desire of power and dominion engrafted in us for that purpose.

from the word for 'man,' if we wish to be men." Cicero, *Tusculan Disputations,* trans.
J. E. King, Loeb Classical Library (London: Heinemann; New York: Putnam, 1927).]

they know they must ascend by degrees to perfection; and that the science, when once they have made any considerable advances in it, will well reward their labour and become easier, and that they are suitably employing <162> their time and talents: so is it likewise in the first steps of virtue, especially if one has bad habits and long indulged, impetuous, passions to grapple with and conquer. But virtue, like science or art, becomes more pleasant as one improves or proceeds in it. When one is become master of his passions, and virtuous inclinations are become, as it were, the bent of the soul, then all goes smoothly and equally on; and in the mean time the gradual advancement recompenses all the labour it requires, because the mind feels itself greaten, feels itself suitably employed, and feels its power and dominion increase. We have already mentioned some good effects of the greatness of our mind, with relation to knowledge; but herein chiefly does its usefulness consist, that it moves us to seek after true strength of mind; and no power, no dominion affords satisfaction to the mind of man equal to that power over ourselves and our appetites, to excite us to endeavour after which the desire of greatness was implanted in us. It is because the natural desire of power must be satisfied in some manner that other power is sought; and it is because this true power, the sweetest and pleasantest of all power, is not earnestly contended for, that the mind, if it is not employed in the pursuit of some false species of power, preys upon itself, frets and sours; and becomes at last quite languid and insensible, or quite cankered and insupportable. But the mind gradually greatning and expanding itself, as it advances in the dominion which virtue gives, is ever pleased and happy; for thus a natural and essential appetite of our nature is gratified, even the desire of power, (*principatus,*[60] as *Cicero* calls it).[a] The extensive

a. We had occasion already to mention the natural greatness of our mind in speaking of knowledge. It is the desire of liberty and power, or the disposition of the mind, to expand and dilate itself and prove its force, which is the foundation of all the great arts, and of all the great virtues. Virtue is really pleasant, because it brings forth the strength of the mind into action, and makes the mind feel its own power to enlarge itself.

60. "Preeminence"—Cicero, *De officiis,* trans. Walter Miller, Loeb Classical Library (London: Heinemann; Cambridge: Harvard University Press, 1938), II.xix.66.

power <163> to which inward independence and self-command is absolutely requisite.

Some other considerations on the same subject, taken from ancient authors. Let me subjoin to all this, in order to illustrate a point of the greatest importance in the philosophy of our nature, the three following considerations, all of which are likewise urged by ancient authors with a beauty and force of expression I am not able to approach.

Virtue saves and delivers from many evils, it brings no pains along with it; it is the only support under accidental calamities, and frequently brings good from them, and converts them into real benefits to ourselves and others. Its enjoyments never fade or become insipid, but on the contrary wax more pleasant and delightful by use and practice. And as true virtue knows no reward, but in the exercises and fruitions of more improved and exalted virtue, so it is pregnant with the most comfortable, joyous hopes.

I. Virtue saves from many terrible evils, the natural concomitants or followers of vice. Ignorance is full of doubts and fears, from which knowledge of nature, or of the real connexions of things, delivers: for he who encreaseth in knowledge, increaseth in strength; the wise man is strong; he is steady and immoveable, but the ignorant are weak and feeble, a reed shaken with every wind. And it is the calm undisturbed empire of reason over the appetites that saves from inward riot and tumult, and preserves the mind in that serene chearful state, without which it is impossible to relish any pleasure in the happiest circumstances of outward enjoyment: that chearful estate which is health to <164> the heart, *and marrow to the bones.* For nothing can please the man who is displeased with himself; and the vicious person cannot bear to see his own image. What vice is not either painful in the immediate exercise, or brings suffering after it, or is in both these respects a great evil and mischief, as well as base and unworthy: for abstracting from the ill consciousness which the vicious mind, ever self-condemned, cannot escape or fly from, does not *envy* torture the mind, emaciate the body, and render one contemptible, or rather hateful, as a common enemy, which he must necessarily be considered to be? Does not *avarice* cark and corrode with the vile double cares of hoarding and guarding, starve the body, and eat up the soul?[a] Does not *intemperance* and *sensuality* surfeit, sicken, and at last destroy the very sense of pleasure, and load the body with wearisome, fatiguing pains? Are not *anger* and *revenge* a boiling, scorching fever? The little pleasure they afford when their end is accomplished, what else is it but a short-lived relaxation from the most tormenting pain, which is quickly followed by remorse and just fears? And *malice,* or *Misanthropy,* is it not misery; universal and constant bitterness of mind? It is an invenomed heart always throwing out its poison, and yet never relieved from the cruel, inward rack-<165>ings of its exhaustless gall and discontent. Now virtue, or well regulated affections, save from all those miseries of body and mind, which vice pulls upon us inevitably, in consequence of the frame of our minds, and the connexions of things, that the mind may fly from every tendency towards the immoral state: that it may guard against vice as its greatest enemy, as well as debaser, and run to virtue as its health and peace, its preserver, upholder and comforter, as well as its exalter and ennobler.

What pain does temperance bring along with it? What disturbance did ever goodness and generosity produce within the breast? Or what

a. This is *Homer*'s phrase speaking of a melancholy person, θυμον κατεδων. *Ipse cor suum edens.* See *Cicero Tuscul. Quest.* B. 3. from whence all these arguments are taken. See *Horace's Epistles,* Lib. III. Epist. 2.

Semper *avarus eget* ———
Invidus *alterius macrescit rebus opimis.*

He uses the same phrase—*Si quid est animum, &c.* Therefore philosophy is called *Medicina mentis. Cicero Tuscul. Quaest.* Lib. III. *Est profecto animi medicina philosophia.* See a fine description of it in *Plutarch de educandis liberis.* See *Horace Epist.* Ep. 1. *Sunt certa piacula, &c.* [Homer, *Iliad,* 6.202: "Eating up the soul." The phrase is used of Bellerephon in his anguish; Cicero, *Tusculanae disputationes,* III.xxvi.63: "Eating his heart out alone"; Horace, *Epistles,* I.ii.56–57: "The covetous is ever in want. . . . The envious man grows lean when his neighbour waxes fat"; ibid., I.ii.38–39: "if aught is eating into your soul, etc." Horace, *Satires, Epistles and Ars poetica,* trans. H. Rushton Fairclough, Loeb Classical Library (London: Heinemann; New York: Putnam, 1926). *Medicina mentis*—"medicine of the mind." Cicero, *Tusculanae disputationes,* III.iii.6: "Assuredly there is an art of healing the soul—I mean philosophy." Plutarch, *De liberis educandis,* 7D: "For the illnesses and affections of the mind philosophy alone is the remedy." Plutarch, *Omnia quae extant opera,* 2 vols. (Paris, 1624). Horace, *Epistles,* I.i.36: "There are fixed charms, etc."]

mischievous consequence, can we say any of the virtues hath naturally and necessarily attached to it? Do regularity, good humour, and sweetness of temper, and generous affection, incapacitate for the pleasures of sense? Do they not rather double them? And what signifies it to be surrounded with all the best means of pleasure, if the mind is uneasy, or galled and fretted by evil consciousness, or by turbulent peevish appetites and passions. If it be dissatisfied with itself, and keenly set upon something without its reach. And what is there within our power, or absolutely dependent on ourselves, besides the regulation of our passions and appetites, and their happy effects within ourselves? It is the joys of virtue only which nothing can take from us. The happiness of the sensualist is as independent upon him as the wind or the tide. For do not *riches make to themselves wings and fly away?*[61] whereas a good conscience abideth for ever. Does virtue either bring diseases upon the body, or introduce uneasiness into the mind? Does it render us hateful to others, or deprive us of their esteem, trust and confidence? Does it not, on the contrary, command respect, and excite love, and trustful reliance, self-approbation, and the gladsome sense of merited affection. Must not the vicious man put on the <166> mask, the semblance of virtue, in order not to be marked out for a common enemy; and to gain his selfish, base ends? Dare he declare his inward thoughts to others? Or can he approve of them to himself? Can we be said to be fitted for luxury, debauches and voluptuousness, since the gratifications of sense, when they exceed the bounds which reason prescribes, produce uneasiness, consume the body, and are not more opposite to the exercises of reason and understanding, or even to the pleasures which imagination, when it is well formed and refined yields, so far superior to those of mere sense; than it is to a continued flow of agreeable bodily sensations? Are not a very great share of the very worst distempers and pains with which the body is sometimes so violently tormented, justly attributed to excessive sensual indulgences? Whence else come broken constitutions? Whence else comes rottenness, corruption and insensibility so early upon those who live in riot and wantonness? whilst the sober, the industrious and temperate, are gen-

61. Paraphrase of Prov. 23.5.

erally healthful and easy, and truly venerable in their old age. The old age in which a well spent life naturally terminates, is full of satisfaction, fit for council, and highly honourable.[a]

II. Virtue is the only support under calamities, but vice adds to every torture. By accidental calamities, I mean all such, as arising either from the laws of matter and motion, or from our social connexions, are inevitable by prudence and virtue. A disease may be entailed by a father on a son. Virtue often suffers in society through the vices of others; and distempers or losses which flow from the constitution of the air, and other material causes which work uniformly and invariably, must <167> happen alike to all men, good and bad: but under such distresses, virtue can alleviate pain, and bear up the mind. It hath many cordials to relieve and strengthen the soul; but whither can the vicious fly for ease and comfort in such cases? since he dares not look within his own breast, without being yet more exquisitely tormented; nor can he have any satisfaction from the sense of merited esteem and love, but must consider every one of his fellow creatures at best as his despisers: and since spurning and fretting but augments his suffering. A man may sustain bodily infirmities, *but a wounded spirit who can bear?*[62] The horrors of a guilty mind are truly insupportable. On the contrary, wherever the virtuous man is able to turn his thoughts, every object, whether within or without him, affords him pleasant matter of reflexion; and his being able to withhold himself from complaining and fretting is itself a very comfortable consciousness of becoming strength of mind, or manly patience. But which is more, wisdom and virtue are able not seldom to extract goods out of such evils, and to convert them into blessings. In distresses that leave room for thought, the virtuous make reflexions which are of great use to the temper: this all the good, who have been afflicted, know; nor can it be doubted by any, seeing even the vicious are often brought by distress to a just sense of things; and come forth out of the furnace of

a. See *Cicero de senectute.*—Sua enim vitia insipientes, & suam culpam in senectutem conferunt, &c. [Cicero, *De senectute,* v.14: "For, in truth, it is their own vices and their own faults that fools charge to old age, etc."]

62. Prov. 28.14.

affliction purified from much dross and corruption: made fitter for the offices of society, better friends and neighbours, more prudent, regular and virtuous in their conduct, and consequently much happier.

III. In fine, the pleasures of virtue never fade or become insipid: who was ever weary of acts of generosity, friendship and goodness? or who was ever disturbed by the consciousness of order, and worth, <168> and of merit, with all good and wise beings? Whence proceed dissatisfaction, fickleness of appetite, and nauseating amidst the greatest affluence of outward enjoyments, but from selfishness and sensuality, from seeking pleasure where it is not placed by nature, and cannot therefore be found; from endeavouring to derive more satisfaction from external objects than they are capable to afford; and from overstraining our bodily senses, while in the mean time the exercises of reason and social affection are quite discarded, and have no place in our pursuits and employments? Ambition of doing good may not have means equal to its generous desires, or may be disappointed; but the inward sense of good intention, sufficiently rewards all its scheming, all its activity. But selfishness is tormented with continual disappointments, and by the want of means equal to its insatiability; and if it reflects upon itself, is yet more so by the inward consciousness of its worthless, base, sordid demands. It has been often justly observed, that with regard to the pleasures of the body and the mind, the virtuous man, or he who is acquainted with the exercises of reason and virtue, is the properest judge to make a decision as to the preference; since none can say the pleasures of sense are less satisfactory to him, and he alone hath fully experimented the other. But we may appeal even to the vicious, the most sensual and selfish, whether their joys are durable, and do not commonly terminate in disgust and discontent? or whether, if at any time they have felt the workings of the good affections excited in them, and they have indulged them for a little, these were not the happiest moments they ever enjoyed; the only moments which they take delight to call to mind and reflect upon. No man is so corrupt, so lost to all sense of humanity, as not to have, on some occasions, felt so much of the pleasure attending virtuous affections, as to be able to <169> judge of the happiness the habitually good must enjoy; how pure, how constant and unchanging it must be: and he who

is thoroughly acquainted with the pleasures of knowledge, of the contemplation of order and beauty, and above all of benevolence, places his happiness so entirely in them, that he can desire no reward, but better opportunities of exercising and improving virtue. The only longings of his soul are after more knowledge, larger views of nature, and better occasions of exercising friendship, goodness, and social love. What other happiness, wholly distinct from this, can be offered to him which he would look upon as a recompence? Would he prefer larger draughts of merely sensual joy to an improved mind, and more entensive insight into the beauty, order, wisdom and goodness in nature? Or would he imagine himself bettered for all his generous, benign, social, public-spirited endeavours, by any change of circumstances, into ease and softness, in which he should never again feel those amiable, transporting workings of a good mind, which are now his supreme delight? Virtue alone can be its own *reward:* There can be nothing in nature superior to virtue, either in worth and excellence, or in pleasure and satisfaction, but higher and more enlarged virtue; and therefore to suppose it recompensed by any other enjoyments, of whatever kind,[a] is to suppose it rewarded by being sunk into a merely animal state, consisting of no higher gratifications than those of sense, without the exercises of reason and generous affection. For all other enjoyments are necessarily as much inferior to virtue, as merely animal or vegetative life is to reason and intelligence.
<170>

In whatever light therefore we consider virtue, it is man's highest excellence and happiness, and the end to which his whole moral structure points and prompts him. Tho' one may suffer by the vices of others, since no evil in society can be single, but as in the natural body, so in every system, where one member suffers, the whole must suffer in some

---

a. Praemia virtutis & officii, sancta & casta esse oportere: neque ea aut cum improbis communicari, aut in mediocribus hominibus pervulgari. *Cicero de inven. rhetorica,* Lib. II. [Cicero, *De inventione,* II.xxxix.114: "that the rewards for heroism and devotion to duty ought to be considered sacred and holy and should not be shared with inferior men nor made common by being bestowed on men of no distinction. . . ." Cicero, *De inventione.* . . . , trans. H. M. Hubbell, Loeb Classical Library (London: Heinemann; Cambridge: Harvard University Press, 1949).]

proportion, the more adjacent parts chiefly. And tho' one may also suffer
with all his virtue by means of the necessary operation of those very laws
on which many portions of his happiness, as a certain species or a part
of a system, depend; yet without virtue no person can have any happiness
of the rational kind, and but very little even in the sensitive way, or by
gratifying common lower appetites. The reason is, as hath been said,
because in the nature of things the happiness of an insect or brute will
only make an insect or brute happy: A nature with further powers must
have further enjoyments; and therefore, man, considering the powers he
is endowed with, must have another happiness, another set of enjoyments, in order to be satisfied, than a being merely consisting of senses
without reason, conscience of merit, a public sense and generous
affections.

All I have been now saying, is most feelingly expressed by our excellent
moral Poet.

> *What nothing earthly* gives, *or can destroy,*
> *The soul's calm sun-shine, and the heart felt joy,*
> *Is virtue's prize:* ———63

And again,

> *Know, all the good that individuals find,*
> *Or GOD and nature meant to meer mankind;*
> *Reason's whole pleasures, all the joys of sense*
> *Lie in three words,* health, peace, *and* competence. <171>
> *But health consists with temperance alone;*
> *And peace, O* virtue! *peace is all thy own:*
> *The good or bad the gifts of fortune gain;*
> *But these less taste them, as they worse obtain.*
> *Say, in pursuit of profit or delight,*
> *Who risque the most, who take wrong means or right?*
> *Of vice or virtue, whether blest or curst,*
> *Which meets contempt, or which compassion first?*
> *Count all th' advantage prosp'rous vice attains,*

---

63. Pope, *Essay on Man,* IV.167–69.

> *'Tis but what virtue flies from, and disdains;*
> *And grant the bad what happiness they wou'd,*
> *One they must want, which is, to pass for good.*
>
> Essay on man, Epist. 4.[64]

Thus then it appears that we are made for virtue; and that it is our truest interest; and that whether we are to subsist after this life or not; it is present happiness, the only present happiness which bears any proportion to our constitution.

Conclusions concerning virtue; that it is interest or private good.

I shall conclude this article with observing, that philosophers, ancient and modern, have taken routs, which at first view appear very different in establishing the nature of human duty and happiness, but all these terminate in the same conclusion. Whether we consider the fitness of things, the truth of the case, our interest or our dignity, 'twill still come out, that virtue is what man is made for. As for the quibling and jangling about *obligation,* it is sufficient for us to remark,

Some observations on the disputes among modern moralists about obligation.

I. If by it is meant a moral necessity arising from the power of a superior to enforce his commands, by rewards and punishments, then obligation being so defined, a man cannot be said to be *obliged* to virtue, but simply in respect of his being under the influence of a superior, who commands him to be virtuous by laws, which he has sufficient power to enforce by rewards and punishments. If by it is meant a moral necessity arising from natural connexions, <172> which make it our interest to behave virtuously, then is man *obliged* to virtue simply in this respect, (that being then the definition of *obligation*) because such is the natural order and establishment of things, that virtue is his interest. If by it be meant the same as more reasonable, more becoming, more perfect, *&c.* then is man *obliged* to virtue for the sake of virtue, or on account of its becomingness and excellency.

II. Now in all these different views may *obligation* be taken if philosophers please. And in all these different senses have philosophers proved man to be *obliged* to virtue: whence it must follow, that when it

64. Ibid., IV.77–92.

is owned, that virtue is fit, becoming, reasonable, and our perfection, if
man is not allowed to be *obliged* to virtue in that sense, it must only be
because *obligation* is thought more properly to mean one or other, or
both of the other moral necessities, and not the last one named; and so
the debate is merely about the use of the word *obligation*.

III. But it is obvious, that in all reasonings to prove that man is *obliged*
to virtue in the first sense, the fitness or becomingness, or the natural
beauty and excellence of virtue, must be laid down as the principle upon
which they proceed and are founded. For how else can we know the will
of the Deity with regard to our conduct; but by knowing what is in itself
best and fittest? For how indeed can we prove the Being of a GOD,
unless we have first formed and established, adequate and clear ideas of
moral excellence and perfection? 'Till we have conceived what virtue or
merit is, we cannot have any idea of GOD, or consequently of what he
wills and approves.

IV. With regard to the other sense of *obligation* in which it means the
same as interest. As all rea-<173>sonings about the obligations to virtue,
which suppose its excellence must be highly assistant to virtue, and consequently are of the greatest importance in moral philosophy; so, on the
other hand, whatever pretences are made to supporting virtue by any
philosophers who deny the dignity of virtue, they are but such adherents
to it as some are said to have been to the doctrines of JESUS CHRIST, who
followed him for the sake of the loaves with which he fed them. I use
this similitude, because if there be a real difference between esteem, love
and friendship, for the sake of one's amiable temper, and great and good
qualities, and that hypocritical pretended affection which only eyes some
selfish advantage, there must likewise be a real difference between the
inward esteem and love of virtue for its own intrinsic beauty, and meer
outward conformity to its rules for the sake of some conveniencies and
advantages, without any inward liking to it.[a] If there be any real differ-

---

a. See *Cicero de finibus*, Lib. 2. No. 22. Nemo pius est qui pietatem metu capit,
&c.—And, *de legibus*, Lib. 1. No. 14. Tum autem qui non ipso honesto movemur,
ut boni viri simus sed, utilitate aliqua atque fructu, callidi sumus non boni, &c. [Cic-
ero, *De finibus*, II.xxii.71: "None is good, whose love of goodness, etc." *De legibus*,

ence in the one case there must be a real one in the other. He alone can be said to do a virtuous action, who does it with delight and complacency in it as such; otherwise one who inwardly hates the person he caresses and flatters in order to get his confidence, and then betray him, is his real friend till the moment he hurts him, notwithstanding his dissimulation and evil intention; and he who abstains from robbing for fear of the gallows is as honest as he who would rather suffer the cruelest torments than commit the least injury to any one in thought, word or deed.

But all that hath been said, (from which it clearly follows, that the laws of our nature with regard to virtue, and private and public good are so fitly <174> chosen) will be yet clearer when we consider our constitution or frame with regard to society. Mean time we may conclude with my Lord *Shaftsbury.* "Thus the wisdom of what rules, and is first and chief in nature, has made it to be according to the private interest and good of every one, to work towards the general good; which if a creature ceases to promote, he is actually so far wanting to himself, and ceases to promote his own happiness and wellfare. He is, on this account, directly his own enemy: nor can he otherwise be good or useful to himself, than as he continues good to society, and to that *whole* of which he is himself a *part.* So that virtue, which of all excellencies and virtues is the chief and most amiable; that which is the prop and ornament of human affairs; which upholds communities, maintains union, friendship and correspondence amongst men; that by which countries as well as private families flourish and are happy; and for want of which every thing comely, conspicuous, great and worthy, must perish and go to ruin; *that single quality,* thus beneficial to all society, and to mankind *in general,* is found equally a happiness and good to each creature *in particular;* and is, *that* by which alone man can be happy, and without which he must be miserable."[65]

I.xiv.41: "furthermore, those of us who are not influenced by virtue itself to be good men, but by some consideration of utility and profit, are merely shrewd, not good."]

65. Shaftsbury, "Virtue" II.ii., conclusion, in *Characteristics,* ed. Klein (Cambridge: Cambridge University Press, 1999), 230.

Another class of laws. Those relative to society and the dependence of human happiness and perfection on social union and rightly united force. Let us consider another law of our nature. "The law of society. In consequence of which all men are not only led to society by several strong affections and dispositions; but man is so framed for society, that private and public happiness and perfection exceedingly depend upon our uniting together in a proper manner, or under proper <175> laws, and a right form of government, for promoting our common happiness, dignity and perfection."

A general view of our social make or form. We are led to society by an appetite after it, which cannot be satisfied without company, fellowship, and social communication: nay, so social is our make, that neither the pleasures of the body, nor those of the mind, separated from society or public affection, can afford us any lasting enjoyment.

> Remember, man, "The universal cause
> Acts not by partial, but by gen'ral laws."
> And makes what happiness we justly call
> Subsist, not in the good of one, but all.
> There's not a blessing individuals find,
> But some way leans and hearkens to the kind.
> No bandit fierce, no tyrant mad with pride,
> No cavern'd hermit, rest self-satisfy'd;
> Who most to shun or hate mankind pretend,
> Seek an admirer, or would fix a friend:
> Abstract what others feel, what others think,
> All pleasures sicken, and all glories sink;

Each has his share, and who would more obtain
Shall find, the pleasure pays not half the pain.
Essay on man, Epist. 4.[66]

We have all the affections which are necessary to the maintenance of society, and to receiving happiness by social correspondence and participation: an inclination to propagate our kind; natural affection to our offspring and to our parents; disposition to friendship; tenderness to the sex; regard to reputation, or desire of fame and esteem; gratitude, sympathy and compassion; delight in the happiness of others, in that particularly which is of our own giving or procuring to them; satisfaction in whatever presents us with the agreeable idea of the power, improvement and perfection belonging to our nature. All these affections and dispositions are deeply em-<176>planted in us, as we may be as sure, or rather surer by experience, than we can be of any properties belonging to external objects of sense. And suitably to these affections and dispositions, men have different turns, capacities, genius's and abilities, insomuch that they are as distinguishable from one another by their different moral features, as by their outward airs, shapes and complexions; and as are dependent upon one another as they can be conceived to be, in order to render society at the same time necessary and yet agreeable or the object of voluntary choice. For if we were not united together at once by such affections, and by such reciprocal wants as necessarily result from diversity of interests, abilities and tempers; society would only be merely necessary or merely agreeable; but being so tied and connected together as we are, society is neither solely necessary, nor is it merely matter of choice; but it is equally requisite and satisfactory.

It is needless to dwell long upon proving, that we are formed and made for society, and dependent one upon another: our very manner of coming into the world, and education to the state of manhood, the source of many endearing relations, and agreeable affections and offices sufficiently prove it. And what can be more obvious, than that no consid-

66. Pope, *Essay on Man,* IV.35–48.

erable improvements can be made in the arts and sciences, or in true grandeur and elegance, without social union and rational virtuous confederacy? In order, however to give a just view of the extent and usefulness of this law, and of the phenomena belonging to it, I shall offer the few following observations.[a] <177>

Man is in as proper a sense made for society as any machine for its end. I. We cannot more certainly pronounce, that a watch or any other machine is formed for a certain end from the consideration of the parts of which it is formed; than we may conclude from all the parts of our constitution, and their mutual references to one another, that we are formed for society and for social happiness; and if it be fit, wise and good that it should be so, then must our constitution as such, be wise and good.

Hardly will any one call into doubt, the fitness, the wisdom and goodness of our being designed and made for society, of our being made one kind, and our having as such a common stock, a common end, a common happiness. One of the greatest objections brought against our frame and constitution is, that society is not natural but adventitious, the meer consequence of direful necessity; men being naturally to one another wolves; that is, not as wolves to wolves for there a kind of union

a. —Quae quidem omnia contingent, si quis remp. bene constitutam nanciscatur. Id quod quidem *Amaltheae* quod dicitur cornu voco. Etenim in recta legum constitutione sunt omnia; neque maximum naturae humanae bonum vel existere absque ea, vel comparatum & auctum permanere possit. Nam & virtutem & ad virtutem viam haec in se continet, quandoquidem in ea partim naturae bona procreantur, partim & mores, studia, leges optime se habent & recta ratio, pietas, sanctimonia, magnopere vigent. Quamobrem qui beatus futurus & feliciter victurus est, eum in bene constituta repub. & vivere necesse est & mori, &c. *Hyppodamus Thurius Pythag. de felicitate.* [Hippodamus Thurius, *De felicitate:* "All these things will happen if people hit upon a well-ordered city. And these things, I say, are what is called the horn of Amalthea. For everything depends upon good order and without it the greatest good of human nature cannot come into existence, nor can it endure if it does come into existence and grows. For good order includes within itself virtue and the road to virtue, since through good order in part the goods of nature are produced and in part so also are our customs. Our endeavors and laws are as good as they can be, and right reason, piety, and sanctity flourish magnificently. Hence someone who wishes to be happy and to live a successful life must live and die in a well-ordered city." In Gale, ed., *Opuscula mythologica, physica et ethica. Graece et Latine.* . . . (Amsterdam, 1688), 662–63.]

and society takes place, but as wolves to sheep, and devourers and destroyers. Men, say they, are made for rapine and plunder; to fight for victory, and to subdue and enslave each as many of his fellow-creatures as he can by force or stratagem. In one word, men, according to this scheme, are made to be a prey one to another: The only natural principle or instinct those philosophers acknowledge in our nature is, the lust of power and dominion, and an insatiable desire of tyranizing: And were this a true account of our nature, and of the state for which our author has intended us by our make, a state of perpetual war;[67] then indeed it would be impossible to conceive a good opinion of his disposition towards <178> his creatures. But so far is this from being a true description of human nature, that nothing is more repugnant to feeling and experience.[a] *Cicero,* indeed, and all the best ancient philosophers, have taken

The fundamental error of *Hobbs* consists in his considering the desire of power which is natural to man as his only natural passion or instinct.

a. See the first Book of *Cicero's offices.* Huic veri videndi cupiditati adjuncta est appetitio quaedam *principatus,* ut nemini parere animus bene a natura informatus velit, nisi praecipienti, aut docenti, aut utilitatis causa, juste & legitime imperanti: ex quo animi magnitudo existit, humanarumque rerum contemptio—Omnino fortis animus & magnus, duabus rebus maxime cernitur: quarum una in rerum externarum despicientia ponitur, cum persuasum sit, nihil hominem nisi quod honestum, decorumque sit, aut admirari, aut optare, aut expetere oportere: nullique neque homini, neque perturbationi animi nec fortunae succumbere. Altera est res, ut cum ita sis affectus animo, ut supra dixi, res geras magnas, illas quidem & maxime utiles, &c. [Cicero, *De officiis:* "To this passion for discovering truth there is added, as it were, a hungering for independence, so that a mind well-moulded by nature is unwilling to be subject to anybody save one who gives rules of conduct or is a teacher of truth or who, for the general good, rules according to justice and law. From this attitude come greatness of soul and a sense of superiority to worldly conditions" (I.iv.13). "The soul that is altogether courageous and great is marked above all by two characteristics: one of these is indifference to outward circumstances; for such a person cherishes the conviction that nothing but moral goodness and propriety deserves to be either admired or wished for or striven after, and that he ought not to be subject to any man or any passion or any accident of fortune. The second characteristic is that, when the soul is disciplined in the way above mentioned, one should do deeds not only great and in the highest degree useful, etc." (I.xx.66). Cicero, *De officiis,* trans. Walter Miller, Loeb Classical Library (London: Heinemann; Cambridge: Harvard University Press, 1938).]

67. Thomas Hobbes, *Leviathan,* ed. Richard Tuck (Cambridge: Cambridge University Press, 1991), pt. 1, chs. 10–13.

Our natural
desire of power
as it is con-
joined in our
frame with
other equally
natural desires
is a most noble
and useful
instinct.
notice of a very laudable *greatness* in the human mind, which makes its
capacity for great virtues and noble efforts, in consequence of its natural
desire of *principatus,* as *Cicero* calls it: that is, of power and rule or independence. But this disposition or instinct is not the only one in our
frame; it is ballanced by several others which serve each in its turn as a
counterpoise to it. All these natural dispositions or instincts are enumerated and explained by *Cicero,* in the first Book of his *Offices* at the
beginning, as the foundation of all the virtues which constitute human
dignity, perfection and happiness, as we have already had occasion to
shew: *viz.* the desire of knowledge, the desire and love of society, and a
moral sense, or a sense of beauty and deformity in affections and characters, analogous, as he observes, to our sense of beauty and proportion
in corporeal forms. Now our desire of power and rule, as it is united
with these other dispositions, is so far from being a hurtful principle in
our nature, that it is of admirable use. It serves to push us on to improve
all our powers and faculties; it impels us to exert ourselves with all our
might to attain to the highest perfection in knowledge, and in every
ability we are capable <179> of. It serves to excite us to take a very high
aim; to despise mean and low objects, and to delight in whatever presents
us with a very high idea of our own capacity, force and perfection. Without such a principle, man would indeed be a low, a timid, unaspiring
creature, incapable of fortitude and magnanimity: incapable of ruling
his sensitive appetites; incapable of great attempts, and of despising dangers for the sake of virtue. But then, on the other hand, were not this
loftiness of mind, this desire of power and rule checked by the love of
society, by generous public affections, and by a sense of beauty in good
affections and actions, it would indeed make every man naturally a tyrant; and produce all the horrible evils, which *Hobbs* says, must be the
product of men's natural disposition, till they resolve to live quietly, and
make a voluntary league for the sake of safety and peace.[68] It is impossible
to have a just idea of any whole by considering any part of it singly or
abstractedly from all the other parts. But if we consider our disposition
to seek after power, as it is joined in our frame with the other equally

Greatness of
mind or love of
power, how
useful in our
frame.

68. Hobbes, *Leviathan,* pt. 1, ch. 13.

natural and strong dispositions in our nature which have been mentioned, we shall be led immediately to *Cicero*'s conclusion, That by these
dispositions, as they are united together in our constitution, we are made
to acquire prudence, to exercise benevolence, and to study order and
beauty in *our moral behaviour,* and for fortitude and magnanimity. This
natural greatness of mind, considered with regard to our equally natural
appetite after knowledge, conduces to prompt us to seek after large and
comprehensive views of nature; knowledge of the most enlarging, en-
nobling and exalting kind; such knowledge as will be most conducive to
increase our power and dominion: It makes us delight in contemplating
great objects; objects which wonderfully fill and delate the mind; objects
which prove its force and put its grasp to the trial: hence the origine of
the sublime in senti-<180>ments, in discourse, and in actions, and of
all the pleasure it gives, as *Longinus* has observed.[69] This natural greatness
considered with respect to our love of society, serves to save it from de-
generating into too tame and simple submissiveness for the sake of ease
and quiet to every proud usurper of dominion: and it excites us to aim
at power in order to do good, in order to spread happiness round us with
a liberal hand. Our natural greatness of mind or desire of Power is indeed the source of ambition: but of what ambition is it naturally the
source; as it is conjoined in our mind with benevolence but generous
affection? Thus it tends to excite the great and God-like ambition of
being able to do glorious and meritorious services to our fellow-creatures:
it excites us to seek after inward liberty and independency. To no other
ambition does it, or can it excite us as it is directed by the love of society,
and the benevolent principle with which it is united in our frame, that
it might co-operate with it. For it is that different springs or movements
may work jointly that they are placed together in any piece of mechanism: and it must be so likewise in moral constitutions. Finally, this natural desire of power and rule, or independency, when it is considered
together with the love of order, and regularity in affections, conduct and
society, prompts us to pursue regularity and good order in all our behaviour, and to subdue all the passions which tend to introduce irreg-

69. This is a major theme of Longinus in his *De sublimitate.*

ularity and disorder into our own breasts, inconsistency and irregularity into our own outward actions, and proportionable disorder and irregularity into society. All these instincts or dispositions therefore as they are contrived by nature to ballance one another, and to co-operate in our minds, make a very beautiful constitution, or a constitution adapted to very noble ends and purposes. If any of them be too strong or vehement, then is the ballance disturbed, and so far is our frame disordered: but that any one of them which is most in-<181>dulged should become stronger than the rest which are less so, is the effect of an excellent general law with regard to temper and habitude of mind already explained. It is just so in natural compositions or machines, in which some particular spring may acquire too much force in proportion to the rest, and the end of the whole, by various causes: and as it is in mechanism, so is it in moral nature. When all the springs and wheels are sound and right, and in a just ballance, then and then only all will go right. The happiness as well as the proper business of man as a rational agent, consists in exerting himself to understand his frame; and understanding it, to give due attention and diligence to keep all his moral springs and movements in their due and proportioned strength, as benevolence and his love of beauty and order direct, and as self-love itself requires for interest's sake: virtue and happiness being the same, as has been proved.

All our affections, not only the public ones, but even the private, respect society, and are formed with a view to it. Our affections, no doubt, one and all of them are often matter of uneasiness to ourselves, and sometimes occasion misery to others; it must be so when any one is indulged and nourished into a degree of strength above its proper tone; but the question is, which of them we could have wanted without greater loss and suffering in the whole. They are by nature ballanced one against another, as the antagonist muscles of the body, either of which separately would have occasioned distortion and irregular motion, yet jointly they form a machine most accurately subservient to the necessities, conveniencies, and happiness of the whole system.[a]

a. See Mr. *Hutcheson* on *the passions,* whose words I here use. [Francis Hutcheson, *An Essay on the Nature and Conduct of the Passions. . . .* (1728); ed. Aaron Garrett (Indianapolis: Liberty Fund, 2002), I.VI.iii.]

We have already observed whence the ultimate necessity arises of adding certain uneasy sensations to all our desires, from which they have the name of passions. [a] And we have a power of <182> reason and reflexion by which we may discern what course of acting will naturally tend to procure us the most valuable sort of gratifications of all our desires, and prevent all intolerable or unnecessary pains, or provide some support under them. Nay we have wisdom sufficient to form right ideas of general laws and constitutions, so as to preserve large societies in peace and prosperity, and promote a general good amidst all the private interests. Now as to take away our passions and affections would be to deprive us of all the springs and motives, all the principles necessary to action, and to leave nothing to our reason to govern and guide; so, on the other hand, to rob us of our reason, would be to deprive us of a guiding principle, and to reduce us to the lowest condition of animals impelled and driven by instinct and appetites, without any foresight, without capacity of chusing, and consequently without all capacity of virtue or merit. As well therefore may one deny that we are made for walking erect, and not to grovel on the ground, as that we are made for society; since all our powers and affections are contrived for the good of our kind. Even those of the private sort are plainly so; for do they not then only work towards private good when they preserve that due proportion which the common good of mankind requires? and becoming too strong or too weak with regard to the general good of our kind, do they not likewise become disproportioned with regard to the private system and its well being? This is plain from the very principle of self-preservation, or the love of life, that becomes unable to answer its end in the private system, producing inability to save ones self when it is too strong; and when it is too weak, is the occasion of equal mischief to ourselves and others. For as the timorous and fearful cannot help themselves and others, so the rash and adventurous do not bring more hurt upon others <183> than upon themselves. Thus therefore the private affections are equally well adjusted to private and publick good. But if they should be said to belong merely to the selfish system, and to have no farther respect in their

a. In the second chapter.

contrivance and tendency, there are however many other affections in
our nature, which do not immediately pursue merely private good, but
which in many cases lead us directly beyond ourselves, violently inter-
esting us in the concerns and for the affairs of others in their adversity
as well as prosperity, and conducing to make us regardless of ourselves,
or at least to make us prefer the interest of our fellow creatures to our
own private ease. What else are our compassion and friendly sense of
sorrow, but the alarms and impulses of kind nature, watchful[a] for the
whole, to engage us in the interest of others, and to prompt us to fly to
the relief of a suffering brother? What are the στοργη; *i.e.* natural affection to offspring, sympathy, friendship, the love of ones country; or,
in one word, all our social feelings, which make up,[b] or lay the foundation for so much of our happiness, but so many necessary ties by which
we are linked together and make one system? By these each private agent,
is originally and independently of his own choice, made subservient to
the good of the whole. And in consequence of this mechanism of our
nature, he who voluntarily continues in that rational union, cultivates
it, and delights in employing his powers and talents for the general good
of his kind, makes himself happy; and he who does not continue this
natural union freely, but voluntarily endeavours <184> to break it and
disunite himself from mankind, renders himself wretched; and yet he
cannot totally burst the bonds of nature. His moral and public sense,
his desire of honour and esteem, and the very necessities of his nature
will continue to make him dependent on his kind, and oblige him to
serve it whether he inclines to it or not.

a. See Mr. *Hutcheson on the passions.* [This doctrine is dealt with throughout
Hutcheson's *Passions,* but see especially section I.III.]

b. See *Cicero, de legibus,* lib. 1. And *de officiis,* lib. 1. No. 7. Sed quoniam ut praeclare scriptum est a platone non nobis—solum nati sumus—in hoc naturam debemus
ducem sequi & communes utilitates in medium afferre, &c.—See how he refutes
towards the end of this book those who held that we are not of a social make. [Cicero,
De officiis, I.vii.22: "But since, as Plato has admirably expressed it, we are not born
for ourselves alone . . . in this direction we ought to follow nature as our guide, to
contribute to the general good, etc."]

II. But let it be observed in the second place, That men could not be made fit for society, or for the social happiness which arises from partnership, from communication and participation, and the reciprocal interchange of friendly offices, without being so constituted that they should mutually stand in need of each other; and hence it follows that in order to society, not only diversity, but inequality of talents, mental as well as bodily, is absolutely necessary;[a] for otherwise there would be

Society or variety of social happiness requires variety of talents and characters.

a. *Cicero* often takes notice of the likeness among mankind to one another in their frame, whence it plainly appears that we are, as he expresses it, *ad justitiam nati.* Id jam patebit si hominum inter ipsos societatem conjunctionemque perspexeris. Nihil est unum uni tam simile, tam par quam omnes inter nosmet ipsos sumus, &c. *De legibus,* lib. 1. But see what he says of our personal differences. *De officiis,* lib. 1. n. 30. Intelligendum est etiam, duabus quasi nos a natura indutos esse personis, quarum una est communis—altera autem quae proprie singulis est tributa. Ut enim in corporibus magnae dissimilitudines—sic in animis existunt etiam majores varietates. He gives instances, and then (which no other moralist hath done) he explains the decorum belonging to every particular character. Admodum autem tenenda sunt sua cuique, non vitiosa sed propria quo facilius decorum illud quod quaerimus retineatur, sic enim faciendum, ut contra universam naturam non contendamus: ea tamen conservata, propriam naturam sequamur, &c. This lays a foundation for great variety of beauty in human life. Hence in poetry what is called *decorum,* as *Cicero* observes in the same place, or truth and consistency of characters, which makes so essential a part of poetical imitation. Let us imagine human society divested of this variety, and by consequence of the different duties and decorums arising from it, and we reduce society to a very uniform lifeless state.—See *Homer's Odyssey,* B. 8. line 185. *Pope's Translation.*

> With partial hands the gods their gifts dispense,
> Some greatly think, some speak with manly sense.
> Here heav'n an elegance of form denies,
> But wisdom the defect of form supplies:
> This man with energy of thought controuls,
> And steals with modest violence our souls;
> He speaks reserv'dly, but he speaks with force,
> Nor can one word be chang'd but for a worse. &c.

How fade and insipid would human life be without that pleasant beautiful variety of colours, which different characters arising from various causes cast upon it. [*Ad justitiam nati* translates as "born for justice." Cicero, *De legibus,* I.x.28–29: "This fact will immediately be plain if you once get a clear conception of man's fellowship and union with his fellow-men. For no single thing is so like another, so exactly its counterpart, as all of us are to one another, etc." Cicero, *De re publica, De legibus,* trans. Clinton Walker Keyes, Loeb Classical Library (London: Heinemann; New York: Put-no dependence, and consequently no place for social affections to exert themselves, or for the mutual contribution toward public good, which is involved in the very idea of society and community. Now this diversity and inequality which part-<185>nership, communication, and social intercourse require, is in our case in a great measure (as has been observed)[a] the necessary result of our being related to a sensible world; or of that mutual union between our minds and bodies which is requisite to our having the pleasures of every kind we are susceptible of in that way, which have been enumerated. So strict and closs is the concatenation of things with regard to our make, that whatever is found to be fit or necessary in one respect, is so in all regards and views. The bodies by which we have a communication with a sensible world, and are capable of enjoying it, must be supported, nourished, and defended by methods which require diversity and inequality of powers; diversity and inequality of situations; superiorities and inferiorities arising from several varieties and differences. Minds united with bodies must be affected with the laws of matter and motion; and their different manners of being affected with these laws must be uniform and fixed, so that like effects may always <186> proceed from like causes and connexions. But all these dependencies on matter are the foundations of social exercises, and necessary to the pleasures and advantages of united social life. So complete then is the whole building, if I may so speak, that if any one part is altered, the whole can no longer stand or subsist, but must fall to the ground. What is necessary or fit for our progress in knowledge, and to our enjoyment of a sensible world, is likewise requisite to our moral

The exigencies of our animal life require diversity.

Moral happiness requires the same diversity.

---

nam, 1928). *De officiis:* "We must realise also that we are invested by nature with two characters, as it were: one of these is universal. . . . The other character is the one that is assigned to individuals in particular. In the matter of physical endowment there are great differences. . . . Diversities of character are greater still." (I.xxx.107). "Everybody, however, must resolutely hold fast to his own peculiar gifts, in so far as they are peculiar only and not vicious, in order that propriety, which is the object of our inquiry, may the more easily be secured. For we must so act as not to oppose the universal laws of human nature, but, while safeguarding those, to follow the bent of our own particular nature, etc." (I.xxx.110).

Homer, *Odyssey,* translated by Pope, VIII.185–92.]
a. In the second and third chapters.

perfection and to social happiness; and reciprocally whatever is necessary to the latter is necessary to the former; for social happiness must in the nature of things be a happiness of participation and communication; it must be a happiness that is reflected, as it were, from one creature to another, and that admits of various changes and modifications. Now different textures of bodies are not more necessary to the various reflexions, refractions, and transmissions of light, which constitute all the visible beauty of the corporeal world, than different structures and modifications of human minds are to the various reflexions and refractions, so to speak, of social happiness, which are requisite to the beauty and happiness of society. The only question with regard to the latter is, Whether they are not the properest to produce in the whole of things as equal a distribution of happiness, as those in the sensible world do of light and heat; that is, as equal a distribution as is consistent with the very nature of reflected happiness itself, and with the other useful laws relative to our frame? But hardly can we conceive better provision made for the equal distribution of reflected and participated happiness consistently with it as such, than by the strength which nature hath originally given to our generous affections and to our moral sense: that is, to our desire of spreading happiness, and to our delight in the contemplation of that beautiful order which the <187> regular exercise of benevolent affections naturally tends to produce.

A variety of different tempers and characters is requisite to make various reflexions or modifications of social happiness.

By means of different moral qualities, tempers, and situations, the same kind of happiness has no less various effects than light by its various reflexions and transmissions in the sensible world. Happiness is thus modified or changed into various appearances and effects no less useful as well as beautiful than the variety of colours which make the harmony of the visible world. But by means of a moral sense and of a social disposition, mankind are as firmly tied together as they can be consistently with the power of regulating themselves, or with the dependence of their temper upon their own care to form it, or upon habits of their own contracting. There can be no society, no mutual dependence, without supposing mutual wants; for all social exercises may be reduced to *giving* and *receiving*. But these two necessarily suppose differences among mankind, and insufficiencies in every one to be happy by himself. And in

All social virtues suppose mutual dependencies and wants, for they may all be

reduced to
these two,
giving and
receiving.

fact, such amidst great diversity is the equality of mankind, that none can ever be without wants which he himself is utterly incapable to supply, however extensive his power of giving may be. But what can be happier than deficiencies and wants, which are the foundation of so many and so great goods; of social union, of love and friendship, of generosity and kindness, gratitude and reliance, and sympathy? If these are removed, what remains in human life worth enjoying? Even the gratifications of sense, as has been observed, dwindle into nothing; as is plain from considering one, which will readily be acknowledged to be none of the least; where the *spes mutui credula animi* [70] is felt to be the principal ingredient.

> *Order is heav'n's first law; and this confest,*
> *Some are, and must be, greater than the rest,* <188>
> *More rich, more wise: but who infers from hence*
> *That such are* happier, *shocks all common sense.*
> *Heav'n to mankind impartial we confess*
> *If all are equal in their happiness:*
> *But mutual wants this happiness increase,*
> *All nature's diff'rence keeps all nature's peace.*
> *Condition, circumstance is not the thing:*
> Bliss *is the same, in subject or in king,*
> *In who obtain defence, or who defend;*
> *In him who is, or him who finds, a friend.*
>   Essay on man, Epist. 4.[71]

And again,

> *Heav'n, forming each on other to depend,*
> *A master, or a servant, or a friend,*
> *Bids each on other for assistance call,*
> *'Till one man's weakness grows the strength of all.*
> *Wants, frailties, passions, closer still allye*

---

70. Horace, *Odes,* IV.i.30: "trustful hope of love returned." Horace, *Odes and Epodes,* trans. C. E. Bennett, Loeb Classical Library (Cambridge and London: Harvard University Press, 1968).

71. Pope, *Essay on Man,* IV.49–60.

The common int'rest, or endear the tye:
To these *we owe true friendship, love sincere,*
Each home-felt joy that life inherits here.
                              Essay on man, Epist. 2.[72]

If we take an impartial view of mankind, we shall find, that with all the
inequalities which social happiness or intercourse of good and kindly
offices require, there is however such an equality, that every man does
in reality bring into the common stock, together with his share of the
natural affections common to all men, a certain *peculium,* something
proper to himself, which is of great use or rather necessity to the common welfare of the kind: and that can be nothing else but some particular ability, or some peculiar modification of the natural and common
affections. This will plainly appear if we distinguish well between what
is natural and what is acquired; and remember that, as nothing could be
acquired were there nothing natural, <189> since art or exercise can only
diversify what was originally of nature's growth or implantation, and
that according to settled methods and connexions fixed by nature for
making acquisitions of any kind by exercise and art possible; so were
nothing left to art and exercise, nothing would of course be left to ourselves to do; we could make no acquisitions at all. There are indeed acquired dispositions which are very prejudicial to society; but these are
affections in themselves exceeding useful, perverted by wrong associations of ideas and bad habits: and what diversity is there among mankind
with respect to ability, genius and temper, that there is ground to think
natural, which is not necessary to the various employments and pursuits
without which there cannot be merit of different kinds, nor a sufficient
variety of happiness and perfection in human life? What natural talent
or turn of mind is not a good foundation to work upon, or may not be
improved to the great advantage of society? Let us but think what an
insipid state ours would be, were there not that diversity of turns and
casts of mind, so to speak, among mankind which now obtains; or if all
men had the same qualities precisely in the same degree; and there were

Marginal note: Natural diversities make dif-
ferent materials
for a variety of
good by our
own improve-
ment, or of
our own
acquisition.

---

72. Pope, *Essay on Man,* II.249–56.

no differences among them at all? Variety is as necessary to general beauty, perfection and good, as uniformity: it is uniformity amidst variety, which produces beauty and good in the sensible world. And it is uniformity amidst variety amongst mankind, which alone could render them capable of similar beauty and good in the moral way; or make them a system of beings in which variety of beauty and good of the moral sort could have place, equal or analogous to that variety of beauty and good, which constitutes the riches and greatness, the magnificence and fulness of the corporeal world. In fine, 'tis as impossible that there can be society amongst mankind without great diversity of powers, abilities, <190> and dispositions, as it is that there can be a whole without parts, of various natures adjusted to one another by their differences, and so making a whole.

Benevolence or social affection naturally works in these proper proportions which the general good of society requires.

It operates like attraction in the material world.

III. Let it be remarked, in the third place, with regard to our natural qualifications for society and social happiness; that the social or uniting principle in us is fitted by nature to operate in those proportions, which are most conducive to the common good of our kind. I cannot better explain this than by comparing the uniting, benevolent principle in our nature to attraction in the material system. It is indeed moral or social attraction,[a] and operates like the other proportionally, as best suits to the upholding of the whole fabric in perfect order: it is strongest and most sensible when close cohesion is absolutely necessary, as betwixt parents and offspring: and it diminishes in proportion as we are removed from one another. Yet so are we framed, that with regard to our whole kind, when that idea is reflected upon or presented to us, it is experienced to be exceedingly warm and strong. We all feel that the general good cannot be considered without such due affection towards it, that there is a disposition and tendency in our breasts to submit all particular con-

a. See an excellent paper in the *Guardian* to this purpose. [*The Guardian,* started by Sir Richard Steele, ran from March to October 1713. Addison, Berkeley, Pope, and Gay were among the contributors. The reference is to no. 126. See *The Guardian,* ed. John Calhoun Stephens (Lexington: University Press of Kentucky, 1982).]

nexions and attachments to it, with a strong conviction of the fitness of such submission. Man must first be able to conceive a large whole, and to consider mankind as one family, before he can feel affection to his kind as such: but as one can hardly think at all without being led to perceive the common relation of men to one another as one kind; so every one soon attains to this idea, or rather it obtrudes itself upon all men whether they will or not; and the idea of one's own child does not more necessarily excite natural <191> affection, than the notion of one kind begets strong public affection toward it as such. Hence it is that no person capable of reflexion is not touched with the distress of a man as man, without any other attachment; and does not, on the other hand, rejoice and perceive pleasure, even at the recital of happiness enjoyed in any part of the world, or at any period of time, however remote from all his private interests. Now this is the cement or attraction towards a common center, which together with the particular attractions between persons nearly joined and related, or particularly adapted and suited one to another, holds the whole system of mankind together, or by which it coheres. This is indeed the natural progress of the human mind.

> *God loves from whole to parts: but human soul*
> *Must rise from individual to the whole.*
> Self-love *but serves the virtuous mind to wake,*
> *As the small pebble stirs the peaceful lake,*
> *The centre mov'd, a circle strait succeeds,*
> *Another still, and still another spreads,*
> *Friend, parent, neighbour, first it will embrace,*
> *His country next, and next all human race;*
> *Wide, and more wide, th'o'erflowings of the mind*
> *Take ev'ry creature in, of ev'ry kind;*
> *Earth smiles around, with boundless bounty blest,*
> *And Heav'n beholds its image in his breast.*
> Essay on man, Epist. 4.[73]

73. Pope, *Essay on Man*, IV.361–72.

The notion of a public good is no sooner formed than due affection arises towards it.

The notion of a public good, or of the universal happiness of our kind, is a complicated idea, which is not immediately apprehended so soon as one sees or feels, but requires some reflexion and a progress of the mind to form it; whereas particular generous affections are immediately excited by their proper objects, some of which are ever assailing the mind; (as in the case of natural affection, properly so called, sympathy with the dis-<192>tressed, and complacency with the happiness of others, naturally dear and near to us.) But nature has fitted the mind to form the idea of our kind, and of its general good; for every particular exercise of the mind in the benevolent social way, naturally tends to beget and establish such a prevalency of good humour, tenderness, and benevolence in the general temperature of the mind; as when it is formed, must naturally dispose it to seek for exercise and entertainment to itself in the most enlarged way; and thus the inclination to extend benevolence growing with every particular exertion of it, the idea of good to be pursued, will naturally expand itself, till it not merely comprehends our own kind, but takes in and embraces all beings in general, or the whole system of nature. As the excitement of every particular object naturally supposes its object present to the mind, either really or in fancy; so the notion of public good must precede the desire and pursuit of it; but in proportion as the temper is sweetned by particular exercises of generous affection, the mind will enlarge and open itself to make more room for benevolence to exert all its benignity; and so a more comprehensive object will naturally be imagined. And when the idea of public good is but once so far extended as to take in our own species as one kind, it naturally, and as it were necessarily inflames the breast with affection, large, extensive and overflowing, in proportion to the greatness and comprehensiveness of the idea which bestirs it.

And our mind is so fitted by nature to form that notion that we cannot avoid forming it.

But benevolence, like other affections, is liable to changes, and may be diminished or strengthened.

This will be strongly felt, if one who hath experienced any of the particular and more limited outgoings of the mind in natural affection, compassion, or friendship, will but ask his own heart.—And if this be duty, what then does my country require at my hands?—Hath the public no claim upon me?—For if he but understands these questions, and can put them to himself; nature will quickly give the <193> answer by a sudden overflowing of the warmest affection towards the public,[a] to which he will feel every other passion submitting itself, as conscious of its fit subordinacy or inferiority to it.

Let it however be remarked, that the analogy between moral and natural gravitation must fail in this respect, that whereas the latter is only a mechanical principle which we cannot change; the former is a moral principle, and therefore subject to diversities superinduceable by ourselves, in consequence particularly of the law of habits and associations of ideas already mentioned; insomuch that benevolence may be exceedingly weakened and diminished, thro' the prevalence of other passions. If therefore in some constitutions benevolence is very weak, and self-love is almost the only prevailing principle, let it be called to mind that in other constitutions self-love is really too weak, and some generous affection is too strong. From hence it follows, that as in the latter case it would be absurd to argue from some few instances, that the principle of self-love had originally no place in our frame; so, by parity of reason, it would be equally absurd to infer from a few particular instances, where self-love is too strong, and benevolence almost quite extinct, that originally there was no social principle in our nature. Such changes are all accountable whether on the one side or on the other, and in general with regard to all passions, in the same way; that is, from different associations of ideas, and different contracted habits. The only inference, experience leads to with regard to them is, "That passions are overpowered by passions; and that passions grow more powerful in proportion as they are indulged; or <194> as circumstances have conduced to excite and employ them; since by repeated acts all passions are proportionably wrought

---

a. See *Cicero's offices,* Book 1. No. 16. &c. Sed cum omnia ratione animoque lustraris, omnium societatum nulla est gravior, nulla carior, quam ea, quae cum repub. est unicuique nostrum: cari sunt parentes, cari liberi, propinqui, familiares: sed omnes omnium caritates patria una complexa est. [Cicero, *De officiis,* I.xvii.57: "But when with a rational spirit you have surveyed the whole field, there is no social relation among them all more close, none more dear than that which links each one of us with our country. Parents are dear; dear are children, relatives, friends; but our native land embraces all our loves."]

It is difficult to
determine the
original forces
of any affec-
tions in our
hearts.

into temper." It may indeed be difficult, perhaps impossible, to determine the original forces of benevolent passions in any particular constitution antecedent to all particular exitements and exercises; since from
the beginning objects which naturally excite and employ them are continually affecting us, and calling them forth into exercises or acts: but
then it is no less so for the same reason to determine precisely the forces
of the private or selfish affections. We see variety in both cases, and we
know how this variety must arise from circumstances of exercise and
action in either case. But he who denies any social tendency in our nature
to our kind, or the original implantation in us of any principles besides
the meer selfish affections, and ascribes all that is social or kindly in us
to education, custom and superinduced habits, is obliged to give an account of moral phenomena, which are absolutely inexplicable upon that
supposition; since we may appeal even to the most selfish person, to him
who has studied and laboured the most to make himself such, and to
extinguish all regards to others, whether he has been able to succeed:
whether he can attain to his ends, so as never to feel any stirrings within
him of social and public affections; and whether he can ever seriously
and deliberately, in conversation with his own heart, approve to himself
such an aim. If benevolence is superinduced, and not originally from
nature, whence comes it universally that this customary and superinduced nature, is stronger than original nature itself; insomuch that, far
from being capable of being totally destroyed, it is ever thwarting the
selfish passions, and creating discontent and remorse in a narrow, sordid
breast. This truly cannot otherwise be explained, (unless it is affirmed
that habits may be contracted by repeated acts, <195> without any design
or appointment of the Author of nature that it should be so) but by
saying, that though nature has not planted in us originally any social
propensions, yet the circumstances of human life are so ordered by the
Author of it, that these propensions must necessarily arise in every mind
to such a degree of strength, that nothing shall be able afterwards to
eradicate them; nay, so much as to hinder them from exciting bitter dissatisfaction with ones self in the selfish mind whether he will or will not;
or at least, from creating horrible disturbance and remorse within such
breasts, as often as they sincerely ask themselves, whether the selfish con-

But it cannot
be asserted that
there is noth-
ing social in
our nature,
without deny-
ing the most
evident truths
or facts.

duct be right or wrong, approveable or disapproveable. If he says, the part that man *ought* or *ought not* to act, *right* and *wrong, fit* and *unfit,* are cheats, or meer words without any meaning, he is not one bit nearer to the solution required of him for the phenomena now under consideration. Because the question still returns, why are human affairs so ordered; if these words express no moral immutable differences of affections and actions, and correspondent obligations, that yet universally every thinking man, as often as he thinks, must approve or disapprove, according to that deceit or false imagination, and cannot possibly approve[a] or <196> disapprove according to any other rule, however he may act? For this is as certain as attraction, elasticity, or any other quality of bodies perceived by our senses, that no person ever can, at any time of life, reflect upon his actions, and approve of falsehood, dissimulation

---

a. See how charmingly *Cicero* argues this point, *de legibus,* Lib. I. No. 15, &c. Atqui, si natura confirmatura jus non erit, virtutes omnes tollantur. Ubi enim liberalitas, ubi patriae caritas, ubi pietas, ubi aut bene merendi de altero, aut referendae gratiae voluntas poterit existere? Nam haec nascantur ex eo, quod *naturâ propensi sumus ad diligendos homines,* quod fundamentum juris est.—Atqui nos legem bonam a mala, nulla alia nisi naturae norma dividere possumus. Nec solum jus & injuria a natura dijudicatur, sed omnino omnia honesta, ac turpia. Nam & communis intelligentia nobis notas res efficit, easque in animis nostris inchoavit, ut honesta in virtute ponantur, in vitiis turpia. Haec autem in opinione existimare, non in natura posita, dementis est. Nam nec arboris, nec equi virtus, quae dicitur (in quo abutimur homine) in opinione sita est, sed in natura. Quod si ita est; honesta quoque, & turpia, naturâ, dijudicanda sunt, &c. [Cicero, *De legibus:* "And if nature is not to be considered the foundation of justice, that will mean the destruction of the virtues on which human society depends. For where then will there be a place for generosity, or love of country, or loyalty, or the inclination to be of service to others or to show gratitude for favours received? For these virtues originate in our natural inclination to love our fellow-men, and this is the foundation of justice" (I.xv.43). "But in fact we can perceive the difference between good laws and bad by referring them to no other standard than nature; indeed, it is not merely justice and injustice which are distinguished by nature, but also and without exception things which are honourable and dishonourable. For since an intelligence common to us all makes things known to us and formulates them in our minds, honourable actions are ascribed by us to virtue, and dishonourable actions to vice; and only a madman would conclude that these judgments are matters of opinion, and not fixed by nature. For even what we, by a misuse of the term, call the virtue of a tree or of a horse, is not a matter of opinion, but is based on nature. And if that is true, honourable and dishonourable actions must also be distinguished by nature, etc." (I.xvi.44–45).]

and dishonesty, not to say barbarity and cruelty: or not approve truth, veracity, candour, gratitude and benevolence, and public spirit.

How the mind is differently affected by any ideas or objects, is matter of experience, and therefore the fact rests upon the same indubitable evidence which ascertains other facts, that is, experience. But in accounting for this fact, it is necessary to resolve it ultimately into our being originally so framed as to be so affected; in which case, the original sociality of our nature is acknowledged; or it must be resolved into a secondary intention of nature, to bring about our being so affected by moral objects, which, so far as it has any meaning at all, must be, to all intents and purposes, the same with a primary and original intention or appointment of nature. There is no middle hypothesis between these two, to explain the matter by. And to say that this, or any influence of objects upon the mind, may be totally the effect of education, custom, exercise, or art, or any cause whatsoever, without any intention or appointment of nature that it should be so, must terminate ultimately in saying, that effects may be produced without causes, or without any appointed manner of their being produced. Now how absurd would it appear to every one, if a person should say, that an artist may work matter into any intended form, any how, at random, without any means, or by whatsoever means he pleases; or that he could do it, though there were no certain knowable way of doing it. This would unanimously be owned to shock all common sense: and yet it is the very same thing that must

The absurdity of supposing social or any affection to be produced by art.

<197> be said by those who ascribe all that is social in our nature to art, custom, and superadded habit, without nature's having at least appointed the way in which art, custom, and superadded habit may produce such an effect. For were there not originally in us certain qualities for art and exercise to operate upon, according to certain fixed methods of nature's institution, there would be no materials for art to work upon; nor no means of operating by any moral art or exercise. In moral nature, as well as in the material world, no quality can be superinduced which is entirely the product of art. All arts of the one kind, as well as of the other, are but certain methods of bringing forth into action qualities naturally belonging to subjects, according to the means appointed by nature for bringing them forth into action, in this or the other degree or proportion, and with these or the other appearances. I shall conclude

this head with an admirable description of nature, our social nature in particular, by the excellent moral poet so often quoted.

> *GOD, in the nature of each being, founds*
> *Its proper bliss, and sets its proper bounds:*
> *But as he fram'd a whole, the whole to bless*
> *On mutual wants built mutual happiness:*
> *So from the first eternal order ran,*
> *And creature link'd to creature, man to man.*
> *Whate'er of life all-quick'ning aether keeps,*
> *Or breathes thro' air, or shoots beneath the deeps,*
> *Or pours profuse on earth; one nature feeds*
> *The vital flame, and swells the genial seeds.*
> *Not man alone, but all that roam the wood,*
> *Or wing the sky, or roll along the flood,*
> *Each loves itself, but not itself alone,*
> *Each sex desires alike, till two are one:*
> *Nor ends the pleasure with the fierce embrace;*
> *They love themselves, a third time, in their race.* <198>
> *Thus beast and bird their common charge attend,*
> *The mothers nurse it, and the sires defend;*
> *The young dismiss'd to wander earth or air,*
> *There stops the instinct, and there ends the care,*
> *The link dissolves, each seeks a fresh embrace,*
> *Another love succeeds, another race.*
> *A longer care man's helpless kind demands;*
> *That longer care contracts more lasting bands:*
> *Reflection, reason, still the ties improve,*
> *At once extend the int'rest, and the love:*
> *With choice we fix, with simpathy we burn,*
> *Each virtue in each passion takes its turn;*
> *And still new needs, new helps, new habits rise,*
> *That graft benevolence on charities.*
> *Still as one brood, and as another rose,*
> *These nat'ral love maintain'd, habitual those;*
> *The last scarce ripen'd into perfect man,*
> *Saw helpless him from whom their life began:*
> *Mem'ry and forecast, just returns engage,*
> *That pointed back to youth, this on to age:*

While pleasure, gratitude, and hope combin'd
Still spread the int'rest, and preserv'd the kind.
                                    Essay on man, Epist. 3.[74]

The necessary dependence of social happiness and perfection on right social union. IV. I shall now take notice of something that is yet more particularly the result of our social make, or of our being formed to promote common happiness by joint endeavours. And it is, that in consequence of such an end, and of the make proper to that end, the perfection and happiness of human society must depend on the aptitude of the union into which it is formed, that is, upon its fitness and propriety to promote that end. If happiness must be promoted by joint endeavours, or united application, as social happiness must be according to the very definition of it, then is uniting necessary to it: but joining or uniting in one method, or according to one form, cannot be so proper to promote the end of union, which is public <199> happiness, as joining or uniting in another form. Need I stay to prove what is as evident, as that there may be a better and a worse mechanism for the end of a watch? Yet if this be true, it evidently follows, that the greatest common happiness and perfection of society cannot be effected, but in proportion to the fitness of the form in which society is constituted, to procure that end. Accordingly, the most remarkable differences among societies are such as result from their political forms, or from the natural tendency of their laws, government, and civil policies. There are, indeed, other differences, as with regard to climate, soil, and other such things depending on physical causes. But are not the chief differences confessed to be such as result from civil constitutions, or the various forms of government? If, for example, the flourishing of all the ingenious arts, of philosophy in all its branches, of poetry, statuary, painting, sculpture, architecture, &c. constitute a very considerable part of the happiness and grandeur of society, as being the properest methods for employing men's noblest faculties, and all the wealth that may be purchased by commerce: If it be true, that it is the polite arts which give taste and lustre to human life, or add elegance and

---

74. Pope, *Essay on Man*, III.109–46.

a due polish to it; that they are the *grandeur and grace,*[a] *and comely pride of mankind, without which wealth rots a nusance:* if this be true, it is at the same time equally certain, that one form of government is fit for promoting these arts, and another is quite the reverse. "Hence it is that these arts have been delivered down to us in such perfection by free nations, who from the nature of their government, as from a proper soil, produced the generous plants; whilst the mightiest bodies and vastest empires, governed by force and despotic power, could, after ages of peace and leisure, produce no other than what was deformed and barba-<200>rous of the kind."[75] It was in consequence of this natural fitness or unfitness of certain moral means with respect to certain moral ends, that the laws of *Lycurgus,* according to the confession of *Aristotle, Plato,* and other wise and observing politicians, tended to make men ferocious, and to prevent their being civilized and polished by the humanizing arts: there was no provision made by that institution for their culture and advancement; but, on the contrary, all was calculated to exclude them; and therefore they could not possibly be engendered, far less could they come to perfection in such a state: whilst, on the other hand, at *Athens* they flourished, because every thing concurred to promote them. But it is not my business now to examine different forms of government. All that belongs to our present purpose is, to remark that men are capable of a very great degree of grandeur and happiness, as we feel by experience, in consequence of our own most happy constitution, and its aptitude to promote public spirit, virtue, and arts, beyond any other in the world: and that the perfection and happiness of mankind must depend upon the natural fitness of the form of government they live under, or of their civil and religious constitution, in order to produce that end, is as certain as that there are proper and improper means with relation to any end; or that no end can be accomplished, but by the means fit to attain it: an universal self-evident truth in moral as well as natural mechanism, or with respect to moral ends as well as natural ones. In conse-

Margin notes: Some states are adjusted to one end, some to another.

Every moral end, as well as every natural one, hath its natural and necessary means, by which alone it can be accomplished.

a. *Liberty,* by Mr. *Thomson.* [James Thomson (1700–1748), *Liberty, a Poem* (1735–36). The quote is a compilation from lines 376–87 of part 5.]

75. Shaftesbury, "Soliloquy" II.ii, in *Characteristics,* ed. Klein, 107.

quence of which it is that the science of politics consists in judging of
the propriety and fitness, moral and political, of means to bring about
and promote the sole end of government, the happiness of subjects. And
hence it is accordingly that philosophers and politicians have been able,
in many instances, to form such true judgments of the different forms
of government, laws and policies, as <201> (like *Polybius*,[a] with regard
to the *Roman* republic) to foretel the revolutions and changes of government which must happen, merely from the exact knowledge of the
necessary effects of moral causes. Here, as well as in the natural world,
effects may be with certainty inferred from their causes; for in both cases,
from a certain concurrence of circumstances or causes, certain consequences necessarily result. To be satisfied of this, one needs only look
into the political reasonings of any good writer on politics, *Aristotle, Polybius,* or our own *Harrington.* So that we may lay down all that is requisite for our purpose to make out as an indisputable truth. That such
is the natural dependence of men upon each other, that they cannot
attain to the perfection and happiness for which they are intended by

Hence it is that politics is a science.

a. Hence it is that the political science is able to amount to what *Cor. Nepos* says
in his Life of *Atticus,* concerning *Cicero's* Letters to him.—Quae qui legat non multum desideret historiam contextam, illorum temporum. Sic enim omnia de studiis
principum, vitiis ducum, mutationibus reipub. perscripta sunt, ut nihil in iis non
appareat: & facile existimari possit, prudentiam quodammodo esse *Divinationem.*
Non enim Cicero ea solum quae vivo se acciderunt futura praedixit: sed etiam que
nunc usu veniunt, cecinit vates. To be satisfied of the truth of this remark, one needs
only look into the sixth book of *Polybius,* and observe from what principles he reasons. And if we consult our own *Harrington,* we shall see from his reasonings in one
single instance, *viz.* about property, how necessarily the happiness of mankind depends upon a good constitution, sagely and honestly administred. [Cornelius Nepos,
Liber de Latinis historicis XXV, *Atticus* XV.16: "One who reads these does not feel
great need of a connected history of those times; for such complete details are given
of the rivalry of the chief men, the faults of the leaders, the changes of government,
that there is nothing that they do not make clear, and it may readily appear that
Cicero's foresight was almost divination. For he not only predicted the events that
actually happened during his lifetime, but, like a seer, foretold those which are now
being experienced." *Cornelius Nepos,* trans. John C. Rolfe (Cambridge: Harvard University Press; London: Heinemann, 1984). Polybius (ca. 203–ca. 120 B.C.) was a Greek
historian whose *History* of Rome covers the period from the first Punic War to the
destruction of Corinth; this is a major theme of James Harrington's *The Commonwealth of Oceana,* in *The Political Works of James Harrington,* ed. and intr. J. G. A.
Pocock (Cambridge: Cambridge University Press, 1977).]

nature, but by their uniting together, in order to promote it by their joint application: and that there are in the nature of things, improper and proper means of acting for obtaining that end. We are certainly intended by nature for whatever happiness and perfection we are qualified to pursue and attain to, whether singly or by united force. But all means and manners of uniting together, can no more be equally proper for attaining to an end in moral combinations of powers or qualities, than in natu-<202>ral ones. And the wisdom and goodness of our Author clearly appears in making us social, and reciprocally dependent; in fitting us for attaining to a very great degree of happiness and perfection in that way; in prompting us by our natural benevolence, and other dispositions, to establish ourselves into the best form for that end; and in directing us to find it out by our moral sense.

This is all the provision nature could make for uniting us together in the properest form, consistently with making our chief interest dependent on ourselves, or happiness to be our own acquisition. And thus nature appears to be exceeding kind, especially when we call to mind, that though social happiness makes social dependence absolutely necessary; yet at the same time, the chief happiness of every private man, as far as it can be acquired singly, or independently of society rightly constituted and modelled, consists in the exercise of the same virtuous temper, which fits for and points to the proper manner of uniting, in order to promote general happiness or perfection; it being in every one's power, considered as one individual, to regulate his affections according to the real nature of things or truth; from which government of opinions and affections no unhappiness results; but from it, on the contrary, do many goods naturally spring, in comparison of which, all other enjoyments are of very little consideration or importance, equally gross and unsatisfactory, as has been already observed. "Thus, then, it plainly appears that we are excellently formed for procuring to ourselves that true perfection and happiness, which must, in the nature of things, be the effect of right government, or well-constituted society." Let us now consider, whether man, who is made for virtue and society, hath any further respect; or whether he is not likewise made for the pleasures of true religion and pure devotion. <203>

Nature could not have dealt more kindly with us than it hath done, by making us social creatures, and by pointing and prompting us to right union by our natural disposition to society, and by our moral sense.

Conclusion.

Man cannot open his eyes to consider the stupendous frame of nature, to contemplate his own make, or indeed any other object which strikes his sense or understanding, without apprehending or conceiving some mighty power that made, upholds and governs all. The idea of a creating and sustaining power or principle immediately presents itself to his mind. He cannot escape forming it; so strongly does nature, every thing in nature, bespeak and proclaim it to him.[a] Hence that idea may be called *innate;* that is, an intelligible form or conception, which offers itself

a. All the reasoning in this chapter is chiefly taken from *Cicero:* See *de legibus,* Lib. I. No. 7. & sequ.—Est igitur, quoniam nihil est ratione melius, eaque & in homine, & in deo; prima homini cum deo rationis societas. Inter quos autem ratio, inter eosdem etiam recta ratio communis est. Quae cum sit lex, lege quoque consociati homines cum diis putandi sumus. Inter quos porrò est communio legis, inter eos communio juris est.—Ut jam universus hic mundus, una civitas communis deorum, atque hominum, existimanda.—Cumque alia quibus cohaerent homines, è mortali genere sumserint, quae fragilia essent, & caduca; animum tamen esse ingeneratum à deo: ex quo verè vel agnatio nobis cum caelestibus.—Itaque ex tot generibus nullum est animal, praeter hominem, quod habeat notitiam aliquam dei: ipsisque in hominibus nulla gens est neque tam immansueta, neque tam fera, quae non, etiam si ignoret, qualem habere deum deceat, tamen habendum sciat. Ex quo efficitur illud, ut is agnoscat Deum, qui, unde ortus sit, quasi recordetur, ac noscat. Jam verò virtus eadem in homine, ac deo est.—Est autem virtus nihil aliud, quàm, in se perfecta, & ad summum perducta natura. Est igitur homini cum deo similitudo. Quod cum ita sit, quae tandem potest esse proprior certiorve cognatio? Quid est enim verius, quam neminem esse oportere tam stulte arrogantem, ut in se rationem, & mentem, putet inesse, in coelo, mundoque non putet? Aut ut ea, quae vix summa ingenii ratione comprehendat, nulla ratione moveri putet? quem vero *astrorum* ordines, &c. Compare *de natura deorum,* Lib. II. Et tamen ex ipsa hominum solertia esse aliquam mentem, & eam quidem acriorem, & divinam, existimare debemus. *Unde enim hanc homo arripuit?* ut ait apud Xenophontem Socrates.—Ut si quis in domum aliquam, aut in gymnasium, aut in forum venerit: cum videat omnium rerum rationem, modum

Another class of laws.

Those relative to religion.

Man is made for religion as well as for virtue.

disciplinam, non possit ea sine causa fieri judicare, sed esse aliquem intelligat, qui praesit, & cui pareatur: multo magis in tantis, motionibus, tantisque vicissitudinibus, tam multarum rerum, atque tantarum ordinibus, in quibus nihil umquam immensa, & infinita vetustas mentita sit, statuat necesse est, ab aliqua mente tantos naturae motus gubernari.—Si enim, est aliquid in rerum natura, quod hominis mens, quod ratio, quod vis, quod potestas humana efficere non possit: est certe id, quod illud efficit, homine melius. Atqui res coelestes—Quid vero? tanta rerum consentiens, conspirans, continuata cognatio, quem non coget ea, quae dicuntur a me comprobare?— Haec ita fieri omnibus inter se concinentibus mundi partibus profecto non possent, nisi ea uno divino, & continuato spiritu continerentur.—Talis igitur mens mundi cum sit, ob eamque causam, vel prudentia, vel providentia appellari recte possit, haec potissimum providet, & in his maxime est occupata, primum ut mundus quam aptissimus sit ad permanendum, deinde ut nulla re egeat, maxime autem ut in eo eximia pulchritudo sit, atque omnis ornatus.—Multae autem aliae naturae deorum ex magnis eorum beneficiis, & à Graeciae sapientibus, & a majoribus nostris constitutae, nominataeque sunt. Quidquid enim magnam utilitatem generi afferret humano, id non sine divina bonitate erga homines fieri arbitrabantur. Itaque tum illud, quod erat à deo natum, nomine ipsius dei nuncupabant.—Tum autem res ipsa, in qua vis inest major aliqua, sic appellatur, ut ea ipsa vis nominetur deus.—Alia quoque ex ratione, & quidem physica, magna fluxit multitudo deorum: qui induti specie humana fabulas poetis suppeditaverunt.—Videtisne igitur, ut à physicis rebus, bene, atque utiliter inventis, tracta ratio sit ad commentitios, & fictos deos? quae res genuit falsas opiniones, erroresque turbulentos, & superstitiones paene aniles.—Haec & dicuntur, & creduntur stultissime, & plena sunt futilitatis, summaeque levitatis.—Sed tamen, his fabulis spretis, ac repudiatis, deus pertinens per naturam cujusque rei—Cultus autem deorum est optimus, idemque castissimus, atque sanctissimus, plenissimusque pietatis, ut eos semper pura, integra, incorrupta & mente, & voce veneremur. *De natura deorum,* Lib. II.—Superstitio fusa per genteis, oppressit omnium fere animos, atque hominum imbecillitatem occupavit.—Nec vero (id enim diligentur intelligi volo) superstitione tollenda religio tollitur.—Esse praestantem aliquam, aeternamque naturam, & eam suspiciendam, admirandamque hominum generi, pulchritudo mundi, ordoque rerum caelestium cogit confiteri. Quamobrem ut religio propaganda etiam est, quae est juncta cum cognitione naturae: sic superstitionis stirpes omnes ejiciendae. *De divinat.* Lib. II.—Sed sic, Scipio, ut avus hic tuus, ut ego, qui te genui, justitiam cole, & pietatem: quae, cum sit magna in parentibus, & propinquis; tum in patria maxima est: ea vita, via est in caelum, & in hunc coetum eorum, qui jam vixerunt, & corpore laxati illum incolunt locum.—*Somn. Scipionis.* Etenim cognitio contemplatioque manca naturae, quodam modo, atque inchoata sit, si nulla actio rerum consequatur. Ea autem actio in hominum commodis tuendis maxime cernitur. Pertinet igitur ad societatem generis humani. Ergo haec cognitioni anteponenda est: atque id optimus quisque re ipsa ostendit, & judicat.—Itaque nisi ea virtus, quae constat ex hominibus tuendis, id est, ex societate generis humani, attingat cognitionem rerum, solivaga cognitio, & jejuna videatur. Itemque magnitudo animi, remota communitate, conjunctioneque humana, feritas sit quaedam immanitas. *De Offic.*

Lib. I.—Ergo hoc quidem apparet, nos ad agendum esse natos; actionem autem genera plura.—maximae autem sunt, primum, ut mihi quidem videtur, consideratio, cognitione rerum coelestium, quas a natura occultatas, & latenteis, indagare ratio potest: deinde rerumpub. administratio, aut administrandi, sciendique prudens, temperata, fortis & justa ratio, reliquaeque virtutes, & actiones virtutibus congruentes, quae uno verbo complexi omnia, honesta dicimus: ad quorum etiam cognitionem, & usum jam corroborati, *natura ipsa praeeunte* deducimur. Omnium enim rerum principia parva sunt, sed suis progressionibus usa augentur, &c. *De finibus,* Lib. 5. Sed praesto est domina omnium & regina ratio, quae connexa per se, & progressa longius fit perfecta virtus. Haec ut imperet isti parti animi, quae obidire debet, id videndum est viro. Quonam modo? inquies. Velut dominus servo, velut imperator militi. Quae sunt ista arma? contentio, confirmatio, sermo intimus cum ipse secum.—Obversantur species honestae animo. It is reason, good sense, or philosophy, that must preside, in order to preserve the human mind sound, governable, and unfantastical. O vitae dux, virtutis indagatrix. *Cic. tusc. quaest.* Lib. V. [Cicero, *De legibus:* "Therefore, since there is nothing better than reason, and since it exists both in man and God, the first common possession of man and God is reason. But those who have reason in common must also have right reason in common. And since right reason is law, we must believe that men have law also in common with the gods. . . . Hence we must now conceive of this whole universe as one commonwealth of which both gods and men are members" (I.vii.23). "For while the other elements of which man consists were derived from what is mortal, and are therefore fragile and perishable, the soul was generated in us by God. Hence we are justified in saying that there is a blood relationship between ourselves and the celestial beings" (I.viii.24). "Therefore among all the varieties of living beings, there is no creature except man which has any knowledge of God, and among men themselves there is no race either so civilised or so savage as not to know that it must believe in a god, even if it does not know in what sort of god it ought to believe. Thus it is clear that man recognises God because, in a way, he remembers and recognises the source from which he sprang. Moreover, virtue exists in God and man alike . . . virtue, however, is nothing else than nature perfected and developed to its highest point; therefore there is a likeness between man and God. As this is true, what relationship could be closer or clearer than this one?" (I.viii.25). "Indeed, what is more true than that no one ought to be so foolishly proud as to think that, though reason and intellect exist in himself, they do not exist in the heavens and the universe, or that those things which can hardly be understood by the highest reasoning powers of the human intellect are guided by no reason at all? In truth, the man that is not driven to gratitude by the orderly courses of the stars, etc." (II.vii.16). Cicero, *De re publica, De legibus,* trans. Clinton Walker Keyes, Loeb Classical Library (London: Heinemann; New York: Putnam, 1928). Compare *De natura deorum:* "Yet even man's intelligence must lead us to infer the existence of a mind, and that a mind of surpassing ability, and in fact divine. Otherwise, whence did man 'pick up' (as Socrates says in Xenophon) the intelligence that he possesses?" (II.vi.18). "When a man goes into a house, a wrestling-school or a public assembly and observes in all that goes on arrangement, regularity and system, he cannot possibly suppose that these things come about without a cause: he realises that there is someone who presides and controls. Far more therefore with the vast movements and phases of the heavenly bodies, and these ordered processes of a multitude of enormous masses of matter, which throughout the countless ages of the infinite past have never in the smallest degree played false, is he compelled to infer that these mighty world-motions are regulated by some mind" (II.iv.15). "If there be something in the world that man's mind and human reason, strength and power are incapable of producing, that which produces it must necessarily be superior to man; now the heavenly bodies . . ." (II.vi.16). "Again, consider the sympathetic agreement, interconnection and affinity of things: whom will this not compel to approve the truth of what I say? . . . These processes and this musical harmony of all the parts of the world assuredly could not go on were they not maintained in unison by a single divine and all-pervading spirit" (II.vii.19). "Such being the nature of the world-mind, it can therefore be correctly designated as prudence or providence; and this providence is chiefly directed and concentrated upon three objects, namely to secure for the world, first, the structure best fitted for survival; next, absolute completeness; but chiefly, consummate beauty and embellishment of every kind" (II.xxii.58). "Many other divinities however have with good reason been recognised and named both by the wisest men of Greece and by our ancestors from the great benefits that they bestow. For it was thought that whatever confers great utility on the human race must be due to the operation of divine benevolence towards men. Thus sometimes a thing sprung from a god was called by the name of the god himself" (II.xxiii.60). "In other cases some exceptionally potent force is itself designated by a title of divinity" (II.xxiii.61). "Another theory also, and that a scientific one, has been the source of a number of deities, who clad in human form have furnished the poets with legends" (II.xxiv.63). "Do you see therefore how from a true and valuable philosophy of nature has been evolved this imaginary and fanciful pantheon? The perversion has been a fruitful source of false beliefs, crazy errors and superstitions hardly above the level of old wives' tales. . . . These stories and these beliefs are utterly foolish; they are stuffed with nonsense and absurdity of all sorts" (II.xxviii.70). "But though repudiating these myths with contempt, we shall nevertheless be able to understand the personality and the nature of the divinities pervading the substance of the several elements. . . . But the best and also the purest, holiest and most pious way of worshipping the gods is ever to venerate them with purity, sincerity and innocence both of thought and of speech" (II.xxviii.71). Cicero, *De natura deorum, Academica,* trans. H. Rackham, Loeb Classical Library (London: Heinemann; New York: Putnam, 1933). *De divinatione,* II.lxxii.148–49: "superstition, which is widespread among the nations, has taken advantage of human weakness to cast its spell over the mind of almost every man. . . . But I want it distinctly understood that the destruction of superstition does not mean the destruction of religion . . . the celestial order and the beauty of the universe compel me to confess that there is some excellent and eternal being,

—————

who deserves the homage and respect of men. Wherefore, just as it is a duty to extend the influence of true religion, which is closely associated with the knowledge of nature, so it is a duty to weed out every root of superstition." Cicero, *De senectute, De amicitia, De divinatione,* trans. William Armstead Falconer, Loeb Classical Library (Cambridge: Harvard University Press; London, Heinemann, 1923).

The *Somnio Scipionis* appears as part of Cicero's *De republica,* VI.xvi: "But, Scipio, imitate your grandfather here; imitate me, your father; love justice and duty, which are indeed strictly due to parents and kinsmen, but most of all to the fatherland. . . . Such a life is the road to the skies, to that gathering of those who have completed their earthly lives and been relieved of the body, and who live in yonder place." Cicero, *De re publica, De legibus,* trans. Clinton Walker Keyes, Loeb Classical Library (London: Heinemann; New York: Putnam, 1928).

De officiis: "for the study and knowledge of the universe would somehow be lame and defective, were no practical results to follow. Such results, moreover, are best seen in the safeguarding of human interests. It is essential, then, to human society; and it should, therefore, be ranked above speculative knowledge. Upon this, all the best men agree, as they prove by their conduct" (I.xliii.153). "And so, if that virtue [justice] which centres in the safeguarding of human interests, that is, in the maintenance of human society, were not to accompany the pursuit of knowledge, that knowledge would seem isolated and barren of results. In the same way, courage, if unrestrained by the uniting bonds of society, would be but a sort of brutality and savagery" (I.xliv.157).

De finibus, V.xxi.58: "It is therefore at all events manifest that we are designed by nature for activity. Activities vary in kind . . . but the most important are, first, according to my own view . . . the contemplation and the study of the heavenly bodies and of those secrets and mysteries of nature which reason has the capacity to penetrate; secondly, the practice and the theory of politics; thirdly, the principles of prudence, temperance, courage and justice, with the remaining virtues and the activities consonant therewith, all of which we may sum up under the single term of morality; towards the knowledge and practice of which, when we have grown to maturity, we are led onward by nature's own guidance. All things are small in their first beginnings, but they grow larger as they pass through their regular stages of progress." Cicero, *De finibus bonorum et malorum,* trans. H. Rackham, Loeb Classical Library (London: Heinemann; New York: Putnam, 1931).

Tusculanae disputationes, II.xxi.47–xxii.51: "but reason, the mistress and queen of the world, stands close at hand and mounting by her own strength and pressing onward she becomes completed virtue. It is man's duty to enable reason to have rule over that part of the soul which ought to obey. How is it to be done? you will say. Even as the master over the slave, or the general over the soldier. . . . What are the weapons he will need? He will brace and strengthen and commune with himself. . . . Let the ideals which a true man honours be kept constantly before his eyes." Cicero, *Tusculan Disputations,* trans. J. E. King, Loeb Classical Library (London: Heinemann; New York: Putnam, 1927).

Ibid., V.ii.5: "O thou guide of life, o thou explorer of virtue. . . ."]

naturally to the mind as soon as it reflects; an idea the mind cannot avoid if it thinks, but that necessarily occurs to every one. That it is so is plain from universal experience; for no fact is more certain, than that no nation ever was so barbarous, but that it acknowledged a supreme, independent, creating power, the father of the world and of mankind. <204>

We are necessarily led by the consideration of our own existence, which is felt to be derived and dependent, to perceive our dependence upon the Author of nature. And our moral sense, so soon as we think of a creating principle, naturally disposes us to ascribe the best disposition and temper to such a mind. So are we framed, that every effect leads us to apprehend a cause; and consequently, the existence of the world leads to apprehend an Author of it. And every thing great, regular or pro-portioned, excites admiration, either towards itself, if we imagine it an-imated; or, if not animated, towards some apprehended cause. No de-termination of our mind is more natural than this; no effect more universal: one has indeed better reason to deny the connexion between the sexes to be natural, than to deny a disposition in man to admire the Author of nature, which is a disposition to religion.[a]

He can hardly avoid forming the idea of a supreme power, upon which he abso-lutely depends.

Our sense of natural and moral beauty necessarily leads us to enquire into and admire the order, beauty, grandeur, wise and good oeconomy of the world; and to apprehend that our disposition to understand and love order and goodness cannot but proceed from an Author whose mind is perfect order and goodness. And, indeed, it is as certain as that we have intelligent powers, and a moral sense implanted in us, that our Creator must have in-<205>telligence, and benevolent, generous affections to-wards public good. For if the contrary is supposed, then are we more perfect than our maker; then have we in our nature a better, a more noble disposition than our Author, the contriver and creator of all our moral powers and dispositions, and of all the beauty, order, and good we see

And our moral sense naturally leads us to ascribe not only intelli-gence, but the love of order and benignity of temper, to the first or original mind.

a. *Hutcheson on the Passions.* [Francis Hutcheson, *An Essay on the Nature and Con-duct of the Passions. . . .* (1728); ed. Aaron Garrett (Indianapolis: Liberty Fund, 2002), I.vi.3.]

and admire. Nay, if the Author of nature has no perception of order, good and beauty, nor no disposition to approve it, then we have an excellent disposition in our frame of which he could not have any idea, and which is therefore blindly and undesignedly implanted in us. This reasoning is not above the reach of any one; it is what every person who thinks at all, is naturally led to by the turn and disposition of the human mind. For how can we avoid saying to ourselves, when we look upon the immense power, wisdom and goodness the creation manifests; when we look into our own minds, and consider our natural delight in analogy, harmonies, general laws, and the good that results from them; that whatever power or excellency, wisdom or order is derived, the Author from whom it comes, must posses such power, intelligence or virtue, in a degree far superior to all his creatures. He who gave us understanding, does he not understand? He who gave us reason, has he not supreme and perfect reason? He who gave us capacity of <206> perceiving order and delighting in it, does he not understand and love order? He who made us so that we must approve truth, veracity, benevolence, greatness of mind, and every virtue, and disapprove the contrary affections, does not he like those virtues, has he not a sense of their excellence? Does he not delight in them? Whence can he have copied the ideas of them but from his own mind? Had he not these excellencies originally in himself, whence could he have formed the notion of them; or whence could he have been moved and determined to give them to us, or to implant them in us? Could he form those, or any dispositions in our natures without having an idea of what he was doing? Or could he have been moved to plant such dispositions in us by a temper quite the reverse of what he was doing? By a temper quite the reverse of all excellency and goodness? We may therefore be no less sure, that our Creator has understanding, reason and benevolence, as well as creating power, in the most perfect, pure, unalloyed, unlimited degree, than we are sure that what we have is derived understanding, reason and benevolence.

Such reasonings are natural to the human mind.

Now these reasonings are not only just, but they are natural to the mind: it as naturally tends to form them, as it tends to delight in any object which is adjusted to its frame, but is not an immediate ob-<207>ject of sense. And indeed all the opinions of philosophers about chance, mechanical blind operation of matter, or whatever other strange hypotheses, if they are not absurd, (as they plainly are) they are at least subtleties, which lie very remote from the human mind, and to which it can never yield. Religion is therefore as natural to the mind as a moral sense. But, like it, or being but a part of it, it must be improved by culture, by contemplation and exercise. Where there is a moral sense, reflexion must soon lead to apprehend an infinitely good mind, the cause of all things. And where there is a moral sense, an infinitely good mind cannot be apprehended, without the highest love and admiration, without supreme complacency and delight: but the idea must be improved to its perfection, like every other object of contemplation, by due consideration, by carefully examining it, lest any thing contrary to it should be associated and mixed with it on the one hand, or on the other, lest it should be too defective and inadequate, or too weak in its influence upon our minds.

If it is asked, how then it comes that such depraved notions of the Deity, so destructive of morality, and therefore so opposite to a moral sense, have always prevailed in the world? To this I answer, 1. That nothing is more plain from history, than that even <208> amidst the prevalence of superstition and idolatry; all the thinking part of mankind have ever had very just notions of the Deity and religion. What one of the personages in *Cicero*'s Dialogues about the gods says, was ever the opinion of all philosophers, a few only excepted, who studied and laboured hard to contrive some other uncommon system: *Namely,* That the doctrine of many gods, unless it be understood allegorically, is glaring nonsense. 2. It seems plain from history, that superstition crept in gradually by means of various artifices; and not improbably, it took its chief rise from, or was principally promoted by tyranny, as it is said in *the book of wisdom.*[76] It seems to be its cruel invention in order to enslave men more effectually, or to make them more easy dupes to its ambitious aims. It is an art invented or promoted by tyrants and their flattering accomplices

Whence then imposition or false religion.

It took its rise with tyranny, or was promoted by it.

76. Wis. of Sol. 14.

who share the prey with them, to instil into the minds of those they
would enthral and hold in compleat subjection to their lawless will, a
notion of divine right communicated to them from above, to bear absolute sway on earth till they take their places among the gods destined
for them. Hence the deification of tyrants and heroes in which idolatry
at first consisted, and from whence it most probably took its origin.

> *The workman from the work distinct was known,*
> *And* simple reason *never sought but* one: <209>
> *E'er* wit *oblique had* broke *that steady light,*
> *Man, like his Maker, saw, that* all was right,
> *To virtue in the paths of pleasure trod,*
> *And own'd a* Father *when he own'd a* GOD.
> *Love all the* faith, *and all th'* allegiance *then;*
> *For nature knew no* right divine *in* men,
> *No ill could fear in* GOD; *and understood*
> *A* sovereign being, *but a* sovereign good.
> *True faith, true policy, united ran,*
> *That was but* love of GOD, *and this of* man.
>   *Who first taught souls enslav'd, and realms undone,*
> *Th'enormous faith of* many made for one?
> *That proud exception to all nature's laws,*
> *T'invert the world, and counterwork its cause?*
> *Force first made* conquest, *and that conquest,* law;
> *Till* superstition *taught the tyrant awe,*
> *Then shar'd the tyranny, then lent it aid,*
> *And gods of conqu'rors, slaves of subjects made:*
> *She, midst the lightning's blaze and thunder's sound,*
> *When rock'd the mountains, and when groan'd the ground,*
> *She taught the weak to bend, the proud to pray*
> *To pow'r unseen, and mightier far than they:*
> *She, from the rending earth, and bursting skies,*
> *Saw* Gods *descend, and* Fiends *infernal rise;*
> *Here fix'd the dreadful, there the blest abodes;*
> Fear *made her devils, and weak* hope *her gods:*
> *Gods partial, changeful, passionate, unjust,*

Whose attributes were rage, revenge, or lust,
Such as the souls of cowards *might* conceive,
And form'd like tyrants, *tyrants would* believe. <210>
Zeal then, not charity, became the guide,
And hell was built on spite, *and heav'n on* pride;
Then sacred seem'd th' aethereal vault no more;
Altars grew marble then, and reek'd with gore:
Then first the flamen *tasted living food,*
Next his grim idol smear'd with human blood;
With heav'n's own thunders shook the world below,
And play'd the God an engine on his foe.

Essay on man, Epist. 3.[77]

Now, If it is asked how men, notwithstanding their moral sense, came to suffer themselves to be so grosly imposed upon to their disadvantage? May I not reply, 1. That such an imposition being not more repugnant to a moral sense and a benevolent principle, than it is to self-love, or a desire of private good and happiness; no argument can be brought from its taking place against a moral sense, that does not equally militate against the reality of self-love in our nature; the being and power of which principle was never on that or any other account called into doubt. 2. It appears from history, that such hath always been the care of providence to save, guard against, or deliver men from such pernicious errors, so contrary at once to private interest and to moral sense, as far as could be done consistently with making knowledge progressive and dependent on ourselves: That in all ages of the world, there have appeared true philosophers of generous public spirit, who taught true virtue and religion, <211> and boldly opposed corruption, superstition, and all enslaving doctrines about government; such were *Pythagoras, Thales, Solon, Lycurgus, Socrates, Plato, Confucius, Zoroaster,* and others: and such must *Moses,* the *Jewish prophets,* and JESUS CHRIST be allowed at least to have been. But leaving those with other objections to another place, I shall

[marginal note:] But no argument can be brought from thence against a moral sense in our nature.

77. Pope, *Essay on Man,* III.229–68.

only add now, that to ask why nature has not prevented all error, all falshood, all imposition, all false opinions and prejudices, all credulity, all wrong associations of ideas and bad habits; is in reality to ask, why nature has not done more than can possibly be done for making us capable of attaining to true knowledge, just ideas and opinions, rational conclusions, improved powers and good habits. For it has been already proved, that we are furnished and qualified for the pursuit of and attainment to knowledge, and for arriving at moral perfection, with all the provision that these ends require in our situation: or with regard to such beings as mankind are and must be, to render the scale of life full and coherent.

Religious contemplation is a very pleasant exercise. | I shall therefore proceed to observe on the head of religion, 1. That every exercise of contemplation, admiration, and love towards an all-perfect creator and governor of the world, is in its nature exceeding pleasant and delightful. All beauty is naturally agreeable to our mind, but chiefly moral beauty. And therefore the contemplation of an all-perfect mind, compleatly wise and good, as well as omnipotent and infinitely removed from all imperfection, <212> must greatly raise, transport and exhilerate the mind. This is the necessary consequence of a moral sense.

And highly improving to virtue. | 2. Such contemplation must be highly assisting to and improving of the virtuous temper. It must strengthen our love of virtue; and redouble our emulation to improve and excel in it. It is indeed nothing but the love of virtue in its highest degree. And how doubly satisfying must the conscience of sincere endeavours to advance in virtue be, when one reflects that it is the way, the only way to be like our Creator, and to recommend ourselves to his favour here or hereafter: That it is imitating him, and acting in concert with him.

But good affections may become too strong or vehement. | 3. But as every self-affection may be too strong as well as too weak, so may every generous affection be.

This is what *Horace* means when he says,

Insani sapiens nomen ferat, aequus iniqui,
Ultra quam satis est, virtutem si petat ipsam.[78]

The best affections may not only be too weak to gain their ends; but by misguidance, or too great indulgence, they may become too strong and vehement. The love of mankind may thus become romantic. And, in like manner, religious contemplation and admiration, tho', on the one hand, it may be too little exercised in order to our happiness, <213> and the improvement of our temper; yet, on the other hand, it may become too ardent; and thus it may degenerate into such excessive delight in raptorious contemplation, as may render averse to action, the great end of knowledge and of religion. And when one abandons the world to give himself up to religious contemplation, mankind being naturally made for social exercise and communication with one another in many acts of benevolence and friendship, the right ballance of the mind will be lost: action not being duly mixed with contemplation, the imagination will become visionary and romantic. And hence it is, that such persons are apt to imagine an extraordinary commerce and peculiar intimacy with the supreme Being; and to fancy all the thoughts or visions, which present themselves in consequence of their devotional contemplation and admiration, to be special dictates from heaven to their minds. It is true, good and just sentiments which are thus excited in the mind, as they are in that respect peculiarly the effects of religious acts, they may, in that sense, be said more especially to be from GOD; but they are not from him in any other way, than as they are the natural fruits of such contemplation and devotion according to the natural frame of our mind: and one cannot be too cautious in guarding against the perswasion of any special communication with the Deity, which pride is so apt, if it is once suffered to enter into the mind, or in the least indulged, to nourish

Into what religious admiration is apt to degenerate.

If any other guide is set up in our mind superior to natural reason, and not to be tried by it, our whole frame is unhinged.

---

78. Horace, *Epistles,* I.vi.15–16, "Let the wise man bear the name of madman, the just of unjust, should he pursue virtue herself beyond due bounds." Horace, *Satires, Epistles and Ars poetica,* trans. H. Rushton Fairclough, Loeb Classical Library (London: Heinemann; New York: Putnam, 1926).

to great extravagance; because in proportion as any other guide is set up in the mind besides reason and moral conscience, in proportion will those our natural guides be abandoned and forsaken by us in favour of that imagined superior one: and thus the <214> whole coherence of the human moral texture will be greatly endangered.

But perhaps there is not so much reason to caution against excesses, into which pious and devout affection may be misguided, as to recommend strongly the pleasure and profitableness to virtue, of devotion rightly governed. And then certainly it is so when we take frequent pleasure in contemplating the divine perfections; and such contemplation produces, on the one hand, chearful submission to the divine pleasure with respect to all things independent of us, or absolutely external to us, and out of our power, from the perswasion that the divine providence does all for the best in the whole. And when, on the other hand, the contemplation and love of the Deity excite us to action, or to seek with delightful attention and care, opportunities of exerting our benevolence, and of doing all the good we can; from a perswasion that it is only active benevolence which can liken or approve us to that infinitely perfect Being, whose happiness consists in communicating his goodness as extensively as Omnipotence can.

The genuine effects of true well moderated devotion, are submission to providence, and activity in doing good.

Conclusion. Thus we see, we are made for religion as well as for virtue; and that indeed in our nature, religion and virtue are one and the same thing: it is the same natural disposition of the mind, employed *contemplatively* in admiring and loving supreme virtue; and *actively* in imitating that model; or in endeavouring to become more and more conformable to it. And as this is the idea which reason gives us of religion and virtue, so it is the idea christianity gives of it. The sum of religion and virtue according to that doctrine, is to love GOD, and to love our neighbour; and according to that doctrine these two good dispositions are inseparable: They must go together. *He who thinketh he loveth God, and loveth not his neighbour, deceiveth himself, for God is love.*[79] <215>

79. This Biblical quote appears to be a paraphrase of 1 John 3.10 and 1 John 4.8.

Having thus considered the chief laws and principles, powers and properties in the human nature relative to our bodily or moral frame, to our sensitive part or our connexion with a material world, relative to knowledge, to virtue, to interest, and to society: I think we may conclude, that human nature is well constituted, and makes an excellent species which well deserves its place in the rising scale of life and perfection: a species of being which shews an Author of perfect wisdom and goodness.

A brief review of the human nature, and its powers and dispositions, and their laws.

Now that all the principal phenomena relating to human nature and mankind, are accountable by reducing them to good principles from which they must result, will appear by casting our eye upon the following *Table of effects,* for these seem to be the principal phenomena belonging to us as men; and they are all reducible to the laws that have been already found either to be necessary, or fitly chosen and established.

Phenomena belonging to the general law of power.

Goods.	Evils.
Having a sphere of power and activity. Liberty and dominion; and so being capable of praise, virtue and good desert: Having great knowledge and proportioned power in consequence of culture or care to improve ourselves.	Want of power through ignorance and neglect of culture, blindness, impotence, slavery, consciousness of acting ill; remorse, shame, a desart and uncultivated, or a corrupt and diseased mind. <216>

A table of the phenomena, good and bad belonging to human nature, or resulting from its contexture.

1. *To the laws of* knowledge.

GOODS.	EVILS.
Science, prudence, philosophy, arts, good sense, good taste, a refined imagination, an extensive understanding; knowledge of the beauty, order and wisdom of nature, and skill in imitating it by various arts.	Ignorance, error, prejudices, narrow views, dull or slow imagination, corrupt fancy, false taste; caprice and fantastical pursuits.

2. *To the laws of the sensible world and our union with it.*

GOODS.	EVILS.
Sensitive pleasures of various sorts; contemplation of nature or natural knowledge, pleasures of imagination, social intercourse about moral ideas, sensitive appetites to be governed.	Sensitive pains, subjection to the laws of matter and motion, false imaginations and pains arising from them. Unruly excessive sensual appetites and passions; uneasy sensations annexed to moral or intellectual desires, as well as to sensitive ones.

3. *To the laws of association of ideas and habits.*

GOODS.	EVILS.
Habitual knowledge, memory and acquaintance with nature, perfection in science, in arts, in every faculty, good taste, invention, advancement toward moral perfection, inward liberty, self-command, free agency.	Wrong associations, fantastic imaginations, bad habits, unimproved faculties, inward slavery, indolence and impotence.

4. *To the laws of our moral sense, reason and moral conduct.*

GOODS.	EVILS.
Reason, a moral sense, beauty, harmony, and consistency of manners, conscious virtue, or a sense of merit, greatness of mind, fortitude, magnanimity.	Depraved taste, remorse and self-condemnation, irregular self-tormenting, self-disapproving affections, lowness of mind, pusillanimity.

<217>

5. To the laws of interest and happiness, or of private and public good.

GOODS.	EVILS.
Generous affections, well governed private affections, social ones, their pleasant effects and happy consequences, the pursuit of private and public good, or virtue and interest the same.	Ungenerous, unsocial selfish affections, disorderly desires, and their unhappy effects and influences; private and public ill, or vice and misery the same.

6. To the laws of society, our social make and our mutual dependence.

GOODS.	EVILS.
Social union, mutual dependencies, derived happiness by communication and participation; confederacy to promote virtue, and the true elegance, grandeur and happiness of society.	Disunion, tumult, disorder, tyrany, rebellion, barbarity, slavery, public lowness and misery.

7. To the law of religion.

GOODS.	EVILS.
True ideas of GOD and providence, true religion, its pleasures, resignation to the Deity, imitation of the Deity, consciousness of conformity to him, and of his favour and approbation.	False ideas of GOD and providence, superstition, idolatry, blind zeal, dread of the Deity, sense of disconformity to him, and fear of his displeasure.

This is a short view of the principal appearances in the human system. Now all the appearances reducible to those laws must be good, the laws being good. And that they are such is evident; for if the preceeding account of our frame, and the laws relative to it be true, it plainly and necessarily follows, 1. "That, in consequence of them, we are made for a very considerable degree of happiness and perfection of the moral sort chiefly." And, 2. "That there is no <218> affection, disposition, power or faculty in our nature which merely produces evil; or which, on the

All these phenomena are reducible to the excellent general laws already considered, which fit and qualify man for a noble end or happiness.

contrary, does not produce very many great goods and no evils, but what are the effects of such a general prevalence of these laws, as makes our constitution a good whole, or adapted to a noble end." But if these con-

Therefore there are no evils absolutely considered arising from our frame.

clusions be true, then are no effects in the human system evils absolutely considered; that is, with respect to the whole frame and constitution of human nature. In order to have a just notion of the government of the world, and of its Author, we need only ask ourselves, towards which kind of phenomena, the good or the opposite bad ones, the natural tendency of our powers and dispositions is; whether it is for the sake of the bad ones, which arises from their misuse or misguidance, that we are endowed with these powers and dispositions which constitute our frame; or for the sake of the good ones towards which these powers and dis-

If we judge in this case, as we do in other like ones, we must conclude that all our powers are given us for a very useful and noble end.

positions naturally operate? Let us judge here as we do in analogous cases with regard to moral agents. Is one thought to have bestowed money, power, or any gift upon one which may be employed to good purposes, that they may be misapplied and abused to bad ones unless we are previously certain of the malignity and wicked disposition and intention of the giver: but ought we not to form like judgments in like cases? But which is more, if we reflect that together with all our powers and dispositions, the Author of nature hath given us a moral sense, to what other purpose can we suppose our powers to be given in this manner, or

Our moral sense cannot possibly be given us for any other reason but to guide us to the right use of all our powers.

so conjoined, but for the best use or the best end; since our moral reason and sense cannot be implanted in us for any other purpose, but to point and prompt us to the best use of all our powers, appetites and affections? For this moral sense is as naturally fitted for directing us right, and for no other end, as a helm is to guide and steer a ship. <219>

How do we judge of any machine natural or artificial? Do we not say, it is fitted for that end to which it is properest to serve; or that to be applied to its most useful purpose, is its perfect and most natural state? Thus we judge of plants, trees, ships, watches, and all sorts of structures, animate or inanimate. Why then should we pronounce or judge[a] other-

---

a. This is the ancient way of reasoning about man analogous to our way of reasoning about all other constitutions natural or artificial. Instances of it have been already quoted from *Cicero* and others; and another shall be added immediately.

wise concerning man and the human system? or can we do so without departing from all the received rules of judging of any thing; all the rules of judging either used in philosophy or common life? Ought we not therefore to reason in this manner with regard to every law of our nature? as for instance, with regard to the law of knowledge; that must be owned to be a good law which is necessary to our being capable of science, prudence, philosophy, arts natural and moral, power, virtue and merit; tho' in consequence of the same power we cannot but be capable of contracting prejudices, forming narrow views, and making false judgments; or tho' in consequence of the very laws and establishments that render knowledge progressive and dependent on ourselves, and by which we have a certain sphere of activity, power and dominion, errors, prejudices, wrong associations, false judgments, and therefore bad choice, and unreasonable pursuits cannot be otherwise avoidable by us, than by the right exercise of our understanding and reason to which we are prompted and directed in the only way we can be so consistently with our own exercising and employing them; that is, by our delight in order, general laws, and the contemplation of public good. Or to give another instance, 2. With regard to the law of society. That must be a good law with regard to the human system, which binds and unites us together, by making our greatest happiness depend upon our uniting <220> together in a proper manner to promote that end; tho' in consequence of that very law our greatest happiness cannot otherwise be acquired or attained than by right confederacy and union; and therefore many miseries must arise from disunion, and from uniting in an unfit or improper manner,—and so on.—For, in like manner, must we reason with respect to all the other laws of our nature that have been mentioned, and their phenomena or effects, which it is needless again to repeat. Now if this way of reasoning be good, then is nature sufficiently vindicated by the account that hath been given of the laws of our nature; for if it be good, then every effect concerning which we can reason in the manner as above, is sufficiently explained and accounted for morally as well as physically; since it is thus reduced to an establishment or general law and principle in nature, necessary to many excellent purposes, for which were not our nature fitted, it would not be so perfect as it is.

Our whole frame is good. For all effects reducible to the law of knowledge,

and all effects reducible to the law of society; or to any other of the laws of our nature above mentioned,

must be sufficiently accounted for, if explication of phenomena hath any meaning at all.

For all the pre-
ceeding reason-
ings about the
fitness of laws
go on in the
same way that
is admitted to
be good in
every other
case.
In natural phi-
losophy in
particular.

But that the reasoning is good, is evident, 1. Since it is that very way of reasoning we admit in every other case to be good, and without admitting which natural philosophy cannot advance one step: for what does, or can natural philosophy do, but reduce natural appearances to general laws, and shew the goodness of these laws. 2. But which is more, it must be true, in general, that no whole can be a good whole in any other sense but this, that its parts, and all the references of its parts, with all the laws according to which these operate or are operated upon, are adjusted to a very good end: Such a whole is a good whole in any proper or conceiveable sense of a good whole. And therefore our structure is such.

The preceeding
account of
human nature
is therefore
strictly
philosophical.

This account therefore of nature is strictly philosophical, or philosophy and the explication of nature hath no meaning. We must admit it, or by parity of reason be obliged to give up with natural philosophy, and say it does not sufficiently explain or <221> account for appearances by reducing them to good general laws; but that something else must be done. Now what that *something more* means no philosopher has yet declared.

A recapitula-
tion of it to
prove this.

The case with regard to our constitution is briefly this. 'Tis impossible to make beings capable of attaining to any qualifications or improvements, and of being happy by so doing, otherwise than by providing them with the powers, faculties, affections, materials, and occasions of attaining to them. And therefore, this being done, a being is duly fitted, qualified or furnished for a certain degree of perfection, and is in its kind of a perfect make, well deserving its place in nature, which, without such a kind, could not be full, coherent and rise in due degree. To demand more to moral perfection than the necessary provision and furniture for such perfection, is to demand in order to sufficient provision and furniture, some thing more than sufficient provision and furniture. It is to demand that moral attainments may be attainments without being attained, acquisitions without being acquired. [a] Wherefore our frame and

a. Animi autem, & ejus animi partis, quae princeps est, quaeque mens nominatur, plures sunt virtutes, sed duo prima genera. Unum earum, quae ingenerantur suapte

make is sufficiently vindicated, when it appears that we are, as has been shewn, excellently provided by nature for very great acquisitions in knowledge, power, virtue and merit, and by that means in happiness and perfection; if we set ourselves to make a right use of our natural abilities, as <222> we are directed and excited to do by our natural instincts, affections or determinations. Natural endowments, properly speaking, are not virtues or moral perfections; they are but the foundation, the capacity of and furniture for moral improvements, acquisitions and virtues; the pre-requisites to moral perfection and happiness. But who dares say to himself, that he has it not in his power to attain to a very high degree of perfection? What man may attain to, we know from many examples in history and in present times; and who can look upon such characters, and not feel that man may arrive at a truly noble degree of dignity and worth? They cast us at a distance indeed, and upbraid us; but why? but because we feel that it is in our power, if we would but earnestly set about it, or if we are not sadly wanting to ourselves, even to do more than they?

That must be the natural end of a being,[a] to the pursuit of which his

---

natura, appellanturque non voluntariae: alterum earum, quae in voluntate: positae, magis proprio nomine appellari solent: quarum est excellens in animorum laude praestantia prioris generis est docilitas memoria: quae ferè omnia appellantur uno ingenii nomine: easque virtutes qui habent, ingeniosi vocantur. Alterum autem genus est magnarum, verarumque virtutum: quas appellamus voluntarias, ut prudentiam, temperantiam, fortitudinem, justitiam, & reliquas ejusdem generis. *Cicero de finibus,* Lib. 5. No. 13. [Cicero, *De finibus,* V.xiii.36: "The mind, on the other hand, and that dominant part of the mind which is called the intellect, possess many excellences or virtues, but these are of two main classes; one class consists of those excellences which are implanted by their own nature, and which are called non-volitional; and the other of those which, depending on our volition, are usually styled 'virtues' in the more special sense; and the latter are the pre-eminent glory and distinction of the mind. To the former class belong receptiveness and memory; and practically all the excellences of this class are included under one name of 'talent,' and their possessors are spoken of as 'talented.' The other class consists of the lofty virtues properly so called, which we speak of as dependent on volition, for instance, prudence, temperance, courage, justice, and the others of the same kind."]

a. Est enim actio quaedam corporis, quae motus, & status naturae congruentes tenet: in quibus si peccetur distortione, & depravatione quadam—contra naturam sunt.—Itaque è contrario moderati, aequabilesque habitus, affectiones, ususque cor-

---

poris, apti esse ad naturam videntur. Jam vero animus non esse solum, sed etiam cujusdam modi debet esse, ut & omneis parteis habeat incolumeis, & de virtutibus nulla desit. Atqui in sensibus est sua cujusque virtus, ut ne quid impediat, quominus suo sensus quisque munere fungatur in iis rebus, celeriter, expediteque percipiendis quae subjectae sunt sensibus. Animi autem *&c. Cicero,* Lib. 5. No. 12. Now it is in this ancient, and only true way of arguing we have proceeded, and therefore we may conclude with him, That man is truly such as he paints him out to be. *De legibus,* Lib. 2. at the end. Nam qui se ipse norit, primum aliquid sentiet se habere divinum, ingeniumque in se suum, sicut simulacrum aliquod, dedicatum putabit; tantoque munere deorum semper dignum aliquid & faciet, & sentiet: &, cum se ipse perspexerit: totumque tentarit; intelliget, quemadmodum a natura subornatus in vitam venerit, quantaque instrumenta habeat ad obtinendam, adipiscendamque sapientiam: quoniam principio rerum omnium quasi adumbratas intelligentias animo, ac mente conceperit: quibus illustratis, sapientia duce, bonum virum, & ob eam ipsam causam cernat se beatum fore. Nam eum animus, cognitis, perceptisque virtutibus, a corporis obsequio, indulgentiaque discesserit, voluptatemque, sicut labem aliquam decoris oppresserit, omnemque mortis, dolorisque timorem effugerit, societatemque caritatis coierit cum suis omneisque natura conjunctos, suos duxerit, cultumque deorum, & puram religionem susceperit, & exacuerit illam, ut oculorum, sic ingenii aciem, ad bona diligenda, & rejicienda contraria: quae virtus ex providendo est appellata prudentia: quid eo dici, aut excogitari poterit beatius? Idemque cum coelum, terras, maria, rerumque omnium naturam perspexerit, eaque unde generata, quo recurrant, quando quo modo obitura, quid in iis mortale, & caducum, quid divinum, aeternumque sit, viderit ipsumque ea moderantem, & regentem paene prehenderit, seseque non omnis circumdatum moenibus, popularem alicujus definiti loci, sed civem totius mundi, quasi unius urbis, agnoverit: in hac ille magnificentia rerum, atque in hoc conspectu, & cognitione naturae, dii immortales, quam ipse se noscet! Atque haec omnia, quasi saepimento aliquo, vallabit disserendi ratione, veri & falsi judicio, scientia, & arte quadam intelligendi, quid quamque rem sequatur, & quid sit cuique contrarium. Cumque se ad civilem societatem natum senserit, non solum illa subtili disputatione sibi utendum putabit, sed etiam fusa latius perpetua oratione, qua regat populos, qua stabiliat leges, qua castiget improbos, qua tueatur bonos, qua laudet claros viros: qua praecepta salutis, & laudes apte ad persuadendum edat suis civibus: qua hortari ad decus, revocare a flagitio, consolari possit afflictos: fataque, & consulta fortium, & sapientium, cum *improborum ignominia,* sempiternis monumentis prodire. Quae cum tot res, tantaeque sint; quae inesse in homine perspiciantur ab iis, qui se ipsi velint nosse, earum parens est, educatrixque sapientia. This is a true picture of human nature, and of our duties. And truly had we not been made by an infinitely wise and good being, man must have been quite the reverse; such an animal, as *Ulysses*'s men were metamorphosed into by *Circes* in *Homer,* the sum of which fiction amounts briefly to this in *Horace*'s words.

> *Sirenum voces, & Circes pocula nosti:*
> *Quae si cum sociis stultus cupidusque bibisset;*

Sub dominâ meretrice fuisset turpis & excors,
Vixisset canis immundus, vel amica luto sus.
Epist. lib. I. Epist. 2.

[Cicero, *De finibus,* V.xii.35–xiii.36: "Again, there is also a certain form of bodily activity which keeps the motions and postures in harmony with nature; and any error in these, due to distortion or deformity . . . is contrary to nature. . . . And so, on the contrary, a controlled and well-regulated bearing, condition and movement of the body has the appearance of being in harmony with nature. Turning now to the mind, this must not only exist, but also be of a certain character; it must have all its parts intact and lack none of the virtues. The senses also possess their several virtues or excellences, consisting in the unimpeded performance of their several functions of swiftly and readily perceiving sensible objects. The mind, on the other hand, etc."

De legibus, I.xxii.59–xxiv.62: "For he who knows himself will realise, in the first place, that he has a divine element within him, and will think of his own inner nature as a kind of consecrated image of God; and so he will always act and think in a way worthy of so great a gift of the gods, and, when he has examined and thoroughly tested himself, he will understand how nobly equipped by nature he entered life, and what manifold means he possesses for the attainment and acquisition of wisdom. For from the very first he began to form in his mind and spirit shadowy concepts, as it were, of all sorts, and when these have been illuminated under the guidance of wisdom, he perceives that he will be a good man, and, for that very reason, happy. For when the mind, having attained to a knowledge and perception of the virtues, has abandoned its subservience to the body and its indulgence of it, has put down pleasure as if it were a taint of dishonour, has escaped from all fear of death or pain, has entered into a partnership of love with its own, recognising as its own all who are joined to it by nature; when it has taken up the worship of the gods and pure religion, has sharpened the vision both of the eye and of the mind so that they can choose the good and reject the opposite—a virtue which is called prudence because it foresees— then what greater degree of happiness can be described or imagined? And further, when it had examined the heavens, the earth, the seas, the nature of the universe, and understands whence all these things came and whither they must return, when and how they are destined to perish, what part of them is mortal and transient and what is divine and eternal; and when it almost lays hold of the ruler and governor of the universe, and when it realises that it is not shut in by [narrow] walls as a resident of some fixed spot, but is a citizen of the whole universe, as it were of a single city— then in the midst of this universal grandeur, and with such a view and comprehension of nature, ye immortal gods, how well it will know itself. . . . And in defence of all this, it will erect battlements of dialectic, of the science of distinguishing the true from the false, and of the art, so to speak, of understanding the consequences and opposites of every statement. And when it realises that it is born to take part in the life of a state, it will think that it must employ not merely the customary subtle method of debate, but also the more copious continuous style, considering, for example, how to rule nations, establish laws, punish the wicked, protect the good, hon-

natural powers are fitted, and <223> the pursuit of which is his soundest, his pleasantest state. But so are we made with regard to moral perfection; the pursuit of it therefore is our natural, our healthful, our sound or happy, as well as perfect state. So that if the preceeding account of man be true, we may justly conclude, "That tho' the Author of nature, who hath filled his creation with all possible degrees of beauty, perfection and happiness, hath made a species of beings lower than angels; yet man, who is this species, is crowned by him with *glory and honour,* and invested with a very large and noble sphere of power and dominion."[80] If the preceeding account of man be true, we are made for progress in virtue. And as any machine must be made for what it is made, tho' it cannot last forever, or whether it last but one day or a thousand years; so man must be made for what he is made, whether he is to last but threescore years, or forever. But having now found for what end man is made while he exists, let us enquire what reason can deter-<224>mine with any probability concerning his duration; or whether there is not good ground to believe that he is made immortal, and consequently for eternal progress, in proportion to his care to improve his moral faculties. Which is the point proposed to be proved by this enquiry.

But before we proceed to that, in order, by a kind of contrast, to give further light to the preceeding reasonings concerning man, let us endeavour to imagine to ourselves an idea of what the workmanship of a malicious creator must have been; in consequence of his malign disposition; for certainly we shall find that human nature must have been

Marginal notes:

Conclusion concerning our nature. *N.B.* See in the notes a true picture of our nature, dignity, happiness, and end, drawn by *Cicero,* and inferred from the same principles we have laid down in this essay. It remains therefore to be enquired how long man is likely to exist; or whether he is not designed for immortality.

But before we proceed, it is proper to oppose to the preceeding account of man, such a

---

our those who excel, publish to fellow-citizens precepts conducive to their well-being and credit, so designed as to win their acceptance; how to arouse them to honourable actions, recall from wrong-doing, console the afflicted, and hand down to everlasting memory the deeds and counsels of brave and wise men, and the infamy of the wicked. So many and so great are the powers which are perceived to exist in man by those who desire to know themselves; and their parent and their nurse is wisdom."

Horace, *Epistles,* I.ii.23–26: "You know the Sirens' song and Circe's cups; if, along with his comrades, he had drunk of these in folly and greed, he would have become the shapeless and witless vassal of a harlot mistress—would have lived as an unclean dog or a sow that loves the mire."]

80. Paraphrase of Psalms 8.5.

the very reverse of what it now is, had it been formed by a malicious Creator, or with vicious and ungenerous intention. "Would we allow room, (says an excellent author) to our invention to conceive what sort of mechanism, what constitution of senses or affections a malicious, powerful being must have formed, we should soon see how few evidences there are for any such apprehensions of the Author of this world. Our mechanism, as far as ever we have yet discovered, <225> is wholly contrived for good, no cruel device, no art or contrivance to produce evil, no such mark or scope seems even to be aimed at: But how easy had it been to have even contrived some necessary engines of misery without any advantage, some member of no use, but to be matter of torment: Senses incapable of bearing surrounding objects without pain, eyes pierced with the light, a pallat offended with the fruits of the earth; a skin as tender as the coats of the eye, and yet some more furious pain forcing us to bear these torments: Human society might have been made as the company of enemies, and yet a perpetual more violent fear might have forced us to bear it. Malice, rancour, distrust might have been our natural temper: our honour and self-approbation might have depended upon injuries, and the torments of others have been made our delight, which yet we could not have enjoyed through perpetual fear. Many such contrivances we may easily conceive, whereby an evil mind could have gratified his malice by our misery; but how unlike are they all to the structure and design of the mechanism of this world, to the mechanism and structure of our minds in particular?"[a]

state of mankind as it is reasonable to suppose must have been the product of a malignant Creator, who had no sense of, nor regard for virtue, or the good and perfection of moral beings.

If we pursue this thought a little further, we shall immediately perceive, that a malignant Author would have made our frame and constitution quite the reverse of what it is. All our senses would have been made so many avenues to pain alone, and inevitably such. Every increase of our understanding would have been tormentful: and we would have been made dependent one upon another, not for our good, but merely for our suffering and torture. Every pain would have been much keener and intenser, and the effects of laws which would have produced very

---

a. See Mr. *Hutcheson on the passions,* whose words these are. [Hutcheson, *Passions,* I.vi.3.]

little if any good. Laws would not have been made general for the greater good, but in order to bring about greater misery in the <226> sum of things, and no pleasure would have been intended but for a decoyer and seducer into pain.

In fine, let us run over in our minds all the laws of our frame which have been mentioned, and we shall plainly see that had we been contrived by a malicious Author for evil, not one of them would have taken place, but on the contrary their opposites: knowledge would have been equally necessary and painful; equally difficult and tormenting, and yet indispensably necessary; we would not have been allured to it by the pleasure of truth, nor fitted for it by a sense of order and a complacency in analogies and general laws. And it would have been impossible for us ever to have attained to facility, readiness and perfection in arts, sciences, or practices by frequent acts; but repeated exercises would have been lost labour, and our toil would always have been to begin again. Instead of a moral sense, we would have had an immoral one; or we would have approved good affections, and yet have suffered by them, and not virtue but vice would have been private interest, that so men might not be otherwise the same kind, than as they were impelled and fitted by their passions and powers more particularly to work one another's misery. No form of society would have tended to produce perfection and happiness; or no other combinations and confederacies would have been possible, but those that result in disorder, ruin and misery. All nature would have filled us with horror and dread; we would not only have hated one another, but have hated ourselves and our being; and yet we should not have been able to put an end to it.

Our frame and constitution is therefore an infringible argument of the wisdom, benevolence, and excellent moral disposition of the Author of our nature, and of the generous administration that prevails over all his works. We are indeed the image of an all perfect Creator; since tho' there be no reason to think that we hold the highest rank in the <227> scale of created intelligence, yet we are endowed with very noble powers, and are placed in an excellent situation for their improvement to a very high pitch of perfection and happiness. And thus, "are crowned with glory and honour, tho' we be lower than the angels."

ʘ CHAPTER IX ʘ

It now remains to enquire what may be fairly and justly concluded from human nature, and the present constitution of things concerning death or the dissolution of our bodily frame? In order to determine which question, we need only state the phenomenon in a true light. And thus it stands. "We are by nature excellently equipped and furnished for attaining to a very considerable degree of moral perfection, or of knowledge and virtue by the due culture of our natural endowments; and are placed in a very proper situation for that effect, even by having relation to, and communion with the sensible world by means of our bodies: but our bodies are made liable to dissolution: they are not made to endure for ever; but must wear out, and may be destroyed while they are yet sound and vigorous, by different kinds of violence, in consequence of their structure and subjection to the laws of matter and motion." This is the truth of the case. What judgment then is it reasonable to form of this phenomenon, or of this state and tendency of things with regard to mankind?

Let us now enquire what judgment ought to be formed concerning death:

The phenomenon fairly stated.

Futurity[a] is wisely hid from us; it is not fit that infants should know whether they are to live to <228> old age and foresee the fortunes of their lives: In general, it is not fit for us to know such good or bad accidents as are to happen us in consequence of the laws of the sensible

Futurity is wisely hid from us.

---

a. See *Cicero de divinatione,* Lib. 2. No. 9. Atque ego ne utilem quidem arbitror esse nobis futurarum rerum scientiam. Quae enim vita fuisset Priamo, si ab adulescentia scisset, quos eventus senectutis esset habiturus? &c. [Cicero, *De divinatione,* II.ix.22: "And further, for my part, I think that a knowledge of the future would be a disadvantage. Consider, for example, what Priam's life would have been if he had known from youth what dire events his old age held in store for him!"]

world, or our social connexions which are in the nature of things unavoidable.

> *Prudens futuri temporis exitum,*
> *Caliginosa nocte premit Deus.*[81]

Or as our own Poet has it,

> *Heav'n from all creatures hides the book of fate,*
> *All but the page prescrib'd, their* present state,
> *From brutes what men, from men what spirits know,*
> *Or who could suffer being here below?*
> *Oh! blindness to the future! kindly giv'n,*
> *That each may fill the circle mark'd by heav'n.*
>
> Essay on man, Epist. 1[82]

We know, or may know enough of the settled order and succession of things for the regulation of our conduct, that is, for the common exigencies of natural life, and for avoiding the bad consequences of folly and vice, and reaping the good fruits of prudence and virtue; and that, it is evident, is all the foresight which is convenient, or can be pleasant to us, and therefore our duty and business is as the Poet expresses it.

> ——— *Quod adest memento*
> *Componere aequus.*[83]

Now for the same wise reasons that future events in this present life are hid from us, the particular events which are to happen to us after death; that is, the various scenes or changes of being we may be intended to pass through after leaving this state, are likewise beyond our forecast. But tho' our future state cannot be fully foreseen by us, because such knowledge would neither be agreeable nor convenient for us; <229> yet

---

81. Horace, *Odes,* III.xxix.29–30: "With wise purpose does the god bury in the shades of night the future's outcome." Horace, *Odes and Epodes,* trans. C. E. Bennett, Loeb Classical Library (Cambridge and London: Harvard University Press, 1968).

82. Pope, *Essay on Man,* I.77–80, 85–86.

83. Horace, *Odes,* III.xxix.32–33: "Remember to settle with tranquil heart the problem of the hour!"

from the present state, we may infer very probably that death is not a total dissolution of our moral powers and their acquirements, but that these do survive our bodies. Because, 1. The dissolution of our bodies is no more than putting an end to our communication with the sensible world, or to one kind of ideas we now receive from without, and the order in which they are conveyed into our minds; and therefore, there can be no reason to infer from hence the total dissolution of all powers. 2. Because this state is but our entrance on life, and having all the appearances of a proper first state of enjoyment, or rather of trial and discipline, for rational beings; it is natural to conclude, that it is but our first state of probation, and not the whole of our existence. 3. Because the ideas of wisdom and good order, which are natural to the human mind, or to which we are led by the consideration of the present state of things wherever we cast our eyes; and in the perswasion of the prevalence of which throughout the universal system, we must be the more confirmed, the more we examine nature, or the fuller view we are able to take of it: All these considerations give us good ground to hope, that beings endowed with such powers as men are, which may survive one method of enjoyment and exercise, were not made to be wilfully destroyed; or are not so totally subjected to the laws of matter and motion, that they cannot subsist any longer than these laws take place. We may indeed fairly put the issue of the question about our future existence upon this footing. "Whether it be more probable, that is, more analogous and consistent with the preceeding account of our make to imagine that we are made with moral powers, merely for the entertainments and exercises which we are capable of receiving from a sensible world by our bodies for the short while they only can last; or that it is but our first state of trial, and to be succeeded by another such existence as good order and wisdom <230> in the whole requires?" For surely, if in what we have seen, by enquiring strictly into our constitution, nothing but good order and perfect contrivance and harmony appear, there can be no reason to apprehend that disorder, far less, that cruel destruction, or wilful annihilation, ever can happen under such a wise and benevolent administration, as the present frame of things strongly and clearly bespeaks.

Yet we have reason to infer that death is not a dissolution of our moral powers.

It is not analogous to our make to suppose that it is.

<table>
<tr><td>It is proper to
consider this
matter more
fully.</td><td>But in order to set an affair, of such consequence to the quiet and satisfaction of every thinking person, in a true light, I would offer the following observations, which are but so many corollaries evidently resulting from the account that hath been given of human nature, and of the general laws to which all the effects and appearances belonging to it are reducible.</td></tr>
</table>

Our present
connexion with
a sensible
world by
means of our
bodies, is arbitrary, not
necessary.

I. We have a thinking part that receives our sensible ideas from without, or upon which they are impressed, according to certain laws. It is not, as ancient philosophers have said, [a] the eyes, or the <231> ears, or any of our outward senses (properly speaking) which perceive: these are only certain methods <232> or orders, according to which, certain sensations are produced in us. Our thinking part therefore, which is properly our-

---

a. The chief arguments from which the ancients inferred the immortality of the soul shall be taken notice of, because some have said, no good arguments are to be found among them, to render it so much as probable. The first was, universal consent: Sed ut Deos esse natura opinamur, qualesque sint, ratione cognoscimus: sic permanere animos arbitramur consensu nationum omnium: qua in sede maneant, qualesque sint, ratione discendum est. Cujus ignoratio finxit inferos, &c. Enim autem in re consensio omnium gentium, lex naturae putanda est. *Tusc. Quaest.* Lib. I. No. 16.

2. The second was, that our connexion with a sensible world, by means of our bodily organization, is not necessary, but arbitrary; and that our thinking part being totally or essentially distinct from our body, may survive it, and cannot otherwise perish with it, than by the will of our Creator that it shall. "Nos enim ne nunc quidem oculis cernimus ea quae videmus. Neque enim est ullus sensus in corpore, sed, ut non solum physici docent, verum etiam medici, qui ista aperta, & patefacta viderunt, viae quasi quaedam sunt ad oculos, ad aureis, ad nareis à sede animi perforatae. *Itaque saepe, aut cogitatione, aut aliqua vi morbi impediti, apertis atque integris & oculis, & auribus, nec videmus, nec audimus:* ut facile intelligi possit, animum & videre, & audire, non eas parteis, quae quasi fenestrae sunt animi: quibus tamen sentire nihil queat mens, nisi id agat, & adsit. Quid, quod eadem mente res dissimillimas comprehendimus, ut colorem, saporem, calorem, odorem, sonum? quae numquam quinque nuntiis animus cognosceret, nisi ad eum omnia referrentur, & is omnium judex solus esset.—Haec reputent isti, qui negant, animum sine corpore se intelligere posse. Videbunt quem in ipso corpore intelligant. Mihi quidem naturam animi intuenti, multo difficilior occurrit cogitatio, multoque obscurior, qualis animus in corpore sit, tanquam alienae domui, quam qualis, cum exierit, & in liberum coelum, quasi domum suam venerit.—Animorum nulla in terris origo inveniri potest: nihil enim est in animis mixtum, atque concretum, aut quod ex terra natum, atque fictum esse videatur—His enim in naturis nihil inest, quod vim memoriae, mentis, cogitationis habeat, quod & praeterita teneat, & futura provideat, & complecti possit praesentia:

quae sola divina sunt. Nec invenietur umquam, unde ad hominem venire possint, nisi a Deo. Singularis est igitur quaedam natura atque vis animi sejuncta ab his usitatis, notisque naturis. Ita quidquid est illud, quod sentit, quod sapit, quod vivit, quod viget, coeleste & divinum est, ob eamque rem aeternum sit necesse est. Nec verò deus ipse, qui intelligitur a nobis, alio modo intelligi potest, nisi mens soluta quaedam, & libera, segregata ab omni concretione mortali, omnia sentiens & movens, ipsaque praedita motu sempiterno.

3. We can separate our minds from our bodies when we will, in a certain sense. Tota enim philosophorum vita, ut ait idem, commentatio mortis est. Nam quid aliud agimus, cum a voluptate, id est, a corpore, cum a re familiari, quae est ministra, & famula corporis, cum a rep. cum a negotio omni sevocamus animum? quid, inquam, tum agimus, nisi animum ad seipsum advocamus, secum esse cogimus, maximeque a corpore abducimus? secernere autem a corpore animum, nec quidquam aliud est, quam mori discere.

4. Their principal arguments were taken from the dignity, the excellent moral powers of our minds, many descriptions of which have been quoted from them. See what is said of them *Tusc. quaest.* Lib. I. No. 25, & deinceps. With which arguments were joined, our natural sense and desire of immortality, our care about futurity, love of glory, and natural pleasure in expanding the mind in the contemplation of eternity. *Cicero, ibidem,* and in the *Somnio Scipionis.* [Cicero, *Tusculanae disputationes:* "But just as it is by natural instinct that we believe in the existence of gods, and by the exercise of reason that we learn to know their nature, so it is that resting upon the agreement of all races of mankind we think that souls have an abiding life, and it is by reason that we must learn their place of abode and their nature. It is ignorance of this that has invented the world below" (I.xvi.36). ". . . in every inquiry the unanimity of the races of the world must be regarded as a law of nature" (I.xii.30). Cicero, *Tusculan Disputations,* trans. J. E. King, Loeb Classical Library (London: Heinemann; New York: Putnam, 1927).

Ibid.: "We do not even now distinguish with our eyes the things we see; for there is no perception in the body, but, as it is taught not only by natural philosophers but also by the experts of medicine, who have seen the proofs openly disclosed, there are, as it were, passages bored from the seat of the soul to eye and ear and nose. Often, therefore, we are hindered by absorption in thought or by some attack of sickness, and though eyes and ears are open and uninjured, we neither see nor hear, so that it can be readily understood that it is the soul which both sees and hears, and not those parts of us which serve as windows to the soul, and yet the mind can perceive nothing through them, unless it is active and attentive. What of the fact that by using the same mind we have perception of things so utterly unlike as colour, taste, heat, smell, sound? These the soul would never have ascertained by its five messengers, unless it had been sole court of appeal and only judge of everything" (I.xx.46). "Let the thinkers who say they cannot understand soul without body reflect upon these considerations, and they will see how far they understand soul while it is actually in the body. For my part, when I study the nature of the soul, the conception of it in the body, as it were in a home that is not its own, presents itself as one much more difficult, much more doubtful than the conception of the nature of the soul when it has quitted the body and come into the free heaven, as it were to its home" (I.xxi.51). "No be-self, is absolutely distinct from all these sensations which it receives from without. And what follows from thence, but that there can be no natural or necessary connexion between the subsistence of our thinking part, and its having its present sensations from without. But if this be true, then may it not only survive the prevalence of the order in which our present sensations are conveyed to us; but it cannot otherwise perish, when that order ceases to take place, than in consequence of a positive

We may therefore survive such a connexion.

appointment of nature that our minds should not survive such an order. I need not dwell long upon this head, since it is owned by all philosophers that our present communication with a sensible world, according to the laws of which sensible ideas are produced in our minds, is but an arbi-

Our perishing totally with it, must be the effect of an arbitrary appointment that it shall be so.

trary connexion. For if this be true, it must necessarily follow, that our minds might have existed without any such communication, and may subsist when it no longer takes place. Nay, it must follow, that as the present connexion between our thinking part and a sensible world, by means of our bodily organization, is but an arbitrary connexion; so if we are totally destroyed when our communication with a sensible world by means of our bodies is at an end, that must likewise be the effect of as positive and arbitrary an institution, as our present connexion with a

---

ginning of souls can be discovered on earth; for there is no trace of blending or combination in souls or any particle that could seem born or fashioned from earth. . . . For in these elements there is nothing to possess the power of memory, thought, reflection, nothing capable of retaining the past, or foreseeing the future and grasping the present, and these capacities are nothing but divine; and never will there be found any source from which they can come to men except from God. There is then a peculiar essential character belonging to the soul, distinct from these common and well-known elements. Accordingly, whatever it is that is conscious, that is wise, that lives, that is active must be heavenly and divine and for that reason eternal. And indeed God Himself, who is comprehended by us, can be comprehended in no other way save as a mind unfettered and free, severed from all perishable matter, conscious of all and moving all and self-endowed with perpetual motion" (I.xxvii.66–67).

Ibid., I.xxx.74–xxxi.75: "For the whole life of the philosopher, as the same wise man says, is a preparation for death. For what else do we do when we sequester the soul from pleasure, for that means from the body; from private property, the handmaid and servant of the body; from public interests; from any kind of business: what, I say, do we then do except summon the soul to its own presence, force it to companionship with itself and withdraw it completely from the body? But is severance of the soul from the body anything else than learning how to die?"]

sensible world is. But what reason is there to fear such a destroying will or humour in nature?

II. The destruction of material beings cannot properly be called destruction, since existence is lost upon matter, considered by itself as an unperceiving substance; and the end of its creation can be nothing else but its being perceived by some thinking beings. When matter therefore is said to be destroyed, all that can be said to be done is, that perceiving be-<233>ings have lost a certain class or order of perceptions, conveyed unto them from without, according to certain laws, which now no longer take place. The rules of analogous reasoning surely do not permit us to infer from the most evident symptoms of the destruction of unperceiving substances, the total destruction of perceiving beings, since these latter are the only ones to whom existence can really be any benefit or blessing? But which is more, when we narrowly examine what we call the destruction of matter, we evidently perceive that it is not properly destruction, but change of form. And certainly, if there really be no destruction at all, even of what is not benefited by existence, there can be no ground to apprehend the destruction of any being that is. The true state of the case, with regard to matter, as far as we can observe its changes, is,

> *Look round our world: behold the chain of love*
> *Combining all below, and all above.*
> *See, plastic nature working to this end,*
> *The single atoms each to other tend,*
> *Attract, attracted to, the next in place,*
> *Form'd and impell'd, its neighbour to embrace.*
> *See matter next, with various life endu'd,*
> *Press to one centre still, the* gen'ral good.
> *See dying vegetables life sustain,*
> *See life dissolving vegetate again:*
> *All forms that perish other forms supply,*
> *By turns they catch the vital breath, and die.*
> Essay on man, Epist. 3.[84]

Marginal notes:

There is no reason to apprehend such an annihilating or destroying humour in nature.

The destruction of matter is not properly destruction.

Wherefore the destruction of a perceiving being cannot be inferred from the destruction of matter.

---

84. Pope, *Essay on Man,* III.7–18.

But there is no ground to think any particle of matter is destroyed: what we call so, is really but change of form.

Now if we ought and must reason from analogy, when we see no examples in nature of destruction, but merely of change, it is only change, and not destruction that can be inferred. It is only from a destroying humour prevailing visibly in nature, that the destruction of perceiving beings can be inferred. And therefore if we do not find plain symptoms of <234> a destroying temper in nature; or of delight, not in frugality and preservation, but in waste, and wilful annihilation, we can have no reason to suspect nature to be a destroyer of moral beings and powers?

A Fortiori there is no reason to think any perceiving being is destroyed.

But whence can we have any ground to entertain such a cruel and gloomy idea of its course and tendency; since it is plain, even unconscious matter, in its seeming dissolution, is not destroyed, but only changed?

All that can be inferred from death is, that a particular order in which certain sensations are now conveyed into our minds, then ceases.

III. In reality, all that can be said to be done, when our bodies are dissolved by death is, that a certain method by which our minds are now affected with sensations and passions, ceases to take place. But can the total destruction of moral powers and beings be inferred from the ceasing of one certain method of being affected, or of receiving sensations from without? According to such a way of arguing, no one sense can be lost; but by parity of reason it might be said, the being who hath lost it can no longer exist. For it would be in vain to say, the present question is not about the dissolution of one organ, but of all our organs; for all of them are as distinct from us, that is, from our thinking part, as any one of them; nay, if any one of them be distinct from it, every one of them must be distinct from it, and consequently all of them together

Whence a destruction of all thinking powers cannot be deduced.

must be different from it. Further, experience tells us, that when all the senses cease to convey sensations from without, imagination, memory and reason can operate, and afford sufficient entertainment and employment to our mind. This happens frequently, not only in sleep, when all the organs of sense are fast locked up; but likewise in serious study, when the mind is intent on the search of truth and knowledge, or conversing with itself about its own actions and duties. How therefore can the destruction of all our moral powers, or of our thinking part, be justly inferred, merely from our ceasing to <235> have communication by our outward organs with a material world? Does any philosopher doubt that certain beings have or may have ideas from without, to which we are utter strangers? Or will any philosopher say, it is impossible even for us to have ideas conveyed to us from without, which we have never yet perceived, and in a quite different way and order from that in which our present ideas of sense are conveyed to us? How then can the total cessation of one way of conveying ideas into the mind from without, prove the total cessation of memory, imagination, reason, and other moral powers, and the absolute annihilation of moral beings! Every presumption which is not founded upon likeness or parity, is allowed in all cases to have no foundation; but what likeness or parity is there, between death, whatever view we take of it, and our total annihilation? Is there any likeness or parity between the destruction of unperceived things not benefited by existence, and perceiving beings, who alone can be said properly to exist, because they alone can properly be said to enjoy? Or is there any likeness, any parity between the constant preservation of inanimate substances, in such a manner that not one particle of matter is lost, but only changes its form, and the total, absolute destruction of perceiving beings? Is there any likeness or parity between the cessation of one manner of being affected with sensations, and the total cessation of all conveyance of ideas into minds from without? Or finally, is there any likeness or parity between the total cessation of all conveyance of sensible ideas from without, and the total destruction of all higher and nobler powers of the intellectual and moral kind? <236>

There is no likeness between death, and total destruction of our being; whatever view we take of it.

IV. That rant of *Pliny* the elder,[a] and of *Lucretius* before him, in which they affect to crowd a great many absurdities together, as resulting from or included in the supposition of our existence after death, does itself terminate in a very glaring contradiction to all sense and reason: for it proceeds upon the supposition of a necessary, physical connexion between the existence of the present material world to us, and the existence

The objections of Pliny *and* Lucretius *against immortality, absurdly suppose that matter can think.*

a. *Pliny* in his *Natural history,* and *Lucretius,* Lib. III

Praeterea gigni pariter cum corpore & una
Crescere sentimus, pariterque senescere mentem, &c.

To which it is sufficient to oppose one excellent passage of *Cicero,* which is so just an account of human nature, and of what may be inferred from it concerning futurity,

of our thinking part. Our bodies and our minds do indeed grow up together, as it is very fit mates should; and when the one suffers in any degree, the other sympathizes with a most tender fellow-feeling, insomuch that when <237> the body is heavily oppressed and disordered,

---

that I cannot chuse but add it to what hath been already quoted, to shew how just notions they had of religion and virtue, of mankind, and the Author of nature. Quid multa? sic mihi persuasi, sic sentio, cum tanta celeritas animorum sit, tanta memoria praeteritorum, futurorumque prudentia, tot artes, tantae scientiae, tot inventa, non posse eam naturam, quae res eas contineat, esse mortalem:—Et cum simplex animi natura sit, neque haberet in se quidquam admixtum dispar sui, atque dissimile, non posse eum dividi: quod si non possit, non posse interire. *Cicero de senectute,* No. 21. These arguments do certainly amount to a very great degree of probability, and must have had a very persuasive influence on minds so well disposed, as to look upon those who taught the mortality of our souls to be *Minuti Philosophi,* because they had pleasure in promoting a doctrine so opposite to the natural greatness of the human mind, and tending to cramp it most miserably: and who were so inclinable to entertain the other chearful and quickening belief, that they could say with *Cicero,* (ibidem) Quod si in hoc erro, *animos hominum immortalis esse credam,* libenter erro: nec mihi hunc errorem, quo delector, dum vivo, extorqueri volo. Sin mortuus (ut quidam minuti philosophi censent) nihil sentiam: non vereor, ne hunc errorem meum mortui philosophi irrideant. [Lucretius, *De rerum natura,* III.445–46: "Besides, we feel that the mind is begotten along with the body, and grows up with it, and with it grows old." Lucretius, *De rerum natura,* trans. W. H. D. Rouse, rev. Martin Ferguson Smith, Loeb Classical Library (Cambridge: Harvard University Press; London: Heinemann, 1975).

Cicero, *De senectute,* xxi.78: "Why multiply words? That is my conviction, that is what I believe—since such is the lightning-like rapidity of the soul, such its wonderful memory of things that are past, such its ability to forecast the future, such its mastery of many arts, sciences and inventions, that its nature, which encompasses all these things, cannot be mortal . . . and since in its nature the soul is of one substance and has nothing whatever mingled with it unlike or dissimilar to itself, it cannot be divided, and if it cannot be divided it cannot perish." Cicero, *De senectute, De amicitia, De divinatione,* trans. William Armstead Falconer, Loeb Classical Library (Cambridge: Harvard University Press; London: Heinemann, 1923).

Ibid., xxiii.85: "And if I err in my belief that the souls of men are immortal, I gladly err, nor do I wish this error which gives me pleasure to be wrested from me while I live. But if when dead I am going to be without sensation (as some petty philosophers think), then I have no fear that these seers, when they are dead, will have the laugh on me!"

Minuti philosophi translates as "petty philosophers."]

the mind is bowed down, and cannot raise itself to its highest exercises. But all this only proves that in this present state, our minds and bodies are united together in the closest and most intimate manner: nay, properly speaking, it only proves, that in this present state our minds are variously affected by the various operations of the laws of matter and motion, according to a certain fixed order. For it is our mind, or thinking part, which perceives, or which is touched and affected: matter or body cannot perceive or feel. Body, or union with body and matter, can, therefore, only mean a certain order or method, according to which the mind is affected. And therefore to say, that mind must cease to exist when body ceases, is indeed to say, that mind must necessarily cease to exist, when one way of its being affected no longer takes place: or it is to say, that mind itself is not distinct from some of its perceptions, and the order in which these are conveyed to it; both which assertions are equally absurd.

They only prove a present dependence of our body and mind, according to certain laws of nature.

To say with the above-mentioned authors, "What probability is there, that we begin to live when we perish; that we become *gods,* or at least *demi-gods,* in comparison of our present state, when we cease to be; or that we are destroyed in order to exist in a more perfect manner?" All this is manifestly begging the question, and taking it as granted that our minds dissolve with our bodies, and consequently, that our thinking part is nothing distinct from its sensible perceptions. But who is not conscious that the principle in him which receives ideas from without, is totally distinct from these passive impressions? Or can any philosopher assert so glaring an absurdity, as to say, passive, unperceiving matter can any otherwise affect a thinking being, than by means of laws appointing a connexion between its operations; or, more properly speaking, operations produced upon it, and certain sensations or <238> passions in minds. But all the idle stuff about matter's acting has been too long ago exploded by philosophers to be now refuted.

V. Let us therefore proceed to such conclusions, as a complete view of our present frame and state suggests, with regard to our surviving the dissolution of our bodies, or the present arbitrary union, by means of our bodies, with a sensible world. Now from what has been proved to

This is a very good first state for such a progressive being as man.

be really our constitution, it is plain that we set out with very good furniture for making considerable progress in knowledge and virtue: our very senses are chiefly given us in order to be instruments and means of virtuous exercises in this present state: what therefore is the natural language resulting from such a frame, but that we are made for continual progress in moral perfection, in proportion to our culture, and our situation for culture, in whatever state or circumstances we may be placed? For because death happens, nothing more can be said on that account, than, "That there is a way at present by which our thinking part is affected, according to certain laws, which ceases upon the

A first state cannot last always, but must give way to another. dissolution of our organical frame by death." It cannot be said, merely on that account, that a Being fitted for moral progress, cannot make progress after such a way of being affected from without no more takes place. The more natural conclusion is, that such a way of being affected ceasing, Beings fitted for progress shall be placed in new circumstances of progress and improvement. A progressive being cannot be made to continue always in the same state; and therefore a being so made has no reason to imagine its first state shall be its only state; or to conclude any thing else, when its first state ceases, than that, as a first state ought not to be, nor cannot indeed in the nature of things be the only state of progressive beings; so accordingly it now goes to another, proper to succeed to its first. <239> This is certainly the conclusion death leads us to, if we take a just view of our moral make; moral powers being

It is therefore reasonable to think that this state only ceases, as the first state of a progressive being ought to do. evidently made for progress, and therefore not for one state: otherwise we must say, that moral powers, which in themselves look to be designed and fit for perpetual cultivation and improvement, must necessarily cease to be, because, though they must have a first state, and are not made always to continue in one state, but for progression, yet this state ceases to be; which is in effect to say, that because our first state ceases, we are not likely to have another, though it must cease, because it is but a first. In other words, it is to argue thus; we must have a first state, being progressive beings, which state can only be a first state; yet if it ceases, we must cease to be. Than which nothing can be more absurd.

It is true, our present state is dissolved with concomitant pains; but what follows from thence? but that it is dissolved in consequence of certain laws of matter and motion, which must, till they have no longer any influence upon us, variously affect us with pains and pleasures: it only follows from hence, that the dissolution comes about analogously to, or consistently with the general laws, according to which we are affected with pain or pleasure from without. These pains are no more a proof of the dissolution of the mind, than any other pains proceeding from the same laws, which the mind survives. And our moral fabric plainly bespeaks only a temporary connexion with matter, as a proper first state, for their formation, exercise and improvement. For even during this connexion, our sensible appetites and gratifications are, according to our fabric, made to submit to our moral powers, in such a manner that unless they are directed and governed by them, they afford no true happiness and enjoyment to us; but rather contrariwise bring pain and < 240 > misery upon us. To illustrate this reasoning more fully, let us consider,

That our death is attended with pain, only proves that the laws of union with body continue to operate till the union is quite dissolved.

VI. There is an evident reason why, in the scale of existence, there should be such a being as man, that is, a moral being connected for a while with a material world; since were there no such being in the world, there would be a great void in nature: such a kind of being is absolutely necessary in the gradation of life and perfection, which makes the riches, the plenitude of nature; because without such a being, nature would not be full and coherent. But there is no reason, on the other hand, why a being made for progress, should always continue in the same state: nay, it is repugnant to the very nature of a progressive being, or a being made for progress toward perfection proportionably to the culture of its powers, that such a being should always continue in that situation which is its beginning or first state. This present condition of mankind, which is requisite in its place to the fullness and consistence of nature, affords us in our first beginning excellent materials and means of improvement in knowledge and virtue, considered as a beginning. And therefore the question is, why it ought not to be considered merely as a beginning? If there is an end to it, as there plainly is by death, what does that prove,

There is a plain reason why there should be such a being as man, or a being with such moral powers united with body.

But there is no reason to think

such an union
should always
continue, or be
the only state
in which our
moral powers
are placed.

but that a beginning or first state of progressive powers does not always last; or that, as it ought not to last, so neither does it? An end to a first state can prove no more, but that it is a first state; its further look must be inferred from the nature of the powers themselves, which make this first state; and therefore it having been found that our powers, sensitive and moral, as they are conjoined in our frame, make an excellent first state, for our formation and improvement in moral perfection; which state is by no means the only state our thinking part, with all its moral powers, can subsist in; it is reasonable <241> to conclude, since this, considered only as a first state, is a very good and proper one, that it is only such. In that view, all is orderly and consonant to the general course and analogy of nature, so far as we can pry into it; and the opposite notion is quite repugnant to the order, beauty and wise administration every where discernible in nature. And therefore this must be the true view of our present state, "That it is indeed our first, which must cease, but not the whole of our existence."

And it is evi-
dent that
union with
body and a
material world
cannot always
last.

VII. But in the next place, as we see a plain reason why the present condition of mankind should take place in nature, which is so fit a state for us to be formed in, or rather to form ourselves in, to a very high degree of perfection, since without such a being as man, nature would not be full and coherent; so we may see a very plain reason, why this state does not always continue: not only a moral reason, why, being a beginning state, it should not continue; but a physical reason why it cannot last always. The existence, that is, the perception of a sensible world, is necessary to the fullness and riches of nature, and the perfection of its works. But this beautiful and useful sensible world, with which we have now communication by means of our bodily organization, must wear out, it cannot last for ever: such is the nature and constitution of matter, or such is the essential law of nature, with regard to all matter that falls within our sense or observation, that it, like artificial machines, is wasted by attrition; all the springs in it decay, become weak, and unable to perform their functions, and at last are quite worn out: nay, this happens to artificial machines, because they are material ones. Such then is the nature of bodies; such is the nature of matter in general. Wherefore the present constitution of our mundan system cannot hold out for ever, its powers will fail, it will at last be no <242> longer able to produce its ends. Or, which is the same thing to us, to all intents and purposes, since the sensible world to us, is the sensible world we are affected by, perceive, and have commerce with; our bodies, by which we have communication with a material world, as they naturally grow up to perfection, so they as naturally decline and dwindle away: nor can we have bodies that must not so waste and consume, composed of any matter we know; or endued with the properties our bodies must necessarily be, to have correspondence with the matter we are acquainted with; since all the matter we know is evidently alterable in its form and texture, by the same laws which render it of any use to us. This all philosophers are agreed in, and therefore we need not insist longer upon it.

This is a plain consequence of the properties of body or matter.

It is owned by all philosophers.

But what follows from this, when we compare our moral powers with this system of matter with which we are now united, which thus perishes; whereas they are of an unperishing nature, and capable of eternal improvement, without any specific alteration of their present make: what follows from thence, but that we are but for a time, and in our beginning state, united with what, though it cannot last for ever, yet while it lasts; or, which is the same thing to us, while our correspondence with it lasts, affords to our moral powers in their first beginnings, very proper objects to exert themselves about; very proper means and occasions for their improvement. This, certainly, is what alone can be rationally inferred from the complex view of our frame, especially if we add to this,

Hence it is reasonable to conclude, that our moral powers, naturally capable of lasting for ever without wearing out, are only united for a time with bodies, in order to the fulness of nature, and because it is a very proper first state for our powers to be formed and improved in.

VIII. That in consequence of the frame of our earth, and the nature of our present united state, all mankind cannot live together on earth; but as it now happens, one generation must make room for another; because the earth would soon be overpeopled, if it were not inhabited as it is, by succes-<243>sions. I need not tell those who have the smallest tincture of natural philosophy, that in order to make our earth more capacious, or a proper habitation for a much greater number of inhabitants of vari-

Men must live upon earth by successive generations.

ous kinds than it now is, that its magnitude must be increased, and consequently the whole constitution of our mundan system, if not of all things that exist, must be changed: for if the proportions of the magnitudes of the bodies which compose it be altered, their distances, orbits, attractions, and in one word, all the laws relative to them, must be changed: and therefore to demand such an alteration with regard to our earth, is in reality to desire, there were no such system in nature as our mundan one, but that its space were entirely void, or filled with another

Our earth could not be rendered more capacious, without altering our whole mundan system, and in all likelihood the whole universe.

system of a different texture: which will be allowed to be a demand that is physically absurd; since, as far as we can carry our researches, or as analogy can lead us to form any notion of things, nature is full and coherent as it is, and cannot be so if any change were made. But since it is so that mankind must occupy the earth by successive generations, and that the earth which is a fit and proper part of our mundan system; which in its space is the properest system with regard to the whole of nature: what follows from this, according to the rules of analogical reasoning, but that though one generation of men gives place to another, and must do so, and things are likely to continue so, while the earth continues to

When our mundan system is able to hold out no longer, there is reason from analogy to think it shall be succeeded by another, proper to succeed to it, perhaps rising out of its ruins.

be a fit habitation for them, which it is likely to be while the laws of our mundan system are able to hold it together in tolerable order; yet our mundan system, and consequently our earth, and all successions of its inhabitants, must have an end at last, and shall be succeeded by another system, formed perhaps out of the ruins of this, which shall be in its place and order of succession, as beautifully, regularly, and beneficially constituted, as this present one is. This is <244> indeed, what present order, and the analogy of things naturally lead us to conceive: for why should we apprehend nature to be exhausted by the present production? What reason have we to believe its fecundity so limited and scanty? Or if this be not its only birth, why should we imagine that its future ones shall be less regular, shapely, and sound? But these things I only mention, to shew how analogy leads us to think of nature in general, or with regard to its general order of production, that we may the better feel the force of the presumptions which arise from analogy, with regard to ourselves.

But if so, we have yet better

For if we have reason to think so of nature in general, as hath been suggested, why ought we not to think of nature with regard to ourselves in like manner? What reason have we to fear that the parent who produced us, hath provided so liberally for us, and set us so well at present, cannot provide another habitation for us, when this fails, as well fitted to us as a second state, as this is as a first state? Hath nature, which hath produced our moral powers, and such variety of entertainment and employment for them, no further power, no further fertility? Is it quite drained, is it quite unable to support us longer, or to make further provision for us?

reason to think this is but our first state, which shall be succeeded by one very proper to follow it.

IX. Before we proceed to other arguments to corroborate all that hath been said, let us add, that the same principle so easily admitted by all philosophers, with regard to our present state, "That without it nature could not have been full and coherent," extends a great deal further than some are apt to imagine. It affords an excellent argument for our future existence. For if mankind cease to be at death, or when their bodies are dissolved, there must necessarily, upon that event, be a chasm or blank in nature; since it is only a transition by man from this to another state, suited to him as coming from the present one, which can continue the chain <245> of being without any interruption or breach. It is, upon supposition of our perishing totally by death, broken and discontinued. This opinion concerning the plenitude of nature, and a rising scale of existence through all possible gradations of being, to the highest, is not only an ancient one, but it is what the contemplation of nature naturally, if not necessarily directs us to: for where do we perceive any void? how nicely, how subtly, or by what imperceptible steps do beings rise to man, the only order of moral agents within our observation in our present state? And if we do not perceive a chasm in the descending gradation of nature, from us to meer vegetative life, why should we dream of any blank in the ascending gradation above us, to which by our imagination (so vast is its expanding power) we can set no bounds. This however is certain, that if the maxim be well founded, and there be no reason to think that there ever can be any void in nature; it must likewise be true, that no perceiving being shall ever cease to exist, but shall continue to be, and to pass through the gradations suited to its kind, and consequently to the riches and fullness which makes the perfection of nature.

If mankind cease to be at death, there will necessarily be a void, a chasm in nature.

That nature is full and coherent, we have reason to conclude from experience and analogy.

Or whatever may be said of merely sensitive beings of the lower order (to whom, however, why should we begrudge immortality, as if the value of ours would be lessened by its being common to all perceiving beings)

Yet that maxim must be false, if man is not made for eternal progress, and ceases to be at death. at least, it must be true that moral agents cannot cease to be, but must continue for ever, and must pass thro' the several gradations naturally suited to them, in proportion to their culture and care to improve. This must be true, because indeed, not only upon the ceasing of any species, but upon the ceasing of any individual of moral agents to exist, there necessarily would be a chasm, an interruption in the chain of nature; a want, a deficiency, instead of fullness. For a moral being, instead of making the progress it is naturally fitted for, would thus stop short, and <246> so leave nature void of that particular progression it, and it alone, can make or fill up. The progress man, as such, is fitted to make in a succeeding state to this, is no less necessary to the complete fullness and perfection of nature, than that which he is fitted for in this present state; for it is only a being so constituted, that is, it is only man, who can make that progress; and all possible progresses in moral perfection are requisite to make nature full and coherent. That idea involves in it the existence of all capacities of moral perfection which can exist, and consequently of all possible progresses, or all the progresses which may be made by moral powers of all sorts, in proportion to the culture, implied in the very notion of moral perfection, of each according to its kind, and in its particular manner. If therefore the riches and perfection of nature

But we have no ground to doubt of the fullness of nature. consists in such fullness, and such fullness really be the end pursued by nature, man is not to perish, but to make for ever progress, in proportion to the pains he takes to improve himself. But, indeed, as we cannot form any other notion of fullness and perfection in nature, but this which hath been described, so the further we advance in the knowledge of nature, the more instances we find of this fullness, riches, and coherence; and consequently, the more must we be confirmed in this opinion of

This idea is natural to the mind; it greatly delights in it. nature, than which nothing can be more delightful. Our mind seems to be formed to conceive it, take hold of it, and rejoice in it with unspeakable triumph. Whence else could it afford us the satisfaction and transport it does; how else could it so wonderfully dilate, expand, and quicken our mind, were we not made to be so affected by it? And if it is naturally so pleasing, so exhilarating to the mind, must it not be true? can it be a delusion? Were not nature really as great as this conception, so natural to the human mind, represents it to be, whence could we have that idea? How could we be so great-mind-<247>ed as to form it; how could nature lead us to it as the most natural sentiment?

It is needless, however, to tell philosophers that this notion concerning the fullness of nature, cannot without manifest absurdity, be extended to signify, "That nature hath always been full;" since created beings must begin to be; and that only hath no beginning which is uncreated, and exists by necessity of nature from all eternity: nor to signify, "that nature hath at all times been full, with all kinds of perfection and happiness, or capacities of them:" since moral powers, the chief of all powers, are in their nature progressive; and progress, in the very idea of it, supposes a time preceeding every acquired degree of perfection, in which that did not, nor could not exist; or, in other words, supposes intermediate steps by which the progress is made. The fullness of nature, therefore, can only mean a continued, unbroken progress towards fullness; if which take place, man must be immortal. For otherwise a certain, possible progress would not take place; and so nature would not be a perfectly full, and coherent progress, which we have so good reason from the analogy of nature to think it is intended to be.

But by fullness of nature can only be meant a full progress.

Which cannot be the case, if man is not immortal.

Hitherto I have only spoken of *nature;* because reasonings from analogy require no more, but that we argue from the observable state and course of things. And according to this way of reasoning, we see that from nature, considered as a whole, as one frame or constitution of things, there is no ground to imagine that the better or nobler parts in it, moral powers, do not, as well as all its other parts, naturally tend towards their highest and noblest end; or that they shall only last for a while, and then be destroyed: there is no appearance of any such imperfection, any such disorder and waste, any such destroying humour and tendency in nature. In this way of reasoning, we have abstracted <248> from all consideration of the temper and disposition of the universal mind; and have considered nature itself just as we would consider and argue from any

Hitherto we have only enquired what ought to be inferred from the course of nature by analogy.

But this course of nature proves the Author of nature to be perfectly well disposed.

machine, by itself, with respect to its ultimate tendency. But since there can be no established course of things without a mind; and such a settled, wise course of things as we have found human nature and the laws relative to it to be, plainly proves the efficiency and superintendency of a powerful, wise and benevolent mind; let us now see how the conclusion will turn out upon changing the phrase: and if instead of arguing from the stated order and course of things, we reason from the nature of the Author, of which that affords a plain and irresistible proof, "Perfect, good and wise contrivance, is the good contrivance of some mind equal to it; it is therefore the contrivance and effect of a very powerful, wise, and good mind." Let us therefore no longer leave the governing mind out of the question; and let us now ask ourselves what it is reasonable to think concerning death, since,

Let us therefore consider how the argument will stand when instead of nature, or the course of things, we say the good and wise Author of nature.

1. Our frame and contexture shews in every respect an excellent moral disposition in our Maker, provided we are not destroyed by death, but are really intended, as our moral powers evidently seem to be, for eternal progress in moral perfection, proportionable to our care to improve in it; or since, could we but conclude that to be the case, there would be no ground at all to doubt of the perfect goodness of our Author, our present state being, upon that hypothesis, a most excellent first state of trial and formation for our moral powers, and consequently a full proof of an infinitely wise and generous superintendency.

Since, 2dly, We not only can exist after our connexion with a material world by means of our bodies ceases, there being no necessary, but only a voluntary or arbitrary connexion between our moral powers and bodies; or a sensible world, and the <249> dissolution of our bodies is but the necessary effect of the very same laws which render a sensible world, which cannot always last, while it lasts, so fit an occasion and subject for the improvement of our moral powers in this their first state.

Since, 3dly, The very nature of a progress supposes a change of state, the cessation of a first, and a transition to another: since, I say, all those principles are true, let us ask ourselves, whether it is not reasonable to look upon this as our proper first state, which shall be succeeded by another, as fit to follow it as this is to be our first state? Let us ask ourselves, whether this is not a reasonable conclusion from these principles; or what else can be supposed, that is so consonant to the nature of things, and to that temper and disposition of the Maker and Governor of the world which it indicates? For the argument in its weakest form must stand thus, "All nature looks well with respect to virtue, provided death does not annihilate our moral powers, and this be but our first state of trial and formation: all but this one doubtful phaenomenon bespeaks an excellent Maker and Governor." Now if this be the case, why does this single fact alarm us, or appear frightful to us, since our communion with this sensible world is but an arbitrary connexion; this sensible world cannot last always, but our moral powers may survive its destruction, and we cannot pass into another state without leaving this, which we only do in the manner necessary, in consequence of the very laws which render our present state, while it lasts, so fit a subject and means for the improvement of our powers. This, I say, is the only probable conclusion we can draw concerning death, from the consideration of our present frame, if our present connexion with a sensible world be only an arbitrary connexion. But the strength of conviction this argument carries along with it, in this shape, will encrease upon us, the more we reason the matter with ourselves, from the account that has been given of <250> our constitution, and of the order of things in this our present situation, relative to our moral powers.

How the argument must then stand in its weakest form.

For, I. If in the present state of mankind, even those laws of matter and motion, in consequence of which death happens, are so well adjusted to our happiness, or our progress in moral perfection, what reason have we to apprehend such bad management and intention toward man, as his total destruction by death plainly imports? It is only confusion and disorder which forebodes greater confusion and disorder: it is only evil dispositions and intentions plainly displayed and evidenced, which can reasonably create fear: present order prognosticates future order; evidences of goodness and kind intention ought to create trust and confidence: seeing therefore man is made for a very noble end here; and since all the laws and powers relative to his situation are excellently fitted to that end, what ground can we have to conceive so ill of the disposition

It gathers strength from several considerations.

It is only from confusion and disorder that confusion and disorder can be reasonably inferred.

of our Author, as to think he had no other design with regard to us, than to equip and furnish us for everlasting progress, merely to have the pleasure of disappointing us, by demolishing our powers almost as soon as he gave us being; or as we had arrived by the course of things, to a tolerable conception of what our powers may attain to by due culture, if they are not wilfully destroyed. We can draw no just conclusion concerning the dissolution of our bodies at death, in consequence of the laws of the material creation, without taking into our consideration the other parts of our present make, and the ends to which they are adapted; for that would be to reason from a very partial view of the object. And therefore the only question with regard to man is, whether there is any ground to think, from the consideration of his many moral faculties, that these are made to be destroyed with our bodily frame; or whether there is not, on the contrary, better reason to think that this state is his first probationary <251> one, or one very fit for him in the beginning of his existence, in order to his being schooled, tried and improved to a very considerable degree of perfection, but not his only one, or the whole of his existence. Now the result of all that has been said of our frame and constitution, and of the laws relative to our present condition prove, that it is an excellent first state, a very proper school for our moral improvement; a state in which we may by proper culture, in consequence of the occasions, materials and means it affords us, arrive at a very considerable degree of perfection as a first state. And why therefore should we think, that when our bodily organization is destroyed, and consequently all the present material objects of gratification or exercise are taken from us, our minds capable of higher pleasures and enjoyments, are also quite destroyed together with what they have only an arbitrary connexion with: a connexion which ought to cease with its end and use; a connexion which cannot in the nature of things always last; and which must of necessity cease if we are progressive beings, as we as plainly appear to be, as any machine appears to be fitted for its end; for a state cannot succeed to another, unless that other give way to it. Would not this indeed be to conclude, that to beings made for progress, and therefore to change states, what may be only a change of state, and what must

Our present state is an excellent first state, considered as such, and therefore it forebodes a good, orderly future state, to succeed it.

happen upon the change of our present state according to its very good laws, is not a change, but destruction of being? Is it not, in short, to say, that what is well conducted as a first part, is for that reason not to be looked upon as a well conducted first part, but as a bad whole?

II. We cannot suppose death to be a transition to another state, but the same pains and other circumstances which now attend it, must likewise accompany it on that supposition: since they are the necessary effects of our bodily constitution, and the <252> laws of matter and motion. But it is most consonant to the nature of our moral powers, and to the provision made for their improvement here, to suppose it not a dissolution of our whole frame, but merely of our bodily part, and a transition into another state; and therefore the presumption must be that it is such. Some may imagine that there would not be so much ground for doubting about our future existence, if all mankind lived till their constitutions were quite worn out in old age, and none were destroyed violently. But what tho' some die in infancy, others in their prime? What tho' death comes upon men at all ages; since it always happens in consequence of laws of matter and motion necessary to many excellent purposes in our present state; and nature may have adjusted the state into which men pass from this, at whatever period of life, or with whatever temperature of mind, so as that a future life shall make with this a very regular, consistent and well adjusted whole; a compleat *drama,* as some of the ancients have not improperly expressed it. The only question is, Whether there is not good reason to think so from the present state of things, and no just reason to fear the contrary? Whether our being does not begin in such a manner as forebodes an orderly and proper progress instead of sudden destruction? Upon supposition that this is not the whole of our being, but that there is a future state; or, (to speak more agreeably to what our moral being presages) upon supposition that we are immortal, it is easy on that hypothesis to conceive how mankind's entering upon a future state, at various ages, may contribute to the happiness, variety and general good of a future state. But death, however it happens, is the effect of the steady operation of the laws of the material system, which

It is no objection again this reasoning, that death comes upon men at all ages.

For as this is the necessary effect of good laws, so it may be requisite to general good in a future state.

are found to be every way well adjusted to it; and it is not inconvenient, but rather necessary to the general well-being of mankind in this state. For which reasons, unless it could be proved that this phenome- <253>non cannot possibly contribute otherwise than to disorder in a future state, it cannot be any ground for calling the good government of the world into question, or of fears with regard to futurity.

To imagine that we are destroyed at death, is to think worse of the Author of nature than we can of any rational creature.

III. In fine, if it be true, as I think it hath been sufficiently proved, that man is made in this state (whether it be his only one or not) for progress in virtue; for governing his sensible appetites by reason and a moral sense, and for the generous pursuit of public good; and that all the parts of his frame concur to fit him for that end, push him to pursue it, or afford him means of pursuing it; and consequently of exerting great virtues: if this be true, then there can be no more reason to apprehend that the Author of such a frame and constitution of things, only designed man to make progress in it for a short time, and after that to cease by being destroyed, than there is reason to imagine that he would have made us for moral perfection, and for happiness by so doing, if he had no pleasure in moral creatures and their virtuous improvements and happiness. And sure no other reason could have induced our Author to indue us with reason and a moral sense, but satisfaction in the improvement and hap- piness of moral beings. But such a motive could never have determined him to set such narrow bounds to our moral improvements, by allowing such a short duration to our existence, as is the case on supposition that we perish with our bodies. Why should we conceive so of our Author; since hardly is there any one among us that would do so, or any thing like it, had we any power analogous to his? For can there be among men goodness surpassing that of the universal parent; benevolence excelling his, who made us capable of forming the idea of benevolence, and de- lighting in it. We may here apply what the Poet says on another occasion, and ask,

> *Heus age, responde, minimum est quod scire laboro,*
> *De Jove quid sentis? est ne, ut praeponere cures* <254>

Hunc cuinam? cuinam? vis staio? an scilicet haeres?
Quis potior judex, puerisve quis optior orbis?

Pers. Sat. 2.[85]

IV. It is true, every part of a whole must be submitted to the greater good of that whole. But what reason can we have to imagine, that the greater good of the whole creation to which we belong as a part, can require our destruction after we have existed for some short time; since we may exist, when our relation to this material world no longer subsists? Hardly will any one say, that there may not be room for us, after the destruction of our bodies, in immense space. And certainly the greater good of intelligent beings, in the sum of things, cannot require the annihilation of any particular species capable of moral or intellectual happiness and perfection. The fewer species there are in nature capable of moral happiness, the smaller quantity of capacity for happiness, and consequently of happiness itself, there must be in nature: that is, the less perfect must nature be: but if the greater good of the whole cannot make it necessary that there should be less good in the whole than may be, it can never make it necessary that mankind, capable of existing in another state, should be annihilated. Can the good of intelligent beings demand, that man should be made for acquiring virtue, to improve in many excellent qualifications, and that only that he might cease to be when he is considerably improved? And yet this is the fate of all men, who have given due pains to add virtue to virtue, and to advance in wisdom and goodness, if men perish with their bodies. What can the greatest good of intelligent be-

The greater good of the whole cannot make it necessary.

85. Persius, *Satires,* II.17–20: "Come now, answer me this question: it is a very little thing that I want to know; What is your opinion of Jupiter? Would you rank him above—'Above whom?'—Above whom, you ask? Well, shall we say Staius? or do you stick at that? Could you name a more upright judge than Staius; or one more fitted to be a guardian to an orphan family?" *Juvenal and Persius,* trans. G. G. Ramsay, rev. ed., Loeb Classical Library (London: Heinemann; Cambridge: Harvard University Press, 1940).

'Tis in vain to say, that we who know but a small part cannot judge of the whole.

ings, or of beings in general, mean, but the greatest aggregate or sum of happy beings? And can the greatest sum of happy beings require that there should be a quantity of happiness wanting which may exist? To assert this, is really the same absurdity as to say, that four is not a greater number than two. 'Tis in vain to say, that if nature had intended the greatest aggre-<255>gate of good which could exist, there would be no degree of pain or misery in nature: For with respect to physical evils or pains, they are the effects of good laws whose uniform operation is absolutely good. And with regard to the greatest aggregate of moral good or happiness which could exist, all that can be done consistently with the very nature and kind of it, was to produce the greatest aggregate that could be of the capacity of it; since moral happiness must, according to its very notion, be a moral progress, a moral acquisition, or the result of the right use moral beings make of their moral powers.

For we are able clearly to determine several truths:

as, that the world must be governed by general laws.

V. It is likewise to no purpose to say, we who know but a part, cannot reason about what the greatest good of the whole may or may not require: For tho' it be very true, that we know but a small part of the immense system of nature, and that our faculties are very narrow, compared with that vast object; yet our knowledge must certainly extend as far as we have clear and distinct ideas, and are able to perceive clearly their agreements and disagreements. And we may form the ideas of a whole, and of universal order and good from the consideration of any part of nature: every part, as for instance, every vegetable, or every animal, being itself a particular whole, tho' a part of a larger system: or we may form these ideas from the consideration of any machine of human invention: and so soon as we attend to these ideas of whole and universal good, we clearly perceive, 1. That all the interests of intelligent beings require that nature should operate according to general fixed laws; and there cannot be beauty, regularity and perfection in a whole, without the observance of general laws in the disposition, oeconomy and operations of the whole. The very notion of a whole, includes in it an aptitude of parts to a principal end, a fixed design, and regular fixed means operating towards that design in the simplest and steddiest way. In like manner may <256> we conclude concerning a whole of intelligent beings. 2. That no effects of the general laws necessary to their good are evil with regard to the whole, since all the inconveniencies of the uniformity of such laws are fully compensated by the particular advantages which result from them, together with the general advantages redounding from the universality and uninterrupted operation of laws. 3. In like manner may we conclude, that something must be wanting to the perfection of a whole of intelligent beings, if any additional quantity of happiness could take place in it. 4. In like manner may we conclude, that a whole, consisting of a variety of moral beings, the happiness of whom is made dependent on themselves, or to be acquired by themselves, is a more perfect whole, than one consisting merely of perceiving beings incapable of reflexion, willing, chusing, approving, disapproving affections and actions; or, in a word, who have no dominion, power or sphere of activity. All these, and many other such general conclusions may be as certainly laid down as any conclusions whatsoever in any science: they are plain corrolaries from the very idea or definition of a whole, and of general perfection and good. Good must mean the good of some perceiving being; and if one perceiving being may be of a higher order than another, (as very different orders, classes and ranks may be conceived) then is moral perfection, or the capacity of attaining to moral perfection, higher than merely perceptive power, that is, meer capacity of receiving sensations. And if so, the greater quantity of happiness producible, must mean no more, than the greatest quantity of capacity for moral happiness.

VI. Nay, tho' we are not able to comprehend the whole of nature, there are yet more particular inferences which we may deduce with as great certainty as these general ones concerning the perfection and <257> good of a whole, with reference to our existence after the dissolution of our bodies. 1. It is only the due care of moral beings that can make a perfect whole; for they are the chief beings in rank and dignity; or their happiness is the object of the greatest importance, the greater good. And therefore it is not consistent with good order, not only to suppose the laws of matter not subservient to them, since matter itself is incapable

That no effects of general good laws are evil.

That a whole cannot be perfect, if any greater, quantity of happiness could take place in it.

That the good of a moral system ought to be preferred to the good of an inanimate system.

of happiness or enjoyment; but it is likewise so, to suppose the greater quantity of moral happiness to be lessened to make room for, or give place to a quantity of merely perceptive enjoyment. 2. The happiness of moral beings, their moral instruction, or their encouragement to the improvement of their moral powers, cannot require that any moral being, who in their first state have made good improvements, or have laid themselves out with all sincerity and constancy to make progress towards moral perfection, should so soon as they have done so be destroyed. 3. Far less can any of these ends require, that they should be moved into another state, in which improvement shall be under very great discouragements and disadvantages, and where moral beings who have made considerable improvements shall have less occasions and means of improving in moral qualifications, than in their beginning state. These ends cannot require, that virtue should be necessarily pushed backwards, forced into decline, or deprived of all opportunities of advancing. Nothing can be more repugnant to the idea of a good governor, and of the pursuit of general good, and of a perfect whole, than such administration. 4. Far less still can these ends require, that beings furnished, prompted and encouraged, as we are in this state by our make and frame to make progress in virtue, should, after having taken due pains to attain to a certain degree of it, be banished into a state absolutely contrived for the suffering and misery of such moral beings. 5. Not on-<258>ly are such propositions diametrically opposite to the notion of a good and perfect whole, and of a wise and perfect governor; but from the very idea of a perfect whole of moral beings, it necessarily follows, that beings who have suffered in their first state by their steady adherence to virtue in spite of all opposition through the vices of others, must have reparation made to them; that is, be placed in such happy circumstances for the exercise and improvement of their virtue, as shall make their reflexion upon their past struggles and sufferings for virtue's sake exceedingly delightful to them, and greatly contribute to stir them up to redoubled zeal to make higher improvements suitable to so generous a recompense from the governor of the world, by placing them in happier circumstances of improvement. In general, we may conclude, that if the greatest good and perfection of moral beings be intended and pursued, the

The greater happiness of moral beings cannot require the destruction of moral powers.

Or discouragement of virtue in a future state.

Far less the absolute misery of virtue.

The general good must make it necessary that tried and improved virtue be promoted.

happy connexions which now take place, in consequence of which virtue is the highest enjoyment or moral perfection, is the greatest happiness, shall not be changed for the worse, or to the disadvantage of moral perfection; nor those which tend to make every degree of vice its own punishment, give place to others, which shall absolutely invite and encourage to vice, and discourage virtuous exercises and improvements. We cannot indeed imagine, that moral beings cease to be agents, or are laid even by way of punishment under a fatal, physical necessity of being irreclaimable; that they can be made utterly incapable of reflexion and reformation, or be tied to vice by any other fetters, besides those arising from habit, which hold the wicked so fast intangled. But then there is no reason to think, that their bad contracted habits will not adhere closly to them, and greatly torment them, all the means and objects of their gratification being removed: much less that there will be such a change in a future state in favour of vice, that it shall not so much as suffer in any way <259> analogous to what it suffers here, by being its own tormenter and punisher: but that it shall immediately become happier than it now is or can be; whilst the hatred of it is quite inextinguishable in our minds.

It cannot require that the present connexions of things should be changed in favour of vice.

In one word, if we are made for virtue, and so to be happy by attaining to it here to as high a degree of perfection as is consistent with a first state; then to apprehend any succeeding state, in which all the present constitutions in favour of virtue, and the discouragements of vice shall be reversed, is contrary to analogy, to probability, and, in one word, to all our methods of reasoning about beings and things. It is to conclude from wise and good administration, that very bad government shall succeed: it is to infer malice from goodness: it is to deduce grounds of distrust and fear from the plainest symptoms of sincere kindness and good-will.

All these reasonings about futurity must hold good, if in the present state, things are so far constituted in favour of virtue and moral perfection, that there is reason to conclude our Maker and Governor sincerely loves and delights in our moral improvements. Were there not indeed manifest tokens in the present oeconomy and government of our Author with relation to us, and to all beings within our observation, of due regard to virtue; suitable care of its education, improvement and hap-

piness, then truly might we with reason dread a succession of worse government, and fear this were but the prelude to complete misery: but if
from what hath been said of human nature, it plainly appears, that while
due care is taken of inferior beings in our system, suitable provision is
also made for us who are capable of very high moral attainments; that
is, for our improvement in many noble moral qualifications, in so much
that all the laws of the material system, to which we are subjected by
our union with a sensible world, are admirably conducive to our moral
improvement and moral happiness; then may we justly not only hope
<260> well concerning futurity, but rest satisfied that such an excellent
first state of mankind shall be succeeded not by a worse, but by a better
with respect to virtue and moral perfection; that is, one suited to tried
and proved beings. To apprehend the contrary, would be to fear where
there is the best foundation for comfortable expectation. It would be to
think worse of the Author of nature than we can think of any man, who
has any degree of goodness, any sparks of wisdom, or any benevolence
in his constitution. For can he be called good among men, nay, or any
thing else than the cruelest of tyrants, who would exercise his power in
the manner such suppositions make the Author of nature, and of all the
goodness men are capable of, to act with regard to his moral creatures?

The only objections against the preceeding train of argument I can
foresee, which deserve our attention, are these two following ones.

Objection I.   I. It may be said, that almost all the knowledge we can acquire here, is
such knowledge of the material world, and of our present connexions
with it, as can only qualify us for living in this state, or in one very similar
and analogous to it: It can be of no use to us in one quite new, or absolutely different from this present condition of mankind. How can our
present state be considered as a school to form and fit us for another
succeeding one, unless we can attain here to such knowledge of our future life as may prepare us for it? For without such instruction, whatever
other knowledge we may acquire, we must be as great novices at our
entrance on a future state, and as much to begin to learn then how to
act or behave ourselves, as we are when we enter upon this present stage.
How can that be called a school for a state, in which we cannot possibly

acquire any notion of its constitution and laws, or be any way made acquainted with it, but to which we must needs go <261> as much at a loss about every connexion and law in it, as if we had had no schooling at all? But what can we know here of our future condition? All we can learn here hath only relation to this state, and is hardly sufficient for our direction in it.

This objection appears at first sight not unplausible. But it will soon evanish when we consider,

I. That those powers which, at our entrance upon life, are and must   Answer. necessarily be but in *embrio,* rude and shapeless as it were, or quite un-formed, may be made very vigorous and perfect here by proper exercise and culture; so as to become fit to be employed about any objects of knowledge of whatever kind, or however different from those which make the present materials of our study and speculation. Insomuch that this state may as properly be said to be a school for forming and perfec-tionating our rational powers, in order to their being prepared and fitted for exercise about higher objects in a succeeding state; as the first part of our education here is called a school for life, or to prepare us for the affairs of the world and manhood, which are objects far above our reach, till our understanding by proper gradual exercise and employment is considerably ripened, or enlarged and strengthened, which is the proper business of liberal education.

II. But not only is it true, that our understanding may be sharpened, invigorated and improved in this state by suitable culture, so as to be rendered fit for progress in knowledge in an after-life, which rational powers cannot be but in a gradual progressive manner, in consequence of due exercise and culture: But which is more, the knowledge and vir-tue; or, in one word, the moral perfection of whatever sort we acquire here, can never be lost labour, or be useless to us, however foreign to the pre-<262>sent state of mankind any other we go into may be. For,

i. Imagination and memory may retain the idea of the present world, and all the knowledge we have acquired of it, so as to be able to compare the new one with it; as a person, who happens to lose his sight after he had attained to a very considerable acquaintance with the visible world, may always retain that knowledge, of which there are many examples. 2. No state into which moral beings can be supposed to pass, can be absolutely, or in all respects so disanalogous to that from which they go into it, but the knowledge of their own powers, or of the fabrick and constitution of their mind; and all the knowledge of moral powers which analogy can lead us to, must be in several regards of very important use to them. Every state of moral beings must be in many respects analogous to every other state of moral beings; because moral beings, however different they may be from one another, must in several respects bear an analogy or likeness one to another. And as that must be true in general of all moral beings; so must it likewise be true, that every new progressive state of the same moral beings must bear a very particular analogy or likeness to the state immediately preceeding it: Therefore, as much knowledge of the common properties, relations and laws relative to all moral beings, and all moral endowments; and as thorough a knowledge of ourselves in particular; that is, as extensive a moral knowledge as we can attain to in this state, must be of very great consequence to us upon our entrance into any new one, however different it may be from the present. 3. Tho', in progress of time, all memory of our present state should be entirely lost or quite effaced; yet beings who have made progress in knowledge, and understand what enquiry into the nature of things means, and how such researches ought to be carried on and pursued, must be so far past schooling, that they shall no more need to learn <263> or be instructed in that art, which however is not only the first and most essential, but the most difficult part of knowledge; without which indeed no progress can be made, and which being acquired, progress is very easy and rather pleasure than toil. This done, the science of advancing in knowledge is mastered, the nature of truth and knowledge is understood; and that being over, the mind is so far very well fitted and prepared for any state, and can never again be such an infant or novice in any state of moral powers, as it must necessarily be at its first existence, before any notion of knowledge, or of the methods and arts of acquiring it is formed; and while its powers are quite weak and uncultivated as moral powers must needs be till they are unfolded and perfected by use and culture. All this will be yet clearer if we reflect, 4. How much is over when beings have learned to reduce appearances to general laws, and to look out for harmonies, analogies and agreements of effects; and are, by practice in induction, become masters of that only way of reasoning by which real knowledge can be attained. For they are thus prepared for unravelling any appearances, and for tracing them to their sources and causes, or general laws; and so are fit for studying any system in order to get the knowledge of its constitution and laws. Into whatever state one may pass, it must certainly be a very high and advantageous preparation for it, to be able to know how to go to work to get real knowledge and to avoid error; to have distinct ideas of general order, beauty and good, and of government by universal laws. Now so far may all advance in this state, who will give due diligence to improve their understanding and reason in the search of nature. 5. Besides, it is evident, that into whatever state one enters, the knowledge of number and proportion must always be of use, since these are properties or relations which must belong to all objects, and to all states. 6. And as for the <264> knowledge of moral duties resulting from moral relations, that science, which of all others is the most becoming moral beings, and ought to be their chief study, it must be of perpetual and unchangeable use. The present virtues and vices must remain essentially the same in every state. Benevolence in all its branches must endure for ever. And what else are all the virtues but acts of generous affection? New relations will produce new obligations and duties; but the nature of moral obligation being well understood, new relations can no sooner present themselves to a mind so well qualified, but the duties resulting from them must immediately be discovered and perceived. 7. And, in the last place, as for the dominion over ourselves, and the inward liberty and power, and all the good habits which may be formed and acquired here by the assiduous study and practice of virtue, to attain to which is our principal business in this our first state, these being once acquired or established, that important work is over; that part of education or schooling, so essential to the happiness of moral beings in whatever state they may be placed, is past; and being accomplished, it must produce its natural good fruits and effects. The happiness resulting from a well-formed mind, and highly improved virtue, cannot take place till virtue is brought by due culture to great maturity and perfection. That is as impossible as it is for any plant to come to its maturity otherwise than by gradual progress, and to yield its fruit before it is grown up to its fruitful state; but when the good seeds of virtue are ripened, then must its happy harvest naturally succeed; then must virtue have its full effect: we must sow before we reap; but as we sow, so shall we reap; such really the constitution of things with regard to us evidently appears to be. So that, in every proper sense, this present state may be called our school, or our state of education for a future state, however new that state may be to us at our first arrival into it: our state of for-<265>mation, discipline and culture, whether with regard to our understanding or our will; whether with regard to science or temper; knowledge or virtue; our rational faculties, or our appetites, affections and passions. But all that hath been said will be still more evident when we have considered the other objection, to which I therefore proceed.

Another objection. II. It is said, why is not virtue compleatly happy here, and vice, on the other hand, compleatly miserable? Or since it is not so, what reason have we to imagine a succeeding state shall not be of the same mixed kind, in which the vicious may have a great share of pleasure, and the virtuous a large share of uneasiness and suffering, and in which goods and evils shall be as promiscuously dispensed as they are here? If we reason from analogy, let us reason analogously, and not conclude a better state from this confused, promiscuous distribution of things, in which virtuous and vicious persons (to say no more) are not distinguished from one another by any remarkable dispensation of favours to the former, and punishments to the latter. For here do not all things happen alike or indifferently to all men? that is, are not external advantages and disadvantages administered either by no rule at all, or at least, in a way which virtue has but little reason to think particularly in her favour and interest?

Answer. Now in answer to this objection, which hath been often urged in various forms, let it be observed that, were not the present condition of mankind a very proper first state for forming and training up moral powers to great perfection, there would, indeed, be no reason at all to think well of the Author of nature, or to hope well concerning futurity. But, on the contrary, if it really appears to be a very proper first state for the education of our moral powers to a very high degree of perfection, then there must <266> be very good ground to entertain a good opinion of our Creator, and to expect such a state to succeed to this, as is proper to succeed to a state of education and discipline. The whole stress of our argument lies upon that.

Now that this present state is a very proper one for the education, exercise and culture of our moral powers, is manifest: For,

1. We have moral powers capable of improvement to great perfection; and this state affords us excellent means, occasions, subjects and materials for their exercise and culture, in order to their very high improvement. And all the laws relative to the growth and improvement, or the degeneracy and corruption of our moral powers are very suitable to the nature of moral powers, and their progressive formation and course, in general; and to our rank and situation, in particular: insomuch that all the goods and evils which happen to us in this life, may very properly be considered as fit means and occasions of improvement in virtue: not the evils only, but likewise the goods; for as adversity is necessary to form, exercise and improve certain virtues, so is prosperity, to exercise, form and improve other virtues: and in a state of trial, formation and culture, various means of exercise, trial and culture are absolutely necessary. Objectors against providence are apt to represent distresses and afflictions only as trials; but those who take a right view of moral powers, and of the natural progress of virtue to perfection, will consider prosperous circumstances in the same light, with regard to beings, whose first end is to be formed to virtue; that is, by means of trial. Nay, those who have thoroughly studied human nature, have not scrupled to pronounce ease and plenty to be a severer searcher, explorer, and prover of the human mind,[a] than <267> the more ordinary and tolerable vexations of human

---

a. So *Salust.* Secundae res animum sapientis fatigant. So *Tacitus,* Hist. lib 1. Fortunam adhuc tantam adversam tulisti secundae res acrioribus stimulis animum explorant. Quia miseriae tolerantur, felicitate corrumpimur, &c. [Sallust, *The War with Catiline,* xi.7: "Prosperity tries the souls even of the wise." *Sallust,* trans. J. C. Rolfe,

life. 2. And yet all the evils complained of in human life, which do not flow from the vices of mankind, and which ought therefore to be considered as its natural and proper bad consequences, it being of the nature of vice to do hurt or mischief: all other evils, I say, do either proceed from the constant operation of the general laws of the material world, which by their steady, unvaried operation, produce an excellent system, without the existence of which, while it can exist, nature would be incomplete and incoherent; an excellent system with respect to our moral powers, and their exercises and improvements, as well as with respect to the sensitive enjoyments it affords us. Or, 3. They are the effects of another most excellent general law; even that universal law of our nature, in consequence of which all moral and natural goods are our own acquisitions; namely, that our industry and application shall gain its end,[a] and that nothing internal or external shall be procured by us, but in proportion to our diligence to acquire it. For the goods of life which are said to be so unequally distributed, fall no otherwise in great abundance to any vicious person, than in consequence of that universal law, so essential to moral beings, and their powers, by which it is, that whatever we set ourselves to acquire is acquired. They fall to one's share in the same way that the philosopher hath his beloved pleasure arising from large and extensive knowledge; and that the virtuous man acquires the treasure upon which his soul is solely bent, even a well regulated mind, and consciousness of merit in the eyes of every wise and good being. Good habits, (and all the virtues are such) are formed and established by our own industry to attain them. And if bad habits are acquired by those who set themselves to form them, it is because it is fit that general law should take <268> place with respect to the fruits of our industry and application, *that as we sow, so shall we reap*.[86] Now it is in no other

---

Loeb Classical Library (London: Heinemann; New York: Putnam, 1920). Tacitus, *Histories,* I.xv: "Thus far you have known only adversity; prosperity tests the spirit with sharper goads, because we simply endure misfortune, but are corrupted by success." Tacitus, *The Histories,* trans. Clifford M. Moore, 2 vols., Loeb Classical Library (London: Heinemann; New York: Putnam, 1925).]
   a. The law explained in the beginning of the first chapter.
   86. Gal. 6.7.

way that external goods fall to the share of any one. It is only because
he sets his heart upon them, bestows all his thought, time and care about
them, and leaves no stone unturned to procure them: and it is a proper
general law, that our goods or evils should chiefly be of our own procurance, or of our own making, and that application should not be suc-
cessless. 4. But when external goods are acquired in great redundance,
they cannot give the true happiness of the rational mind. That can only
proceed from improved virtue; and virtue, in order to be formed and
improved, must likewise be earnestly contended for and sought after; or
due pains must be taken to advance and raise it to perfection. How happily is all this, (which follows so clearly from the account that hath been
given of our nature and frame in this Essay) expressed by our incomparable Poet.

> *"Whatever is, is right."*—*This world, 'tis true,*
> *Was made for* Caesar,—*but for* Titus *too:*
> *And which more blest? who chain'd his country, say,*
> *Or he, whose virtue sigh'd to lose a day?*
> *"But sometimes virtue starves while vice is fed.*
> *What then? is the reward of virtue, bread?*
> *That, vice may merit; 'tis the price of toil:*
> *The knave deserves it when he tills the soil,*
> *The knave deserves it when he tempts the main,*
> *When folly fights for Kings, or dives for gain,*
> *The good man may be weak, be indolent,*
> *Nor is his claim to plenty, but content.*
>
> *What nothing earthly gives, or can destroy,*
> *The soul's calm sun-shine, and the heart-felt joy,*
> *Is virtue's prize.—*
>
> *O Fool! to think, God hates the worthy mind,*
> *The lover, and the love, of human kind,* <269>
> *Whose life is healthful, and whose conscience clear;*
> *Because he wants a thousand pounds a year!*
> Essay on man, Epist. 4.[87]

87. Pope, *Essay on Man*, IV.145–56, 168–70, 189–92.

Here is, in a few words, (in a short, clear, but most extensive reasoning) a full solution, to all who are able to pursue it in their thoughts throughout all its consequences, of all the objections brought against the present distribution of goods and evils; a *full vindication of the ways of God to man.* 5. But let it also be considered, that as education must precede perfection, and virtue cannot be formed but by degrees and in proportion to culture; so the fruits of improved virtue arising from its proper exercises, cannot take place till virtue is brought to its maturity. That is as impossible as it is in nature for harvest to precede seed-time and due husbandry. Virtue cannot yield the fruits and advantages of complete virtue, nor be fit for the exercises and employments from which its happiness must arise, till it is such. The good habits, whence the felicity is to arise, must first be formed or acquired before the happiness which can only result from their proper exercises can take place. The foundation must be laid before the superstructure can be raised. But proper exercises to form, school, discipline, try and improve moral powers, having the suitable degrees of enjoyment attending them as such, as properly or naturally prognosticate a harvest of virtue, a moral ripeness and its fruits, as such, to succeed to this state of moral culture, as seed-time and industry promise a harvest in the natural world. 6. And finally, as no state can be blamed in which the after-reaping is proportionable to, and of a kind with the sowing, or in which it is the general law of nature with respect to moral beings, that their future perfection and happiness shall be in proportion to the foundation they lay by their moral improvements: so, on the other hand, no happiness, but on the contrary, mi-<270>sery alone can be looked for from the total corruption of the mind by vice, from confirmed evil habits and passions, especially after the external means of sensual gratification fail, or are quite removed from them; which is the case, so soon as our minds are divested of our bodies, and separated from a material world. If there be any essential or established differences between virtue and vice, or the improvement and abuse, the perfection and corruption of moral powers; the final effects of these must be as different or contrary, as the roots from which they proceed, are. But these two opposites cannot have their full effect till a certain time of culture, formation and probation is past; because a moral building must advance gradually, as well as a material one; or because a moral harvest requires as necessarily a progress towards it, as a natural one. We must either deny, that the proper adequate happiness of a moral being must be the result of his perfection, or of the high exercises for which greatly improved moral powers are qualified, which is absurdly to distinguish the proper happiness of a rational being from its proper perfection: Or, if we ask, why virtue is not compleatly happy while it is but in a state of formation; we really absurdly ask, why education must precede perfection. But if complete rational happiness must be the natural effect of highly improved virtue suitably placed and employed, what can be expected from a degenerated corrupted mind in a state far removed from all material objects, but the natural effects of disorderly passions, depraved habits, and the consciousness of deformity and guilt: a harvest of corruption and proportionable misery?

Thus therefore, in whatever light we consider our present state, there is good reason to think it our first state only, and a very proper one as our first state: our moral seed-time to which our after-harvest shall be proportioned. For this is evidently the law of nature with regard to us, That as we sow, so <271> we shall reap. The moral improvements, from which alone the happiness truly suited and proportioned to our moral frame can spring, must be acquired by due culture and exercise. They cannot have their complete and perfect effect till they are arrived to perfection: But a proper state for their education to perfection, plainly betokens a succeeding state, in which effects shall be congruous and proportionate to the culture passed through, and its fruits.

Let us only add to all this, that the hope or presentiment of future existence is natural to man: and whence else can this proceed, but from the care of our Maker, who will not disappoint any instinct, desire, or hope he hath implanted in his creatures? It is Heaven that points out *an hereafter, and dictates eternity to mankind;* 'tis Heaven hath inspired us with this pleasing hope, *this longing after immortality,* which is so noble a spur and excitement to virtuous labours and deeds. And search all nature throughout, and shew one instance, if you can, where it works in vain; or merely to disappoint even bodily instincts, much less well governed rational affections and desires.

> *What future bliss, he gives not thee to know,*
> *But gives that* hope *to be thy blessing now.*
> Hope *springs eternal in the human breast;*
> *Man never is, but always* to be *blest;*
> *The soul uneasy, and confin'd at home,*
> *Rests, and expatiates, in a life to come.*
>
> Essay on man, Ep. 1.[88]

And again,

> *For him alone,* hope *leads from gole to gole,*
> *And opens still, and opens, on his soul,*
> *'Till lengthen'd on to* faith, *and unconfin'd,*
> *It pours the bliss that fills up all the mind.*
> *He sees, why nature plants in man alone*
> *Hope of known bliss, and faith in bliss unknown?*
> (*Nature, whose dictates to no other kind*
> *Are giv'n in vain, but what they seek they find*) <272>
> *Wise is her present: she connects in this*
> *His greatest* virtue *with his greatest* bliss.
> *At once his own bright prospect to be blest,*
> *And strongest motive to assist the rest.*
>
> Essay on man, Ep. 4.[89]

Conclusion. Man therefore is made for eternal progress in moral perfection proportionally to his care and diligence to improve in it. And with respect to death, we have reason to say with an excellent Ancient, "Eo *itaque simus animo, ut horribilem illum diem aliis, nobis faustum putemus: Non enim temere, nec fortuito sati & creati sumus; sed profecto fuit quaedam vis quae generi consulerit humano: nec id gigneret, aut aleret, quod cum exanclavisset*

---

88. Pope, *Essay on Man,* I.93–98.
89. Ibid., IV.341–52.

omneis labores, tum incideret in mortis malum sempiternum—portum po-
tius paratum nobis & perfugium putemus.[90]

The End of the First Part. <273> <274>

90. Cicero, *Tusculanae disputationes,* I.xlix.118–19: "let us all the same make up
our minds to regard that day as auspicious for us, though to others it seems terrible.
. . . For not to blind hazard or accident is our birth and our creation due, but assuredly
there is a power to watch over mankind, and not one that would beget and maintain
a race which, after exhausting the full burden of sorrows, should then fall into the
everlasting evil of death: let us regard it rather as a haven and a place of refuge prepared for us." Cicero, *Tusculan Disputations,* trans. J. E. King, Loeb Classical Library
(London: Heinemann; New York: Putnam, 1927).

The Principles of Moral Philosophy

Being
A further vindication of HUMAN NATURE; in which the
chief objections made against it are examined, and proved to
be absurd.

Quod si mundi partes naturâ administrantur, necesse est
mundum ipsum naturâ administrari: cujus quidem administratio nihil habet in se, quod reprehendi possit. Ex iis enim naturis,
quae erant, quod effici potuit, optimum, effectum est. Doceat
ergo aliquis potuisse melius, sed nemo unquam docebit, & si quis
corrigere aliquid volet, aut deterius faciet, aut id quod fieri non
potuit desiderabit.

Cicero de natura Deorum, Lib. II.[1]

Respecting man, whatever wrong we call,
May, must be right, as relative to all.
Essay on man, Epist. I.[2] <275>

---

1. Cicero, *De natura deorum,* II.xxxiv.86–87: "But if the parts of the world are
governed by nature, the world itself must needs be governed by nature. Now the
government of the world contains nothing that could possibly be censured; given the
existing elements, the best that could be produced from them has been produced.
Let someone therefore prove that it could have been better. But no one will ever prove
this, and anyone who essays to improve some detail will either make it worse or will
be demanding an improvement impossible in the nature of things." Cicero, *De natura
deorum, Academica,* trans. H. Rackham, Loeb Classical Library (London: Heinemann; New York: Putnam, 1933).

2. Pope, *Essay on Man,* I.51–52.

The Principles of Moral Philosophy

✂ PART II ✂

Introduction

In the former part of this enquiry, we have proved from the direct consideration of our frame and constitution, that it is good; or that we are made for an excellent end. But because this subject is of the last importance, it is well worth while to consider the objections which are made against human nature, and the present state of mankind.

How it is proposed to answer objections.

Now before I examine particular objections, it is proper to premise in general,

I. That objections which necessarily terminate in demanding impossibilities, are absurd. And such <276> are all those which imply in them as direct a contradiction, as if it were demanded that man should be, and not be, at the same time.

II. Such objections are likewise absurd which demand any alteration to the worse; or a change from which greater inconveniencies would necessarily follow than those complained of. For a more inconvenient law would certainly be a worse one.

Objections which end either in demanding an impossibility, or a change to the worse are absurd.

It is necessary to premise these two plain truths in an Essay, wherein it is proposed to shew, that the objections brought against our present state, do, if not at first sight, yet when closely pursued to their ultimate meaning and tendency, terminate either in demanding an impossibility, or a change to the worse. But they are also premised, because a great many imperfections and evils in the world, are resolved by some ancient philosophers into what they call *inhability or obliquity of the subject, and necessity of nature.* By which I am apt to think, they meant imperfections and evils which are, in the nature of things, absolutely unavoidable upon

What the ancients meant by the inhability or obliquity of a subject.

the supposition of the existence of certain subjects, as being absolutely inseparable from them. And, without all doubt, the objections which terminate in demanding some law or property in a material being; for instance, which it cannot in the nature of things admit of, are absurd for that very reason, if there is a moral fitness, that there should be a material creation. I give this example,[a] because those philosophers had recourse to the inhability or obliquity of the subject, and the necessity of nature chiefly in accounting for apparent evils of the physical kind, that is, apparent evils resulting from the properties of matter, and the laws of corporeal motion. But we may justly call inhability of the subject and necessity of nature, all natural or essential incapacity in any subject, moral or material of any demanded per-<277>fection. For certainly all such appearances are sufficiently vindicated, which are shewn to be the necessary result of the essential qualities of a subject, natural or moral; or all such objections are sufficiently refuted, which are shewn to demand something incompatible with the essential properties of a subject, provided it can be proved to be morally fit and good that such a subject should exist.

Thus all objections against the material creation, which necessarily terminate in demanding that matter should be active and not passive, are certainly absurd. If it be morally fit that matter should exist: since matter is essentially, or as matter, passive and inert. In like manner, all objections against a moral creature, which necessarily terminate in demanding impeccability in such creature; or a physical impossibility of its forming any wrong judgment, or chusing unreasonably, must be absurd, if it be morally fit and good that such a moral creature should exist; since impeccability or absolute impossibility of erring is incompatible with the moral powers and properties which constitute a moral creature. All such demands terminate in an absurdity, because they require what the subject cannot admit of; what is contrary to its nature, that is, what is really impossible and contradictory.

a. *Plutarch* de procreatione animae. [Plutarch, *De procreatione animae*. Possibly a reference to passages at 1014D–E, 1015A, 1026D–E, or 1027A. Plutarch, *Omnia quae extant opera*, 2 vols. (Paris, 1624).]

Now inhability of a subject, or necessity of nature, as we have explained it, supposes no limitation of creating, unless the impossibility of working contradictions; as for instance, of making a thing to be and not to be at the same time, or of making the same subject possess at the same time repugnant and incompatible qualities, be a limitation of creating power, which cannot be asserted. Nor does inhability, or necessity of nature, as we have explained it, presuppose the necessary existence of any subject previous to and independent of the mind that created the world; it only supposes, that subjects of a certain nature, if they be created, must be created with <278> that particular nature, or with the properties which belong to it; and that properties which are absolutely in their essence repugnant to co-existence in the same subject, cannot be made to co-exist in the same subject. And that is, not to suppose creating power limited by any thing, or subjected to any thing, since the impossibility of making contradictions to be true, is no limitation of power.

In what sense inhability of the subject supposes no limitation of the divine power.

II. The other proposed method of solving objections made against human nature, and the present state of mankind, by shewing, that they terminate in demanding a change to the worse; or that would be attended with more or greater disadvantages than those complained of, does not involve in it any limitation of creating power; since power cannot be said to be limited or confined, because it is directed by wisdom and goodness; and is only employed to produce that from which greater good, in the sum of things, must necessarily ensue. Nay, if we rightly consider the matter, it will be found, that this last way co-incides with the former; and that such demands, as well as the former, terminate in requiring a natural impossibility. For, so certainly do all demands terminate, "which require the general advantages of a general law without the general prevalence of that law"; "or the goods of one law by means of another law"; "that an end should be produced without means proper and apposite to its production"; "or that such and such a law should be general, and yet several necessary effects of its general operation be hindered from taking place." To require a change of any law on account of the inconveniencies which attend it, if these be compensated by the good effects of that law,

Objections that terminate in demanding a change to the worse, are absurd.

is an absurd demand; since all the interests of intelligent beings require, that the laws by which they are regulated, or which are fixed for their regulation of themselves, should be general and prevail uniformly: and to re-<279>quire that a being should be progressive, without the consequences which necessarily redound from progressiveness, is plainly an absurd demand. But all this will become clearer, when we consider particular objections. And whatever ancient philosophers meant by the inhability of the subject, and necessity of nature, we shall see that the greater part of the objections against man, do necessarily terminate in some contradictory, or very unreasonable request, and that in this sense, "*Si quis corrigere volet, aut deterius faciet, aut id quod fieri non potuit desiderabit.*"[3]

---

3. Cicero, *De natura deorum,* II.xxxiv.87: "anyone who essays to improve some detail will either make it worse or will be demanding an improvement impossible in the nature of things."

✂ CHAPTER I ✂

Let us first consider the effect of complaining that man is so perfect as he is; or that he has the powers and affections he is really endowed with; and, secondly, the effect of complaining that he is not more perfect than he is.

I. All objections which tend to cut off and retrench any perfections which man is endowed with by nature; any of his senses, appetites, affections, or capacities of pleasure, his reason, activity, moral agency, power and liberty, or any other property, are objections against his perfection; they are complaints against the Author of our nature for making him so perfect as he is. For which of them is not exceeding useful; the source of very noble enjoyments; the foundation of many excellencies and virtues? Our discerning, distinguishing, judging and reasoning powers, are evidently the foundation of our being capable of rational exercises and enjoyments: and as for our appetites and affections, they are either of private or public use, or both. We <280> may call the private ones modes of self-love, for they are all moved by a prospect of real or apparent good to ourselves. But can a perceptive being exist without a principle of self-preservation; or without the love and desire of pleasure; or can the love and desire of pleasure in a sensible being be less extensive than its ideas of good and pleasure? The public ones we may call modes of benevolence or social love; for they are all moved by the specious shew of public good: and is it not fit that rational creatures should be endowed with such affections as unite and bind them together, and without which there can be no merit, no society, no happiness by communication and participation; which would be the case, were we not endowed with a principle of benevolence, and the social affections which spring from it?

Some objections against man, are really objections against his perfection.

For all our powers, dispositions and affections are capacities of happiness and perfection.

303

All appetites and affections, of whatever kind, may be rendered weaker or stronger than they ought to be by habit; but such active, be-stirring principles, as appetites and affections, are necessary in our constitution, to be the springs of motion, to prompt, to impel, or rather to drive us into action: not the private only, lest we forget the public, and reason should not be sufficient, or have force enough to persuade us before it is too late, to mind that interest, which, though in one sense it be foreign to us, is in reality our most natural or best good. Nor yet the public only, lest by being wholly taken up abroad, we should entirely forget home affairs, and soon become incapable either to look abroad, or to take care at home to any advantage. It is, indeed, hard to say, whether the social without the private, or the private without the social, would be more pernicious to us. And not only is it necessary, if either the one or the other have any considerable degree of force in our frame, that the other should likewise have considerable force, in order to preserve a just ballance; but it is requisite that both should have a considerable degree of force, that they may <281> be able to move us, and that we may have pleasure and satisfaction in our pursuits; for without affections and appetites there can be no enjoyment. Reason itself can only give us satisfaction by its exercises, whether in searching after knowledge, or in acting agreeably to the nature of things, in consequence of our having in our nature an appetite after knowledge, and a moral sense of the fitness of actions.

So are all the laws with regard to them. The law of habits in particular.

Now as for appetites and affections, their being diminished or strengthned in their force by habit; this is necessary, in order to our being really benefited by the exercises of our faculties; or to their being bettered and improved by our diligence to improve them. For what is any habit, but a faculty or affection brought to great force and vigour by repeated acts? Without such a constitution, we could never attain to perfection in any science, art or virtue. And which way more honourable or advantageous to us could have been contrived for improving all our different powers and affections to their greatest perfection, and for keeping them in due order, than besides the natural controul which those of one kind are to those of another, to have given us a cool and sedate principle, to deliberate, advise and govern them: our reason, which also becomes stronger or weaker, in proportion as it is exercised; and soon becomes master as it ought to be, if it has but fair play allowed it, or if it is not violently opposed and born down. For reason, by frequently exercising our powers and affections aright, forms many good and perfect habits in us.

Let us examine all our senses, all our appetites and passions, and then let us say which of them we would not have to take place in our frame: not those which impel us to take care of ourselves, for why should the private system not be preserved? or can the public system be sufficiently taken care of by nature, unless each private part of the whole be <282> furnished with what is necessary to its preservation? Not those which lead us to partnership and union; for how can individuals make a whole, without a common feeling, and cementing affections? Reason cannot be left out of our frame, and we continue rational; and if there were no affections and appetites in our frame, what improvements would we be capable of; what would reason have to govern; or what would spur us to action? All the proper exercises of any of our affections, whether private or public, are certainly pleasant; and if the improper ones are either mischievous to ourselves or others, or equally so to both, how can we have the pleasures in the one way, without the pains in the other; otherwise than by the right government of them the consciousness of which is itself the greatest pleasure we are capable of? Did the passions move within us necessarily, just as it is proper and convenient for ourselves and our kind that they should, without the interpositions of our reason as a governor, or independently of our own choice and direction, then would we be good animals, but we could not be called virtuous or moral beings: that higher rank and character supposes in its very idea, reason to govern affections and appetites agreeably to a natural sense of right and wrong, of fit and unfit: without them therefore we would be deprived of all the enjoyments and advantages which now belong to us, as beings of a higher order than merely sensible, passive creatures; capable of ruling our appetites and passions to good purposes, if we but set ourselves in earnest to do so: that is, we would be less perfect than we are.

But hardly will any one object against our Author for providing us with so large a capacity for pleasures of various sorts, or for making us so perfect as we are. And yet, on the other hand, <283>

The objections against man's imperfection are no less absurd.

II. All objections which are made against our constitution, because we have not greater and higher natural capacities, or a larger stock of faculties, are absurd; because such objections cannot stop, while man is less than the very highest order of created perfection. These objections, if they have any meaning at all, must prove that no creature ought to exist, but that which is of the most perfect nature a finite and created being can be. In reality, to use the words of a very good author,[a] "The demands made when man is objected against because he is not a complication of all perfections, are as absurd, as to demand why a fly is not made a swallow, every swallow an eagle, and every eagle an angel; because an angel is better than any of the other creatures named. There must, says he, be a gradual descension and ascension of the divine fecundity in the creation of the world, to make it a full demonstration of the fullness of his power and bounty." The ancients answered these objections in like manner, by telling us, that the riches and perfection of nature consists in its being filled with different kinds of being and perfection from the lowest to the highest. Such objections, in truth, ultimately come to this, Why man at all? or rather, why any creature, which is not as perfect as a creature can be? And sure it is sufficient to oppose to such like questions, the following more generous ones: Why should there be any discontinuity or void in nature, *which unless it be full cannot be coherent?* Why should any system be wanting which the first cause can produce, the natural tendency of which, according to its constitution, is to greater good in the sum of things? Why not all possible kinds, orders and ranks of beings? Why not as rich a manifestation of the Creator's power and goodness, as <284> the most immense variety of being, perfection and good, can shew forth? If angels, why not arch-angels? And why not, likewise, in the descending scale of life, man; since he hath made him but *a little lower than the angels, and hath crowned him with glory and honour, and given him a very large dominion* natural and moral.

Objections then, which demand that man should be more perfect than he is, are absurd, because they can never stop; and they are really

They terminate in demanding an impossibility.

They know no stop.

a. *Henry More's Divine Dialogues.* [Henry More, *Divine Dialogues* (Glasgow: Foulis Press, 1743), 236.]

objections against the general perfection of nature. This is their absurd
language,

> Why is not man an angel, earth a heav'n?
> Who ask and reason thus, will scarce conceive
> GOD gives enough, while he has more to give:
> Immense the pow'r, immense were the demand;
> Say, at what part of nature will they stand?
>
> Essay on man, Epist. 4.[4]

But there is likewise a physical contradiction in these demands or objections. For with regard to the moral, as well as the natural world, it is
necessarily true, that every species of being must have its determinate
nature and constitution, with which certain other qualities are absolutely
incompatible. With respect to corporeal beings it is manifest, that flying,
swiming, walking upright, and all other such various qualities, require
a particular organization to be maintained and preserved in a particular
way, with which other structures are as inconsistent as being streight is
with being crooked. Nor will it be less evident if we think a little upon
the matter, that every moral being must have some certain determinate
constitution, with which the qualities of any other mental fabric is as
inconsistent, as one bodily organization adapted to one chief purpose,
is with that adjusted to another: a moral being can no more have two
different mental structures, than one and <285> the same material being
can have two different bodily structures. It is equally absurd in the moral
and in the natural world, that one and the same being should be two
different beings. It is therefore a contradiction to demand, why any being
is not a complication of all perfections: it is to ask, why a being has not
at the same time all various structures and constitutions: it is to ask, why
it is made for an end that requires a certain fabric adjusted to it, and why
at the same time it is not made for another end, that requires another
distinct fabric adjusted to it.

There is plainly a physical absurdity in them.

---

4. Pope, *Essay on Man*, IV.162–66.

Hence we may
see what must
be the only
question with
respect to our
make.
Now from this it plainly follows, that the only intelligible question, with regard to any constitution or fabric, must be, to what end is it adapted, and whether that end be worth while; could it be better adjusted to its end, or ought the end to which it is adjusted, to have place in nature? So that all the objections made against man must vanish, if it appears that he is made for a very noble end. For (though there are, no doubt, higher orders of beings in nature than man) yet if he be so made, he well deserves his place in a gradation which could not exist without him; but, did he not exist, would necessarily be interrupted and incoherent. But to be satisfied that man is made for a very noble end, let us only consider what our own hearts tell us, upon serious reflection, our end is. For if to be made to make progress in moral perfection to the degree we are capable of arriving, by due diligence to improve ourselves, be not a noble and worthy end, what can be such? Is it not worth while to attain to that perfection we know men can arrive at by due diligence, whether we look within, and enquire what we are made for; or whether we recal to mind certain sublime characters in history which cast us at a distance, and reproach us, because we are able, if we set about it, even to do more than they have done. Man hath, indeed, noble, honourable and glorious powers, <286> capable of being improved, even in this their first state, to a wonderful height of excellency and merit, if we are not wanting to ourselves, whatever our circumstances or situation may be. And that these powers are immortal, and shall afterwards be placed in circumstances well suited to the use that has been made of them here, must be certain, if there be any thing immortal in the creation; if all things are not made merely to be soon annihilated; if the Author of nature does not take more pleasure in pulling down and destroying, than in building up and communicating happiness; if capacity for enjoyment of the noblest kind, is not made merely to be disappointed; if it is not made merely to be able to conceive what the Author of nature will not be so generous as to give; or, in fine, if the Author of nature is but as good as man is by his own natural disposition, which he owes to him.[a] Man <287> hath,

a. See what *Plutarch* says of the dignity of man, and the extent of his power and dominion, in his excellent treatise *de fortuna*. Finge vero aliquem nostrum sic dicere:

fortuna praestat ut videamus, non visus & oculi, quos luciferos Plato dicit. Fortuna audimus non facultate ictum aeris apprehendente qui per aures ad cerebrum fertur. Quis non vereatur hoc modo sensibus detrahere? Atqui visum auditum, gustatum olfactum, reliquas item corporis facultates atque partes natura nobis dedit, ut earum ministerio prudentia uteretur, mens enim videt, mens audit, reliqua caeca sunt & surda. Et sicut sole sublato quod ad reliqua sidera attinet, perpetuam haberemus noctem ut Heraclitus dixit: ita praestare reliqui sensus non possent absque mens esset & ratio, ut reliquis animalibus anteiret homo. Nunc quod potiores sumus iisque imperamus, non casu aut fortuitu fit, sed Prometheus, id est, rationis usus hoc efficit.

Foetus equorum, asinorumque & boum genus
Munera rependens, quae nostris laboribus
Subeant—ut est apud Aeschylum.

Alioqui sui ortus natura & conditione pleraque bruta sunt quam nos meliora. Alia enim cornibus armantur, dentibus stimulis, &c.—Solus homo, ut ait Plato, nudus, incrinis, sine calceis & tegmine est a natura relictus.

Unum sed haec largita, emollit omnia.

Scilicet rationis usum & industriam ac providentiam,

Vires exiguae sunt mortalium
Sed calliditate multiplici,
Belluas maris, & terrestria,
Et sub coelo volitantia
Omnia homo domat.

Nihil agilius equo nihil velocius; sed hominibus currunt. Ferox est animal canis & iracundum: sed homines custodit—Faciunt enim eo, ut discamus quo hominem attollat ratio, & quibus rebus eum superiorem faciat, utque omnia in suam redigat potestatem.—Peritia autem, memoria, sapientia & arte secundum Anaxagoram omnia quae ipsa habent bruta in nostros vertimus usus: favos apum colligimus, lac mulgemus, &c.—Enim vero in humanis rebus haud dubie censendum est etiam artificum opera & fabrorum qui metalla cudunt, qui domos aedificant, qui statuas faciunt, &c.—Mirum itaque sit, cum artes ut suum finem consequantur nihil indigeant fortunae opera, artem omnium maximam & perfectissimam quae humanae gloriae & officii summam continet nullam esse, &c. [Plutarch, *De fortuna*, 98B–99C: "Suppose indeed that one of us says that it is chance that is responsible for our seeing and not the faculty of sight and our eyes, which Plato calls 'conveyers of light,' that it is by chance that we hear and not by a faculty which takes up a vibration of the air which is conveyed through the ears to the brain. If this were how things were, who would not be fearful of relying on their senses? But nature has given us sight, hearing, taste, smell, and the other faculties and parts of the body so that practical wisdom should make use of their ministerial possibilities. For mind sees, mind hears, everything else is blind and deaf. And, just as if the sun were removed from the world then, despite the continuing existence of the stars, we would be in perpetual night as Heracleitus

by his reason, power to make every element, every piece of matter, every
inferior creature, greatly subservient to him; and if he is not wilfully
destroyed by his Maker, through delight in destroying, which there is
no reason to apprehend from any thing in nature, nothing but himself
can stand in the way, as he is constituted, of his making eternal progress
in perfection. And is not such a being worthy of his place in nature? He
is furnished by nature for moral improvements, in the only way he can
be furnished for such: he hath all the faculties necessary for advancement
in knowledge and virtue;[a] faculties, which, by use and exercise, soon be-

---

says; so also even if a human being had the other senses, but did not have mind and
reason, he would be no greater than the other animals. But we are greater than they
and have dominion over them, not fortuitously or by chance, but instead it is because
of Prometheus, that is, it is brought about by the use of reason. 'The offspring of
horses, of asses, and of bulls take on our roles and undertake our labors'—as Aes-
chylus says. Yet by the nature and condition of their birth most animals are better
provided for than we are. For some are armed with horns, with sharp teeth, etc. . . .
Only man, as Plato says, naked, hairless, unshod and without covering, has been
forsaken by nature. 'But by nature's gift one thing softens everything,' namely the
use of reason, attentiveness, and foresight.

> Mortals have meager powers;
> But by his wide-ranging cleverness
> Man dominates all things,
> Monsters of sea and land,
> And the birds of the air.

Nothing is more nimble than the horse, nothing faster, but it is for men that they
run. Dogs are courageous and irascible, but they watch over men. . . . The point is
that we thereby learn to what extent reason elevates man, and learn what those beings
are over which reason gives him a superior position, so that all things are in his
power. . . . By experience, memory, wisdom, and art we put to our use, according to
Anaxagoras, everything that the beasts have. We take honey, milk, etc. . . . Moreover,
without doubt among 'human activities' there are to be included the work of artificers
and handymen who work with metals, build dwellings, make statues, etc. . . . It would
be a matter for wonderment if, when the other arts do not need good fortune to secure
their goals, the greatest and most perfect of all arts, the one which includes the peak
of human glory and duty, were a nothing without good fortune."]

   a. Natura enim hoc corporis tabernaculum veluti instrumentum composuit ut &
obediens sit, & ad omnes vitae rationes concinno quodam aptoque modo par esse
possit. Animus quoque ad convenientes virtutes conformandus est atque instituen-
dus: nimirum ad temperantiam, veluti corpus ad sanitatem: ad prudentiam vero veluti
ad sensuum subtilitatem: ad fortitudinem veluti ad robur & vires: ad justitiam veluti

<288>come strong and vigorous; and he is surrounded not only with inexhaustible subjects of the most entertaining enquiries, but with excellent means, materials and occasions of exercising every great and noble virtue, having a very large extent of power and dominion in the material as well as the moral world. What therefore can be objected against him, if it be indeed no objection, as it certainly is not, to say he is not the top of the creation; that there are beings much higher than he; or that though he hath a noble nature, yet it is not the very noblest that can exist? Is it not sufficient to take off all these objections, that we have good reason, from the analogy of nature, and the consideration of the temper and character of the supreme being our Maker, which is so clearly imprinted upon the whole of nature, as far as we can pry into it by all our research to conclude, "That the highest pitch of perfection any among mortals have ever arrived at, howsoever great it be in comparison

---

corpus ad pulchritudinem. Harum virtutum primordia quidem sunt ex natura: media, vero & fines, in diligentia: in corpore videlicet gymnastices adjumento & medicinae: in animo autem eruditionis & philosophiae beneficio. Hae enim facultates nutriunt & roborant, &c. *Timaeus Locrus de anima mundi.*

Hoc opus sapientiae mihi videtur ad quod natus & constitutus est homo, atque ad quod instrumenta & facultates Deo accepit. Homo in hoc natus & constitutus est, ut naturae rationem in universo contempletur: & cum ipse sit sapientiae opus, speculari prudentiam quae in existentibus reperiretur, &c. *Archytae libro de sapientia.* [Timaeus Locrus, *De anima mundi:* "For nature has set up this tent like an instrument so that it should be obedient to, and appropriate for, all of life's goals. The mind too must be made to conform with the virtues for which it is constructed: to conform with temperance, as the body conforms with health; with prudence as the body conforms with a sharpness of the senses; with courage as the body conforms with strength and vigor; with justice as the body conforms with beauty. The origins of these virtues are in nature, the means and ends are due to diligence; in the case of the body the virtues are owing to the help of gymnastic exercises and medicine; in the case of the mind the virtues are due to the good work of instruction and philosophy. For these powers nourish and invigorate, etc." In Gale, ed., *Opuscula mythologica, physica et ethica. Graece et Latine.* . . . (Amsterdam, 1688), 564.

Archyta, *De sapientia,* in Gale, *Opuscula,* 733: "This seems to me the work of wisdom, the work for which we have been born and constituted, and for which we have received from God our organs and powers. We have been born and composed for this, in order that we should contemplate rational nature in the universe and, because we are the work of wisdom, we should investigate the practical intelligence which is found in existing things, etc."]

of our state at our first setting out in infancy, is however as nothing, when compared to the superior perfection those so improved and exalted men shall attain to, by their continued care to improve themselves, in another state; and, in fine, that at every period of their future existence, the perfection arrived to will be the same nothing, so to speak, in respect of that superior excellence still before them, and in their power to attain to." <289>

To this question a sufficient answer hath been given in the principles. This is what I have been endeavouring to prove to be the case, in the first part of this essay; and that no doubt may remain with relation to it, I shall go on to consider, first of all, two of the most material objections made against the present state of mankind; and then I shall conclude, by endeavouring to make every objector against the government of the world feel the absurdity of all objections against it; or clearly perceive that whatever change he can possibly desire or imagine, would make a very bad state of things, could it possibly take place.

The two great objections made against the state of mankind are, I. The prevalence of vice; and II. The unequal distribution of the goods of fortune, as they are called, or external goods.

I shall therefore, in the first place, lay a few observations together, in such an order as seems to me to give full satisfaction, with regard to the prevalence of vice in the world.

The chief objections confuted.

First of all let it be observed, that[a] "Here men are apt to let their imaginations run out upon all the robberies, pyracies, murders, perjuries, frauds, massacres, assassinations, they have either heard of, or read in history, thence concluding all mankind to be very wicked: as if a court of justice were a proper place to make an estimate of the morals of mankind, or an hospital of the healthfulness of a climate. But ought they not <290> to consider, that the number of honest citizens and farmers far surpasses that of all sorts of criminals in any state; and that the innocent or kind actions of even criminals themselves, surpass their crimes in numbers. That it is the rarity of crimes, in comparison of innocent or good actions, which engages our attention to them, and makes them to be recorded in history, while honest, generous, domestic actions are over-looked, only because they are so common; as one great danger, or one month's sickness, shall become a frequently repeated story, during a long life of health and safety."

The objection taken from the prevalence of vice among mankind.

Not so much vice as is generally imagined.

Cicero[b] mentions a book written by a famous Peripatetic philosopher, *Dicaearchus,* to shew that more mischiefs are brought upon mankind by the hands of men themselves, than by earthquakes, deluges, pestilences,

a. See Mr. *Hutcheson* on the *Passions,* whose words these are. [Francis Hutcheson, *An Essay on the Nature and Conduct of the Passions. . . .* (1728), ed. Aaron Garrett (Indianapolis: Liberty Fund, 2002), I.VI.iv.]

b. *De Offic.* Lib. 1. [Cicero, *De officiis,* II.v.16.]

devastations of savage beasts, or any other such causes. But we ought, says *Cicero,* to set over-against these evils, the innumerable benefits which men receive from men. The vast advantages which redound from rightly constituted society, from arts and sciences, from philosophy, from oratory, from prudence and virtue.

Let not the vices of mankind be multiplied, or magnified; let us make a fair estimate of human life, and set over-against the shocking, the astonishing instances of barbarity and wickedness, that have been perpetrated in any age, not only the exceeding generous and brave actions with which history shines, but the prevailing innocency, good nature, industry, felicity and chearfulness, of the greater part of mankind at all times, and we shall not find reason to cry out, as objectors against providence do on this occasion, that all men are vastly corrupt and vicious, and that there is hardly any such thing as virtue in the world. Upon a fair computation, the fact does <291> indeed come out, that very great villanies have been very uncommon in all ages, and looked upon as monstrous; so general is the sense and esteem of virtue.

In consequence of the excellent laws of our nature, some vices are unavoidable, because narrow views and wrong associations of ideas are unavoidable.

II. But, in the second place,[a] It is easy to conceive, how false opinions, wrong notions of things, prejudices, misleading associations of ideas, narrow views, and unreasonable pursuits must spread, if they are once introduced among any part of mankind, in consequence of these most useful principles and laws in our constitution; "our dependence upon one another"; "the docility and pliableness of our infant minds"; "our regard to our parents, teachers and superiors"; "the influence of example, and our disposition to imitate." In consequence of these excellent dispositions in our minds, 'tis impossible, but errors, false judgments, and correspondently wrong actions must gain ground, if they ever begin or take place. No person in such a state as ours, can be single in his false opinions, bad taste, or hurtful pursuits. In the political as well as the natural body, when contagion enters, it must spread. On the other hand, in a state of beings entering upon the world, with minds formed for gradual progress in knowledge and virtue, in sciences, in arts, and every

a. See the corolary to the Chapter, *on the association of ideas and habits;* Part I.

moral perfection; it is morally impossible, but some must form false opinions, and be influenced by narrow views. It is our imagination and judgment, or our opinion of things, that chiefly guides our conduct, and adds strength to one sort of affections by taking from the force of others: and therefore, if narrow views, false judgments, and wrong associations of ideas take place: vicious pursuits must likewise take place. But how is it possible to conceive any state of beings formed <292> to make gradual progress in perfection, in proportion to their diligence to improve themselves therein, absolutely secured against acting upon any views that are not true; or absolutely secured against rashly conceiving any false opinions? This is certainly to demand an impossibility with respect to any infant or first state of progressive beings, in whatever situation they may be placed. And if it be to demand an impossibility with regard to any infant state of beings: what must such a demand be with respect to beings capable of receiving pleasures from external objects; and consequently of sollicitations from their senses before their reason can grow up even by any degree of culture to very great maturity and strength? Now it is to demand an impossibility with regard to any first state of progressive beings. For it is in reality, either to demand a physical or a moral impossibility that such beings should ever err. But to demand a physical impossibility, in this case, is certainly to demand, that their progress should nowise depend upon themselves, which is, in other words, to demand that they should not be progressive beings, or beings to be formed to perfection in knowledge and virtue, by their own application to improve themselves. And to demand a moral impossibility, that beings so made should ever err, what is it but to demand, that it should not belong to the nature of moral agents, to be able to assent to any opinions that are not true, or to be determined in their conduct by any views that are false. And both these demands are equally absurd in any sense that can be put upon them, but this alone: That such ought to be the nature of things, that truth only can have the full and complete distinguishing evidence of truth, and right only can have the distinguishing characteristics of right, which every one will readily own to be necessarily and immutably the case with regard to truth and right, whatever false judgments or wrong choices any one may precipitantly make.

And according to the excellent laws of our nature, vices when they begin, will spread.

Illustrations upon this argument.

<293> These demands, if taken in any other sense, require that moral beings should be so formed, as that either something else should be necessary to perswade and determine them, than the appearances of things to their minds, and what that should be, is absolutely inconceiveable: Or that their making true judgments and acting rightly, should be in their own power some other way, than by their being furnished with the faculties, senses and dispositions necessary to make true judgments and right choices; and by its depending on themselves to exert and employ these faculties and dispositions as they ought, in order to distinguish truth and right from vice and falshood; which is also quite inconceiveable. There is absolutely no middle between these two states; beings with a certain sphere of activity, or a certain dependence of effects upon their own application of their own faculties to this or the other purpose; and beings who have no power, no sphere of activity, or upon whose will there is no dependence of effects as to their existence or non-existence: Beings, whose right and wrong use of their faculties is in their own power, and beings who have no active powers, no dominion.

Further illustrations on this argument.

In order to set this in another light, let me but just ask any one, whether it is possible to conceive beings made for progress in knowledge and virtue, all of whom do from the very beginning, and during the whole course of their lives, form just judgments in all cases, where choice and determination is immediately necessary, without ever erring; without ever mistaking their interest or duty? Or to keep close to our state, which is that now under consideration; let me ask, whether it is possible to conceive all men, even in their most infant and unimproved state, ever acting under the influence of right views, and with due proportionate affections to the values of objects, without any one's ever mistaking his true interest and the nature of things in any point; without any <294> one's ever yielding rashly to any sollicitations of inviting pleasure; or without his having certain appetites oftner called forth into action, by certain concurrences of circumstances, than any others, and thus made stronger in his constitution by frequent exercise, than those which, tho' equally natural to him, are not so frequently solicited by their proper objects? Whether, in one word, he can conceive all men as they are now formed, ever so acting, and so influenced to act by circumstances, which must necessarily excite certain affections to a certain degree, that none, (for instance) shall conceive too high an opinion of power over the rest; an inclination to have it; or having it, not be disposed to exert it otherwise than to the greatest advantage of others in all respects, without abusing, deceiving, or hurting any one in any degree. I believe every one will readily grant this to be inconceivable or morally impossible. But if any one, upon granting it to be so, should urge, why then man is made; or why is there such a state at all. He does really ask either. 1. Why there is any affection, faculty or appetite in our constitution, which in the nature of things is capable of being the source of bad. Which is to ask, why there is any affection, faculty or appetite in our nature at all. Since there can be no faculty, no affection, or appetite even of the social or benevolent kind, which may not by misguidance become the source of evil. Or, 2dly. Why any circumstances are allowed to take place, which may invite faculties, appetites or affections to operate in any way that is vicious or hurtful. To which question, the only proper answer is to ask, what circumstances in life happen antecedent to, or independent of all wrong exercises of human powers, affections and appetites, which are not the consequences of some general law relative to our frame and state, which is of excellent use; nay, necessary to our perfection and happiness: and what circumstances in life happen consequently to mankind's own wrong exercises of <295> their powers, which are not likewise the fit and proper consequences of their being made for happiness and perfection, proportionally to their right use of their powers and faculties: Or to ask in general, what effect belonging to human nature may not be reduced to some general law, either of the natural world, or of the moral kind, which is itself of the greatest utility, if not necessity to our happiness and perfection. Now it hath been proved over and over again in this Essay, that every faculty, appetite, and affection in our nature, and every law relative to their exercises, is of admirable use.

No objection can be fetched from hence that does not terminate in an absurdity.

In fine, to infer from our being so made by nature, that our affections, appetites and faculties, which are of very great use, may be perverted and abused, or wrongfully employed; to infer from thence, that we have a very bad make and constitution; or that our make and constitution is

very improperly situated and placed; is not only to argue against the
utility of a thing from the perversion of it, which is allowed in every
other case to be an absurd way of reasoning; but it is to infer that we are
badly made, because we are made capable of turning a very large stock
of powers, faculties, appetites and affections to very good account; in
such a way as we may have the merit of it, and the pleasure arising from
the consciousness of such merit. For it is self-evident, that were it not
the order and constitution of nature with regard to us, that right use and
bad use of our natural stock should depend on ourselves, we could make
no acquisition; we could not be capable either of praise or blame, good
or ill desert, because nothing would be ours in any proper sense of that
word. Observing the connexions of things, in order to act wisely or
agreeably to them, could not be our employment, or the source of our
happiness, as it is at present: We would only be capable of receiving a
succession of meer sensations, external or <296> internal, without any
of the interpositions of our own reason or will, which being our own
interpositions, give us a title to the character of moral active beings; and
are the source, as such, of all the noblest pleasures we enjoy.

> *Two principles in human nature reign,*
> *Self-love to urge; and reason to restrain;*
> *Nor this a good, nor that a bad we call,*
> *Each works its end, to move or govern all.*
> *And to their proper operation still*
> *Ascribe all good; to their improper, ill.*
> *Self-love, the spring of motion, acts the soul;*
> *Reason's comparing Ballance rules the whole;*
> *Man, but for that, no action could attend,*
> *And but for this, were active to no end.*
> *Fix'd like a plant, on his peculiar spot,*
> *To draw nutrition, propagate, and rot;*
> *Or meteor-like, flame lawless through the void,*
> *Destroying others, by himself destroy'd.*
>
> Essay on Man, Ep. 2.[5]

5. Pope, *Essay on Man*, II.53–66.

We may illustrate all that hath been said by this obvious similitude. Does not every one rest satisfied, that the right culture of his garden depends absolutely on himself, tho' notwithstanding a sense of harmony, beauty, and of true imitation of nature be natural to all men, yet one must have improved that sense very much, and have studied gardening before he can be able to lay out fields with good taste: and tho' it be morally impossible, some amongst mankind should not fall into a wrong taste of imitating nature, or of beauty in laying out fields, or in other imitative arts, notwithstanding the natural sense of beauty common to all mankind, capable of being improved by all to a perfectly good taste. Does any one think his gardens independent on him, because his fields are not so made, that nothing can succeed, but what is done according to right taste, and tends to make a good <297> whole; or because negligence and wrong taste have bad effects, and it is only good culture and good taste, that can make a well-disposed garden, suitably furnished with all that is useful and delicious, wholesome and beautiful? Would any one have our taste in this, or any other of the elegant arts, not to depend upon our own improvement of our natural faculties, or to be acquirable otherwise than it is by us? Does not every one take the acquisition of such a taste to be sufficiently in his power, as things are constituted; and is he not sensible of the abridgement, nay, total destruction of the pleasures the elegant arts now give; that would necessarily ensue, if improvements in them were not made as they now are?

We must admit this solution to be good; or say, that good taste ought not to be an acquirable perfection.

But if this be owned, it must by parity of reason be acknowledged, that the right culture of all our other natural powers and dispositions, and of the mind, in general, is sufficiently in our power as we are now constituted; and that, in any other way, our improvement would not be our own acquisition, nor by consequence give us the pleasures it now does, by being our own work and acquisition. Let not men therefore contradict themselves, and call that unreasonable and unfit in one case, which they allow to be proper and very well ordered in another precisely parallel or like case: but let it be remembered, that the way of the human mind's operation towards its improvement, ought to be uniform; that the way to one improvement ought to be analogous to the way of improvement

Which none will say.

in every other case: or that it is fit there should be an universal fixed order with regard to the manner of attaining to perfection of whatever kind; that is, of whatever faculty, disposition, taste or affection in our nature, *viz.* that it should be in proportion to our diligence and care to improve our knowledge and taste.

Vices are but the corruptions or degeneracies of good and useful affections.

III. All this will be yet plainer, if we consider the vices of mankind in their true light, or trace them <298> to their real springs; for we universally find, "that no man acts from pure malice; that the injurious person only intends some interest of his own without any ultimate desire of our misery; and that he is more to be pitied for his own mean selfish temper, for the want of true goodness, and its attendant happiness, than to be hated for his conduct, which is really more pernicious to himself than to others. There is no reason to think, there is any such thing as pure disinterested malice in the most vicious of mankind."[a]

Some of self-love which is absolutely necessary.

And, in reality, if we trace vices to their sources, we shall find, that they are all the corruptions or degeneracies of highly useful and noble affections. This point is exceedingly well handled by *Plato* in his *Gorgias,*[6] but I shall only on this subject, excerpt two observations from two excellent modern writers upon it, which are sufficient to shew us from what springs all vices proceed, or to what causes they ought to be ascribed. Dr. *Henry More,* in his *Divine Dialogues,*[7] speaking of vices, says, "They are the spawn of self-love, which, if we eye narrowly, we shall find to be very useful, nay, a very necessary mother in society. Self-love is absolutely necessary: nay, it is no more than the desire of pleasure and happiness, without which a sensitive being cannot subsist: and if rightly conducted, it would lead us to the pursuit of virtue as our interest. Yet wrath, envy, pride, lust, and the like evil passions, are but the branches and modifi-

a. See *Hutcheson on the passions,* whose words I here use. [Hutcheson, *Passions,* I.VI.iv. The last sentence of the quote is not included in this passage, but appears to be a version of a sentence in I.III.v.]

6. This is a major topic in the lengthy discussion between Socrates and Callicles in Plato's *Gorgias,* 477E–481B.

7. More, *Divine Dialogues,* 219–20.

cations of this fundamental necessary disposition towards good and happiness; for what is wrath, but self-love edged and strengthened for fend-
ing off the assaults of evil? What is envy but self-love grieved at the sense
of its own want, aggravated and made more sensible by the fullness of
another's enjoyment? What is pride, but self-love desiring to be the best,
or aspiring for the best, <299> and partly triumphing and glorying that
it is now become none of the least? He quotes an excellent saying of
Socrates[8] to this purpose, that the wicked man really pursues, by a fatal
mistake, that which is worst for himself; that he himself is the greatest
sufferer; and that therefore, with the wise and good he can be no object
of envy, but of pity and compassion."

Such indeed was the opinion of all the wiser and better ancients[a] concerning vices. A philosophy as much more tender and humane, as it is
truer than <300> the prevailing modern philosophy, which delights in

This was the
opinion of the
best ancients.

---

8. Plato, *Gorgias,* 477E–481B.
   a. See *Plutarch de virtute morali.*—Multo autem his utiliores sunt affectuum foetus, rationi praesto ubi sunt, eique ad virtutem enitenti opem ferunt. Sic moderata
ira fortitudini adjumento est, odium in malos justitiae, ac justa indignatio adversus
nullo suo merito rebus secundis elatos, quando hi dementia simul atque petulantia
inflammatis animis coercitione opus habent. Jam ab amicitia naturalem ad diligen-
dum propensionem, ab humanitate misericordiam, a vera benevolentia gaudere una
atque dolere, ne si velis avellere ullo modo possis. Praeterea si peccant qui una cum
insano amore omnem tollunt amorem: equidem non recte agunt, qui propter avaritiam omnes etiam alias damnent appetitiones. Sed perinde agunt ac si quis curren-
dum, quod aliquando impingatur, aut jaciendum neget, quia nonnunquam a scopo
aberretur; aut canendum quod inscite canatur.—Adde quod si omnino evelli ex animis affectus possint multorum eorum ratio hebetior fieret atque ociosior, sicut gu-
bernator vento cessante non admodum habet quod agat. Atque haec ut apparet, ob-
servantis legumlatoris in civitate ambitionem, aemulationemque excitant, &c.—Non
enim tam recte cum Xenocrate dixeris, mathematicas disciplinas esse ansas philosophiae: quam hoc, affectus istos verecundiam, cupiditatem, poenitentiam, voluptatem, dolorem, ansas esse adolescentium: quas salutari atque concinna opportunitate
ratio & lex apprehendentes, eos cum profectu in rectam perducant viam, ut non male
professus fuerit *Laco* ille paedagogus effecturum se, ut puer gauderet honestis, ac mo-
leste ferat turpia, quo liberalis institutionis fine neque major potest ullus, neque pul-
chrior nuncupari.
   Virtus est rationis prudentia, irae fortitudo, cupidinis temperantia, & totius animi
justitia.—Vitium ex oppositis; rationis insipientia, irae pavor, cupidinis intempe-

exhibiting man in the blackest colours. There certainly is implanted in our nature that desire of power and dominion which *Hobbes* takes notice of and from the degeneracies, corruptions and perversions of this natural appetite, many woful evils do indeed arise. But *Hobbes*'s error consists in his considering, that desire of power and dominion as the only principle of our nature, and not taking along with it the other equally natural appetites with which it is united in our frame, and with which it is therefore intended to co-operate; and in the just ballance of which

---

rantia, totius denique animi injustitia. Virtutes ex recta vivendi ratione, rectaque educatione; vitia ex contrariis. *Salusti philosophi de diis & mundo,* Cap. 10. [Plutarch, *De virtute morali,* 451D–452E: "But of much greater use than these [i.e., horse, ox, boar, hound] are the offspring of the passions when they are helpful to reason, and contribute to making virtue shine forth. Thus moderate anger is an aid to courage. Hatred of wicked people is an aid to justice. And righteous indignation is an aid against flourishing but meritless people, when their souls are inflamed with madness and wantonness and they have to be punished. And surely even if you so wished you could not separate from friendship a natural propensity for love, nor separate pity from humaneness, nor joy and sorrow from true benevolence. Moreover, if those people are wrong who reject all love along with crazy love, so also are those incorrect who, because avarice is a kind of desire, therefore condemn all desires. They behave in the same way as those who would ban running because people sometimes trip up, or would ban throwing because sometimes one misses the target, or those who would ban singing because some sing out of tune. . . . Furthermore if the passions could be entirely plucked out of the mind, the reason of many people would become weaker and less occupied, just as a pilot does not have anything to do when the wind stops blowing. And legislators, evidently seeing these things, stir up ambition and rivalry in the state, etc. . . . For it would not be so correct to call the mathematical sciences 'the occasion for philosophy' (in Xenocrates' phrase) as it would be to use the phrase of the passions of the young, namely shame, greed, repentance, lust, and grief. If reason and law grasp these passions as constituting an advantageous and suitable opportunity, they will lead the young to the right road on which to start their journey; so that the Spartan teacher spoke well when he said that he would see to it that a boy in his care would rejoice at what was honorable and would be hostile to the dishonorable. No greater or finer end of a liberal education could be pronounced than these words by the Spartan teacher." Plutarch, *Omnia que extant opera,* 2 vols. (Paris, 1624). Sallust, *De diis et mundo,* §10: "The virtue of reason is prudence, of anger is courage, of desire is temperance, of the whole mind is justice. Vice is from the opposite. The vice of reason is stupidity, of anger is fear, of desire is intemperance, and of the whole mind is injustice. Virtues derive from a right idea of life and from a correct upbringing. The vices derive from the opposite." See *Sallvstii Philosophi De Diis et mvndo,* ed. Gabriel Naudus (Rome, 1638). (A.B., trans.)]

kept and maintained by the presiding authority of reason, virtue or the health and perfection of the mind consists. Now these other appetites and dispositions are our love of knowledge, and our delight in truth, or our desire of knowing the real connexions, relations and values of things: our love of society and public good: and our moral sense or our determination to approve or disapprove affections, actions and characters, according as they are conducive to public good or public mischief. My Lord *Shaftbury*[9] refutes this gloomy pernicious doctrine of *Hobbes,* in the truly philosophical, pleasant and good natured way, of which we have several examples among the ancients when they are reasoning against the same tenets. We find *Arrian* just arguing in the same way in his commentaries upon *Epictetus* against that opinion, as Lord *Shaftbury* does against *Hobbes. Cicero* often treats the same opinion in the same pleasant manner: and those excellent authors do indeed set a noble example before us, that ought to be imitated in all disputes and controversies, even of the most important kind. For what can be of greater moment than the question about the human make, whether it argues a good or a bad disposition in its Author: and yet even upon this subject, they shun invectives and use kindly terms, preferring hard arguments to abusive words. <301>

They set us an excellent example of the best manner of confutation.

It was certainly, as Lord *Shaftbury* observes,[a] an extreme dread of anarchy and licentiousness, that frightened *Hobbes,* into his system of absolute monarchy and passive obedience: the fright he took upon the sight of the then governing powers, who unjustly assumed the authority of the people, gave him such an abhorrence of all popular government, and of the very notion of liberty itself, that to extinguish it for ever, he recommends the very extinguishing of letters, and exhorts princes not to spare so much as one ancient *Greek* or *Roman* historian. His quarrel with religion was the same as with liberty; the same times gave him the

a. See his *Essay on the freedom of wit and humour.* This passage is quoted as an example of good natured refutation. [What follows is a selection of quotes from Shaftesbury's "Sensus communis," II.i, in *Characteristics,* ed. Klein (Cambridge: Cambridge University Press, 1999), 42–44.]

9. Shaftesbury, "Sensus communis," II.i, in *Characteristics,* ed. Klein, 42–45.

same terror in this other kind: he had nothing before his eyes besides the ravages of enthusiasm, and the artifices of those who raised and conducted that spirit. Hence likewise his quarrel with human nature. But what should we say to one of these anti-zealots, who in the zeal of such a cool philosophy, should assure us faithfully, "that we were the most mistaken men in the world to imagine there was any such thing as natural faith or justice? For that it was only force and power that constituted right. That there was no such thing in reality as virtue; no principle of order in things above or below; no secret charm or force of nature, by which every one was made to operate willingly or unwillingly towards public good, and punished and tormented if he did otherwise." Is not this the very charm itself? Is not the gentleman at this instant under the power of it?—"Sir, the philosophy you have condescended to reveal to us is the most extraordinary. We are beholden to you for your instruction. But, pray, whence is this zeal in our behalf? what are we to you? are you our father? or if you were, why this concern for us? is there then such a thing as natural affection? if not, why all this pains? why all this danger on our account? why not keep this secret to yourself? or what advantage is it to you <302> to deliver us from the cheat? the more are taken in it, the better. 'Tis directly against your interest to undeceive us, and let us know that only private interest governs you, and that nothing nobler, or of a larger kind should govern us whom you converse with. Leave us to ourselves, and to that notable art, by which we are happily tamed and rendered thus mild and *sheepish*. 'Tis not fit we should know, that by nature we are all wolves. Is it possible, that any one who has really discovered himself such, should take pains to communicate such a discovery?"

But mere vices are the degeneracies of benevolent affections by misguidance. II. But this leads me to another observation upon the springs and sources of human vices; the great disturbers of human life, and on account of which the human make is subject of complaint, or rather railery among some philosophers; and it is this, "a great many evils are not so properly the product of self-love wrong directed, and of our desire of power, which are, however they may be perverted in themselves, very suitable; nay, necessary affections or dispositions in our nature: but they are really the degeneracies of benevolence itself"; for as the noble Author just now quoted, observes,[a] "Does not *Philanthropy,* or the love of mankind, by a small misguidance of the affection become pernicious and destructive? A lover of mankind becomes a ravager: a hero and deliverer becomes an oppressor and destroyer. But if we consider matters rightly, it is not strange, that war, which of all things appears the most savage, should be the passion of the most heroic spirits. For it is in war that the knot of fellowship is closest drawn. 'Tis in war that mutual succour is most given, mutual danger run, and common affection most exerted and employed. The generous passion is no where so strongly felt, or vigorously exerted, as in actual conspiracy or war; in which the highest genius's are often known the forwardest to employ themselves. For the most <303> generous spirits are the most combining. They delight most to move in concert, and feel, if I may so say, in the strongest manner the force of the confederating charm."

The same Author furnishes us with another example in caballing or cantonizing. "How the wit of man, saith he, should so puzzle this cause as to make civil government and society appear a kind of invention, and creature of art, I know not. For my own part, methinks this herding principle and associating inclination, is seen so natural and strong in most men, that one might readily affirm, 'twas even from the violence of this passion, that so much disorder arose in the general society of mankind.

"Universal good, or the interest of the world, in general, is a kind of remote philosophical object. That greater community falls not easily under the eye. Nor is a national interest, or that of a whole people, or body politic, so readily apprehended. In less parties, men may be intimately acquainted or conversant, and acquainted with one another. They can there better taste society, and enjoy the common good and interest of a more contracted public. They view the whole compass and extent of their community; and see, and know particularly whom they serve, and

---

a. See *Charact.* T. 1. p. 115. whence this excellent observation is taken. [What appears to be a single long quote is an out-of-order selection of quotes from "Sensus communis," III.ii, in *Characteristics,* ed. Klein, 52–53.]

to what end they associate and conspire. All men have naturally their share of this combining principle, and they who are of the sprightliest and most active faculties, have so large a share of it, that unless it be happily directed by right reason, it can never find exercise for itself in so remote a sphere as that of the body politic at large. For here, perhaps, the thousand part of those whose interests are concerned, are scarce so much as known by sight. No visible band is formed; no strict alliance; but the conjunction is made with different persons, orders, and ranks of men; not <304> sensibly, but in idea; according to that general view, or notion of a state or common-wealth.

"Hence other divisions amongst men. Hence, in the way of peace and civil government, that love of party and subdivision by cabal. For sedition is a kind of cantonizing already begun within a state. To cantonize is natural, when the society grows vast and bulky: and powerful states have found other advantages in sending colonies abroad, than merely that of having elbow-room at home, or extending their dominion into distant countries. Vast empires are in many respects unnatural, but particularly in this, that be they ever so well constituted, the affairs of many must, in such governments, turn upon a very few; and the relation be less sensible, and in a manner lost, between the magistrate and people, in a body so unwieldy in its limbs, and whose members lie so remote from one another, and distant from the head.

" 'Tis in such bodies as these that great factions are apt to engender. The associating spirits, for want of exercise, form new movements, and seek a narrower sphere of activity, when they want action in a greater. Thus we have *wheels within wheels.* And in some national constitutions (notwithstanding the absurdity in politics) we have one empire within another. Nothing is so delightful as to incorporate. Distinctions of many kinds are invented; religious societies are formed; orders are erected; and their interests espoused and served with the utmost zeal and passion. Founders and patrons of this sort are never wanting. Wonders are performed in this wrong social spirit by these members of separate societies. And the associating genius of man is never better proved, than in these very societies, which are formed in opposition to the gene-<305>ral one of mankind, and to the real interest of the state.

"In short, the very spirit of faction, for the greatest part, seems to be no other than the abuse and irregularity of that social love and common affection, which is natural to mankind. For the opposite to sociableness is selfishness. And of all characters, the narrow, selfish one is the least forward in taking party. The men of this sort are, in this respect, true men of moderation. They are secure of their temper, and possess themselves too well, to be in danger of entering warmly in any cause, or engaging deeply with any side or faction."

Thus we see that almost all the vices of mankind are nothing else but the degeneracies of good and useful affections; or good, useful affections influenced by narrow views. I do not say this to extenuate the guilt or deformity of vice, but to shew how we ought to judge of our make and constitution, notwithstanding all the vices which have or do prevail in the world. For sure that ought not to be imputed to the Author of nature, which is in reality a perversion of the qualities he has endowed us with for excellent purposes. Properly speaking, the original stock is his, and what alone he is accountable for; the use or abuse of our affections is ours, if there be any being in the world who hath any thing that can be called its own; or if there can be, with regard to any being, any foundation for approving or blaming itself.

All this is delightfully illustrated by the excellent moral poet so often quoted, in several parts of his truly philosophical, as well as poetical, essay on man.

> *Better for us, perhaps, it might appear,*
> *Were there all harmony, all virtue here;*
> *That never air or ocean felt the wind;*
> *That never passion discompos'd the mind:* <306>
> *But all subsists by elemental strife;*
> *And passions are the elements of life.*
> *The gen'ral order, since the whole began,*
> *Is kept in nature, and is kept in man.*
> *What would this man? Now upward would he soar*
> *And little less than angel, would be more;*
> *Now looking downwards, just as griev'd appears,*
> *To want the strength of bulls, the fur of bears.*

Made for his use all creatures if he call,
Say what their use, had he the powers of all?

Essay on man, Epist. 1.[10]

And with regard to the passions implanted in our nature,

As fruits ungrateful to the planter's care,
On savage stocks inserted, learn to bear;
The surest virtues thus from passions shoot,
Wild nature's vigour working at the root.
What crops of wit and honesty appear,
From spleen, from obstinacy, hate, or fear!
See anger, zeal and fortitude supply;
Ev'n av'rice, prudence; sloth, philosophy;
Envy, to which th' ignoble mind's a slave,
Is emulation in the learn'd and brave:
Lust, thro' some certain strainers well refin'd,
Is gentle love, and charms all womankind:
Nor virtue, male or female, can we name,
But what will grow on pride, or grow on shame.
    Thus nature gives us (let it check our pride)
The virtue nearest to our vice ally'd;
Reason the byass turns to good from ill,
And Nero *reigns a* Titus, *if he will.*
The fiery soul abhorr'd in Cataline,
In Decius *charms, in* Curtius *is divine,*
The same ambition can destroy, or save,
And makes a patriot, as it makes a knave.

Essay on man, Epist. 2.[11] <307>

Nature could not possibly have done more for us than it has. IV. But to clear up this point yet further, let us reflect what we would have done by nature to set us right, and to prevent our abuse of our powers and affections; or what we can conceive possible for nature to have done for that effect, which it hath not done.

10. Pope, *Essay on Man*, I.165–78.
11. Ibid., II.181–202.

It appears from what has been said of vices, that none of them take their rise from affections or appetites in our nature, merely implanted for evil purposes, or to qualify us for vices. No vice takes it rise from a passion or affection absolutely hurtful, and not fitted for very good purposes. Even the love of power, as hurtful as it is by some effects of it, is in itself a most noble principle in our nature, as being the foundation of greatness of mind, and of many lofty and excellent virtues. Without it, the human mind would have been timorous, submissive, low and groveling; it could never have risen to great attempts, or have been capable of great sentiments. Magnanimity, despight of danger, and public spirit, could not possibly have been virtues within our reach, without such an original greatness of mind, as supposes the desire of extending our abilities and our sphere of activity. But if this is really the case, nature acted a kind part with regard to us, in implanting in us this principle; it certainly intended our good and perfection by it. Or would any man chuse to have had mankind secured against the bad effects of wrong-turned ambition, at the expence of our being utterly destitute of a capacity of noble and worthy ambition, of high ideas, great sentiments, and suitable actions?

How, therefore, can we conceive mankind to be secured by its Author against the vices which really spring from affections necessary to our good and perfection, influenced and directed by false and narrow views, till they are become very strong and powerful; nay, are quite wrought into temper by repeated acts, in consequence of the useful law of habits: how, I say, can we conceive mankind se-<308>cured by our Author against such vices, and their hurtful effects, otherwise than by his originally well proportioning the forces of the affections implanted by him in our nature, to one another, and to the general good of the whole system; and by giving us reason, together with a sense of order and just subordination, in the regulation of all our natural affections, to enable us to direct and guide them to their best ends. This is certainly the only conceivable way, consistent with our being reasonable beings, our having any moral sphere of activity, or our being capable of approving ourselves and our conduct. For nothing can be more evident than that it is the power of governing appetites, affections and actions by reason, and a

The original forces of affections stand right.

sense of right and wrong, that makes the order of beings called rational creatures; an order, confessed to be superior in rank and dignity to such as have no sense of right and wrong, no power over their perceptions, motions and choices; or rather, no power of chusing, prefering and acting.

I. Now with respect to the original forces of our affections, it is well observed by an excellent author,[a] whom we have often quoted, that to assert, "That men have generally arrived to the perfection of their kind in this life, is contrary to experience. But on the other hand, to suppose no order at all in the constitution of our nature, or no prevalent evidences of good order, is yet more contrary to experience. We actually see such degrees of good order, of social affection, of virtue and honour, as make the generality of mankind continue in a tolerable, nay, an agreeable state. However, in some tempers we see the selfish passions by habits grown too strong, in others we may observe humanity, compassion and good nature sometimes raised, by habits, to excess. <309>

Illustration on this argument. Were we to strike a medium of the passions and affections, as they appear in the whole species of mankind, to conclude thence what has been the natural ballance, previously to any change made by custom or habit, which we see casts the ballance to either side, we should, perhaps, find the medium of the public affections not very far from a sufficient counter-ballance to the medium of the selfish; and consequently the over-ballance on either side, in particular characters, is not to be looked upon as the original constitution, but as the accidental effect of custom, habit, associations of ideas, or other such causes; so that an universal increasing the strength of either, might, in the whole, be of little advantage. The raising universally the public affections, the desires of virtue and honour, would make the hero of *Cervantes,* pining with hunger and poverty, no rare character. The universal increasing of selfishness, unless we had more accurate understandings to discern our nicest interests, would fill the world with universal rapine and war. The consequences of either universally abating or increasing the desires between

---

a. Mr. *Hutcheson* on the passions. [Hutcheson, *Passions,* I.VI.vii.]

the sexes, the love of offspring, or the several tastes and fancies in other pleasures, would perhaps be found more pernicious to the whole, than the present constitution. What seems most truly wanting in our nature, is greater knowledge, attention and consideration; had we a greater perfection this way, and were evil habits, and foolish associations of ideas prevented, our passions would appear in better order.

But while we feel in ourselves so much public affection in the various relations of life, and observe the like in others; while we find every one desiring indeed his own happiness, but capable of discerning by a little attention, that not only his external conveniency, or worldly interest, but even the most immediate and lively sensations of delight, of which his nature is susceptible, immediately flow from a <310> public spirit, a generous, humane, compassionate temper, and a suitable deportment; while we observe so many thousands enjoying a tolerable state of ease and safety, for each one whose condition is made intolerable, even during our present corruption: how can any one look upon this world as under the direction of an evil nature, or even question a perfectly good providence? How clearly does the order of our nature point out to us our true happiness and perfection, and lead us to it, as naturally as the several powers of the earth, the sun, and air, bring plants to their growth, and the perfection of their kinds? We, indeed, are directed to it by our understanding and affections, as it becomes rational and active natures; and they by mechanic laws. We may see that attention to the most universal interest of all sensitive natures, is the perfection of each individual of mankind. That they should thus be, like well-tuned instruments, affected with any stroke or touch upon any one. Nay, how much of this do we actually see in the world? What generous sympathy, compassion, and congratulation with each other? Does not even the flourishing state of the inanimate parts of nature, fill us with joy? Is not thus our nature admonished, exhorted, and commanded, to cultivate universal goodness and love, by a voice heard through all the earth, and words sounding to the ends of the world?"[a]

a. This author makes another observation to the same purpose, page 177, which the reader may consult.

Now what is the result of all this excellent reasoning from the experience of all mankind, but that there is ground to think, our affections stand originally in our nature very well proportioned to one another, and to the ultimate end of them all, the general good of the kind, and the private good of every individual, so far as the good of the kind <311> admits the private good of every individual to be consulted; or that all the variety, with respect to the human affections, there is any reason to imagine to be original, is well adjusted to the public good. These conclusions do certainly ensue from the experiences above narrated. And indeed, the most considerable inequalities that are observed in human life, with respect to the forces of the affections, of whatever kind, do plainly take their rise from what hath been proved to be of admirable use in our nature, *viz.* the way and manner in which habits are generated or produced. It is by habit only that any appetite or affection is strengthened, or wrought into temper.

II. Now there being ground to think that the affections originally stand right, or in due proportion in our original nature, what more could nature have done for us, in order to their being preserved in a due ballance, for private and public good, than to have given us reason, and a sense of right and wrong, to govern them by?

And nature hath given us a guiding principle.

That we have such a power or faculty is indisputable; and how this faculty may gain strength, is no less evident to experience: even by exercise, as all our other faculties, powers and principles do. But to say, why hath not nature made reason stronger in us, or to grow up faster, is indeed to ask, why reason is a faculty improvable into strength and vigour by exercise. It is to ask, why it does not acquire force and authority, otherwise than by due culture. It is therefore to ask, why it is reason. It is known to be early in our power to bring reason to very great perfection, with regard to the management of our passions; for, as corrupt as man is, we have many instances of such perfection: this is in our power, in any sense that any thing can be said to be in our power, and if we do not cultivate reason, it does not arrive at due perfection, for this very good <312> cause, "That nature designed and willed that the cultivation of our reason should be a progressive work, dependent on ourselves." I am obliged often to have recourse to this principle, this law of our nature, because it is universal, or runs through the whole of our composition.[a]

All this is beautifully expressed by our excellent moral poet.

> *Most strength the moving principle requires,*
> *Active its task, it prompts, impels, inspires;*
> *Sedate and quiet the comparing lies,*
> *Form'd but to check, delib'rate, and advise.*
> *Self-love yet stronger, as its object's nigh;*
> *Reason's at distance, and in prospect lie;*
> *That sees immediate good by present sense,*
> *Reason the future, and the consequence;*
> *Thicker than arguments, temptations throng,*
> *At best more watchful this, but that more strong.*
> *The action of the stronger to suspend,*
> *Reason still use, to reason still attend:*

a. Animi constitutio sic se habet, ut una sit ejus pars ratio, altera iracundia, tertia cupiditas. Ratio cognitioni, ira robori, cupiditas appetitui praeest. Cum igitur haec tria una compago in unum redigantur, tum virtus in animo gignitur & concordia: cum per seditionem inter se dividuntur, vitium oritur atque discordia. Sunt autem virtuti haec tria necessaria, ratio, facultas & consilium. Jam ratione animae praeditae virtus est prudentia, quoniam judicii & contemplationis particeps est habitus: iracundiae autem fortitudo, quandoquidem resistit, & gravia perfert hic habitus: cupiditatis vero temperantia, posteaquam corporis voluptatum quaedam est moderatio: totius denique animi justitia, &c. *Ex Theage Pythagorio, in libro de virtutibus.* [Theages Pythagoreas, *De Virtutibus,* in Gale, *Opuscula,* 688–89. The sentence beginning "Sunt autem" is from Metopus Pythagoreus, *De virtute* (Gale 685), and the remainder of the passage is a paraphrase of Theages Pythagoreus (Gale 689–90). "The constitution of the mind is such that one of its parts is reason, the second is irascibility, and the third is desire. Reason governs thinking, anger governs strength, and desire governs appetite. When therefore these three things are reduced to one by a single link then virtue and concord arise in the mind. When they become divided by dissension then vice and discord arise" (Gale 688–89). "But there are three things that are necessary for virtue, reason, ability, and deliberation" (Metopus, Gale 685). "Now, the virtue of the mind that corresponds to reason is practical wisdom, since that is a disposition to both judgment and contemplation. The virtue corresponding to irascibility is courage, since it withstands things, and the disposition secures weighty aims. Temperance is the virtue corresponding to desire, since it acts to moderate the pleasures of the body. Justice briefly is the virtue of the whole mind" (Theages, Gale 689–90). Gale, ed., *Opuscula mythologica, physica et ethica. Graece et Latine.* . . . (Amsterdam, 1688).]

Attention, habit and experience gains,
Each strengthens reason, and self-love restrains.
Essay on man, Ep. 2.[12]

I shall only now add one thing with respect to it, that has hitherto been but just suggested, namely, that men never hesitate in admitting it to be a good <313> account of nature, with respect to any of our external powers, or their subjects, to shew that the right management of them depends upon ourselves; for that we are free with regard to them, they never doubt. Thus no man thinks of blaming nature, because one does not manage his eyes, or any other of his senses or members, to the best advantage for his conveniency and pleasure, in the way of merely animal life: that is readily said to be one's own fault, when the person is at his own disposal, and free from external violence of every sort. Here every such an one is immediately pronounced free: no person is at a loss to understand what this freedom means: and none who understand what it means, do not think, that in these matters, nature has done well to put our interest or good in our own power, and to make them dependent upon our selves. Every one will say, that not to have made man so, would have been to have made him a mere sensitive brute; and that such an one, though he should never feel any pain, but be entertained with a constant flow or succession of agreeable sensations, would, however, be but a mere animal, quite passive, and far inferior to a being capable of foreseeing and acting, or of pursuing ends by his own choice. But if this be owned with respect to external objects, and our sphere of activity in the natural world, how comes it not to be owned with regard to moral objects, and our sphere of activity in the moral world? Such a freedom with regard to the latter, must be freedom with regard to them, as much as the freedom with regard to external objects just defined, is freedom with respect to them. And if freedom with regard to external objects be any excellence: freedom of the same kind, with regard to moral objects, must be at least an equal excellence. Let metaphysicians quibble and wrangle about freedom as long as they please, it is certain, that in the

12. Pope, *Essay on Man*, II.67–80.

same sense that we can be said, and are unanimously said to be <314> free, with respect to eating, drinking, walking, sitting, or any such external acts; we are likewise free with respect to many internal or moral acts, such as thinking upon this or the other subject, indulging or crossing this or the other affection, &c. Nay, which is more, with regard to moral acts, we have really more freedom than with regard to any of our operations upon external or material objects. For who is not sensible, that the cultivation of his mind depends more upon himself than the cultivation (for instance) of his garden; for it is subject to fewer letts and impediments than the other: the cultivation of our mind depends only upon our setting ourselves in earnest to do it; whereas the cultivation of our garden depends upon many causes we cannot oppose or controul.

All that I aim at by this is, that if we are but allowed to be free with regard to the operations of our minds about our affections, in the same sense that we are said to be free with regard to any external actions, or operations upon material objects; it must follow, that nature is not to be blamed for our mismanagements in the one case, more than for our mismanagements in the other, which nobody thinks of doing.

If our having natural power be no ground of objection, having moral can be none.

> *Account for moral, as for nat'ral things:*
> *Why charge we heav'n in these, in those acquit?*
> *In both, to reason right, is to submit.*
>   Essay on man, Epist. 1.[13]

Indeed, to blame nature in either of these cases, is to say, nature has done wrong in giving us any sphere of activity at all, or in making us creatures capable of acting by foresight and choice. But objections against man are sufficiently answered, if they are shewn ultimately to terminate in demanding, "Why nature hath made any order of beings of that kind, or made any creatures with such a <315> sphere of dominion, as raises them above creatures who do not at all guide themselves, or chuse for themselves, having no guiding principle in their constitution."

13. Pope, *Essay on Man,* I.162–64.

If it is said, that several men's minds are like certain spots of ground, uncapable of cultivation to any good purpose. It might be answered first of all, that it is not certain that there is any such spot of ground, which by a full knowledge of soils acquireable by man, if he gives due pains, and takes right methods to attain to such knowledge, may not be managed to a very useful purpose: we must first be able to say, the science of nature cannot be carried farther than it hath been, before we can affirm any soil is absolutely useless. But however that be, it may be justly affirmed, that there is no ground to think there is any such mind amongst mankind, otherwise than in consequence of some law of matter and motion necessary to the good of the natural world, our union with which, and consequently our dependence upon the laws of which, makes so proper a state of being in the fullness of nature, as has been already proved. I believe all naturalists will agree with me, that there is reason to think from experience, that the incapacities of ideots and changelings is such a phenomenon as distortion in the members of the body, and owing in like manner to natural causes. And in the third place, however even that may be, it is certain, on the one hand, that such examples are very rare; and, on the other, that great variety of talents, not only with respect to strength and quickness, but even in species, is requisite to the happiness and perfection of mankind: though all talents, faculties and genius's are not alike useful, yet there is none we know of which is not useful, or capable of being employed to very good purposes. Nay, on the contrary, the care of mankind about their happiness is certainly very deficient in this very article, in not taking due pains to manage educa-<316>tion in a manner suited to explore, bring forth and improve every various talent and temper in mankind; all these being so many materials nature has liberally laid to our hands, as a rich stock for the improvement of society into goods. And to this we may add, that human life absolutely requires that many should be more fitted for bodily exercise, than for the employments of the understanding; more for the labours of the hands, than for those of the head. But it is sufficient to our purpose to observe, that the fact in universal experience with regard to mankind is, that it is difference with regard to improvement and culture of natural powers and affections that makes the most remarkable differences[a] and inequalities amongst mankind; insomuch that it may be justly said, "that to attain to a good <317> temper of mind, and to light sufficient for his right conduct in the more ordinary circumstances of human life, is in every man's power."

> *Take nature's path, and mad opinions leave,*
> *All states can reach it, and all heads conceive;*
> *Obvious her goods, in no extreme they dwell,*
> *There needs but thinking right, and acting well,*
> *And mourn our various portions as we please,*
> *Equal is* common sense, *and* common ease.
>   Essay on man, Ep. 4.[14]

a. This objection would quickly evanish, if we would but reflect, 1. How necessary variety of talents and characters among mankind is.

> *There's some* peculiar, *in each leaf and grain;*
> *Some unmark'd fibre, or some varying vein:*
> *Shall only man be taken in the gross?*
> *Grant but as many sorts of mind, as moss.*

And, 2. Whence this variety proceeds.

> *That each from other differs first confess;*
> *Next, that he varies from himself no less:*
> *Add nature's, custom's, reason's, passion's strife,*
> *And all opinion's colours cast on life.*
> *Yet more; the diff'rence is as great between*
> *The optics seeing, as the objects seen.*
> *All manners take a tincture from our own,*
> *Or come discolour'd thro' our passions shown,*
> *Or fancy's beam enlarges, multiplies,*
> *Contracts, inverts, and gives ten thousand dies.*
>
> *'Tis education forms the common mind*
> *Just as the twig is bent, the tree's inclin'd.*
>
> *Nature well known, no miracles remain,*
> *Comets are regular, and* Clodio *plain.*
>   Mr. *Pope,* Ep. Eth. B. 2. Epist. to Lord *Cobham.*

[Pope, *Moral Essays,* Epistle I, To Sir Richard Temple, Lord Cobham, lines 15–22, 31–36, 149–50, 208–9. Alexander Pope, *Pope: Poetical Works,* ed. Herbert Davis (London: Oxford University Press, 1966).]
14. Pope, *Essay on Man,* IV.29–34.

Reason, as
such, must
depend on
culture.

'Tis true, very many who call themselves *philosophers,* have taken great pleasure; a very odd unaccountable pride, in declaiming against human reason: some have even gone such a length, as to say, that the brutes are happier without it than man is with it; or can be, considering how weak it is and feeble; how easily it is deceived by any false semblance of good, and how easily it yields to every corrupt affection or headstrong appetite; or rather how tamely it is driven before them; for so they speak who make this objection, and so may we say of many persons. But to what does all this amount, if it be true, as we have endeavoured to prove from experience, 1. That all our affections stand rightly in our nature. 2. That it is fit habits should be contracted by repeated acts. And, 3dly. That it is fit, reason should depend as to its strength upon our culture or care to exercise and improve it? What do all those objections prove, if these propositions be true, but that some do not take care to improve their reason, and therefore their reason is weak; and that some have, by indulging their passions in a wrong way, instead of governing them by reason, very strong hurtful passions. It does not prove, that the way in which nature designed we should improve in knowledge or in virtue, is not a good way. In order to make <318> their objection militate against the Author of our make, they must either prove, "that to have sensations without the power of chusing, or any sphere of activity, is a nobler, a better state, than to have the power of chusing, a guiding principle, and a sphere of activity:" Or they must prove, "that it is a very bad state of things to make perfection of any kind only attainable by care to improve one's faculties, powers and affections." For tho' it will be readily granted to them, that philosophers (that is, some who are commonly so called) are frequently greater slaves to passions than others; yet what can be inferred from hence, but that the government of the affections requires not only the knowledge of right and wrong, but constant and steady discipline. A man may not only have made very great advances in several parts of learning and science, without having much considered the nature of the human mind, and the right conduct of human affections; but one may even have that latter sort of knowledge in theory to great perfection, and yet be a slave to some bad appetite for want of setting himself to subdue it, and to disenthral himself from its tyranny by proper means. We have had again and again occasion to observe, that it is by repeated acts alone, that new habits are produced, or that old ones are destroyed: and we have not only many examples before our eyes, even among the illiterate part of mankind, to convince us what perfection may be attained to, by right discipline in the conduct of the passions; but we have each of us something within us, which tells us on every occasion, that it is in our power to conquer any bad habit, any impetuous unruly appetite, and to attain to the mastership of all our affections and desires; and that it is at once our interest, and our duty, to set ourselves to obtain this inward liberty, this self-command, this best and noblest of dominions. <319>

V. But, in the fifth place, we might just as well argue from the vices which prevail among mankind, that there is no such thing as self-love in our make, as that there is not a principle of benevolence in our nature. For what vice is contrary to the well-being of our kind, or of society, which is not likewise contrary to the private good of every individual? The three greatest moral evils, in human life, are ignorance, superstition and tyranny. Now let us consider each of these, 1. Ignorance. No doubt, a vast many bad effects arise from it; but what better provision could nature have made than it has done for our improvement in knowledge? Man, indeed, through the defect of natural knowledge is not half the lord of the universe he would be, were he at due pains to improve his knowledge: all the lordship he hath, all the advantages he enjoys, are owing to his knowledge of nature; but what vast fields of natural knowledge lie yet quite uncultivated! Men in their studies and researches go too far beyond or above themselves; not that the knowledge of any part of nature is not worthy of pursuit, but because the interests of mankind chiefly require acquaintance with our earth, with soils, with climates, with air, with water, with fire, and other subjects, more immediately relating to us and our advantages, to the preservation of our health, the abridgement of our labour, and other conveniencies. It chiefly concerns us to know these elements; and if they are not understood, so far as to be able to make them as subservient to our purposes as they might be rendered; whence is it, but from what hath made all the progress we have been able to make

We may as well pretend to infer, that there is no such thing as self-love in our nature from the vices that prevail among mankind, as to pretend to prove from them, that there is no benevolence in our nature.

This reasoning applied to ignorance

in natural knowledge, so late and slow; to our not studying nature itself? Now, benevolence indeed, if we would but listen to it, calls upon us for the sake of mankind to apply ourselves to this study: it calls upon societies to set about and encourage these enquiries: it calls upon magistrates and rulers of states to take proper <320> methods of having this science cultivated and pursued; because all the interests of mankind are deeply concerned in the advancement of such knowledge. But does self-love less strongly excite to what is so evidently the interest of the whole, and of every private person. And why then should the neglect of this study be imputed merely to the want of benevolence in our nature, since all our private interests are no less concerned in it, than public good? If we neglect what self-preservation or self-interest prompts to, is it allowed to be an argument, that there is no self-love in our nature, or that it is too weak? And if that be not allowed, how can the neglect of what benevolence urges to, be reckoned a proof that there is no benevolence, no social principle, no virtue in our composition: or why should the Author of our nature be accused for not having dealt well with us, in not giving us a strong enough desire of public good, merely because public good is not sufficiently attended to; more than be accused for not having planted in us a strong enough principle of self-preservation, since true self-interest is not sufficiently attended to, which is never done. For if it be fair to make the one accusation, it must be so to make the other. And if it be sufficient to vindicate nature, in the one case, that we are well endowed with the powers and means of knowing our interest; it must be sufficient, in the other case, to vindicate nature, that we are sufficiently provided with the power and means of knowing the public interest. Indeed our being so provided is a sufficient justification of nature in both cases, because the chief enjoyments any beings are capable of, are those which arise from the gradual improvement of their own powers, by proper care to improve them: this, I say, is a sufficient vindication of our nature, especially if it be added to the account, "that private and public good, are in the nature of things, the <321> same, or, at least, inseparably connected, and therefore, that to be rightly selfish is true wisdom."

II. The same reasoning may be applied to moral knowledge, because it can only be acquired in the same way as natural; that is, by experience and observation, or by the study of moral objects, as the other by the study of material ones; and because self-love no less strongly dictates to us the study than benevolence does; a thorough knowledge of ourselves, and of our interests and pleasures, being evidently the interest of every particular person, as much as it can be the interest of the public. But then with regard to moral knowledge, it is worth while to observe further, that tho' the acurate knowledge of the human mind be a part of science which has never been so much cultivated as it ought, yet the common duties and offices of human life have always, or at all times, and in all ages been sufficiently understood. This plainly appears from the history of mankind; for in all ages of the world, and in all countries, there have been proverbs in every one's mouth, which sufficiently express the greater part, or, at least, the more important parts of morality.ᵃ The ignorance and barbarity of certain nations and times have been studiously magnified by some travelers and historians, to serve I know not what purposes: but from others we learn, that hospitality, justice, gratitude, candor, temperance, and all the <322> virtues have been found very general, even in nations called the most barbarous. Insomuch that no country has ever wanted its proverbs, as has been just said, expressing very fitly the advantages of them, and the obligations to them: not even the countries the most corrupted and perverted by superstition and tyranny: the two other great evils complained of in human life; and which are indeed the two greatest obstacles to the progress of useful knowledge;

a. That temperance is the best preservative of health, and that honesty is the best policy, are universal proverbs in all countries, and they ever were so; and are not these a complete system of morals. For every one becomes soon enough acquainted with his constitution to know what disorders or discomposes him; and, in order to know, what honesty requires in any particular instance, one needs only suppose himself in the case proposed, and ask himself, what he would desire or expect to be done to him in it. But which is more, in all countries there are prevailing fables known to the vulgar, that express in a very strong manner, all the more important duties and rules of life.

the great sources and supports of all the ignorance that has prevailed, or still prevails among mankind.

III. Now with regard to them, we may observe, that though we want very much a history of superstition, faithfully collected, it seems evident that if tyranny be not the inventress and mother of superstition, yet at least, they have always gone hand in hand, kept pace, and acted as it were in concert. Tyranny, no doubt, says a noble author, has a natural tendency to corrupt mens notions of the Deity, and of religion and morals.[15] "Morality and good government must go together: there is no real love of virtue without the knowledge of public good. And where absolute power is, there is no public. Accordingly, they who live under tyranny, and admire its power as sacred and divine, are debauched as much in their religion as in their morals. Public good, according to their apprehension, is as little the measure or rule of government in the universe as in the state. They have scarce any notion of what is good and just, other than as mere will and power have determined. Omnipotence, they think, would hardly be itself, were it not at liberty to dispence with the laws of equity, and change at pleasure the standard of moral rectitude."

"But, notwithstanding the prejudices and corruptions of this kind, 'tis plain, there is something still of a public principle, even where it is most perverted and depressed. The worst of ma-<323>gistracies, the mere despotic kind, can shew sufficient instances of zeal and affection towards it. Where no other government is known, it seldom fails of having that allegiance and duty paid it, which is owing to a better form. The eastern countries, and many barbarous nations have been, and still are, examples of this kind. The personal love they bear their prince, however severe towards them, may shew how natural an affection there is towards government and order among mankind. If men have really no public parent, no magistrate in common to cherish and protect them, they will

15. This sentence and the following lengthy quote are from Shaftesbury, "Sensus communis," III.i, in *Characteristics,* ed. Klein, 50.

still imagine they have such a one; and, like new-born creatures, who have never seen their dam, will fancy one for themselves, and apply (as by nature prompted) to some like form, for favour and protection. In the room of a true foster-father and chief, they will take after a false one; and, in the room of a legal government and just prince, they will obey even a tyrant, and endure even a whole lineage and succession of such."

All this is very true with regard to tyranny and its natural tendency; so that the greatest corruptions among mankind, either in morals or in religion, may be ascribed to it as their source and first cause: but surely, tyranny, and its dismal effects, are not more repugnant to benevolence, than they are to self-love and self-interest. For at what would we think should self-preservation make us spurn and rebel more zealously, than the cruel usurpations of despotic will and lawless power? But if the rise of superstition, or false religion, should not be thought sufficiently accountable, by supposing it the device of tyrants to carry on their ambitious schemes[a] of enslaving <324> mankind more easily and success-

To superstition which is found to go hand in hand with tyranny.

a. A late author, (*Hist. du Ciel*) in my opinion, hath rendered it exceeding probable, that superstition or idolatry took its rise from the misinterpretation of the symbolical language in practice amongst the *Aegyptians* more especially, the first meaning of which, after the invention and common use of letters, was soon forgot. But, at the same time, he shews, that the worship of dead heroes was the earliest species of idolatrous worship; ancient symbols that were originally used, to signify the proper occupations of the different seasons and months of the year, and to mark out the returns of feasts, having been, after their proper use was forgot, first interpreted to signify the inventions or actions of deceased benefactors, heroes or kings. And nothing is more plain from history, than that ambitious men were at great pains to promote the custom of *Apotheosis,* in concert with those employed about sacred things, who found their account in it on many considerations. In fine, we may judge how idolatry was introduced and kept up in ancient times, from the way in which false religion is now supported. Tyrants, and corrupt priests, mutually finding their interest in it, cordially league and unite to uphold it by all the arts they can devise. 'Tis the divine right of these two to enslave the rest of mankind, and to live luxuriantly upon their industry, or rather drudgery, that is the chief end of all the mixed policy of arbitrary power and superstition. But the success of such cruel policy, so evidently contrary to the well-being and happiness of every individual in such tyrannies, must first be allowed to be a good argument against our being naturally sensible to misery and happiness, before it can be brought as one to prove, that we have in our nature no social feeling, no disposition toward society and union. [Noël Antoine Pluche,

fully; or whatever may have been the rise of it, sure any barbarous usages which have been established by it, are equally repugnant to the love of ourselves, and to the love of one another. From all which, it follows, that nothing can be inferred from any vices which have ever reigned among mankind, but that men are capable of falling into sad corruptions, if they do not use their natural powers rightly. To which it ought, on the other hand, to be opposed, that mankind are capable of great perfection and happiness by the right use of their powers. And this being the case, it can never remain a question, whether man is well formed by nature, with those who think the greatest of all happiness and perfection is that which is attainable by a being itself, in proportion to its care to improve its natural stock of powers and <325> affections. To what hath been said, we may just subjoin, that almost at all times, and in all ages and countries, even among the most barbarous, enthraled and superstitious, there have not been wanting some persons who not only had arrived, by the due exercises of their faculties, to just notions of religion, morality, and mankind's true interests; but who likewise thro' public spirit, boldly bore testimony to the truth, and called upon mankind but to open their eyes, that they might see the happiness and perfection for which nature hath kindly designed them. For this fact is sufficiently attested by history.

Without a mixture of good and evil, there can be no place for prudence, &c.

VI. But I proceed to another consideration, in order to shew the absurdity of the complaints made against human nature, on account of the vices to which it is liable. We have often had occasion to desire it to be observed and remembred, that moral ends and effects must have their stated means and causes, as well as natural ones; otherwise there could be no such thing as moral connexions, moral order, and moral knowledge: let those therefore who object against the human make, and the present state of things, on account of physical and moral evils which spring from certain causes, consider well the ultimate result of their objections; whether by them they do not demand causes without their effects, or effects without their causes, both which are equally absurd; both

Histoire du ciel considéré selon les idées des poètes, des philosophes et de Moïse (Paris, 1738–39, translated by J. B. de Freval as *The History of the Heavens* (London, 1740).]

which are owned to be grosly absurd with respect to natural causes and effects: and both which must, by parity of reason, be absurd with regard to moral effects and causes. 'Tis certainly absurd to wish to have the capacity of foreseeing the consequences of things in the natural world to any degree, and the power of procuring goods to ourselves, of avoiding evils, or of turning evils into goods, in consequence of that capacity; and, at the same time, to desire that there were no bad consequences, no evils to be guarded against, or turned <326> into goods. Now the same must likewise hold true with respect to moral connexions, and our capacity of foreseeing moral goods or evils, and our power in consequence thereof, of shunning or warding off such evils, or of turning them into goods. Nature, in both cases, has designed to make procuring goods and avoiding evils dependent on ourselves, in order to make the study of nature our employment, and our happiness in a great measure our own work and acquisition. And therefore, if on the one hand, we think such conduct of nature necessary with regard to us, in order to our enjoying the pleasures of knowing nature's laws and connexions, of foreseeing consequences, and of exerting ourselves wisely, as it certainly is, then let us not blame nature for having so constituted things, that knowledge and foreseeing might be necessary; or that there might be place for such a thing as acting wisely, and chusing well, since these could not take place, were there no evils to be avoided or converted into good by wisdom and virtue. If, on the other hand, we do not like the conduct of nature, which lays a foundation for wisdom and virtue, good and prudent action, foresight and self-approbation; let us speak out plainly the ultimate meaning of our complaint against nature; and say, nature hath dealt unkindly by us in making our happiness depend in any measure on ourselves, and in making us capable of the pleasures of knowledge, foresight, self-direction, and good management.[a] <327>

a. See this subject finely treated in *Plutarch de fortuna.* Vitam regit fortuna, quidam dixit, non sapientia. Quid ergo? neque justitia, neque equalitas, neque temperantia, neque modestia res humanas dirigunt? Sed a fortuna & propter fortunam factum est ut in sua perseveraret Aristides paupertate cum parare divitias sibi posset? Et Scipio, &c.—Jam consilii dexteritate sublata, par est neque considerationem ullam rerum relinqui; neque investigationem utilitatis—Quid enim invenire aut discere homines possent homines si fortuna omnia dirigantur?—Ita prudentia neque aurum est, neque argentum, neque gloria, neque valetudo, neque robur, neque pulchritudo. Quid ergo ea est? Id quod recte his omnibus uti potest, ac singula horum jucunda facit, laudibilia, utilia, cum sine hac inutilia, sterilia, damnosaque sint, & molestiam dedecus possidenti ea adferant. Praeclare itaque Prometheus apud Hesiodum praecipit Epimetheo.

————Ne munera magno
   Ab Jove missa unquam accipiat, sed habere recuset.

Nimirum de fortunae bonis loquens: perinde ac si musicae ignarum canere fistula, aut recitare indoctum, aut equitare ignarum equi gubernandi vetant: ita eum hortans ne magistratum gerat cum imprudens sit, neve sit dives animo praeditus illiberali. Non enim duntaxat res secundae indigno oblatae occasionum stultis exhibent malorum consiliorum, ut Demosthenes dixit; sed & prosperitas merito major imprudentibus calamitatum ansa & origo est.

The substance of all this account amounts briefly to this. If the moral and natural world are not governed by general laws, they are governed without order in a desultory indeterminable manner, which is chance, or equivalent to it: and if, according to the general laws by which the world is governed, there are not evils to be avoided, as well as pleasures to be pursued; there can be no such thing as prudence and folly. Which is as plain, as that there can be no such thing as an art of avoiding, where there is nothing to be avoided; or an art of procuring happiness, where happiness cannot be the object of search and pursuit. This reasoning goes further than it is necessary to my purpose to pursue it. It is difficult to handle the necessity of evil in such a manner, as not to stumble such as are not above being alarmed at propositions which have an uncommon sound. But if philosophers will but reflect calmly on the matter, they will find, that consistently with the unlimited power of the supreme cause, it may be said, that in the best ordered system evils must have place. But because some will easily grant that with respect to physical evils, I would only suggest here to such, one thing that I have purposely avoided in this enquiry, which is, that whatever way moral good and evil be considered, or from whatever source they are derived, moral evil supposes physical evil to be the effect of certain actions in consequence of the laws of nature. The deduction of moral obligations from the essential difference of actions in respect of beauty or fitness (which must be the basis whatever other method is taken) necessarily supposes physical evils to be the consequence of certain methods of action. Suffer me, however, to propose one question to philosophers, the consequences of which, whatever way it may be determined, reach very far. "Whether all constitutions or connexions of things can be indifferent to the first independent mind, the creator of all things; that is, equally agreeable to him, of whatever temper he may be supposed to be, good, or bad." Every one will easily perceive, that to say, if he is good, he must like what is best, is no answer at all; because if there be no goodness or badness, but what is of his appointment, whatever he appointed would have been good, if he had appointed it to be such. The same question may be put thus, in other terms, "was the first mind determined to chuse by any meliority in what

Before we object against a state of rational creatures, because evils do result from certain combinations of things, as goods do from others, according to fixed laws, ascertainable by them, in order to be the rule of their choices, conduct, and pursuits; we ought to be sure whether it is possible in the nature of things, that there can be rational creatures capable of the pleasures resulting from choice and wise pursuit, were there not evils resulting from certain choices and pursuits, in consequence of the connec-<328>tions of things; or if not positive evils, at least what may be called evils, that is, pleasures very inferior to other pleasures; but that is so far from being possible, that we cannot possibly conceive how there can be any such thing as place for right or wrong choice, wisdom or virtue, but in such a state; nay, we clearly see there cannot be place

---

he chose; or would any other frame of things have been equally good, if he had appointed that to be the frame of things." Wherever choice is made, there is better and worse independent of choice. Whether a mind be necessarily determined in his choices by motives or not; deliberation itself supposes something to be preferred. [Plutarch, *De fortuna,* 97C–100A: "Someone said that it is chance, not wisdom, that governs life. Is it therefore neither, nor equality nor temperance, nor modesty that controls human affairs? But was it through chance and on account of chance that Aristides persevered in his poverty when he could have obtained great wealth? And Scipio etc. . . . But if skillfulness in practical thought is removed, then likewise there will not be any reflection on human affairs nor an investigation of the advantage of certain acts. . . . For what could men discover or learn if everything is governed by chance? . . . Practical wisdom is not gold, silver, renown, health, vigor, or beauty. What then is it? It is that which can make appropriate use of all these things, and makes all these things agreeable, praiseworthy, and beneficial. For without it they are useless, unproductive, and damaging, and they bring trouble and dishonor to their possessor. And Prometheus gives Epimetheus fine advice:

> He should never accept gifts sent by Jove, and instead should refuse to take them.

He is of course speaking about gifts which are the good things that come by chance; just as if he were forbidding a person ignorant of music to play on a pipe, or forbidding a person who is uneducated to give a recitation, or a person who cannot control a horse to ride. Thus he exhorts him not to be a state official if he lacks practical wisdom, nor to be rich if he is mean. For not only is the prosperity of one unworthy of it likely to give wrong ideas to the stupid, as Demosthenes says, but prosperity that goes beyond what is merited is an occasion and a cause of distress to the unwise." Plutarch, *Omnia quae extant opera,* 2 vols. (Paris, 1624).]

for wisdom and virtue, good and bad conduct, but in such a state; for right and wrong choice, with respect to whatever mind, even with respect to the creating mind, necessarily suppose connexions productive of happiness, and connexions productive of evil, or at least of less good. There is therefore an absolute ne-<329>cessity in the nature of things, that in order to the existence of agents capable of good and bad choice, there should be, at least, very high goods to be obtained by certain pursuits, in comparison of others, to be obtained by other pursuits. And is not this coming very near to admitting an absolute necessity of connexions from which evils result, in order to the very being of rational creatures, and their distinguishing excellence and happiness. But if we are obliged to go so far, in admitting a necessity of evil in a comparative sense, ought we not to be very cautious how we object against any evils which take place: or can we, indeed, reasonably object against evils, unless we can clearly prove, that they are not at all necessary to the happiness and perfection of rational creatures; for till we can prove that, (a necessity of comparative evil being once admitted) the presumption will lie with respect to any particular evils, that they may be necessary to good, the greater good of rational beings: but as such, they are goods, and not evils.

Several virtues necessarily presuppose not only physical but moral evils. But, having but just suggested this general observation, I shall now go on to shew, from particular instances, that many of the evils complained of in human life, moral as well as natural, are, in the nature of things, necessary, absolutely necessary to many goods, without which human life could have no distinguishing excellence, nor indeed any considerable happiness; which instances will confirm, *a posteriori,* our arguing, as we have just done, abstractedly, from the nature of things, for the necessity of evil in general.

I. Not only is it true in general, as has been already observed, that there can be no rational creatures, capable of right and wrong choice, good and bad conduct, wisdom and virtue, unless there be, with regard to them, connexions which are productive at least of lesser and greater pleasures, to be <330> the objects and rule of their conduct and pursuits. But with respect to man, it is certain, that several vices and imperfections,[a] as well as physical pains and wants, are absolutely necessary to the very being and exercise of certain virtues, which are the highest glory of human life, and afford men their best pleasures and enjoyments. Not

a. The whole dissertation of *Plutarch de capienda ex inimicis utilitate* is a proof of this. Vis inimico ut egre sit facere, noli ei exprobare lasciviam, molitiem, intemperantiam, illiberalitatem, ipse fortis esto, castus, verax, humanumque & aequum iis cum quibus tibi res est te praebe. Quod si ad maledicendum, &c.—Si illiteratum, studium discendi tuum laboremque intende: si timidum, excita fortitudinem tuam, si lascivum dele ex animo si quod restat delitescens libidinis vestigium.—Atque hoc modo licet in inimicitia mansuetudinem & malorum tolerantiam demonstrare. Simplicitati & magnanimitati atque bonitati plus loci hic est, quam in amicitiis. Non enim tam pulchrum est, bene amico facere quam turpe non facere id, cum necessitas ejus requirit. Ceterum oblata occasione ulciscendi inimicum, eum missum facere aequanimitatis est. Qui vero & miseratur inimicum afflictum & opem infert indigenti, & filiis ejus ac familiae adverso ipsorum tempore operam suam studiumque defert; hunc qui non amat ob animi humanitatem neque probitatem laudat, Huic pectus atrum est atque adamantinum.—He concludes with a most generous remark. Qui vero non excaecatur odio inimici, sed vitam ejus, mores, dicta, factaque ut incorruptus spectator contemplatur, is pleraque eorum, quorum sinistra aemulatione correptus est, intelliget ei diligentia, providentia, probisque actionibus parta esse: eodemque contendens, studium honestatis, gloriaeque suum augebit; vanitate & socordia affectuum amputatis, &c. [Plutarch, *De capienda ex inimicis utilitate:* "Should you wish to upset your enemy do not reproach him with being licentious, soft, intemperate, or mean. You yourself be strong, pure, truthful; be humane and fair with those with whom you have to treat. If for cursing, etc. . . . If you say your enemy is illiterate, intensify your studying and your hard work. If you say he is timid, kindle your courage. If you say he is licentious, erase from your mind any trace of lechery that may remain there. . . . And in this way it is possible, in our dealings with our enemies, to show mildness and tolerance of wicked people. There is more room for guilelessness, magnanimity, and goodness here than in our dealings with our friends. For it is less fine a thing to behave well toward a friend than it is a bad thing not to behave well toward him when he has need of your kindly act. But to let pass an occasion to take revenge on an enemy is to perform an act of impartiality toward him. Indeed a person who has pity for an afflicted enemy and helps him in his need, and works industriously on behalf of his enemy's children and household during this difficult time for them—one who does not love him for his humane spirit and does not praise him for his uprightness has a heart which is black and hard" (88C–91A). "But someone who is not blinded by hatred for his enemy but instead, as an uncorrupted spectator observes his enemy's life, morals, affirmations, and actions, will come to understand that most of the things of which the enemy has been accused as a result of perverse envy, have been produced in consequence of his enemy's diligence, foresight, and honest acts. And so, striving toward this same goal, he will intensify his striving for honor, repute, and renown, and will make an end of his idleness and indolence, etc." (92C–D).]

only are darkness, doubts, ignorance, narrow views and false conceptions, as necessary, in the nature of things, to give a high relish to knowledge, truth,[a] instruction, recovery from error, and the breaking in of
light upon the mind, as hunger, thirst, and other urgent appetites are to
the exquisiteness of the pleasure sensible gra-<331>tifications afford; insomuch that the one could not be without the other: but which is more,
several moral diseases, imperfections and vices, make the materials and
subjects of many excellent virtues, they make place for them, they call
them forth into action, they give them occasion to exert themselves,
prove their force, and display all their beauty. As without distresses,
wants and afflictions of the natural kind, there could be no room for
patience, fortitude, compassion and charity; so without moral evils to
combat with, or to remedy, there could be no place for heroism, for
generous instruction, for noble efforts to reform mankind from errors
and vice, for struggling against corruption and tyranny; in one word, for
any of the noble, public-spirited, generous virtues, which add such lustre
and glory to human life; and often render it a scene not unworthy of
higher orders of rational beings to contemplate.[b] Here then is not only

a. So *Cicero,* in a fragment preserved by *D. Aug.* Lib. IV. cap. 2. *de Trinitate.*—
Nec enim fortitudinis indigeremus, nullo proposito aut labore aut periculo: nec justitia cum esset nihil, quod apeteretur alieni: nec temperantia quae regeret eas, si nullae
essent libidines: nec prudentia quidem egeremus nullo delectu proposito bonorum
& malorum. [Augustine, *De trinitate,* XIV.ix.3: "For we would not need courage
where neither travail nor danger confronts us. Nor would we need justice where there
was nothing of another's that was coveted. Nor would temperance govern the passions where there were no passions. Nor would we need prudence where there were
no goods to delight us, nor any evils either." (A.B., trans.)]
b. See *Seneca.* Quare bonis viris mala accidunt quum sit providentia. He perhaps
goes too far, when he says, Nobis interdum voluptati est, si adolescens constantis
animi irruentem feram venabulo excipit, si leonis incursum interritus pertulit, tantoque spectaculum est gratius, quanto id honestior fecit. Non sunt ista quae possunt
Deorum in se vultum convertere, sed puerilia & humanae oblectantia levitatis. Ecce
spectaculum dig. num, ad quod respiciat intentus operi suo Deus. Ecce par Deo dignum, vir fortis cum mala fortuna compositus, utique si & provocavit. Non video
inquit, quid habet in terris Jupiter pulcrius, si convertere animum velit, quam ut
spectet Catonem?
He makes, however, very good reflections upon this subject. Vir bonus omnia
adversa exercitationes putat. Quis autem, vir modo, & erectus ad honesta, non est

laboris appetens justi & ad officia cum periculo promptus? Cui non industriae otium poena est? Athletas videmus quibus virium cura est cum fortissimis quibusquam confligere.—Marcet sine adversario virtus. Tunc apparet quanta sit, quantum valeat polleatque cum quid possit, patientia ostendit.—Magnus es vir; sed unde scio, si tibi fortuna non dat facultatem exhibendi virtutis?—Nemo sciet quid potueris; ne tu quidem ipse. Opus est enim ad notitiam sui experimento.—Gaudent magni viri rebus adversis, non aliter quam fortes milites bellis.—Ad quam rem non opus est aliqua rerum difficultate? Gubernatorem in tempestate, in acie militem intelligas.—Ipsis, Deus consulit, quos esse quam honestissimos capit, quotiens illis materiam praebet aliquid animose fortiterque faciendi. Calamitas virtutis occasio est.—Hos itaque Deus quos probat, quos amat, indurat, recognoscit, exercet:—Hanc itaque rationem dii sequuntur in bonis viris, quam in discipulis suis praeceptores: qui plus laboris ab his exigunt, in quibus certior spes est.—Quid mirum si dure generosos spiritus Deus tentat? Nunquam virtutis molle documentum est,—Ignis aurum probat, miseria fortes viros.—Hoc est propositum Deo, quod sapienti viro ostendere haec quae vulgus appetit, quae reformidat, nec bona esse nec mala. Apparebunt autem bona esse, si illo non nisi bonis viris tribuerit, & mala esse si malis tantum irrogaverit.—Omnia mala ab illis removet. Scelera & flagitia & cogitationes improbas & avida consilia, & libidinem caecam & alieno imminentem avaritiam. Isti quos pro felicibus aspicitis, si non qua occurrunt sed qua latent, videritis, miseri sunt sordidi, turpes, ad similitudinem parietum suorum extrinsicus culti. Non est ista solida & sincera felicitas: Crusta est, & quidem tenuis.—Cum aliquid incidit, quod disturbet & detegat, tunc apparet quantum altae ac verae foeditatis alienus splendor absconderit. Vobis dedi bona certa mansura: quanto magis versaverit aliquis, & undique aspexeritis, meliora majoraque permisi vobis, non egere felicitate felicitas vestra est. [Seneca, *Moral Essays* I, *De providentia:* "Why, though there is a providence, some misfortunes befall good men." Then: "We men at times are stirred with pleasure if a youth of steady courage meets with his spear an onrushing wild beast, if unterrified he sustains the charge of a lion. And the more honourable the youth who does this, the more pleasing this spectacle becomes. But these are not the things to draw down the gaze of the gods upon us—they are childish, the pastimes of man's frivolity. But lo! here is a spectacle worthy of the regard of God as he contemplates his works; lo! here a context worthy of God—a brave man matched against ill-fortune, and doubly so if his also was the challenge. I do not know, I say, what nobler sight the Lord of Heaven could find on earth, should he wish to turn his attention there, than the spectacle of Cato . . ." (II.8–9). "All his adversities he counts mere training. Who, moreover, if he is a man and intent upon the right, is not eager for reasonable toil and ready for duties accompanied by danger? To what energetic man is not idleness a punishment? Wrestlers, who make strength of body their chief concern, we see pitting themselves against none but the strongest" (II.2–3). "Without an adversary, prowess shrivels. We see how great and how efficient it really is, only when it shows by endurance what it is capable of" (II.4). "You are a great man; but how do I know if fortune gives you no opportunity of showing your worth" (IV.2). ". . . no one will know what you can do—not even yourself. For if a man is to know himself, he must be tested" (IV.3).

an <332> excellent use of these moral evils, which are however, as we
have seen, nothing but the corruptions and perversions of affections,
which in themselves are of the highest importance to our dignity and
perfection: but here is plainly a necessity of imperfections and vices, to
the very existence of many virtues, or to their formation, trial, exertion,
and glorious efforts. Imperfections and vices do indeed give force and
heightening to good qualities and virtues, as the shades in a picture set
off the brighter and more enlightened parts. It is not possible that there
can be an agreeable variety of beauty in the moral world, without foils
and contrast, any more than in the natural; for whatever is raised, heightened, or made conspicuous in nature, must be rendered such by shade
and contrast; And let us but think how dull the history of mankind
would be, or how low, untouching, insipid and <333> groveling a show

---

"Great men, I say, rejoice oft-times in adversity, as do brave soldiers in warfare" (IV.4).
". . . and to this end they must encounter some difficulty in life. You learn to know
a pilot in a storm, a soldier in the battle-line. . . . God, I say, is showing favour to
those whom he wills shall achieve the highest possible virtue whenever he gives them
the means of doing a courageous and brave deed" (IV.5). "Disaster is virtue's opportunity" (IV.6). "In like manner God hardens, reviews, and disciplines those whom
he approves, whom he loves" (IV.7). "And so, in the case of good men the gods follow
the same rule that teachers follow with their pupils; they require most effort from
those of whom they have the surest hopes" (IV.11). "Why, then, is it strange if God
tries noble spirits with severity? No proof of virtue is ever mild" (IV.12). "Fire tests
gold, misfortune brave men" (V.10). "It is God's purpose, and the wise man's as well,
to show that those things which the ordinary man desires and those which he dreads
are really neither goods nor evils. It will appear, however, that there *are* goods, if these
are bestowed only on good men, and there *are* evils, if these are inflicted only on the
evil" (V.1). "Evil of every sort he keeps far from them—sin and crime, evil counsel
and schemes for greed, blind lust and avarice intent upon another's goods" (VI.1).
"The creatures whom you regard as fortunate, if you could see them, not as they
appear to the eye, but as they are in their hearts, are wretched, filthy, base—like their
own house-walls, adorned only on the outside. Sound and genuine such good fortune
is not, it is a veneer, and that a thin one . . . when, however, something occurs to
overthrow and uncover them, then you see what deep-set and genuine ugliness their
borrowed splendour hid. But to you I have given the true and enduring goods, which
are greater and better the more any one turns them over and views them from every
side. I have permitted you . . . your good fortune is not to need good fortune"
(VI.4–5). Seneca, *Moral Essays*, vol. 1, trans. John W. Basore, Loeb Classical Library
(London: Heinemann; New York: Putnam, 1928).]

to ourselves, human affairs would be, without the magnanimous contests, and heroic achievements of virtue contending with vices. But this is not all the vices serve for, merely to illustrate virtues, and to display their charms to advantage: for benevolence, magnanimity, gratitude, patriotism, public spirit, and all the other virtues, which are the great ornaments of mankind, could not take place, were there no wants among mankind to supply, or distresses to be relieved, no monstrous passions to bear down and subdue, no savage enemies to combat and destroy, no great goods to bring to mankind, or no great evils to deliver them from. A *Hercules* could not have ascended among the gods, and acquired everlasting fame, had there been no cruel tyrants, that ravaged mankind like furious tygers, to conquer and extirpate. Nor could an *Orpheus* have done the most glorious work that can fall to the share of mere mortal, by civilizing a people, and bringing in wholsome laws, philosophy, arts, and good taste among them, had he not found a nation that was yet living like the wild beasts, and quite a stranger to all the high enjoyments of well polished humanity. All this is as evident, as that supplying supposes wants, and delivering supposes distress. They, therefore, reason most absurdly, who would have human life distinguished by glorious virtues, and yet those virtues not have subjects, materials and occasions to exert and prove themselves upon.

II. But in the second place, if objectors attend to human nature, to the nice ballance and dependence of human affections, and to the natural tendency and course of things, they will plainly see an absurdity in many of their complaints against human nature, on account of the vices to which it is liable, unless they think that mankind ought not to form themselves into societies, and endeavour to make the <334> bodies into which they form themselves, great, opulent and powerful, by encouraging manufactures, trade, and the polite arts. If they think that mankind ought not to do so, but would be happier in small bodies, without any arts, but such as are necessary to mere subsistence; or by foregoing all worldly power and grandeur for simplicity and quiet, or rather indolence. It is sufficient to answer, that men may do so if they please: they are made for society, and they may chuse for themselves, their end

Every state of the body politic, as well as of the body natural, is incident to particular diseases or vices

and form in contriving society. Though they cannot attain to any end by any means, no more than a machine can be well formed for a certain end, without a fabric adjusted to that end; yet they may chuse their end, and the means to that end, if they will but content themselves with that end, and expect no advantages from it, but what it is fitted in the nature of things to produce.

But, to expect the advantages and benefits which arise from large bodies, who set themselves by proper means to make a great, an opulent and polite society, from small bodies that have no such aim, and do not therefore take the ways and means to attain to it; or to expect to avoid the inconveniencies which naturally arise from this or the other manner of combination, or from the pursuit of this or the other end by its proper means, is as absurd as to eat our cake and cry for it.

Of the vices to which the opulent state is subject.

III. But having premised this general answer, in order to be convinced of the absurdity of complaints against our make, on account of the many vices mankind are obnoxious to, when formed into great societies, whose end is wealth, power and politeness; I would desire the reader to attend to the following very evident maxims.

1. On the one hand, worldly wealth, power, greatness, when attained, necessarily give more occasions to the affections to take a strong turn and <335> bent towards the pursuit of external gratifications, than their contraries, indigence, weakness, and obscurity do. Affections and appetites must necessarily be strongly sollicited by objects and means proper to gratify them, if these are continually present to the mind; and affections much sollicited, much called upon, and frequently indulged, must grow stronger and stronger as they are so. Whence it follows, that according to the nature of things, inordinate appetites and affections towards external goods, must be very prevalent in opulent, powerful and great states. It is unavoidable.

2. On the other hand, worldly power, wealth and greatness, cannot be obtained by a state, but by the pursuits of the individuals; for what else is a state but an assemblage of many individuals; or its goods, but the sum or aggregate of the goods obtained by the pursuits of the individuals? But it is impossible that external advantages can be obtained,

if they are not very keenly pursued; or be keenly pursued, if they are not highly valued. And it is extremely difficult for individuals to value so highly as to pursue keenly, any external goods, and still preserve their affections from all the inordinancies and irregularities, to which keen and strong affections towards external goods are liable, and which would prove the ruin of society, if they were not restrained to a certain degree by right policy.

3. On the one hand, as riches and plenty cannot be obtained without industry; so without very great consumption industry cannot be encouraged or maintained: but whatever contributes to consumption, must, as such, conduce to promote and encourage industry: and there will necessarily be most encouragement to industry, where there is most consumption; but there will be most consumption of external goods, where there is most sensual gratification, and consequently there will be most encouragement to industry, where there is more affection <336> to sensual gratification, than where there is less. The pains taken to procure goods will be in proportion to the demand for them.

4. But on the other hand, as it is certain that wealth and greatness cannot be procured by a state, unless they are sought and pursued; so it is certain, that opulence and plenty when procured, by affording for a time the means of sensual gratification, to a very great degree of voluptuousness, tend to make men averse to the toils and hardships, to the labour and assiduity, by which alone continual consumption can be supplied and reinforced with fresh stores, in order to the continuance of opulence and plenty. The temper and spirit necessary to acquire them is lost by great indulgence in the enjoyment of them. So that as a nation cannot be opulent, unless there be the consumption by sensual gratifications, necessary to maintain the industry requisite to procure them; so opulence and plenty cannot long subsist, unless, notwithstanding the indulgences necessary to consumption, the spirit of industry be kept up amidst that indulgence and consumption.

5. From these positions it follows, that the formation and maintenance of a society, which shall pursue and attain to wealth and grandeur, requires the nicest administration, a very curious adjustment, many counterpoising regulations, and with all, the most watchful, delicate at-

tention and interposition.[a] Such a society must, in the nature of things, be <337> a composition of contrary qualities, from which harmony and general good are to be educed; which must require very skilful management, very accurately contrived laws, and a very dextrous administration.

a. Ut in fidibus, ac tibiis, atque cantu ipso, ac vocibus concentus est quidam tenendus ex distinctis sonis, quem immutatum, ac discrepantem aures eruditae ferre non possint, isque concentus ex dissimillimarum vocum moderatione concors tamen efficitur & congruens: sic ex summis & infimis, & mediis interjectis ordinibus, ut sonis moderata ratione, auctus consensu dissimillimorum concinit, & quae harmonia a musicis dicitur in cantu, ea est in civitate concordia arctissimum atque optimum omni in repub. vinculum incolumitatis; quae sine justitia nullo pacto esse potest. *Cicero de rep. l. 2. Ex Aug. de civit. dei. l. 2. c. 21.*

Statuo esse optimi constitutam rempublicam quae ex tribus generibus illis regali, optimo, & populari confusa modice, nec puniendo irritet animum immanem ac ferum, nec omnia praetermittendo, licentia cives deteriores reddat. *Cicero de repub. l. 2.*

Resp. res est populi, cum bene ac juste geritur, sive ab uno rege, sive a paucis optimatibus, sive ab universo populo. Cum vero injustus est rex, quem tyrannum voco: aut injusti optimates, quorum consensus factio est: aut injustus ipse populus, cui nomen usitatum nullum reperio, nisi ut etiam ipsum tyrannum appellem: non jam vitiosa, sed omnino nulla resp. est; quoniam non est res populi, cum tyrannus eam, factiove capesset: nec ipse populus est, si sit injustes, quoniam non est multitudo juris consensu, & utilitatis communione sociata. *Cicero de rep. frag. Ex Aug. l. 2. c. 21. de civitat. dei.*

Debet enim constituta sic esse civitas, ut aeterna sit. *Ibid.* [Augustine, *De civitate Dei*, II.xxi: "As, when lyres or flutes accompany the voices of singers, a kind of harmony should be maintained out of separate sounds, and the trained ear cannot endure any false note or disagreement, and such harmony, concordant and exact, may be produced by the regulation even of voices most unlike, so by combining the highest, lowest and between them the middle class of society, as if they were tones of different pitch, provided they are regulated by due proportion, the state may produce a unison by agreement of elements quite unlike. The agreement that musicians call harmony in singing is known as concord in the body politic. This is the tightest and best rope of safety in every state, and it cannot exist at all without justice." Augustine, *The City of God Against the Pagans*, vol. 1, bks. 1–3, trans. George E. McCracken, Loeb Classical Library (London: Heinemann; Cambridge: Harvard University Press, 1957).

Cicero, *De republica*, II.xxiii.41: "I consider the best constitution for a state to be that which is a balanced combination of the three forms mentioned, kingship, aristocracy, and democracy, and does not irritate by punishment a rude and savage heart . . . nor by overlooking every thing does it leave the citizens worse off in the face of licentiousness." The final seven Latin words do not appear in modern editions, but

But, 6. That such an adjustment and administration of society is possible, our own constitution, to go no further, is a sufficient proof; since were but a few things changed, it would necessarily produce the continuance of great opulence and power, great industry and noble arts, glorious virtues, and great general happiness: it would produce consumption necessary to the maintenance and encouragement of industry, without the decrease of the industrious spirit, which is, and must be the great secret, in order to the getting and preserving of opulence and greatness. It would not be free from vices; but all vices being duly curbed and restrained, out of the vices that did prevail would be educed great goods by the virtues to which such a constitution would naturally give due vigour and force.

IV. This reasoning is certainly true, but if it is so, then it inevitably follows, that all objections against man, on account of the vices his nature is liable to in certain combinations of men and things are absurd. For mankind must certainly be well made, "since <338> we are made capable of pursuing various ends, and of forming ourselves into different combinations for attaining various ends with foresight and choice"; "since bad constitutions of society, or unnatural combinations, not proper to attain to any good end, must be miserable and cannot long subsist, but must dissolve like a diseased body"; "and since by means of good gov- Men may
chuse their
state, but every
state hath its
natural and
necessary
consequences.

---

they are in the 1661 *Opera Omnia* from which Turnbull was quoting; see Cicero, *Opera Omnia*, ed. Cornelius Schrevel, 4 vols. (Amsterdam, 1661), 4:1314A. The words are given by Schrevel on the authority of Nonius Marcellus; see *De compendiosa doctrina*, under "modicum."

Augustine, *De civitate Dei*, II.xxi: "a people'd estate exists when there is good and lawful government whether in the hands of a monarch, or of a few nobles or of the whole people. When, however, the monarch is unlawful—I use the term 'tyrant'— or the nobles are unlawful—I call their mutual agreement a faction—or the people itself is unlawful—for this I found no current term if I am not to call it too a tyrant— then the state is no longer merely defective . . . but . . . does not exist at all. For there was no people's estate when a tyrant or a party takes over the state, nor is the people itself any longer a people, if it is unjust, since in that case it is not a throng united in fellowship by a common sense of right and a community of interest. . . ."

Cicero, *De republica*, III.xxiii.34: "for a state ought to be so firmly founded that it will live forever."]

ernment, societies may be extremely happy, not only notwithstanding any excesses or degeneracies, to which the affections implanted in us, or that can be ingrafted upon us, are liable; but in great measure, at least, even in consequence of the inordinate affections and concupiscences which are necessary to the procuring worldly wealth and greatness, or which they naturally tend to engender; these being counter-poised or counter-worked by the virtues, a good constitution of society as naturally tends to produce, as any well contrived machine works to its effect, while all its springs and wheels are in due order." This being the case, no objection can be made against our make and frame, which does not terminate in asking, either why we are made to arrive at any considerable end by uniting our forces in the social way, which is to object against our being social creatures, and made for fellowship, communication and participation; or, in asking, why our forces must be rightly combined and exerted in order to gain a certain good end, which is indeed to ask, why means are requisite to an end; or why an effect must be produced by its causes, than which there cannot be a greater absurdity in physics or in morals; or, lastly, in asking, why the goods in any combination of qualities in order to attain them may not be effects of another calculated to attain other goods, which is likewise absurd. For it is no less impossible, that the advantages of a simple state of mankind without arts only aiming at quietness, and mere subsistence, can belong to a state calculated to advance in opulence and greatness, by <339> the arts and means requisite to that end; than 'tis impossible, that fire should have at the same time, the properties of fire and of water. Men are capable of both states and conditions, but they cannot have the goods of both at the same time. Each hath its peculiar advantages and disadvantages, which must go together.[a] <340>

a. See an excellent paper on this subject, Vol. VI. No. 464. that is concluded with a very pretty alegory, which is wrought into a play by *Aristophanes,* the *Greek* Comedian. It seems originally designed as a satyr upon the rich, though in some parts of it, it is like the foregoing discourse, a kind of comparison between wealth and poverty.

Chremylus, who was an old and a good man, and withal exceeding poor, being desirous to leave some riches to his son, consults the Oracle of *Apollo* upon the sub-

As the natural so the political body hath its infancy, childhood, manhood and decline; and in both equally each of these stages, as it hath its peculiar advantages and pleasures, so it hath its peculiar diseases. Nay, as every habit of the natural body is incident to certain particular dis-

---

ject: The Oracle bids him follow the first man he should see upon his going out of the temple. The person he chanced to see, was to appearance, an old sordid blind man, but upon his following him from place to place, he at last found by his own confession, that he was *Plutus,* the God of riches, and that he was just come out of the house of a miser. *Plutus* further told him, that when he was a boy, he used to declare, that as soon as he came to age, he would distribute wealth to none but virtuous and just men; upon which, *Jupiter,* considering the consequences of such a resolution, took his sight away from him, and left him to strole about the world, in the blind condition wherein *Chremylus* beheld him. With much ado, *Chremylus* prevailed upon him to go to his house, where he met an old woman with a tatter'd raiment, who had been his guest for many years, and whose name was *Poverty.* The old woman refusing to turn out so easily as he would have her, he threatened to banish her, not only out of his house, but out of all *Greece,* if she made any more words upon the matter. *Poverty,* on this occasion, pleads her cause very notably, and represents to her old landlord, that should she be driven out of the country, all their trades, arts and sciences would be driven out with her; and that if every one was rich, they would never be supplied with these pompous ornaments and conveniencies of life, which made riches desirable. She likewise represented to him the several advantages which she bestowed upon her votaries in regard to their health, their shape, and their activity, by preserving them from gouts, dropsies, unwieldiness and intemperance. But whatever she had to say for herself, she was at last forced to troop off. *Chremylus* immediately considered how he might restore *Plutus* to his sight; and, in order to it, conveyed him to the temple of *Esculapius,* who was famous for cures and miracles of this nature. By this means the deity recovered his sight, and begun to make a right use of it, by enriching every one that was distinguished for piety towards the gods, and justice towards men; and at the same time, by taking away his gifts from the impious and undeserving. This produces several merry incidents, till in the last, *Mercury* descends with great complaints from the gods, that since the good men were grown rich, they had received no sacrifices, which is confirmed by a priest of *Jupiter,* who enters with a remonstrance, that since this late innovation, he was reduced to a starving condition, and could not live upon his office. *Chremylus,* who in the beginning of the play, was religious in his poverty, concludes it with a proposal, which was relished by all the good men who were now grown rich, as well as himself, that they should carry *Plutus* in a solemn procession to the temple, and instal him in the place of *Jupiter.* This allegory instructed the *Athenians* in two points: first, as it vindicated the conduct of providence in its ordinary distributions of wealth; and, in the next place, as it shewed the great tendency of riches to corrupt the morals of those who possessed them. [*The Spectator,* no. 464, 1712.]

orders; the corpulent to one sort, for instance, and the meager to another; so every form of society and government hath its peculiar evils as well as goods naturally growing out of it. The rich and opulent state hath its evils. But the poor mean one hath likewise its no less pernicious or disagreeable ones.

It belongs therefore to man to chuse. He cannot alter the nature of things, but ought to direct his conduct according to them. And to desire that his Creator should have made him capable of chusing for himself and conducting himself, and yet not have made variety of better and worse for the exercise of his thought and choice; is it not to desire matter of choice without any difference in things? Nay, to demand that all connexions of things should be equally beautiful and <341> good, it is not only to take away from a rational creature all subjects of choice, but it is to demand, that all different things, and combinations of things should have precisely the same relations, qualities and effects: A physical absurdity too gross not to be perceived by the most ordinary understanding. Thus then it is visible, that when we trace objections against the make and frame of man, and the connexions he stands in, to the bottom, they end in contradictory demands.

But the objections brought against mankind, on account of the vices they are liable to, being chiefly fetched from the vices which prevail in great and opulent states: it is not improper, before I leave this head, to add two or three remarks upon them.

Several things are misrepresented; luxury, for instance, is declaimed against in a very vague sense.

I. The complaints which are made against such states, in the general confused way of declaiming against luxury, have many of them no meaning at all, or a very absurd one. For luxury is often taken by those declaimers in such a vague, indeterminate sense, that, in reality, every thing which agrandizes a nation, may be said to be luxury, and in such a sense, not only poetry, painting, statuary, sculpture, architecture, gardening, music, and all the fine arts, even philosophy itself are voluptuous pursuits, and encouraging them is luxury; but trade also, and all its imports, are a nusance, a plague.

Now to put an end to such confused railery or morality, let it be called which you will, I would only ask those who have any understanding of

human affairs, 1. Whether under a wise administration, a people may
not only enjoy all the polite arts in great perfection, but even enjoy all
the goods of other countries which their own product can purchase,
without being impoverished by it? If they would have no trade, then let
us live upon the product of our spot: for sure, if they would have <342>
trade encouraged, they would have foreign goods imported in exchange
for our own product; and would they have them imported and not enjoyed? And as for the polite arts, what do they do, but employ the wealth
of a nation to the best purposes in the best taste, or with the greatest
elegance? What indeed is wealth without these, must it not be a nusance?
2. I would ask, whether under a wise administration, where military affairs are duly taken care of, or where a spirit of bravery and skill in military discipline are kept up by proper methods; a wealthy nation may not
live in all the ease and plenty imaginable, and in many parts of it shew
as much pomp and elegance, and delicacy of taste, as human wit can
invent, and at the same time be formidable to their neighbours? Is there
indeed no way of becoming brave and masculine, without being poor,
without abandoning trade and all polite arts, and giving ourselves up
entirely to martial exercises, and becoming a nation of mere soldiers?
Here sure there is a medium, which several nations have hit upon, otherwise there would never have been a nation at once, wealthy, polite and
brave. It is indeed commonly said, that the polite arts soften and enervate
a people, but if that be absolutely true,[a] is it not as certain, on the <343>

> The fine arts
> do not
> effeminate.

> But other arts
> must be united
> with them to
> make a brave as
> well as a polite
> people.

a. See the different effects of arts described by *Plato,* together with the gymnastical
exercises, which make a truly liberal education. *De Rep.* Lib. 3. Nonne animadvertis
inquam at animum afficiant, qui gymnasticam per omnem vitam exercent, musicam
non attingunt, vel qui contra faciunt? Qua de re, inquit loqueris? De feritate inquam
& rustica quadam duritie, & contra molitie & mollitate & comitate. Novi equidem
eos inquit, qui mera simpliceque utuntur musica plus aequo agrestiores evadere. Qui
contra musica duntaxat molliores, quam quod sit illis decorum. Atqui vis ipsa ag-
grestis ad iracundae naturae animositatem, granditatemque pertinet quae in recta educatione instituitur, in fortitudinem abit: sin autem praeter id quod decet extenditur
atque excrescit, ferox, ut consentaneum est, ac dura;—Quid vero? Nonne philosophica natura vim habet quandam mitem atque comem, quae si nimium remissa fuerit,
plus aequo mollior redditur: sin praeclare educata atque instituta, praeclarum aliquod
modestiae & comitatis exemplum solet existere.—Nonne igitur oportet illas inter se
aptas conspirare atque consentire? Ejusque animus qui hoc temperamento aptatus

other hand, that without these arts, human life is very rude, savage, un-
polished, and hardly one remove above that of the brutes which just
breath, eat and drink? Were it indeed a dilemma, one part of which must

---

est atque affectus temperans est atque fortis.—Quicunque igitur sinit musicae cantus
perpetuo circumsonare animo suo, eamque per aures veluti per infundibulum, con-
centibus illis quos supra dulces, molles appellavimus perfundit.—Tandemque liquat
& dissolvit animum, donec omnis illa animositas contabuerit penitus, eamque veluti
nervos ex animo exciderit, segnemque bellatorem effecerit.—Quod si quis gymnastices victui se totum tradat musicae & philosophiae studiis neglectis, primo quidem
firmum corporis habitum consecutus, animos sumit, & granditate seipsum replet
ipseque seipso fortior evadit. Quid vero? Quandoquidem nihil aliud agit, neque illi
quicquam cum musis est commune, neque ullum discendi studium in ipsius animo
inest quippe qui ne supremis labris quidem ullam disciplinam gustarit.—Neque ullam
aliam musicae partem, infirmitas quaedam, & visus, & auditus hebitudo dominatur:
quum ipsius sensus neque exsuscitentur, neque nutriantur, neque ullo modo expur-
gentur: Hispidus quidem & importunus homo, omnis eruditionis ac comitatis expers
mihi videtur, &c. See *Aristot. Polit.* Lib. 8. 3, 4, 5, 6, *&c.* where the character of the
Lacedemonians is shewn to be the natural effect of their education. [Plato, *Republic*,
410C–411D: " 'Surely you have noticed,' I said, 'the effect on the mind made by those
who do gymnastic exercises throughout their lives, and who do not concern themselves with music, and the effect on the mind of those who live the opposite kind of
lives?' 'What do you mean?' he said. 'I mean a certain wildness and coarseness, and
on the contrary side, a gentleness and courteousness.' 'I have noticed,' he said, 'that
those who listen to plain, simple music more than they should, become more wild.
Those who listen only to music become softer than is right for them. And there is a
wildness if the boldness turns into courage. But if it grows beyond what is fitting,
then, as is agreed, it becomes fierce and hard.' 'And so?' 'Surely a philosophical nature
has a certain kindly and gentle force which, if it were too weak, would become too
soft. But if it were rightly instructed and composed it would have a disposition of
exemplary modesty and kindness. Should not these two natures combine and work
harmoniously? And the mind which has become suited to and qualified by this temperament is self-controlled and strong. Whoever allows music to resonate forever in
his soul, pours through his ears as through a funnel the sweet, soft songs to which we
have already referred. At length it melts and dissolves the mind until all that wildness
has wasted away completely, as if he has cut out the nerves from his mind and made
himself a lazy fighter. . . . But if someone works hard at gymnastics and eats heartily,
and if he does not work at music and philosophy, then he becomes physically strong
and also lively in spirit, and he acquires a certain grandeur and a greater courage.'
'Surely he does.' 'But if he does nothing other than this, nor has anything in common
with the Muses, nor goes in for any studying, he will not taste any instruction at the
highest levels nor will taste any other part of music. A certain weakness and a dullness
of sight and hearing reigns, for his senses are neither stimulated nor nourished nor
in any way purified. He seems to me to be a rough and unfit man, a stranger to all
learning and to courteous living.' "]

be the case, who would hesitate which to chuse; whether to be as the fierce savage *Lacedemonians,* or as the intelligent polite *Athenians?* But there is far from being any dilemma in the case, for were not the *Athenians* as brave as they were polite? However, not to enter into historical discussions which would lead us too far from our point; who ever dreamed, that men could maintain a masculine, hardy, martial spirit, or have the courage and skill war requires, without any care taken upon them to nourish and keep up that spirit; and to exercise them for that effect in the arts and discipline of war? But why may not the qualities, resulting from the polite arts be united with those which result from war-<344>like exercises; may not the two be conjoined; is it not the conjunction of the two seemingly opposite qualities, *viz.* the soft and the masculine, that we admire in the *Athenians?* Is it not this conjunction that makes the truly amiable hero? It was this made a *Scipio.* And it is this that will make a people, at the same time brave and polite, humane, social, generous, tender, and bold, formidable, inconquerable. To produce which great and lovely character, a rightly model'd education in a state, otherwise well constituted and governed, would be as infallibly effectual, as any means in the natural world are to produce and effectuate their end.

II. Another observation I would make is, that as it is virtue alone that can make any particular person truly happy; so it is virtue alone that can be called the basis and cement of society, or that makes it happy. For tho' vanity, prodigality, debauchery, and other vices, promote consumption, and consequently trade, yet they tend to destroy the spirit of industry: they would effectually dissipate and waste opulence and the means of worldly grandeur and power, were they not counterpoised by other vices on the opposite extreme, such as avarice, superstitious abstemiousness, and excessive contempt of all sensible gratification: no goods can arise from vices, without the aids of public wisdom and many virtues; and if not restrained within certain bounds, they would effectually ruin and destroy all society. Private vices are therefore really to society, what ordure and filth is to land; they are equally abominable and nauseous in themselves; and, like it, are only made useful by skilful, sagacious and industrious management. They are the excrements of what is really

[marginal note:] It is virtue alone that is the cement of society.

[marginal note:] It is virtue and political wisdom that educes good out of evil.

useful, and can only be turned into use as natural ones are. Excrements of the one kind as well as the other, will abound most in opulent places where there is plentiful consumption; and in this also are they both alike, that they are in themselves of a poisonous, pestilential <345> nature, and tend to produce plagues, which would soon destroy mankind, or make them very miserable: In great quantities they are pernicious to good soil, and choak the good seeds thrown into it, bringing forth nauseous weeds in greater plenty than useful grains: without skilful tillage and husbandry, and sound wholesome seed, they would never produce any good at all: and, in fine, as manure is chiefly necessary to poor, barren or exhausted soil, so vanity, prodigality, debauchery, and other vices only can serve as a counterballance to such vices of the opposite extreme,[a] as avarice or penuriousness in all its branches and modifications, which, like poor ground, would but swallow up the seed thrown into it, and yield no crop. The similitude holds exactly in all these instances. And if that be the case, then can vices, in no proper sense, be said to be beneficial to society, though goods may be educed from them by virtue and political wisdom; unless it can be said, that a good crop is owing to excre-

Excrements may be made useful, and so may vices. ments chiefly, and not to good seed and right husbandry; which cannot be said even with respect to soil that requires manure to change its barren nature, and render it fertile. But if it be really so with regard to vice and virtue, then there can be no doubt about the truth I am now endeavouring to establish: for then our argument stands thus. "All the vices of men are but the corruptions, the degeneracies and perversions of affections implanted in our nature for most excellent purposes, and without which, as they are grafted in us to be managed by our reason, we could not be capable of any share of that dignity and perfection to which we now can by that means raise and advance ourselves. But even these vices,

a. Extremes in nature equal good produce,
   Extremes in man concur to general use.
      Eth. Ep. l. 2. Ep. 3.

[Pope, *Moral Essays,* Epistle III, to Allen, Lord Bathurst, lines 161–62. Alexander Pope, *Pope: Poetical Works,* ed. Herbert Davis (London: Oxford University Press, 1966).]

by good management in the public, and the counter-working of many virtues exerting themselves to that effect, <346> may be converted into benefits; insomuch, that societies, notwithstanding all the vices human nature is liable to in any circumstances, may be rendered very happy, very great and powerful, by good government and administration."

Now this defence of human nature must be admitted to be good, if what we have often said of the absurdity of objecting against the dependence of the happiness of society upon a right form of government be called to mind, *viz.* that it is objecting against our being made social creatures. But,

III. Let it be just added on this article, that supposing it to be granted that vices are necessary in the moral world, in the same sense that excrements are in the other; equally unavoidable, or if you will, mechanical effects; what will follow from this concession, but that, as such is the constitution of the material world, that the excrements which are unavoidably necessary or mechanically so, that would poison or corrupt the air, and produce diseases were they not carried off, may by skill be rendered useful at manuring the ground; so such is the constitution of the moral world, that the evils which are absolutely unavoidable in consequence of the human make, that are in themselves plagues and miseries, may be converted by skill and good management into goods. This, I say, is all that could be inferred upon granting that vices are necessary in the same sense that animal excrements are necessary; and therefore good order would still stand upon the same footing with respect to the moral world, as it does with respect to the material, where an objection taken from filth that can thus be turned into profit, would be justly stiled silly and ridiculous: there would still, even according to that way of reasoning, be the same difference between virtue and vice, as between excrements and good seed, and right husbandry.

Supposing vices to be necessary, yet good being educed out of them, the wisdom of the moral world will stand on the same footing as the wisdom of the natural.

But what hath been supposed cannot be granted: <347> the similitude between vice and excrement fails in this respect. The former is absolutely a mechanical effect, whereas the other depends, as we feel by experience, upon ourselves; it being in every man's power to govern his affections,

But vices are in no proper sense mechanical effects.

and to prevent them from running into enormities and irregularities. In the one case, it only depends upon us to prevent the bad effects, or to turn into good; in the other, it depends upon us to prevent our affections from being extravagant, and to manage them well; and it likewise depends upon us, by joining in right society, to turn the bad actions of the wicked and vicious into good uses, or to restrain them within certain bounds. We have therefore in the last case a double power, or there is a double dependence on ourselves. And for that reason, whatever necessity there may be for evils in order to goods, no evil can be said to be necessary, in a sense that implies any necessity upon any person not to act right, or not to govern his affections well. We are not more sure that certain effects in nature, within and without our bodies, are absolutely independent upon our will, than we are sure, each of us for ourselves, that the government of our affections and actions depends upon ourselves: this is a difference between things that must remain, while our nature and the present constitution of things exists, that some things are not in our power, and that others are: it cannot be altered. And so plainly is that difference felt in moral things, that whatever objections may be made against providence, and the human make, all objectors find that they cannot chuse but blame themselves, and think they suffer justly, when they act amiss. We may arraign nature as much as we please, in order to throw a share of our own faults upon nature, providence, or something external to us and independent of us, but when we have done all we can thus to extenuate our guilt in doing wrong, to ourselves we are still conscious that the guilt lies at our own door. <348>

We shall now consider the objections taken from the physical evils which prevail in the world; the various distresses and calamities that vex human life, and what is called an unequal distribution of external goods, such as riches, power, &c.

Now I think the following observations will sufficiently evince the absurdity or unreasonableness of all such complaints against providence in the government of mankind, and shew that there is no reason to object against the pains and troubles of human life, or the distribution of external goods; but on the contrary, good ground to approve the excellent laws, according to which all is brought about; or to conclude that all is brought about according to most useful general laws, none of which can be changed, but to the worse. But let it be remembered, before we go further, that it is impossible to consider the laws of the material world, and those of the moral separately. Man being indeed, as some philosophers have well expressed it, *Nexus utriusque mundi;*[16] or it being a nice blending and interweaving of natural and moral connexions and their effects, that constitutes our present state, or makes us what we really are. If this be kept in mind, the reader will easily see that repetitions upon this subject are unavoidable, since we must ever be having recourse to the same laws and principles in our nature, whatever the difficulty, question or objection about man may be. This being premised, to prevent cavilling at repetitions, which, however, I shall endeavour to avoid as much as the nature of the subject admits; I would observe, that in order to treat distinctly and <349> clearly of the miseries and vexations com-

> Objections taken from physical evils.

---

16. "A binding of both worlds."

plained of in human life, it is necessary to separate or distinguish three sorts of them.

These evils classed.

I. Such as totally arise from the laws of matter and motion; or in other words, the laws of the sensible world, such as earthquakes, storms, &c.

II. Such as arise from social connexions. Of which kind are all sufferings on account of disorders in the society we belong to; or such as arise partly from our social connexions, and partly from the laws of matter and motion; of which sort are, for instance, diseases and misfortunes descending from parents to their children. And,

III. Such as spring partly from our own follies and vices, and partly from the laws of the corporeal world. Of this kind are diseases brought upon ourselves by intemperance, &c.

I shall therefore treat of these three classes of evils separately, yet not so as to confine myself so strictly to any of them, as not at the same time to take notice under each of them, of certain evils, which though they do not strictly belong to that class, yet may be accounted for from the same principles as those which are properly of it.

Unless there is a mixture of good and evil, there can be no prudence or folly; there cannot be good and bad choice.

I. With respect to evils of all sorts in general, or to those which flow from the steady and uniform operation of the general laws of the sensible world, in particular, let not a principle already mentioned be forgot, namely, connexions producive of evils are necessary, in order to our having matter of foresight and choice: for if all connexions produced equal goods, we would have no occasion for studying nature, no use for foresight, no matter of deliberation and choice. It would be all one to us what happened, <350> we might fold our arms, and let things take their course. If it is fit there should be creatures whose goods and enjoyments are to be in any measure of their own procurance, it is absolutely necessary, with regard to such beings, that there should be some things to be avoided, as well as some things to be desired and sought after; matter of bad as well as of good choice; actions which tend to bring pain, as well as methods of acting which tend to bring pleasure and happiness. In fine, unless it can be doubted whether it is worth while to be endowed with the power of studying nature's laws and connexions, and to have happiness dependent in any degree on one's self; it cannot be doubted, but it must be fit that choices and actions should have different consequences, some producing good, and others evil; and to desire that there should be any such beings existing as we are, capable of chusing and acting, and whose happiness is dependent in a great measure on our choices and pursuits, where there is nothing evil to be avoided, is really to demand a state, in which there shall be beings capable of chusing, without any matter or subject of choice in that state.

2. With regard to physical evils, or such as flow from the laws of the sensible world in particular, to object against our state because there are such evils in it, involves this absurdity in it: it is to demand our bodies were so made, that every object, whatever its texture is (for every particular object must have its own particular one) might be congruous to their structure or organization. Now let objectors explain, if they can, how any body can affect another agreeably, without being proportioned and adjusted to it, without tallying with it, so to speak; for their objections suppose that to be possible. It is certain that physical goods ought to be produced according to some general law, or in some fixed, unvarying order: and this is found by experience to be the gene-<351>ral law with regard to us (and to all animals that fall within our observation) that whatever external objects tend, by any application, any effluvia, or in whatsoever way, to hurt our bodily contexture, alarms us by a sense of pain;[a] and the sense of pleasure is produced by influences of external objects which suit our organization, or no wise tend to destroy or hurt it. Now to ask why we should have any sense of pain, when external objects are really prejudicial to us, or tend to destroy our bodies, is to ask, why nature gives us warning what to avoid? And to ask, why any external objects are hurtful to our bodies, is either to ask why we have a

Physical evils are absolutely necessary, if beings have particular textures, and are subject to general ascertainable laws.

---

a. Quicunque igitur motus sunt qui naturam excedunt, dolorem pariunt: quicunque vero ad ipsam restituuntur voluptates nominantur, &c. *Timaeus locrus de anima mundi.* [Timaeus Locrus, *De anima mundi:* "Hence whatever changes there are that go beyond what is natural, cause pain; and whatever changes there are that restore things to their natural state are called pleasures." In Gale, ed., *Opuscula mythologica, physica et ethica. Graece et Latine. . . .* (Amsterdam, 1688), 557.]

particular organization, or why there is any variety of external objects? Nay, it is to demand, that even the same external object, applied to the same bodily organization, at whatever distance, with whatever force, or in one word, in whatever manner, should always be congruous to it, and never tend to hurt it in any degree. The objection really results in demanding, that sensible pleasures should not be produced in us by external objects which have a certain aptitude to our organization, which aptitude may be found out by studying our structure, and the various textures of bodies; for if there be such a thing as aptitude or congruity, there must be likewise such a thing as inaptitude and incongruity: it really results in demanding that sensible pleasures should be produced in us in no order or method, by no intermediate steps, progress or means: for if they are produced in some order or method steadily, each recess from or contrariety to that order, must unavoidably produce an effect different from or contrary to what is produced by the order tending to give pleasure. One order cannot be another order. One <352> train of causes and effects cannot be a different one. Every thing must have its determinate nature and properties; and every determinate nature or composition of properties, must, as such, have its determinate influences, consequences and effects, with regard to every other determinate nature or composition of properties. All this is self-evident; or what can knowledge and study of nature mean?

We must think we have quite exhausted natural knowledge, before we can say that several evils are absolutely unavoidable by prudence and art.

3. But in the third place. With regard to physical evils let it be observed, that as general laws producing goods and evils, are necessary to the existence of beings capable of activity and prudence, and of happiness acquired in that way; so we cannot possibly determine, that all physical evils we complain of are quite inevitable by prudence and art, till we are sure that we have quite exhausted the science of nature, and have gone as far by the study of it, as our knowledge can extend, with regard to avoiding evils, or turning them into goods. The further we advance and improve in the knowledge of nature, the more we are able to subdue earth, sea, and every element; or to make them subservient to our advantage. And though there are, no doubt, many hurtful effects of the laws of the sensible world, which are absolutely unavoidable or unal-

terable by us, yet it is no less sure, that the study of nature is far from its being at its *ne plus ultra,* and that it may be yet carried much farther than it is, in order to abridge human labour, to surmount the barrenness of soil, to provide remedies and antidotes against diseases occasioned by a bad constitution of air, pestilential exhalations, and other physical causes; to make navigation and commerce less dangerous; and in a word, to produce many goods we are not yet able to produce, and to prevent, or at least to alleviate, many evils in human life we cry out against. But as far as evils are owing to our ignorance, or the narrowness of our knowledge, through our neglect of studying nature in a right manner; so far we can <353> have no just reason of complaint, unless it be such, that our happiness is made to depend upon our own prudence and activity; that is, unless it be a just cause of complaint that we are rational beings.

4. But what is of principal consideration in this question is, "That natural philosophers have been able to shew, that almost all the physical evils complained of in human life, flow from the general laws, by which we have and enjoy, and can only have and enjoy, all the pleasures and advantages a sensible world affords us in our present state, which cannot be changed but to the worse." Dr. *Henry Moore,* in his *Divine Dialogues,* insists much upon the necessity of general laws; and in answer to the objections taken from the falling of rain in the highways, *&c.* says, the comical conceit of *Aristophanes,* in explaining rain by *Jupiter*'s pissing through a sieve, is not so ridiculous, as considering the descending of rain like the watering of a garden with a watering pot by subaltern free agents.[17] The objections taken from earthquakes, storms at sea, irruptions of fire in vulcano's, pestilences, and other such phenomena, terminate in a like absurdity: they demand that the sensible world should be governed by those general laws, to which we owe all the pleasures and benefits arising from our present commerce with a sensible world, without any of their hurtful effects. That is, they terminate in demanding general laws, without all their effects. When we murmur at the evils which happen by the qualities of air, fire, water, and other bodies, in

But which is principal, they all proceed from good general laws.

17. Henry More, *Divine Dialogues* (Glasgow: Foulis Press, 1743), 153.

consequence of gravitation, elasticity, electricity, and other physical powers, we certainly do not attend either to the innumerable good and useful effects of these qualities or powers, and their laws; or to the fitness in the whole, that qualities or powers, and their laws, should be general, that is, operate uniformly and invariably. If we reflect upon this, we would not rashly conclude, to use the words of some author <354> on this subject, for instance, "That the wind ought not to blow unfavourably on any worthy design of moral agents: but think better, and say more wisely, that the good laws of nature must prevail, tho' a ship-full of heroes, patriots, worthies, should perish by their invariable uniformity."

Illustration. If we consider the beautiful order of the sensible world, and the vast extent of those few simple laws which uphold it, we can by no means think it strange, says an excellent author, "If either by an outward shock, or some internal wound, particular animals, and sometimes man himself, are deformed in their first conception, and the seminal parts are injured and obstructed in their accurate labours. It is, however, then alone that monstrous shapes are produced. And nature, even in that case, works still as before, not perversly or erroneously, but is over-powered by some superior law, and by another nature's justly conquering force. Nor need we wonder, if the soul or temper partakes of this occasional deformity, and suffers and simpathises with its close partner. Why should we be surprized either at the feebleness and weakness of senses, or the depravity of minds inclosed in such feeble and dependent bodies; or such pervertible organs, subject, by virtue of a just and equal subordination, to other natures and other powers, while all must submit and yield to nature in general, or the Universal System." But every one may find full satisfaction with regard to the laws of a sensible world, in several excellent treatises on this subject; in Dr. *John Clarke*'s discourses at *Boyle*'s lecture (in particular) upon the origine of evil; and therefore referring my readers, on this head, to such writers, I shall just add, that from the late improvements in natural philosophy it plainly appears, as an admirable philosopher excellently expresses it, "That as for the mixture of pain or uneasiness which is in the world, pursuant to the general laws of nature, and <355> the actions of finite, imperfect spirits: this, in the state we are in at present, is indisputably necessary to our well-being. But our prospects are too narrow: we take, for instance, the idea of some one particular pain into our thoughts, and account it evil; whereas if we enlarge our view, so as to comprehend the various ends, connexions and dependencies of things, on what occasions, and in what proportions we are affected with pain and pleasure, the nature of human freedom, and the design for which we were put into the world, we shall be forced to acknowledge, that those particular things, which, considered in them-selves, appear to be evil, have the nature of good, when considered as linked with the whole system of beings."

> *We just as wisely might of heav'n complain,*
> *That righteous* Abel *was destroy'd by* Cain,
> *As that the virtuous son is ill at ease,*
> *When his lewd father gave the dire disease.*
> *Think we like some weak prince th' Eternal Cause,*
> *Prone for his fav'rites to reverse his laws?*
>   *Shall burning* Aetna, *if a sage requires,*
> *Forget to thunder, and recall her fires!*
> *On air or sea new motions be imprest,*
> *O blameless* Bethel! *to relieve thy breast?*
> *When the loose mountain trembles from on high,*
> *Shall gravitation cease, if you go by?*
> *Or some old temple nodding to its fall,*
> *For* Chartres' *head reserve the hanging wall?*
>   Essay on Man, Ep. 4.[18]

5. But before I leave this head, in order to lead the reader to attend to the wonderful concatenation of causes and effects throughout nature, throughout all, in particular, that regards mankind; and to observe how necessary the present mixture of evils and goods is to our well-being, and how impossible it is to conceive any change but to the worse; I can-not <356> choose but suggest another observation to him, almost in the words of an author, who does not seem to have designed to defend prov-

Let those who object against evils as abso-lute evils, well consider the concatenation of things natu-ral and moral, and how things must hang together in nature.

---

18. Pope, *Essay on Man*, IV.117–30.

idence, and yet has made several observations, which, when pursued to their real result, do effectually prove its wisdom and goodness; which observations, were this the proper place for it, I could easily shew to have no dependence upon certain principles with which he sets out, and of which he seems excessively fond. "The necessities, the vices and imperfections of man, together with the various inclemencies of the air, and other elements, contain in them the seeds of all arts, industry and labour: it is the extremities of heat and cold, the inconstancy and badness of seasons, the violence and uncertainty of winds, the vast power and treachery of water, and the stubbornness and sterility of the earth, that rack our invention, how we shall either avoid the mischiefs they may produce, or correct the malignity of them, and turn their several forces to our own advantage a thousand different ways; whilst we are employed in supplying the infinite variety of our wants, which will ever be multiplied as our knowledge is enlarged, and our desires encrease."[19] No man needs to guard himself against blessings, but calamities require hands to avert them. Hunger, thirst and nakedness, are the first tyrants that force us to stir; afterwards our pride, sloth, sensuality and fickleness, are the great patrons that promote all arts and sciences, trades, handicrafts and callings; whilst the great task-masters, necessity, avarice, envy and ambition, each in the class that belongs to him, keep the members of the society to their labour, and make them all submit, most of them chearfully, to the drudgery of their station, kings and princes not excepted.

Illustration. The greater the variety of trade and manufactures, the more operose they are, and the more they are divided in many branches, the greater numbers may be contained in a society, without being in one ano-<357>ther's way, and the more easily they may be rendered a rich, potent and flourishing people. Few virtues employ any hands, and therefore they may render a small nation good, but they can never make a great one. To be strong and laborious, patient in difficulties, and assiduous in all businesses, are commendable qualities; but as they do their own work, so

19. Bernard Mandeville, *The Fable of the Bees,* 4th ed. (London, 1725), 424–25.

they are their own reward, and neither art or industry have ever paid their compliments to them: whereas the excellency of human thought and contrivance has been, and is yet, no where more conspicuous, than in the variety of tools and instruments of workmen and artificers, and the multiplicity of engines, that were all invented, either to assist the weakness of man, to correct his many imperfections, to gratify his laziness, or to obviate his impatience.

It is in morality as it is in nature: there is nothing so perfectly good in creatures, that it cannot be hurtful to any one of the society, nor any thing so entirely evil, but it may prove beneficial to some part or other of the creation. So that things are only good and evil in reference to something else, and according to the light and position they are placed in.

And thus, saith he,[20] what we call evil in this world, moral as well as natural, is the grand principle that makes us sociable creatures, the solid basis, the life and support of all trades and employments; without exception, there we must look for the true origine of all arts and sciences; and the moment evil ceases, the society must be spoiled, if not totally dissolved.

This author brings a very proper instance to illustrate this, from the advantages and different benefits that accrue to a nation on account of shipping and navigation, compared with the manifold mischiefs and variety of evils, moral as well as natural, that befal nations on the score of sea-faring, and <358> their commerce with strangers, and that are the very foundation of trade and commerce; which the reader may consult at his leisure.[a]

There are several other reasonings and examples in this author, which might very well be applied to our present purpose, to shew what is the result upon the whole, of the mixture of pains, that is so greatly mur-   Illustration.

a. *Fable of the bees.* [See notes 19–20.]
20. Ibid., 428.

mured at in human life, and how absurd such murmuring is, when we take a large view of the connexions and dependencies of things. But as for the main end that author had in view, which was to prove, "that there is nothing social in our nature, and that it is direful necessity only that makes us sociable creatures; and that all the so much exalted moral virtues, are nothing else but the offspring of political flattery, begot upon pride";[21] I need not stay here to refute them, since in the former part of this essay, we have fully proved the very contrary to be true, or that we are social by nature, and have a principle of benevolence very deeply inlaid into our nature, and likewise a moral sense of the beauty and deformity of affections, actions and characters. *Cicero* hath long ago, in several parts of his philosophical works, charmingly proved the absurdity and falshood of such corrupt doctrines concerning human nature, and the rise of society, towards the end, in particular, of his first book of *Offices,* where he borrows a very apt similitude from the bees. My lord *Shaftsbury* hath shewn us what we ought to think of this kind of philosophers, and how we ought to deal with them, in the passage above quoted. And a little after he more particularly examines this philosophy, tracing it through all its subtle refinements; a piece of excellent reasoning, that well deserves our closest attention. "You have heard it (my friend) as a common saying, that *Interest governs the world.* But I believe, whoever looks narrowly into the affairs of it, will find that passion, humour, caprice, zeal, faction, and a thous-<359>and other springs, which

These reasonings have no necessary connexion with the principles of the author from whom they are taken.

are counter to self-interest, have as considerable a part in the movements of this machine. There are more wheels and counterpoises in this engine than are easily imagined. It is of too complex a kind to fall under one simple view, or be explained thus briefly in a word or two. The studiers of this mechanism must have a very partial eye, to overlook all other motions besides those of the lowest and narrowest compass. It is hard, that in the plan or description of this clock-work, no wheel or ballance should be allowed on the side of the better and more enlarged affections; that nothing should be understood to be done in kindness or generosity,

21. Ibid., 37.

nothing in pure good-nature or friendship, or through any social or nat-ural affection of any kind: when perhaps the main springs of this ma-chine will be found to be, either these very natural affections themselves, or a compound kind derived from them, and retaining more than one half of their nature.

But here (my friend) you must not expect that I should draw you a formal scheme of the passions, or pretend to shew you their genealogy and relation, how they are interwoven with one another, or interfere with our happiness or interest. It would be out of the genius and compass of such a letter as this, to frame a just plan or model, by which you might, with an accurate view, observe what proportion the friendly and natural affections seem to bear in this order of architecture.

How such principles ought to be refuted.

Modern projectors, I know, would willingly rid their hands of these natural materials, and would fain build after a more uniform way. They would new frame the human heart; and have a mighty fancy to reduce all its motions, ballances and weights to that one principle and foun-dation, of a cool and deliberate selfishness. Men, it seems, are unwilling to think they can be so outwitted and imposed on by nature, as to be made to serve her purposes, rather <360> than their own. They are ashamed to be drawn thus out of themselves, and forced from what they esteem their true interest.

There has been, in all times, a sort of narrow-minded philosophers, who have thought to set this difference to rights, by conquering nature in themselves. A primitive father and founder among these, saw well this power of nature, and understood it so far, that he earnestly exhorted his followers, neither to beget children, nor serve their country. There was no dealing with nature, it seems, while these aluring objects stand in the way. Relations, friends, countrymen, laws, politic constitutions, the beauty of order and government, and the true interest of society, and mankind, were objects which he well saw would naturally raise a stronger affection, than any which was grounded upon the bottom of mere self. His advice, therefore, not to marry, nor engage at all in the public, was wise and suitable to his design. There was no way to be truly a disciple of this philosophy, but to leave family, friends, country, and society to cleave to it.—And, in good earnest, who would not, if it were happiness to do so?—The philosopher, however, was kind in telling us his thought. 'Tis a token of his fatherly love of mankind.

> *Tu pater & rerum inventor! tu patria nobis*
> *Suppeditas praecepta!* ———[22]

But the revivers of this philosophy in later days, appear to be of a lower genius. They seem to have understood less of this force of nature, and thought to alter the thing, by shifting a name. They would so explain all the social passions and natural affections, as to denominate them of the selfish kind. Thus, civility, hospitality, humanity towards strangers, or people in distress, is only a more deliberate selfishness. An honest heart is only a more cunning <361> one; and honesty and good nature, a more deliberate, or better regulated self-love. The love of kindred, children, and posterity, is purely love of self, and of one's immediate blood; as if, by this reckoning all mankind were not included; all being of one blood, and joined by intermarriages and alliances, as they have been transplanted in collonies, and mixed one with another. And thus, love of one's country, and love of mankind, must also be self-love. Magnanimity and courage, no doubt, are modifications of this universal self-love! For courage, (says our modern philosopher) is constant anger. And all men (says a witty poet) would be cowards if they durst.

That the poet and the philosopher both were cowards, may be yielded perhaps without dispute. They may have spoken the best of their knowledge. But for true courage, it has so little to do with anger, that there lies always the strongest suspicion against it, where this passion is highest. The true courage is the cool and calm. The bravest of men have the least of a brutal bullying insolence; and in the very time of danger, are found the most serene, pleasant and free. Rage, we know, can make a coward

---

22. Lucretius, *De rerum natura,* III.9–10: "Thou, father, are the discoverer of truths, thou dost supply us with a father's precepts." Lucretius, *De rerum natura,* trans. W. H. D. Rouse, rev. Martin Ferguson Smith, Loeb Classical Library (Cambridge: Harvard University Press; London: Heinemann, 1975).

forget himself and fight: but what is done in fury or anger, can never be placed to the account of courage. Were it otherwise, womankind might claim to be the stoutest sex: for their hatred and anger have ever been allowed the strongest and most lasting.

Other authors there have been of a yet inferior kind: a sort of distributers and petty retailers of this wit; who have run changes and divisions, without end, upon this article of self-love. You have the very same thought spun out a hundred ways, and drawn into motto's and devices to set forth this riddle; 'that act as generously or disinterestedly as you please, self still is at the bottom, and nothing else.' Now if these gentlemen, who delight so <362> much in the play of words, but are cautious how they grapple closly with definitions, would tell us only what self-love was, and determine happiness and good, there would be an end of this enigmatical wit. For in this we should all agree, that happiness was to be pursued, and, in fact, was always sought after: but whether found in following nature, and giving way to common affection; or, in suppressing it, and turning every passion towards private advantage, a narrow self-end, or the preservation of mere life; this would be the matter in debate between us. The question would not be, 'who lov'd himself, or who not'; but, 'who lov'd and serv'd himself the rightest, and after the truest manner.'

'Tis the height of wisdom, no doubt, to be rightly selfish. And to value life, as far as life is good, belongs as much to courage as to discretion. But a wretched life is no wise man's wish. To be without honesty, is, in effect, to be without natural affection, or sociableness of any kind. And a life without natural affection, friendship, or sociableness, would be found to be a wretched one, were it to be try'd. 'Tis as these feelings and affections are intrinsically valuable, and worthy, that self-interest is to be rated and esteemed. A man is by nothing so much himself, as by his temper, and the character of his passions and affections. If he loses what is manly and worthy in these, he is as much lost to himself, as when he loses his memory and understanding. The least step into villany or baseness, changes the character and value of a life. He who would preserve life at any rate, must abuse himself more than any one else can abuse him. And if life be not a dear thing indeed, he who has refused to live a villain, and has preferred death to a base action, has been a gainer by the bargain."[a] <363>

Such evils as result from social dependence are goods.

II. But I proceed to consider a second class of evils in human life objected against; those which arise from our social connexions, or partly from them, and partly from the laws of the sensible world. Now upon this head I need not insist long, since evils, as far as they are resolvable into the connexions of things, which make the sensible world, or the laws of matter and motion, have been already considered. And as for our suffering in consequence of our social relations and dependencies; as by the misfortunes of others, their want of health, infirmity, death, or their external losses by bad weather, storms, shipwrecks, and other physical causes, it is plainly the result of our reciprocal union and connexion; that is, of our being made for society, and by consequence mutually dependent: Can a finger ake or be hurt, and the whole body to which it belongs not suffer? If therefore it is not unfit that we should be one kind, made for participation and communication, it cannot be unfit that we should be linked and cemented together, by the strongest ties, by mutual wants and indigencies; or that we should make one body. For to demand society, social pleasures, social happiness, without that closs and intimate dependence which makes us one body, is indeed to desire society without society. And it being as impossible, that a certain number of men should be congregated together in a certain form politic, called *a state or constitution,* without certain effects resulting from it; as that any number of bodies should be mixed, without producing certain effects; nature is justly deemed very kind to us, since it prompts, directs, and points us, by our generous affections, and our inward sense and love of public order and good, to associate ourselves in the way and manner, by which alone, in the nature of things, general good, beauty and happiness can be attained. For this is all that could be done consistently with the dependence

a. *Characteristicks,* T. 1. [The long quote, running from pp. 376 to 380, is from Shaftesbury, "Sensus communis," III.iii, in *Characteristics,* ed. Klein (Cambridge: Cambridge University Press, 1999), 53–56.]

of <364> our happiness on ourselves, to put us into the road to true happiness.

III. In the third place therefore, it remains to consider those evils which flow from follies and vices of whatever kind; whether the laws of matter and motion have any share in the effect, as they plainly have in the diseases brought upon us by excesses in eating, drinking, and other external indulgencies; or whether our social connexions have any share in the effect, as they likewise must have in many cases; since 'tis impossible, for example, man can have the advantages of good reputation and conduct in society, without having, at least, the semblance of the qualities that deserve it; and since, whatever sets us in a bad situation with regard to the favour and love of mankind, must impair our happiness: Or whether, in the last place, they are wholly mental, and spring from the natural ballance and dependence of our affections, in consequence of the anatomy, so to speak, of the mind; as many plainly are: for what are the diseases of the mind, the worst of all diseases, such as choler, envy, peevishness, madness, &c. but disorders naturally introduced into the mind, in consequence of its fabric, by excessive passions, and wrong associations of ideas. Now with regard to all these evils, I would observe, that it must be highly unreasonable to complain of them, unless it be absolutely unfit that vice should be its own punishment, or bring its own chastisement, either along with it, or after it in any degree; or unless it be unfit, that there should be such a thing as prudence and imprudence, wisdom and folly, right and wrong conduct. For what can these mean, if different passions and actions have not different conse-<365>quences?

On the one hand,[a] it is absurd to object against providence, or the

Vices punish themselves according to the natural course of things.

a. There is an excellent treatise of *Plutarch, De his qui sero a numine puniuntur,* well worth our attention, in which he gives several answers to this important question, Why the wicked are not immediately and visibly punished in this life, but often suffered to flourish. First, he quotes *Plato,* Plato in nobis visum a natura fuisse accensum dicit, ut spectandis admirandisque coelestium corporum motibus anima nostra amplecti condocefacta decorum & ordinem odium conciperet incompositorum & vagorum motuum, temeritatemque & casui fidentem levitatem fugeret tanquam omnis vitii & erroris originem. Non est enim major alius fructus quem ex Deo capere possit homo, quam quod imitatione pulchrorum & bonorum quae divinae naturae insunt, virtute potiatur. Propterea Deus malis interposita mora ac tarde poenas infligit. Non

government of the world, because some goods fall to the share of the vicious. For persons guilty of many vices, may yet have several excellent qualities, and do several prudent, nay good actions. Very few, if any are totally vicious, or quite deprived of every good quality. And good actions and qualities will be good actions and qualities with whatever vices they are mixed. But is it a bad constitution of things in which acts of prudence, industry and virtue have their good effects? Nay, on the contrary, is it not a most excellent general law, that prudence and industry should be in the <366> main successful and obtain their ends? Is it unreasonable or unjust, that internal goods should be procured by certain means? And what are the means, by which they are attained to, according to the connexions of things in the government of the world? Is it not industry

Goods fall to the share of the vicious according to the excellent general laws of industry.

---

quod vereatur, ne accelerando supplicio erret aut committat cujus poenitentia aliquando ducatur. Sed ut in vindicandis aliorum peccatis saevitiam & vehementiam nobis hoc exemplo suo eximat.—Caute in hoc genere versari & mansuetudinem graviumque laesionum tolerantiam pro divina habere virtutis parte, quam Deus nobis demonstrat, puniendo, paucos emendantem, tarde puniendo multos juvantem atque corrigentem, &c. The other reasons he adds seem very nearly to coincide with what our Saviour says in answer to this question, *Wilt thou then that we go and gather up the tares? But he said, Nay; lest while you gather up the tares, you root up also the wheat with them:* And with what St. *Peter* says, *Be not ignorant of this one thing, that one day is with the Lord as a thousand years, and a thousand years as one day. The Lord is not slack concerning his promise, as some men count slackness, but is long-suffering toward us, not willing that any should perish, but that all should come to repentance. Account therefore that the long-suffering of our Lord is salvation.* [Plutarch, *De his qui sero a numine puniuntur,* 550D–F, 551C: "Plato says that sight was awakened in us by nature, so that by looking at and admiring the motions of heavenly bodies our mind would love their beauty and regularity, would conceive a hatred for irregular and undirected motions, and would flee from what happens by chance and by accident as the origin of all vice and error. For there is no greater benefit that a man can gain from God than that by imitation of the beautiful and good things which are inherent in the divine nature he can come to acquire virtue. God therefore imposes punishment in a slow unhurried way. It is not that he is afraid that if he punishes with greater haste he will make a mistake or will come to repent of his acts. Rather it is that in not hurrying to punish the sins of people he would by his example take from us our cruelty and violence. . . . Consider things in this area with caution and take the mildness and strong tolerance which God reveals to us to be a divine part of virtue, a part which improves a few people by punishing them, and helps set right many by being slow to punish, etc."

Matt. 13.29; 2 Pet.3.8–9, 15.]

employed to get them, that purchases them? And can there be a better rule with regard to acquisitions of all sorts, than that they should be made by industry, diligence and labour to make them? Thus the philosopher attains to the knowledge which is his delight. Thus the virtuous man attains to the virtuous qualities his soul is solely or chiefly bent upon. And in no other way do any goods fall to the share of any person than by setting himself to attain to them.

On the other hand, it would certainly be a great absurdity to object against providence, that according to the connexions and order of things, vice is in a great measure its own punisher by the evils it brings upon the wicked. And yet if we look cautiously into things, we shall find, that the far greater part of the evils and miseries complained of in human life, are the effects and consequences of vicious passions, and their pursuits. Whence else is it that honesty is so universally pronounced the best policy; and dishonesty, folly? The plain meaning of this maxim is, that according to the natural tendency and course of things, there is no solid security for the best goods and enjoyments of life, but by virtuous conduct; and that a vicious one is the most unwise, because the most unsafe, dangerous course, all things considered, even with regard to this life only. This maxim is readily assented to by all upon the slightest review of human affairs, or when the more visible and obvious effects of good and bad conduct only are attended to. But the more accurate observers of things have found reason to carry the maxim still further, and to assert, *"omnis homo suae fortunae artifex est."*[23] Or, as it is otherwise expressed, *"sui cuique mores <367> fingunt fortunam."*[24] i.e. Every man's happiness or misery is chiefly owing to himself; insomuch, that what is vulgarly called good or bad luck, is really and truly at bottom good or bad management. Many, very many of the evils of human life, which to superficial observers appear accidental, are indeed originally

Vice always produces misery.

23. "Every man makes his own fortune."
24. Cornelius Nepos, *Atticus,* XI.16: "Tis each man's character his fortune makes." *Cornelius Nepos,* trans. J. C. Rolfe (Cambridge: Harvard University Press; London: Heinemann, 1984).

owing to wrong judgments or excessive passions. If we attend to faithful history, or to what *Aristotle*[a] calls a better instructor than history, to good, that is, probable poetry, in which human life and the natural consequences of passions and actions are justly represented: if we attend to these teachers, we shall quickly perceive, that many more of the miseries of mankind are owing to misconduct, to some wrong step, to some immorality, than we are generally aware of; or, at least, than the objectors against providence seem to have sufficiently attended to. Every good dramatic piece is a proof of this. The reason why the tragic plots, which according to *Aristotle* are the best,[b] move our fear and pity without raising any dissatisfaction, or repining in our minds at providence, is because they exemplify to us the fatal consequences into which one little error, any too vehement passion, any the smallest immoral indulgence, may plunge those who are possessed of many excellent, highly estimable, truly amiable qualities. But how could this be done; or how could we be moved by such representations, were they not natural? And in what sense can they be called natural, unless the whole progress of the representation be according to nature; that is, unless the effects represented be according to the structure of the human mind, and the regular established course and influence of things?[c] "Tragedy hath indeed chiefly for its object the distresses of the great: <368> the high genius of this poetry, consists in the lively representation of the disorders and miseries of the great, to the end that the people and those of a lower condition may be taught the better to content themselves with privacy, enjoy their safer state, and prize the equality of their guardian laws."[d] But how does it, or can it conduce to that excellent end, but by shewing in what greater miseries than lower life can ever be plagued with, the great are often involved by the vices to which their high circumstances only expose, as they can only so severely punish. No such representation could move,

History and
poetry prove
this.

a. Aristotle *ars poetica*, cap. 9. [Aristotle, *Poetics*, 1451A36–1452B4.]

b. Ibid. cap. 13. [Ibid., 1453A.]

c. See this observation illustrated by Mr. *Hutcheson, in his conduct of the passions.* [Hutcheson, *Passions*, I.III.v.]

d. *Characteristics*, T. 1. advice to an author. [Shaftesbury, "Soliloquy," II.i, in *Characteristics*, ed. Klein, 98.]

unless it were natural. And it cannot be natural, unless nature, that is, the constitution of things with regard to virtue and vice, be such as the imitation represents. In fine, we must give up all pretensions to beauty, truth and nature in moral poetry, that is in fiction or imitation of moral life, unless it be true, in fact, that the least vicious excess, or the smallest immoral indulgence, may and commonly does involve in a long train of miseries.

In reality, poetical probability, beauty, justice, truth or nature, if they are not words without a meaning, suppose the account that hath been given of human nature in this essay to be true.

They suppose, 1. That there is a social principle, and a sense of beauty in actions and characters deeply interwoven with our frame, and improveable to a very high pitch of perfection. For how else could we be moved by the struggles between virtue and passion, which make the sublime and the pathetic too of sentiments in such compositions? Or how could we possibly not only admire but love virtue even in distress; be charmed with its firmness and beauty, and prefer its sufferings to the most triumphant circumstances of the villain? 2. They suppose such a nice ballance and dependence of our affections, <369> that every vicious passion produces great disorder, horrible tumult and riot in the mind, and sadly endangers its health, peace and soundness. 3. They suppose, that the smallest immoral indulgence often, nay, almost always involves in the most perplexing difficulties, the most awful miseries. There, in particular, do we see the truth of what the satyrist observes.

> ——— *Nam quis*
> *Peccandi finem posuit sibi? Quando recepit*
> *Ejectum semel attrita de fronte ruborem?*
> *Quisnam hominum est, quem tu contentum videris uno*
> *Flagitio? Dabit in laqueum vestigia noster*
> *Perfidus* ———
>
> Juv. Sat. 13.[25]

25. Juvenal, *Satires*, XIII.240–45: "For who ever fixed a term to his own offending? When did a hardened brow ever recover the banished blush? What man have you ever seen that was satisfied with one act of villainy? Our scoundrel will yet put his

If these principles are not true, poetry can have no foundation in nature, it cannot be true imitation and please as such; it cannot be natural: Truth, consistency, beauty, a natural plot, and right and wrong conduct in such compositions and representations are words without a meaning. But, on the other hand, if the premises concerning the imitative arts are true, as they must be, if there is truth in poetry, or indeed in any other imitative art; how excellently is human nature constituted, and what reasonable objection can be brought against it? For which of those principles of human nature, which have been mentioned as the foundation of poetical truth, and as the source of all the pleasures moral imitations afford or can afford us, is not a most useful and noble one: an unexceptionable proof that we are indeed the workmanship of an infinitely wise Being, who is, as he was called by the ancients, *perfect reason, perfect virtue?*

In objections external goods and evils are much magnified.

But to proceed, in the objections against providence, on account of the distribution of external goods and evils; are not these goods and evils exceedingly magnified? It is certainly fair to reduce <370> them to their true values and measures before we pronounce any judgment concerning them. Now what are those goods which are said to be so unequally divided? Or what are their opposite evils which are so loudly complained of? The goods may be all reduced to one, wealth, for it includes them all in it, that is, it is the means of procuring all that voluptuousness desires, or rather, lusts after; and the opposite to that is poverty, or mediocrity of circumstances; a fortune that can afford little or nothing toward the gratification of sensual appetites. But what is wealth, if, in reality, there be more greatness and sublimity of mind in despising it than possessing it? And if those are indeed the most amiable and glorious characters among mankind, who prefer virtue, not only in poverty, but under violent persecution, to flourishing redundant vice; and who look upon the consumption of wealth in mere gratification to selfish sensual concupiscence as sinking and degrading the man; as acting a beastly, a vile,

---

feet into the snare. . . ." *Juvenal and Persius,* trans. G. G. Ramsay, rev. ed., Loeb Classical Library (London: Heinemann; Cambridge: Harvard University Press, 1940).

abominable part? And yet what else is it, but such a virtuous contempt
of merely sensual enjoyments, that makes the sublime of sentiments and
actions in life, in history, or poetry?

If we attend to the objections made against providence, or the doubts
which crowd into our minds in melancholly hours, we shall find that we
are apt to make several mistakes: the goods of sense are over-rated, and
the pains magnified; for what are all these goods in comparison with
those, which our reason, and a refined imagination, our moral sense, and
such other powers, far superior to our external senses, afford us? And
what are all the evils and pains in the world, compared with the agonies
of a guilty mind? Besides, we are ready to apprehend every person to be
miserable in those circumstances which we imagine would make ourselves miserable; and yet we may easily find, that the lower rank of mankind, whose only revenue is their bodily labour, <371> enjoy as much
chearfulness, contentment, health, quietness, in their own way, as another in the highest station of life. Both their minds and their bodies are
soon fitted to their state. The farmer and labourer, when they enjoy the
bare necessaries of life, are easy. They have often more correct imaginations, thro' necessity and experience, than others can acquire by philosophy. This thought is indeed a poor excuse for a base, selfish oppressor, who, imagining poverty a great misery, bears hard upon those in a
low station of life, and deprives them of their natural conveniencies, or
even of bare necessaries. But this consideration may support a compassionate heart too deeply touched with apprehended miseries, of which
the sufferers themselves are insensible.

The pains of the external senses are pretty pungent; but how far short,
in comparison of the long tracts of health, ease and pleasure? How rare
is the instance of a life, with one tenth spent in violent pain? How few
want absolute necessaries; nay, have not something to spend in gaiety
and ornament? The pleasures of beauty are exposed to all, in some measure. Those kinds of beauty which require property to the full enjoyment
of them, are not ardently desired by many; the good of every kind in
the universe is plainly superior to the evil. How few would accept of
annihilation, rather than continuance in life, in the middle state of age,
health and fortune? Or what separated spirit, who had considered hu-

man life, would not, rather than perish, take the hazard of it again, by returning into a body in the state of infancy.

——— *Who would lose*
For fear of pain, this intellectual being?[26] <372>

External goods depend in general on industry, which is a good institution of nature. Again,[a] Let us consider that external goods must (as it hath been observed) fall to the share of those who set themselves to procure them; they are the purchase of industry and labour. They may be got by fraud or violence. But they are naturally the product of virtuous labour and diligence to get them. They may fall by succession or gift into the mouths of the indolent and lazy, but some one must have taken pains to procure them. And is it then any wonder, or any just cause of complaint, that things are so constituted that wealth shall be purchased by industry, or riches fall to the share of any one who leaves no stone unturned to attain them? Do not all goods, of whatever kind, thus depend upon our setting ourselves to purchase them; the goods of the mind as well as external ones? But, which is more, when external goods fall to one's share, can **They cannot make happy alone, or without virtue.** they alone make him happy? Who is it that truly enjoys them, but the good, the generous man, whose supreme delight is in making others happy? Truly,[b] the happiness of man does not consist in the abundance of the things he possesses. Else, whence is discontent and uneasiness more frequent among those placed in the most favourable circumstances

a. Most of these observations are given in Mr. *Hutcheson's* words, in his excellent treatise *on the conduct of the passions.* [Rather than being "in Mr. Hutcheson's words," the preceding paragraph and what follows are paraphrased in Turnbull's words; see Hutcheson, *Passions,* IV.iv.]

b. See *Plutarch's* excellent treatise *De virtute & vitio,* where he reasons at great length to prove that the greatest abundance of worldly wealth, or the happiest circumstances of outward enjoyment, are absolutely insufficient, without virtue, to produce peace and contentment of mind, or to make happy; and on the other hand, that virtue is an unspeakable support in adversity. [The subject of Plutarch's entire treatise *De virtute et vitio* is indicated in Turnbull's comment.]

26. Milton, *Paradise Lost,* 2.146–47. "Though full of pain" is given in place of "For fear of pain." Turnbull appears to have lifted the quote from Hutcheson, who has the same wrong wording (*An Essay on the Nature and Conduct of the Passions. . . .* (1728); ed. Aaron Garrett (Indianapolis: Liberty Fund, 2002), VI.iv).

of outward enjoyment, than others in more disadvantageous ones? And if many want and are distressed, are there not many likewise, who, being able to relieve them, deprive themselves of the highest joy riches and power can afford, to wipe tears from mournful eyes, and to bid misery be no more? <373>

Further; the pleasures of wealth or power are proportioned to the qualifications of the desires or senses, which the agent intends to gratify by them; now "the pleasures of the internal senses, or of the imagination, are allowed by all who have any tolerable taste of them, as a much superior happiness to those of the external senses, though they were enjoyed to the full; so that wealth or power give greater happiness to the virtuous man, than to those who consult only luxury or external splendor. If these desires are become habitual or enthusiastic, without regard to any other end than possession; they are an endless source of vexation, without any real enjoyment: a perpetual craving, without nourishment or digestion: and they may surmount all other affections, by aids borrowed from other affections themselves. The sensible desires[27] are violent, in proportion to the senses from which the associated ideas are borrowed; only it is to be observed, that however the desires may be violent, yet the obtaining the object desired gives little satisfaction, the possession discovers the vanity and deceit, and the fancy is turned towards different objects, in a perpetual succession of inconstant pursuits."[a]

When "we have obtained any share of wealth or power, let us examine their true use, and what is the best enjoyment of them.

a. *Quod petiit, spernit: repetit quod nuper omisit:*
Aestuat, & vitae disconvenit ordine toto:
Diruit, aedificat, mutat, quadrata rotundis.
Hor. Epist. Lib. 1. Epist. 1

[Horace, *Epistles*, I.i.98–100: "scorns what it craves, asks again for what it lately cast aside; when it shifts like a tide, and in the whole system of life is out of joint, pulling down, building up, and changing square to round?" Horace, *Satires, Epistles and Ars poetica,* trans. H. Rushton Fairclough, Loeb Classical Library (London: Heinemann; New York: Putnam, 1926).]

27. In this quote from Hutcheson, *Passions,* I.V.ix, Turnbull has "sensible desires" in place of Hutcheson's "Fantastic desires."

———— *Quid asper*
Utile nummus habet? patriae carisque propinquis
Quantum elargiri decet? ————

Persius.[28]

What moral pleasures, what delights of humanity, what gratitude from persons obliged, what ho-<374>nours may a wise man of a generous temper purchase with them? How foolish is the conduct of heaping up wealth for posterity, when smaller degrees might make them equally happy; when the great prospects of this kind are the strongest temptations to them to indulge sloth, luxury, debauchery, insolence, pride, and contempt of their fellow creatures; and to banish some noble dispositions, humility, compassion, industry, hardness of temper and courage, the offspring of the sober dame poverty? How often does the example, and almost the direct instruction of parents, lead posterity to the basest views of life! How powerfully might the example of a wise and generous father, at once teach his offspring the true value of wealth or power, and prevent their neglect of them, or foolish throwing them away, and yet inspire them with a generous temper, capable of the just use of them."[29] Education, in order to make wise and happy, ought to fix early upon the mind those two important truths, 1. That it is not indeed riches which can make happy, but that he only who can be happy without them, can have true happiness from them. 2. But yet it is fit that industry should gain its end: vicious industry its end, as well as virtuous industry its end. These two truths well understood, and deeply rooted in the mind by right instruction and education, could not fail to produce a quiet, easy, contented mind, and industry wisely placed.

All this reasoning is excellently set forth by the incomparable poet often quoted.

28. Persius, *Satires,* III.69: "What good is there in fresh-minted coin; how much should be spent on country and on your dear kin?" *Juvenal and Persius,* trans. G. G. Ramsay, rev. ed., Loeb Classical Library (London: Heinemann; Cambridge: Harvard University Press, 1940).
29. Hutcheson, *Passions,* II.VI.vi.

"Whatever is, is right." *This world, 'tis true,*
Was made for Caesar—*but for* Titus *too:*
And which more blest? who chain'd his country, say,
Or he whose virtue sigh'd to lose a day?
"But sometimes virtue starves while vice is fed."
What then? is the reward of virtue, bread? <375>
That vice may merit; 'tis the price of toil:
The knave deserves it when he tills the soil,
The knave deserves it when he tempts the main,
Where folly fights, for tyrants, or for gain.
The good man may be weak, be indolent,
Nor is his claim to plenty, but content. ————

   What nothing earthly gives, or can destroy,
The soul's calm sun-shine, and the heart-felt joy,
Is virtue's prize: a better would you fix?
Then give humility a coach and six,
Justice a conqu'ror's sword, or truth a gown,
Or public spirit its great cure, a crown:
Rewards, that either would to virtue bring
No joy, or be destructive of the thing.
How oft by these at sixty are undone
The virtues of a saint at twenty one! ————
———— *'Tis phrase absurd to call a villain great:*
Who wickedly is wise, or madly brave,
Is but the more a villain, more a knave.
Who noble ends by noble means obtains,
Or failing, smiles in exile or in chains,
Like good Aurelius *let him reign, or bleed,*
Like Socrates, *that man is great indeed.*
                        Essay on man, Epist. 4.[30]

But having sufficiently insisted in the former part of this essay upon the happiness which virtue alone can give; I shall just subjoin two or three more reflexions upon the present distribution of goods and evils.

---

30. Pope, *Essay on Man*, IV.145–56, 167–72, 181–84, 230–36.

The punishment of vice is wisely left in some measure to society.

I. As many of the goods of life are by our social constitution dependent upon the right government of society; so, on the one hand, many of the evils complained of arise from a disorderly or ill-administred state; and, on the other hand, many of the sufferings and punishments due to vice are likewise left to be the effects of rightly governed socie-<376>ty. All these things are too evident to need much illustration. The progress of knowledge, and all the elegant pleasures, which the due encouragement of ingenious arts are able to afford to mankind, plainly depend upon the care of society, to promote and encourage the arts and sciences. And therefore, if society is deprived of many enjoyments of these sorts, so superior to merely sensual gratification, 'tis owing entirely to the wrong government of society, the narrow views and bad pursuits of its administrators. And just so, on the other hand, if all manner of vice is not duly restrained, curbed, and chastised, and consequently vice is more prosperous and triumphant than it ought to be; to what is that owing, but to society's not taking suitable measures to promote general happiness? But the fitness or moral necessity of such dependence of general happiness upon the right government of society, a good politic constitution, and the impartial execution of good laws, has been again and again handled in this discourse.

Unless we suppose a mixture of goods and evils dependent on other causes than virtue; or if we suppose external motives to virtue according to the course of things; there could be no true or pure virtue in the world.

II. Let us consider a little what would be the consequence, if the encouragement of virtue, and the discouragement of vice, were not in some degree left to society, to mankind themselves; but if such were the constitution of things, that vice was always discovered and pointed out by some extraordinary calamity inflicted upon it in this life; and virtue, on the other hand, was sure of having its merit distinguished by some remarkable external favour. 'Tis evident, that the present constitution of things, by which the procurance of external goods is the effect of skill and industry to attain them, is absolutely inconsistent with such a state and connexion of things, and could not take place with it. But besides, in such a constitution of things, virtue would not be left to be chosen for its own sake, that is for the enjoyments which virtuous exercises, toge-<377>ther with the sense of having acted rightly, afford: There would then be another motive to virtue, arising from a positive external reward, the very being of which would necessarily lessen the merit and the excellence of virtue, by removing the trial of it, which the present state gives occasion to.

For then only indeed is a person truly virtuous, when his sense of the dignity and excellence of virtuous conduct, is able to make him adhere to virtue, whatever other pleasures he may forego, or whatever pains he may suffer by such adherence. I do not say, that there is no virtue, but where this virtuous fortitude[a] is quite insurmountable: few attain to it in such a degree. But one is only virtuous in proportion as he hath this noble strength of mind. And invitation to this pure love of virtue does not require a positive connexion between it and any external badges of the divine favour: it can, on the contrary, only take place, in a state where there is no external bribe to virtue, or nothing to excite to it, besides the pleasures of the rational and moral kind accompanying it, and the consciousness of its excellence. The fortitude in which the perfection of virtue consists, cannot be formed but in a state where there is a mixture of goods and evils to try and prove it, to give it occasions, subjects and means of exerting itself. And therefore, at least, till that fortitude be formed and attained to, its fit that rational beings should be placed in a state fit for forming and improving it. But, which is more, how <378> can virtue be supposed to be rewarded, in consequence of a positive arbitrary institution, by enjoyments distinct from the exercises of virtue,

---

a. So all the ancients define the virtuous man. See *Plutarch, De virtutibus moralibus.* And, *De animi tranquillitate.*—So *Cicero* frequently. See particularly, *De legibus,* Lib. 1. Quod si poena si metus supplicii non ipsa turpitudo, &c.—So even the poets.

Cautus enim metuit foveam lupus accipiterque
Suspectos laqueos, & opertum milvus hamum.
Oderunt peccare boni virtutis amore.
                Hor. Epist. Lib. 1. Epist. 16

[Cicero, *De legibus,* I.xiv.40: "But if it is a penalty, the fear of punishment, and not the wickedness itself, etc." Cicero, *De re publica, De legibus,* trans. Clinton Walker Keyes, Loeb Classical Library (London: Heinemann; New York: Putnam, 1928). Horace, *Epistles,* I.xvi.50–52: "For the wolf is wary and dreads the pit, the hawk the suspected snare, the pike the covered hook. The good hate vice because they love virtue."]

and its natural fruits in the mind, without supposing something superior
to all those enjoyments which are the natural effects of virtue itself? For
virtue is the love of virtuous pleasures: but a pleasure given by way of
reward for acting virtuously, must mean a pleasure superior to that which
attends virtuous behaviour. Wherefore in any proper sense of reward,
virtue can only be said to be its own reward: it can only be rewarded by
higher attainments in virtue. I am afraid, those who demand such a connexion of things, as has been mentioned in favour of virtue, desire such
a connexion in its favour, as should at last reward the virtuous man for
his virtuous conduct, by giving him the means of wallowing in sensual
pleasures. If this is not their meaning, let them explain themselves, and
name the positive reward they would have annexed to virtue in this life
different from all that is rational and virtuous: and if they mean such a
reward: as, to desire any reward to be given virtue before it be formed to
very great perfection, if they are for allowing virtue at all to take place,
and to be formed, is to desire it too soon; so to desire such a reward after
virtue is formed, is to desire a reward to formed virtue, which would
destroy it after it is formed. But if they do not mean such a reward as
would destroy virtuous affection, but a reward consistent with it, and
that not till it is arrived at very great perfection, let them say at what
time, or at what period of virtue they would have it bestowed; and, above
all, let them name the reward they would have, that we may see whether
it can be bestowed in this life on virtue, without altering the state of
things in this life that is necessary to form and try virtue, and to bring
it to perfection. If by their reward to virtue, they mean higher improvements in virtue, and better and more enlarged means of exerting its
excel-<379>lence, let them shew us, that this state does not afford means
of higher improvements, and of larger exertions of the virtuous dispositions, than any, the most virtuous or perfect man, has made all the
advantage of in his power; let them shew us, why a first state of virtue,
which ought to be a mixed one, should not have its boundaries; or how
it possibly cannot have its *ne plus ultra*. And let them shew us, that it is
better and wiser not to place virtue first in a forming state, and afterwards
in a state suited to its improvements, than to do so. For all this they

ought to prove, in order to make their objection against this state of any force; for till they prove all this, it will remain exceeding probable, that this state is very well adapted to form and improve virtue; since any other connexions in favour of virtue than now take place (as by positive rewards different from its natural and inseparable fruits) would make this an improper state for the education, trial and improvement of virtue; that is, for forming rational beings to the love of moral perfection or virtue for its own intrinsic excellence, and its own rational fruits.

When all the sufferings which virtue now and then meets with in the world, all its oppositions and persecutions are laid together, what do they prove, but that in this state, occasions and means now and then arise of calling forth and exercising very great virtues? And how glorious! how eligible are such circumstances to true, high-improved virtue! Who would not rather be the distressed sufferer than the prosperous persecutor? What do all these sufferings prove, but that a noble trial falls sometimes to the share of virtue; and that it is then it appears in all its fortitude, majesty and beauty? And what is the result of this, but that this is a proper first state for virtue, and that we are indeed made to be virtuous, since the case of suffering virtue is so eligible to every mind able to discern its <380> beauty; since the toils, the struggles, the hardships of virtue are so inviting to us, that while the greatness of virtue in suffering bravely for truth and goodness is present to the mind, none can chuse but prefer such a state to all the triumphs of prosperous, insolent vice? What is the natural language of all this, or what does such a constitution of things prognosticate, but care for ever to give virtue suitable occasions of exerting, and thereby rewarding itself; and that when this state of formation and trial comes to an end, virtue shall be placed in circumstances suited to its improvements, in which it shall be, more than it can be in its forming state, its own reward? In fine, whatever violence, opposition, cruelty or barbarity virtue may meet with in this state, what can be inferred from thence, but that this state is not the whole of our existence, but a part, our entry on being; and that the future state of virtue and vice shall clear up many difficulties, which cannot but appear

The evils that happen to the virtuous, are occasions and materials of great virtues.

Some reflex-
ions on the
arguments for
a future state
from present
inequality with
respect to vir-
tue and vice.

dark and intricate, till the *drama* is further advanced. Very good arguments are drawn from the present state of things to prove a future state,
which have been often repeated by divines and philosophers, and I shall
not therefore now insist upon them. Two cautions, however, with regard
to some such arguments are not unnecessary, since, in fact, many are led
by them into mistakes. The first thing I would observe on this head is,
that in the warmth of some reasonings on this subject, several good men
are often led to represent the case of virtue here as very deplorable, and
the administration of things as very disorderly; and thus to magnify the
distresses and evils of human life, and to undervalue its blessings and
advantages, in order to prove the necessity of reparation, or juster distribution in a future state. But surely future order cannot be inferred
from utter present disorder and confusion. 2. In the warmth of such
reasonings, several expressions are used, which are liable to be miscon-
<381>structed into an opinion of future rewards, distinct from rational
pleasures, nay, contrary to the exercises of virtue, and of the sensual kind.
But surely nothing can be more excellent, or more great than virtue; and
what is inferior, not to say repugnant to it, cannot be its reward.

I do not make these observations, which greatly merit our attention,
with any view of derogating from any writer, far less with an intention
to suggest that the reasonings taken from the present flourishing of vice,
and suffering of virtue, to prove a future state, are not conclusive; but
merely to prevent any one's being misled by inaccuracies of language or
rhetorical arguments, into opinions very contrary to truth, and to the
sense of those writers themselves who have laid the great stress of the
evidence for a future state upon what they have called an inequality with
regard to virtue and vice in this life. When providence and the present
state of mankind are fairly represented, the argument for a future state

The true state
of the case or
argument.

stands thus, and is unanswerable. We are so constituted, that the exercises of virtue, and the conscience of it, are our highest[a] enjoyment; and
vice, whatever pleasure it may afford of the sensual kind, always creates

a. See a fine sentence of *Cicero* to this purpose preserved by *Lactantius,* Lib. 5.
cap. 19. Vult paene virtus honorem: nec est virtutis ulla alia merces, quam tamen illa
accipit facile, non exigit acerbe. Sed si aut ingrati universi, aut invidi multi, aut inimici

bitter remorse, and almost always great bodily disorder: but such a constitution must be the workmanship of <382> such a perfectly virtuous and good Creator, as all the other parts of nature prove its Author to be, in proportion as we advance in the knowledge of it. And therefore we have just reason to think, that beings capable of improvements in virtue, are not made merely to exist in a state, which, though it be very fit for the trial and formation of virtue, yet cannot be thought to be contrived for any other purpose, but to be a first state of trial and formation. Were a state of trial and formation the only state in which moral beings exist, nature would be but a very imperfect, nay, a bad system: but as it cannot be such, if the Author of nature be infinitely good and perfect, which all the other parts of nature, as far as we can search into them, proclaim him to be; so there is no reason to apprehend it to be such, from any such appearances as are by no means symptoms of imperfect administration, but upon supposition that this is the only state of mankind: for to infer so, purely on that account, is to conclude that there is no future

---

potentes suis virtutem praemiis spoliant, nec illa se tamen multis solatiis oblectat, maximeque suo decore seipsam sustentat. With regard to vice, there is another fragment of *Cicero* preserved by the same author, *Lib. 6. cap.* 8. which is exceedingly beautiful. Est quidem vera lex, recta ratio, naturae congruens, diffusa in omnibus, constans, sempiterna—Unusque erit communis quasi magister, et imperator omnium Deus, ille legis huius inventor, disceptator, lator: cui qui non parebit, ipse se fugiet, ac naturam hominis aspernabitur, atque hoc ipso luet poenas maximas, etiamsi caetera supplicia, quae putantur, effugerit. See a charming description of virtue, and the happiness it brings along with it, in *Juvenal*'s Prayer, *Satyre* 18. See what he says of the punishment of vice by itself, *Satyre* 13. And there are many beautiful passages to the same purpose in *Plato*, particularly *De Republica*, Lib. 1. [Lactantius, *The Divine Institutes*, bk. 5, ch. 18.4: "Virtue almost has a claim on honor, nor does virtue have any other reward. But she accepts it with ease and does not demand it with bitterness. Yet if all the ungrateful people or the many who are envious or the powerful hostile people rob virtue of its rewards, she will nevertheless delight in so much consolation and will sustain herself particularly with her comeliness." Lactantius, bk. 6, ch. 8: "The true law, right reason, is indeed congruent with nature, diffused through all things, constant, everlasting. . . . And one God will be as it were a common master and commander of all. He will be inventor, judge and proposer of this law. Whoever will not submit to him will put himself to flight and will spurn his nature as a human being. He will thereby suffer the greatest penalty even if he escapes other punishments which are being considered." (A.B., trans.)]

state, merely because the first state looks to be what a first state ought to be, namely, a state of trial and formation; which is absurd.

If we do not exceedingly depretiate virtuous enjoyments, and excessively magnify external gratifications, we must own some care about virtue here; a care proper to its state of education and discipline: but if we do, it is reasonable to expect future care and concern about it. If separately, from the consideration of certain goods which fall to the share of vice, and of certain evils which sometimes fall to the share of virtue here, we have very good reason <383> to think well of nature; or, that all bespeaks a good Author and Governor; then is it highly probable there is a future state of mankind, to which this is a well adjusted prelude. To shew it is not probable, it must be proved, that such is the fate of virtue and vice here, that this state hath not at all any appearance of being a proper first state, but is so irregular, and contrary to good order, that whatever all other things may seem to prove, considered separately, yet when the circumstances and connexions with regard to virtue and vice are taken into the account, all the other signs of wisdom and goodness prove nothing, and the present state of virtue and vice clearly evidences such utter confusion, irregularity, and hatred of virtue, that from it no future good can reasonably be hoped for. Either this must be proved, or a future state is certain. But who can think so harshly of nature, if he but opens his eyes to the manifold instances of wisdom, benevolence, and love of virtue, which every where appear throughout its administration!

The present question chiefly turns upon this single point, Whether, since it is reasonable to think that the first state of rational beings should be a state of formation and discipline, there is not, all things considered, more reason to think that this our present state is but a first state of trial and formation, than to think it is our whole existence? Now if it be true, that all the evils in this state are not only proper to a first state of trial and formation, but do arise from general laws, the steady operation of which is absolutely fit, and which produce much greater goods than evils, goods of the highest and noblest kind: and if it be true, that the further we look into any parts of nature, and into the connexions and dependencies of things relative to man in particular, the more reason we find to think well of nature, and consequently of its Author: if all this, I say, be true, as I think we have sufficiently proved it to be, what then can be concluded, with any shew of reason, but that, as <384> there ought to be a first state of rational beings, so this is our first state, and not the whole of our existence: and that, as the progress of things, or the scheme of government advances, so in proportion, shall all perplexing difficulties with regard to nature open to us, be cleared up and unravelled? If the *drama* be not compleated here, then we see but a part: and if we see but a part, it is no wonder if we are considerably in the dark. But do we not see enough of order, and goodness, and excellent conduct, to persuade us that we are only in the dark, because it is but a part that we can see? For must not virtue be formed before it can be perfect? And must it not be perfect, before it can reap the fruits of its perfection? Can the effect precede or take place without the cause; or the end prevent the means?

CHAPTER IV

But to go through more objections separately would but oblige me to repeat very often the same principles, from which the solutions given to those that have been mentioned are brought, the principles fully explained in the first part of this enquiry. I shall now, therefore, take as complete a view of the human state as I am able, and endeavour to shew, that no change can be demanded, which is not either impossible or unreasonable; that is to say, for the worse.

A complex view of the objections made against human nature and of the absurdities resulting from them, or in which they necessarily terminate.

Let us, I say, take as full a view of our nature as we can, and impartially enquire, what it is in our constitution and frame we would have altered; or strictly examine the tendency and meaning of our objections and demands, whether they do not necessarily terminate, when they are closely pursued to <385> their last result, in requiring something very absurd, or very inconvenient and disadvantageous.

Would he who is not pleased with our present make have no gradation of perfection in nature? Or would he have a gradation in nature from the lowest to the highest species of created perfection without man? Would he have nature as full of life, perfection and happiness as may be; and yet such a species as man wanting? Or would he have mankind to exist, and to make a proper species in the rising scale of existence, that fills nature and makes it coherent, and yet not be that very species necessary to such gradation and fullness? Why does not man deserve his place in being? Or in what respect is he wrong placed? Would he have earth without inhabitants, or would he have no earth in our mundan system? Or can we alter that mundan system in any respect, without altering it entirely, that is, without making quite another system, and consequently without allowing this one a place in nature? This no person, who has any tincture of natural philosophy, will propose.

Would the objector have man a merely passive being, without any power, dominion or sphere of activity allotted to him; only impelled by appetites and affections, succeeding to one another in their turns, independently of his own choice and direction, and driving him irresistibly to ends he cannot foresee, or foreseeing, cannot prevent or avoid? Would he have man to have been made only capable of certain passive gratifications, without any power of judging, willing, chusing, deliberating and ruling; without any thing committed to his charge and management; without any objects or subjects to regulate, work upon, and command? Would he have man to have been created incapable of acquiring and procuring goods to himself or others, incapable of reflecting upon himself, as one able to be useful or hurtful to his kind as he pleases; incapable of distin-<386>guishing between good and evil, beneficial or hurtful, and of approving or disapproving his conduct? Would he have man formed without a moral sense, without the capacity of perceiving fitness and unfitness in affections, actions, and characters; and without the capacity of receiving pleasure from the consciousness of having acted a fit and becoming part? Or can there be a sense of right and wrong, fitness and unfitness, unless there be essential differences of things as to right and wrong, fit and unfit? Can objects co-exist, without having certain relations to one another? Or a mind designed for chusing and acting, and to whom a certain sphere of activity is assigned, ought it not to be capable of discerning the relations and differences of objects; moral ones in particular? Would we have been more perfect without any power, without any dominion? Or can there be power and dominion without subjects? Ought our power to extend only to natural objects and not to moral, or to moral and not to natural ones? Is it too large? Or is it too small, because we are not omnipotent? Hardly will it be said it is too large. Yet to say, that there must be a gradation in nature, and no inferior as well as superior species to us, is manifestly absurd. But how are intelligent beings superior to others, but in knowledge, power and dominion, or an intelligent sphere of activity? Nor is it less absurd to say, that any species can exist without having its determinate nature, capacity and extent of power. The only question therefore is, whether our sphere of activity has not an extent that constitutes a very noble species of being,

Continued.

worthy, as such, of a place in the scale of existence? Let us therefore examine a little its reach and extent. Is not progress in knowledge to infinity, or beyond any assignable bounds dependent upon ourselves; that is, is it not in our power to be continually advancing in a field of science, which is absolutely exhaustless? And does not our dominion in nature en-<387>crease with our knowledge of nature; our dominion over material objects with the knowledge of the material creation, or of the laws and properties of bodies; and our dominion over moral objects with the knowledge of ourselves, or of the nature and ballance of our affections, and of the qualities of the objects suited to them? What known property of bodies has not been made subservient to some use by science and arts? Practical arts, which are all imitations of nature, advance with real knowledge. And thus our dominion in nature is enlarged, and is continually enlargeable by ourselves. And as for our affections and appetites, is it not in our own power to regulate them according

Continued.   to our reason and moral conscience, or conformably to the natural agreements and disagreements of things? For these two ways must mean the same thing. Now, would the objector have us capable of acquiring dominion, either natural or moral, previously to knowledge; or knowledge not to be dependent on, or acquirable by ourselves; but have judgments to spring up in the mind, without our knowing whence they proceed, how they are formed, or why they are right, and may be relied upon; or, in one word, without our having the pleasure of attaining to science by our own diligence, by our own application to get it, by the voluntary right use of our faculties? Sure no objector against the imperfection of our make would have us more perfect, and yet not active. But can we otherwise be active, than by moving, exerting and employing our faculties by choice? Far less sure would any objector have man so formed, that he could not arrive at perfection or improvement of any sort by all his repeated labour; but that he should always be obliged to begin anew, and never acquire any facility, readiness or perfection in sciences or actions, by all the repeated exercises of his powers. Would he have man incapable of attaining to the deliberative habit; or to the habit of thinking well <388> before he determines? Or would he have him to attain to it, without repeated acts, without endeavours to acquire it? Would he have man formed without affections; and so have no springs to move him, no motives to action, and no capacity of pleasure? But how can we have pleasure without affections; or what but a sense of pleasure and pain can stir us to action and choice? Or would he have us formed with affections and appetites, without objects suited to them; would he have man capable of pleasures, without senses of pleasures and appetites after pleasures; or would he have us indued with appetites and senses, and no objects fitted to gratify them? Or would he have objects fitted to gratify them, and yet these objects have no congruity with one another; or have congruity without having particular determinate natures; or have particular determinate natures, and not operate according to them; or operate according to their determinate natures, without operating within certain fixed limits and boundaries; or can objects and appetites have determinate natures and operate according to them, only within certain *Continued.* boundaries, and yet there be, with regard to perceiving beings, no transitions from pleasure to pain, and alternately from pain to pleasure; no stated rules with regard to agreeable and disagreeable sensations and perceptions, no blending of good and ill, or bordering of the one upon the other? Is it not this to demand, that an object may be determined and yet undetermined, congruous and incongruous in the same respects? Is it not to demand, that white may be also black, that a triangle may be a circle?

Would the objector against man, have him formed without private affections, without self-love and the other appetites necessary to self-preservation; or without those which regard others, and knit us to society, and merely with the few narrow contracted ones which terminate in ourselves? Would he have man capable of sensible and private pleasure, and likewise capable of social happiness, without both these kinds of affections to ballance one another? Or <389> of which of these kinds of happiness would he have us incapable? Would he have the soundness of a mind indued with these kinds of affections not to depend upon the just ballance of them; or the ballance to be necessary to happiness, and yet not to depend upon our own regulation of our affections; or would he have the ballance impaired or incroached upon, and that diminution or encroachment not felt by sensation, but merely perceived by reflexion, without any uneasiness; whilst the effect of each rightly governed and ballanced affection is pleasant in itself, by way of sensation? Or would he have us perceive affections operate within us without any sensation of pleasure or pain? One or other of these he must demand; or our affections must continue to work as they do. But to demand the last, is to require that affections should not at all affect us, or be perceived by us. And to demand the other, is to require that an affection in its due proportion should be pleasant, and yet not be disagreeable when it is out of that due proportionate state; which is to require, that things should be proportionate and disproportionate at the same time in the same respect; congruous and incongruous to the same thing; tally and not tally with it? Would he have our frame of body or mind to be disordered, or threatened with hurt, and we have no warning of our danger; or would he have all things to have the same relation to, the same agreement with the same texture? Would he have every man so framed, as to have no relation to other men, no dependence upon the rest of his kind? Would he have men to constitute one kind, without a

Continued. common stock, a common interest? Or would he have a common dependence, without reciprocal ties and affections? Would he have men so framed as to be related to one another, and mutually connected and dependent, and yet their common happiness not be dependent upon good union and joint endeavours <390> rightly directed and governed? Or would he have the common happiness of mankind to be dependent, and yet the happiness of individuals not to be dependent in any measure upon right union and duly confederated force? Would he have one kind of union as fit to promote the common happiness as any other; disunion as fit as union? Would he have ends gained without means, or all means to be equally fit for accomplishing and effectuating any end whatsoever? Would he have mankind to constitute one kind, without being like to one another in the fabric and temperature of their minds, as well as in that of their bodies? Or would he have mankind constitute one species, whose greatest good and perfection should depend on social, virtuous union, and yet there be no differences amongst men in talents, dispositions, genius's and abilities? Would he have all men precisely the same in every respect; all of them placed in one point of time, place and sight, altogether equal, as so many pieces of matter of the same magnitude, form, size and weight? Can there be a whole without parts? Can there be unity and harmony of design without variety, either in the natural or in the moral world? Or is it only in the natural world, that diversity of parts and qualities can shew power and wisdom, or that uniformity amidst variety can produce beauty and good, and so evidence wise and good design? Would any objector have man begin to be, and not set out; to be a progressive creature, and not begin and proceed? Would he have man to attain to perfection gradually, and yet not to aim at it, advance towards it, and arrive at it by intermediate steps; attain to it without means, by any sort of means, or by contrary means? Would he have man to be formed to attain to moral perfection, without moral powers, or without exerting these powers; that is, acquire otherwise than by acquiring: For is not moral perfection, a perfection and happiness that is acquired by moral beings <391> themselves? In fine, let any objector take a just and full view of the natural aptitude and tendency of all our faculties, as sensitive, as understanding, as moral, as social beings, and say, whether all these are not fitted together to attain to an excellent end; a very considerable portion of sensitive and of rational, moral and social happiness. Let us but imagine mankind, with their common wants and indigencies, and their different talents and dispositions, acting with regard to themselves and others, as far as their mutual power and influence reaches, conformably to their reason and moral sense, in all their pursuits, employments and exercises; and then let us say, whether mankind in such a situation, would not shew a very beautiful variety of moral perfection and happiness; or make a very orderly, beautiful and happy kind? Let us consider, how orderly, beautiful and happy, any consociation of mankind is in proportion as it approaches to such a state; and then let us say, where the blame is to be laid, if mankind be not a very happy, orderly and beautiful system. The question, as far as the end of our make designed by our Author is concerned, is, what we are capable of being in this state, what we are sufficiently framed and provided for; and consequently what is the natural aptitude and tendency of all the inferior parts of our frame, considered as commited to the guidance and management of our reflecting powers, to be directed according to our

Continued.

moral sense of right and wrong. This is the only fair way of judging or pronouncing sentence concerning mankind, the end of our being, and the intention of our Author; because this is the only fair way of judging of any whole, or of any author and contriver. Would it not be absurd to say, a watch is not a good watch because it is not a ship, or a fire-engine, or is only fitted for what it is fitted? And would it not be absurd, in like manner, to say, a watch is not well contrived because it can be broken and disordered? But it is no less absurd to say, mankind is not a <392> good system because it is not another system; or that mankind is not well constituted for its end, because men may disappoint that end: the very end for which we were made, being a certain degree of perfection and happiness to be acquired by our proper care to attain to it. That only can be called natural to any intelligent being to which its nature regularly tends; and by deviating from which, proportionable disorder and unhappiness are produced. Let us therefore consider by what deviations it is, that disorder and unhappiness are produced among mankind; and then, say, if virtue, if moral perfection be not our natural end. But how closely we are pushed and prompted by nature, to pursue that end, and not to deviate from it in any degree, will sufficiently appear to every one, if he will but ask his own heart, whether he is ever difficulted

Continued. to find out his duty, and what it becomes him to do, if he but consults his moral conscience, looks within himself, and seriously enquires about it. Notwithstanding all attempts to silence moral conscience, and bear it down or impose upon it, it often, uncalled upon, bears testimony for truth; for right, and against wrong, even in the most corrupted mind, to its great disquietment. And this moral conscience is never consulted or called upon, but it immediately gives sentence against vice and folly, and clearly points out truth, fitness and goodness. Let the most abandoned, hardened, callous debauchee, retire but a moment within his own breast, and tell himself, if he dare, that it does not.

> *This* light *and* darkness *in our chaos join'd,*
> *What shall divide? The God within the mind.*
> *Tho' each, by turns the other's bounds invade,*
> *As in some well wrought picture, light and shade,*

And oft so mix'd the difference is too nice,
Where ends the virtue, *or begins the* vice.
Fools! Who from hence into the notion fall,
That vice *or* virtue *there is none at all* <393>
If white and black, blend, soften, and unite,
A thousand ways, is there no black and white?
Ask your own heart, and nothing is so plain;
Tis to mistake *them costs the* time *and pain.*

Essay on man, Ep. 2.[31]

Can our duty, our dignity, our happiness be more clearly or more strongly pointed out to us? Or can we indeed make any wrong step without blaming ourselves, without being conscious it is our own fault? And is not virtue our supreme happiness? Where else can we find it? And is not this happiness within our power, within every one's reach? Is not virtue most glorious, most lovely, when it is most severely tried; and is not trial necessary to its formation, necessary to its education, and to displaying all its charms, beauty and force? Can there be trial and formation, without means, occasions and subjects? Or is it not fit, nay, necessary to the being of virtue, that it be schooled, proved and severely searched? Ought not rational beings to be placed in such a state? And does not such a one naturally forebode another more perfect state of formed and improved virtue to succeed it? Must immortal moral powers necessarily perish when the first means and objects of their exercises cease? Or is there ought in nature that gives ground to apprehend, that this first state of our existence is our only one? Are we formed to acquire virtue, and yet hardly have time with all our diligence to make great advances in it till we are utterly destroyed? Or is it a good reason to think Continued. no other state succeeds to this, because this hath all the appearances and symptoms of such a state of trial and formation, as our first state ought to be? Is it a good reason to think, that it is the whole of our being, because some things appear as dark to us, as they must necessarily do, if this be but a part of our being? Whence could we have ideas of virtue,

31. Pope, *Essay on Man*, II.203–4, 207–16.

a sense of its beauty, a strong attachment to it, <394> if our Author had
no ideas of it, no perception of its beauty, no attachment to it? Or what
is there in nature we understand, that does not clearly evidence the goodness, the perfect goodness of its Author? But if he be good, what have
the virtuous to fear, here or hereafter? All things must work together for
the good of the virtuous, for their good is the chief object worthy the
Author of nature's care and concern; he can love or approve them only.
But that all things may work to their good, to this state of trial, another
state must succeed, so fitted to beings, who have passed through their
first state of trial, as will best conduce to the general happiness of all
moral beings; to the happiness of the virtuous, or of such as are at due
pains to improve in the moral perfection their nature is capable of. That
there is order, and wisdom, and goodness prevailing in nature, all nature
cries aloud: And if there be, the Author of nature must love and pursue
the general order, happiness and perfection of his system. But if he does
so, what hath his own image to dread? And surely well improved reason
and virtue is such. If we are not to subsist hereafter, it must be because
there can be no provision, no entertainment for us after our commerce
with this sensible world is at an end; or because, tho' there can be, yet
the Author of nature is not disposed to make any other provision for
those excellent powers with which he hath furnished and adorned us.
But what reason have we to imagine so cruelly of him who hath so well
provided for us here? If we have none other but the mixture of pains
and evils with goods in this state, we have none at all; for the goods, are
by far superior to the evils; the evils all flow from principles and laws
necessary to the highest goods and enjoyments; and a mixture of evils
is absolutely necessary to the forming, schooling, proving, and perfec-
tionating reason and virtue. <395>

Can the full fruits of virtue take place till virtue is become perfect?
Can the happiness which results from a greatly improved mind, from
ripened and well formed powers and good habits, exist before powers
are duly formed and improved, and good habits are contracted and established? Can an effect precede or prevent its cause? Can harvest be
before spring? Or must there not be a moral spring before a moral harvest, as well as a natural spring before a natural harvest? Whatever may

be said of the order in which natural effects are produced, it is certain, that moral powers cannot come to their full maturity, or consequently bring forth their fruits, and have their full effect, till they are duly cultivated and improved. To suppose it, is a downright contradiction.

What else then can any one, who impartially considers things, con- Continued. clude, but with *Socrates, "Nec enim cuiquam bono mali quidquam evenire potest, nec vivo, nec mortuo, nec unquam ejus res a diis immortalibus negliguntur."*[32]

In all the reasoning hitherto, I think I have not supposed the Being of a GOD, and a divine providence proved from any arguments *a priori:* but if I have, let such suppositions be entirely laid aside, as they ought to be in an attempt to prove divine providence *a posteriori,* or from the state and condition of things; and let every one ask himself, what it is most natural to conclude concerning man from the account that has been given of the human nature; what it is most reasonable to conclude concerning a being so furnished for progress in knowledge as man is, so fitted for society and happiness in the way of participation and communion; a being with such an extent of dominion and power in the natural and in the moral world, and so capable of delighting in order, wisdom, truth of design, and general good: whether it is more likely that he is the workmanship of a wise and good Creator, <396> and under a perfectly wise and good providence and administration, than otherwise; and whether, in fine, it is more natural to imagine, that this present state of mankind is our whole existence, or that it is but our first state of formation and trial; since all appearances are very accountable upon that supposition. For the question comes to this, "Whether all the parts of our complex frame, and all the laws relative to it, are really so good as we have shewn; that is, whether they do not really produce exceeding great goods, and no evils for the sake of evil?" And to that question the first part of this essay is designed to be an answer.

32. Plato, *The Apology,* 41C–D: "No evil can happen to a good man, either in life or after death. He and his are not neglected by the gods."

The excellent poet we have so often quoted, hath clearly shewn, in one of his *Ethic Epistles,*[a] how difficult it is to judge of the motives by which men are influenced to act, from the actions; because the same actions may proceed from contrary motives, and the same motives may influence contrary actions: and therefore to form characters, we can only take the strongest actions of a man's life, and try to make them agree, in which there must be great uncertainty, from nature itself, and from policy.

But whatever difficulty or uncertainty there may be, in judging of the springs of particular actions, human nature and its Author are sufficiently vindicated, when it appears, that all the powers of man, and all the springs which move him, are given him for excellent purposes: and that all the variety of <397> characters among men must be resolved into certain mixtures or blendings of appetites and affections, which are all of them of the greatest use in our frame, and which all operate, or are operated upon, mix and combine, grow and improve, or contrariwise degenerate and corrupt, according to most excellent general laws. We have not attempted in this essay to draw or paint particular characters, or to account for any particular characters, by analysing them into the original ingredients of which they are compounded; because it was enough to our purpose, to point out the constituent parts, by the various combinations of which, all different, nay opposite characters are composed; and to shew, that not only all these are very useful particles in our constitution, but that they cannot mingle and blend, be strengthened

a. *Ethic Epistles,* Book II. Epist. 1. to Lord *Cobham.* [Pope, *Moral Essays,* Epistle I, To Sir Richard Temple, Lord Cobham. Alexander Pope, *Pope: Poetical Works,* ed. Herbert Davis (London: Oxford University Press, 1966).]

or diminished, improve or degenerate, otherwise than according to certain rules or laws, which are very fitly established. But let any one take
any character in *Homer, Virgil, Horace, Terence,* in any epic poem, in any
tragedy or comedy, in history, or in natural, that is, probable fiction, and
try whether all the ingredients in it are not resolvable into those powers
and affections belonging to human nature, treated of in this enquiry;
and the particular mixture forming that character into the operations of
the general laws, by which all the various modifications of human powers and affections are brought about, which have likewise been here explained and vindicated.

In other words, the design of this enquiry being *to vindicate the ways
of God to man,*[33] by accounting for moral as for natural things, we cannot
help thinking it is accomplished, if we have proved that all the instincts,
appetites, affections and powers given to man, are so placed, that they
have proper materials, occasions, means and objects for their exercise
and gratification; and that all the laws relative to their growth and improvement, or degeneracy <398> and corruption, to their strengthening
or diminution, their intermingling or jarring; and consequently all the
laws relative to our pain or enjoyments, to happiness or misery, to virtue
or vice, are excellent general laws, none of which can be changed but for
the worse. For thence it follows, that *Order is kept in man* as well as *in
nature:* or, that in both, the universal interest is steadily pursued by general laws, beyond all exception, good. Now this, we think, is done; because, though all the particular appetites and passions, or rather all their
particular workings, are not particularly specified and defined, yet the
capital sources whence all the diversity in human life proceeds, are
pointed out, and the final causes of these powers and affections are discovered to be exceeding good or beneficial.

> *On life's vast ocean diversly we sail,*
> *Reason the card, but passion is the gale:*
> *Nor GOD alone in the still calm we find;*
> *He mounts the storm, and* walks upon the wind.

33. Pope, *Essay on Man,* I.16.

> *Passions, like elements, though born to fight,*
> *Yet mix'd and softned, in his work unite:*
> *These, 'tis enough to temper and employ,*
> *But what composes man can man destroy?*
> *Suffice that reason keep to nature's road,*
> *Subject, compound them, follow her and GOD.*
>   *Love, hope, and joy, fair pleasure's smiling train,*
> *Hate, fear, and grief, the family of pain,*
> *These mix'd with art, and to due bounds confin'd,*
> *Make, and maintain, the ballance of the mind:*
> *The lights and shades, whose well-accorded strife*
> *Gives all the strength and colour of our life.*
>
> Essay on man, Ep. 2.[34]

Every virtue (as an excellent author hath observed),[a] hath some vice nearly allied to it, or <399> springing, as it were, from the same root: for every vice is some useful affection misguided or misplaced. But there is no misguidance, abuse or corruption in the human mind, whatever its evil effects and consequences may be, which does not happen according to some law of our nature, which, did it not take place, we could have no dignity, no excellence, no freedom, no power, no virtue, no moral happiness. Man, therefore, is well constituted and well placed here at present. And shall not the work advance as it begins? If order prevail now, shall it not prevail for ever? Universal good is now pursued, and will therefore for ever be pursued. To conclude otherwise, is indeed to forsake all reason; for it is wilfully to reason contrary to all appearances of things, or to the whole analogy of nature.

As in the material world, while one hath no notion of reducing effects to general laws, he cannot but be lost, bewildered and amazed, amidst a chaos of seemingly odd and whimsical, independent effects: so must it likewise happen with respect to the moral world. For regularity and order can never be apprehended, but in proportion as effects are reduced

---

a. *Cicero de Inven. Rhet.* Lib. II. No. 55. *Ed. Schrivelii.* [See Cicero, *De inventione*, II.liv.165. Cicero, *De inventione. . . .* , trans. H. M. Hubbell, Loeb Classical Library (London: Heinemann; Cambridge: Harvard University Press, 1949).]

34. Pope, *Essay on Man*, II.107–22.

to general laws; or when they are considered as the effects of such. When one objects against eclipses, meteors, comets, earthquakes, vulcano's, and a thousand other phenomena, which indeed appear very uncouth, while considered by themselves singly, as arbitrary effects, produced without any rule; or while one merely reflects on the mischiefs they produce; what does the philosopher, what ought he to do, or what indeed can he do, to remove such objections against nature, but shew, if he can, the general laws whence these seemingly evil effects proceed, and the fitness of these general laws: or, if he cannot do that, shew that we can trace nature, in so many instances, to operation, by excellent general laws, that there is good ground to <400> think nature works universally by good general laws, and never by partial arbitrary wills. And in the same manner, when one objects against particular appearances in the moral world, the philosopher certainly gives a satisfying answer, when he shews, that we can trace the far greater part of the appearances in the moral world to powers, and general laws of powers, wisely and fitly chosen and established, in order to promote the general good of the human system. It will not be easy to name any effects which may not be reduced to one or other of the general laws here defended. But if some appearances should be inexplicable, that is, if the general laws from which some particular phenomena arise, should not be ascertainable; yet seeing in very many, or rather almost all instances, general laws can be assigned which are unexceptionably good, it is highly reasonable to conclude, that nature works throughout all by good general laws; and consequently, that even the appearances which cannot be explained, because their general laws are not known, must be the effects of good general laws. For to conclude otherwise, is to argue in downright opposition to analogy, or to all rules of judging concerning any system or whole.

In other words, whatever disorder and confusion there may appear to be in the material world, whilst one stops at particular effects, or considers them as single, unconnected incidents; yet all must appear very orderly, when one represents to himself the necessity of its being governed by general laws, and accordingly is able to represent to himself all its effects, as proceeding from such general laws, as gravity, centrifugal force, attraction, elasticity, electricity, &c. For in proportion as he comes

thus to see effects, seemingly evil, whilst they are considered as the effects
of particular wills, to be in reality good, as being the effects of operation
by good general laws, he must in proportion begin to think <401> well
of nature, and persuade himself that all effects in it are owing to good
general laws, and must therefore be all, for that very reason, good effects.
But if this way of reasoning, with respect to the material world, be just:
it must likewise be good reasoning with regard to the moral world, to
conclude in like manner concerning it, that all its effects proceed from
good general laws, provided in many instances we can trace its effects to
good general laws. And accordingly, let any one, instead of suffering his
mind to wander through the various appearances in the moral world,
from phenomena to phenomena, as single, detached, unconnected parts,
represent to himself the powers and affections belonging to human nature, and the laws relative to the different operations, influences and effects of these powers, as one whole; and then, let him say, whether it is
not a system formed to produce a quantity of good, that well deserves
its place in nature. It is to help one to take such a review of the moral
world, that the general laws of our nature have been pointed out in this
enquiry. For that being done, it only remains to every one to remove
himself, as it were, at a distance from it, and to consider it as a whole,
governed by these general laws, in like manner as we may and ought to
do, in order to have a just idea of our material system; to construct it to
himself in his imagination, and thus making a whole of it, consider the
general laws by which it is governed. It requires but a very small degree
of reflexion to find out that there is no other way of judging concerning
either. And whoever carefully attends to what hath been said of the general laws relating to our powers, and their operations, must soon see,
1. That all the laws of matter and motion, or of the material world, are
either necessary, or very proper to afford suitable materials, means, occasions and objects, to the exercise, employment and gratification of our
powers <402> and affections; and consequently, that no circumstances
happen in consequence of the general operation and prevalence of these
laws, which are evils, absolutely considered. And, 2. That as our powers
and affections themselves are necessary to our happiness and dignity, so
all the laws relative to their various operations, and all their changes,

modifications, influences and consequences, are likewise necessary to our dignity, happiness and perfection. But what else is there to be accounted for, with regard to mankind, but the affections and powers belonging to our composition, and their operations in various circumstances; and the variety of circumstances which excite or bring them forth into action, according to fixed laws in certain manners.

Whatever powers creatures have, they must be powers which operate, or are operated upon, according to certain fixed methods. But if the powers be good, and all the laws according to which they work, or are worked upon, be good, the system composed by these powers, and laws of powers, must be a good system. If therefore the laws relative to our external circumstances, that is, the laws of the sensible world; and the laws relative to our moral faculties, to our advancement in knowledge, in power and liberty, to association of ideas and habits, to virtue, to private and social happiness, that is, all the laws relative to our moral perfection; if all these laws be good, be well adjusted to one another, and none of them can be altered without sinking and degrading the rank and condition of man, or without diminishing his capacity of happiness and perfection, then is the human system a good system. Or it must be said, that the human system, though contrived and formed very fitly to produce a very good whole, ought not to take place in nature, because other powers placed in other circumstances, would make, not indeed the human system, but a comparatively better system. To which I <403> know no answer can be given, but this one, That there is a very good reason why there should exist in nature every kind of system which makes a good whole; for thus alone can *nature be full and coherent;* thus alone can infinite benevolence exert itself, and be happy, by communicating happiness in the amplest or the most unbounded manner.

If a system be the contrivance and production of a perfect mind, it must be a perfect work. There can be no evil in it. We may clearly see, on that supposition, how it comes about in such a system, that those who know but a part, are not able to account for every phenomenon; or why some things may appear to such, imperfections, nay, disorderly and evil effects. For that must needs be the case, with regard to those who have only a partial view of a system. But in such a whole there can be no real evil, or absolute imperfection; that is, there can be nothing that is not necessary to the general order, perfection and good of the whole system. Wherefore, if the Author of the system of which we are a part, be perfectly good, that system must be perfectly good. But since we can see but a part, it is not strange that some things should appear to us imperfect or unaccountable. Nay, it is impossible in such a situation that some things should not appear to us to be such. What then ought those who are persuaded of the being of a God, and of a perfect over-ruling providence, by arguments brought *à priori* to prove it; what ought they to conclude, but that if we had a larger view of our system, we should see more order and perfection in it, than we can possibly perceive in a limited view of it. The goods we perceive in it, we may be sure, were intended by the Author of nature; and the causes, means, or laws which produce them, may likewise produce other greater goods, which we cannot discern, till we have a more full and comprehensive knowledge of the system. But the seeming evils for < 404 > which we cannot account, because we do not comprehend enough of the system to be able to account for them, cannot be real evils, but must be, with respect to the whole, good, if the Author be perfect in wisdom, goodness and power. For what is produced by such a mind, must be good in the whole. This is the conclusion which necessarily follows from the arguments brought *à priori* for a divine all-perfect providence. Now how compleat, how full, must our conviction of this truth be, when we find by enquiring into our system, that the farther we are able to carry or extend our researches into it, the more marks and evidences we discover of wisdom and good order prevailing throughout all in man as well as in nature, agreeably to what the arguments fetched *à priori* prove, must needs be the case.

The arguments *à priori* have been set in so many various lights by excellent writers, Dr. *Samuel Clarke* and Mr. *Woolaston* particularly,[35] that I need not now insist upon them, in an essay merely intended to

35. See Samuel Clarke, *A Discourse Concerning the Unchangeable Obligation of Natural Religion* (London, 1706), and William Wollaston, *The Religion of Nature Delineated* (London, 1724).

reason *à posteriori.* Let me, however, just observe, that these arguments are far from being so intricate as some are pleased to represent them. They, on the contrary, must be very obvious to every one, who but understands what power and effect of power, contrivance and production, whole and part mean. For those ideas to which the consideration of any animate or inanimate being, or indeed any artificial machine, naturally leads us, being distinctly conceived, all the reasoning *à priori* (as it is called) to establish the being of a God, and the reality of an all-perfect providence, turns upon the few following self-evident principles.

1. That whatever is contrived is contrived by some contriver; and whatever is produced is produced by some producer, possessed of power sufficient to produce it. <405>

2. That all power, not only of contriving, but of producing, all power belonging to mind; or nothing being active but mind by its will, it is a mind only that can contrive and produce.[a]

Observations on the arguments *à priori.*

3. That nothing can be an original ultimate source of derived power, but a mind whose power is not derived.

4. A mind which produces by power not derived, produces by power eternal and uncreated, between the exertion of which and its effects, there is an essential, necessary, independent, immutable connection; a connexion not established by the will of any other being, but which cannot but take place.

5. One system is one effect, but one effect can have but one cause or producer; it cannot be totally produced by two causes.

6. There must be some likeness, proportion or parity, between the manner in which a being exists, and its essence, or all its qualities and attributes. And consequently, a being which exists in an independent and unlimited manner, must be in every respect independent and unlimited: or, in other words, a being which exists in the most perfect man-

a. See this important truth fully and clearly explained by Mr. *Locke,* in his chapter on power. *Essay on human understanding.* [John Locke, *An Essay Concerning Human Understanding,* ed. Peter H. Nidditch (Oxford: Oxford University Press, 1975), bk. 2, ch. 21.]

ner, must be in every respect essentially and absolutely remote from all imperfection, that is, perfect.

To corroborate this last proposition, involving in it an absolute necessity for the essential moral perfection of an independent mind, it is justly added,

I. That there can be no malice but where interests are opposite. But a first universal mind can have no interest opposite to that of its own workmanship, and therefore can have no malice. "If there[a] be a General Mind, it can have no parti-<406>cular interest; but the general good, or the good of the whole, and its own private happiness, must of necessity be the same. It can intend nothing beside, nor aim at any thing beyond, nor be provoked to any thing contrary; so that we have only to consider, whether there be really such a thing as a mind which has relation[b] to the whole or not. For if unhappily there be no mind, we may comfort ourselves, however, that nature has no malice. But if there really be a mind, we may rest satisfied, that it is the best-natured, the best-disposed, the most benevolent one in the world."

II. It may be added, that there cannot be a disposition in creatures more perfect than the disposition of their Maker. If therefore, there is such a thing in our nature as delight in universal good, there must be such a disposition belonging to our Maker: He must have it in its most perfect degree, unalloyed and incorruptible.

Now all these propositions being very evident, we have thus a very clear evidence before we enter into a particular examination of effects, that the one eternal mind, the Author of the system of which we are a part, must be perfect in wisdom and goodness, as well as in power. And by the preceeding enquiry into the human make and situation, man is found to be such a being, that the further we are able to carry our researches into his frame and state, the more reason have we to be satisfied

---

a. This reasoning often occurs in the *Meditations of Marcus Antoninus Philosophus.* See it explained, *Characteristicks,* T. 1. *Essay on enthusiasm.* [Shaftesbury, "Letter Concerning Enthusiasm" V, in *Characteristics,* ed. Klein, 21.]

b. That there must be a mind which has relation to the whole, is evident, because a whole must be contrived and produced.

with respect to the wisdom and good intention of his Maker. Thus therefore we have arguments, *à priori* and *à posteriori,* exactly tallying together to confirm beyond all exception that most comfortable truth, "That there is an infinitely perfect GOD, who <407> made and rules his whole creation, of which we are a part, in the most perfect manner, whom it is therefore our duty to love, adore and imitate." But as this is the doctrine of reason, so it is the doctrine of the christian religion, confirmed to us by another kind of truly philosophical evidence. For JESUS CHRIST gave a proper and full proof by his works, of a far more comprehensive knowledge of the universe in all its parts, that is, of GOD's providence and government of the world, natural and moral, than we can attain to; and at the same time, full evidence of his integrity and good intention. But such information or testimony hath all the qualities necessary to create trust, or render it credible. The truth of the testimony of JESUS CHRIST concerning a divine providence, immortality and a future state, (which yet does not encroach upon reason, but leaves sufficient room for all philosophical researches into nature, and leaves the proper evidence of every other kind of reasoning entire) depends upon a no less simple self-evident maxim than this, "That samples of knowledge are samples of knowledge, and samples of integrity are samples of integrity; that these two evidence an honest and well qualified informer, and that a well qualified honest informer ought to be credited and relied upon."[a]

Reason therefore, and revelation concur to assure us, that we are made by, and are under the direction of an infinitely perfect Author, who loveth virtue, and who will make it happy: that man is framed by him to make immortal progress in virtue, in proportion to his diligence to improve in it.

And that virtue or moral perfection, when it is brought by proper exercise and culture to due maturity and vigour, shall then be rendered complete-<408>ly happy by those higher employments for which it cannot before that be qualified: the capacity for great moral happiness must

---

a. See this fully handled in my *philosophical enquiry concerning the connexions between the doctrines and works of Jesus Christ.* [*A Philosophical Enquiry Concerning the Connexion Between the Doctrines and Miracles of Jesus Christ* (London, 1731).]

first be formed or acquired before that happiness can be enjoyed: but when the capacity is acquired, then shall the happiness for which it is fitted, be attained.

It is usual in treatises of this nature and length to conclude with a brief recapitulation of the whole. But the contents shall be digested into a regular summary to serve that purpose; and because of the momentuousness of the subject, I rather chuse to finish this *vindication of human nature, or of the ways of God to man,* by giving in a few propositions such an united view of the human state, as will immediately be perceived by every intelligent reader to make a very coherent and comfortable system, and to carry (not to say any more of it) a much greater degree of probability along with it, than the contrary to it, and that by itself, or independently of any other considerations.

Another view of the human state.
I. As a material world can only be good or bad, that is, useful or hurtful with respect to beings made capable of perceiving it, and of being affected by it; or is really to all intents and purposes, nothing, while it is considered as absolutely unperceived: so it is obvious to every one, who can think at all, that the material world, with which mankind and other perceptive beings are so closly and intimately united in this present state of things wherein we exist, must be considered as making one whole; or a system, all the parts of which have a mutual connexion and dependence. This connexion and dependence is very manifest wheresoever we cast our eyes. And the parts which have this coherence may very properly be divided in general, into moral and natural parts, that is, perceptive beings, and their powers, capacities and affections, and material objects perceived by perceptive beings, and variously affecting them. <409>

II. Now where parts have mutual respects, and are so connected, as evidently to make one system, if general laws are found by induction to prevail in many instances in that system, the presumption must be, that general laws prevail throughout all the parts of it, or throughout the whole system. If they are found to prevail in many instances in the material part, that is, in the effects of the material part upon perceptive beings; it is presumable, not only that they prevail universally with regard to the material part, but universally with regard to all the parts of the same system. But the presumption that all is governed by general laws, must be yet stronger, if general laws are found in any considerable number of instances to prevail also in the moral part, that is, with respect to other effects distinct from those of the material kind, such as the improvements of understanding, reason, temper, &c. and the pleasures and pains arising from these and the like sources.

III. By parity of reason, if the general laws, to which effects are reducible, as far as we are able to go in tracing or deducing them, be good, the presumption must be that all is governed by good general laws. If we may not reason in this manner concerning effects, there is an end to all enquiries into effects: there is, there can be no such thing as knowledge.

In reality, unless effects proceed from general laws, and may be traced to them, we cannot possibly understand them, or form any rules of conduct to ourselves from them: there is no order; and science is a vain absurd attempt. But, on the other hand, if we find general laws prevailing and ascertainable in any instances, then we have encouragement to go on in our enquiries: and if in going on, we find good general laws prevailing as far as we go, then may we most reasonably presume, that we may ad-<410>vance further by due diligence in finding out good general laws; and that in proportion as we advance in this knowledge, the more goodness and wisdom we shall find in the constitution and government of things.

IV. And accordingly, philosophers have found by their enquiries into the material part, as far as they have been able to carry their researches, order, beauty, and general good, arising from the general laws by which it is governed; or according to which appearances in it are produced. They have not only been able to ascertain several general laws, by operating conformably to which, or in imitation of which many very useful arts have been invented to the great advantage of human life: but they have found the general good of perceptive beings to be pursued and effected, and therefore intended by the operation of these general laws; the good of mankind more particularly. Since the knowledge of the material world hath been brought to such great perfection by Sir *Isaac New-ton,* many excellent treatises[a] have been written to prove, that the material part is governed by excellent general laws, or general laws admirably adjusted to produce the greatest general conveniency or advantage with respect to the perceptive beings, which inhabiting it are capable of receiving pleasures from it. The result of his and all other researches into the material system, (commonly called *nature*) carried on in the same way of induction from experiments, and of resolution[b] of appearances into laws deduced from experience, is, that the Author of nature does nothing in vain, but works by the fewest, that is, the simplest means, steadily and uniformly, or always <411> analogously for the general good and perfection of the whole.

V. Now this being the result of all proper methods of enquiry into nature, we have not only great encouragement to go on in our researches into the material part, but we have likewise great encouragement to go on as Sir *Isaac Newton*[c] proposes, and to enquire in the same manner into the moral part, or the appearances which properly relate to our moral powers, that is, to our improvements, as beings capable of reflexion, reasoning, acting, and of uniting in society for the advancement of our common happiness and perfection. That we have reason, and the power of acting and chusing, and certain moral affections belonging to our nature, cannot be called into question: Nor can it be doubted, that powers and affections of whatever sort, sensitive or moral, must have their various degrees of perfection and imperfection; and that a power is intended to be advanced to the highest degree of perfection to which it can be. But, in order to the advancement of any power to its perfection, there must be certain means and methods of advancing it to its perfection: and if there be certain means and methods, by which a power may be advanced to its perfection, there must necessarily, on the other hand,

a. Many of the discourses at Mr. *Boyle*'s lecture are of this kind. Those of Dr. *John Clark* in particular.

b. *Analysis* and by *Synthesis.*

c. In his *optics* towards the end. [Isaac Newton, *Opticks,* 4th ed. (1730); reprint, pref. I. Bernard Cohen (New York: Dover Publications, 1952), bk. 3, query 31.]

be certain means and methods, by which a power cannot but degenerate
and corrupt, or become depraved: for the means and methods contrary
to the perfecting means will be such. Our business therefore is to enquire
into these fixed means, or general laws relative to our powers and affections, according to which they may be raised to their perfection, and
into their contraries producing opposite effects, in order to know them,
and see whether, as in the material part, so likewise in the moral part, all
the laws, as far as we can trace them, be not contributive to the <412>
general good, or such as cannot be changed in any respect without the
greatest inconveniencies or disadvantages.

VI. But if we give any attention to our make and situation, we shall
plainly find, that by the powers and affections bestowed upon us, and
the laws relative to their exercises in our situation, we are fitted to attain
to a very considerable degree of moral perfection and happiness, consisting in, or arising from the dominion of reason over our sensitive appetites, or their just subordination to a well-improved sense of order,
fitness, right and public good implanted in us, to be duly improved in
order to be our guide and ruler. By a little attention to our constitution
and circumstances, we shall find, that being endued with a principle of
reason, and capable of forming the ideas of general order and good, and
of delighting in the contemplation of it, our union with a material
world, by means of our bodies, affords us matter of most agreeable contemplation and study; and that being endued with a social principle, and
a sense of public good, and of moral order and decency, that the highest
satisfaction we are capable of is, that which results from our being able
to moderate and govern the sensitive appetites and faculties, by which
we are made susceptible of pleasures from material objects, as a just view
of public good, and a right sense of moral order and decency requires;
while at the same time, such are the laws relative to our sensitive pleasures
and pains, or the laws according to which material objects affect us, that,
in general, not sensitive pleasure, but sensitive pain is the proportional
effect of departure from the dictates of reason with respect to the government of our sensitive appetites. Either there is no such thing as perfection and imperfection with respect to any power or quality; but these
words have absolutely no meaning: or the regular and constant presi-

dence of our reason over our sensitive appetites and faculties, <413> and over all our choices, actions and pursuits; is the perfect state of those powers, sensitive and rational, which constitute us what we really are. And as indeed, it is a contradiction to suppose in any case the happy state of a being not to be of a kind with, to result from, and be proportioned to the perfect state of that being: so, in our case, our self-enjoyment, greatest peace, pleasure and happiness, result from and are proportioned to that which hath been said to be our perfect state, and must be such in any proper sense of perfection: or in the same sense, that we say the perfection of any constitution of whatever sort is such or such.

VII. Now since intelligent pursuit supposes knowledge guiding the pursuit, and knowledge cannot but be progressive; and what is not acquired by the application of a being with choice, to acquire it cannot be its own acquisition, or give it any pleasure as such, it is plain the perfect state of our powers and affections, in order to give us the pleasure of self-approbation and a sense of merit, must be gradually formed and acquired by ourselves, or by the intelligent and diligent pursuit of such a state, according to the methods by which it may be attained to, in consequence of the laws of our nature and circumstances. Which method will immediately be found, upon a little reflection, to be no other than exercising our reason, not only to know the boundaries of pain and pleasure, their moments or quantities, the effects of different exercises and gratifications, with regard to the happiness of our kind, and the rules of truth, fitness and decorum, with respect to all our exertions of our affections, and all our actions; but likewise to regulate our affections, choices, actions and pursuits, agreeably to the dictates of this knowledge. For as habits of any kind can only be acquired by repeated acts, so this habit of governing all our affections and <414> conduct by reason, and agreeably to the just views of things, acquired by its due application to have right information, can only be attained by repeated acts of reason, in order to get knowledge, and to establish itself into full power and command. Knowledge to direct to what is right and fit can only be attained by taking due pains to know. And the habitual authoritative power of reason, by which it becomes our steady ruler, can only be acquired by its assiduity to exert and keep its command. And consistently with this method of attaining to our perfect moral state, it is the universal law of our nature with respect to all acquirements, internal and external, that they shall be purchased by application to purchase them, according to certain methods easily discoverable by us. Were there not certain methods of our attaining to external goods established by nature, they could not be purchased by us. And in like manner, were there not certain methods of our acquiring internal qualities or goods established by nature, they could not be acquired by us. Now as the methods of attaining to external advantages by application and diligence agreeably to them, are easily discoverable by all who will but look a little about them, and reflect upon the connexions in nature which every day present themselves to all: so the methods of attaining to the internal dominion of reason, our most perfect state and chief good, are very obvious, since it only requires our having made this reflexion, that it is our perfect state and chief good, and our setting ourselves, in consequence thereof, assiduously and steadily, to exert our reason as our guiding principle.

VIII. But this being the case with regard to all acquisitions, external or internal, it is evident, that men are upon the equallest footing they possibly can be, not only with respect to external advantages, but, which is principal, with respect to their attain-<415>ment of their chief good. For thus acquisitions of both kinds are as dependent upon every one's intelligent and assiduous application and pursuit, as may or can be consistently with certain differences among mankind, which are absolutely necessary. For different circumstances with respect to situation for taking in views of the connexions of nature, and with respect to situation for receiving social assistances in our pursuits, must make differences with regard to situation for making acquisitions by our application or industry. But all men cannot be placed in the same circumstances; nor can community and society take place, or all men be mutually useful, and at the same time mutually dependent, without various powers, or (which will amount to the same thing, with different original talents) without our being placed in various situations, which produce divers turns of mind, different extent of powers, and various use and application of powers. Such differences which are the result of our make as social individuals, or are the effects of the laws of nature, properly so called, that is, of the laws of the material world, are the only limitations upon the general law, with respect to our acquisitions by our industry: so that it may be said, that according to the general law of acquisitions, all men are upon as equal a footing as possible, with respect to external advantages, it being the general law with respect to the acquirement of them, that they are to be the purchase of industry to attain to them. And as for moral happiness and perfection, every man is upon as equal a footing as may be, it being according to the general law and establishment of moral things, in every man's power to have that supreme satisfaction, which arises from the sense of due pains to keep and maintain, or rather improve, his reason, in its capacity and authority, to guide and rule his conduct. <416>

IX. And what is the effect of all the differences among mankind, proceeding from the sources which have been just mentioned; but that hence arise means, occasions and subjects, for the education, trial, exertion and improvement of many eminent moral excellencies. There is no ground to think that the powers and affections in all men do not stand originally so rightly proportioned to one another in force, that by due culture a great degree of moral perfection may be acquired by every one. The most remarkable moral differences among mankind do arise from negligence and culture, from right use and abuse of powers and affections; for by diligence to cultivate do powers and affections only gain strength and vigour, and arrive to perfection. But the exercises necessary to perfect faculties and affections, and establish good habits, cannot take place without certain proper objects or materials. And such really is the result of all the differences among mankind, whencesoever they arise, that they afford suitable means, opportunities and objects for the exercises necessary to bring forth several virtues into action, and thereby to work them into perfect habits. All the virtues may be reduced to benevolence; they are nothing else but so many different exertions of social love or benignity on different occasions, or in different circumstances. And without many differences among mankind, variety of benevolent affections and actions could not have place, they could not have subjects: there could not be that variety of circumstances which is requisite to their various exertion, to their trial and formation, their discipline and culture, and a due diversity of their beautiful pleasant employments.

X. Now if this be the state of mankind, all the evils complained of in human life, must either be owing to the steady operation of the laws of the ma-<417>terial world, which laws are sufficiently justified and vindicated by natural philosophers: or to our suffering sensitive pain, in consequence of our not governing our sensitive appetites, and their pursuits and gratifications by the rules of right reason, which is an excellent law in the moral world; or to our not bestowing proper culture upon our powers and faculties, to bring them to their proper perfection; and yet that right and wrong use, improvement and neglect, pains to perfect, and labour to deprave, should have the different effects in the moral world they have, is likewise an excellent general law: or lastly, they must arise from differences among mankind, all the sources of which are necessary to the general good, and which differences are in themselves a very proper means of forming and improving virtuous habits. So that upon the whole we may justly conclude; that mankind are endued with powers capable of being advanced to great perfection; and are at present very well placed, in order to the schooling, the education and discipline of these powers. It is therefore a very orderly and well constituted state of existence, which well deserves its place in nature.

XI. But if it be a proper state for education, to a very great degree of moral perfection, in which happiness, inward happiness, advances proportionably with moral perfection: is it not highly reasonable to conclude, that it is really intended for a state of moral education? It is plainly our first setting out; and if it be a proper state to set out in, or to begin the pursuit of moral perfection and happiness, what reason can there be to conclude that it is not such only; or that it is the whole of our existence? From a proper state for the formation and improvement of moral powers to great perfection, what ought we to expect or look for, but proper care afterwards to place well-improved powers in circumstances suited <418> to them, or in which they shall have proper enjoyments by proper exercises. To make compleatly happy, two things must concur, powers or capacity, and objects suited one to another. Powers or capacity cannot make happy, without suitable objects; nor can objects bring happiness, where the powers or capacity is wanting. Capacity must be formed, before objects only suited to capacity, formed to a certain pitch of perfection, can be means of happiness. But if suitable care to form a capacity for great moral perfection be taken here, by furnishing us with the proper materials or subjects of exercise, in order to its improvement; and if the gradual advances in improvement by proper exercises reward themselves, or are a very great degree of happiness, what can we induce ourselves to think shall be the state of highly improved capacity of moral happiness, when the state of formation and trial is at an end, but such an one as shall afford it full happiness, by exercises adequate to it? Virtue and vice cannot be idle unmeaning words, unless use and abuse, corruption and improvement, perfection and degeneracy of powers, be insignificant terms. But if they are not, highly improved virtues or moral powers, brought by due culture to their perfection, and corrupted minds, or depraved faculties and powers, must have very opposite effects. Nothing but tormentful appetites, and a direful conscience of guilt and deformity, can be the result of a vitiated mind, in a state far removed from all the means of sensual gratification, and where the employments and entertainments necessarily require moral powers greatly improved, a prevailing love of moral exercises and enjoyments, and full dominion and mastership over sensual appetites. But how can we imagine that man, who by his frame and make cannot, even in the most luxuriant circumstances of outward enjoyment, attain to any solid contentment or satisfaction of mind, but in propor-<419>tion as he is conscious to himself of his giving due diligence to improve all his rational faculties to their proper perfection, and to maintain his reason in full power over all his desires, appetites and passions; how can we imagine that man, who is so made, when this state, which is only fit for educating and cultivating moral powers to a certain degree of perfection, and which cannot possibly always last, does cease, shall not pass into another state, in which care shall be taken of virtue, proportioned to the improvements it hath made! This state being really wisely and benignly constituted and governed, we may justly promise ourselves, that order shall prevail for ever; and that, as it is really the effect of perfectly wise and kind contrivance and administration, so whatever we can clearly conceive to be necessary to equally good administration in an after state, shall certainly take place there. And therefore we may reasonably conclude, that though here many die before they have had time and opportunity of attaining to any very great degree of moral perfection, yet since that happens in consequence of laws very well adapted to general good in the present state, it can be no ground of objection against providence; because, if a good disposition is but beginning to exert itself, moral powers may be placed, upon their removal from this state, in circumstances very advantageous for their speedy improvement. And though all have not here the same advantages for moral improvements, yet since the differences whence that inequality proceeds, arise from excellent causes, and are themselves exceeding useful, this can be no just ground of objection against providence, because minds duly improved by proper culture, in proportion to the circumstances they are placed in for improvement, may be placed after death in a very happy situation for quick and great improvement: and thus, as it were, compensation may be made to them. In one word, if this be an <420> orderly first state, in which the general good is steadily intended and pursued by its Author, we have all the reason in the world to rest satisfied, that a future state shall likewise be a very orderly one, in which the happiness of every well-disposed mind shall likewise be pursued, as far as is consistent with the universal good of rational beings. And we may be as sure as we can be of any thing, "That if the universal good of rational beings be intended and pursued, this is the law of the government of the universe with regard to mankind, and all rational beings, that their happiness shall advance with their moral perfection, which can only advance in proportion to the care of moral agents to improve their moral powers."

I think it is impossible to take an impartial view of mankind, and not clearly see that this is the real state of the case, with regard to us; or to imagine, that we are not here in a very proper station for arriving to a very great capacity of moral happiness, by attaining to a great degree of moral perfection.

And sure nothing can be more delightful than this opinion of mankind; or more gloomy, horrible and dispiriting than the contrary notion.

One's mind must indeed be in a very corrupt state, before he can possibly take pleasure in persuading himself that man is not made to aim at and attain to moral happiness hereafter, by duly improving his moral powers here; if to take pleasure in it be at all possible, as I, indeed, can hardly conceive how it can be. The mind of man is so made, that the idea of attainment to great happiness hereafter, by the suitable culture of his mind here, is no sooner presented to it, than it gladly takes hold of it, and indulges itself with truly laudable complacency in the great and cheering hope; nay, it triumphs and exults in it, and thereby feels itself rise to the noblest ambition, and swell with the most elating expectation. And if it be so, then indeed is man made for virtue, and he is in-<421>deed the workmanship of an infinitely perfect being; for is not a mind, animated with such virtuous desires, resolutions and hopes, truly the image of a Creator, who is complete moral perfection, complete reason and virtue? Whence else could such capacity proceed? How could man, were not his Creator infinitely perfect, have been capable of such a great idea, and so divine an ambition?

Would a person really have a strong, a truly great soul, this is the belief which alone can produce it. He who hath this persuasion duly rooted and established in his mind, by frequent meditation upon it, must indeed rise in his affections above all sensual enjoyments, and look down with contempt upon every pleasure that is repugnant to integrity and virtue: nay, he will be able to surmount, with sedate fortitude, the cruelest sufferings by which virtue ever was or can be proved, and come forth from them doubly brightened and perfected.

Surely no one who duly considers the moment of this doctrine I have been endeavouring to establish; or with what noble comfort, with what fulness of joy, with what great and elevating hopes, it is pregnant, will wonder that I have laboured to the utmost of my abilities to set it in various lights; and that I can hardly part with it, but am at the end of every different view I am capable of giving of it, fond to begin again, and to try to set it yet in some other light, that may better suit some one or other's understanding.

For it is of the greatest importance to every thinking person's solid happiness to be firmly persuaded of it. Without being convinced of it, what can one who thinks enjoy! Or how can he be easy? For if it be not true, how gloomy, how frightful is the state of things! Discontent, horror, despair, must needs be the never ceasing tormentors of every one who thinks mankind are not under the kind care of an all-perfect mind. But the doctrine of a good providence over-ruling all, and of a future <422> state of immortal happiness to the virtuous, is as true as it is comfortable. For even the very small part of the vast scheme of providence we here see, tho' it be but a small, a very small part, is full of the riches of the wisdom and goodness of its Author, in imitation of which lies, according to our make, our only true happiness; for the happiness of a man consisteth not in the abundance of the things which he possesseth, but in the practice of virtue, and the hopes of attaining to complete happiness, by attaining to perfect virtue: and our happiness being so placed, as to be found there alone, that is itself a full proof, that he who made us, and placed us here, is perfectly happy only in consequence of his absolute moral perfection.

XII. Those who search into the works of GOD, have indeed reason to say with an ancient, "He hath garnished the excellent works of his wisdom, and he is from everlasting to everlasting: unto him may nothing be added, neither can he be diminished; and he hath no need of any counsellor. O how desirable are all his works! and that a man may see even to a spark. One thing establisheth the good of another; and he hath made nothing imperfect; and who shall be filled with beholding his glory? By his word all things consist, and all his visible works praise him. But there are yet hid greater things than these be, for we have seen but a few of his works." The same writer after a long discourse upon the works of GOD, and the wonderful conduct of providence towards all his creatures, towards man in particular, breaks forth into this most animated address to all good men.

"Hearken unto me, ye holy children, and bud forth as a rose growing by the brook of the field: and give ye a sweet savour as frankincense, and flourish as a lily; send forth a smell, and sing a song of praise, bless the LORD in all his works. Magnify his name, and shew forth his praise with <423> the songs of your lips, and with harps, and in praising him you shall say after this manner: All the works of the LORD are exceeding

good, and whatsoever he commandeth shall be accomplished in due season. And none may say, What is this? Wherefore is that? For at time
convenient shall they be sought out.—He seeth from everlasting to lasting; and there is nothing wonderful before him. A man need not to say,
What is this? Wherefore is that? For he hath made all things for their
uses.—For the good are good things created from the beginning: so evil
things for sinners. The principal things for the whole use of man's life,
are water, fire, iron, and salt, flour of wheat, hony, milk, and the blood
of the grape, and oil, and clothing. All these things are for good to the
godly: so to the sinners they are turned into evil.—All the works of the
Lord are good, and he will give every thing in due season. So that a man
cannot say, this is worse than that; for in time they shall all be well approved. And therefore praise ye the Lord with the whole heart and
mouth, and bless the name of the Lord."

I have in the marginal notes quoted many passages from ancient authors, to prove the antiquity and universality of the belief of an universal
good providence, and of the immortality of mankind, and of all rational
beings. And I need not tell any who are acquainted with the sacred writings, how clearly these truths are there asserted. But I cannot chuse but
take notice of what is said of a future state, in a book of the same class
with that from which I have just now transcribed so beautiful a part.

Righteousness, saith that writer, is immortal.

He represents the reasoning of the ungodly with themselves in this
manner. "Our life is short and tedious, and in the death of a man there
is no remedy: neither was there any man known to have returned from
the grave. For we are born at all adventure; <424> and we shall be hereafter as though we had never been: for the breath in our nostrils is as
smoke, and a little spark in the moving of our heart; which being extin-
guished, our body shall be turned into ashes, and our spirit shall vanish
as the soft air, and our name shall be forgotten in time, and no man shall
have our works in remembrance, and our life shall pass away as the trace
of a cloud, and shall be dispersed as a mist that is driven away with the
beams of the sun, and overcome with the heat thereof.—Come on therefore, let us enjoy the good things that are present, and let us speedily use

the creatures like as in youth. Let us fill ourselves with costly wine and ointments,—let none of us go without his part of voluptuousness; let us leave tokens of our joyfulness in every place; for this is our portion, and our lot is this.

Let us oppress the poor righteous man, let us not spare the widow, nor reverence the ancient gray hairs of the aged. Let our strength be the law of justice; for that which is feeble is found to be nothing worth. Therefore let us lie in wait for the righteous, because he is not for our turn, and he is clean contrary to our doings; he upbraideth us with our offending the law, and objecteth to our infamy the transgressings of our education. He professeth to have the knowledge of GOD; and he calleth himself the child of the LORD. He was made to reprove our thoughts. He is grievous unto us even to behold; for his life is not like other men's, his ways are of another fashion. We are esteemed of him as counterfeits; he abstaineth from our ways as from filthiness; he pronounceth the end of the just to be blessed, and maketh his boast that GOD is his Father. Let us see if his words be true, and let us prove what shall happen in the end of him. For if the just man be the son of GOD, he will help him, and deliver him from the hand of his enemies." <425>

After this truly natural picture of a vicious mind and its language, he adds, "Such things they did imagine; for their own wickedness hath blinded them. As for the mysteries of GOD they know them not: neither hoped they for the wages of righteousness; nor discerned a reward for blameless souls. But GOD created man to be immortal, and made him to be an image of his own eternity.—The souls of the righteous are in the hand of GOD, and there shall no torment touch them. In the sight of the unwise they seemed to die: and their departure is taken for misery, and their going from us to be utter destruction: but they are in peace. For tho' they be punished in the sight of men, yet is their hope full of immortality. And having been a little chastised, they shall be greatly rewarded; for GOD proved them, and found them worthy for himself; as gold in the furnace hath he tried them, and in the time of their visitation they shall shine. They shall judge the nations, and have dominion over the people, and their LORD shall reign for ever; but the ungodly shall be punished according to their own imaginations. For whoso despiseth

wisdom and nurture, he is miserable, and their hope is vain, their labours unfruitful, and their works unprofitable. But glorious is the fruit of good labours, and the root of wisdom shall never fall away. The unrighteous tho' they live long yet shall they be nothing regarded; and their last age shall be without honour. Or if they die quickly, they have no hope, neither comfort in the day of trial. And when they cast up the accounts of their sins, they shall come with fear, and their own iniquities shall convince them to their face. Then shall the righteous man stand in great boldness before the face of him who afflicted him, and made no account of his labours. For the righteous live for evermore, their reward also is with the LORD, and the care of them is with the most High."
<426>

I have quoted this beautiful passage, as a further proof to shew how ancient, the comfortable belief of a future state is. And with regard to the doctrine of the christian scriptures concerning a future immortal state, I shall only beg leave to observe, 1. That no positive account can in the nature of things be given of the order, constitution, and laws of a future state, but so far as it is analogous or like to our present one; and therefore being a new state, very different from this, which can only be like to it in a few general respects, a positive account of it can only be given in these few general respects; and the many more things in which it is different from it, can only be declared to us negatively, or by negative propositions, signifying that it differs from, or is not like to our present

Observations on the account given of a future state in the christian religion.

state, in such and such respects. Wherefore to object against christianity, that the account given of a future state, consists chiefly of negative propositions, is to object against it for not giving an account of a future state, that cannot possibly be given to us, unless our intelligence could reach further than our ideas, or our ideas extend beyond experience, and analogy to our experience. I need not tell philosophers, that a great part of what is called *science* is but negative knowledge. It is sufficient to the present purpose to remark, that the few positive and many more negative declarations relative to a future state in the gospels and epistles, if they were carefully collected together under their proper heads, would be found to amount to such a discovery of the nature of a future state, as well deserves the most serious attention of all who have just notions of

GOD, and of the dignity of human nature. 2. I would observe, that according to the scripture doctrine concerning the happiness of a future state, it arises from moral perfection suitably exercised and employed. It is described to be the natural and proper effect, fruit or harvest (in consequence of the laws of GOD's <427> moral providence and government) of highly improved virtues, good habits, or a well formed and pure mind, and its suitable exercises about objects adequate to its capacity and disposition; it is said to be the consequence of having sown to the spirit, that is, of having laid a foundation by the improvement of our moral powers and affections for spiritual employments, and the happiness resulting from them; as the misery of the vicious is, on the other hand, represented to be the natural effect, harvest and fruit of a vitiated and depraved mind, or of degenerated corrupted powers and bad habits, or of having sown to the flesh and corruption. A great part of the happiness of a future state is said to arise from more perfect knowledge; that is, from larger, juster, and more clear and comprehensive views of the divine wisdom and goodness in the government of rational beings, than we can now attain to in our present situation, or till the great scheme of providence is advanced to that period; and from those devout and pious affections, which such knowledge must excite towards the all-perfect Creator and Governor of the universe. Yet the whole of the felicity of that state is not represented as consisting in contemplation and pious adoration; but it is described as an active state, a state of service to GOD, and of mutual service to one another: for it is represented to be a city, a state of high and noble activity; a state of active benevolence; a state of rule, trust, power and dominion. And indeed the happiness of the superior orders of beings to man mentioned in the sacred writings, is likewise set forth there, as chiefly resulting from their being ministering spirits, employed in carrying on some noble, generous ends, in the administration of GOD, for the universal good of all rational beings. But it is not my present business to enquire more particularly into the christian doctrine concerning a future state. I have only mentioned these few things, <428> in order to shew the consistency between what is said of it in revelation, and what reason naturally leads to conceive concerning it. In the scripture, it is expresly affirmed, that this is the unchangeable law of GOD in his government of all rational beings, of mankind in particular, that "as they sow so shall they reap." And this we find, by enquiring into the constitution of man, and into the nature and means of all the acquisitions he is found capable of making, to be the rule. It is the rule here, and will be the rule for ever; and that rule being observed in the administration of moral beings, it must be right, just, good, reasonable administration: the ways of GOD towards man are perfect.

The chief thing aimed at in this essay, is to prove from the consideration of our affections, and powers, and of the laws relative to them, natural and moral, which constitute our present state, that man is made by an infinitely wise and good being for immortal progress in moral perfection and happiness. But in the marginal notes several remarkable passages of ancient authors are quoted, or referred to, not to make an ostentation of reading; but to shew, that the way in which human nature is considered in this enquiry, and the inferences deduced from it are very ancient; because some late writers have contended, that among the ancients, no good reasonings are to be found about divine providence, the end of man's creation, and a future state; and to shew the contrary is not merely to do justice to ancient philosophers; it is doing justice to truth and to human nature. For had even the most thinking and enquiring part of mankind, for many ages, never been able to form a just idea of the end or perfection for which man is made; of his relation to a supreme Author and Governor of infinite excellence; and of our duties and interests resulting from our moral powers, and their relations, connexions, and tendency or aptitude, mankind must <429> certainly have been all that time in a most forlorn, dark and miserable situation; as incapable of attaining to their true end, as if they had been created for no such end. We are exceedingly indebted, on many important accounts, to divine revelation in all its different periods and dispensations, which will be found by every careful, impartial observer, to make a very beautiful, progressive part in the system of providence; or one continued connexion and series, one uniform design and analogy carried on for many ages, to its completion in the appearance of JESUS CHRIST in the world, very consistent with all the laws of the moral world. But surely, to assert that without revelation, men have no law, rule or guide; or which is to all intents and purposes the same thing, are unable to discover any law, rule or guide, to direct them in the pursuit of their proper end, perfection and happiness, is to affirm, that men, without a revelation, are incapable of attaining to that knowledge, which alone can enable them to judge rightly of a revelation when it is given to them.

As well may a house stand in the air without a foundation, as revelation be supposed not to be built upon some certain principles of reason or natural religion, clearly discernible by their own intrinsic light and evidence. But because it will be said, that this question is simply about fact, that is, whether previously to revelation, or without its assistance, enquirers into nature had been able to reason well concerning the being of GOD, a future state and human duties: I have therefore taken care, as I have gone on in this enquiry concerning man, to point out several passages from ancient authors, where the nature of man, of divine providence, and of human perfection and happiness, are not only well defined, but accurately deduced from solid principles in a truly or strictly philosophical manner. <430>

It is a very considerable satisfaction to a well-disposed mind, to imagine that good sense hath always been very universal in the world. Nay, in truth, it is hardly possible to vindicate moral providence, or the ways of God to man (in the persuasion of the equity and goodness of which all the comfort of a thinking person is bound up) upon the contrary supposition. And, in fact, there have almost never been wanting some among mankind, who, in the main, had just notions of human dignity and perfection; and who, actuated by a due sense of it, laid themselves out with all diligence to instruct others in that important knowledge. It does not appear that there were more scepticks, who took pleasure in puzzling and perplexing clear truths, in ancient than in later times; or that such were then looked upon by the wiser part of mankind with less contempt, or rather pity, than they now are, on account of the illiberal cast of mind, from which alone a zealous propagation of doctrines tending to discourage virtue, and throw a most gloomy damp upon all truly noble and generous ambition, can proceed. And what though speculative men in former ages had recourse to various hypotheses; and in pursuing some particular one; which, as all false suppositions when they are

pursued far must do, led them into odd subtilties to avoid glaring contradiction, reasoned sometimes very weakly and childishly; can it be inferred from thence, (as, I think, a late author does in express terms) that
these philosophers never reasoned well, or were absolutely incapable of
reasoning well, about the very first principles of natural religion and
morality? I cannot help thinking, that it would be very bad logic to say,
that the great design of revelation cannot even now be discovered, because many pursuing strange hypotheses, reason, even now, very wildly
and incoherently about it: or that, even now, morality is not capable of
being set in a clear light because very different, not to say repugnant,
me-<431>thods are even now taken, in order to explain it; and among
many writers very uncouth suppositions are still admitted and reasoned
from. It might easily be shewn, that there is no hypothesis made use of
by any ancient moralist, in order to account for providence, and the
present state of mankind, which hath not been adopted, nay, pursued
very far, and had great stress laid upon it, by some very modern writer.
But what would that prove? Surely, to bring it as an argument that, even
now, morality is quite darkness and uncertainty, would justly be reckoned very childish and silly. And yet, if such reasoning be not true now,
it can never be in any case, that is, with respect to any time, good reasoning. If any thing be clear, this must be so: That good reasonings are
good reasonings, though, not only at the time they were produced others
reasoned weakly and foolishly about the same things, but even the very
same persons did, on other occasions, admit and push far some odd hypotheses, and so reasoned very wildly and foolishly about the same matters, concerning which they at other times express very just sentiments,
with great clearness, propriety, elegance, and force of argument. So
strangely do some still go to work in their defences of a cause, which
standeth indeed upon a very plain, as well as sure foundation; that I could
not chuse but say thus much in behalf, not merely of ancient philosophy,
but of the clearness and certainty of rational morality, that is, morality
easily deducible from obvious principles of reason and common sense.
Nay, I cannot but add, that, so fully and clearly are all the principles and
doctrines of morality explained in the writings of ancient moralists, that
there is no conclusion, and almost no reasoning, in any of the best mod-

ern writers upon morality and natural religion, that is not to be found in some ancient philosopher, if not in all of them. None who are acquainted with *Puffendorf* and *Grotius,* and their <432> commentators, and the other most esteemed authors of this class, can call this assertion into doubt: for in these writers, most beautiful passages from ancient authors are on every occasion quoted. What is principally aimed at in this essay, is to call upon philosophers to take the ancient way of considering human nature, and the care of providence about man in moral affairs, which is the same late philosophers have agreed to take in the investigation of natural effects, and in accounting for them, as the only proper method of coming at the knowledge of nature. And all the best, or most useful observations in this treatise, concerning human nature, and the ways of GOD to man, are taken from ancient authors: it was by them, or by modern authors who have rendered justice to them, that I was led to these reflexions. All indeed I have any right to pretend to, is to have attempted to dispose very ancient observations upon mankind and moral providence, into the order that natural philosophers, after Sir *Isaac Newton,* follow, in accounting for material phenomena, which in moral philosophy was the ancient method. It is in the knowledge of the natural world that we surpass the ancients. And if it may be justly wondered at, that the ancients never thought of searching for general laws in the material system, but imagined it almost impossible to attain to any certainty in phisiology, though they plainly had very just notions of moral providence, or of the care of heaven about mankind; and accounted for moral effects, by reducing them to powers and their laws, or manners of operation, which they perceived to be excellent beyond all exception; may it not with equal reason be justly wondered, that modern philosophers, who have found so remarkably the advantage of tracing material effects to powers and general laws of powers, should not think of carrying on their enquiries into moral phenomena in the same manner? The reason why *Socrates* despised the <433> phisiology of his time, was because it did not reduce effects to general laws, and shew the wisdom, fitness or goodness of those general laws, from which effects proceed. And those who will take the trouble to look into his philosophy, as it is delivered to us by his scholars, must soon see, that his way of reasoning concerning human duties, consisted in pointing out the perfections to which our several moral powers are capable of being advanced, according to the laws of our nature; and that his way of vindicating moral providence, or the ways of heaven to man, was by reducing effects in the moral world to good powers, and excellent laws of these powers, constituting the human capacity of moral perfection and happiness.

But after all that hath been said of the perfection of moral philosophy among the ancients, I think the following truths, with respect to its farther improvement, in order to carry on right education to the best advantage, very obviously follow, from the sketch of its design and aim, and fundamental principles, which hath been delineated in this enquiry; and they may therefore be added to it, as so many Corolaries.

Corolary I

From the idea of moral philosophy delineated in this enquiry, it plainly appears that physiology and moral philosophy are (as the ancients have often observed) in the nature of things, quite inseparable. The material world was certainly created for the sake of the moral world; they make one strictly, connected system. And indeed, the material world, considered apart from its effects upon perceptive beings, hath no existence, or at least, cannot be said to merit existence; it is neither good nor bad, beautiful nor deformed, useful nor hurtful; it cannot be <434> said to have any properties, but bare existence, which, by consequence, would, in that case, be thrown away upon it. Now hence it follows, that enquiries into the beauty, order and goodness of the material world, can only mean, enquiries into the effects, material laws and connexions have, by the appointment of the Author of nature, upon perceptive beings, and the good final ends answered by such effects. But in this sense, not only is natural philosophy a part of moral, but a very essential part of it, in order to form a just judgment of our Creator, and his disposition towards us; or, at least, to have a full and satisfactory idea of his wisdom and goodness.

COROLARY II

Not only is this true in general, but we are so united in our present state with the material world, that we may justly be said to be a kind of being constituted by a certain blending and intermingling, or mutual dependence of moral powers and laws of matter and motion. This we plainly feel to be our present state and rank. And therefore the knowledge of ourselves must be perfect or imperfect, in proportion to the justness and adequateness of the ideas we have of that mutual dependence, and of the parts so blended and connected: This must be true of what is called *moral knowledge* with respect to us, or the knowledge of human nature; because it is obviously true in general. "That to know any frame, constitution, or whole, of whatever sort, is to know its parts, and those mutual respects of its parts, which make it one whole adapted to a certain end or ends." < 435 >

COROLARY III

It is therefore very much to be desired, that philosophers would carry on their researches into human nature, as a being composed by the mutual respects of moral and material parts: And while these researches are pursued, it would be of great use to youth, if the more important observations, and reasonings from observations, which have hitherto been made concerning the human nature, and the material world with which it is united, so as to make one system, were ranged into such order, as would best serve at once to give them early right notions of man's great end, or of the chief perfection and happiness for which he is intended and made; and of the care of GOD, the Father of all rational beings, about mankind; and to put them into the right road of pursuing such important enquiries for the further advancement of true knowledge. Such a system of moral philosophy for the instruction of youth, would certainly be of the greatest use. The great happiness of every man, depends upon his being early convinced, by good and solid reasoning, of his being under the care of an infinitely wise and good providence, and

made to pursue, by proper culture, the moral perfection of which his
nature is capable, in order to complete happiness. Without such early
instruction, all other science is comparatively vain and unprofitable. *The
proper study of mankind is man.* And a system of this knowledge proper
for youth is greatly needed. The necessary materials are not wanting: the
work is well worth the labour of some genius adequate to it: and several
noble steps have been made towards it; but a great deal remains to be
done, to accomplish such a body of moral knowledge, as would fully
answer the ends which have been mentioned. <436>

COROLARY IV

It is very evident from what hath been found to be true concerning human nature; and indeed, it is obvious to every one who thinks at all, that
mere instruction of the best kind is not sufficient to effectuate the great
end of education; but together with it, early and uninterrupted, right
usage or accustomance is absolutely necessary. For the deliberative temper, or a fixed unalterable disposition to act with judgment, and after
due deliberation, can only be acquired or established in the mind, like
all other habits, by use, custom, or often repeated acts. And yet until this
temper or habitual power of acting deliberately and judiciously be
formed, one acts precipitantly or blindly, and is not master of himself
and his actions: he is really not a reasonable agent. Education ought
therefore to be contrived, and calculated to produce betimes this self-
command, this freedom and mastership of the mind. But tho' it be absolutely necessary, that by proper instruction, young minds should early
be richly replenished with just opinions and judgments concerning all
the pleasures and pains in human life, or which may attend human actions; and concerning what is fit and unfit, true, just and good, or contrariwise in every various kind of conduct in all circumstances: yet of
how little use will these judgments laid up in the mind be, unless from
the moment one is capable of imbibing any of them by any methods
of instruction, he is likewise inured to have recourse to them to direct
him in his choices and determinations. It is only by the last method, that
theoretic principles can become practical ones; and that the deliberative

habit can be formed in the mind; which being formed, it would almost be impossible to err, so strongly doth pure undebauched nature point out to every <437> one in every case what is fit and becoming; or, at least, what is base and unworthy. How defective education commonly is in this respect is but too evident. And how much of the viciousness and misery of mankind is owing to its being so, will appear by considering the same part of human nature in another light.

Corolary V

For how is it, according to the preceeding analysis of human nature, that we are guided in our actions; or how are our affections variously moved, strengthened or diminished? Is it not by our opinions of things, or by the associations of ideas which prevail in our minds? And how do false ones become so strong and fixed, that they can hardly be altered, but by allowing them to operate upon us very long without examination or controul? If our happiness chiefly depends upon our opinions of things, and the associations of ideas which excite our affections, it must be of the last importance to accustom youth by right education and discipline, often to examine their opinions of things, and call their associations of ideas to a strict account; to break them into pieces, or resolve them into their constituent parts, and impartially to consider how these parts come to be united together into one idea, opinion or judgment; upon what foundation, or for what reason, that is, whether justly or unjustly. For thus alone can one acquire, or having acquired, maintain the ruling power of reason over his opinions and associations; or be sure of not becoming a mere dupe and slave to any the most foolish unaccountable fancy. But that our happiness, as far as it depends on ourselves, chiefly depends upon our opinions of things, and the associations of ideas which rule in our minds, is evident; for <438> tho' we cannot alter natural qualities and connexions; tho' pleasures and pains are fixed and immutable things, yet there are almost no pains human life is incident to, which we may not very considerably alleviate by dissociating from the ideas of them, several opinions connected with them by association, contrary to reason and truth, which greatly aggravate them. Nor are there any pleasures which truly deserve to be pursued with very great affection, which may not, on the one hand, be very much diminished in our opinion, by some false and unreasonable association; or, on the other hand, very much heightened, by a true and just or well founded opinion of them, or by uniting with them, by frequent association, such complete ideas of them, that is, of their influences, tendencies, consequences and connexions, as properly belong to the account, in a fair and true estimation of their full value. Nothing can be more true, than that our affections are excited by and correspondent to the complicated appearances of things to our minds. And it is certainly true, that a very large share of the vexation and misery, as well as folly and wickedness of mankind, is owing to want of a full and strong view of the dignity and excellence of steady consistent virtuous conduct; or of just and complete associations of ideas with respect to right actions; and to the very false opinions of the pleasures arising, from certain mere vanities, in consequence of false ideas of good connected or associated with them. To lead youth therefore to right opinions, and to form and fix in their minds just and true associations of ideas, is the great business of education; the principal part of which end is accomplished by inuring them often to examine their opinions and associations of ideas; and, in general, to let no idea of happiness or misery enter, or, at least, settle in their mind, till it hath been soundly examined; for, notwithstanding the prevalency of false opinions in the world about happiness, <439> were the examining temper early established by right practice, so powerful is nature and truth; so powerful is the language of genuine, uncorrupted nature, that just ideas of pleasures and pains would as it were spontaneously present themselves to the mind: The truth of this appears plainly, if we but reflect how unavoidably the true notions of virtue and vice haunt even the most vicious to their great disquiet. In vain do they chase them away, fly from them, or endeavour to keep them out.

Here the maxim holds true,

Naturam licet expellas,[36] *&c.*

---

36. Horace, *Epistles*, I.x.24: "you may drive out nature. . . ." Horace, *Satires, Epis-*

The many artifices men contrive to put some fair shew to themselves upon their vices, are clear proofs, that the sense of virtue and vice is natural and hardly eradicable: every vice is originally so hateful to every man, that he naturally thinks himself at first absolutely incapable of ever yielding to it: it is by slow degrees, not without violent struggling, and by means of many deceitful artifices to palliate things, or give them false colours, that any man ever becomes reconciled to vice in any degree: But if a person once suffers himself to listen to the subtle language of false pleasure, and to be deluded by its guileful devices into precipitant compliance, instead of calling upon his reason and moral conscience, to exert their proper authority, who can tell where such a one may stop! 'Tis for this reason, that all good moralists speak so seriously of the *deceitfulness of sin,* and warn us with so much warmth, to guard with the utmost watchfulness against yielding or indulging in any case, till we are sure there is no deceit, but that all is strictly agreeable to honour, virtue and integrity. <440>

> *Vice is a monster of so frightful mein,*
> *As to be hated, needs but to be seen;*
> *Yet seen too oft, familiar with her face,*
> *We first endure, then pity, then embrace.*
> Essay on man, ep. 2.[37]

It is in some such way only, that men become villains. And therefore the only preservative against gradual corruption of the heart, is strict and uninterrupted care to maintain and uphold our reason in the habitual practice of governing all our passions, and of examining strictly all the subtle pretexts with which they are so fertile.

Corolary VI

But more particularly with regard to instruction in the science of man, it is evident from the preceeding introduction to moral philosophy, that

---

tles and Ars poetica, trans H. Rushton Fairclough, Loeb Classical Library (London: Heinemann; New York: Putnam, 1926).

37. Pope, *Essay on Man,* II.217–20.

it may proceed two ways. Either by laying open to view the powers belonging to human nature, and the laws relative to these powers in our present situation, and by tracing effects to these powers and laws of powers, as their sources, and shewing their good final causes. By *powers,* I would here be understood to mean, not only the active faculties belonging to man, more properly called *powers;* but, together with these, all the affections and appetites belonging to our nature. And in this sense I have often used the word *powers* in this essay for brevity's sake. Now, in such an analysis of man, human duties will naturally present themselves to our view; for what else can the duties of man mean besides the proper exercises of his several powers; the several perfections to which they are capable of being advanced by suitable exercises; and the apposite means, according to our frame and situation, for attaining to the highest degree of excellency our powers are sus-<441>ceptible of. The end, the dignity, the perfection, and the happiness of a being, must necessarily mean the same thing. And as it can only be inferred from the consideration of the make and situation of a being; so these being known, it must obviously appear, or be very easily discoverable.

Or moral philosophy may proceed to shew directly, that certain manners of acting, in certain circumstances, are human duties. Now if it goes this way to work, it is manifest, not only that it ought to advance gradually from one class of duties to another, according to the simplest order, and to advance in demonstrating the duties of each class from the simplest, to more and more complex cases gradually; but it is likewise very evident, that in such a demonstration of duties, recourse must every where be had to our real frame and constitution, and to our real situation, and the real connexions of things upon which we in any degree depend. It will therefore ultimately terminate in a true analysis of human nature, from which the care of Heaven about mankind, and the provision made for their advancement to perfection and happiness, will plainly appear.

Corolary VII

An ethical system, in either of these methods, in the latter more particularly, would not only be exceedingly embellished, but greatly enforced by pointing out the various devices of ingenious arts, in order to paint out, and recommend with force to the mind, moral truths, or all the discoveries of reason concerning human duties, the beauty and advantages of every virtue, and the deformity and evil consequences of every vice; and the wise and good order observed by the Author of nature in all his works. For what, indeed, properly speaking, <442> are all the ingenious arts, or their productions, which are called works of taste and genius, (poetry more especially in all its branches) but so many languages by which truths may be conveyed into the mind, so as to reach our affections, and move them at once usefully and agreeably?

But which is more, in such ethical systems, the principal powers of the mind, and their operations, cannot be fully explained, without having recourse to the imitative arts, because there is a very remarkable class of effects produced on our minds by these arts, in consequence of certain powers belonging to our nature. Their influences upon the mind, the sources of these influences; and the rules which must be observed in compositions of various sorts, in each agreeably to its particular kind and end, in order to its perfection, must be laid open; or a very considerable part of our frame would be neglected and left out of the account. And accordingly, in ancient treatises upon morals, these arts and their delightful effects, are frequently taken notice of and illustrated. And in many ancient authors, the use that might be made of them in education, and the fitness of instructing youth early in their principal aim and true excellence, are often inculcated with great earnestness.[a] <443>

---

a. See *Plutarch de audiendis poetis.*—Non ergo fugienda sunt poemata philosophaturis: sed adhibenda poematibus philosophica consideratio, adsuescendumque ut in eo quod delectat utilitatem quaeras & eam amplectaris.—Enim vero sicut in picturis color plus afficit quam linea, propter similitudinem corporis & fallendi aptitudinem: ita in poematibus mendacium probabilitate temperatum magis percellit & gratius est apparatu carminis & dictionis fabula & figmento carentis.—Magis quoque adhuc cautum eum reddemus, si simulatque eum ad poemata applicamus, ipsam poeticam ei describamus; artem nimirum esse imitatricem, pingendique arti quasi ex altera parte respondentem. Neque id modo auditum habeat omnium sermone tritum, quo loquentis picturae nomine poesis, pictura tacentis poesis afficitur. Sed praeterea quoque eum doceamus quod pictam lacertam aut simiam, aut Thersitae faciem videntes delectamur, miramurque non pulchritudinis sed similitudinis causa. Suapte enim natura fieri id quod turpe est pulchrum non potest: imitatio, sive pulchrae, sive turpis rei similitudinem exprimat laudatur: eademque rursus, si pulchram turpis corporis imaginem effingat, decorum non servaverit. Pingunt etiam quidam actiones absurdas—in his adolescens est maxime assuefaciendus ut discat rem quae imitatione expressa est, non laudari: sed artem quae id quod propositum erat, recte representaverit. Quando igitur poetica ars—idcirco eum admonebimus, indignum esse, si honestatis pulchrique studiosus, & non hoc, sed doctrinae capiendae causa poemata legens obiter negligenterque percipiat quae ad fortitudinem, temperantiam aut justitiam declamantur in iis—qualia sunt, videre hominem prudentissimum in mortis periculo cum tota multitudine communi constitutum, non mortis sed turpitudinis metu duci, animo adolescentis ad virtutis studium motum afferet.—*After many virtuous lessons from the poets, he adds,* Nonne haec demonstrationem habent eorum quae de devitiis & externis bonis tradunt philosophi, ea sine virtute nihil possessoribus prodesse?—*He concludes,* Itaque cum propter haec, tum praedictorum causa omnium, adolescenti in lectione poetarum bona opus est gubernatione; ne sinistra suspicione occupatus, sed praecedente potius institutione formatus, placidus ita familiarisque & amicus a poesi ad philosophiam deducatur. [Plutarch, *De audiendis poetis:* "So poems should not be shunned by budding philosophers. Instead philosophical thought should be given to poems, and you should form the habit of seeking and embracing the beneficial in that which delights you" (15F–16A). "For just as, in the case of pictures, color is more affecting than line because of color's resemblance to bodies and because of its tendency to take people in, so also a poem containing plausible falsehoods is more striking and more gratifying than is a work which has poetic form and vocabulary but lacks a story line and is unimaginative" (16B–C). "We shall make the budding philosopher still more cautious if, when we turn his mind to poetry, we describe the poetic art to him as an imitative art corresponding to the art of painting and, as it were, from another part of the mind. And he should not just be given the trite description that is on everyone's lips: 'Poetry is a vocal picture and a picture is silent poetry'" (17F). "But we should also teach him that we delight in, and admire, a painting of a lizard or a monkey or of Thersites' face, because of the likeness achieved and not because of the beauty of the model. For that which is ugly by nature cannot be made beautiful. But if a painting resembled a thing, then whether the thing was beautiful or ugly, the painting would be praised. If, to the contrary, the painting was a beautiful image of an ugly body, propriety would not have been maintained. Some painters even paint crazy acts" (18A). "In these things, the young man should, through instruction, become accustomed to the fact that what is to be praised is not the thing which has been copied, but the art itself which has accurately represented the object that was copied. When therefore the art of poetry . . ." (18B). "So let us advise him that it is not right if a person who is keen on what is honorable and beautiful, and who reads poems for the sake of gaining instruction, should only incidentally and negligently notice the elements in poems that speak of courage, temperance, and justice. To see that a most prudent man, in danger of death along with the entire multitude, is led on by fear not of death but of disgrace will bring the young man to the study of virtue" (30D–E). Then: "Surely these things are

COROLARY VIII

Early instruction in the true beauty and perfection of poetry, and its sister-arts, is not only necessary to render liberal education complete, because a right taste of them adds greatly to human happiness, and because that is the only proper method of preventing the bad effects, which these arts, being misapplied, have upon the morals of youth: But besides, right instruction in the foundation and rules of these arts, and the proper ends they ought to pursue, and cannot arrive to their beauty and perfection without pursuing, must really terminate in a very full examination or analysis of human nature. For whence else can the effects of these arts be deduced, but from nature? This is acknowledged, as of-<444>ten as the conduct of a good poem or of a good picture is pronounced to be just and beautiful, because it is natural. And, in fact, the pieces left us by the ancients upon poetry and rhetoric, and several justly esteemed discourses of the same kind by moderns, are indeed truly moral treatises, and afford very great insight into human nature. But having sufficiently considered this matter in my treatise on *ancient painting,* I shall go on to another remark, which may be inferred from this introduction to *moral philosophy.*

COROLARY IX

In explaining moral duties, in the various circumstances of human life, in those which more frequently occur in particular, the necessity of bringing examples from history, or probable fictions, in which actions and characters are naturally represented, from the former more especially, will be readily acknowledged by all who have duly attended to the

---

a demonstration of what philosophers conclude as regards riches and external goods—they are worthless to a possessor who lacks virtue" (36C); and finally: "Given these points and all the ones that precede, a young man needs sound guidance on the reading of the poets; so that not preoccupied with dark distrust, but instead informed by prior instruction, he may be drawn, in an amiable, familiar, and friendly mood, from poetry to philosophy" (37A–B). Plutarch, *Omnia quae extant opera,* 2 vols. (Paris, 1624).]

power and efficacy of example upon the human mind, or our natural strong disposition toward imitation. Examples of the virtues and vices, beautifully expressed or pointed out by being opposed to one another, do, like contrast in a picture, wonderfully strengthen, heighten and set off a moral lesson: it is thus the beauty of virtue, and the deformity of vice appear in the most conspicuous shining light. And as examples take a firmer hold of the imagination and memory than bare precepts;[a] <445> so instances of good and praise-worthy conduct laid up in the memory, are ready at hand, not only to point out duty to us in a stronger and clearer language, than a general rule, without particular exemplifications of it, can possibly do; but likewise to work immediately upon our imitative disposition, exciting a truly noble and laudable emulation in us. For the same reasons, it would be a very useful exercise for youth, to employ them in frequently giving their judgment of particular actions recorded in history, with reasons to support their opinion: and also to accustom them to determine what virtue requires to be done in certain given cases, which ought always to be such as have, or may occur in real life; and at first ought to be such as more frequently occur in, and are most suited to their own age and its common incidents, much in the manner *Xenophon* describes in his account of the education of *Cyrus*.[38]

a. *Hence these and such like sayings so frequent among the ancients,*
   Nihil recte docetur sine exemplo.   *Columella.*

   Facilius quid imitandum vitandumve sit docemur exemplis.
   Longum iter est per praecepta, breve & efficax per exempla.
                                                        Seneca.

[Columella, *De re rustica,* XI.i: "Nothing can be taught correctly without an example." Columella, *On Agriculture:* X–XII, *On Trees,* ed. and trans. E. S. Forster and Edward H. Heffner, Loeb Classical Library (Cambridge and London: Harvard University Press, 1968). Seneca the Elder, *Controversariae,* IX.2.27: "it is easier for us to learn by example both what to imitate and what to avoid." The Elder Seneca, *Declamations,* trans. M. Winterbottom, vol. 2, *Controversariae,* bks. 7–10 (Cambridge: Harvard University Press; London: Heinemann, 1974). Seneca the Younger, *Ad Lucilium epistulae morales,* I.vi.5: "the way is long if one follows precepts, but short and helpful, if one follows patterns." Seneca, *Ad Lucilium epistulae morales,* trans. Richard M. Gummere, 3 vols., Loeb Classical Library (Cambridge: Harvard University Press; London: Heinemann, 1917).]

38. Xenophon, *Memorabilia,* II.ii.10–11.

Corolary X

As moral instruction ought to be carried on very gradually, by proceeding from simpler to more and more complex cases; so certainly, in the education of those of the higher ranks in life more especially, it ought to advance to the most complex and difficult of sciences, politicks. I do not merely mean, that part of it which treats of the general duties of magistrates, and the duties and rights of subjects; nor even that which treats of the duties of separate independent states, one to another; but that still more complex part, which enquires into the nature and effects of different constitutions and forms of government, and compares them together. It is not more absurd to assert, that different mixtures and combinations of sensible qualities have not each its peculiar effects, in consequence of the properties of bodies, and the laws of matter and <446> motion; than it is to assert, that different mixtures and combinations of moral qualities or causes, have not each its peculiar effects, in consequence of the nature of moral causes and their laws. Both assertions do equally terminate in affirming, that what results from a certain combination of qualities or causes, happens by chance, and is not the natural effect of the combination of qualities and causes. And if that affirmation be absurd with respect to physical qualities, or causes, and their combinations, it must likewise be absurd with respect to moral qualities, or causes, and their combinations. For quality is in no other sense a quality, but as it hath fixed, certain influences in certain cases. The words *natural* and *moral,* can make no difference in that respect. As a natural quality must mean a property of a body, which hath certain effects, so a moral quality must mean some quality of a mind which hath certain effects. If combinations of moral qualities or causes hath not their natural effects, as well as combinations of physical qualities, then there could be no political science, since that only means a collection of just conclusions concerning the natural effects arising from certain moral causes: even as there could be no physical science, did not physical causes or qualities produce certain effects, since that only means a collection of just conclusions concerning the operations of physical qualities in various circumstances or combinations. Better or worse, more or less inconvenient, cannot be acknowledged, or indeed have any meaning with respect to civil constitutions, but upon supposition that different internal principles of government (as they are very properly called by political writers) have naturally different effects. But if they have, and therefore there really be such a science as politicks, it ought certainly to make a principal part in the education of youth, of the more distinguished ranks in life, who are, as it were, born, to be public guardians, that is, <447> they ought early to be directed into the proper method of making right judgments about different constitutions, and the various effects they are liable to, in consequence of the natural effects of their internal principles in various circumstances; and of studying history in that view: and to prepare them for such study, they ought early to be made acquainted with the authors who have reasoned best upon these subjects. And indeed the more I have looked into history, and into such authors, the more reason have I found to conclude, all the effects produced by different internal principles of government or civil polity, to be proofs of the wisdom of the laws, which constitute and govern the moral world: and, at the same time, the more reason have I found to conclude, that a great deal more is owing to the natural operation of internal principles than is commonly imagined.

It is pity, that historical registers of natural phenomena have not been carefully kept from the beginning of the world, in all times and countries. Had that been done, it is reasonable to think, natural knowledge must have been long ago brought to very great perfection; and, by consequence, man would have been, long before this time, that master of the world he was certainly intended to be by science, and can only be in that manner. But tho' that method of enlarging human dominion and happiness be yet exceedingly neglected, notwithstanding all the pains Lord *Verulam,* and other great genius's have taken to recommend and chalk it out to us; tho' it be not set on foot as it ought, even now when it is universally acknowledged by all philosophers to be the only method, and an infallible one, of getting at the knowledge of nature, of the advantages of which to us no one can doubt: tho' this is really matter of regret, yet it is a great happiness to mankind, that the history of moral affairs from the most ancient times is so exactly transmitted to <448>

us as it is: and indeed, in this case, the only thing that seems wanting, is the art of making the proper uses of such experimental registers. It were therefore to be wished, that more persons of abilities for it, would apply themselves to such calculations and deductions, for the benefit of human society, as these moral records afford proper materials for.

As it is natural to think, that very like circumstances of mankind, in the more capital or important respects, must frequently recur, because all men, in all ages, are actuated by the same springs, *i.e.* by the same affections, and have nearly the very same powers, and the very same connexions and dependencies: so, in fact, almost no circumstances now happen to any society, of which ancient history doth not afford some example, so similar in many material points, that by it a very right judgment may be made of their tendency, according to the natural operations of moral causes; and of the proper means to be used or interposed to give them any demanded turn.

This must have been the case ever since history deserved to be recommended, not merely for amusement, but for our instruction in the various tendencies of moral causes, and in the arts of government. 'Tis only on this account, that history merits to be called not barely, *"Testis temporum & nuntia vetustatis;"* but, *"Lux veritatis & magistra vitae."*[39]

It could not be of use in that way, were it not for that likeness of times to times, and events to events, arising from the likeness of men to men, or that sameness of human nature in all times and ages of the world, which history puts beyond all doubt. But human affairs appearing by history to be really such, it acquireth thereby a right to be appealed to, to confirm or refute any political reasonings, as we do in philosophy to experiment; and thus to be <449> deemed the best, the most useful of all studies, and the surest teacher and guide in matters of society and publick concern. No doubt, men acquainted with history and human

---

39. Cicero, *De oratore,* II.ix.36: *Testis temporum*—"bears witness to the passing of the ages"; *nuntia vetustatis*—"bears tidings of ancient days"; *lux veritatis*—"sheds light upon reality"; *magistra vitae*—"gives guidance to human existence." Cicero, *De oratore, Books I and II,* trans. E. W. Sutton, completed by H. Rackham, Loeb Classical Library (Cambridge: Harvard University Press; London: Heinemann, 1942).

nature, might carry on moral investigations about moral qualities, and combinations of moral qualities, and their effects, a much greater length than hath been yet done. And till youth are acquainted with making proper reflexions upon, or useful deductions from events, as from moral experiments, they cannot possibly study history in the only profitable way.

But, however that be, it is obvious, to use the words of a very great author often quoted, "That as low as philosophy is now reduced, if morals be allow'd belonging to her, politicks must undeniably be hers. For to understand the manners and constitutions of men in common, 'tis necessary to study man in particular, and know the creature, as he is in himself, before we consider him in company, as he is interested in the state, or join'd to any city or community. In order to reason rightly concerning man, in his confederate state and national relation; as he stands engaged to this or that society by birth or naturalization; we must first have considered him as a citizen or commoner of the world, and have traced his pedegree a step higher, or have view'd his end and constitution in nature itself."[40]

Philosophy does not proceed to its principal part, till the nature of human society, the end of government and laws, and the various tendencies of different moral combinations in social respects, or with regard to publick happiness, are thoroughly weighed and understood. But it must begin at considering man in the abstract, or his natural state and constitution; since to deduce any moral duty, or to know the perfection or imperfection of any creature whatever, it is requisite first of all to understand what condition and relation it is placed in, <450> and what is the proper end and purpose of its being.

Corolary XI

If any one should ask, what is the properest way and time of beginning in the instruction of youth? The answer seems obvious from the preceeding account of human nature. It may be delayed too long, but it

40. Shaftesbury, "The Moralists," I.i, in *Characteristics,* ed. Klein, 232–33.

cannot be attempted too soon.[a] For the sooner our faculties are invited by proper methods to disclose themselves, the sooner they begin to operate, and by proper working, they quickly gain considerable strength, and arrive to great maturity: our moral sense, together with our delight in analogy and similitude, soon discover themselves, if they are duly tried. And one of the properest means of improving both these faculties, or rather determinations of our nature, is very early to convey into young minds the more simple and obvious moral truths, by apposite fables and allegories. Here poetry is of admirable use; for whatever principles, max-

---

a. Quintilian *gives a very important advice to this purpose, founded on a very true observation.* Igitur nato filio, pater spem de illo primum quam optimam capiat, ita diligentior a principiis fiet. Falsa enim est querela paucissimis hominibus vim percipiendi quae traduntur esse concessam; plerosque vero laborem ac tempora tarditate ingenii perdere. Nam contra, plures reperias, & faciles in excogitando, & ad discendum promptos: quippe id est homini naturale. Ac sicut aves ad volandum, equi ad cursum, ad saevitiam ferae gignuntur: ita nobis propria est mentis agitatio atque solertia, unde origo animi coelestis creditur. Hebetes vero & indociles, non magis secundum naturam hominis eduntur quam prodigiosa corpora, & monstris insignia. Sed hi pauci admodum fuerunt. Argumentum quod in pueris elucet spes plurimorum, quae cum emoritur aetate manifestum est, non naturam defecisse sed curam. Praestat tamen ingenio alius alium concedo: sed ut plus efficiat aut minus. Nemo tamen reperitur, qui sit studio nihil consecutus, &c. *Quin, Inst.* l. 1. c. 1. [Quintilian, *Institutio oratoria,* I.i.1: "I would, therefore, have a father conceive the highest hopes of his son from the moment of his birth. If he does so, he will be more careful about the groundwork of his education. For there is absolutely no foundation for the complaint that but few men have the power to take in the knowledge that is imparted to them, and that the majority are so slow of understanding that education is a waste of time and labour. On the contrary you will find that most are quick to reason and ready to learn. Reasoning comes as naturally to a man as flying to birds, speed to horses and ferocity to beasts of prey: our minds are endowed by nature with such activity and sagacity that the soul is believed to proceed from heaven. Those who are dull and unteachable are as abnormal as prodigious births and monstrosities, and are but few in number. A proof of what I say is to be found in the fact that boys commonly show promise of many accomplishments, and when such promise dies away as they grow up, this is plainly due not to the failure of natural gifts, but to lack of the requisite care. But, it will be urged, there are degrees of talent. Undoubtedly, I reply, and there will be a corresponding variation in actual accomplishment: but that there are any who gain nothing from education, I absolutely deny." Quintilian, *The Orator's Education,* ed. and trans. Donald A. Russell, 5 vols., Loeb Classical Library (Cambridge and London: Harvard University Press, 2001).]

ims, or precepts can <451> be so conveyed, both strike the mind more strongly at first, and are more easily retained by it afterwards.

But, in order to form the attentive habit, and strengthen and whet reason and the perceptive faculties; or to beget at the same time the love of knowledge, and a just notion of acuracy and coherence in reasoning, geometry hath ever been acknowledged by all philosophers to be the proper instrument, if I may so speak. *Quintilian* tells us, in a few words, what opinion the best ancients had of it in these respects. *"Fatentur esse utilem teneris aetatibus, agitari namque animos atque acui ingenia & celeritatem percipiendi venire inde concedunt. Sed prodesse eam non ut caeteras artes, cum perceptae sint, sed cum discantur, existimant."*a

But there is another reason, tho' that be sufficient, why it ought to make an early part of education, namely, because it is the key to that true natural philosophy, which shews so plainly the wisdom of GOD in all his administration; and so naturally leads the mind to the study of order, beauty, wisdom and goodness, which cannot be contemplated without being loved, nor loved without being imitated.

I shall only add to this, that by the proper methods of instructing youth in any language, their tender minds will be early let into, and replenished with the knowledge of the beautiful and truly wonderful analogies and harmonies, which prevail throughout the whole of nature. For were not only all sensible ideas analogous, in many respects, one to another, but all moral ideas likewise analogous in many respects to almost all sensible ideas, if there could be any such thing as language at all, which I much doubt, yet it is plain, at least, that languages could not abound so much as they do in <452> metaphorical words. But that being the case, early instruction in the beauty, propriety, elegance and force of metaphorical words, must not only improve the imagination, but it must really fill the mind betimes with very useful and agreeable knowledge.

a. *Instit.* l. 1. c. 17. [Quintilian, *Institutio oratoria,* I.x.34: ". . . it is admitted that some parts of it [geometry] are useful for young children, because it exercises the mind, sharpens the wits, and generates quickness of perception. But it is thought that the advantages come not (as with other arts) when it has been learned, but only during the learning process."]

All this is as true and as manifest, as it is that a metaphor must be lost upon one who does not fully and clearly comprehend the analogy signified by it, and that makes it a proper or well chosen one.

Corolary XII

From this specimen of moral philosophy, and the preceeding corolaries, it is visible, that the ancients had very good reason to say, that all the sciences are one, even as nature is one; and that they ought not to be violently torn asunder from one another in education; but ought, on the contrary, to be united together in it agreeably to their natural connexion and one common end.[a] <453>

a. *See what is said on this head from* Plato *by* Cicero. Ac mihi quidem veteres illi majus quiddam animo complexi, multo plus etiam vidisse videntur, quam quantum nostrorum ingeniorum acies intueri potest, qui omnia haec, quae supra & subter, unum esse & una vi, atque una consensione naturae constricta esse dixerunt. Nullum enim est genus rerum, quod aut avulsum a ceteris per seipsum constare, aut quo cetera, si careant, vim suam atque aeternitatem conservare possent—Est etiam illa Platonis vera & tibi, Catule, certe non inaudita vox, omnem doctrinam harum ingenuarum, & humanarum artium; uno quodam societatis vinculo contineri, ubi enim perspecta vis est rationis ejus, qua causae rerum, atque exitus cognoscuntur, mirus quidam omnium quasi consensus doctrinarum, concentusque reperitur. De *Orat.* 1. 3.

So pro Archia poeta: *Orat.*

—Etenim omnes artes, quae ad humanitatem pertinent, quoddam commune vinculum & quasi cognatione quadam inter se continentur, &c. And nothing can be more just than what is said by one of the persons in the third book, *De finibus,* towards the close, in order to shew the mutual connexion and dependence of natural and moral philosophy. Physicae non sine causa tributus est idem honos: propterea quod qui convenienter naturae victurus sit, ei & proficiscendum est ab omni mundo & ab ejus procuratore. Nec vero potest quisquam de bonis & malis vere judicare, nisi omni cognita ratione naturae & vitae etiam deorum, & utrum conveniat, necne, natura hominis cum universa—Atque etiam ad justitiam colendam, ad tuendas amicitias, & reliquas caritates, quid natura valeat, haec una cognitio potest tradere. Nec vero pietas adversus Deos, nec quanta his gratia debetur, sine explicatione naturae intelligi potest, &c. [Cicero, *De oratore,* III.v.20–vi.21: "And in my own view the great men of the past, having a wider mental grasp, have also a far deeper insight than our mind's eye can achieve, when they asserted that all this universe above us and below is one single whole, and is held together by a single force and harmony of nature; for there exists no class of things which can stand by itself, severed from the rest, or which the

All the liberal sciences into whatever different classes they may be distributed, do indeed make but one body; and none of them can be fully understood separately, or apart from all the rest; no more than a limb can be, without referring it to the whole body of which it is naturally a member.

This is plain, because in reality, that which is the only object of real knowledge, *viz.* nature, is truly one indivisible object, all the parts of which are strictly coherent. All that we can study, or have to study, is our own constitution and situation; our own make, and the relation we stand in to the system of which we are a part, and its author. And all the liberal arts and sciences are really but so many different languages, by which the various connexions which make our system may be pointed out, expressed, embellished, recommended or enforced on the mind: as other inferior ones are but so many arts of imitating certain laws and connexions in nature, for the convenience or ornament of human life and society. But having sufficiently illustrated this point in my *essay on ancient painting*,[41] I shall not now insist longer upon it.

---

rest can dispense with and yet be able to preserve their own force and everlasting existence . . . there is also the truth enunciated by Plato, which you, Catullus, have undoubtedly heard, that the whole of the content of the liberal and humane sciences is comprised within a single bond of union; since, when we grasp the meaning of the theory that explains the causes and issues of things, we discover that a marvellous agreement and harmony underlies all branches of knowledge." *Pro Archia poeta,* I.2: "Indeed, the subtle bond of a mutual relationship links together all arts which have any bearing upon the common life of mankind, etc." *De finibus,* III.xxii.73: "The same honour is also bestowed with good reason upon natural philosophy, because he who is to live in accordance with nature must base his principles upon the system and government of the entire world. Nor again can anyone judge truly of things good and evil, save by a knowledge of the whole plan of nature and also of the life of the gods, and of the answer to the question whether the nature of man is or is not in harmony with that of the universe. . . . Also this science alone can impart a conception of the power of nature in fostering justice and maintaining friendship and the rest of the affections; nor again without unfolding nature's secrets can we understand the sentiment of piety towards the gods, or the degree of gratitude that we owe to them, etc." Cicero, *De oratore, Book III, De fato, Paradoxa Stoicorum, De partitione oratoria,* trans. H. Rackham, Loeb Classical Library (London: Heinemann; Cambridge: Harvard University Press, 1942).]

41. Turnbull, *A Treatise on Ancient Painting* (London, 1740), ch. 7.

I shall conclude with observing, that the moral philosophy here de-lineated, will not suffer its students to give themselves up entirely to contemplation and admiration, but will vigorously push and <454> prompt them to virtuous activity as their main end, in fitting us for which the whole merit of science consists. They will soon perceive, as *Cicero* observes, 1. That the active mind of man when it is once inured to serious meditations and profitable enquiries, can be very busy about these while the body is intent upon, or entirely occupied in walking, riding, or other such exercises. 2. And every step one advances in moral researches, he must have this important truth more and more deeply enforced upon him, that man is made for society and action. *"Virtutis laus omnis in actione consistit."* [a] I cannot better explain this doctrine, which is the plain language of our whole frame and contexture, than *Cicero* hath done in his *offices.* [b] I shall therefore give his opinion of it in the words of his *english* translator.

"The principal of all the virtues is that sort of wisdom which the *Greeks* call σοφια; (for as to *that* sort which they call φρονησις and we *prudentia,* it is a thing of a perfectly different nature, as being no more than *the skill of discerning what it is that we ought, or ought not to do:*) But that sort of wisdom, which I said was the principal is, *the knowledge of things both divine and human;* and so comprehends the society and relation of men with the gods, and with one another. If then this, as most certainly it is, be the greatest virtue; it follows, that the duties which flow from society must as certainly be the greatest: for the deepest knowl-edge and contemplation of nature, is but a very lame and imperfect busi-ness, unless it proceed and tend forward to action: now the occasions wherein it can shew itself best, consist in maintaining the interests of men, and of consequence belong to the society of mankind: from whence it follows, that the maintain-<455>ing of this, should in reason

---

a. First book of the *offices,* toward the beginning. [Cicero, *De officiis,* I.vi.19: "The whole glory of virtue is in activity." Cicero, *De officiis,* trans. Walter Miller, Loeb Classical Library (London: Heinemann; Cambridge: Harvard University Press, 1938).]

b. First book of the *offices* towards the end. Edit. Schrv. No. 43, 44. [Ibid., I.xliii.153–xliv.158.]

take place before learning and knowledge. Nor is this any more than
what all good men shew they judge to be true by their actions and practices: for who is there so wholly addicted to contemplation and the study
of nature, as that, if his country should fall into danger, while he was in
one of his noblest researches, he would not immediately throw all aside,
and run to its relief with all possible speed; nay, though he thought he
might number the stars, or take the just dimensions of the whole world?
And the same would he do in the case of any danger to a friend or a
parent. From all which things it undeniably appears, that the duties of
knowledge and searching after truth, are obliged to give way to the duties
of justice, which consist in upholding society among men; than which
there is nothing we should be more concerned for. Nay, those very men,
who have spent their whole lives in philosophy and learning, have yet
always endeavoured, as much as they could, to be serviceable to the interest and good of mankind. For many brave men, and very useful members of their several states, have in great part been made such by their
institutions. Thus *Epaminondas,* the famous *Theban,* was indebted for
his education to *Lysis,* the *Pythagorean: Dion* of *Syracuse,* for his to *Plato;*
and the same may be said of a great many others; even I myself, whatsoever service I have done the republick, (if at least it may be said that
I have done it any service) must wholly ascribe it to that learning and
those instructions I received from my masters. Neither is their teaching
and instructing others determined to the time of their living here; but
they continue to do it even after they are dead, by the learned discourses
which they leave behind them: for there is no one point they have left
unhandled, relating either to the laws, customs, or discipline of the commonwealth: so that they seem to have sacrificed their leisure and <456>
opportunities of study, to the benefit of those who are engaged in business: and thus we see how those men themselves, whose lives have been
spent in the pursuit of wisdom, have nevertheless endeavoured by their
learning and prudence, to be some way profitable to the community of
mankind. And for this one reason, persuasive speaking, if joined with
prudence, is a greater accomplishment than the acutest thinking, if destitute of eloquence: for thinking is terminated in itself alone, but speaking reaches out to the benefit of those with whom we are joined in the

same society. Now as bees do not therefore unite themselves together, that so they may the better prepare their combs; but therefore prepare their combs, because they do by nature unite themselves together: so men, and much more, being creatures that naturally love society, in consequence of that, seek how they may find methods of living happily in it. From hence it follows, that the knowledge of things, unless it is accompanied with that sort of virtue, which consists in defending and preserving of men, *i.e.* in the maintenance of human society, is but a barren and fruitless accomplishment; and even greatness of soul, without a regard to this society and conjunction, is very little better than savageness and barbarity. Thus we may see, that the getting of knowledge is a duty of much less concern and moment, than the preserving this society and union amongst men. It is a very false notion, that hath been advanced by some people, that necessity alone was the motive to this society, which we have so often mentioned; and that men would never have associated together, but that they were not able, in a solitary life, to furnish themselves with the necessaries of nature; and that every great and exalted genius, would providence supply him with food and the other conveniences of life, would withdraw from all business and intercourse with mankind, and gave himself <457> wholly to study and contemplation. This is not so; for he would avoid solitude, endeavour to find a companion in his studies, and always be desirous of teaching and learning, of hearing and speaking. From all which it is abundantly evident, that the duties belonging to human society, should in reason take place before those which relate to unactive knowledge."

All I have been endeavouring to prove, in the text to be true, and in the marginal notes to have been the constant opinion of the best ancient philosophers, concerning human nature and the present state of virtue, is delightfully expressed by *Cicero,* in his first book of laws, where it is likewise fully explained and demonstrated. *Animal hoc providum, sagax, multiplex, acutum, memor, plenum rationis & consilii quem vocamus hominem, praeclara quadam conditione generatum esse a supremo Deo. Quid est, non dicam in homine, sed in omni caelo, atque terra ratione divinius? Quae cum adolevit, atque perfecta est, rite sapientia nominatur. Est igitur, quoniam nihil est ratione melius, eaque & in homine, & in Deo; prima homini cum Deo rationis societas. ——— Jam vero virtus eadem in homine ac Deo est, neque ullo alio ingenio praeterea. Est autem virtus nihil aliud, quam in se perfecta, & ad summum perducta natura. Est igitur homini cum Deo similitudo. Quod cum ita sit, quae tandem potest esse proprior, certiorve cognatio. ——— Nec est quisquam gentis ullius, qui ducem naturam nactus ad virtutem pervenire non possit.*[42]

42. Cicero, *De legibus:* ". . . that animal which we call man, endowed with foresight and quick intelligence, complex, keen, possessing memory, full of reason and prudence, has been given a certain distinguished status by the supreme God who created him. . . . But what is more divine, I will not say in man only, but in all heaven and earth, than reason? And reason, when it is full grown and perfected, is rightly called wisdom. Therefore, since there is nothing better than reason, and since it exists both in man and God, the first common possession of man and God is reason" (I.vii.22–23). "Moreover, virtue exists in man and God alike, but in no other creature besides; virtue, however, is nothing else than nature perfected and developed to its highest point; therefore there is a likeness between man and God. As this is true, what relationship could be closer or clearer than this one?" (I.viii.25) "In fact, there is no human being of any race who, if he finds a guide in nature, cannot attain to virtue" (I.x.30).

ADVERTISEMENT

So soon as the AUTHOR's Health permits, will be published, CHRISTIAN PHILOSOPHY: or, *The* CHRISTIAN DOCTRINE *concerning* PROVIDENCE, VIRTUE, *and a* FUTURE STATE, proved to be perfectly agreeable to the PRINCIPLES of MORAL PHILOSOPHY. In a Discourse given by St. *Paul, of the divine* MORAL GOVERNMENT, in these Words: *Be not deceived, God is not mocked, whatsoever a man soweth, that shall he also reap.*